Phillip Kerman

{ ActionScripting in FLASH™ }

201 West 103rd St. • Indianapolis, Indiana, 46290 USA

ActionScripting in Flash

International Standard Book Number: 0-672-32078-9

Library of Congress Catalog Card Number: 00-108995

Printed in the United States of America

First Printing: April 2001

04 03 02 01 4 3 2

Trademarks

All terms mentioned in this book that are known to be trademarks or service marks have been appropriately capitalized. Sams Publishing cannot attest to the accuracy of this information. Use of a term in this book should not be regarded as affecting the validity of any trademark or service mark.

Warning and Disclaimer

Every effort has been made to make this book as complete and as accurate as possible, but no warranty or fitness is implied. The information provided is on an "as is" basis. The author and the publisher shall have neither liability nor responsibility to any person or entity with respect to any loss or damages arising from the information contained in this book.

Executive Editor
Jeff Schultz

Development Editors
Kate Small
Alice Martina Smith

Managing Editor
Charlotte Clapp

Project Editor
Carol Bowers

Copy Editors
Michael Henry
Alice Martina Smith

Indexer
Sheila Schroeder

Proofreader
Daniel Ponder

Technical Editor
Lynn Baus

Team Coordinator
Amy Patton

Interior Designer
Alan Clements

Cover Designer
Alan Clements

Page Layout
Ayanna Lacey
Heather Hiatt Miller
Stacey Richwine
DeRome

Overview

Contents

Foreword

The upgrade to Flash 5 turned an already compelling medium (Flash animations) into something truly amazing. The inclusion of a new version of the ActionScript language means that Flash 5 can do almost anything. If you just organize your goals and translate them to the language of a programmer, you can make Flash do precisely what you imagined. But therein lies the problem: Translating goals into a programming language is not easy for everyone.

This book targets the reader who can assemble a basic Flash movie and who knows what he or she wants to achieve. I'll help you divide your goal into individual tasks that can then be translated into ActionScript. Naturally, this will involve teaching you how to "program" (and even think like a programmer). This book is not, however, a general programming book; *every* topic is related to and applied to Flash. Naturally, if you are already an experienced programmer, you might find parts of this book to be a review. But for you programmers, I'll show you how to apply your programming knowledge to make Flash perform. All the programming skill in the world (whether I teach it to you or you bring it with you) won't help you if you can't apply it to Flash.

This book definitely does not shy away from advanced topics. But it isn't an exhaustive reference to every detail in the ActionScript language either. The truth is that there are countless other resources for advanced programming topics. That's not what this book is about. It's about giving you the skills so that you can apply any idea you have to Flash. When you're equipped with the knowledge I cover, you'll be able to meet any challenge. It might involve researching an esoteric formula for physics or applying a unique math calculation. If that means you have to research a specific topic, this book will give you the skills to figure out how to apply it to Flash.

I started this book having just finished *Sams Teach Yourself Macromedia Flash 5 in 24 Hours*. Although this isn't a continuation of that book, there isn't much repeated content either. I said earlier that you'll need to be able to assemble a Flash movie (for example, I'm not going to teach you how to draw in Flash). The first chapter, "Flash Basics," goes over the prerequisites. It's important that you come with this basic knowledge. Don't worry, I won't go so fast that you can't keep up, but everyone should start at this base level.

The book is organized in two parts. The foundation chapters are like a textbook. Plenty of examples are interspersed, but you won't need to follow along with Flash running. (I suspect, however, that you'll often want to try things out when inspired.) The workshop chapters are all hands-on tutorials. It's a chance to apply what you learned in the foundation part. If you prefer, you can jump right into the workshops as references are made to the foundations when further explanation might be helpful. You'll find the workshops to be quite useful. In some of them, I even guide you down the wrong path so that we can discuss the solution that follows. I find that this is more true-to-life than some tutorials that seem to prove only that it's *possible* to achieve a particular result with very few steps. Real life is often frustrating and perhaps the simulated reality of these workshops will help you avoid frustration when you go on your own.

One last note before we get rolling. Flash 5 was such a change from Flash 4 that I chose to cover *only* Flash 5. It turns out that there are a few ancillary mentions of Flash 4 in this book, including a good part of Appendix A, "Equivalents." By and large, however, this book is for Flash 5 only. The first workshop provides information about ensuring that your users have the correct Flash player. Naturally, you'll be shown how to upgrade those users so that they can see your Flash 5 creations.

Now get ready to transform yourself from a Flash user to an ActionScripter!

About the Author

Phillip Kerman is an independent programmer, teacher, and writer specializing in Macromedia products. His degree in Imaging and Photographic Technology from the Rochester Institute of Technology was earned back when "multimedia" had a different meaning than today. One of Phillip's internships, for example, involved programming multiple slide projector presentations with dissolves synchronized to a sound track—the multimedia of the 1980s. In 1993, he found Macromedia Authorware a natural fit for his interest and skills. After getting his start at The Human Element, Inc., he moved back to Portland, Oregon to work on his own.

Phillip has transitioned his expertise from Authorware to Director, and now, to Flash. Over seven years, he has had to adapt to a total of 13 version upgrades—Flash 5 being the most significant of them all! In addition to retooling and building his own skills, Phillip finds teaching the biggest challenge. He has trained and made presentations around the world, in such exotic locations as Reykjavik, Iceland; Melbourne, Australia; Amsterdam, Holland; and McAlester, Oklahoma. He wrote *Sams Teach Yourself Macromedia Flash 5 in 24 Hours* (that is the title, not how long it took to write). His writing has also appeared in such publications as *Macworld*, *Macromedia User Journal*, and his self-published *The Phillip Newsletter* (`www.teleport.com/~phillip/newsletter`).

In addition to showing others how to create multimedia, Phillip has had plenty of opportunities to get his hands dirty in programming. Last century, Phillip programmed the all-Flash Web site `www.m-three.com` for Paris France Inc. This site was included in both *Communication Arts Interactive Design Annual* and the *British Design & Art Direction Annual* in 2000. The latest version of the M3 site won the navigation category at the London Flash Film Festival.

Feel free to email Phillip at `flash5@onemain.com`.

Dedication

Dedicated to my entire family including our newest member, Savannah. And the canine Kerman, Max, who deserved more walks than he got during the writing of this book.

Acknowledgments

The hardest part of writing a book is attempting to acknowledge all those who helped, but knowing that you'll fail to mention everyone. Here is my attempt to acknowledge everyone.

First, the people at Sams Publishing. You'll find a list of the key players in the credits column on the copyright page, but even they would acknowledge that others helped them. After seeing my first book become a reality last year (with the same team), I realized that even if I could write a perfect book on my own (which, of course I can't), it would never get printed because there's so much work involved in preparing the files for the printer. Although I can't say I know how every publisher works, I can say that Sams is professional, responsive, and fun. Of particular note, Kate Small made the book flow. Everything seemed to make sense when I wrote it, but after Kate reorganized parts, it made much more sense. Lynn Baus used her Flash experience both to ensure that technical details were correct and exercises could be performed, as well as to suggest countless additional facts that were included in the text. Copy editors are doubly valuable as they both eliminate errors that would otherwise make the book difficult to read and they also make me a better writer! Reviewing their edits is like a free English class. The production team led by Carol Bowers turns the manuscripts into a real book. Obviously, there are many others who work behind the scenes for whom I am grateful.

Macromedia continues to amaze me with its forthcoming and approachable style. The company is totally involved in email lists and Flash community sites. The folks who seem to go way beyond the call of duty by providing help to all include Brad Bechtel, John Dowdell, Gary Grossman, Erica Norton, Peter

Santangeli, and Eric J. Wittman. Others who provided specific help for this book include Jeremy Clark and Matt Wobensmith.

I subscribe to many e-mail lists, but four in particular have been most helpful—those run by Darrel Plant, Branden Hall, Jon Warren Lentz, and Robert Reinhardt. There are countless instances when a thread on one of these lists has helped me.

One last acknowledgment for some authors of other Flash books. I'm proud of this book, but it contains only my style of communication. For some different perspectives on Flash, check out books containing contributions by the following authors:

Joshua Davis, Brendan Dawes, David J. Emberton, Bruce Epstein, Derek Franklin, Garo Green, Branden Hall, Andreas Heim, Jon Warren Lentz, Colin Moock, Darrel Plant, Robert Reinhardt, Crissy Rey, Gary Rosenzweig, Glenn Thomas, Phillip Torrone, Bill Turner, and Samuel Wan.

I can't vouch for books I haven't reviewed, but I can say these folks know their stuff. They've also provided direct help on various Flash related matters to myself and others for years.

Tell Us What You Think!

As the reader of this book, *you* are our most important critic and commentator. We value your opinion and want to know what we're doing right, what we could do better, what areas you'd like to see us publish in, and any other words of wisdom you're willing to pass our way.

You can e-mail or write me directly to let me know what you did or didn't like about this book—as well as what we can do to make our books stronger.

Please note that I cannot help you with technical problems related to the topic of this book, and that due to the high volume of mail I receive, I might not be able to reply to every message.

When you write, please be sure to include this book's title and author as well as your name and phone or fax number. I will carefully review your comments and share them with the author and editors who worked on the book.

Fax: 317-581-4770

E-mail: `graphics@samspublishing.com`

Mail: Mark Taber
Sams Publishing
201 West 103rd Street
Indianapolis, IN 46290 USA

{Part I}

Foundation

{ Foundation } Introduction

The following 14 chapters cover practically every detail of ActionScript. Although the content is organized like a textbook, I've included several examples along the way. You are encouraged to break from the reading and try out any topic that interests you. Generally, however, this is the part of the book that you read. In the second half (the workshops), you can follow along with the 21 detailed tutorials.

Here's a quick rundown of the topics explored in this part of the book:

1. "Flash Basics" includes the prerequisites that I expect every reader to bring with him or her. Even if you consider yourself a Flash expert, you should read this chapter as both a review and an insight into some of the terms that I'll use throughout the book.
2. "What's New in Flash 5" introduces you to the key features in Flash 5 that pertain specifically to ActionScript. In addition to changes in the programming language, features that affect how you build a Flash movie are discussed. Finally, this chapter includes a quick rundown of previous knowledge (that you might have acquired in older versions of Flash) that is best forgotten.
3. "The Programmer's Approach" is a very general chapter that lays the groundwork for your programming career. Topics such as writing specifications, prototyping, and exactly what "good style" means are covered.
4. "Basic Programming in Flash" introduces you to the terminology and basic elements of ActionScript, such as data types and variables. It's impossible to discuss these elements without showing how they work, but the goal is to simply introduce all the pieces that will be incorporated in later chapters.

5. "Programming Structures" is a huge chapter that explains all the ways ActionScript is structured. If Chapter 4 was the building materials (like wood, bricks, and concrete), this chapter is the framework and architectural styles. You also get a peek at both the Math and Number objects because they're so integral to the structural elements covered.
6. "Assigning Values" offers a chance to catch your breath (after Chapter 5) and take the time to learn ways to ensure quality programming before you go too far in the wrong direction. The new Flash Debugger is explained, as well as some general programming techniques to avoid or remove bugs.
7. "The Movie Clip Object" introduces a familiar component of Flash, but in a way that will help you understand other "objects" that come up in later chapters. In this way, you can leverage your existing knowledge when learning advanced topics.
8. "Functions" shows you how to use the built-in functions as well as how to write your own functions. It turns out that homemade functions prove to be much more involved than the ones that come with Flash. This is possibly the most valuable chapter because it can save you a ton of time.
9. "Selecting Text, Trapping Keys, and Manipulating Strings" looks at ways to control text both on the screen (such as HTML text and input text) as well as off the screen (such as cleaning up strings before the user sees them). Also, you'll learn how to use the Key object to "trap" user interaction with the keyboard.
10. "Arrays" explores how to make, access, and manipulate arrays, which are simply a great way to organize complex information.
11. "Objects" introduces the general form of objects, shows you how to use the built-in objects Sound, Color, and Date, and teaches you new ways to use the familiar Movie Clip.
12. "Homemade Objects" shows you how to apply knowledge you already have to make complex objects in Flash. If arrays are a way to store complex information easily, objects are a way to store *really* complex information.
13. "Smart Clips" walks through all the ways to build and use Smart Clips, from ways of making standard Smart Clips work for you to creating Custom User Interfaces (Custom UIs).
14. "Interfacing with External Data" shows you many ways Flash can "talk" to outside applications. Topics include reading text files, interacting with server applications, exchanging XML-structured data, invoking and being controlled by JavaScript, and interacting with the host applications Authorware and Director. I didn't have time in this chapter to actually show you how to use all these other tools, but it shows you practically everything else.

It's amazing to think that there's so much to say about Flash and I don't even say it all. I could probably double the size of this book and there'd be still more! However, I'm sure that if you grasp all the content I've organized in these 14 chapters, you'll be able to adapt quickly to any new situation that arises.

{ Chapter 1 }

Flash Basics

Flash professionals are a strange breed. Some have traditional animation and graphics skills. Others come to Flash from a programming background. Still others are so young they don't have *any* professional background—they're straight out of college (or younger)! It doesn't matter where you come from because Flash is approachable and powerful.

For this book to serve as the bridge between intermediate Flash and advanced programming, it is best if you start at the same level. Intermediate Flash users, who are familiar with drawing, tweening, and sound effects, are about to embark on programming; already experienced programmers are about to apply their skills to Flash. But we all need to start at the same level.

This chapter is an important link to the material that follows. It isn't a recap of drawing, tweening, and sound effects; rather, it's a quick overview of foundational knowledge unique to Flash scripting. If this material looks familiar, good. If not, you should make sure that it all makes sense before attacking the rest of the book.

Specifically, this chapter covers

- The timeline hierarchy of nested Movie Clips
- The Stage coordinate system
- Traditional Flash tricks such as invisible Buttons and empty Movie Clips
- The places where scripting occurs

I'd like to think most of this chapter is a review, but it's alright if some material is new to you. If nothing else, you should begin to approach the concepts in the way they're presented here. For example, if you've never heard of invisible Buttons, that's fine—just try to start using them.

Timeline Hierarchy

A key concept that is critical to understanding Flash is nested timelines. Any time you select a shape and Insert, Convert to Symbol… (F8), the shape is placed in the Library and you're left with an instance of the symbol on stage. You can also select an instance of a symbol and Insert, Convert to Symbol…, which places an instance of the selected symbol inside a new symbol. The main thing to remember is that F8 takes whatever is selected and places it in the Library as a new symbol (even if you have a symbol instance selected). Such nesting of symbols has implications for both programming and animation structure.

Implications for Animation and Filesize

To see how nesting symbols applies to animation, consider how to create a symbol of a car containing moving wheels. First, draw a wheel and convert it to a Graphic Symbol. To create a rotating wheel symbol, you must convert an instance of the wheel Graphic Symbol to a Movie Clip. Then edit the contents of the Movie Clip by making a simple Motion Tween that rotates the wheel symbol. Because only symbol instances can be used in a Motion Tween, the extra step of placing the wheel symbol inside the "wheel in motion" symbol is necessary. Finally, use two instances of the "wheel in motion" clip inside a third clip, "car." Then you can animate the car across the main timeline.

In the end, your car is a symbol containing two instances of the "wheel in motion" clip, which both contain an instance of the plain wheel. When building such nested symbols, it's usually best to work from the "inside out" or "specific to general." However you approach it, be sure to monitor the address bar that appears above the stage as shown in Figure 1.1. The address bar begins with the name of the scene that you're currently editing, and shows the hierarchy of symbol nesting as well. In Figure 1.1, the address bar indicates that you're editing the "Wheel" symbol inside "Wheel in Motion," which in turn is nested inside "Car." Of course, you can make more complex nested symbols than a car with rotating wheels—you just have to keep track of what you're doing.

Figure 1.1 *The address bar shows the hierarchy of nested symbols.*

Besides enabling complex effects, nested symbols can reduce your movie's filesize by recycling graphic components. You can actually take this seeming advantage too far and it will begin to work against you. For example, take the absurd example of a single-pixel symbol that is recycled and nested to make a line…and then four lines are used to make a square…and so on. Generally, however, the benefits of recycling symbols are significant.

In addition to filesize savings, careful use of symbols generally (and Movie Clips specifically) can help your productivity. For example, when a change is made to the master symbol, that change is reflected in each instance already in use. Also, when you duplicate a shape that hasn't been converted to a symbol, you encounter two problems: the obvious filesize contribution and the fact that Flash might not render the "identical" shapes the same way. Because you can position graphics in fractional locations, Flash often needs to round off when drawing every pixel. The bottom line is that two different shapes of the same size can easily appear slightly differently whereas multiple symbols look the same (unless they're scaled differently).

Implications for Programming

Finally, nested symbols can be useful for programming tasks. Consider, for example, how a simple draggable Movie Clip is created. If you want to write a script that responds when the user begins to drag (mouse press), you can use a button. But you can't make a button that's draggable—only Movie Clips are draggable. Instead, you simply nest a button inside a Movie Clip. The script attached to the button says, effectively, "drag me" but it's really the clip containing the button that is dragged. It's not always required that you nest symbols to achieve a particular effect (as in the case of dragging), but often it's desirable because it makes your Flash file more modular and manageable. Imagine if our entire money supply were based in pennies. It would certainly be possible to carry out any transaction, but it'd be a pain. You could nest one hundred pennies in a "dollar" symbol. A ten-dollar bill is like 10 instances of the "dollar" symbol. Sometimes such nesting is simply more convenient.

Targeting

When creating nested symbols, it's important to pay attention to the address bar. When programming, it's just as important to understand the concept of *targeting*. That is, which clip you want to affect. In the case of a button inside a draggable Movie Clip (as earlier), the "drag me" instructions really target the clip in which it is contained. By default, if you don't indicate otherwise, the "current clip" (the one in which the script is contained) is targeted. If you want to target a different clip, you just need to clarify which clip.

One way to envision targeting is to think of the folder (and subfolder) structure on your computer. You can have folders inside folders just like symbols inside symbols. (I'll use this analogy throughout the description and tie it to Flash at the end of this section.) If you are browsing one folder and you want to open a file in a subfolder, you simply "target" the subfolder you want to browse. When you decide to target another file or folder, you have two basic ways to do so: relatively and absolutely. Take a quick look at Figure 1.2. Starting from the folder "Flash 5," if you want to go into a folder "Help" and then into a subfolder "UsingFlash," the relative target can be expressed as *go into the folder "Help" and then into the subfolder "UsingFlash."* Consider that you can only be "in" (browsing) one folder at a time, so when you begin by saying *go into the folder "Help,"* you're assuming there's a folder called "Help" present within the current folder. This is relative targeting because it's relative to where you are.

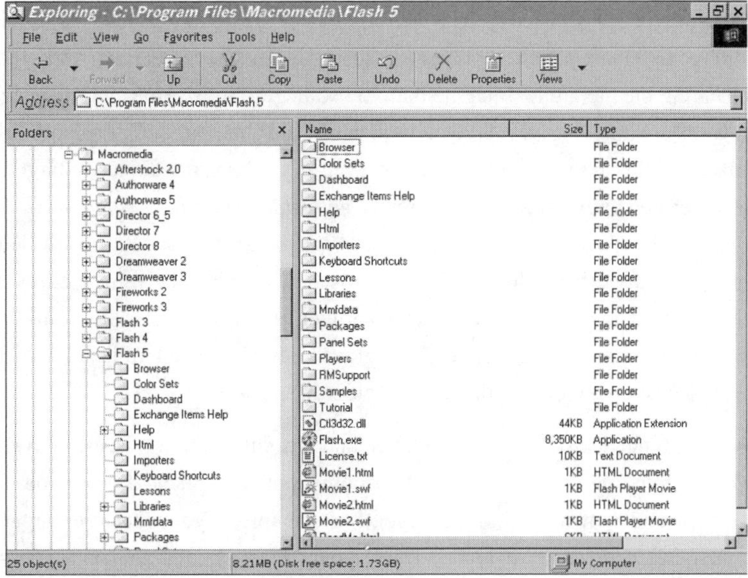

Figure 1.2 *Relative and absolute targeting are similar to browsing files and folders on your computer.*

In addition to relative targeting that "dives" down into subfolders, relative targeting can go up, too. That is, if you're inside one folder (or Movie Clip), you can refer to the folder that contains the folder you're in. For example, if you were browsing the "Flash 5" folder inside the "Macromedia" folder, you could refer to the "Macromedia" folder with a relative target: "go up one level" (the same way you could click "Up" in Figure 1.2). In Flash, such a relative reference involves the term `_parent`, and in HTML, the characters `../` are used. You'll learn these later this chapter, but the important concept is that relative references can go "up" or "down."

Absolute targeting is an alternative to relative targeting. Absolute targets specify the entire address of the item (or folder) that you're targeting. As such, absolute references are unaffected by which folder you're currently "in." In the case of browsing folders, an absolute path would include the drive letter. For example: C:\Program Files\Macromedia\Flash 5 is an absolute path. You can also compare a phrase such as "next door" or "down the street" to a relative target, and "1234 SW Whatever St., Portland, OR 97214" to an absolute target.

It's a subjective decision as to which references are better: absolute or relative. But, generally, relative references are desirable because you aren't restricted in changing the hierarchy. Imagine that you wanted to move your "Flash 5" folder to a different hard drive? All of a sudden, the absolute target C:\Program Files\Macromedia\Flash 5 won't work. However, if you're using a relative target, such as Macromedia\Flash 5 (which is really *go inside the folder "Macromedia"—adjacent to where I am—and then go into the folder "Flash 5"*), it isn't tied to any particular drive or folder. The only disadvantage of relative references is that they require you to be "in" a particular folder (in this case, the "Program Files" folder). The absolute reference C:\Program Files\Macromedia\Flash 5 works no matter where you are (as long as the folder hasn't moved).

Although the decision between relative and absolute targeting is subjective, you'll often find that relative targets become quite complicated when you have to go "up" and "down" to find the target. For example, if you wanted to target the folder called "Flash 3" (which is inside your "Macromedia" folder) if you were in the "Flash 5" folder, a relative target would be *go up one folder, and then down into "Flash 3."* It's not impossible to make relative references that change direction like this, but an absolute target is often easier.

Just so we don't drift too far from Flash, let's look at targeting in Flash. You target clip instances (and their timelines). Using the earlier car example, if I were in a "wheel," I could use a relative target to target the car in which I was contained. It helps greatly to name the instances of each nested Movie Clip. For example, if I wanted to target the front wheel instance inside my car, I would want to make sure that both the car and the wheel had an instance name. Consider that you could have two instances of the master "car" symbol on stage. You can target only one clip instance at a time—so you'd have to specify which car instance you were targeting.

Relative targeting in Flash is pretty simple. You just use the instance name of the clip you're targeting. If the instance name is "BigCar," that's all you need to use! To target instances inside instances, you simply separate each instance name with a dot (that is, a period "."—but people say *dot*). `BigCar.FrontWheel` will target the "FrontWheel" instance inside the "BigCar" instance. If you are writing a script from inside the "FrontWheel" instance and want to target the "BigCar" instance, use `_parent`. The term `_parent` means the clip that contains the clip

I'm in. You can also use `_parent._parent` (and so on) to "go up" more than one level at a time. You can also target an instance that's "up one level." Say, from inside the "FrontWheel" instance, you want to target "BackWheel" (which is contained in "BigCar," the same clip containing "FrontWheel"), you can use `_parent.BackWheel`.

Absolute targets in Flash almost always begin `_root`, which targets the main Timeline. For example, `_root.BigCar.FrontWheel` will target the instance named "FrontWheel" inside "BigCar," which is in the main Timeline. The only exception to beginning absolute targets with "_root" is when targeting levels. Using Load Movie, you can play .swf files inside clips or level numbers. To target a clip (or the entire .swf) absolutely that's been loaded via Load Movie, begin with `_level1` (use `_level2` for level 2, `_level3` for 3, and so on).

Targeting clips might sound like an exercise in futility, but there are actually several reasons to do so. You can target a clip to change one of its properties. For example, you could target the front wheel in the car to change its alpha property. For example, the script `_root.BigCar.FrontWheel._alpha=50` would set the front wheel's alpha to 50%. Not only can you change properties, but also you can make Actions affect individual instances. For example, `_root.BigCar.FrontWheel.gotoAndStop(10)` will go to frame 10 (in the FrontWheel instance) and stop. When you apply an Action to an instance in this way, the Action is called a *method* of the instance. We'll discuss both changing properties and using methods (plus much more) in Chapters 4, "Basic Programming in Flash," and 7, "The Movie Clip Object." It's just important to understand *why* you'd need to target a clip in the first place.

This section provides the basics of targeting. However, you might want to practice. A great way to learn is through Flash's Target Path Editor. Any time you see the Insert Target Path button (shown in Figure 1.3), you can explore your entire file and Flash will write the target reference for you. What's more, you can experiment with both relative and absolute targets.

Finally, although the old "slash" reference is also supported (and might be familiar to those with HTML experience), I recommend using only the dot notation. You can see the Target Path Editor in Figure 1.4.

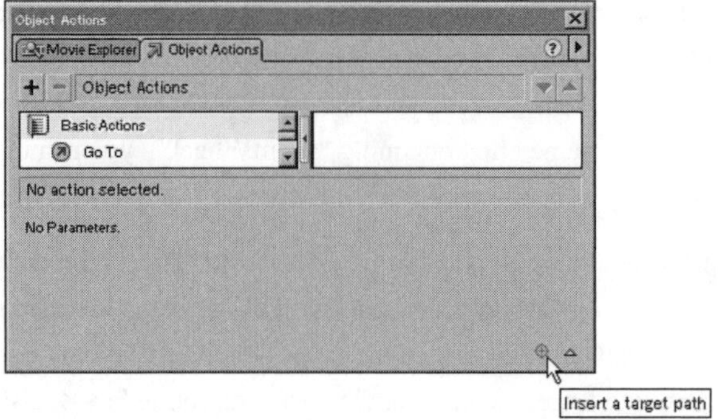

Figure 1.3 *The Insert Target Path button helps you compose a target path.*

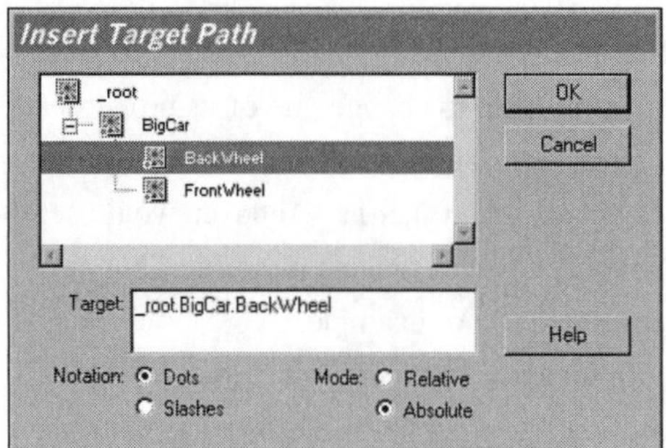

Figure 1.4 *The Target Path Editor enables you to choose between relative and absolute paths and dot and slash notation.*

Script Locations

All your scripts are written in the Actions panel, but there are three places you can attach scripts: keyframes, button instances, and Movie Clip instances. You can also place scripts inside a master Movie Clip, but still attach scripts only to keyframes, button instances, and clip instances that are inside the Movie Clip. Flash is "event-driven," meaning that events trigger scripts to execute.

Keyframe scripts are probably the easiest to understand. You simply select a keyframe and open the Actions panel to create a script. The event that triggers a frame script is that the frame is displayed. That is, if you put a script on frame 10, it will execute when the playhead reaches frame 10. Keep in mind that Flash executes the script first and then draws the onscreen contents. This becomes important if your script's instructions are to jump to another frame; you might never see the onscreen contents of the frame where the script is written.

Button and Movie Clip scripts are attached to instances of buttons or Movie Clips—but not contained inside the master symbol of a button! If you place a script anywhere inside a button's symbol, it will be ignored. If you place a script inside a Movie Clip symbol, it will work fine; but consider such a script is placed in a keyframe, button instance, or nested clip instance. To attach a script to a button or clip instance, select an instance onstage and then use the Actions panel to write a script. Button and clip instance scripts differ from frame scripts in one interesting way: They are always contained within an event. Buttons respond to mouse events (such as Press, Release, and Roll Over) and clip instances respond to clip events (such as Load, Unload, and EnterFrame). So, whereas keyframe scripts execute in the event that the frame is reached, button scripts respond to mouse events, and clip instance scripts respond to clip events. For example, you can't simply make a button `gotoAndPlay(1)`. You have to specify exactly what event will trigger that script—a Press mouse event…a Roll Over event…or other? Events are further discussed in Chapter 4, but you should have a clear understanding of these three script locations.

One other very important concept related to targeting is that button and keyframe scripts both perform as if you were "in" the timeline in which they reside. Scripts attached to clip instances perform as if you were "in" the movie clip's timeline. For example, if your script `gotoAndStop(1)` were attached to a keyframe or button (within a mouse event), it would cause the playback head to jump to frame 1 within the timeline in which the button or keyframe resides. If the same script were attached to a clip instance, the playback head would jump to the first frame *within the clip* unless you changed the script to `_parent.gotoAndStop(1)`. This topic will be fully explored in many of the workshop portions of this book.

One last point about script locations. The Actions panel can be displayed in Normal Mode or Expert Mode. This is set—per object (keyframe, button, or clip)—through the Options Arrow at the top right of the Actions panel (which I often call the "Mystery Arrow," and which is shown in Figure 1.5).

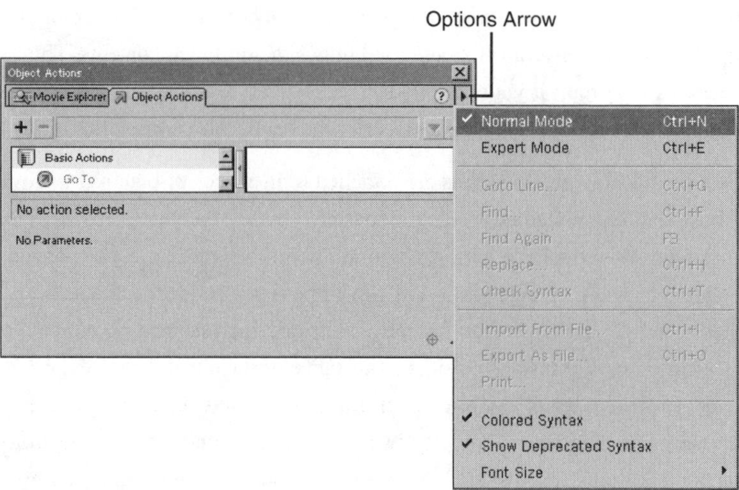

Figure 1.5 *The Options Arrow (or Mystery Arrow) enables you to change from Normal to Expert Mode.*

You can set the default mode under Edit, Preferences, General tab. Personally, I like switching between Expert and Normal Modes quite often. In Normal Mode, Flash helps you build scripts with parameters that appear in the bottom of the Actions panel. For example, instead of getting mixed up as to whether the mouse event is called "mouseDown" or "press," if I just set the Actions panel to Normal Mode, I'll see all the appropriate choices in the parameters area. Additionally, because I know that button and clip instance scripts are always enclosed in either a mouse event or clip event, Normal Mode eliminates the need to type "on (press)" or "onClipEvent (mouseDown)". Instead, if I simply add *any* script while in Normal Mode, it will be automatically surrounded by the appropriate event type. Select a clip instance and, with the Actions panel in Normal Mode, click once in the script area. Now press (and release) the Esc key, followed by the E key and then the V key (this is a keyboard combination to insert the "evaluate" Action). The blank line for the evaluate Action is inserted just as if I had selected it from the Toolbox list on the left of the Actions panel, but it is automatically surrounded by a default clip event (see Figure 1.6).

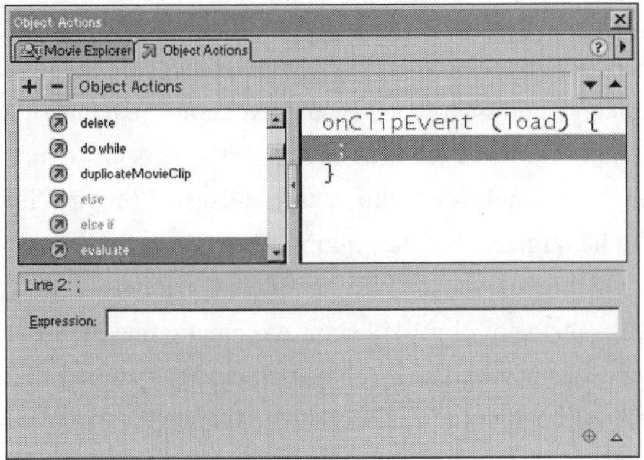

Figure 1.6 *While a clip is selected, Actions can only be surrounded by clip events.*

Always Movie Clips

Every time you create a symbol, you have a choice between Movie Clip, Button, or Graphic behavior. Selecting the Button symbol is often convenient because an instance automatically causes the cursor to change to a "finger" (for the user), and the symbol has provisions for various visual states plus a "hit" state. Buttons are great when you need buttons.

The choice between the Graphic and Movie Clip symbols isn't as clear. I used to believe, incorrectly, that Graphic symbols were appropriate for static graphics and Movie Clips for multi-frame clips. A Graphic symbol should be used in one of only two cases: when you're creating a multi-frame clip that you want locked to its parent timeline (so that you can scrub—by dragging the red current frame marker—to preview its behavior) or when you're planning to take advantage of one of the special loop settings available only to Graphic symbols (as shown in Figure 1.7).

Figure 1.7 *Use a Graphic symbol only when you need to preview in the Timeline or use one of the Loop options found in the Instance panel.*

Basically, if neither of those cases exists, use Movie Clips. Only Movie Clip instances can be named, which means that only clip instances can be targeted to have their properties changed or ascertained (you must know the name of a clip to target it, after all). There are other features of clip instances—just remember the cool stuff that can be done only with clip instances. Nested Movie Clips not only have the ability to be targeted, but they almost always contribute less to filesize. A simple test in which you compare nesting Graphic symbols inside Graphic symbols to clips inside of clips will show a dramatic filesize difference. To offer a bit of balance, nested Graphic symbols will tend to perform slightly better but this is usually of negligible benefit compared to the filesize bloat they cause.

Realize that the behavior you select when you make the symbol or if you change a Library symbol's properties later will only affect the default behavior for created instances. Through the Instance panel, you can change a particular instance's behavior as shown in Figure 1.8. A symbol that was originally a button can "act" like a Movie Clip, for example. Changing an instance's behavior makes that instance perform as selected—the only difference is that the original symbol (and subsequent instances) might have a different default behavior.

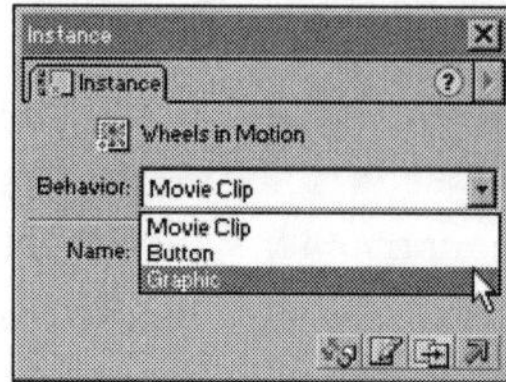

Figure 1.8 *You can change the behavior of any instance on stage through the Instance panel.*

Coordinate System

On the Stage, Flash considers the x and y coordinates to begin at the top-left corner. The x coordinate increases as you move to the right. The y coordinate increases as you move down. This might be familiar to you, and you just accept that "0 0" is the top-left corner. In the case of clip instances, position is based on the center registration point of that clip. If you use `someClip._x=100`, the center of the clip will move to x position 100. Whenever you're inspecting the coordinates of clips on the Stage, use the Info panel and be sure to click the center box as shown in Figure 1.9 (so that you're not viewing the top-left corner of the clip).

Use center point

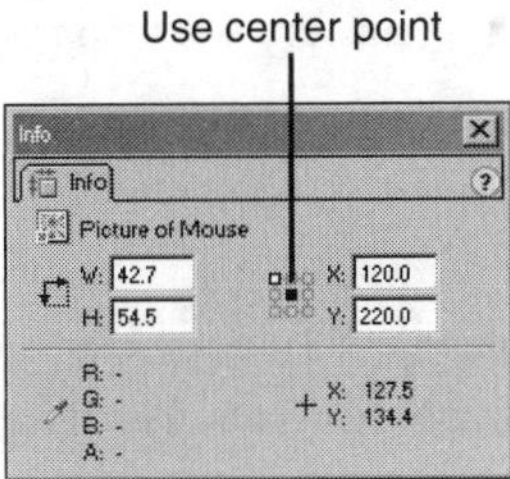

Figure 1.9 *The center option on the Info panel reflects the location a clip will move to when using ActionScript.*

Similarly, when you are inside a clip, "0 0" is the center of the clip, as shown in Figure 1.10. The best way to understand coordinates is to select View, Rulers and edit a symbol by double-clicking the symbol item in the Library.

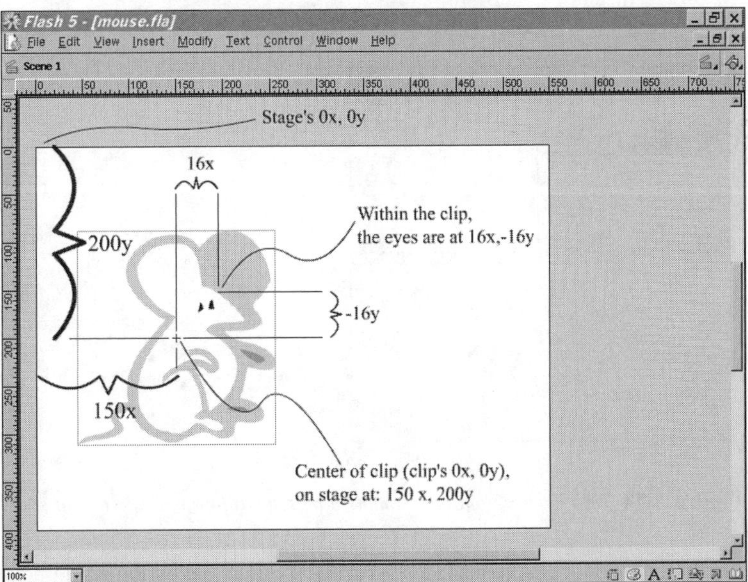

Figure 1.10 *The position of objects on the Stage is based on the top-left corner being 0x 0y. Within Movie Clips, objects are based on the center being 0x 0y.*

Tricks of the Trade

As I mentioned, Flash-heads tend to be strange characters. Perhaps they've turned out that way while developing creative and resourceful solutions to control Flash. Some of the tips I'm about to disclose might seem very wacky on first look, but they're all very useful.

Invisible Buttons

Buttons are cool because you can automatically create an Over and Down state. However, they also offer something else: access to mouse events. There are situations when you want or need access to a mouse event (such as Roll Over, for example), but you don't need or want all the pretty graphic features of a button. An invisible button is perfect for this. What's an invisible button? Simple: a button that has no graphic contents except a shape in its hit state (as shown in Figure 1.11). I don't know how many times I've drawn a shape, converted to a button symbol, and then double-clicked the button instance to edit its contents by dragging the first frame to the hit state—but it's a lot of times! The coolest part of invisible buttons is that Flash will display (while authoring) a semi-transparent cyan shape, so it's easy to position the button.

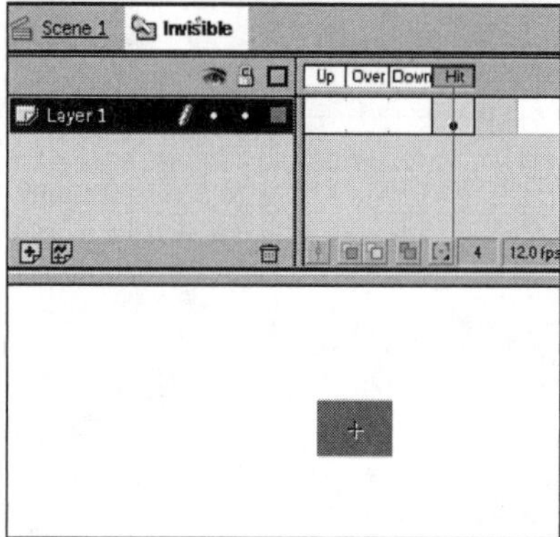

Figure 1.11 *An invisible button is simply a button with graphics in the hit state only.*

Let me give you a couple examples of when an invisible button might be useful. Say you have several words that you intend to perform as clickable buttons. It would be easiest to have a separate button for each word, but to nest the text inside the button would be clumsy. Each word would be a separate button, editing the words would require going into the button, and each one would need a hit state that's larger than the word (or they would be hard for the user to click). Compare this to having several instances of an invisible button that contains a rectangle in its hit state. All the text can be in the main timeline where it's easy to edit, you can resize the invisible buttons as needed, and overall it will be easier to maintain.

Invisible buttons can also be used in conjunction with clip instances. I often find that a button with just an Over and Down state isn't enough—sometimes a "selected" state is necessary to show the user which buttons have been selected. One Movie Clip could contain different frames for Up, Over, and Down (similar to a button). Additionally, the clip could contain graphics to communicate "selected" (perhaps a checkmark). Just place an invisible button in the clip (or on top of the clip) and by jumping to the appropriate frames within the clip, you could make a much more sophisticated button. We'll explore these techniques (and more) in the following exercises in the Workshop Creating a Multistate Button.

I can think of many more times when invisible buttons would be useful. Any time you simply want something "clickable," but you don't want to put all the graphic content inside a button, invisible buttons can help.

Empty Movie Clips

Similar to the reasons for invisible buttons, empty Movie Clips are useful when you want to take advantage of some benefit of a Movie Clip, but you don't have a need or desire for any graphics. A Movie Clip can do "Movie Clip things" regardless of whether the clip has any graphic contents. You can put extra frames and keyframes within an empty clip to write scripts; you can attach scripts to instances of empty Movie Clips; you can even give names to empty clip instances so that they can be targeted. The easiest way to create an empty Movie Clip is to select Insert, New Symbol; name it; and click OK. When you're taken inside the clip to edit its contents, just return to your main scene. The trick to remember is that you'll need to drag an instance of this empty clip from the Library window. Unlike invisible buttons, empty Movie Clips are displayed as a white dot while authoring (shown in Figure 1.12).

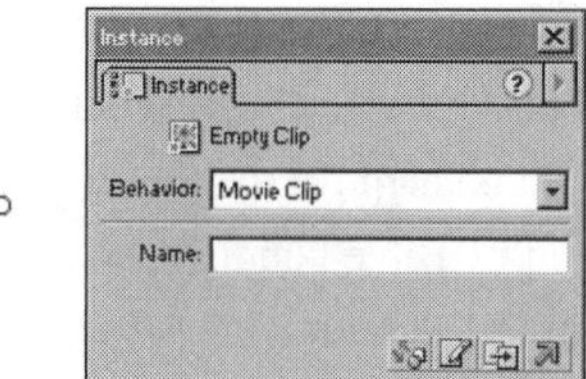

Figure 1.12 *Empty Movie Clips appear as a small white dot when on stage.*

There are two main reasons people resorted to empty Movie Clips with Flash 4: to ascertain the position of the user's cursor and to continually monitor changes. Both these applications have become practically obsolete with Flash 5 (as you'll learn in the "Previous Knowledge Worth Forgetting" section next chapter). You can still use empty Movie Clips any time you don't have any visuals but want access to the clip events unique to clip instances—`enterFrame` and `mouseMove` in particular. For example, to monitor the mouse's location, you could attach a script to an empty clip that—on the `mouseMove` clip event—checks to see where the mouse has moved. In this situation, you could cause several other clips to respond to the mouse movement. The idea is that the empty clip is the "brains of the operation" and the other clips just respond to the clip event.

Another use for empty Movie Clips is as a storage location for variables. As you'll learn in Chapter 5, variables are contained in clip instances. If you always want access to a certain set of variables, you could store them all in an empty Movie Clip called "globals". Then, any time you want access, just use `_root.globals.`*`varName`* (where "*varName*" is the variable name you want access to). Like I said, you'll learn more about variables later, but just remember empty Movie Clips are a place to store variables.

Finally, perhaps even more common than empty Movie Clips are Movie Clips that have contents in all their frames *except* the first frame. While authoring, such a clip appears like an empty Movie Clip; that is, a white dot. (Actually, because the dot is so cryptic, I often place *something* in the first frame of every clip—I just move it offstage so that the user won't ever see it, but I'll be able to grab it while authoring.) There are situations in which you don't want to display the contents of a clip until a certain event occurs. Just create a blank keyframe in the first frame of the clip with a stop Action. Then, perhaps when the user clicks the correct button, you can use a script like `_root.clipInstanceName.play()`, which causes the instance (called "clipInstanceName" in this case) to play. You'll see exactly how this works in more detail in Chapter 4, but you should have an idea how such clips can be used.

Empty Layers and Keyframes

A really great technique is to create an extra layer for no other purpose than to contain blank keyframes. These keyframes are strategically placed wherever you want a label or Action. You could actually have one layer for all your keyframe Actions and another for all your labels. It's nice to separate these keyframes from your graphics (and tweens) because they won't disrupt anything visual. For example, if you want a keyframe Action that stops your animation right in the middle of a tween, inserting a keyframe action on the same layer as the tween will disturb your tween. Instead of just two keyframes (one at the beginning and one at the end), you'll have three keyframes. If, later in the project, you want to move the middle keyframe (where the stop occurs), you can't do it without changing the tween. Putting a stop Action on a dedicated Actions layer solves this problem. Figure 1.13 shows a real project with separate layers for Actions and labels.

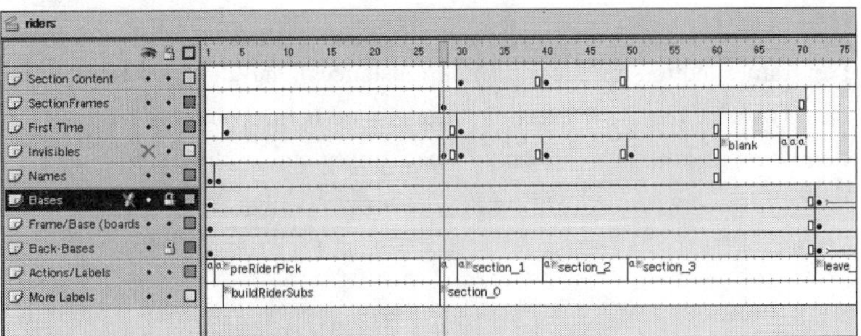

Figure 1.13 *A typical project's timeline will include layers that contain only labels and Actions.*

I have another trick that combines layers with empty Movie Clips. Empty clips are difficult to select because you need to grab a tiny white circle (shown in Figure 1.12). If you have several empty clips near each other, it can be impossible to select the correct one. To keep things organized, I often create a new layer for each empty clip (or group of clips). Because I know that when I click the layer in the timeline it will select all the contents of that layer on stage, I can quickly determine which empty clip is which by clicking the layer that I've named to match the clip. The nice thing about layers is that they don't add to the exported .swf's filesize.

Throughout this book you'll find many more tips and tricks where appropriate. I expect the tricks I've shown so far, however, are familiar if not "old hat" to you. At least make sure that you understand how they work and why they're helpful.

Summary

Depending on your past experience, this chapter was either a review, all new, or a mix thereof. In any case, this is the starting point from which we will program advanced Flash scripts. It's fair to assume that you know how to draw and animate in Flash. However, I think this chapter was a good way to get everyone oriented. If some of the material was new to you, that's fine. If it's all new to you, I suggest first reading a basic Flash book such as *Sams Teach Yourself Macromedia Flash 5 in 24 Hours,* which I wrote before this book.

The critical concepts that you really must understand to get the most out of this book include timeline hierarchies (nested clips), targeting, script locations (keyframes, button instances, and clip instances), and the coordinate system. In the "Tricks of the Trade" section, you learned helpful (but not required) information about making invisible buttons and empty movie clips. Additionally, a method to use a whole layer for keyframes containing Actions or labels was also discussed.

{ Chapter 2 }

What's New in Flash 5

Even if you're experienced in Flash 4, it's likely that some of the Flash basics covered last chapter looked unfamiliar because they're new to Flash 5. The tremendous changes in Flash 5 have made even the most proficient programmers look like dinosaurs. I think it's pretty safe to say that every minute you spend learning a new feature in Flash 5 will be generously paid back in hours of time savings. This chapter will look at the key features that make programming in Flash 5 much different (and better).

Specifically, in this chapter you'll learn the value of advanced features such as clip events, Smart Clips, external scripts, functions, and objects. Additionally, you'll undergo de-programming in which I'll help you to forget traumatic ActionScript elements such as `Tell Target` and `Eval`.

Advanced Features Making Programming Easy

There are so many new features in Flash 5 that it's hard to even start this section. Instead of describing *everything,* I'll concentrate on the benefits of each feature. The rest of the book will show you how to apply the new features, but for now let's just look at how easy our future programming in Flash will be.

Clip Events

As you saw last chapter, a new place where you can attach scripts are clip instances. On the surface, this fact simply means you're given a third place to write scripts (in addition to keyframes and button instances). But so what? The real benefit is that along with clip scripts, you're given a whole new set of clip events. This means you can have scripts that respond to previously unnoticed events. For example, you could always write a script that executed when a particular frame was reached (keyframe script) or when a button was pressed (button script), but it was impossible to make a script execute the moment that data from external variables loaded into memory. It was also impossible to write a script that executed as soon as a clip was removed from the screen! The new clip events (such as the one shown in Figure 2.1) simply provide a way to "trap" events that were impossible or required tricks to catch previously.

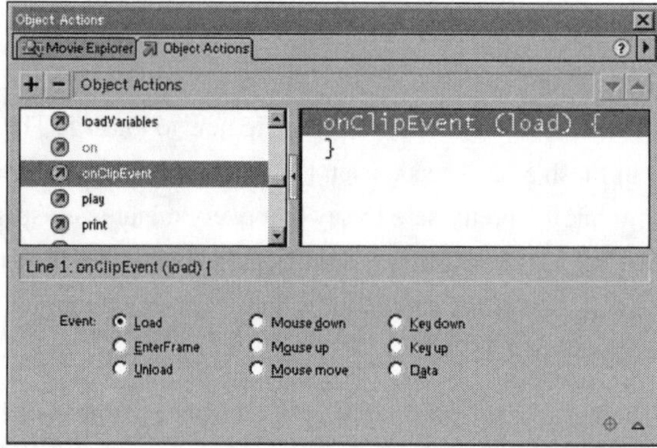

Figure 2.1 *Placing scripts on clip instances gives you access to a new set of events.*

Smart Clips

Each instance of a Movie Clip on stage maintains its own unique properties and variables. For example, the _x position of one clip instance can be different from another instance. Additionally, if you used variables within a clip, they could change independently. However, to initialize variables contained in clips required setting each variable by hand in a script.

If you try to initialize variables from within a Movie Clip, the script will be identical for each instance and therefore each instance will be initialized identically.

In Flash 4, you could be very sneaky and write a script (inside a clip) that would modify initial variables based on its own instance name. For example, clips named "init_1" and "init_3" could have the same script—effectively saying *get the fifth character in my name*—which could initialize themselves uniquely. This was a big pain and is now unnecessary in the light of Smart Clips, introduced in Flash 5. A Smart Clip is a way for you to establish that certain variables will be accessible through the Clip Parameters panel (shown in Figure 2.2). This means any homemade variable used within a clip can be set via an easy-to-use panel.

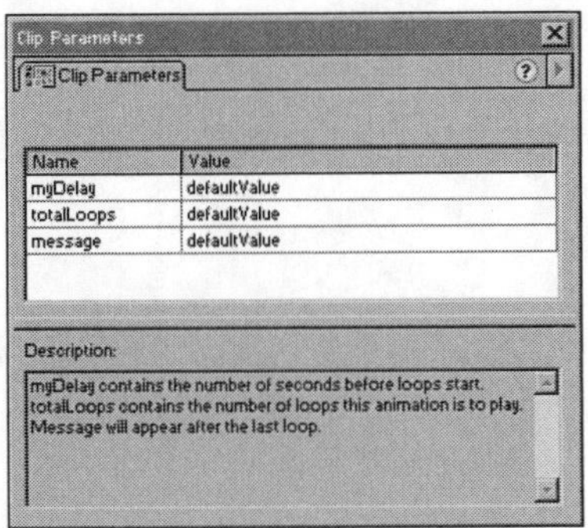

Figure 2.2 *Through the Clip Parameters panel, you can set parameters (variables) uniquely for each Smart Clip instance.*

Smart Clips can be used in several ways. I see the most immediate value as a way for you to initialize variables uniquely for each instance as described earlier. In my work, I make Smart Clips that I'll use throughout a project. However, as you'll see in great detail in Chapter 13, "Smart Clips," you can also use Smart Clips as a way to insulate certain team members from the code contained in a clip. For example, you can create a complex Smart Clip that others can simply insert from the Library, set a few parameters (that is, variables), and never need to touch the code. You can make the process even more digestible and easier by creating a Flash movie that replaces the default Clip Parameters panel as shown in Figure 2.3. More about this in Chapter 13. For now, just realize Smart Clips are a way for the author to further customize each clip instance uniquely.

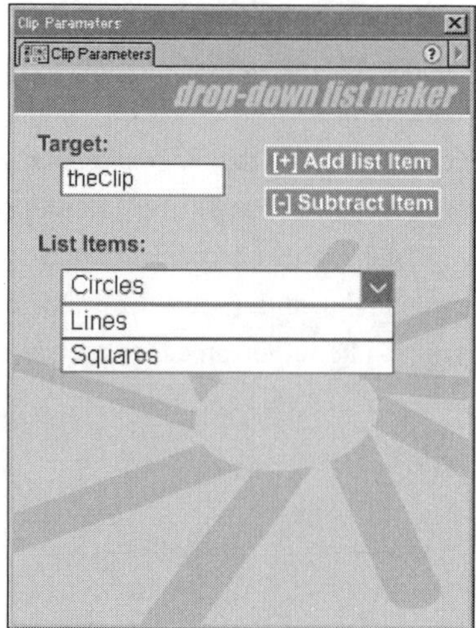

Figure 2.3 *The Clip Parameters panel can be customized with another Flash movie.*

External Scripts

Flash 5 adds a feature that enables you to keep your scripts in external files instead of embedded within your .fla file. Although the ramifications are indeed great, they're not as wonderful as you might expect because external scripts are automatically included when you export your movie (as a .swf). The process involves keeping scripts in external text files to which your .fla file points. At the time of export, the scripts are copied into the .swf. Even though this means you can distribute your .swf without needing to include the text file with the scripts, you can't make updates and fixes to your online .swf files simply by replacing the external script files.

The limitation I mention is relatively minor. The benefit of external scripts is that anywhere you would have written a script in Flash, you can instead point to an external file. In this way, several movies can point to the same file, or you can point to the same file from many places within in one movie. If you find that you want to change or fix a problem in the script, you need to do it only once—in the original external text file. It's sort of like a shared library containing a script. In Chapter 6, "Debugging," and Chapter 14, "Interfacing with External Data," you'll learn the details of this feature. In case you want to get a jump on it, the "include" Action is all you need to use to point to an external file. Macromedia suggests that you use .as (for "ActionScript") instead of .txt—but that's simply a suggestion for a convention and not required. (I've simply associated the .as extension with my favorite text editor.)

Custom Functions

Before custom functions, it was hard to call Flash a "programming language" without laughing. Functions enable you to write one script to perform the same (or a similar) task repeatedly instead of copying the same code in multiple locations. In the past, the only thing close to functions was the "call" Action. Although the "call" Action does enable you to execute a particular frame's script from anywhere in Flash (repeatedly if you want), that is only half the benefit of a function. True functions (such as Flash's built-in functions) have the ability to accept parameters and return values. If you don't know what this means, you'll be introduced to functions in Chapter 4, "Basic Programming in Flash," explore them in detail in Chapter 8, "Functions," and have plenty of practice in the Workshop portion of this book. (If you do know what "accepting parameters and returning values" means, you're probably quite excited—I know I am!)

Objects

Objects are a feature that exists almost exclusively in ActionScript—so they're difficult to visualize because they often have no physical evidence. Although objects can often seem vague or imaginary, their effects can be great. For example, when you use the Sound object you can control the volume and pan of a sound using scripting. This means at runtime a sound can change based on the user's interaction—for example, the user can use a slider to change the sound. You probably already know more about objects than you realize because clip instances are objects. Clip instances are an easy object to understand (because there is physical evidence in each instance you drag onstage) and this will make learning other objects easier. You'll get to explore objects in much more detail in Chapter 11, "Objects," and Chapter 12, "Homemade Objects."

Just to give you a preview of objects now, let me walk you through what you can do with some of Flash's built-in objects. Two of the most profound objects are the Color object and the Sound object. With the Color object, you can tint a clip instance using scripting. The Sound object enables you to start or stop a sound and control its volume or pan (among other things). The XML object is similarly powerful; it enables you to import data that's structured in XML format. This means an entire database can be easily imported and individual records and fields can be used in your movie. Another object—Date—is pretty useful because you can use it to ascertain the current time and date.

All these objects I mentioned require two steps: you first instantiate the object (by placing it into a variable) with the `new` constructor, which is the keyword to construct a new object instance, and then you can use the various methods built into the type of object. For example, the following code puts a Sound object into the homemade variable "mySound":

```
mySound = new Sound();
```

From that point, you use any of the methods (that is, functions that perform a particular effect) of the Sound object, such as:

```
mySound.attachSound("musicItem");
mySound.start();
```

Later, you could change the volume like so:

```
mySound.setVolume(40);
```

Even without understanding the code, you should understand that after the object is assigned to the variable (`mySound` in this case), you can perform the features of the object by referring to that variable. We'll cover all this in later chapters.

Some objects don't require the instantiation step (that is, the `new` constructor). Some of the predefined objects that work this way include String, Math, and Selection. Basically, you can just start using these objects without too much thought. If you need to determine the third character in a particular string, you can use `myString.charAt(2)` where `myString` contains a string and `2` is the index (location within the string) from which you want to draw the individual "character at."

Without getting into the necessary detail to *really* understand objects now, just realize there are objects that enable you to perform useful maneuvers. Those useful maneuvers include extracting a particular character (with the String object), calculating the cosine (with the Math object), and finding out which field is currently selected (with the Selection object). We'll cover much more, but feel free to snoop through the Objects section of the Actions panel to see them all.

HTML Text

The last feature we'll look at (as applied to scripting) is HTML text. Quite simply, a Dynamic Text field in Flash 5 can optionally display text formatted with HTML. Dynamic Text fields always display one variable at a time. You can write a script to change the variable and if you use *basic* HTML tags (such as `<b>` for bold), you can affect the style of the displayed text. In the past, you had to manually select the text you wanted to display as italic or bold. The problem was that this method left the text exactly as you formatted it. HTML text can change during runtime. Although it might seem cheesy to actually let the user *watch* text change, you can use this feature in very effective ways. For example, onscreen text can include the user's name within a sentence with just her name appearing in a different color. Additionally, because you can include the `<a href>` tag that creates a hyperlink, you can have links within a block of text. Compared to the old method of placing invisible buttons on top of certain words, this is a big leap forward. We won't spend a ton of time on this feature, but you will see its application in Chapter 9, "Selecting Text, Trapping Keys, and Manipulating Strings."

Previous Knowledge Worth Forgetting

It's sometimes true that the less you know, the better off you are. In the case of learning Flash 5, there is a great deal of knowledge you might have acquired in Flash 4 (or earlier) that will only get in the way. Luckily, Macromedia has officially deprecated specific elements of ActionScript; those elements are being phased out. In addition, there are elements that have lost their usefulness and, in some ways, *should* be deprecated. Finally, many techniques that might have been necessary or useful in past versions are completely unnecessary in the light of new Flash 5 features. Let's look at all three things to forget (deprecated code, code that should be deprecated, and old tricks no longer needed).

Deprecated ActionScript

Deprecated ActionScript refers to elements that are best avoided because—even though they are still supported and work fine— alternatives are available that should be used instead. It's not that the new way is necessarily better (although often it is), but rather that the old ActionScript is being phased out. Luckily the Actions panel highlights all deprecated elements in green. Another similar, and possibly confusing, feature is yellow highlights on certain ActionScript components. These are elements that aren't supported in the Flash version you're targeting. To see the yellow highlights, first select File, Publish Settings and choose Flash 4 or lower from the Flash tab. Figure 2.4 shows how you can tell which code is deprecated.

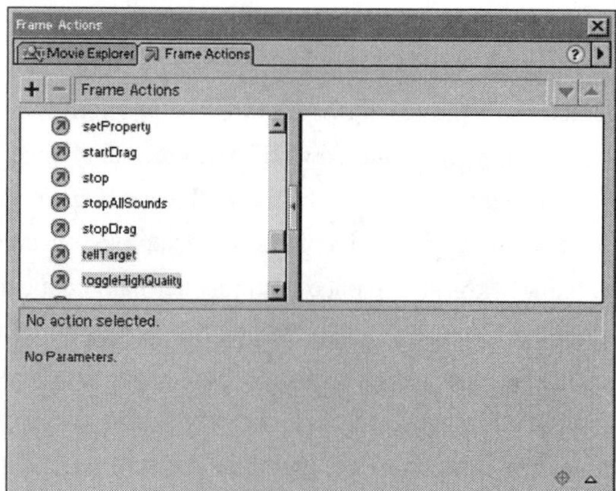

Figure 2.4 *Deprecated code is highlighted in green to clearly show which elements are being phased out.*

The first step is to recognize which ActionScript is deprecated (that's easy, it's highlighted green); the second step is to find alternatives. In the Flash help files, each deprecated element includes a reference to the replacement. You can also find a list and extensive explanation of many in Appendix A, "Equivalents." Let me point out just a few now.

The biggest deprecated element is `Tell Target`. If you don't know `Tell Target`, consider yourself lucky that you'll *never* need it. (Those with such memories, just try to forget.) To target a particular clip and "tell" it to perform an Action or other operation, you don't need anything fancy—just dot syntax. The way dot syntax works is detailed in Chapter 4, but it's so simple! For example, simply use `slideShow.gotoAndStop(10);` if you want a clip named `slideShow` to jump to frame `10`. In the past, you had to first target `slideShow`, and then (in an extra line) *tell* `slideShow` to go to frame 10, and finally remember to close the target you opened. So, generally, `Tell Target` has been deprecated in light of the fact you really don't need it! The dot syntax can be a bit unwieldy when you want to do more than one task. For example:

```
slideShow._alpha=50;
slideShow.gotoAndStop(10);
slideShow.curSlide=slideShow.curSlide+1;
```

A new Action called "with" can perform the same operation (similar to what Tell Target would have done) like so:

```
with (slideShow){
    _alpha=50;
    gotoAndStop(10);
    curSlide=curSlide+1;
}
```

Although the replacement of Tell Target is probably the most profound, a ton of mathematical and string manipulation operations are deprecated, too. For example, someNumber=int(someNumber) was used in the past to convert a number in the variable someNumber to an integer. Now there's an entire suite of math functions. Use someNumber=Math.floor(someNumber) as an alternative to int(). Even though the new alternative is no better, when you see all the other math functions, you'll like the new way much better. In Chapter 5, "Programming Structures," you'll start using the math functions.

All the string controls (functions and operators) are deprecated. Therefore, subString(), gt (greater than), and lt (less than) are all gone. In their place is a suite of string functions. Actually, the "suite of string functions" (and the math functions, for that matter) is a built-in object. You'll be introduced to objects in Chapter 5, and specifically learn how the string object works in Chapter 9. The good news is that after you learn one object type, you'll be able to apply that knowledge to any object.

There are other specific deprecated ActionScript elements. Refer to Appendix B for more.

Non-Deprecated ActionScripts That Should Be

When you really understand the dot syntax way of doing almost *everything* in Flash, you'll see that several ActionScript components are no longer needed. It's not so much that they are deprecated, but that they're superfluous. For example, "Set Variable." In the past, you first selected "Set Variable" and then entered both the name of the variable and the value you wanted to set it to. You can still use the Actions panel in this way, and I suppose there's some value to being walked through the necessary parameters (see Figure 2.5).

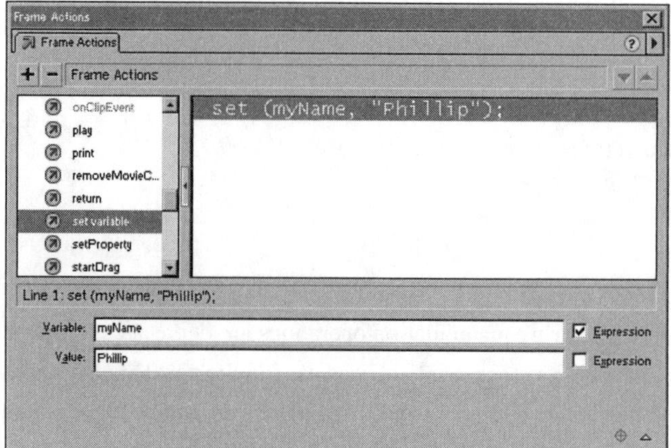

Figure 2.5 *While the Actions panel attempts to make scripting easier, it can actually get in the way.*

However, I think this approach tends to be even more complicated than just getting in there and doing it by hand! Even the resulting code is weird:

```
set ( myName, "Phillip");
```

You can much more easily write this:

```
myName="Phillip";
```

So, when you understand the purpose of "Set Variable," you won't need it because you can write the second line of code shown.

Similar to "Set Variable," the ActionScripts "Set Property" and "Get Property" are unnecessarily cumbersome. Trust me; when you see how to set and access properties of clips in Chapter 4, you'll never use these again!

One of the most powerful Actions in Flash 4 was "call." This Action enabled you to store scripts in a keyframe and then to execute that code from anywhere in the movie. As mentioned earlier, "call" has been replaced with homemade functions. Not only can functions be used in a similar way, but they can do much more.

Old Tricks That Are Old News

It's sometimes depressing to think about all the acquired technical knowledge that is eventually discarded because there's a better way. I suppose the improvements should be embraced because they're useful—but I still want to use the old techniques. Here are just a few old tricks resourceful Flash 4 programmers developed that will all be forgotten in Flash 5.

Two-Frame "Updater" Clips

To continuously monitor activity while a movie played, you could create a two-frame movie clip with an Action in frame 1 and a `gotoAndPlay(1)` in frame 2. Because you could only write scripts in keyframes and buttons, this was the only way to execute a script repeatedly (instead of waiting until the user clicked a button or reached a keyframe at the end of the timeline). This trick is no longer needed because you can now place scripts on clip instances and the new EnterFrame clip event executes 12 times a second (if the framerate is 12 fps).

The two-frame updater technique might still be convenient when you don't want to place your code on a clip instance, but it's safe to say that you don't *have* to use this old trick ever again.

Finding Cursor Position

In Flash 4, you could not ascertain the position of the user's cursor. However, you could "Get Property" of a clip instance (that is, *get* the `_x` and `_y` positions). To get around this, the resourceful Flash programmer would create an empty clip and, in the first frame of the movie, start dragging the clip. Normally, you'd expect to drag something when you clicked (that is, on press), but this trick caused the movie to be dragged at all times even though the user never clicked. This way, any time you wanted to know where the cursor was, you just got the `_x` and `_y` properties of the empty Movie Clip that was being dragged.

The new `_xmouse` and `_ymouse` properties enable you to determine the location of the cursor at any time. One little tip for using these properties: They return the position of the mouse relative to the timeline you target. For example, within a Movie Clip, `_xmouse` is counted from the center point of the clip, but from the `_root` timeline, the top left is used as the origin. Review targeting and the coordinate system from Chapter 1, "Flash Basics," if necessary. The "Custom Cursor" workshop covers this technique.

Eval for Pseudo Arrays

Even though `eval()` is not entirely useless, nor is it deprecated, the most common way it *used* to be used is no longer necessary. Flash 5 supports arrays, meaning that you can store many bits of information into one variable. In Flash 4, each variable could contain only one value. Therefore, if you needed a lot of different numbers saved, you needed lots of different variables. To keep track of the variables, you could name them logically, such as "loc_1," "loc_2," "loc_3." Then you could refer to them logically by using an expression such as `"loc_"&curLoc` (where if "curLoc" were 1, you'd get `"loc_1"`). Because it wasn't the *name* `"loc_1"` that you were looking for, but rather the value, you needed to evaluate the expression, like this: `eval("loc_"&curLoc)` (In Flash 4, the ampersand "&" was used to concatenate a string; Flash 5 uses the plus "+".) The fact that you can simply store all the values in one variable (an array such as `allLocs=[100,125,175]`, for example) has all but eliminated the need for `eval()`. You can extract any element in an array by index (that is, slot in the array). You'll learn all about arrays in Chapter 10, "Arrays." In Chapter 4, you'll see how placing an expression between the brackets next to an associative array will effectively do an `eval()` on the expression. For example, `_root ["clip_"+curNum]` will refer to a clip named `clip_1` (if `curNum` is `1`). Note this refers to the *value* that is the clip itself—not just the name of the clip, as `"clip_"+curNum` by itself would. I just wanted to demonstrate that `eval()` was no longer needed—you can learn more details about this in later chapters.

Summary

The changes in Flash 5 are so great that I could probably extend this chapter endlessly. However, I just wanted to walk through the elements directly related to scripting—all of which you'll see later. If you consider yourself a proficient programmer in Flash 4, review this chapter as needed. If you're new to Flash, just consider yourself lucky!

{ Chapter 3 }

The Programmer's Approach

This chapter might appear to be the most ambiguous and vague in the book. However, it's probably the most valuable chapter because it can save you time. Effective programming requires more than just brute force, math skills, and technical ability (which are all important); you must also be efficient. For any programming task, you can do it the hard way or you can do it the easy way. This chapter will help you find the easy way. I don't want to suggest that there are always shortcuts that make anything easy. Only that avoiding overly complex solutions can save you a lot of grief.

This chapter explains conventional programming philosophies to help you

- Write specifications
- Prototype your creations quickly for initial review
- Develop good style
- Keep code and data separate

Specification

It might sound cavalier, but after you finish a detailed specification, 95% of your work is through. When a client asks me whether something is possible, I always answer that if he can describe it in detail, I can program it. That's all a specification is—a detailed description of exactly how the Flash movie is to appear and perform. A good specification can take a lot of time and work, but when it's finished it serves as the blueprint from which to work. It's like creating an outline for a term paper. After you know where you're headed, it's just a matter of filling in the outline.

One person's idea of the necessary level of detail might vary from another's. But the more detail, the better. When you invest additional work upfront, it not only saves time down the road, but it reduces the chances of rework because everyone involved presumably reads the "spec" and raises necessary objections early. Another value of a specification is that it makes estimating total cost easier because the task is clearer.

As you'll see in the following section on prototyping, the problem in writing a super-detailed specification is that you will fail to fully describe the final program because a written spec's form is different from the final media. That is, it's impossible to describe the colors in a painting using just words or the sound of a song without some kind of musical device—there's a translation error. This doesn't mean you should simply forgo the specification process entirely. Rather, just write enough detail to get rolling. In addition, be sure to leverage previous work of your own, and the work of others. For example, part of your specification might say that you're going to build something "like the project we did last year," but with these differences. Do whatever you need to make it clear. Include tables, figures, and pictures—whatever helps.

Writing specifications takes practice. An interesting exercise to improve your specification writing skills is to go back and look at any description or specification you were given early in a project that is now finished. Identify the types of details that were missing or would have helped were they given to you. Without providing a lesson on how to write specifications, let me simply say those details make a big difference.

Prototyping

A good specification makes you more efficient because it defines the course you'll take before you start. Even though this means that you want to wait to start programming, there is one type of programming that can start early, even while you write the specification: prototyping. A *prototype* is a quick and dirty sample that's created in Flash simply to get an idea of how the final project might look and feel. No matter how great a specification on paper might be, it will never compare to the real thing. It's sort of like learning to fly an airplane. You can read all the books, use a flight simulator, even hang out at the airport—but eventually, you'll have to actually go up in the airplane and fly! Prototypes are the best "simulation" of your final movie because they are produced in Flash.

One way to produce a great site involves first roughly defining the objectives and then starting the prototyping right away. You make a few quick prototypes and then analyze the results. Let everyone play with the prototypes so that they can get a feel for the direction the site is taking. Then go back to the drawing board and elaborate on your specification. This cyclical process (defining, prototyping, redefining, and so on) might seem slightly inefficient, but it usually results in a better end product.

If ever there were a place where being sloppy is alright, it is while prototyping. The goal while prototyping is to quickly get something up and running. The prototype doesn't have to be pretty. Just check out Figure 3.1, which shows an early prototype of part of a larger project.

Figure 3.1 *A prototype doesn't have to be pretty—it just has to communicate the idea. You can even use a picture of your dog as a placeholder.*

Your prototypes will not only look rough, but you can allow the programming to slip a bit, too. Let's look at a few prototyping techniques that—during any other stage of programming—could be considered bad style.

Hard Wiring

Hard wiring is generally a big no-no. *Hard wiring* is using an explicit value instead of a variable or reference to other values. For example, imagine that your program is supposed to display a message "Welcome <User>," where "<User>" would be replaced by whatever name the user used when logging in. Instead of actually doing the work to display the user's name dynamically, you could hard wire the screen to read "Welcome Phillip" and then any time you demonstrate the prototype, you make sure to log in as "Phillip." Of course, if you logged in differently, the program would still display "Welcome Phillip" because it's hard wired. This is perfectly acceptable because likely everyone can just imagine how this will work in the final project. Sometimes you'll want your prototype to really do the work—especially if you're sending the prototype to a client who might not understand that it's just a prototype. Depending on who is judging the prototype, you can do more or less hard wiring as appropriate. Just remember the term "hard wiring" because in later chapters I'll refer to it as a bad thing—ideally everything is dynamic.

Pseudo-Code

Unlike hard wiring, pseudo-coding is always a good thing. The only problem is that you'll need to replace all your pseudo-code eventually. Pseudo-coding is the process of writing scripts using your own words, not the ActionScript language, as instructions. Then you can replace your completed pseudo-code with components of ActionScript. The truth is that really detailed and clear pseudo-code can be quickly and easily translated to functioning ActionScript. I often say that if you can pseudo-code well, you can get a monkey to clean it up ("cross all the *T*s and dot all the *I*s," as it were). You might find that you can clearly state what you want your interactive movie to do, but you need help from an experienced programmer to translate your pseudo-code. But the process of pseudo-coding actually makes you a better programmer by forcing you to sort out the details of the task you're solving.

Pseudo-code should be very detailed and written in clear English. That is, you want to say *everything* necessary, but you don't need to use any words from the ActionScript language. For example, imagine you plan to program a button that will convert a dollar amount from one field and display the equivalent value in Euros in another field. (By the way, the preceding description is suitable as part of a specification—it provides enough information to start programming.) The pseudo-code for such a button might look like this:

```
When user presses button
    dollars=text in field
    exchangeRate=.5
    euros=dollars multiplied by exchangeRate
    euros=euros rounded off to two decimal places
    put euros into another field
end
```

After you know a little bit of ActionScript, you can easily translate this pseudo-code into a working script. The first step, however, is to sort things out in your own words.

Good Style

If this chapter is ambiguous, this section is downright subjective. *Good style* means programming in a way that's easy to maintain. Your code should be easy enough for anyone to understand. Not because others need to see what you've programmed (which could happen), but so that you can quickly interpret what you've produced when you need to make adjustments or fix bugs. It's easy to get carried away trying to build something and ignore good housekeeping practices. Before you know it, your code resembles a plate of spaghetti (hence the term *spaghetti code*). In fact, haste makes waste, so you should always try to follow the rules of good style.

Even though the value of good style is easy to understand, the concept itself is subjective. Here are a few characteristics of good style; call them *rules* if you want.

Less Is More

Consider that every line of code you read has to be translated in your mind. You have to figure out what it really means. The fewer lines you must read the better. Generally, any time you can do something in fewer steps or less code—do it. It's almost never too late to use less code. For example, I often start programming and then come up with a better (more concise) solution while implementing the original idea. Even if it means going back and starting over, it's usually worth the resulting compact code. Compare the two code segments in Figures 3.2 and 3.3—both achieve the same effect, but the code in Figure 3.3 is much more concise.

```
on (release) {
 setProperty ("highlight", _x, getProperty ("highlight", _x )+10);
 tellTarget ("highlight") {
  gotoAndStop (getProperty("",_currentFrame)+1);
 }
}
```

Figure 3.2

```
on (release) {
 highlight._x+=10;
 highlight.nextFrame();
}
```

Figure 3.3 *The script in Figure 3.2 achieves the same effect as the script in Figure 3.3, but with unnecessary complexity.*

You can take this rule too far. The appeal of concise code should not outweigh legibility. It's easy to get carried away and end up with code you can't even read. I would never fault a finished piece of code that worked—so, really, that's the number one priority. Second, your code must be maintainable by you. Remember to write code that you can read. For example, in Chapter 4, "Basic Programming in Flash," you'll learn that `count++;` is equivalent to `count=count+1;` Although the latter takes more typing, it might be easier for you to read. By all means, use what you understand. If this occasionally means that your code is a little bit wordier, so be it. Take it one step at a time and you should see your code shrinking in size.

Comments

Comments are lines of code that are ignored by Flash. Text preceded by `//` is ignored. Actually, if you start a block of text with `/*`, all lines are ignored until `*/` is reached. The idea is that you can write notes to yourself (or anyone reading your code) that explain—in normal English—what's going on in the code. Actually, you'll often find that comments help you discover bugs. You might see a comment that says `//loop through all the answers` and then notice that the code doesn't really do that!

I suppose that I'm a bad boy because I often don't fully comment my code until right after I get a program running. However, it's important for me not to delay this step because I will forget everything about the code days after writing it. Without comments, code is much more difficult to interpret. So, just take the time to comment your code, even if it's after you've finished and when the incentive to do so is reduced. Compare the uncommented code in Figure 3.4 to the same code with comments in Figure 3.5. Even though you might not understand the details of the code, if there were a problem, you could easily identify the portion containing the problem.

```
onClipEvent (keyUp) {
    if (Key.getAscii() == 13 | Key.getAscii() == 0) {
        return;
    }
    if (Key.getAscii() == 8) {
        if (cur.charAt( cur.length-2)==" "){
            _root.wordsThisTime--;
        }
        cur = cur.slice(0, cur.length-2)+mbchr(8);
        if (_root.wrongPlaces[_root.place-1] == "X") {
            _root.wrongPlaces.pop();
            _root.wrongs--;
        }
        _root.place>0 && _root.place--;
        return;
    }
}
```

Figure 3.4

```
onClipEvent (keyUp) {
    //ignore these characters
    if (Key.getAscii() == 13 | Key.getAscii() == 0) {
        return;
    }

    // if they click backspace
    if (Key.getAscii() == 8) {
        //remove a blank space?
        if (cur.charAt( cur.length-2)==" "){
            _root.wordsThisTime--;
        }
        //remove the last character (but put the box at the end)
        cur = cur.slice(0, cur.length-2)+mbchr(8);

        // did they fix a mistake?
        if (_root.wrongPlaces[_root.place-1] == "X") {
            _root.wrongPlaces.pop();
            _root.wrongs--;
        }
        // set place back one
        _root.place>0 && _root.place--;

        //and leave
        return;
    }
}
```

Figure 3.5 *Before being commented, the code in Figure 3.4 is difficult to understand. Figure 3.5 shows how a few comments can make things clearer, even if you don't understand the underlying code.*

Finally, comments are of great assistance while creating a prototype. Instead of building *everything,* you can simply place a comment that says something like `//check their answers here` and then come back later to actually write the code that does. This technique also exposes errors in logic flow. Remember that specifying exactly what a Flash movie is supposed to do is most of the work. A comment can be a way of specifying the tasks that need to be implemented.

Magic Numbers, Constants, and Variables

A "magic number" is an explicit value used within a formula. For example, to calculate the page count for any chapter in this book, I use this formula: characters/1900=pages. I know there are approximately 1900 characters per printed page. Of course, if the margins or page size were different I'd have to use a different magic number than 1900 in my formula. An example of a constant is pi. To calculate the area of a circle, use pi times radius squared (πr^2). Generally, magic numbers should be avoided because they're dangerous. At a minimum, they should be commented.

Consider what happens if I use my magic number for characters per page in many places and then the book layout changes—maybe we change the paper size. I would need to replace every instance of 1900 with the new number. The ultimate solution in this case is to use a variable (discussed in Chapter 4) like a constant. At the very beginning of my movie, I could establish a variable "charsPerPage" as 1900 (`charsPerPage=1900;`). Then, instead of using `1900` in several locations, I could use `charsPerPage` instead of my constant. If `charsPerPage` were to change, every instance would reflect the change. Compare magic numbers to a `gotoAndPlay(2)` Action (where 2 is the magic number). A better solution is to use a frame label (which you can think of as a constant), as in `gotoAndPlay("loopFrame")`. If you move the "loopFrame" label, you won't need to go and fix your scripts in any way.

It's very easy to think a magic number will *never* need to change, so it doesn't seem worth the effort to create a variable that can be used like a constant. In reality, magic numbers are not evil. It just takes a bit of foresight to realize whether such a number could potentially change—in which case, you should use a variable instead.

Repeated Code

To put it simply: Every programming task should appear only once in your movie. If you have the same code in two places, that means you'll have twice the work to make updates or fix bugs. You'll learn ways to achieve this—such as keeping scripts in the library, in functions, or external to the movie itself—but for now, just make sure that anytime you copy and paste code, a bell rings in your head to notify you there must be a better way.

You'll probably develop more techniques that exemplify good style. Remember, it's subjective and based on personal preference. Although there are definitely methods that *should* be employed by all programmers, you only need to acquire skills as you become comfortable. I know that if I looked at anything I programmed even just a few months ago, I'd question the approach I took—but that's because I'm always improving. If you waited until your skills were perfect, you'd be waiting a long time. Just jump in, but take the time to be self-critical so that you can improve.

Code Data Separation

All programmers should strive to keep code (that is, the programming scripts) separate from the data (or the project-specific content such as text and graphics). By keeping code separate from data, you enable all your programming efforts to transfer easily to other projects. Similarly, when you want to make a major change to the content—say, redo the entire project in a different language—you just need to replace data without touching (or breaking) the code. It's a great concept that is sometimes difficult to achieve.

Imagine a factory that produces furniture with a wide selection of fabric upholstery. Likely the upholstery (think "data") is kept separate from the furniture and padding (think "code") until an order is placed. The benefit of code data separation (in this analogy) is that the factory can easily produce furniture as its customers request it and never have additional stock that's already upholstered. Applying this to Flash isn't much different. Assume that your Flash site has graphic buttons that display a floating tool tip whenever the user places his cursor over the button. If you kept the code (the script that makes the tool tip appear) separate from the data (the actual text or words that appear in the tool tip), you could easily translate this to another language by replacing the text for the tool tips. Ideally, you would keep *all* the text for all the tool tips in one location to make translation that much easier. The main idea is that you want to be able to make significant changes to either the code or data without affecting the other.

You can think of code data separation as a form of modularization. There are other forms of modularization—including Flash's `LoadMovie()`, which enables you to play separate .swf files within a larger movie. Modularization has many benefits in addition to those mentioned for code data separation. For one thing, by modularizing your Flash movie, users won't have to wait for the entire site to download. They can selectively download just the portions in which they are interested. Also, modularizing makes working with others easy and efficient. Consider that if you just had one master file for the entire site, only one person could work at a time. So, there are a ton of benefits to code data separation and other kinds of modularization. Without providing a lot of details now, just realize that throughout this book I'll try to emphasize solutions that exhibit such modular attributes.

Summary

This chapter explored the attributes that make up the "programmer way." In my experience, it seems that programmers tend to fit the same profile. For example, they often work in darkened offices that lack windows and subsist on soft drinks.

You don't have to become a geek to be a good programmer. Just concentrate on the approach discussed in this chapter. Try to develop a good style by striving to write concise code with lots of comments and avoid magic numbers and repeated code. Realize, too, that your programming style should continually improve. The best programmers in the world know they have room to improve further.

The process you undertake can also make programming easier (and better). Creating a specification and quickly producing prototypes might seem like additional up-front work, but they will save you time later. Finally, always try to separate code from data. In no time, you'll start "feeling it" and before you know it, you can call yourself a "programmer" with pride.

{ Chapter 4 }

Basic Programming in Flash

Although you don't have to know traditional programming concepts to use ActionScript, they will help you greatly in Flash. If you're experienced in another programming language, this chapter might look familiar to you. Flash's ActionScript language is based on the same standard used by JavaScript (called *ECMA-262**). As such, many aspects are similar or identical. This chapter is a good introduction for both experienced programmers as well as those with basic Flash skills. I'll explain some general programming concepts, but with specific attention to how they apply to Flash.

In this chapter, you will

- Learn basic programming terms
- Recognize built-in script elements
- Get an overview of traditional concepts such as variables and data types

Terminology, Special Characters, and Formatting

The terms and rules in programming are very strict. This can actually be helpful. Unlike in English where the meaning of a sentence can be ambiguous or vague,

---

**ECMA stands for The European Computers Manufacturers Association (see* `www.ecma.ch`*).*

in programming there are absolutes. After you fully understand what a "property" is, for example, you never need to wonder what kind of property—as you would with the word *property* in English, which has multiple meanings. Not only do terms in programming have absolute meanings, but they're usually closely related to the word's meaning in English. Be careful though: Sometimes your first impression of a term could carry special meaning to you that is unrelated to the true meaning. Luckily, most terms are very easy to learn.

Events

Everything that happens in Flash is the result of an event that causes a script to execute. Even for such a simple example as the user clicking a button that causes the movie to skip ahead, the instructions (to skip ahead) resulted from the click "mouse event."

There are three types of events in Flash: keyframes, mouse events, and clip events. Notice that these correlate to the three places you can place scripts (keyframes, button instances, and clip instances). If a script is placed in a keyframe, the script will execute as soon as Flash reaches the keyframe. In the case of buttons, you must always specify the mouse event to which you want to respond. Similarly, scripts on clip instances need to include a clip event. Figure 4.1 shows the available mouse events and clip events.

I like to think of an event as the wrapper of the scripts that it contains. Consider that you can't just have a `stop()` Action attached to a button—it must be wrapped within a mouse event. I suppose that it makes sense to think the `stop()` Action *follows* the mouse event. But because you can have several Actions follow one event (maybe the button causes both `stop()` and `stopAllSounds()` to execute), you need some indication of where the event ends. In Flash, the event wrapper starts with an opening curly bracket (`{`) and ends with a closing curly bracket (`}`). Sort of like a "script sandwich" with two curly brackets for bread and scripts in the middle. Even if that corny analogy doesn't help, you should see that scripts are wrapped inside events. (See Figure 4.2.)

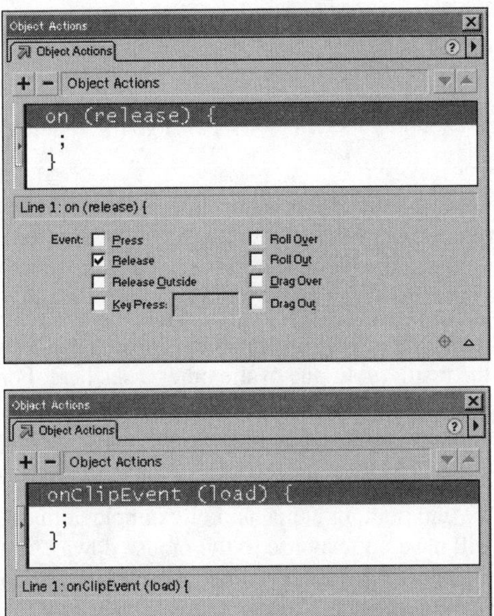

Figure 4.1 *The mouse events (for buttons) on the top and the clip events (for clips) on the bottom include all the events available in Flash.*

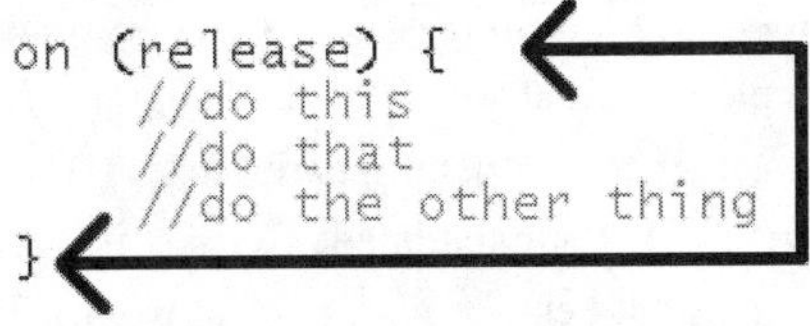

Figure 4.2 *Everything between the two curly brackets will be performed when the event occurs.*

Results of Events

After an event happens, a script is executed. The instructions that Flash follows can range from simple to complex. Let's start by thinking about the results of events in very general terms. First, we'll look at the five types of tasks that happen as the result of an event:

- One: A script can do something that is invisible or unimportant to the user (such as add to a counter that is tracking how many times a button is clicked).
- Two: The script can do something visual (such as change the rotation of a movie clip).
- Three: The script can trigger another script to execute—effectively behaving like a homemade event. Perhaps the script attached to one button causes another script to rotate a movie clip. In this way, several buttons can trigger the same "rotate the clip" script and your code can be modularized.
- Four: Scripts can "ask" other scripts for information (the part that's said to be "returned") and use the result to do one of the other tasks here. For example, one script could ascertain the current exchange rate from another script and use that information to translate a price from yen to dollars.
- Finally, the fifth result of an event is nothing. That might seem funny, but events happen all the time and nothing happens. For example, a linear movie with no buttons will have no response to the mouse down event (despite the fact that it happened). It's kind of like a tree falling in a deserted forest. That's an event despite whether anyone reacts to it.

Terms

We can't go much further without defining a few terms.

Syntax

Syntax is the way any sentence is organized. In programming, a "sentence of code" is called a *statement*. The syntax, or the form of your statements, must adhere to strict syntax rules. One simple rule (that works in English, too) is that any parenthetical statement that you start with an opening parenthesis ("(") must be followed by a closing parenthesis (")"). If your statement's syntax isn't correct, your code will perform unexpectedly (at best) or not at all (at worst). There are many ways that Flash helps you follow perfect syntax.

While in Normal Mode, the Actions panel will all but ensure that your syntax is perfect. Actually, as soon as your statement contains an error, it is highlighted in bright red. An explanatory message appears to guide you along. Figure 4.3 shows a statement that isn't complete. Remember that even after your syntax is perfected, it doesn't mean your Flash movie will play the way you want it to. The script could still contain logical errors. The first step is to get the syntax fixed, and then you can ensure that it performs correctly.

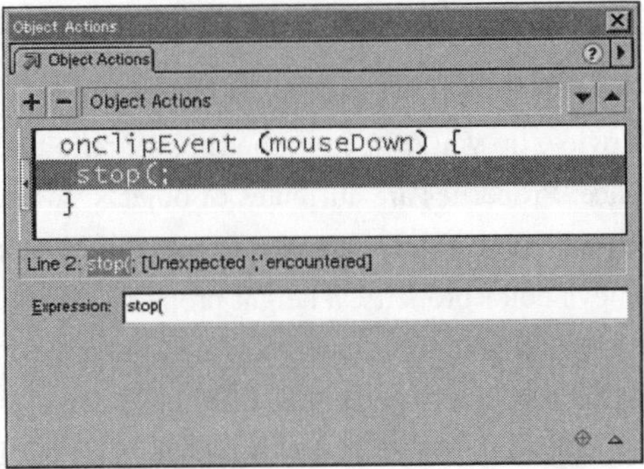

Figure 4.3 *While editing your script, errors are highlighted while typing.*

Another way that Flash helps you produce perfect syntax is by color-coding certain terms. The Colored Syntax option in the Action panel's Options menu is a great way to learn to type (and spell) terms correctly. Keywords and identifiers (which, for now, simply consider built-in terms of ActionScript) are colored blue. Properties (such as `_x` and `_y` or `_currentFrame`) are always green (not highlighted green the way deprecated ActionScript is, but the text itself is green). Comments (which are ignored by Flash to provide you a way to write notes to yourself or others reading your code) are always pink. Finally, anything you type between quotation marks is gray. This is particularly useful because you must remember to end any quotations you start (just like parenthetical statements). If you start a quotation, everything that follows will turn gray until you type another quotation mark. You'll find out more about keywords, properties, comments, and strings later this chapter.

I wanted to mention the Colored Syntax feature because it's a great way to learn. For example, when you look through someone else's finished code, it's easy to separate the elements that are built-in to Flash (they'll be blue) from the code that's created by the programmer (left in black). Additionally, if you want to type a particular property but are unsure of your spelling, you can tell you've typed it correctly when it turns green. Possibly the most frustrating syntax rule in Flash is that all keywords are case sensitive. For example, `goToAndPlay(2)` won't work (only `gotoAndPlay(2)` will work). Throughout this book you'll see many places where syntax is important. Colored Syntax is just one little helper available to you.

Objects, Instances, Instance Names, and Properties

In Flash, there are many types of objects, but the easiest kind to understand are Movie Clip instances. Every Movie Clip you drag from the Library onto the Stage becomes a separate instance. Properties are attributes of objects. In real life, you could compare properties of objects to personal attributes and characteristics of people. People have an eye color property, a height property, a weight property, and so on. If you have two instances onstage, they're both based on the original master symbol but each is most likely positioned differently—that is, they'll have different _x and _y properties. Not only can you change properties of individual clip instances while editing, but through scripting you can change each instance's properties at runtime. This is easiest if the clip instance has been given an instance name (via the Instance panel). In pseudo-code, you'd say something like this: *Set the _x property of the instance named "box_1."* Just remember that it's the instance name that matters (not the master name in the Library).

After you fully understand how to access clip instance properties, it will be easy to understand other objects. In Chapter 7, "The Movie Clip Object," you'll learn how to access instance properties. You will use the same techniques in Chapters 9, "Selecting Text, Trapping Keys, and Manipulating Strings," 10, "Arrays," and 11, "Objects," to control the sound object, string object, and color object (among others). Finally, in Chapter 12, "Homemade Objects," you'll create your own objects. The reason the Movie Clip is so much easier to understand is that it's the only object that you can see and touch. All the other objects are just as real, but you'll never grab one with your mouse or see it onscreen. It's sort of like how you can have a picture in your mind. Think of a physical printed photograph as the Movie Clip object—you can fold it, frame it, hang it on the wall. Now, consider a picture in your mind as any of the other objects. Even though there's no physical evidence, you can still manipulate the picture in your mind—picture it being folded, framed, and so on.

Statements, Expressions, and Operators

The entire block of text in the Actions panel is a script, where each line is a statement. As mentioned earlier, statements are "sentences of code." It's not so critical if you interchange the terms *script* and *statement*. But if a statement of code is like an entire sentence in speech, an expression is like a phrase. In speech, you might use the phrase *slow as molasses*. First of all, you'd create an entire sentence (a statement) such as *His computer is slow as molasses*. You can see that the expression (or phrase) is only part of the statement.

Expressions in Flash are evaluated. For example, an entire statement might read: `halfprice=price/2`. The part on the right of the equal sign is an expression and it will be evaluated (that is, a result will be placed in that spot). If it helps, think of evaluated expressions as having "math" done on them. Now, imagine that "slow as molasses" is an actual speed (say 1 mile-per-hour). If you evaluated the expression, you'd be left with the result "1 MPH." The original sentence would become *His computer is 1 MPH*. This analogy is beginning to fall apart, but it's a good way to learn about statements and expressions (plus the terms *evaluate* and *result*).

Finally, operators perform specific (usually math) operations. They always need at least one number, called an *operand*, on which to work. For instance, "+" is an operator that performs addition. The "+" addition operator requires two operands to work. Get it? There's the operator (doing the work) and the operands (getting work done on them). The thing to remember is that operators are used within expressions. Therefore, they're evaluated and their results appear in their place. For example, saying `whatever=2+2` is the same as saying `whatever=4`. The expression on the right is evaluated and turns into 4. This might seem simple. Just think of expressions morphing into their results.

Operators are pretty easy to understand when you consider familiar math operators (such as multiplication "*", division "/", subtraction "-", for example). Others aren't so easy to figure out and might even seem arbitrary. For example, one deceptively useful operator uses the percent sign ("%"), but not to calculate a percent. It's called the *modulo* operator and results in the remainder of two numbers. `10%2` is evaluated into `0`. Ten divided by 2 has 0 for a remainder. This can be useful to determine whether a number is odd or even (or evenly divisible by any other number, for that matter)—that is, if the number % 2 is 0, it's an even number because it's evenly divisible by 2. Anyway, I don't recommend memorizing all the operators. We'll use many of them in the Workshop section especially when we make sliders and the currency exchange calculator. However, after you understand the form—that operators create an expression that's evaluated and they always require at least one operand—you can learn them gradually.

Actions and Functions

In Flash, "Actions" have many meanings. I think it's best to think of Actions as Flash-unique commands that execute specific tasks. For example, the `stop()` Action is a command that causes the playback head to stop. The `gotoAndPlay("framelabel")` Action is another command that jumps to a frame number or label and plays. These Actions do things specific to Flash. However, the Actions panel lists many "Actions" that are, technically, statements (or elements of statements). Figure 4.4 shows some Actions that are really statements. For example, `if` is a piece of code that creates a statement. You have to specify additional details (such as, "if *what*?"), but `if` was around way before Flash—and in my book, it's a statement. For the sake of understanding, I'll try to avoid the term "Actions" completely.

Keep in mind that although the term "Actions" is made up, Actions behave in a consistent manner. All the Actions in Flash are one of two types. They're either specific Flash commands (such as `stop`, `duplicateMovieClip`, and `play`), or they are statements (such as `if` or `break`). (Actually, you'll learn in the next chapter that a more common name for many actions is *method.*) Many Actions (of either type) need additional parameters provided—for instance, `gotoAndPlay()` requires a frame label or number. Another consistent attribute of all Actions is that they're never evaluated; they do things. Actions have consequences (and to avoid confusion, don't call them results). The script you create using Actions doesn't morph into a result the way expressions do. Actions simply "do things." Either they help construct a statement or they do a Flash-unique task.

Flash's built-in functions are easy to confuse with Actions, but they are different in a profound way. A function always returns a value. That is, a built-in function's job is to calculate an answer. Similar to how an expression is evaluated, a function "returns" a value which, in turn, is placed where the function was called. For example, the function `getTimer()` returns the total number of milliseconds elapsed since the movie started. It's almost like a "what time is it?" function. But consider if you asked someone, "What time is it?" That person might look at her watch, but unless she "returns" the answer, you might never know what time it is. Similarly, if you just wrote the script `getTimer()`, it would be meaningless. The `getTimer()` would turn into a number—maybe 10200, but so what? If, however, you wrote `elapsedTime=getTimer()/1000 + " seconds"`, the `getTimer()` part would turn into 10200 and the expression on the right side of the equation would evaluate as "10.2 seconds."

All the built-in functions behave this way. Consider these real-life activities as Actions: drive a car, stop the car, fill the car with gas. Now consider these as functions: get today's price of gas, determine how many liters fit in my 20-gallon gas tank, determine how many yen are equal to 10 dollars. The functions always result in an answer (which can be used within a bigger calculation). Notice, too, that some functions just provide an answer (such as "getTimer" or "get today's price of gas"). However, other functions (such as "convert gallons to liters") require additional data to be provided (that is, "How many gallons?"). In these cases, you need to provide a parameter.

Figure 4.4 *All the "Actions" in Flash are actually a mix of statements and Flash-unique commands.*

In Chapter 8, "Functions," you'll learn all about functions—both the built-in functions and homemade functions. For now, just understand Flash Actions are either Flash-unique commands (also called *methods*) or statements, and that built-in functions always return values. The big difference is that an Action can be used by itself and a function is always used within a larger script.

Special Characters and Formatting

As part of the many syntax rules in Flash, certain characters have special meaning. Additionally, the layout or format of your scripts must follow some rules. Parentheses are a perfect example of this point. Any parenthetical statement must start with an opening parenthesis and must always end with a closing parenthesis. The reason this is important is that you can have nested parentheses like this: `((6+2)*3)/2`, which results in 12. That's different than `6+((2*3)/2)`, which is 9. The innermost expressions are evaluated first, followed by expressions in outer parentheses. The point is that anything you start, you have to finish. For example, `((6+2)*3/2` will cause an error because there's an extra open parenthesis.

There are identical rules for quotation marks (`"`), brackets (`[` and `]`), and curly brackets (`{` and `}`). Quotation marks are a little different because apostrophes will work the same as quotation marks. This way you can nest quotations in quotations. You can't mix and match, however. For example, all of these are legitimate:

```
"This is 'cool' "

'Flash version "5" is better than "4"'

"Phillip's dog is named Max."
```

But these won't work:

```
"What you "start" you have to "finish""

"Mixing will not work'
```

It's interesting because in the case of `"Phillip's dog..."`, you might think that the apostrophe would cause problems. It works fine, however. Also, nested quotation marks are different than nested parentheses. You can have two open parentheses in a row, and as long as you close what you open, they will work fine. However, two quotation marks in a row will cause Flash to think that the second one is closing what the first one opened. So, if you have to nest quotations in quotations, you must use quotations for one and apostrophes for the other. (By the way, the curly, or "smart," quotation marks “ and ” won't work in the Actions panel.)

Generally, spaces and return characters (at the end of a line) are ignored by Flash. If you start a parenthetical statement and close it five lines later, there's no problem. Because you can't simply create a new line to represent a new thought, every line of code can be terminated with a semicolon. For example, look at this piece of code:

```
if (age>18){
    voter=1;
    draftable=1;
}
```

Even though we haven't looked at the if-statement yet, you can see that the open curly bracket is followed (three lines later) by a closing curly bracket. Also, there are two separate lines of code, each ending with a semicolon. Actually, the following is totally legitimate:

```
if (age>18){voter=1;draftable=1;}
```

The first example was easier to read. In either case, the semicolon clearly ended individual statements. Occasionally you can be sloppy and, based on context, Flash will figure out what you intended, but it's best to deliberately use semicolons to end each line.

Finally, one of the best character sequences to learn is the double forward slash `//`, which creates a comment. Comments are ignored by Flash, so you can write anything you want. You can use comments as notes to yourself (or anyone else who might be viewing your code). The phrase "commenting your code" means that you include all the information necessary to make sense of your code through comments. Also, comments are useful to cause Flash to temporarily ignore part of your code—effectively removing the code, but leaving it so that you can restore it easily.

Everything that follows `//` is ignored. You'll see the commented text turn pink, which makes it very easy to recognize. The following code sample includes comments:

```
//This button makes the movie stop
on (release) {
    stop(); //don't go any further
}
```

Normally, comments automatically end at the end of a line. (Notice that there's no "closing" comment mark in the code.) However, you can use `/*` to start a block of comments that will continue until a `*/` is reached.

```
/* Comments:
    This is a comment.
    This is another comment.
*/
```

We'll encounter other special formatting and new terms throughout this book, but this should give you a good start. Now, with the terms and other technical matters out of the way, we can move on to variables and how to use them.

Data Types and Variables

It's difficult if not impossible to discuss either data types or variables without mentioning the other. We'll discuss both here.

Variables' Names and Values

Variables are a way that you can safely—yet temporarily—store data. Think of variables as individual whiteboards. You can write someone's phone number on one whiteboard and refer to it later. You can easily change the phone number on the whiteboard. Variables are similar in that you can store information in a variable for later reference or change it any time. You can have as many variables as you choose. To return to our whiteboard analogy, you could have one for phone number and one for address. Every variable has two parts: a *name*, so that you can keep track of which variable is which, and a *value*, or what is stored in the variable. For example, the name of our phone number whiteboard (or variable) could be "phonenumber," but the value might be "800-555-1212." To assign the value of `phonenumber`, you could write the script `phonenumber="800-555-1212"` (which, translated, reads "the variable named phonenumber is assigned the value "800-555-1212"). We'll discuss variables at length later in this chapter, but you really just need the concepts of value and name first.

String and Number Data Types

The type of data that is stored in a variable's value is important. The type of data that goes into a variable can be one of many types. Just as you can store paper in an envelope, you can also store paper clips, money, even sand. This concept is easiest to understand when you compare two common data types: string and number.

A string is always expressed between quotation marks. "Phillip", "David", and "Kerman" are all strings. (Remember that we're talking about the values contained in a variable—not the variable's name.) You can do interesting maneuvers with strings, such as converting them to all uppercase letters and determining the number of letters in a string (using the techniques you'll learn in Chapter 9.

Numbers (such as 13 and 35) are a different data type. They are as difficult to compare to strings as apples are to oranges. You can also do interesting things with numbers, such as add them together and find their difference. However, you can't mix them. "Phillip" plus 35 doesn't make sense.

The good news about Flash is that it's *untyped*—meaning that you don't have to decide ahead of time the data type for each variable's value. From context, Flash figures it out. If you said `username="Phillip"`, Flash would treat the value of `username` like a string because "Phillip" is contained within quotation marks. If you said `age=35`, Flash would treat `age` as a number. (No, Flash doesn't know what a username or age is—it just figures out the data type from how you've used the word.) Because ActionScript is untyped, you can change the data type in a variable. Maybe in the first frame you said `score="untested"` (at which point the value in the `score` variable would be a string: `"untested"`). Later, you could say `score=85` (and `score`'s value would become a number). Despite the freedom to change data types, it's still important to understand each data type.

More About Strings

In Chapter 9, you'll learn all about manipulating strings. There are two tricks you should understand now. Concatenating two strings is simply a matter of using the *concatenate* character `+`. For example, `"Phillip"+"Kerman"` would evaluate as `"PhillipKerman"`. A more practical situation might be that you have an input text field onscreen (with the variable name "username"), and after the user types her name, you could use the script `message="Welcome " + username + "!"` and make sure to display a dynamic field containing the variable `message`. Notice the variable `message` is having its value set to a string that combines the word "Welcome " (with an extra space) plus the value of `username` plus an exclamation point. Figure 4.5 shows part of such a "Hello World" exercise.

Figure 4.5 *Dynamic text (based on user input) can appear by modifying strings.*

Another interesting trick to understand is how to include characters that would otherwise be difficult or impossible to include inside a string. For example, what if you want your string to contain a double quotation mark, such as `"Phillip is "old""`? Forgetting for a moment the way you learned to nest quotation marks (inside apostrophes), the difficulty here is that the quotation mark right before the letter "o" would act like an end-quote for the quotation mark at the beginning. Instead of letting Flash get confused, you can use a backslash in front of any quotation mark you want to be used verbatim. So, `"Phillip is \"old\""` works fine. This is called an *escape sequence* and on page 43, of Macromedia's Flash 5 ActionScript Reference Guide, you'll find a table of escape sequences. For example, `\r` creates a return and `\t` makes a tab.

More About Numbers

Manipulating numbers will probably look more familiar to you because it works the same as traditional math. Something simple like `10-2` evaluates to 8. It might seem strange that `10+2` evaluates to 12 because we just learned the plus sign is the concatenation character for strings. The plus sign acts as an addition operator when the two operands are numbers. But, something odd like `"Phillip"+2` evaluates to "Phillip2", because one of the operands is a string, so the plus sign concatenates the two. Often, depending on context, Flash will use the same symbols differently.

Other number operators are pretty easy to figure out. Common operators such as `/` (divide) and `*` (multiply) are all listed in the operators section of the Action panel. Remember that an expression by itself won't do anything. For example, `2+2` evaluates to `4`—but so what? If, however, you wrote `myAge=2+2`, the variable `myAge` would be assigned the value `4`. You can also use variables within expressions, as in this example: `myAge=myAge+1`. The right side is evaluated first and the result is placed in the value of `myAge`. That is, `myAge` is incremented (one more than it is currently).

It is good to know a few powerful shorthand operators for numbers. They're not called "shorthand," but these operators perform complex tasks including assignments with very little typing. One operator (the double plus sign, ++) is used to increment a variable. For example, `myAge++` increases `myAge` by one. To decrement, use `--` (for instance, `myAge--`). Consider that both these statements can be written in "long hand" as such:

```
myAge=myAge+1  //performs the same thing as myAge++

myAge=myAge-1  //same as myAge--
```

Finally, if you want to increase or decrease a variable's value by more than one, you can use `+=` or `-=`. `myAge+=5` adds five to the current value of `myAge` (`myAge-=5` subtracts five).

By the way, `"3"` and `3` are different—one's a string and the other is a number. Consider the following example:

```
myAge="3";
myAge=myAge+1;
```

The variable `myAge` would become the string `"31"` (because the plus sign concatenated the string). This situation would easily happen if `myAge` were a variable associated with an Input Text field. The contents of Dynamic Text and Input Text are always treated as strings. Without fully exploring functions, I will introduce one that lets you convert any variable into a number. It's pretty simple: `Number(myAge)` will result in a number version of `myAge` (or whatever you put in the parentheses). So, to be sure that you have a number, you could use the assignment statement `myAge=Number(myAge)+1`. This example should really demonstrate how data types make a difference.

Other Data Types

There are only a few other data types to learn. Boolean is one that's fairly easy. The values in Boolean variables are either `true` or `false`. Perhaps you start your movie with `passedTest=false` and then after the user finishes the test you write the script `passedTest=true`. There are slight efficiency benefits to Booleans. You only need to consider them, however, when appropriate. Examples where Booleans make sense include `PassedTest`, `seenIntro`, and `SoundOn`.

Primitives Versus Reference

The data types discussed so far (string, number, and Boolean) are all considered *primitive* (sometimes called *value variables*). The other data types you're about to see (array and object) are called *reference*. Understanding the difference between primitive and reference is good for more than impressing people at parties.

A variable in a primitive data type (say a string `username="Phillip"`) copies the actual value into the variable. A variable of the reference data type only holds a pointer to the actual data. It's sort of like the way a shortcut on Windows (or an alias on Macintosh) works —it doesn't contain the actual data; it contains only a reference to the real thing. The difference becomes important when you begin to copy the contents of one variable into another. If the data type is primitive, copying duplicates the contents of the variable at the time of copying. If you change the original variable's contents, the new variable remains unchanged. In the case of a reference type, if you copy a variable and then change the original, the copy also changes. Look at the following example of copying by value (that is, using primitive data types):

```
myPaint="brown";        //myPaint contains "brown"
myHouseColor=myPaint; //myHouseColor contains "brown"
myPaint="blue";         //now myPaint contains "blue"
                        //but myHouseColor is unchanged (it's still "brown")
```

Now, consider this example of copying by reference:

```
myFavoriteFoods=["Pizza", "Hot dogs", "Waffles"];
childhoodFoods=myFavoriteFoods;
/*childhoodFoods now contains a reference to myFavoriteFoods
(which currently contains "Pizza"...etc.)
*/
myFavoriteFoods=["Tiramisu", "Bitter Chocolate", "Falafel"];
/*
Not only does this mean that myFavoriteFoods has changed, but since a
reference to myFavoriteFoods is contained in childhoodFoods (not a copy
but a reference) childhoodFoods now contains "Tiramisu" etc.--and will
change any time myFavoriteFoods changes again.
*/
```

There are other subtle differences between primitives and reference data types, but if you simply understand how "copying by value" (primitive) and "copying by reference" (reference) works, you will understand the important difference.

Objects and Arrays

You might have noticed in the examples of primitive and reference data types above that the `myFavoriteFoods` variable was given a value containing more than one item (pizza, hot dogs, and waffles). That's another data type called *array*. An array simply contains several items. If you think of most variables as an empty whiteboard onto which you can write a value, an array is like a whiteboard with permanent horizontal lines separating many pieces of information. The cool part is that you can selectively find out what's in each spot, add items, sort all the items, shuffle them, and so on. Usually, the different items are accessed by their *index* (that is, the position in the array). You'll discover all the ins and outs of arrays in Chapter 10 but there are a couple points we can cover now so that you become familiar with what arrays look like.

You can create an array with a statement as simple as `myFirstArray= ["Phillip", "Kerman", 35]`. In this case, we're creating the array and populating it all in one move. Notice that the creation process simply involves surrounding the data with brackets and separating each item with a comma. Also, notice that any data type can go into any index; I have two strings and one number. (You'll see in Chapter 10 that you can even put arrays into arrays to create a matrix.) Finally, if you're not sure what items you plan to put in the array, but you want to create an empty array that can be populated later, you simply use `new Array()` as in `myFirstArray=new Array()`.

There's a simple technique to manipulate arrays. You might want to access certain items in an array (by index), change the value in a particular index, or simply insert a value in a specific index. The form is `arrayName[`*`index`*`]`. But watch out: Arrays' indexes start counting with zero. The first item is 0, and then 1, and so on. So, to write an expression that returns the third item in `myFirstArray`, you can write `myFirstArray[2]`. (Remember that because this is just an expression, it evaluates as `35` in this case…but by itself it doesn't really *do* anything.) To change the third item, you could say `myFirstArray[2]="age"`. Finally, you can insert an item in the 99th index position by saying `myFirstArray[98]="way out"`. This will create at least 98 blank positions if necessary. Now, just to leave you with a tiny applied script, here's a case in which I'm going to increment the value in the third index. I have to first access the item in the third position (to increment it) and set the value in the third position.

```
myFirstArray[2]=myFirstArray[2]+1;
//also could have used: myFirstArray[2]++;
```

The last data type is *object*. It is similar to arrays in that you can store more than one piece of data in an object. Where arrays use indexes to contain multiple items, an object contains *properties* and *methods*. The big difference between objects and arrays is that when you put data in an array, there's just one copy of that array. If you change the contents in an index, it changes in the one copy. After you design an object and the properties and methods it will contain, you can make as many duplicates as you want. Even though each instance of an object is based on the same design, each instance can maintain different values for each property.

Remember that movie clip instances are really objects. It's easy to understand how each clip instance has unique properties. For example, each instance of a clip onstage can have a different `_x` property and `_y` property. There are several built-in properties of clips that can vary between each instance. Objects also have methods. Methods are commands that operate on an individual object instance. A great example of a method is the `gotoAndStop()` Action. If you said `someClip.gotoAndStop(2);` the clip instance named "someClip" would jump to frame 2. `gotoAndStop()` is a method of the Movie Clip object.

As stated earlier, there are other built-in objects and even a way for you to create your own objects, but none has such a physical presence as a clip instance. To use the other objects, you first create an instance of the object (called *instantiating*) by setting the value of a variable to an object data type. Maybe `oneObject=new Color()`. Then you can change properties of the `oneObject` instance or apply methods to it. (Color happens to be one of the built-in objects and it comes standard with many properties and methods.) If you were making your own object, you'd first have to define the properties and methods you plan to have. It gets very involved, which is why I have several chapters on the subject. But the usage of objects is always the same: You put the object data type into a variable, and then you act on that variable instance. If you want more copies of the object, just stuff them into other variables. Each variable's value is an object. It's pretty weird because you never "see" anything. Just return to the concept that a clip instance is an object and you should have an easier time.

Using Variables

After you stuff a particular data type into your variable's value, there are only a few things you can do with the variable. You can access its value (just to look at it or use it within an expression), change its value (that is, *assign* a new value—which is really what you do when you set its initial value), compare its value with another variable or expression, or pass the value to a function for the function's use. It might sound like that's a lot of maneuvers to learn but it's really not that bad.

Assigning and Accessing Variables

You've already seen how to assign values to variables many times in this chapter, but it doesn't hurt to go over the details. The most common form is `variableName=`*`newValue`*. You can translate this to read "the variable named "variableName" *is assigned the value of* newValue." If, when you read the equal sign, you say to yourself, "...is now equal to..." or "...is assigned the value of..." it should make sense. This means that no matter what the value the variable (on the left side) contains before this statement is encountered, it is now assigned the value of whatever is on the right side. If an expression such as `price/2` is on the right side in the code `halfPrice=price/2`, the right side is evaluated first and the result is placed in the variable on the left.

You actually saw another way in which variables are assigned values. Namely, with assignment operators such as `++` (which increments the variable to the left of the operator). The confusing part is that many operators don't actually change the contents of their operands. For example, `discountPrice= (0.15*originalPrice)` won't change the value of `originalPrice`—`originalPrice` is just being accessed so that it can be used within an expression. But a statement such as `age++` will change the value of `age` by increasing it by one. The most common way in which variables are assigned values is through the equal sign—just don't forget the assignment operators (`++`, `--`, `+=`, and `-=`).

One last point to remember when assigning values. If you want to copy the value of one variable into another (for instance, `myName=username`), just remember the difference between primitive and reference data types. If `username` contains a string (primitive), a duplicate of its contents is placed into the value of `myName`. However, if "username" contains an array (that is, a reference data type), only a reference is placed into the variable `myName`. After that, if `username` changes, so does the value in `myName`.

Accessing variables can be very simple. You just use the variable's name. Variables are evaluated wherever they're used. That is, if you say `username`, the value of `username` is used in that place. Just as `3+2` evaluates to `5`, using a variable's name evaluates to its value. This might seem very simple, because it is! The tricky part is making sure that you're referring to the right variable name (which is covered in more detail later in this chapter).

Comparing and Passing Values

Quite often, you'll find the need to compare or check whether a variable's value either matches, is greater than, or is less than another variable's value. Sometimes you compare a variable's value to an expression, such as

```
if (age>17){
    canVote=true;
}
```

In this case, we're simply checking whether the value of `age` is greater than `17`. (We'll cover the if-statement in detail next chapter.) Consider that, in this case, `17` is "hard wired." What if the minimum age to vote changes? If you expect there's a chance of changes, you could first assign the value to another variable `minimumAge` and create a slightly more dynamic solution:

```
minimumAge=18;
if (age>minimumAge-1) {
    canVote=true;
}
```

In this case, we're comparing the value of `age` to the expression "minimumAge minus 1". You'll do lots of this kind of thing in any programming language, but there are two important concepts to remember. First, such comparisons never change any variables' values. If you're checking whether two variables happen to be equal, use:

```
if (oneVariable==otherVariable){
//then... do whatever
}
```

The double equal sign doesn't change `oneVariable` or `otherVariable` (the way an assignment operator—"="—does). The second concept to remember is that when comparing two primitive variables, the contents of each are compared—number for number or letter for letter. (This is likely the way you expect.)

However, if you're comparing two variables that contain (references to) reference variable types, the comparison checks only whether both variables point to the same original. For example:

```
oneArray=["Phillip", "Kerman"]
anotherArray=["Phillip", "Kerman"]
oneRef=oneArray;
//this line only places a reference to "oneArray" in "oneRef"
otherRef=anotherArray;
if (oneRef==otherRef){
//they match!
}
```

The expression after the if-statement's condition (`oneRef==otherRef`) evaluates as false. Even though the actual contents of both variables look identical, they're pointing to two different arrays (which, remember, are reference data types). The entire subject of "primitive versus reference" might seem esoteric (and, I suppose, it is in many ways). However, you'll find arrays so powerful that the last thing you'll need is to hunt down a bug that's caused by this (less than intuitive) behavior. The two points to remember from this section so far are that comparing variables in an expression doesn't actually change them, and that different data types behave differently.

Finally, passing variables. When we write our own functions in Chapter 8, you'll see that there's an opportunity to write a function that accepts parameters. This concept is similar to how `gotoAndStop()` requires that you provide a parameter—namely, a frame number or label name to *go to*. Often you'll write functions that will act differently depending on parameters that are received. For example, you might write a custom `exchangeCurrency()` function that accepts one price and determines the price in another currency (like we'll do in the Currency Exchange Calculator workshop). To use this (yet to be created) function, you'd simply say: `exchangeCurrency(1.95)`. If you provided a different parameter (the part in the parentheses) such as `exchangeCurrency(14.50)`, you'd get a different answer. Instead of a hard-wired number, you could *pass* a variable instead; for example, `exchangeCurrency(currentPrice)`. In this case, the value for `currentPrice` would be passed. As long as the value of `currentPrice` contained a primitive data type, the original would never be changed by the function. If the `currentPrice` were a reference data type, you *can* program the function to change the original value. Only reference type variables can be changed in this way. Most often you'll pass variables of the data type (as we will in the Currency Exchange Calculator) and hence only pass copies of the variable. However, in

"Working with Odd-Shaped Clickable Areas," Workshop 7, you'll actually pass references to movie clips (which is a reference data type—objects). In that exercise, changing the parameter received will most definitely change the original movie clip instance. (You'll learn much more about functions in Chapter 8.)

Scope and Variable Collision

I said earlier that when you place a variable's name in a script, the variable's value is used in its place. I said it was easy as long as you used the correct variable name. Certainly, you'll need to remember which variable is which. It's just as if you have several children with different names: You need to keep track of which one is which. With kids, it's pretty easy because you memorize their names. You can name your children (and your variables) anything you want. Although some people name their children with their own name, most people tend to use a unique name for each child. You can imagine the problems that would arise if you named two of your children with the same name. In Flash, you can't exactly get away with giving two variables the same name—but almost.

The *scope* of a variable (either local or global) defines the area in which that variable has influence—sort of like a sheriff's jurisdiction is his scope. Variables, unless otherwise noted, are *global*, meaning that there is only one version of each named variable. If, in one part of your script, you say `username="Phillip"` and in another part of your script that's encountered later, you say `username="Joe"`, in the end the one-and-only `username` variable would have the value `"Joe"`. If that's not what you intended, this error is called *variable collision*.

Global Variables

The general implication of global variables is that each variable must have a unique name. It's probably easiest to think of a global variable this way, but what makes it tricky is that a variable's name is tied to the Timeline where it's used. Think of how the _y property of one clip instance (`oneInstance._y`) can be uniquely different than the _y property of another instance of the same clip (`otherInstance._y`). Anywhere inside a Movie Clip, referring to _y refers to the _y of that clip. There's only one version of _y anywhere inside the clip, but as soon as you need to write a script outside the clip (with a different timeline), you need to specify *which* _y property is being used.

Think of `thePresident` as a global variable. Anywhere in the United States, you can refer to `thePresident` and the value (that is, who the president is) is the same. However, imagine you belong to Flash Users Group that elects a president. When in your group, saying `thePresident` could have mixed meanings. Is it `thePresident` of the group or `thePresident` of the United States? Although variables are global in Flash, you can have two versions of `thePresident` as long as they're kept inside a particular clip's timeline (or the main timeline itself). Within either the main timeline or the clip, you could simply say `thePresident` and you'd be referring to `thePresident` of the main timeline or the clip, respectively. However, if (in a script you write in the main timeline) you want to refer to `thePresident` of the clip instance named `myClub`, you could say `_root.myClub.thePresident`. This way, two instances of that clip could each have their own `thePresident` variable (just like each clip can have unique properties). If you want to refer to `thePresident` of the main timeline, you can always say `_root.thePresident`. Although both these absolute references are identical to property references, you can also use relative references just as you can with properties. For example, if you're writing a script inside the `myClub` clip, you could refer to `thePresident` one level up (in the main timeline) with `_parent.thePresident`.

Variable collision occurs from human error. You can avoid the issue entirely if you use unique names for every new variable. However, the most likely error occurs when you try to use a variable in one timeline (maybe the main timeline) and then you try to access that variable (by name) from within a clip. For example, if you were trying to keep track of the total times the user clicks one button (in the main timeline), you could have the script `counter++` inside a mouse event. But inside a clip named `myClip`, you might have another button that should also add to `counter`, so you use the script `counter++` again. Even though `counter` is a global variable, there are really two, noncolliding variables: `_root.counter` and `_root.myClip.counter`. This is a case of using two different variables as if they're one. Even though they have the same name, the two variables are in different timelines so they're not the same one. Obviously a human error, but one that's frustrating nevertheless.

Finally, I should note that keeping variables with the same name inside multiple clip instances could be very useful. Think of such variables as similar to the properties unique to clip instances. For example, assume that you create a movie clip that uses the variable `speed`. You can drag multiple instances of that clip onstage and each instance will have its own `speed`, just as each instance maintains its own `_alpha` property, `_x` property, and so on. The only concern is to be clear which clip's variable you're referring to so that you don't get mixed up.

Local Variables

Even though most of your work will probably involve global variables, there are also local variables. They are used within custom functions and exist only for the short duration while they're used. The benefit is that local variables are always removed from the user's computer memory when they're not being used. Global variables take up space in RAM and will never "let go" of that memory unless you use `delete`, as in `delete someVarName`. You can also just assign a value that's practically insignificant, such as `someVarName=0`, which isn't the same thing but perhaps easier to understand. Local variables have to first be declared, either:

```
var counter;
```

or

```
var counter=0;
```

In the second case, not only is the local variable (`counter`) created, but it's assigned a value from the start. In the first example, you'd have to eventually assign a value to the variable before it could be used. Just remember that such a variable is still useful to temporarily hold a value to be used later, but it only "lives" within the function (that is, between the { and } curly brackets). You can practice with local variables when you learn all about functions in Chapter 8.

Dot Syntax

Flash scripting uses what's called *dot syntax*. You've already seen this in effect throughout this chapter. When we used `someClip._y`, it could be translated to "someClip's _y property." In this way, the dot separates a clip instance name from its property. If you have clips nested inside of other clips, you can use dots to separate the nested clip names; for example: `_root.someClip._y` or `someClip.subClip._y`. You can also use dots to separate clip names from their respective variables. (This fact is probably easiest to learn if you think of variables as custom properties.) Finally, the dot is used to separate a clip name from the method (or action) when you want to apply the method to an individual clip. For example, `someClip.gotoAndPlay(2)`.

If you study the form of dot syntax, it's interesting because it always reads left to right, from general to specific. In speech, we usually refer to things from specific to general. For example, "the age of the mayor in Portland, Oregon" reads from specific to general. If these were nested clips in Flash, it would read the other way: `Oregon.Portland.Mayor.age`. Depending on whether your target path is relative or absolute, the length might change, but it's always general to specific.

Dot syntax is quite easy to learn. Just remember that you can't name variables or clips with periods in their name. Also, although you're allowed to name clips with spaces (but you shouldn't), you can never name variables with spaces in their names. You might imagine if your clip name were "clip.one" there would be no way to tell whether `clip.one._y` referred to the _y property of the clip "one" inside the clip "clip" or the _y of a clip named "clip.one". Avoid periods and spaces in clip and variable names, and you avoid this issue.

Summary

This chapter has consolidated practically every component of ActionScript. Naturally, it's more of a starting point rather than the last word. It's fair to say that everything covered will be revisited—in much more detail—throughout the rest of the book.

Of course, everything was important in this chapter, but a few concepts in particular should be retained. For example, you should be comfortable with all the terms used, even if you don't fully understand their application. You should understand the basic purposes of "events," "properties," "syntax," "statements," and "expressions." The concept of data types is very important, but the good news is that you'll hear more about it later. Regarding variables, if you only grasp that they are a safe—yet temporary—storage mechanism, you'll be fine.

Just treat this chapter as an overview of the basic programming skills that you're about to develop.

{ Chapter 5 }

Programming Structures

I suspect that the overview of programming from the previous chapter has made you eager to start scripting. (I hope so anyway.) The last chapter briefly touched on practically every concept from ActionScript. In this chapter, we'll start by exploring the structural elements necessary to write any script. Just as a house is built from the ground up by first laying down the foundation and then the framework, Flash scripts require a design and a framework. We're about to explore the structural elements of ActionScript that hold your scripts together.

This chapter covers

- How to write expressions and statements
- How to use operators in expressions
- Conditions (such as "if") and loop structures
- Practice using this knowledge

Statements, Expressions, and Operators

To quickly review, statements are complete "sentences of code" that usually do something. Expressions are more like "phrases" because they don't *do* anything by themselves but rather are used within statements. Expressions also result in a value when they're evaluated. For example, if you were to evaluate the expression "slow as molasses," it would have an actual value (perhaps 1" per hour?). It works the same in Flash—the expression `price/2` results in a value. Finally, operators, as part of an expression, perform an operation (often math) on one or more operands. For example, the "plus" operator (+) performs the addition operation on two numbers (operands). The expression `2+2` results in a value (`4`). Finally, the statement `quad=2+2` actually *does* something (namely, assigning the value of 4 to the variable "quad"). Now that we know the terms, we can explore each concept in detail.

Writing Expressions

The key to writing expressions is to always remember you're only writing part of a larger statement. By themselves, expressions don't *do* anything—rather, expressions result in a value because they are evaluated. That is, expressions are evaluated and become their result. An expression from real life might be "the shirt's price minus the discount." If you said, "My credit card's balance is now increased by the cost of the shirt (minus its discount rate)," it becomes a statement that does something. After you can write expressions (segments), you'll have no trouble writing statements.

Let's use the discounted shirt price for practice. Imagine that you previously assigned the variable "price" to the cost of the shirt. It doesn't matter what the price was—but let's just say $25; that is, `price=25`. Also, consider that the discount rate is 10%. Interestingly, I'll bet everyone who's ever gone shopping already knows the shirt will cost $22.50, which just goes to show you can write expressions! One step at a time. Say the variable containing the discount rate is called "discount" (or `discount=.1`). The final expression looks like this:

```
price-(price*discount)
```

You can think of this as a mathematical formula. No matter what the values of "price" and "discount" are, the formula works. It always results in the discounted price.

Precedence

We'll get to statements in the next section, but there's more to learn about expressions. Notice in the earlier expression about price, I placed parentheses around `price*discount`. In the version with no parentheses (`price-price*discount`), you might think that Flash will execute the first two elements (`price-price`) first—the result of that portion would be zero. Then zero multiplied by `discount` would always equal 0 (what a sale... "All Shirts $0"). So, putting parentheses around the expression `price*discount` tells Flash to execute this expression first. It turns out this wasn't necessary. The expression `price-price*discount` results in the same value as `price-(price*discount)`. That's because the precedence for multiplication is greater than subtraction—multiplication is executed first, and then subtraction.

Of course, if you want to force Flash to execute the subtraction operation in first you could rewrite the expression as `(price-price)*discount`. Personally, instead of memorizing the precedence for each operator, any time there's a question as to how Flash will interpret my expression, I simply place parentheses to make the expression not only clear when reading, but crystal clear to Flash despite the fact the extra parentheses are unnecessary. Flash always executes the expressions in the most-nested parentheses first. Look up Operator Precedence and Associativity in Flash's ActionScript Reference (from the Help menu).

Interestingly, operators each have an associativity of either "right-to-left" or "left-to-right," which determines the order of execution when two of the same operators appear and therefore have the same precedence. For example, because addition has left-to-right associativity, `2+3+4` is the same as `(2+3)+4`. Although this example doesn't demonstrate a different result, remember that parentheses can override associativity (as in `2+(3+4)`). Associativity is not usually a critical issue, but it's covered in Flash's ActionScript Reference along with all the operators and their precedence.

Balancing Parentheses

Parentheses in an expression must balance. That is, for every open parenthesis you must have a closing parenthesis. This holds true for the entire statement—but that doesn't mean you can't create errors within an expression. If you're in Expert Mode, you need to ensure that the parentheses balance. One way you can do that is to read your scripts (from left to right) and count up for every opening parenthesis and count down for every closing parenthesis. After reading the entire statement, your count should be at zero proving everything balances. When in Normal Mode, any errors in balance will highlight red and Flash will provide limited information about the error in the parameters area as shown in Figures 5.1 and 5.2.

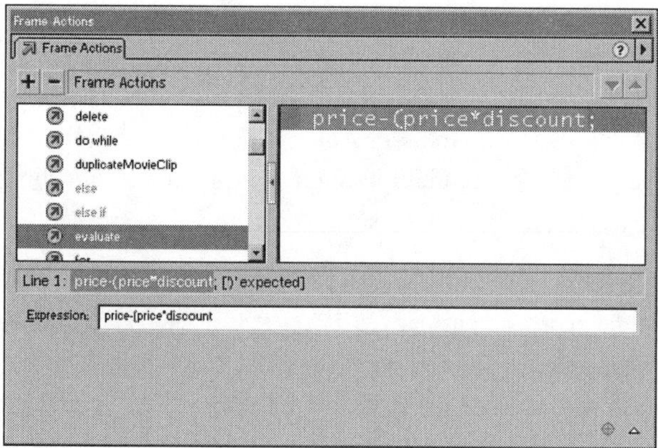

Figure 5.1 *The Actions panel will draw your attention to missing parentheses when in Normal Mode.*

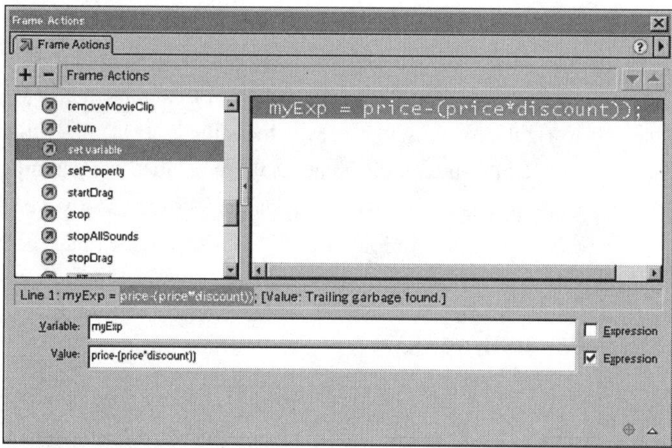

Figure 5.2 *An extra closing parenthesis causes the Actions panel to point out the error.*

It is important to understand that just because you balance your parentheses, there's no guarantee that your code will work as expected. For example, the expression `(price-price)*discount` balances just as well as `price-(price*discount)`, but with entirely different results. So, balancing parentheses is just a technical requirement (like spell-checking a document)—making your code logical or work for your purpose is still necessary. Often, any time I type an open parenthesis I immediately type a closing parenthesis and then backspace to complete the parenthetical portion of the expression. This way I'm sure to balance all parentheses. Finally, everything just discussed about parentheses also applies to quotation marks (`"` or `'`), brackets (`[` and `]`), and curly brackets (`{` and `}` —also called *braces*).

Using Operators in Expressions

Instead of listing every operator here, we'll first look at how operators work, and then explore the ones that operate within expressions (the operators I'll call *arithmetic* and *logical*). Finally, after the upcoming section on statements, we can look at operators that perform assignments.

I've said several times that operators operate on one or more operands. To be technical, when an operator operates on a single operand it is called *unary* (like "uni-cycle"). When operating on two operands, it's called a *binary* operator. Finally, one operator (`?:`) is considered *ternary* because it operates on three operands—but because there's just one such operator, "ternary" may only come up on a quiz show for geeks. What makes this important is that *some* operators can act as either unary or binary. One example is `-`, which is both a "unary minus" and a "subtract" operator. When used on a single operand (as with `-direction` or within a statement such as `oppositeDirection = -direction`), it simply results in an inverse (or minus version) of its operand. But as a binary operator (as in `price-couponValue`), the entire expression is converted into the result of subtracting the second operand from the first.

The fact is that operators operate differently depending on the context. Even though it's pretty easy to see and understand how operators act differently based on the number of operands because you can quickly see how many operands are present, some operators also perform differently based on the data type of their operands. That is, the same operator can perform a different operation on different data types. Recall from Chapter 4, "Basic Programming in Flash," that the value of a variable can be one of several data types. Let's just consider numbers and strings (probably the most common and familiar data types). The `+` operator is either an addition operator or a concatenate (meaning to connect) operator, depending on its operands. If one or both operands are strings, `+` is a concatenate operator, as in

```
first="Phillip";
last="Kerman";
wholeName=first+last;
```

The expression `first+last` results in `"PhillipKerman"`.

If both the operands are numbers, the + performs the addition operation, as in

```
previousScore=10
currentScore=2
totalScore=previousScore+currentScore;
```

The expression `previousScore+currentScore` results in `12`.

This issue can become quite frustrating if you think a variable (say "previousScore") contains a number, but it actually contains the string, say "10". The expression `previousScore+2` will result in the *string* "102" because + acts as the concatenate operator when one or more of the operands are strings. This is likely to happen in Flash when you use a Dynamic (or Input) Text field to display the value of a variable. Even though the field might read `10`, it's actually the string `"10"` because the data type of fields is string. By the way, in Chapter 8, "Functions," you'll learn how to treat a string like a number with the "number" function. Also, later in this chapter, you'll see how certain operators will actually change the data type of their operands.

There's no need to get freaked out about operators. Just remember that operators often behave differently depending on their position in an expression and on their operands' data type. In practice, you'll usually select the correct operator without fail. Just learn to recognize the symptoms of such problems. For example, if the numbers you were expecting to grow end up getting longer (like `10` turning into `101`) or if your strings are appearing as `NaN` (meaning "not a number"), you're likely mixing data types or using the operators incorrectly.

Finally, even though an operator only operates on one or two operands, the operand could actually be an expression. This might have been particularly obvious when we discussed parentheses earlier. The example `price-(price*discount)` has the minus operator operating on the result of an expression (the multiplication part in the parentheses). Figure 5.3 shows how an operand can actually be an expression.

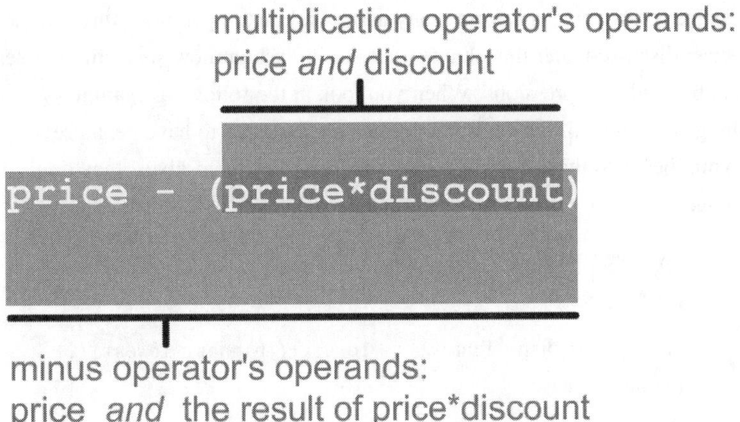

Figure 5.3 *An operand can be the result of an expression.*

Arithmetic Operators

Let's look at the operators used to perform simple arithmetic. These won't change their operands and (when used on number operands) will have expected results.

- Add numbers (+) results in the sum of two number operands.
- Multiply numbers (*) results in the product of two number operands.
- Subtract numbers (-). As a binary operator (that is, with two operands), it results in the difference by subtracting the second number from the first. It can also be used as a unary operator (on one operand) by placing it before the operand (as in `-myNum`), in which case it will result in the inverse of the operand. If it's positive, the result is negative; if it's negative, the result is positive.
- Divide numbers (/) results in the quotient of two numbers. That is, it divides the first number by the second.
- Modulo (%) results in the remainder when you divide the first number by the second. For example, 20%7 results in 6 because after you divide 7 into 20 (two times), you're left with a remainder of 6.

In addition to these, there are two operators (++ and --) that also perform simple arithmetic. Because they both *change* their operands, I've decided to discuss these in the "Assignment Operators" section later in this chapter.

Flash enables you to perform many additional math operations through the Math object discussed later this chapter, but don't discount how such simple operators can be used in expressions. When you look at the following examples keep two things in mind: All the variables' values are assumed to have been previously set to numbers and these are just expressions—so, by themselves, they don't do anything.

Average (mean):	`sum/total`
Half:	`full/2`
Average (median—that is, the midpoint):	`lowest+((highest-lowest)/2)`
Price when discounted:	`price-(price*discount)`
Compounded interest:	`principal+(principal*interestRate)`
Seconds (with milliseconds known):	`milliseconds/1000`

These examples all use simple arithmetic operators on homemade variables. You can certainly combine built-in properties in expressions (for instance, `_currentFrame+1`). You'll see more of this in Chapter 7, "The Movie Clip Object."

Finally, I didn't provide any examples of the modulo (`%`) operator —but it is one of the most powerful operators available. It seems so innocuous, the remainder. But consider how you determine whether a number is even—it has to be evenly divisible by 2. Or, when divided by 2, the remainder is 0. Similarly, to see whether something is evenly divisible by 3, there just has to be no remainder when dividing by 3. This is where Modulo can help. If you just use `anyNumber%2` and find the expression results in `0`, you know the number is even. Later in this chapter (in the "Applied Expression Writing" section), you'll see an example of where Modulo will make a loop execute every *other* time (that is, when `loopCounter%2` equals 0).

Comparison Operators

Comparison operators are used to write expressions that evaluate to either true or false. That's it. You might understand the need for such expressions if you remember that they'll usually reside within a larger statement. For example, by itself the word "true" doesn't mean anything. However, an entire statement that makes sense might be "If your age is greater than 21, you can purchase alcohol." The expression "is greater than 21" always evaluates as either true or false. To make the statement even more explicit, you could say "If the expression 'your age is greater than 21' is true, you can purchase alcohol." This example is a conditional statement. Such statements are covered in detail later this chapter in "Conditionals and Loop Structures."

The comparison operators by themselves are pretty easy to understand. All these operators require two operands in the form *first operator second* (such as `12>4`, where 12 is *first*, > is the *operator*, and 4 is *second*). Let's look at them all.

- Greater than (>) results in true when the first number is greater than the second.
- Less than (<) results in true when the first number is less than the second.
- Greater than or equal to (>=) results in true when the first number is greater than or equal to the second.
- Less than or equal to (<=) results in true when the first number is less than or equal to the second.
- Not equal to (<>) results in true when the first number is not the same value as the second.
- Is equal to (==) results in true when both the first and second number are equal.

The most practical examples of the comparison operators will be seen later in this chapter, but there are several interesting points to make now. Remember that the result of any expression you write with these operators is always either true or false. That is, they can result in nothing except true or false, *and* false is a perfectly fine possibility. An expression such as `12<25` is perfectly legitimate—it just happens to evaluate to `false`.

It's interesting that true and false are the two variations of the Boolean data type. However, you can use them within expressions as if they were numbers. True is 1 and false is 0. For example, the expression `score*(timesCheated<1)` will automatically reduce the value of "score" (no matter what it is) to 0 if the "timesCheated" variable is greater than 0. That is, the portion `timesCheated<1` evaluates to either true or false (1 or 0). If `timesCheated` is 0, that portion is true and "score" is multiplied by 1 and thus is unaffected. If `timesCheated` is not less than 1, that portion is false and multiplies "score" by 0 (bringing it down to 0). This is a form of a conditional statement—but much simpler.

The "equal to" operator is formed by two equal signs. A single character (=) is a different operator entirely. The single equal sign performs an *assignment* (as you'll see later in this chapter). That is, the variable to the left of = is assigned the value of the expression on the right. It actually creates a complete statement (because it *does* something) rather than an expression as the == operator does. Not only does this mean that the variable on the left side changes, but if you intended to create an expression that resulted in true or false, you'd find it always results in true. That is, `age=21` assigns `21` as the value of `age` and this statement will be evaluated as true. On the other hand, `age==21` will be either true or false (depending on what the `age` variable's value happens to be). In addition, `age` will not change value when you use ==. The first case said, "`age` now equals 21"; the second said, "does `age` happen to equal 21?" You'll see more about assignments, but just don't forget this operator is a "double equal."

Finally, string manipulation is covered in much more detail in Chapter 10, but it's worth mentioning that the comparison operators work perfectly well on strings. To work intuitively, both operands must be strings. But the expression `"a"<"b"` evaluates as true because "a" is earlier in the alphabet. (Uppercase letters are considered less than lowercase, which might be counterintuitive.) The truth is, you'll see such amazing ways to manipulate strings in Chapter 10, "Arrays," that it's not worth discussing much here. Just don't expect the comparison operators to act differently depending on the data type of their operands (the way that many of the arithmetic operators do).

Logical Operators

Logical operators are used to compare one or two Boolean values—expressions that result in true or false. (Operators "and," "or," and "not equal" use two operands, whereas "not" uses one.) They let you to extend these comparison operators to make compound expressions such as "age is greater than 12 *and* age is less than 20" ("and" being the logical operator in this case). You're actually comparing two expressions, but the result of each expression must be true or false. If you use these logical operators on non-Boolean values (such as numbers), any number except 0 will be considered true. If you use them on strings, each string will be true too.

- and (`&&`) results in true if both operands are true.
- or (`||`) results in true if either (or both) operands are true.
- not (`!`) results in true when the operand (following `!`) is false.

- not equal to (`!=`) results in true when the two operands are not equal. This is effectively the opposite the behavior of the == operator. `!=` is not officially a logical operator, but I think it makes most sense to discuss it here.

Here are a few common examples:

True if `age` is a "teen":	`(age>12) && (age<20)`
True if either `age` is greater than 15 or `"accompaniedByAdult"` is true:	`(age>15) || (accompaniedByAdult==true)`
True if `age` is anything except 21:	`!(age==21)`
True if `age` is not a "teen":	`!((age>12) && (age<20))`
True if `age` is not equal to 21:	`age != 21`

Even though these expressions should be easy to figure out, there are some interesting elements to note. I included additional parentheses to make these expressions clear. But because the logical operators have very low precedence, the expressions on each side will be evaluated first. That is, `age>12&&age<20` works just as well as `(age>12) && (age<20)` although it might not be as easy to read. Also notice that both operands of the "and" and "or" operators must be a complete expression. For example, `age>12 && <20` won't work. It sounds okay in speech as in "age is greater than 12 and less than 20," but in ActionScript, you want to say "age is greater than 12 and age is less than 20."

Finally, there's one trick that is commonly used to abbreviate scripts—but it might not be intuitive to you. The expression `accompaniedByAdult==true` is the same as `accompaniedByAdult` (by itself). So, in this example, I could have said `age>15||accompaniedByAdult`. If you don't say "==true", it's implied. Of course, you can still get messed up (in either case) if the value of `accompaniedByAdult` is a number or string—but that's another issue (discussed earlier).

You'll get plenty of practice writing expressions. Remember that they'll always be contained within bigger statements. These concepts should begin to make more sense as you write statements. The best way to learn to write statements and expressions is to first write your objectives and then start to program in pseudo-code (as discussed in Chapter 3, "The Programmer's Approach"). You might notice that in many of my examples, I actually include the pseudo-code version as well.

Types of Statements

As I've mentioned countless times, statements *do* things. Often statements do one of two things: either assign values or compare values. A statement could assign a value to the variable `score`. Another statement might compare the user's score to a set of values to determine a grade. Realize that when comparing values, the end result of a statement could be that no action is taken. For example, a statement could compare the user's score to a minimum and then, if the score is not high enough, do *nothing*. Only when the score is high enough would this comparison (or "conditional") statement *do* something—perhaps display a message. We'll look at such conditional statements (that is, the kind that compare values) in the "Conditionals and Loop Structures" section later in this chapter. There's a lot of material to discuss related to assigning values.

Using Assignment Operators to Create Statements

The granddaddy of assignment operators is the equal sign (`=`). When this operator appears in a statement, you can read `=` as "…is assigned the value of…". That is, `username="Phillip"` can be translated and read aloud as "username *is assigned the value of* 'Phillip'." The truth is that you don't need any other assignment operator other than `=`. The others simply make certain tasks easier. For example, the increment assignment operator (`++`) can be used to increment its operand, as in `age++`. That's the same as saying `age=age+1`. So, if you just understand how the plain old `=` assignment operator works, the others are simply variations on the same theme.

Here are the basic assignment operators:

- Assignment (`=`) places the value of the expression on the right into the variable on the left.
- Increment (`++`) increments the variable on the left by 1.
- Decrement (`--`) decrements the variable on the left by 1 (that is, it's reduced by 1).

- Addition and assignment (+=) increases the variable on the left by an amount equal to the expression on the right. (`counter+=10` will increase `counter` by `10`.)
- Subtraction and assignment (-=) decreases the variable on the left by an amount equal to the expression on the right.
- Multiplication and assignment (*=) multiplies the variable on the left by an amount equal to the expression on the right.
- Divide and assignment (/=) divides the variable on the left by an amount equal to the expression on the right.
- Modulo and assignment (%=) assigns the variable on the left a value equal to the remainder of dividing the value of the expression on the right into the value of the variable on the left. It sounds worse than it is—it just tries dividing the second number into the first and assigns the variable on the left what's left over. For example, if your variable "counter" happens to equal 10, `counter%=3` will assign `counter` the value `1` because 3 goes into 10 three times (3*3=9) with 1 left over.

If these are starting to seem a bit complicated, remember that you only *need* =. All the other operations can be achieved with =. For example, `counter+=10` will increase `counter` by 10—but so will `counter=counter+10`. It's not important that you memorize these now. Ultimately, the only thing that matters is getting your movie to do what you want. After you sort that out, you can reach for whichever operators you want.

Possibly the best thing about the assignment operators is that they actually change the operand being assigned (usually on the left side) to a number data type. Realize that all these operators except the plain equals (=) don't serve double duty (that is, they perform only mathematical assignments and don't work with strings). As such, they try to convert their operand into a number. For example, if you had a variable `count` that contained a string `"12"` and you wrote the script `count++`, the value of `count` would become `13` (the number, not the string). So, unlike some operators that operate differently based on the data type of the operands—these attempt to convert operands to numbers.

Although the data type of operands won't make these operators perform different operations—the operator's placement (before or after) the operand does make a difference. You can actually place the ++ or -- in front of or behind the operand, as in `++counter` or `counter++`. The difference is subtle but important. Placing the operator after the operand (called "post increment"—`counter++`) increments `counter` but "returns" the value of the operand *before* the increment happened.

When your entire statement is only `counter++`, this issue doesn't matter. However, when you say `otherVariable=counter++`, `otherVariable` will turn into the value of `counter` *before* it gets incremented. On the other hand, if you say `otherVariable=++counter`, `otherVariable` turns into the incremented (higher) value of `counter`. It's not that one variation is better than the other; it just depends on your intent.

Although the difference between pre and post decrement and increment might seem very subtle, there's actually a particular situation in which you might have to use the pre decrement or pre increment option. When the operand is a value that you're not allowed to change, only pre decrement or pre increment makes sense. For example, the `_totalFrames` property of a Movie Clip cannot be changed with ActionScript. If you want to use a value that's one less than `_totalFrames`, you must use `--_totalFrames`. Although Flash "wants" to decrement `_totalFrames`, it can't, but at least the expression results in a number that's one less than `_totalFrames`. Realize that both pre and post options do two things: change the value of the operand *and* return the value (either before or after the change). Even if the operand is an unchangeable value (like `_totalFrames`), the pre increment or pre decrement options will still return the value as if it could change. Consider these two statements:

```
oneMore=_totalFrames++;
oneMore=++_totalFrames;
```

In either case, `_totalFrames` won't change. But only the second statement will assign the `oneMore` variable a value that's one greater than `_totalFrames`.

Here are a few examples of typical statements that assign values. (Notice that I've thrown in plenty of expressions within the statements.)

- Reduce price to half: `price=price/2;` (You could also use `price/=2;`)
- Calculate a percent correct based on a number of questions: `percentCorrect=(numberCorrect/totalQuestions)*100;`
- Apply a discount to price if age is greater than 64: `price=price-(discount*(age>64));`

Notice that I ended each statement with a semicolon. Flash understands the end of your statement is reached when the semicolon is used. You can't just type a return at the end of the line because both blank spaces and returns are ignored when Flash reads your script. You could actually run all your code along one long (difficult-to-read) line if you separated distinct statements with semicolons.

The Thought Process

Writing statements takes the same skill as writing expressions. Similarly, the skill will come with practice. Most people write any such code in segments. That is, it's difficult to write a statement in the same way that you might compose a sentence in speech (in which you almost talk without thinking—let alone thinking about the composition of your sentence). Rather, to write a script statement, first think of your general objective, write it out in pseudo-code, and then break down your pseudo-code into discrete elements that can be expressed in script. For example, it's unrealistic to simply think "double score when they get the bonus question" and then immediately type: `score*=(1+(bonusQuestion==true))`. Even though this example is intentionally complex, you're unlikely to create such a statement without breaking down the task into smaller parts. Your thought process might follow this order:

"Okay, I want to double their score if they got the bonus question right. Well, what if they got it wrong? In that case, just leave `score` alone. What can I do to `score` that will leave it untouched? Either add 0 or multiply by 1. Since doubling involves multiplying by 2, I've got an idea: I'll either multiply by 2 or multiply by 1 (depending on the outcome of the bonus question). So far, I have the statement `score*=` in mind. That is, `score` is assigned the value of `score` multiplied by blank. I want "blank" to be either 1 or 2. That is, either `1+0` or `1+1`. For the second number (`+0` or `+1`), I can simply write an expression that evaluates as either false or true. The expression `bonusQuestion==true` will always evaluate as 0 (when `bonusQuestion` is *not* true) or 1 (when `bonusQuestion` *is* true). The part of the right (`(1+0)` or `(1+1)`) can be replaced with `(1+(bonusQuestion==true))`. So, the entire statement `score*=(1+(bonusQuestion==true))` makes complete sense now."

Perhaps your brain works differently than mine, but this was just a sample of my thought process. By the way, the same exact task could be expressed with countless variations of statements—this is just one solution. You'll get more practice writing expression and statements at the end of this chapter.

Built-in Statements

Although I've probably said "statements *do* things" enough times so that you'll never forget, what I failed to mention is that there are built-in statements that also do things. Consider that ActionScript and JavaScript are practically identical, but there are a few Flash-centric Actions that only ActionScript contains, such as gotoAndPlay(). The term *Actions* is left over from older versions of Flash. Realize that everything listed in the Actions section of the toolbox list (some of which are shown in Figure 5.4) is either a Flash-centric feature (either a command or method) or a built-in statement. Think of them all as statements if you want. (By the way, another way in which ActionScript and JavaScript vary is in the events to which they respond—Flash has on(release) and JavaScript has onClick, for instance.)

Figure 5.4 *Flash Actions are either Flash-specific features or actually built-in statements.*

We don't need to step through each statement now. You'll pick them up as you write blocks of code. For example, you'll see both `return` and `break` in the following section about conditional and loop statements. The point is that all built-in statements are listed under Actions—and that some of them are unique to Flash.

Simple Objects in Statements

It's only fair to introduce you to objects now. Even though there are five other chapters dedicated to the finer points of objects (Chapter 7, "The Movie Clip Object"; Chapter 9, "Selecting Text, Trapping Keys, and Manipulating Strings"; Chapter 10, "Arrays"; Chapter 11, "Objects"; and Chapter 12, "Homemade Objects"), there are a couple of simple objects that will help you immensely as you write statements. Namely, the Math object and the Number object. Instead of providing detailed information about objects here, I'll simply show you how to use the Math and Number objects. They're so easy, you really can use them without fully understanding objects. When you get to the workshop section you'll find the Math Object useful in almost every exercise. You'll use it to help determine the percentages (when building Horizontal Slider) and angles (when building the Circular Slider). In fact, you'll find the Math Object invaluable if you ever want to go beyond simple addition, subtraction, multiplication, and division.

Using the Math Object

The Math object will give you access to both common mathematical functions as well as constants (such as pi). The functions in the Math object (called "methods") are almost like the buttons on a scientific calculator—actually, they're practically identical. For example, my calculator has a square root button (that looks like this: √). If I first type a 9 and then press the square root button, my calculator "returns" (into the display field) the square root of 9—that is, 3. Within an expression in Flash, you can also type a 9 (or a variable whose value happens to equal 9) and use the Math object's square root method to return the square root into the expression where you used it. The expression looks like this: `Math.sqrt(9)`. (Remember that as an expression, this evaluates to 3, but it doesn't do anything unless you use it in a statement such as `answer=Math.sqrt(9);`.)

The form for all the Math object methods is `Math.methodName()` where "methodName" is the function that you want to use. The parentheses are required for all methods because they often accept parameters. For example, you can't just say `Math.sqrt()`. Flash needs to know "square root of what?". You put the number (or expression that evaluates out as a number) into the parentheses: `Math.sqrt(9); Math.sqrt(6+3); Math.sqrt(oneVar+((someExpression*2) +whatever))`. Flash will take the result of the expression in the parentheses, calculate the square root, and finally put the answer in place of the entire expression. (Remember that it's an expression.)

In addition to methods that perform mathematical operations, the Math object has constants. You can tell them apart from the methods because they're listed in all uppercase letters such as `E` (Euler's constant—for use in natural logarithms) and `PI` (the ratio of a circle's circumference to its diameter—used in trigonometry and geometry). They're used like methods except that because they don't accept parameters, the parentheses aren't used. That is, `Math.PI` (not `Math.PI()`) turns into 3.14159… and `Math.E` into 2.718…. You could probably live your entire life without ever really *needing* constants. For example, you could just hardwire 3.14159 every time you needed to use pi in a formula (for example, if you wanted to calculate the circumference of a circle, `PI` times radius). It's just that the constants are built into ActionScript and they're very accurate—so you might as well use them when you need them. Just remember the constants are all uppercase and don't need or accept parameters, therefore they don't use parentheses.

Instead of going through all the Math object features (shown in Figure 5.5)—effectively providing a recap of the last trigonometry course you took (and possibly awakening the long repressed anxieties associated)—we'll just start using them in statements. Here are a few fun examples of the Math object:

- `Math.abs(number)` (absolute value) returns a non-negative version of *`number`*. For example, `Math.abs(startPoint-endPoint)` returns the distance between `startPoint` and `endPoint`, and it will always be a positive number even if the `endPoint` is a greater number (which would otherwise cause `startPoint-endPoint` to be a negative number).
- `Math.max(x,y)` returns the value of either `x` or `y` (whichever is greater). For example, the statement `bestScore=Math.max(writtenScrore, verbalScore);` will assign the value of `bestScore` to equal the value of either `writtenScore` or `verbalScore` (whichever is greater).

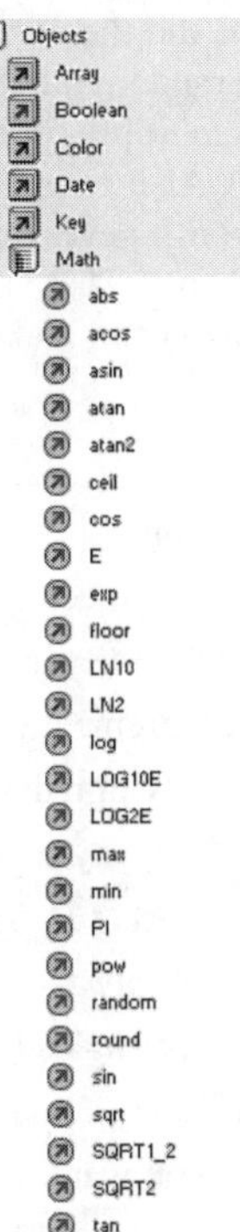

Figure 5.5 *You'll find all the components of the Math object under Objects in the Actions panel's toolbox.*

- `Math.floor(number)` returns the integer portion of a number (that is, it rounds it down). For example, given the number of minutes I've worked on this chapter, I can calculate how many full hours that is `hours=Math.floor(minutesWorked/60);`. I can combine this with the modulo (`%`) we looked at earlier to express a string that shows the total time in hours and minutes (instead of just minutes): `Math.floor(minutesWorked/60) + " hour(s) and " + (minutesWorked%60) + " minute(s)"`.

- `Math.random()`returns a random decimal number between 0 and 1 (but not including 0 or 1—that is, literally *between* 0 and 1, not inclusive). For example, if you want to return a number between `1` and `100` (inclusive), first set `min=1` and `max=100` and then use this expression: `Math.floor(Math.random()*((max-min)+1))+min`. This might not be easy to read, but the idea is that you multiply the random decimal number by `100` (that is, the difference between the `max` and `min` plus `1`—that's the part that reads `Math.random()*((max-min)+1))`. Assume that `Math.random()` returns `0.56899`. It will turn into `56.899` when multiplied by `100`. You take that whole expression and strip off the excess decimals (using the `Floor` method) resulting in `56`. Finally, you add the min (at the end of the expression) because it's quite possible the random number could be `0.00000000001`, which turns into `0` even after you multiply by `100` and use the `Floor` method (and that's lower than our `min`). Also consider that if you multiply the random decimal by `100` (the max) you'll never quite get to `100` because the random number is always *lower* than `1`. That last `+min` eliminates the possibility of going lower than the min (`1`) and makes sure that it's possible to reach the max (`100`).

Just to make things fun, the Math object's trigonometry functions (`Math.sin (`*`angle`*`)`, `Math.cos(`*`angle`*`)`, and `Math.tan(`*`angle`*`)`) expect the angle provided to be expressed in radians (not in degrees with which you might be more familiar). Radians and degrees are simply different measurement units—like miles and kilometers. A half-circle has 180 degrees but only pi radians (a whole circle is 360 degrees or 2 pi). (See Figure 5.6.) Therefore, any time you need to convert degrees to radians, you must *multiply* by `Math.PI/180`. That is, 90 degrees is `(Math.PI/180)*90` radians (or 1.57…). (Just multiply your degrees by `Math.PI/180` to get radians.) Where the trig functions accept angles (in radians, not degrees), the inverse functions (`Math.asin()`, `Math.acos()`, and `Math.atan()`) return angles (naturally, in radians as well). If you want to convert a value represented in radians to degrees, just *divide* by `Math.PI/180`. That is, `1.57` radians is `1.57/(Math.PI/180)` degrees (or `90`). Even though all this might seem like a sick joke from a sadistic mathematician, the truth is that you can usually do all your calculations in radians. You might never need to convert between radians to degrees. An exception would be if you want to display—for the user—a found angle in degrees, or you want to set the `_rotation` property of a clip to an angle you calculated. Generally, do all the calculations in radians and then (if you need to) convert the values to degrees at the last minute. If nothing else, just be aware of the difference.

There's one trig function that Flash provides that you might have never seen in math class: `Math.atan2()`. As you might know, the plain `Math.atan()` function (or "arc tangent") will help you determine the angle of a corner in a right triangle. Just provide the length of the triangle's opposite side divided by the length of the adjacent side, and `Math.atan()` will then return the angle. For example, if one side is `70` pixels and the other side is `200` pixels, the angle is `30` degrees (well, `.528` radians, because `Math.atan(70/120)` returns `.528`). Figure 5.7 has a couple examples.

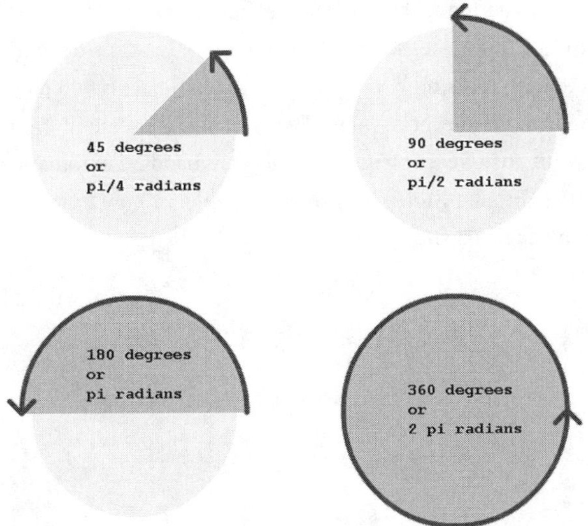

Figure 5.6 *A full circle contains 360 degrees or 2 pi radians—two units of measure that can lead to confusion.*

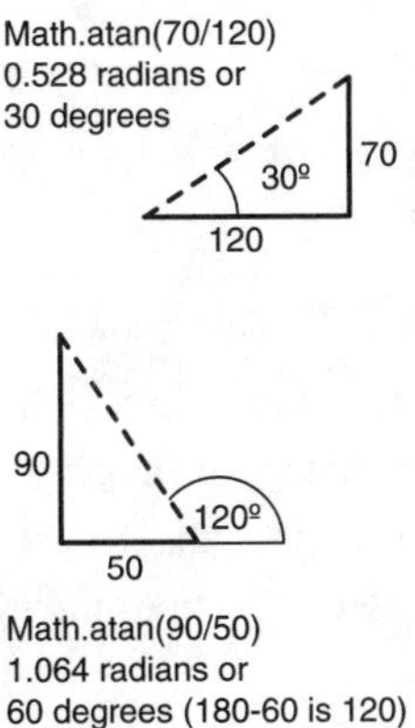

Figure 5.7 *The regular arc-tangent function (`Math.atan()`) enables you to calculate angles given two sides of a right triangle.*

The plain `Math.atan()` is all fine and dandy when you're in the real world (where moving up increases values). But consider the coordinate system in Flash. The y values decrease when you go up! If you consider the second example in Figure 5.7, both the x and y are really negative numbers. Plus, you have to remember in that case to subtract the value you find from 180. It becomes even more of a hassle when you move into the other quadrants (from 180 degrees to 270 degrees and from 270 degrees to 360 degrees). Luckily, `Math.atan2()` resolves the entire mess! You simply provide `Math.atan2()` with two parameters, one for the y value and one for the x value. That's it. You'll notice in Figure 5.8 that all the issues with positive and negative values are handled automatically by `Math.atan2()`. In the Circular Slider workshop, you'll learn how `Math.atan2()` can make calculating angles a snap.

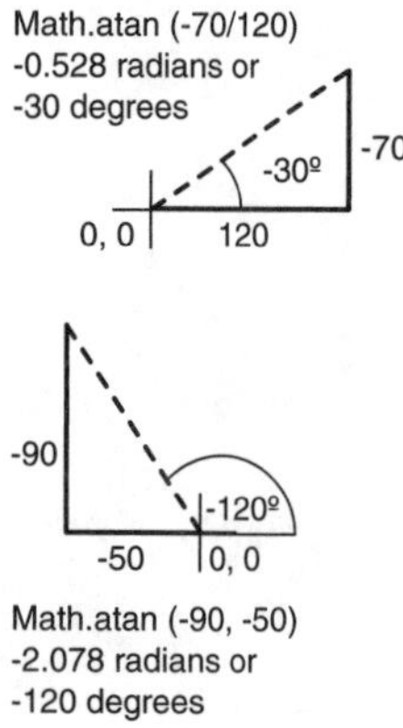

Figure 5.8 *When you consider Flash's coordinate system,* `Math.atan2()` *is a lifesaver because it handles all issues with positive and negative numbers.*

Hopefully you see how the Math object's methods can be used within expressions. Basically, you're given a suite of mathematical functions through this object. It's pretty easy to use the Math object, but that doesn't mean all your expressions will be easy to write. It also doesn't mean all the other objects are as easy either. For now, just realize you're given many useful functions through the Math object.

Using the Number Object

The Number object and Math object are similar in that both can be used in expressions without an intimate understanding of objects. You simply say `Number.methodName()` or `Number.CONSTANT_NAME`. As you can see in Figure 5.9, the Number object is mainly constants (uppercase items). I suspect that you'll most often use the Number object for its constants only, so at this point we'll focus on them. (When we discuss objects in Chapter 11, the Number object's methods—`toString()` and `valueOf()`—will be covered.)

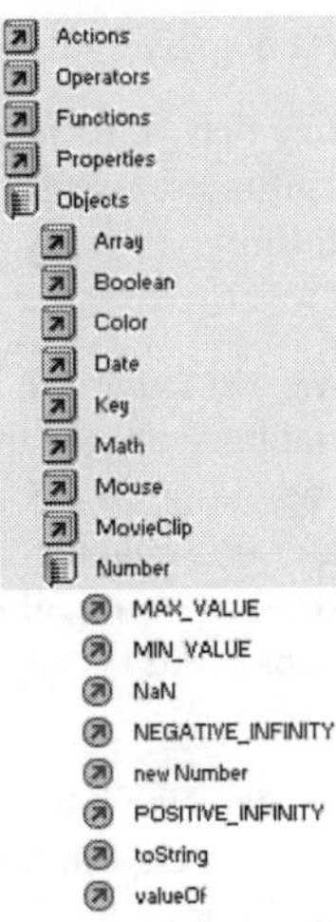

Figure 5.9 *The Number object is primarily used for the constants (all listed in uppercase).*

I've included this brief discussion now, however, because—in addition to being a simple object—there's another part of ActionScript with the *same* name. In addition to the Number object, there's a function called `Number()` that we touched on earlier this chapter. Even though we won't discuss functions fully until Chapter 8, using the `Number()` function is easy: `Number(expresionOrVariable)` attempts to convert the value of `expresionOrVariable` into a number and return the result. So `myNum=Number("100")+1;` will convert the string `"100"` to a number, add 1 to it, and place `101` into `myNum`. Remember that the addition operator will act differently if one operand is a string (and in our case, turn `myNum` into `"1001"`). Because the word *Number* is used in both the case of a Number object and the Number function, it can be confusing. The weird part is that if you use the `new` constructor in front of `Number()`, you'll be creating a new instance of the Number object. A different thing entirely, and something that you probably don't want to do. (At least wait until you learn all about objects in later chapters.)

The Number object's constants are easy to use, albeit not particularly exciting. Here they are

- `Number.MAX_VALUE` is the "largest representable number," meaning a very high number, but one from which you can subtract. For example, you might initialize a variable to equal `MAX_VALUE` (as in `bigNumber=Number.MAX_VALUE`). Then you could subtract from your variable (for a very long time—but not forever).

- `Number.MIN_VALUE` is the smallest number (actually a negative number).
- `Number.NEGATIVE_INFINITY` is so far into the negative that you can't even add numbers to ever get out. You can use this constant in comparison expressions, but you can't perform operations on "infinity" the way you can with `Number.MAX_VALUE` and `Number.MIN_VALUE`.
- `Number.POSITIVE_INFINITY` is like `Number.NEGATIVE_INFINITY` but positive. Because you can't perform calculations on variables that contain `Number.POSITIVE_INFINITY`, the most likely usage would be in a comparison expression (such as an if-statement discussed later this chapter). For example, you could check whether a variable or expression is equal to `Number.POSITIVE_INFINITY`. For example, 1/0 is `Number.POSITIVE_INFINITY`.
- `Number.NaN` means "Not a Number." You'll probably see "NaN" by accident more often then you'll need to select it by choice. When you try performing a math operation on a string, you'll get "NaN" for an answer—meaning the operation failed. `Number.NaN` can be used in comparison expressions such as `(aVariable==Number.NaN)`. Often, however, there are alternatives that might work better. For example, `undefined`, which all variables have for a value before you ever use them. Also, the function `isNaN(`*`expression`*`)` will return false if "*`expression`*" is a number (or true if it's not a number). Because variables all equal `undefined` before they are assigned, you can use a conditional (for example, an if-statement) to check whether a variable is `undefined`—in which case, you could take corrective action like assigning it a legitimate value.

We've looked at a lot this chapter! Expressions, statements, and the operators that hold them together. Also, the Math object was included because it gives you a different set of operators. There's more. Despite the fact that we've seen some perfectly complete statements, we haven't looked at conditional statements (that execute only when certain conditions exist) or loop structures (that repeatedly execute scripts). Loops and conditionals will round out your knowledge and then you can start practicing everything at the end of the chapter.

Conditional and Loop Statements

Flash executes every line of script that it encounters. If a script is never encountered, it's never executed. And, if a script is encountered repeatedly, it is executed over and over. Using conditionals, you can control what part of your script is executed or skipped. Obviously, if you place a script on a button and the user never clicks the button, the script won't execute. However, after a button is clicked, a conditional can control what portion of the contained script executes. This way, you can write scripts that behave differently depending on outside conditions.

Looping is a way to make a particular script execute repeatedly—either a certain number of times or until a condition is met. This is helpful when you have a lot of code to process, but also when you're not sure how many times the code needs to execute. In the upcoming section on loops, you'll find that loops can save you a lot of typing. Compare these two pseudo-code descriptions in which a loop would help:

The long way:

```
Attention Dasher; Attention Dancer; Attention Prancer; Attention Vixen;
Attention Comet; Attention Cupid; Attention Donder; Attention Blitzen.
```

Using a loop:

```
All reindeer... Attention.
```

Although this might not explain the ActionScript syntax (it's just pseudo-code), the second choice (the loop) is obviously easier to use.

Conditional Statements: `if`, `if else`, `if else if`

These three structural conditional statements are really variations on the same concept—if a condition is true, Flash should execute a block of code. At the core of all three variations is "if" and it's the easiest. Consider my wife instructing me, "If they have jellybeans, get me some." The condition is that "they have jellybeans" and the result—if they do—is that I'm supposed to "get some" for her. More technically, *if* the condition "they have jellybeans" is true, I execute the second part of my wife's instructions.

A plain "if" statement will execute the consequences only when the statement is encountered and the condition is true—nothing more. Realize that unless my wife specifies what to do in the event that they're out of jellybeans, I don't need to do anything (of course, I know better). Had she said, "If they have jellybeans, get some; otherwise, get some chocolate," it's clear that I'll be purchasing one item or the other. If the condition is false (that is, if they don't have jellybeans), I am to automatically follow the second part (the "otherwise" or the "else," if you will). In reality, I can't get chocolate unless they have some, but that's not at issue. In this case, when the initial condition is false, the second part (the "else") is executed every time.

You can make the "else" conditional, too. That is, "If they have jellybeans, get some; otherwise, if chocolate is on sale, get some of that." Realize that there's a distinct possibility that I will come home empty handed. A plain "if" can skip part of the code; an "if else" will do one or the other instructions; and an "if else if" could easily skip all the code. Let me just show the three real-life statements in actual ActionScript—using a few homemade variables.

Plain "if":

```
if (jellybeans>0) {
    // buy some
}
```

Regular "if else":

```
if (jellybeans>0) {
    // buy some
} else {
    // get chocolate
}
```

An "if else if":

```
if (jellybeans>0) {
    // buy some
} else if (chocolate == "on sale") {
    // get chocolate
}
```

Even though you *can* write an "if" statement with the Actions panel in Normal Mode, I'd recommend (if just temporarily) going into Expert Mode to do so. I always start by typing the structure of the "if" statement—no conditions, no results… just a skeleton. Like this:

```
if (condition){
}
```

This way I won't forget to satisfy any parentheses or curly brackets I start. Then I go back through and replace "condition" with an expression that results in true or false (1 or 0). Then, finally, after the open curly bracket I make a new line and type the script I want executed (when the condition is true).

If I decide I need to add an "else" catch-all when the condition is not true, I'll add "else {}" at the end. That is, the code

```
if (jellybeans>0){
    //buy some
}
```

can have an "else" provision added, like this:

```
if (jellybeans>0){
    //buy some
} else {
}
```

Then I'll go back through and make a new line after the curly bracket that follows the "else." Adding an "else if" is not much different. Simply add "else if (condition){}" instead of "else {}."

Finally, "else if" statements can be nested. That is, when one condition is not met (because it's false), another condition is not met, and you can keep adding "else if" *ad infinitum*. As such, nested "else if" statements can become unwieldy. Although it's not as eloquent (or efficient for the computer), I recommend avoiding deeply nested "else if" statements and instead using a series of independent "if" statements. For example, you could use all three "if" statement in sequence:

```
if (jellybeans>0){
    //buy some
}
if (!(jellybeans>0)){
    //buy chocolate
}
if (chocolate=="on sale"){
    //buy chocolate
}
```

There's a logical problem with this code as *each* "if" statement is encountered (and potentially entered) meaning that it's possible that I come home with both jellybeans and chocolate. (Not necessarily a problem, but remember that this is supposed to serve as an alternative to a nested "if else if" statement.) If the various conditions were exclusive—that is, when one is true, the others are necessarily false—then there's no problem with this method. Notice that's the situation with the first two conditions. That is, there's no possible way that `(jellybeans>0)` and `!(jellybeans>0)` could both be true—they're mutually exclusive. However, the first and third conditions could both be true, and thus both conditional scripts would be executed. In the case of nested "if" statements, if one condition is met, the others aren't even considered—they're simply skipped.

Even if multiple "if" statements aren't all exclusive (which is the problem here), you can still use this more readable format with a little extra work. The statement `return` will cause Flash to bypass the rest of the script in a block of code. Realize that the code could be enclosed within a larger block of code—perhaps within an `on (press){ }` mouse event of a button. As soon as Flash encounters `return`, it will skip the rest of the code. So, if you type `return` right before the closing curly bracket in each "if" statement, you can be assured that once an "if" statement's condition is met, the rest will be ignored.

My suggestion for a series of "if" statements is beginning to look like a real pain considering that even *after* one condition is met, you want the rest of the "ifs" skipped but you might have more code (at the end) that you want to execute—therefore, you can't simply use `return` within each "if" statement. Just to carry this through, one solution would be to set a "flag" variable. That is, above all the "ifs," you can type `notDone=1;`. Then each condition can be expanded from `if(mainCondition){}` to read `if((mainCondition)&¬Done)){}`. This script says that if *both* the original condition (such as `jellybeans>0`) *and* the condition `notDone==1` then execute the code. Finally, instead of using `return` within (but at the end of each) "if" statement, use `notDone=0;`, which will effectively cause Flash to skip the rest of the conditions. The result would look like this:

```
notDone=1;
if (jellybeans>0){
    //buy some
    notDone=0;
}
if (!(jellybeans>0)&&notDone){
    //buy chocolate
    notDone=0;
}
if (chocolate=="on sale"&&notDone){
    //buy chocolate
    notDone=0;
}
//the rest of the code
```

(Recall that the expression `notDone` is the same as `notDone==1`.) I'll be the first to admit that this solution is not eloquent, nor is it particularly efficient for the computer. I would argue, however, that compared to a deeply nested "if else if" statement, it's probably easier to read. The sacrifice of making slightly less concise code is worth it if it means the code is more readable. Feel free to use `else-if` when you're able to keep track of everything. Keep in mind that this discussion hasn't been wasted because we got to talk about the `return` statement plus a little bit about solving a problem.

You'll get more practice at the end of the chapter, but for now I recommend that you study the skeleton form of each version of the "if" statement.

Loop Statements: `for`, `for in`

Any loop will execute the same script as many times as you specify, or until a condition you specify is met. Often you don't know exactly how many times you need the code to execute, but you can still refer to the number of loops by reference, such as "keep rinsing the spinach until there's no more dirt in the water" and "for every envelope in that stack please address, seal, and stamp each one." If there are 100 envelopes, you'll repeat the process 100 times—but you don't have to explicitly specify 100 iterations. You'll see how to specify the number of iterations this way. In addition, realize that you won't always execute the same exact code repeatedly. For example, when you address, seal, and stamp several envelopes, you're following the same instructions (the same "script," if you will), but with slight variations. You don't put the same address on each envelope, but you do put *some* address on each envelope. When structuring the loop you're writing, consider two issues: How many times should the script execute and how do I write the script (that executes) so that it behaves differently for each iteration?

If you only learn one loop statement, it should be the "for" loop. Here's the skeleton:

```
for (init; condition; next) {
    //do statement(s) here
}
```

Here's an example we can draw upon for discussion:

```
for (n=1; n<11; n++) {
    trace("Current iteration is "+n);
}
```

Just to dissect the skeleton form of this "for" loop, you can read it this way: Starting with *init*, repeat the following while *condition* is true, and on each iteration, do *next*. So, for the example, it says: Starting with `n=1`, keep doing the `trace` Action while `n<11`..., each time incrementing `n`. The `trace` Action is executed ten times in a row, but the string that is formed looks slightly different on each loop. Into the output window, you'll see "Current Iteration is 1", and then "Current iteration is 2", and so on. Imagine walking through this loop—the init says "n starts at 1," so the first time the trace is encountered, n is 1. Look at the "next" expression to see what will happen the next time through and you'll see n++ (meaning that n is incremented by 1) and n becomes 2. The trace Action is executed again. It keeps doing this while the condition—n<11—is true. When n reaches 10, the condition is still true. The next time through, n is 11, so the condition is false and Flash jumps past the closing curly bracket to continue any scripts that follow.

One tip (just like writing "if" statements) is you should start by typing the skeleton and then replace `init; condition; next`. Another tip is to remember the `condition` is the condition that keeps them *in* the loop—not the condition to get out of the loop. That is, repeat *while* the condition is true, not repeat *until* the condition is true. In the earlier example, we wanted to repeat until n reached 11, but the following changed script has a problem:

```
for (n=1; n==11; n++) {
    trace("Current iteration is "+n);
}
```

The problem is that n starts at 1, but the condition is looking for 11, so it doesn't have a chance to ever get to 11. The entire loop is skipped.

Probably the biggest warning I can give you is to make sure that your loops eventually finish. It's easy to accidentally produce a script that, in theory, loops forever. While testing a movie, if Flash ever gets stuck in a loop for more than 15 seconds, it displays a warning to the user as shown in Figure 5.10.

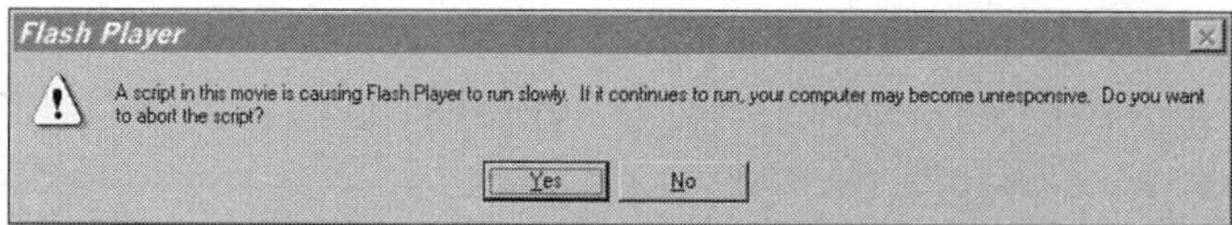

Figure 5.10 *When the Flash player gets stuck in a script for more than 15 seconds, this dialog appears.*

Because each iteration of a script takes a tiny fraction of a second, 15 seconds is a very long time! Generally, being stuck in a script long is likely a symptom of an infinite loop. Here's a perfect example of just such a loop:

```
for (n=1; n>0; n++) {
    //anything because this is an infinite loop!
}
```

The condition (n>0) is true from the beginning and remains so forever! If the "next" expression *decremented* n instead of *incrementing* it—this would not be a problem.

Another way to inadvertently create an infinite loop is to forget how = differs from ==. Only "init" and "next" are assignments (and therefore they're statements), but "condition" is just an expression. Therefore, this example probably doesn't do what the programmer intended (unless she was trying to make an infinite loop):

```
for (n=1; n=11; n++) {
    //Help, I'm stuck in an infinite loop
}
```

Notice the problem is that "condition" is n=11 (an assignment). The entire n=11 statement, if evaluated, is 1 (or true). This code loops forever because the condition (n=11) is true and remains so forever. (This mistake messes me up all the time!)

As I mentioned, learning the plain "for" loop is all you really *need*. However, the variation "for in" is also useful. Unlike "if," "if else," and "if else if," the "for in" loop is not an extension of the plain "for" loop. The two are entirely different statements. To fully utilize "for in," it's best to understand arrays and objects—two subjects covered in later chapters. The idea is that the loop will continue to loop "for all the items in the object." Here's an example: "For all the envelopes in that box, do whatever." I'll just show you the skeleton form and one example without fully explaining arrays or objects.

Form:

```
for(iterant in object){
    //do statement(s) here
}
```

Example:

```
allNames=["Dasher", "Dancer", "Prancer", "Vixen", "Comet", "Cupid",
➥"Donder", "Blitzen"]
```

```
for(n in allNames){
    trace("On "+allNames[n]);
}
```

In the form, there are two elements for you to replace: "iterant" and "object." You simply give iterant any name you want and it becomes a variable that automatically increments from the highest down to the lowest. If there are eight things in your object (as in my example), it starts at 7, returns the value of the 7th item in the array (in my example: Blitzen), and decreases in every loop until it reaches 0. (Because arrays start counting from 0, the range is 7 down to 0 instead of 8 to 1 as you might expect.) "Object" is the name of your object or array (in this case, the variable "allNames," which happens to contain an array of eight items). You don't have to understand arrays fully to imagine how this example works. For now, notice that one way to populate a variable with an array is shown in the first line of the example (use brackets and separate individual values with commas). If you ever need to grab individual elements from an array, you can use the form: `arrayName[index]` where index evaluates as 0 through the total number of items in the array (minus 1, because arrays count 0,1,2,3, and so on).

Unlike the plain "for" loop, "for in" doesn't require that you specify what is supposed to happen on every loop (that is, the "next"). That's because the variable name you use for the iterant automatically goes through all the items in the object (starting at the highest and incrementing down). The two advantages of "for in" are that you don't have to define the "next" and you don't have to specify a condition to control how many times the loop repeats. Here's an example of using a plain "for" loop to achieve nearly the same result as the "for in" example I showed. Notice it's not quite as clean—but it works basically the same way.

```
allNames=["Dasher", "Dancer", "Prancer", "Vixen", "Comet", "Cupid",
➥"Donder", "Blitzen"]
for(n=0; n<8; n++){
    trace("On "+allNames[n]);
}
```

(By the way, instead of hard-wiring `8` in the condition, I could have used `allNames.length`, which returns the length of the array—but that's something you'll learn in Chapter 10.) Do notice that this example is equivalent to, but not the same as, the "for in" loop. The "for in" version effectively goes in reverse order (starting with "Blitzen" instead of "Dasher," as is the case here).

Let's look at the statements that execute every time loop repeats. You can put any statement (or statements) within the loop. You don't have to use the iterant at all. But if you want the statement that executes to vary every time the loop repeats, the trick is to *use* the iterant within the statement. All my examples use a plain `trace` command. However, the string that appears is different in every iteration because the iterant variable is used. It is used either explicitly, as in `trace ("Current iteration is "+n);` or within an expression, as in `trace("On "+allNames[n]);` (This won't reveal the value of `n`; rather it uses `n` to extract an element in the `allNames` variable.)

Also realize that you can include as many statements as you want within a loop. You could even make your own iterant or counter that you maintain. You can nest other statements like "if" statements. See whether you can figure out the result of this nested statement:

```
for(n=1; n<11; n++){
    if(n%2==0){
        trace(n+" is even");
    } else {
        trace(n+" is odd");
    }
}
```

The variable `n` starts at `1` and iterates through `10`. If the expression `n%2` happens to equal `0` (that is, there is zero remainder from trying to divide `n` by `2`), the `trace` command displays "n is even" (but `n` is replaced by the value of `n`). Otherwise, the `trace` command "n is odd" appears. By the way, I wrote out this example by first typing the skeleton of the "for" loop, and then inserting a skeleton of the "if else." Then I finally came back through and filled in the data. (And naturally, I had to test it a couple times to weed out bugs—one of the semicolons in the "for" was a comma, and my "if" condition was mistyped as an assignment: `n%2=0`.)

while

If nothing else, "while" loops are the easiest to accidentally turn into infinite loops. Basically, you say "repeat while this condition is true." If the condition never becomes false, you'll repeat forever. You have to make sure that the condition eventually turns out false. The "while" loop is *not* suitable for repeating statements while you wait for the user to do something (or stop doing something). For example, "while the user has the mouse pressed" is a perfectly legitimate concept, but you have to use a different solution for that objective—"while" loops are simply not made for that. A "while" loop gives you a way to write a script that will repeatedly execute a statement, but because you might not know exactly how many times it is supposed to execute, you can use a "while" loop *while* a condition is true. Remember, both "for" and "for in" required that you specify the number of loops—even if that specification was in reference to a variable, length of an array, or number of items in an object. If, for example, the task is that you keep looping while a variable called `found` is 0 (or `while(found==0)`) the "while" loop is perfect. (Just make sure that `found` will eventually become something *other* than 0 or you'll be stuck in the loop forever.)

Here's the form:

```
while ( condition ) {
    //do this statement
}
```

Here's an example that shows you must take precautions to ensure that the condition eventually becomes false (so that you can get out of the loop):

```
allNames=["Dasher", "Dancer", "Prancer", "Vixen", "Comet", "Cupid", ➥ ➥
➥"Donder", "Blitzen"]
found=0;
n=0;
while (found==0 && n<allNames.length){
    if (allNames[n]=="Rudolf"){
        found=1;
    }
    n++;
}
if (found){
    trace("Rudolf found in spot " + n);
}
```

The form is simple: Statements will repeatedly execute while the condition is true. The example I showed is a bit complex, but instead of contriving an unrealistically simple example, this accurately shows the types of provisions necessary when you use "while" loops.

Basically, I want the loop to repeat until I find the string "Rudolf"—so the initial condition is simply `while found==0` (or false). Before the loop, both `found` and `n` are initialized. Because my basic condition is that `found==0`, I want to make sure that it's `0` from the start. The variable `n` serves as an iterant (you'll almost always need your own iterant in "while" loops). This iterant must be initialized before the loop, so that I can increment `n` at the end of each statement in the loop. The "if" statement simply checks whether the `n`th index of `allNames` contains the string "Rudolf". If so, `found` is set to `1`—and that gets us out of the loop. Notice that even if `found` were set to `1`, the last statement in the loop (`n++`) would still execute once before getting kicked out of the loop on the next iteration. So, if `n` were 4, when Rudolf was found, `n` would be 5 by the time the loop was exited. I'm taking advantage of the fact `n` is always greater than the index where Rudolf was found. My trace doesn't refer to the array index where Rudolf was found but rather to the made up term "spot" which is more intuitive than array's indexes (that count 0,1,2…). Finally, it's quite possible that "Rudolf" is never found! To ensure that the loop would exit after each index was checked, I added `&&` `n<allNames.length` to the condition (`found==0`). Translated, the entire condition reads: "while both `found` is zero and `n` is less than the total number of items in `allNames`." (Notice that I didn't have to say `n<=allNames.length` because the length is `8` and I only needed to check through the last item—at index `7`.)

The previous example shows how "while" loops require extra maintenance in the form of your own iterating variable that you first initialize and then increment. This is almost always necessary, although occasionally you don't need to do it. For example, if you're trying to create two random numbers, the following statement should work fine:

```
oneNum=0;
otherNum=0;
while (oneNum==otherNum){
    oneNum=Math.random();
    otherNum=Math.random();
}
```

There's a theoretical possibility that on every iteration, both `oneNum` and `otherNum` will be assigned the same random number. The two variables contain the same value at the start (`0`) and will then repeat while they remain the same. Likely this loop will only execute once, but even if the two random numbers came out the same, it would only take a fraction of a second to loop a thousand more times. On my 450MHz Pentium III, for example, a loop like this will iterate more than 10,000 times a second! The point is, there's a high likelihood that two different random numbers will be found before Flash reaches its 15-second timeout. But unless you include a "way out" in the condition, a "while" loop could try looping forever (this just means Flash will reach the timeout dialog shown in Figure 5.10—but that is a bad thing because the user sees the dialog).

A couple last points about loops. The user won't see any visual change onstage *during* the loop. For example, consider this statement:

```
for (n=1; n<6; n++){
    someClip._x= n*5;
}
```

You might expect to see someClip's x position appear at 5, 10, 15, 20, and then 25. It actually does move to those five locations, but you won't see it move. When the loop is finished, you'll see it in the final resting position of 25—but the stage does not refresh after each loop. (By the way, you can certainly animate a clip with scripting as we'll do in the workshop portion of this book—but you just can't do it using a loop.)

Finally, there are two interesting statements that change the flow of a loop. Similar to the way `return` will skip out of any function or enclosed event (such as `on(press)`), both `break` and `continue` can make a loop change course. Specifically, `break` will jump out of any loop (actually, it jumps to the end of the loop) and `continue` will immediately jump to the top of the loop (that is, iterate) by skipping any further statements within the loop.

Here's an example that shows how `continue` jumps to the top of a loop:

```
for (n=1; n<6; n++){
    if (n==3){
        continue;
    }
    trace ("A number that's not three is " + n);
}
```

If the condition (n==3) is true, the `continue` jumps to the top of the loop (to continue) while bypassing the `trace` statement below. The `continue` statement effectively says, "skip the rest of the statements but continue looping."

This example shows how `break` will jump out of a loop:

```
n=1;
while(true==true){
  //do something
  if (n>10 && n%2==0){
    break;
  }
  n++;
}
trace ("The first even number past ten is "+n);
```

Without the `break` statement, this loop would repeat forever. When `break` is executed, Flash jumps to the end of the loop where it is currently enclosed (that is, to where the `trace` statement appears in this example). This is just a quick way to get out of a loop. Notice, too, that `break` will jump past the `n++` statement. Compared to `return`, `break` only jumps past the end of an enclosed loop where `return` jumps out of the function or the event that started it all (as with `on (press)`)—most likely skipping a lot more code than a `break` statement will. For example, if `return` were used in this example instead of `break`, the `trace` statement would be skipped as well.

Applied Expression Writing

This chapter is packed with concepts that relate to composing scripts. You've seen a couple previews of concepts that will come up later (such as arrays and functions), but for the most part, everything in this chapter had to do with writing expressions and statements. The remaining pages provide a chance to practice writing more complex expressions. I'll provide the objective and you should at least try to write the pseudo-code and then (if you can) the actual script. I'll provide my solution with a translation. There are two things to remember as you work through these challenges. First, my solution is just one of countless possible solutions. You might very well find a better way to solve the problem. Second, I include many made-up variables. In a real project, these variables would necessarily have their values set earlier or within a different part of the movie. For example, I might use the expression `score>=80`. The idea is that the variable `score` is one that I've been tracking. Perhaps, attached to the button for each correct answer, I used the script: `score=score+10;`. I'm just assuming that such variables have had their values set properly. You can make up variables to use in expressions—just realize that you'll have to take care of them by changing their values as necessary.

Objective: Given a minimum (x location, let's say) and a maximum, write an expression that uses a given percent to return an integer midpoint based on percent. That is, if the west coast is at 100 miles latitude and the east coast is at 3100 miles latitude, a location 50% across the country would be at latitude position 1600 miles. Even though most people can figure that out in their head, it's more difficult to write the expression (using variables named `high`, `low`, and `percent`).

Solution:

```
low+ Math.floor((high-low)*(percent/100));
```

Translation: Calculating 50% of 3000 is easy. Just use `3000*(50/100)`. To determine the width of the United States, for example, you can subtract the latitude of the east coast (`high`) from the west coast (`low`). Our formula so far: `(high-low)*(percent/100)`. That will usually result in a decimal answer, and using `Math.floor()` returns the integer portion. Finally, the entire expression is added to `low` (or the west coast) because you'll want to start counting from there. For example, if the latitude of west coast is 5000 and the east coast is 8000—50% of the difference is still 1500, but if you want to end up in the middle of the country, you need to add 1500 to 5000 (that is, 6500 by counting from the west coast). See Figure 5.11.

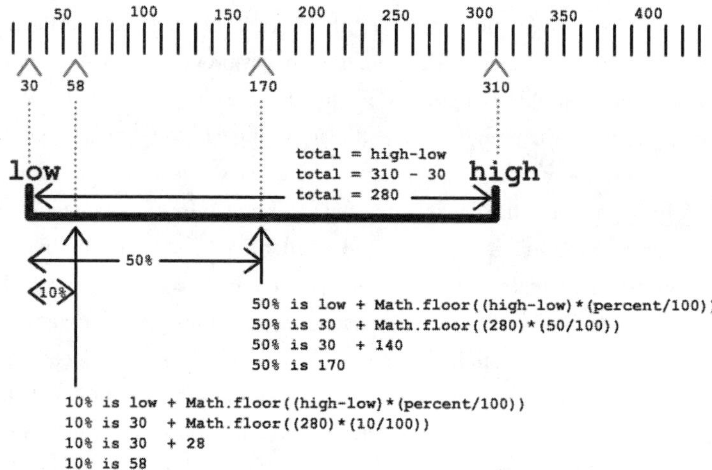

Figure 5.11 *A visual representation of the problem might help you solve the expression for percent.*

Objective: Build an array containing the days of the week, like this:

```
daysOfWeek=["Sunday","Monday", "Tuesday", "Wednesday","Thursday",
➥"Friday", "Saturday"];
```

Then write a loop that displays all the days of the week in the output window (using the `trace` statement).

Solution:

```
daysOfWeek=["Sunday","Monday", "Tuesday", "Wednesday","Thursday",
➥"Friday", "Saturday"];
for (n=0, n<7, n++){
    trace(daysOfWeek[n]);
}
```

Translation: After populating the array, our "for" loop initializes `n` to `0` (because, remember, the first item in an array is in index 0). Then, while `n` is less than `7` (the last item in the array is at index 6), our `trace` statement displays the `n`th item in the array. Notice how the following also works, but displays the days in reverse order:

```
for (n in daysOfWeek){
    trace(daysOfWeek[n]);
}
```

Objective: Write a statement (using if, if else, or if else if) that sets a variable called `grade` to A, B, C, D, or F, based on a variable called `score` using a scale in which 90–100 is an A, 80–89 is a B, 70–79 is a C, 60–69 is a D, and 0–59 is an F.

Solution:

```
grade="F";
if (score>=60){
    grade="D";
}
if (score>=70){
    grade="C";
}
if (score>=80){
    grade="B";
}
if (score>=90){
    grade="A";
}
```

Translation: Granted, this isn't the eloquent solution—there are many other possibilities. The way I solved it was to first award an F (sort of discouraging, I suppose), and then if `score` was high enough (`score>=60`) I give a D, and so on. Even though this isn't super efficient—after all, if a score is 95, the grade is assigned F, D, C, B, and then finally A. I used this solution because it's easy to read and not because it shows off every component of ActionScript.

Summary

What a chapter! Believe it or not, there's more. However, the topics covered in this chapter cover almost all the typical programming tasks that you'll be doing day in and day out. Although many upcoming chapters have interesting and valuable information, this chapter summarizes the core skills.

{ Chapter 6 }

Debugging

Bugs are fact in any programming. Even if you could write code that—by itself—was bug-free, outside influences can cause your movie to fail. Such basic issues as the user's computer configuration, the operating system, the browser, and even the Flash player all have *some* bugs. Of course, you don't need any help creating bugs because if you're human, you'll create many on your own. Actually, you, not the underlying software, will likely be the source of most bugs. Bugs can be a flaw in your flow of logic or they can be an error in the syntax of an expression. Regardless, bugs will crop up with unpredictable results that are invariably undesirable.

Debugging, or finding bugs and fixing them, poses an interesting dilemma. The premise of debugging is that you (the one who created the bug in the first place) are supposed to uncover where the flaw in logic or syntax error appears. Naturally, this is quite difficult because it requires that you find a problem in a script you thought was perfectly logical and legitimate at the time you wrote it. Despite this difficulty, there are both practical methods and built-in features of Flash to help you squash bugs.

In this chapter, you will

- Interpret syntax errors that Flash provides
- Develop methods to identify and document bugs

- Learn conventional debugging techniques
- Use the Flash debugger to watch properties and variables

Compared to last chapter's intensity and length, this debugging chapter should be pretty mild. You should find it a good reprise.

General Approaches to a Bug-Free Life

While programming Flash, your life will never be truly "bug-free." But there are many steps you can take to uncover bugs, fix them, and ensure that there are no obvious ones waiting to reveal themselves at the least opportune time. Most of these quality assurance techniques apply to any process—not just Flash programming. We'll cover built-in Flash features later this chapter in the section on using the Debugger. Let's first look at general ways to find, define, fix, and prevent bugs.

Finding and Defining Bugs

The first—and most important—step in debugging is to find the bug. Some bugs will prove to be elusive. Others will be so significant that you won't be able to make the movie run. I'd categorize three types of bugs as follows: those that prevent the movie from even starting, those that cause the program to effectively stop running, and those with an error in logic that—while allowing the program to run—display inaccurate results. The first type is easiest to find, whereas the third type is most difficult.

Find the Bugs That Prevent Your Movie from Starting

When you select Control, Test Movie, Flash will export a .swf. But if there are any syntax errors (or other critical problems) in your script, you will see a full listing of the problems in the output window (shown in Figure 6.1). Although the offending script will be ignored (after all, Flash simply can't figure out what you meant), other scripts might still work. Regardless, the appearance of any syntax error is effectively a "show stopper." A script you wrote is not being interpreted and that is a problem that must be fixed.

These errors in the output window usually look worse than they are. Sometimes something as simple as a missing semicolon at the end of a line will display a long-winded error message that's easily fixed. Let me explain some of the more common errors you're likely to see and how they're resolved.

```
Scene=Scene 1, Layer=Layer 1, Frame=1: Line 2: Unexpected ';' encountered
     err((;

Scene=Scene 1, Layer=Layer 1, Frame=1: Line 3: ')' expected
     }

Scene=Scene 1, Layer=Layer 1, Frame=1: Line 1: Statement block must be terminated by '}'
     onClipEvent (load) {

Scene=Scene 1, Layer=Layer 1, Frame=1: Line 4: Syntax error.
```

Figure 6.1 *On testing your movie, all syntax errors will appear in the output window.*

First, to digest an error message, you should understand the form shown in Figure 6.2. The exact location in your script where the error occurs is shown first. You can fix the problem only when you track down the script's scene, layer, frame, and line number—luckily, it's all listed clearly. After the address, the generic Flash error message describes the nature of your problem. Some of the more common errors are described in the text following Figure 6.2 (you'll find all the error messages in a table in Flash's ActionScript Reference manual and help documents). Finally, on a new line, a quote or partial quote of your script is shown.

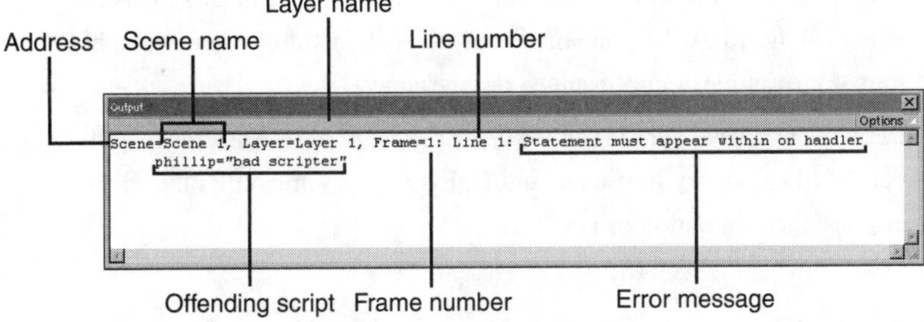

Figure 6.2 *Error messages are detailed, including where the error occurred and the nature of the problem.*

Here are the errors that seem to appear most often.

Balancing Errors

As you learned in Chapter 5, "Programming Structures," anything you start (such as a quote or parenthetical statement) must finish properly. You'll see one of the following errors if you follow this rule.

`string literal was not properly terminated`

`')' expected`

`';' expected`

`Unexpected '}' encountered` (This is usually caused by forgetting to include a semicolon at the end of a line.)

`Statement block must be terminated by '}'`

Right church, wrong pew

These errors appear when you have script—which might be perfectly legitimate—but it's in the wrong place. For example, you can't use an "onClipEvent" anywhere except clip instances. An "onClipEvent" used on a button or keyframe will give you an error.

`Statement must appear within on handler` (This occurs when you place a script on a button without surrounding it with an "on" mouse event.)

`Statement must appear within onClipEvent handler` (This occurs when you place a script on a clip instance without surrounding it with an "onClipEvent.")

`Mouse events are permitted only for button instances` (This occurs when you try to use an "on" mouse event on something other than a button—for example, a clip instance or keyframe.)

`Clip events are permitted only for movie clip instances` (This occurs when you try to use an "onClipEvent" on something other than a clip instance—a button or keyframe.)

Catch all

Although several other specific error messages are available, if your problem doesn't clearly fit into one of those, this catch-all message will appear.

`Syntax error`

Simply fixing the problem is usually easy after you know the cause. Keep in mind that often several errors will appear in the output window. Instead of trying to fix them all, just repair one at a time (starting at the top of the list). You'll find that fixing one problem often resolves others.

By the way, the same error messages will sometimes appear in the output window while authoring. This will happen either when you try pasting a bogus script (from your clipboard) into an Actions panel set to "Normal Mode," or when you attempt to set an Actions panel (that contains a bogus script) from "Expert Mode" to "Normal Mode." When the error is in your clipboard, the "address" of the error is shown as "Clipboard Actions" instead of the familiar scene, layer, and frame format. Additionally, there's a "Check Syntax" (Ctrl+T) feature in the Actions panel's options menu that will provide a similar listing of errors.

Any errors that reveal themselves in the output window are critical and should be dealt with before moving on to other tasks. Also, be sure to clear the output window before each test movie because you're only checking whether the error has been fixed (and it's easy to be distracted by old errors that could have been fixed).

Repeat and Isolate the Bug

The syntax errors that appear in the output window might seem overwhelming, but such errors will—in the long run—prove to be the least of your problems. It's just that they're critical, so you have to deal with them first. Most of your bugs will simply cause your movie to play incorrectly or display erroneous data. Because these errors appear only as you're testing your movie (maybe you click a button and nothing happens), you might believe they are intermittent. Very rarely is a bug truly intermittent and usually only when something outside your control (such as an Internet server or user's computer hardware) is the cause. Even though bugs might appear to be intermittent, to fix them you need to learn the cause, and to find the cause, you must be able to repeat the bug.

I know it sure helps when a client describes precisely how they caused a bug to appear. Often, a good description of the cause will enable me either to think of the solution on the spot or at least to have a good idea of which script I need to resolve. Spending time both to repeat a bug and to clearly specify the steps necessary to make that bug appear is time well spent. It's easy to fool yourself though. The *post hoc, ergo propter hoc* ("after this, therefore because of this") fallacy can mess you up. For example, if you wash your car and then it rains, you could use *post hoc ergo propter hoc* reasoning to mistakenly attribute washing your car to causing the rain to fall.

While tracking the cause of a bug, try to find the fewest steps necessary. For example, imagine that you're testing a movie you made and, after twice clicking a button you labeled "help" followed by a click of the "sound off" button, you find that your "search" doesn't work. You might be super clear those were the steps that caused the problem, but you should start over and try just the last step (pressing the "search" button). That could be the only problem! If the "search" button works, start over and try again by just clicking "sound off"… and then "search." This is really just basic troubleshooting. However you do it, just make sure that you can repeat the bug because the next step is to clearly document the bug.

Document and Analyze the Bug

This is probably the stage that will require the most restraint. The natural tendency when a bug is found is to try to fix it. Don't! It's possible, I suppose, when the bug is acute and clear to simply fix it. More often, when you prematurely attack a bug, you'll find yourself opening a can of worms. It's like starting to bake without a recipe or assemble shelves without reading all the directions first. You want to first have a clear plan of attack, know where you're headed, and then you'll likely fix the bug accurately and efficiently. This is achieved by documenting the bug you've found.

Simply knowing the bug is half the work. Depending on whether you uncover the bug early or late in a project, you should usually attempt to fix the bug with the least disruption to the rest of the code. Obviously, if the bug is rampant or fundamentally intertwined in your program, you'll want to consider rebuilding from scratch. Consider that fixing one thing often causes other things to break. Therefore, when you narrow the bug you'll be able to fix it better. Imagine you have a toothache. Surely, the dentist could simply remove the tooth and place a crown in its place, but this would probably be unnecessary. If a precise location of a cavity were found, the dentist could instead fill that cavity.

Realize also that with any problem, doing *nothing* is a viable alternative. This comes up all the time in medicine when performing an operation is too great a risk compared to doing nothing. The same is true with bugs. Not only should you implement just the necessary changes and nothing more, but you should always consider doing nothing as a suitable option. Every bug should be documented and categorized. Some bugs might be critical and prevent the movie from functioning. Other bugs might occasionally cause a display to blink for a second. Certainly I would always prefer to fix every bug, but you can viably opt to "punt" (just not fix a bug) if the bug isn't very important compared to a looming deadline or if fixing the bug will potentially break many other parts of the movie. I can't establish a set of guidelines for you to use, but if you first document and categorize each bug, you'll be able to set a course of action that is appropriate.

Fixing Bugs

An entire chapter on debugging and only now we talk about fixing bugs? Yep. I can't stress enough that after you know exactly what your objectives are, you can swiftly achieve them. It's true with converting detailed pseudo-code and it's true when you fix bugs. Sincerely, that's all there is to it. Of course, I have a couple tips for *how* you should fix bugs, but the truth is that if you know what the bug is, you're 95% of the way to fixing it.

Have the Humility to Call Yourself a Fool

Most bugs are the result of a stupid mistake. You need to have the humility to realize that you could be overlooking something obvious. I once heard that the majority of the tech help calls to a sound card manufacturer were resolved by simply turning up the volume. Just because a bug is causing you a great deal of grief, it doesn't necessarily require a lot of work to fix. Later in this chapter, you'll learn how to use Flash's Debugger to watch variables and properties change. When you walk through the steps that reveal the bug, leave no stone unturned. That is, don't take for granted the "easy" scripts. They're just as likely to have an error that causes the bug.

Try Being a Cynic

Not only do you need humility, but a good dose of cynicism will also help. The best quality assurance people often come across as cynical people. When applied to finding and fixing bugs, this is a good personality trait. Don't believe *anything* unless it can be proven. Just because it appears that part of your movie is working, a cynic will find a way to trip it up. For example, the movie might start with the user typing his name and pressing a "continue" button. When looking for a bug, you should try everything to break the movie! What happens when you type nothing and click "continue"? What if you press the Enter key—does it make a new line and move the first thing typed out of view? It's like you're *trying* to make it break. Good programmers can do most of this themselves, but because of the need for this cynical attitude, it sometimes helps for someone else to test your creation.

This cynicism can help do more than just uncover bugs. When you're trying to fix a bug, step through the entire code and question the logic every step of the way. Don't simply try to translate the code to English because you'll likely just repeat the intention you had in the first place. Rather, read each line with cynicism—as if someone were trying to trip you up and you have to find the flaw in the logic. If a line can be justified, move to the next line. If a block of code stands the "is it logical?" test, you can move on. It's difficult because you're effectively calling yourself a liar. Opposite to the United States' courts, your code is guilty (of bugs) until proven innocent.

Assuring All Bugs Are Squashed

The joy you feel when a bug is fixed is a feeling like no other. However, don't get too happy (remember, you're a cynic). I think the greatest error programmers make is they don't retest after fixing a bug. Because it's quite possible that fixing one bug causes other bugs to appear, consider retesting everything after you implement a supposed fix. It's difficult because in the process of fixing a bug, you've developed a pattern of steps to re-create the bug. The tendency is simply to follow those exact steps to see whether the bug is still present. Consider that after fixing one bug, if another bug was created you'll probably have to follow a different set of steps to see it. Although it might be impossible to retest everything after every minor bug is fixed, you should at least consider testing at logical milestones. You can also send the file back to your trusty cynic. Realize that even if you tell the testy testing person to check only whether certain bugs are fixed, if he does a good job, he'll actually test everything—not just the things that are supposed to be fixed.

Preventing Bugs

I suppose it's obvious that your life programming in Flash will be better if you simply prevent any bugs from the start. Even though this is wishful thinking, if not pure fantasy, there are several steps you can take while working in Flash that will reduce the likelihood of bugs.

Version Control

One form of documentation that's helpful while programming is version control. Although there are sophisticated software packages that some people use, you can still take advantage of the benefits of tracking versions as you develop a Flash site. The simplest form of version control is to simply do a "Save As" periodically. For example, you can start each day by saving a copy of your movie with the date in the name plus a letter of the alphabet (starting with "a")—such as "17_December_2000-a.fla". Every time you add a feature or squash a bug, save the movie with the next letter of the alphabet ("17_December_2000-b.fla"). If you're really organized, you'll keep a paper log that documents exactly what features were added or bugs were fixed in each revision. That way, if you find that a major bug has appeared that wasn't in an older version, you can go back through the revisions to find the latest version without the problem. Then you can redo the same edits—and test after each one. You'll uncover what caused the bug and your document will help you restore everything else.

Avoiding Bugs in the First Place

A related technique is to build new scripts and resolve bugs "offline." For example, if you intend to add a sophisticated feature to a Flash movie, you can try to work out the solution in a new separate file. After you get it working in the new file, you can add the script you developed to the main file. Sometimes working offline involves so much extra work just in laying the foundation that you might consider using the main file. However, before going wild trying different solutions, you should first save the main file, and then save as "working.fla". Do what it takes to find a solution, but when you do, go back to the original and carefully implement the scripts you developed (in "working.fla"). Even though this seems like extra work, realize that in the process of trying different solutions you might make several attempts that don't work. Even though you might *think* you were careful to dispose any failed attempts, there's a chance they're still present. By determining the solution "offline" and then implementing it "online," you're more likely to create a script that's more streamlined and less buggy. Compare this process to the way an artist will work on several "studies" before creating his masterpiece. (Remember that this technique is useful both for building scripts and for fixing broken scripts.)

The only other tip I can offer that tends to avoid bugs is to build your movies in pieces. No matter how large the task, it's always just a collection of subtasks. When you approach a large Flash project, try to break it down into pieces. Get each element to work before moving on to the next task. You can even modularize scripts by using functions (as you'll see in Chapter 8, "Functions,") and build building blocks of code by using objects (as you will in Chapters 11, "Objects," and 12, "Homemade Objects"). Regardless of the technical solution you apply, you should try to break down your task into pieces.

Using the Debugger

When it comes to finding the bugs you've created, Flash does offer help in the form of the Debugger. Through this special window, you can view variables or properties while a movie plays. In addition, you can change most properties of any movie clip. The name "debugger" might be deceptive. It won't "de-bug"; that is, remove bugs from your movie. Also, it's not exactly what programmers expect from a debugger. "Real" debuggers have options such as setting break points (which are points in the script where the program will pause) and step over/step into (which enable you to selectively skip parts or the script or execute just one line at a time). Flash's Debugger is useful, but be careful when calling it a true debugger. (You can find examples of full-fledged debuggers in Macromedia Director and Dreamweaver 4, as well as in many other programs such as Microsoft Visual Basic.)

Despite the fact that the Debugger won't *fix* your problems and lacks many features that traditional debuggers possess—it's still very useful. We'll first look at how to use the Debugger, and then we'll consider strategies to apply its features.

Viewing and Setting Properties and Variables

Flash's Debugger enables you to view and set both properties and variables. This is done while the movie plays. To view the debugger, select Control, Debug Movie (instead of Control, Test Movie). The first time you try the Debugger, it might appear that it isn't working. That's because the debugger window has to have been present the last time you tested the movie. It's weird because you'll often need to use Debug Movie once, leave the Debugger open but close the movie you're testing, and then use Debug Movie again. You'll know that the Debugger is working when you see—at least—`_level0` listed at the top of the Debugger (as shown in Figure 6.3).

After you have the Debugger working, you'll see a hierarchy of your movie and all its movie clip instances in the white area at the top. To view properties or variables, first select the clip instance that you want to analyze. Selecting `_level0` will enable you to see properties of and variables in the main timeline. Unnamed clips will appear with the seemingly arbitrary names that Flash assigns to them. Regardless, each clip in the hierarchy appears with its full path, always starting with `_level0` (except, of course, movies that you've loaded into other level numbers appear starting "_level*x*"—where "x" is the level number). Despite how complex your hierarchy becomes, all you do is select the clip (or `_level0` for the main timeline) and then view properties or variables from the tabs below.

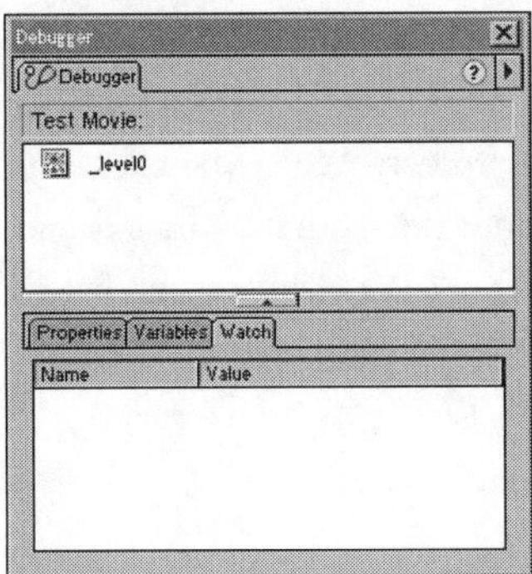

Figure 6.3 *You'll know the Debugger is working when you at least see* `_level0`.

You can test it out by following these steps:

1. Create a text field with some text in it and use the Text Options panel to set the field to Dynamic Text. Also, specify a variable name other than the default `TextField1`—maybe `someVar`. Leave this text on the main timeline.

2. Draw a box and convert it to a symbol (Movie Clip). Use the Instance panel to give it an instance name "box" and use the Effect panel to set the alpha to 50%.

3. Finally, create another Dynamic Text field with text in it and specify a memorable variable name (I used "anotherVar"). Use the Brush Tool to draw a rough circle around the text. Select both the text and the drawn circle and covert to symbol (Movie Clip). Give this instance the name "text."

4. Now, Debug Movie. (The hierarchy should look like Figure 6.4.) You might need to close the movie you're testing—but leave the debugger up and debug again. Also, remember that any time you're done debugging, only close the movie (not the Debugger) or next time you'll have to select Debug Movie twice.

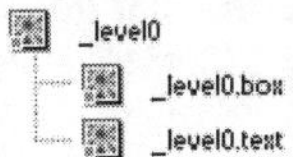

Figure 6.4 *The hierarchy of our exercise includes the two clip instances "box" and "text."*

At this point, you can first select a clip and then click either the Properties tab or the Variables tab. For example, if you click the `_level0.box` clip instance and then view its properties, you'll see `_alpha` listed as `50`. Because the `_alpha` property is not grayed out, you can change it. Double-click the `50`, type a new number, and then press Enter. You should see the clip change onscreen. Select the instance of `_level0.text` and change the `_y` property. When you click enter you should see the property change onscreen. Notice that both the `_xmouse` and `_ymouse` properties are grayed, meaning that you can't change them, but while you move your cursor around the movie, you'll see these properties update. See Figure 6.5.

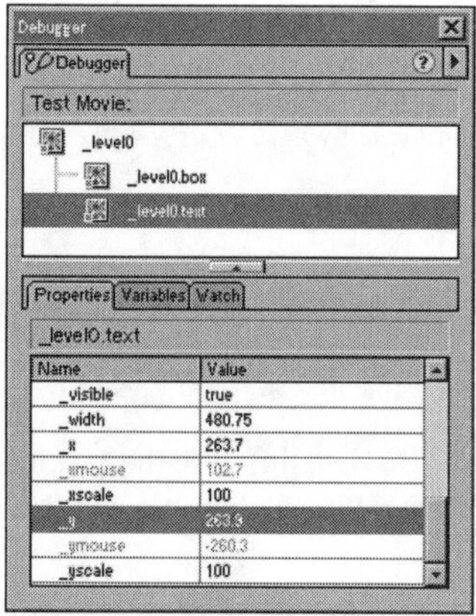

Figure 6.5 *Selecting an instance enables you to view properties, including the current* `_y` *as shown.*

Now, try viewing and changing the custom variables. Select `_level0`, click on the Variables tab, and you should see the name and value of your variable `someVar`. If you want to change this variable's value, remember that because this variable is a string, you need to include the quotation marks or it won't work. (You can view the variable contained in your `_level0.text` clip—but don't try changing the variable because you'll do that in the next section.)

Just to review, the basic process is to select the clip you want to inspect and then select either the Properties or the Variables tab. In practice, the idea is that you might expect to see a clip's `_alpha` change and you should be able to (while the movie plays) see this property change. Or, if there's a variable in a clip (which isn't always shown to the user in a text field), you might want to monitor the current value—that is, make sure that it's changing when you expect. You'll see how this will be useful later in this chapter and in many of the workshop exercises.

Watching Variables

Selecting individual clip instances is a necessary step before viewing their properties or variables because the debugger can show you only one clip's _x property at a time (because different clips might have different values for this property). It was easy in our case because we just had two clips plus the main timeline. In a real project, it can be a lot more complex. Figure 6.6 shows how complex a real project can become.

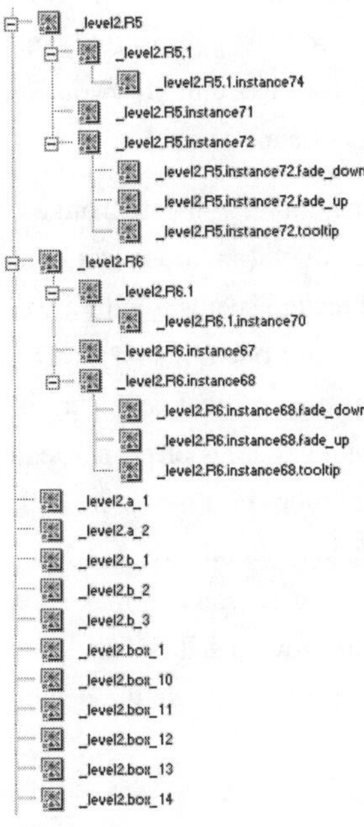

Figure 6.6 *A real project can become quite complex with countless clip instances.*

So, instead of weaving through a complex hierarchy, the Debugger enables you to "watch" certain clip's variables. All you need to do is select the variable that you want to monitor and either right-click it (Control+click on a Macintosh) and then select "watch," or select "watch" from the Debugger's option arrow. You'll see a blue dot next to the variable. Also, when you select the Watch tab, your variable will be visible at all times (regardless of what clip you happen to select at the top of the debugger). Under the Watch tab, you can also select "add watch" (or simply "add") then type the path and variable name you want to watch. But because the Debugger uses the old "slash" notation, I think it's easiest to first find the variable you want to watch (under the Variables tab) and add it from there.

If you want to test it out, just create two buttons and two Movie Clip instances. Name one clip instance `box1` and the other `box2`. Then attach a script on one button that reads `box1.count++` and have the other button's script read: `box2.count++` (both scripts will need to be within a mouse event such as `release`). Now when you Debug Movie, even though you the user won't "see" each clip's `count` variable, you'll be able to with the Debugger. In addition, you can monitor both count variables if you first use the Debugger to find `box1`, select `count` and then "add watch." Do the same for `box2` and you won't need keep finding `box1` or `box2` to view their respective `count` variables.

It seems that the Debugger itself has bugs! For example, you can change variables contained in clips only if you first set up a watch (and do it from the Watch tab). Changing variables' values from the Variables tab seems to edit a variable (of the same name) in the main timeline. If there isn't one already, the Debugger adds it. This, and other minor issues, really aren't that critical considering that the end user will certainly never be able to change variables or properties in this way. You can still use the Debugger to accurately monitor a movie as it plays—I just wouldn't count on it letting you make changes to the movie. Keep in mind too, that the debugger is a runtime-only feature. That is, you can make changes while your movie plays, but if you re-export your movie (that is Test Movie) all variables will reinitialize regardless of the changes you made in the debugger the last time it ran.

Remote Debugging

One of the coolest features of the Debugger is that you can debug movies playing in a browser. This means that even after you upload a finished movie, it's possible to debug it remotely. When you see the steps involved for this to work, you might think it's a pain but the steps are necessary for good reason. For example, you might not want others to be able to debug your movies.

To remotely debug a movie, the following conditions must be set:

- The original `.fla` needs its Publish Settings set to Debugging Permitted. Optionally, you can also specify a password. See Figure 6.7.
- You must be viewing the movie on a machine with the Debug version of the Flash player installed (which comes automatically with the purchased version of Flash). This player can be found in the Players folder (in a folder called Debug) next to your installed version of Flash.
- Finally, the Debugger (while debugging a movie) must have the option set to Enable Remote Debugging.

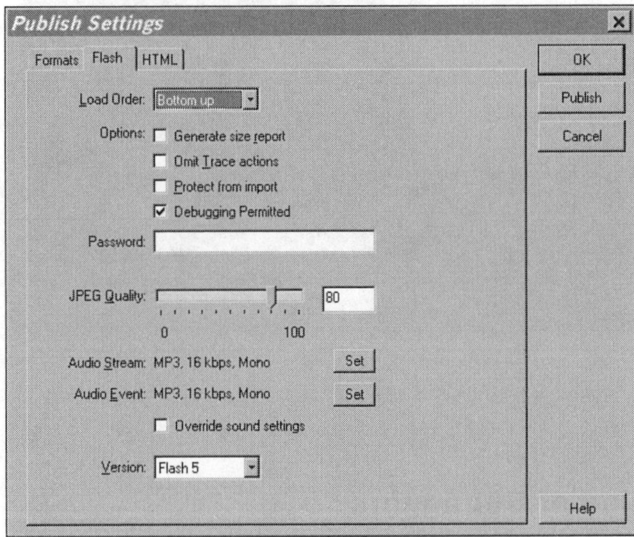

Figure 6.7 *The movie's Publish Settings must allow for debugging.*

To debug a movie, first make sure that Flash is open, and then just launch your browser and right-click a movie that has been set to permit debugging. If you're running the correct version of the Flash player (the Debug version), you can select Debugger from the menu that appears (users who have downloaded the free player from Macromedia won't even see this option). After you enter the password (or simply click OK), you'll be able to debug the movie. One frustrating fact is that Flash removes all panels when it is not the active application. Therefore, when you click the movie in the browser to interact with it, all of Flash's panels—including the Debugger—disappear. Just move the Flash application out of the way, but leave the Debugger in the middle of the screen (as in Figure 6.8). If you need to click on the Web page you're testing, the Debugger goes away, but it's not unworkable.

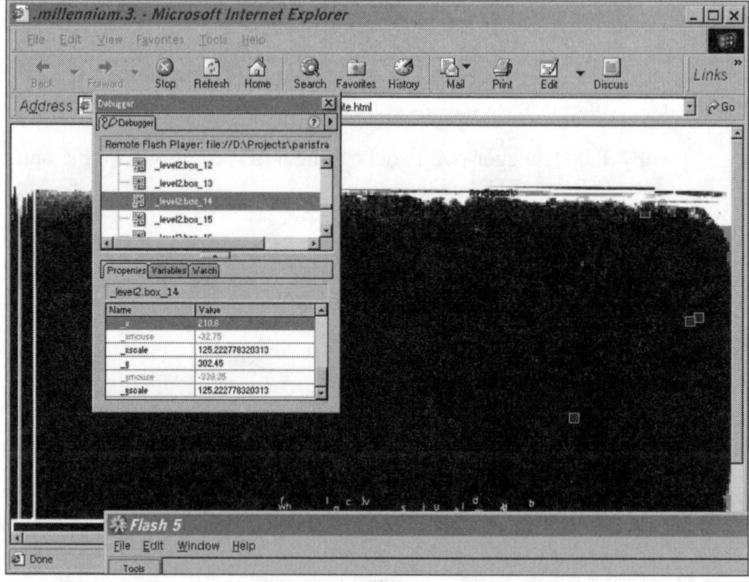

Figure 6.8 *Although Flash must be the active application to perform remote debugging, you can move it down and out of the way so that you can see your browser.*

Strategies of Debugging

After you've found, documented, and determined to fix a bug, the approach you take can involve many different avenues. You can't just select Debug Movie and expect the solution to fall into your lap. You have to be deliberate in your quest. If you need to see whether a variable or property is changing as you expect, the Debugger is great. However, you often need to first determine that a script you wrote is being encountered at all, and then you must determine that it's producing the expected results. There are several ways to check your scripts.

The Trace Command

Sometimes you'll have a script that—for the life of you—appears to be perfect. But that script has to be encountered in order to execute. Often, the script isn't even being reached. Perhaps it's contained within an "if" statement whose condition is false. Or, you keep checking a script that's inside a movie clip that isn't used onstage. There are many ways for this to happen, so you need a quick way to confirm that a script is reached. The trace command is the perfect solution.

If you're testing a movie (or debugging, for that matter), any time Flash encounters `trace("whatever")` the output window will pop up (if it's not already open) and display "whatever." If you place `trace("hi")` inside a loop that repeats 10 times, you'll see `hi` appear 10 times in a row. So, if you have a block of script that appears to be ineffectual, just throw a `trace("hi mom")` right before the script. It's sort of a sanity check to see whether a script is even being used. For example, assume that you have the following script attached to a button:

```
on (release) {
    if (age<12&&age>21) {
        age++;
    }
}
```

Now say that you've tested the movie with the Debugger and noticed that `age` doesn't increment (as you expect) when the button is pressed. So, you can insert `trace("I'm incrementing here")` at the beginning of the if statement like so:

```
on (release) {
      if (age<12&&age>21) {
    trace("I'm incrementing here");
            age++;
      }
}
```

When you test or debug the movie again, if the script is reached, an output window pops up and displays, "I'm incrementing here." To your surprise (or maybe not), the output window doesn't appear. At this point you know that, whether or not the `age++` statement is legitimate, it doesn't matter because it's not even being encountered. What's interesting about the trace statement is that you can actually put an expression in the parentheses (instead of a hard-wired string). For example, if the statement `trace("Age is "+age)` is reached, the output window will show the result of the expression `"Age is "+age`. The problem at hand, however, is that our trace statement is never reached. Try the following script instead:

```
on (release) {
  trace("Age is "+age);
  if (age<12&&age>21) {
        age++;
      }
}
```

This will display the value of the expression `"Age is "+age` (that is, `"Age is "` followed by the value of `age`). This way, the message that appears in the output window will be much more informational. (Remember the "+" operator concatenates when the operands are strings.) You could keep trying different expressions, such as:

```
trace("age: " + age + " part a: " + (age<12) );
trace("age: " + age + " part b: " + (age>21) );
```

Eventually, you should narrow down the crux of the bug (that `age` can't be both less than 12 and greater than 21 and, therefore, our if-statement's condition is never true and we never reach the part that reads `age++`). Granted, this bug was rather obvious, but the idea was to simply show the process of using trace. Trace is a great way to quickly see that a script is being reached as well as displaying the results of an expression right in the output window. You can use trace quite liberally and your audience will never see the output window after you publish the movie. (There's an option in the Flash tab under Publish Settings that enables you to "Omit Trace actions" when you test the movie.)

Using Dynamic Text to Watch Variables or Expressions

The Debugger is great for watching variables and properties change, but you need to make an effort to first activate the Debugger, select Debug Movie, and then find the clip whose variables or properties you want to watch, and then set up a watch. Often, you'll have a specific variable that you need to watch quite a lot and it will become a hassle to always use the Debugger. Also, the Debugger enables you to watch only a single property or variable. What if you want to "watch" an expression? You'll need to devise another way to monitor the values that interest you.

You can quickly monitor any variable by simply creating a Dynamic Text field. (Remember, you'll likely have many variables that won't be visible to the user—this is a case where you want to temporarily view these variables.) If you want to "watch" a variable named `score` in a Dynamic Text field, you simply associate that variable name in the Text Options panel. Of course, the text needs to be placed in the timeline or clip that you want to monitor. If you want, you can even precede the name of the variable (in the Text Options panel) with the path to that variable—such as `_root.score` or `_root.someClip.score`—depending on where the variable is located. Keep in mind that creating a Dynamic Text field will initialize the variable as a string (even if you type a number into the text field). You might need to make sure that the variable gets converted to `0` or some other number immediately after such a field is displayed onscreen. Because the Dynamic Text field will try to make a variable a string, you can place a script in the first frame that reads `score=Number(score)` to reassign the variable to a number data type. The weird part is that a Dynamic Text field will properly display the value of a number (so, you never need to change it back to a string).

This technique of watching variables in text fields works great. If you keep all such variables in a separate layer, it's easy to effectively remove them before publishing by simply changing the layer to Guide (see Figure 6.9). This way, you can just as quickly restore all the variables that you were watching by resetting the layer to Normal.

Figure 6.9 *Keeping dynamic fields in a separate layer allows for quick (yet nondestructive) removal when the layer changes to Guide.*

In addition to convenience, Dynamic Text fields have another benefit over the Debugger. Namely, you can use them to constantly monitor the current value of an expression—not just a variable. Unfortunately you can't simply type an expression in the Text Options panel. Rather, you can use this simple workaround:

1. Create a Dynamic Text field associated with a variable named `result`.
2. Use the Arrow Tool to select the text field and covert to a Movie Clip symbol.

3. Attach a script to the instance of your movie clip now onstage that keeps setting `result` on the enterFrame event. For example, try this script:

   ```
   onClipEvent (enterFrame) {
        result=_root._ymouse;
   }
   ```

Although this example—to monitor the _y property of the mouse—isn't performing anything you couldn't do with the Debugger, consider you can set the `result` variable to anything you want. A much longer expression could show the result of an expression that calculates the user's current average, using variables called `sum` and `questionsAnswered`:

```
onClipEvent (enterFrame) {
    result=_root.sum/_root.questionsAnswered;
}
```

Again, this is a rather simple expression—but it doesn't have to be. Keep in mind that because this script is attached to a clip, it behaves as if it were *in* the clip. You'll need to pay special attention to the target paths for variable names. If you can keep that straight, this is a great way to monitor complex expressions. Because this is just for testing purposes, you can ignore the fact that using the enterFrame event might put a heavy load on the computer processor.

Here's another example. On a button, attach this script:

```
on (release) {
    lastClick=getTimer();
}
```

Then on the movie clip containing the Dynamic Text field displaying the variable `result`, attach this script:

```
onClipEvent (enterFrame) {
    result=Math.floor((getTimer()-_root.lastClick)/1000);
}
```

You'll constantly monitor how long (in seconds) it has been since the user clicked the button. In the `release` event our custom variable `lastClick` is assigned the value of `getTimer()`, which is the precise number of milliseconds since the movie started. Then in the `enterFrame` clip event (which executes repeatedly), we assign the variable `result` the value of `getTimer()` (that is, the current time) minus `lastClick` (the start time). It doesn't matter when you started, you can always determine the elapsed time by finding the difference between the current time (`getTimer()`) and the start (`lastClick`). Finally, we divide by 1000 (which converts milliseconds—for which each second has 1000—into seconds). Finally, the whole expression is inside a `Math.floor()`, which returns the integer portion of the expression.

Quality Assurance and Productivity Scripts

It might be discouraging to find a bug, but when you're aware of a bug (and what causes it) you can at least take the time to address the bug ("the devil you know is better than the devil you don't"). Compare that to bugs you don't find. They're worse because the user might be the first to uncover them. Ideally, you can provide some level of assurance that the quality of your movie is high—that is, has few if any bugs. As you'll see, it's possible to write scripts that provide a level of quality assurance.

A quality assurance script is a script that serves no purpose except to prove the program is working. For example, imagine you're making a reference site with information about the Olympics. Assume that your interface includes a column of 10 buttons for 10 different years and a row of buttons for 10 different events plus three buttons ("photos," "stats," and "winners"). The user could click any year and any event to see photographs, statistics, and medal winners for each combination. The 100 combinations of year/event, multiplied by the three bits of content means a total of 300 discrete pieces of information. Although you don't have to step through 300 combinations to test that it's basically working—you will need to proof all 300 pages of content. Instead of stepping through every combination by hand (and probably missing a few due to human error), you can write a script that does this for you! I would use a couple of temporary buttons ("reset" and "next") plus a Dynamic Text field that constantly displays the combination of year/event/media-type (for "photos," "stats," or "winners"). To proof all the content, you simply click "reset," and then keep clicking "next." If you find a page that has bogus information or doesn't work, just note the data in the Dynamic Text field. Figure 6.10 shows what I have in mind.

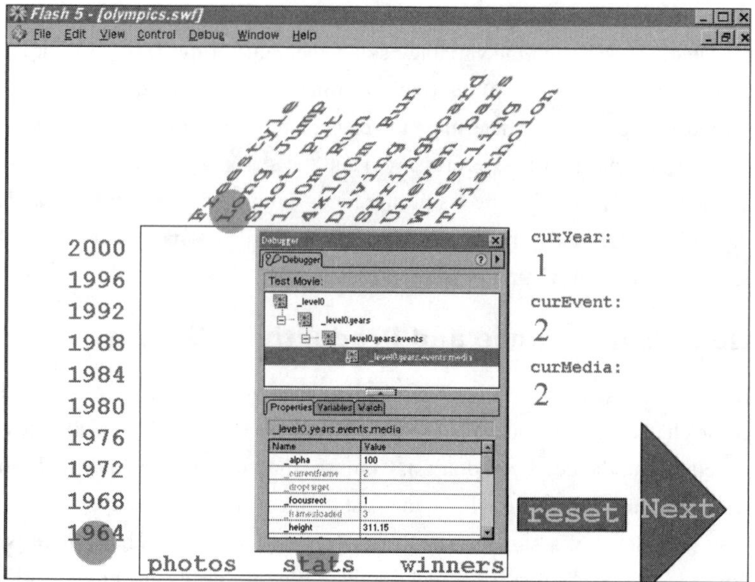

Figure 6.10 *The multitude of options in this matrix calls for a quality assurance script that steps through all 300 combinations.*

To construct this script requires using homemade functions, which we haven't discussed yet (we'll get to that in Chapter 8). By using functions, you can access the same function from several buttons including the "next" button. Without explaining the code, imagine that all the content is in a clip called `years`. The `years` clip contains 10 frames, one for each Olympic year. Every frame in `years` has a unique master clip (with content from a different year) but all clip instances are named `events`. Finally, each `events` clip contains 10 frames for the 10 different events. On each frame of each events clip there's a clip called `media` containing three frames—one each for photos, stats, and winners. Every clip in this movie has a `stop()` script in the first frame. Figure 6.11 shows a portion of the hierarchy in the Movie Explorer.

Here's the script that can be placed in the main movie's first keyframe:

```
reset();
function reset(){
    curYear=1;
    curEvent=1;
    curMedia=1;
    goUpdate();
}
```

```
function goNext(){
    curMedia++;
    if (curMedia>3){
        curMedia=1;
        curEvent++;
    }
    if (curEvent>10){
        curEvent=1;
        curYear++;
    }
    if (curYear>12){
        curYear=1;
    }
    goUpdate();
}
function goUpdate(){
    _root.years.gotoAndStop(curYear);
    _root.years.events.gotoAndStop(curEvent);
    _root.years.events.media.gotoAndStop(curMedia);
}
```

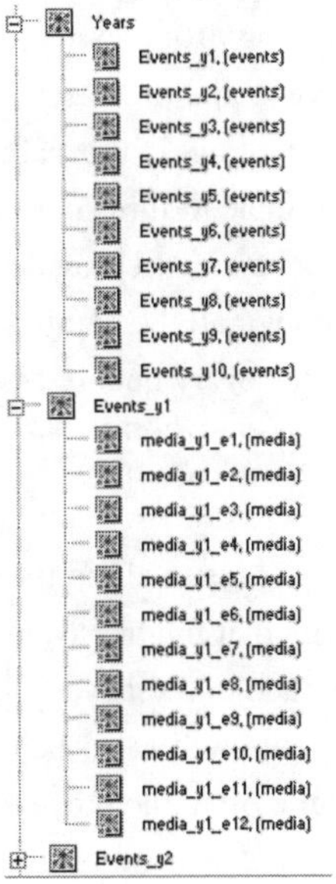

Years
Events_y1, (events)
Events_y2, (events)
Events_y3, (events)
Events_y4, (events)
Events_y5, (events)
Events_y6, (events)
Events_y7, (events)
Events_y8, (events)
Events_y9, (events)
Events_y10, (events)
Events_y1
media_y1_e1, (media)
media_y1_e2, (media)
media_y1_e3, (media)
media_y1_e4, (media)
media_y1_e5, (media)
media_y1_e6, (media)
media_y1_e7, (media)
media_y1_e8, (media)
media_y1_e9, (media)
media_y1_e10, (media)
media_y1_e11, (media)
media_y1_e12, (media)
Events_y2

Figure 6.11 *The Movie Explorer shows the basic architecture used for the Olympics example.*

The `reset()` function (which is executed at the very start) simply sets the variables (containing current year, event, and media) to `1`. Then, it calls the function `goUpdate()`. This is the same function that is called when the user clicks any button (year, event, or media)—but after the variable for `curYear`, `curEvent`, or `curMedia` is set. For example, if the user clicks year 2000, `curYear` is set to `10` and the `goUpdate()` function is called. If the user clicks the Freestyle event, `curEvent` is set to `1` and the `goUpdate()` function is called. When the Next button is pressed, the quality assurance function (`goNext()`) tries to go to the next media element. If doing so puts `curMedia` higher than `3` (for three types of media), it's set back to `1` and `curEvent` is incremented. If `curEvent` is greater than `10` (the total number of events), it's set back to `1` and `curYear` is incremented. Basically, the `goNext()` function starts in the first year and steps through all the media in the first event, and then through all the media of the next event. When it's done with the events in one year, it moves on to the next year.

Even though you might not understand every detail of this script, the concept should start to make sense. You can write a script that serves no other purpose than to aid in the testing process.

It's easy for me to say, "Oh, just write a quality assurance script." Obviously, this will take additional effort, which might seem like time away from your main goal. In fact, the time investment necessary isn't that great, and if it means that you can save time on another stage of the production (proofing, in this case), it's likely worth the investment. In this not-so-contrived example, it turns out this script could have another use. Maybe you think it might be nice to provide the user with an "auto slide show mode" that steps him through all the combinations. You'll already have the script. I don't want to suggest that every quality assurance script will turn out to have other value, but even if it doesn't, it's probably worth the investment.

Another reason why you might want to write an extra script is to aid in the production of your project. Unlike a quality assurance script that might have practical use in the final movie (the way the "next" button turned out to have a secondary use as a slide show), a productivity type of script will *never* be useful in the final movie—but it can still be very valuable. Quite often the process of assembling a project can be tedious. It's possible to invest a little bit of time writing a "productivity script" that will pay back in time saved later.

I had a great opportunity to write a productivity script when I programmed part of the 2000 edition of the site `www.m3snowboards.com`. In one section, individual letters would scatter and assemble themselves to spell the name of each snowboarder on the team (Figure 6.12 shows a sequence of the movie). Each letter was a separate movie clip. Without explaining how I made each letter move, it's obvious that I needed to know the x and y coordinates of each letter in the final arrangement for each snowboarder. With all the different team members and the multiple use of several letters (that is, there weren't just 26 letters—letters like "s" were used many times), the total number of coordinates was more than 1,400!

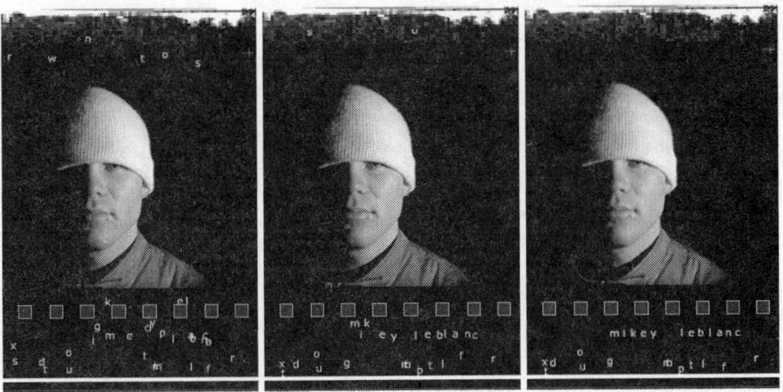

Figure 6.12 *Because each letter arranges itself, I needed to gather the coordinates for each snowboarder's name. From* `www.m3snowboards.com`*—screen shots courtesy of Paris France Inc., copyright MLY Snowboards.*

You can see just half of one page (of five pages) of data in Figure 6.13. At first, I thought that someone would simply need to position the letters in the arrangement he wanted and then—one by one—use the Info panel to ascertain the x and y positions. Then that person (I sure didn't want to be the one) would simply type these numbers into the text file (the result for which is shown in Figure 6.12) and that would be loaded using Flash's load variables Action. Calculating the 1,400 individual coordinates by hand would not only be tedious, but fraught with potential errors. Instead, I wrote a productivity script that would make the process relatively simple.

I made a separate Flash movie that enabled the production author to individually align—by hand—each letter visually. Then the production author would test the movie and press a button in Flash that ran my script. My script would loop through every letter and ascertain the x and y property of each one. This data would be formatted the way the external text file needed to be (URL encoded, as you'll learn in Chapter 14, "Interfacing with External Data"). Finally, the script would use the trace statement to display all this data in the output window. The production author simply copied this text and pasted it into a text file.

```
co_a_1x=549.15&co_a_1y=79.5&co_a_2x=392.6&co_a_2y=364.05&co_b_1x=509.05&co_b_1y=
399.25&co_b_2x=460.55&co_b_2y=405.4&co_b_3x=561.9&co_b_3y=392.95&co_c_1x=372.4&c
o_c_1y=364.1&co_c_2x=419.45&co_c_2y=73&co_d_1x=402.55&co_d_1y=364.05&co_e_1x=455
.65&co_e_1y=363.35&co_e_2x=522.6&co_e_2y=78.8&co_f_1x=507.3&co_f_1y=393.7&co_g_1
x=442.55&co_g_1y=77.65&co_h_1x=382.5&co_h_1y=364.2&co_i_1x=291.1&co_i_1y=404.55&
co_i_2x=449.3&co_i_2y=77.3&co_i_3x=488.5&co_i_3y=396.8&co_j_1x=286.9&co_j_1y=404
.6&co_k_1x=348.35&co_k_1y=78.9&co_l_1x=526.65&co_l_1y=399.4&co_l_2x=534.75&co_l_
2y=397.65&co_l_3x=433.6&co_l_3y=79.25&co_m_1x=513.55&co_m_1y=363.5&co_m_2x=505.5
5&co_m_2y=401.75&co_n_1x=437.15&co_n_1y=404.25&co_n_2x=586.7&co_n_2y=238.4&co_o_
1x=426.7&co_o_1y=363.35&co_o_2x=503.9&co_o_2y=363.35&co_p_1x=451.45&co_p_1y=74.2
&co_q_1x=491.3&co_q_1y=400.35&co_r_1x=464.8&co_r_1y=363.5&co_r_2x=493.75&co_r_2y
=363.5&co_s_1x=474.85&co_s_1y=363.35&co_s_2x=289.9&co_s_2y=75.8&co_s_3x=424.6&co
_s_3y=397.95&co_t_1x=445.95&co_t_1y=363.4&co_t_2x=484.55&co_t_2y=363.4&co_t_3x=4
36.3&co_t_3y=363.4&co_t_4x=217.15&co_t_4y=292.6&co_u_1x=411.9&co_u_1y=400.8&co_v
_1x=460.7&co_v_1y=394.1&co_w_1x=548.25&co_w_1y=402.6&co_x_1x=219.95&co_x_1y=230.
35&co_y_1x=580.6&co_y_1y=255.05&co_z_1x=375.9&co_z_1y=71.6&mm_a_1x=549.15&mm_a_1
y=79.5&mm_a_2x=341.2&mm_a_2y=364.45&mm_b_1x=513.2&mm_b_1y=399.95&mm_b_2x=460.55&
mm_b_2y=405.4&mm_b_3x=561.9&mm_b_3y=392.95&mm_c_1x=332.45&mm_c_1y=364.5&mm_c_2x=
382&mm_c_2y=364.25&mm_d_1x=216.8&mm_d_1y=253.3&mm_e_1x=545.85&mm_e_1y=403.15&mm_
e_2x=522.6&mm_e_2y=78.8&mm_f_1x=507.3&mm_f_1y=393.7&mm_g_1x=389.8&mm_g_1y=364.7&
mm_h_1x=350.1&mm_h_1y=365.2&mm_i_1x=325.95&mm_i_1y=364.6&mm_i_2x=396.55&mm_i_2y=
364.35&mm_i_3x=417.85&mm_i_3y=364.35&mm_j_1x=286.9&mm_j_1y=404.6&mm_k_1x=348.35&
mm_k_1y=78.9&mm_l_1x=526.65&mm_l_1y=399.4&mm_l_2x=534.75&mm_l_2y=397.65&mm_l_3x=
352.2&mm_l_3y=405.6&mm_m_1x=317.5&mm_m_1y=364.6&mm_m_2x=374.65&mm_m_2y=364.35&mm
_n_1x=410.95&mm_n_1y=364.35&mm_n_2x=403.45&mm_n_2y=364.35&mm_o_1x=286.05&mm_o_1y
=80.6&mm_o_2x=383.25&mm_o_2y=406.1&mm_p_1x=537.1&mm_p_1y=379.35&mm_q_1x=518.45&m
m_q_1y=400.35&mm_r_1x=585.6&mm_r_1y=247.85&mm_r_2x=258.55&mm_r_2y=81.35&mm_s_1x=
230.95&mm_s_1y=402.3&mm_s_2x=271.85&mm_s_2y=80.6&mm_s_3x=432.25&mm_s_3y=404.9&mm
_t_1x=454.5&mm_t_1y=403.55&mm_t_2x=390.45&mm_t_2y=405.55&mm_t_3x=278.95&mm_t_3y=
80.65&mm_t_4x=424.1&mm_t_4y=364.25&mm_u_1x=431.4&mm_u_1y=403.6&mm_v_1x=453.75&mm
_v_1y=405.95&mm_w_1x=530.15&mm_w_1y=403.3&mm_x_1x=219.95&mm_x_1y=230.35&mm_y_1x=
432.2&mm_y_1y=364.15&mm_z_1x=375.9&mm_z_1y=71.6&boxA_1x=619.45&boxA_1y=360.05&bo
```


Figure 6.13 *1,400 individual coordinates is a lot of data to type by hand—the production script meant we didn't have to.*

The process was repeated for each snowboarder—but it was a simple process: Just line up all the letters while authoring in Flash, test the movie, press the button, and copy and paste the contents of the output window. Multiply that process by each team member and you can well imagine that it is way less time (and more accurate) than using the Info panel to determine the coordinates of 1,400 letters! It might have taken an hour or two to write the script—but that investment was well worth it.

Summary

This chapter introduced you to many debugging techniques. If you've ever done any kind of troubleshooting, this chapter was not all new. Even though the focus was on applying such skills to fixing or preventing bugs in Flash, it's not much different than fixing or preventing problems with your VCR. In any case, there are no hard-and-fast rules, but rather a general approach you must take.

Finding and documenting bugs was is always the first step. You learned how to use the Debugger, but you must first know what you're looking for before you can fix it. I suggested that you can try to develop personality attributes (such as cynicism and humility) that make finding or testing for bugs easier. Ultimately, you'll develop skills that will reduce bugs in the first place. Writing quality assurance scripts and productivity scripts is one way.

By the way, the workshops that deal with topics from this chapter in detail include "Offline Production," and "Fixing Broken Scripts." Of course, you'll get plenty of practice fixing bugs because they're just a fact of programming. Perhaps realizing this will make the process more part of the entire production rather than something extra that you hadn't expected to do.

{ Chapter 7 }

The Movie Clip Object

The Movie Clip object is the most prevalent and most understandable of all Flash objects. Even the most novice Flash user knows more about objects than he might realize. Although you might not use the words *instance*, *class*, and *object*—those are the concepts you've experienced. By dragging a movie clip on stage, changing its alpha, and then dragging another one and scaling it, you experience the concept of multiple instances of the same master—each with different properties. Each instance (clip on stage) of the class (the master symbol) is an object that has properties (such as alpha and scale).

We'll cover all these details in this chapter. After you understand the Movie Clip object, you'll not only be able to change any property of a clip with scripting, but you'll understand objects generally. As you read this chapter, don't think "now I'm learning the complicated concept of objects"; rather, think "now I'll be able to modify every aspect of a movie clip using scripting!" Although you are indeed learning about objects, it's the application of making movie clips do cool things that's most interesting.

In this chapter, you will

- Access and modify built-in properties of clip instances
- Create custom variables that act like homemade properties
- Learn the concept of, and how to use, "methods" of clips
- Begin to refer to clips dynamically in addition to direct and relative targeting

Properties of Clips

When you drag a Movie Clip from the Library onto the stage, you have already set the _x and _y (position) properties of the instance created. Each instance on stage will have its own set of properties. The available built-in properties are the same for every instance, but the actual settings for each varies. Properties such as scale, rotation, and alpha are examples of other built-in properties that you can modify. Although you can set properties of instances of Graphic symbols and Buttons, you can only access properties of Movie Clip instances with scripting. You can both ascertain the current values of a clip's properties and change them through scripting.

Here's the form that a script takes to access a clip's properties:

```
clipInstanceName.theProperty
```

Notice that this is only an expression that results in the value for whatever property you put in the position "theProperty."

To set a clip's property, the form is

```
clipInstanceName.theProperty=newValue;
```

The form is always "object-dot-property." Even though you can often refer to the object (that is, the clip instance) by its instance name (which is set through the Instance panel), you'll want to make sure that such a clip has been targeted correctly. If you want to, you can precede "clipInstanceName" with a relative or absolute target reference. We'll cover this in more detail later in this chapter, but realize if you don't qualify the instance name with a target path, Flash requires the clip to reside in the same timeline in which you write this script.

The property (shown as `theProperty` earlier) is whatever property you want to reference. The list of built-in properties (shown in Figure 7.1) is available in the Actions panel.

You'll notice that all the built-in properties start with an underscore (as in `_alpha`—not `alpha`). So, an actual script that changes the alpha of a clip named "box" to 50% would look like this:

```
box._alpha=50;
```

Pretty simple, eh? It really is. After you understand the concept of "object-dot-property," you'll understand a lot of other topics that come later in the book.

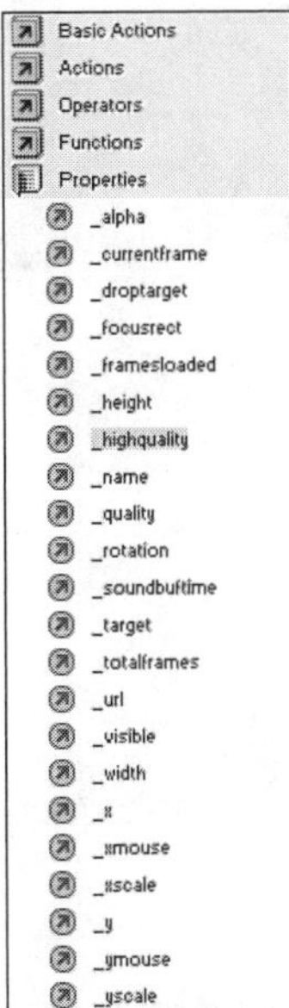

Figure 7.1 *Flash's built-in properties as listed in the Actions panel.*

You Can Get Them All, But You Can't Set Them All

One issue that might be initially frustrating is that although you can *always* ascertain the value of any property of a particular clip—you can set the values of only certain properties. For example, you can set the `_alpha` property of a clip (as in `box._alpha=50`), but you can't set the `_currentFrame` property of a clip. The best way to learn which properties are both "set-able" and "get-able" is to look at the Properties tab of the Debugger. As you can see in Figure 7.2, the properties in gray are only available to view (but not change). This makes sense when you look at a property such as `_totalframes` (which contains the total frames in a clip) because you can only add frames to a clip while authoring—not while watching a movie. Other non-settable properties don't make sense though. For example, I constantly find myself trying to *set* the `_currentframe` property of clips, as in `box._currentframe=12`. As much as I try, it doesn't work because `_currentframe` is simply one of the properties you can only ascertain and cannot set. By the way, you achieve the same result by using the method `box.gotoAndStop(12)`, which is covered later in this chapter.

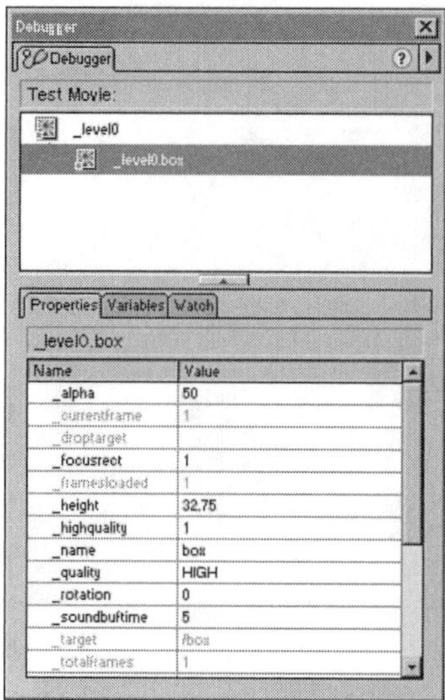

Figure 7.2 *The Debugger displays properties that are unchangeable in gray.*

Anonymous Targeting

I mentioned that you can refer to a clip's property (for example, *instanceName.property*) only when the instance (*instanceName*) is in the same timeline in which this script is written. Otherwise, you must target the clip instance by preceding its name with the path to that clip. We'll discuss targeting clips in more detail later this chapter, but what about referring to a property without specifying a clip at all? That is, what will `_alpha=10` do?

It's actually quite simple. When you refer to a property with no clip name, Flash assumes that you are referring to the clip where you are currently. If you're in the main timeline, you can actually set and get properties *of* the main timeline. Think of real life. You can say "the hair color of that kid" like `kid.haircolor`, if you will. (This assumes that there's a "kid" right in front of you—otherwise, you'd have to precede your reference with a target such as "look across the street at the kid's hair color.") But if you just said "hair color" or "hair color is brown" without specifying an object (or clip instance), you'd assume that it was the person speaking whose hair color was in question. The main point I'm making here is that if you don't use "object-dot-property" and just use "property," you'll be referring to the property of the timeline in which the script resides. Remember, too, from Chapter 1, "Flash Basics," that scripts in keyframes or buttons are "in" the timeline in which the button or keyframe resides, but scripts attached to clip instances are "in" the clip itself (not the timeline in which the instance resides).

The idea of anonymous targeting is that you simply leave off the object part of the form object-dot-property. By doing this, you're implying that you want the current timeline to be used. An explicit way to refer to the "current timeline" (that is, the instance you're in) is to use the keyword `this`. It might seem silly that `this._alpha` has the same meaning as simply saying `_alpha` (because `this` is implied). However, you'll see in later chapters, as well as in the "Dynamic Referencing" section later in this chapter, that you often need `this` to identify the current clip and to refer to the object that you are currently "in." In the case of clip instances, each instance is an object. You'll see other kinds of objects in which `this` can be similarly used to point to the current object. You probably won't need `this` to target clips anonymously, but just realize that you are implying it when you leave it out.

Variables in Clips (or "Homemade Properties")

If you understand how the built-in properties of clips can be ascertained and often changed through the dot syntax (object-dot-property), you'll have no problem understanding how to reference the variables you create in clips. Actually, you should think of homemade variables (in clips) as homemade properties of those clips. Not only is the syntax similar (object-dot-variable), but variables are conceptually the same as properties. Built-in properties include `_x` and `_alpha`. If you use a variable inside a clip, say `age`, you can think of the age property of that clip. Of course, you could say `box.age=21` in the same way that you could say `box._alpha=50`. The only difference is all your variables (oh, I mean "homemade properties") can be both seen and changed (unlike properties, some of which can only be seen and not changed). In addition, it's not necessary to name your variables with an underscore.

Variables exist inside clips as soon as you start using them. If on the first keyframe inside a clip, you had the script `age=1;` every instance of that clip would have its own "age." This is identical to how every clip has its own `_alpha` (and every other property). You have to create and maintain the custom variables, whereas properties are built-in, but the concept is the same. Say you had two instances of this clip (with the `age=1` script in frame 1). From the main timeline, if you name one instance "brother" and the other "sister" and then select

Debug Movie, you would be able to see each clip's variables (as in Figure 7.3). Back on the main timeline, you can place a button that includes the script `sister.age=12` (within a mouse event, of course). Then perhaps another button with `brother.age=sister.age-2`. Notice that both are statements that assign a value to the age variable unique to one clip. The second example assigns brother's age to the result of the expression `sister.age-2` (or two less than sister's age). These examples don't have an immediate and clear practical use, but they serve to show how custom variables can be treated just like properties.

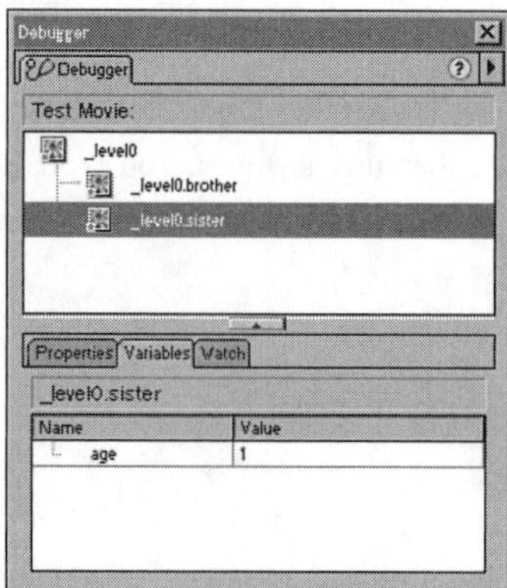

Figure 7.3 *Custom variables can be thought of as homemade properties despite the fact the Debugger lists them as variables.*

Just to sneak in a quick example of how you might apply this, consider a script attached to a clip that reads:

```
onClipEvent (enterFrame) {
    _x+=speed;
}
```

Every time the screen refreshes (12 times a second if the frame rate is 12 fps), this will assign the _x property to "speed" more than it is currently (that is, `_x+=speed`). First, whose _x property? When you don't specify a clip (that is, leave it blank), the script refers to the _x property of the timeline in which it resides—or, inside the clip itself. So, _x is simply the _x property of the clip itself. Because it's anonymous, the same script will work on as many instances that you attach this script to. Second, `speed` is a custom variable. Because it's being used "inside" the clip (remember that scripts attached to clips act as though they are inside the clip), the variable `speed` is this clip's `speed` (like this clip's `_x`). If `speed` is not defined anywhere, it will evaluate as 0 and have no visual effect (as adding zero to the clip's `_x` property will have no effect). However, if you had two clips with this script (with instance names `thing1` and `thing2`, respectively), you could place a script in the first frame of the main timeline that reads:

```
thing1.speed=5;
thing2.speed=10;
```

Now, the movie should move the two clips to the right. The one with a higher "speed" will appear to go faster (that is, bigger steps). You can think of speed either as a variable or a property—I don't care. Because it behaves and follows the same syntax of properties, maybe it's just easier to think of variables as properties unique to the clip where they're used.

Methods of Clips

This is really starting to get fun! After you understand the concept of object-dot-property, you can use the same syntax on variables. Now you're going to learn how methods follow a similar syntax: object-dot-method. A method is easy to confuse with a property, but they are quite different. Think of real-life properties first: hair color, height, weight, tooth count…whatever. Although these properties can change, at any instant they're basically static. As humans, we are given these properties and they can change (sort of like the built-in properties or custom variables in Flash). There's not much more to say about properties.

As humans, we also have certain activities that we can perform. For example, combing our hair, brushing our teeth, running…whatever. The point is that these behaviors are analogous to the concept of methods. A method performs an operation on an individual object. Even though "brushing teeth" is a method, it can be applied to you or me. The method does its "thing" on me or on you. I brush my teeth; you brush your teeth.

In Flash, it's even easier to understand. The simplest method (of clips) is `gotoAndStop()`. By itself, a script that says `gotoAndStop(3)` will jump to frame 3 in the timeline where the script is written. However, that's just because there's no object specified. If the script says `box.gotoAndStop(3);`, the clip with the instance name "box" jumps to frame 3. Does it look familiar? Object-dot-method is the same as object-dot-property and object-dot-variable! You're pretty much done with the book now. Obviously, there's more, but after you get it, you *really* get it.

There are many built-in methods made for clip instances. Most are listed under Actions in the Actions panel—but remember that many "actions" are really statements. Most of the methods for clips are probably very familiar to you: `stop()`, `play()`, `gotoAndPlay(`*`num_or_label`*`)`, `gotoAndStop(`*`num_or_label`*`)`, `nextFrame()`, `prevFrame()`. I'll bet you've used most—if not all—of these. But now you know that they're methods that can apply to unique clips, as in `box.stop()` or `slideShow.nextFrame()`.

One thing you should notice is that all methods have parentheses that follow the method name. This is required (and a good way to recognize methods). Some methods accept parameters between the parentheses—as in `gotoAndStop(12)`. You can't just say `gotoAndStop()`—you have to specify which frame number (or label name) you want to go *to*. The concept of parentheses for parameters will come up again when you learn functions in the next chapter. The word *function* is probably better suited to thinking of human functions such as brushing teeth or combing hair. Think *method* or *function*—it doesn't matter. The difference is that methods are functions that apply to one object (or clip, in this case) at a time. (If you think the list of methods for clips is short, just wait until next chapter, when you write your own functions that can be used as methods of clips.)

Although you'll find only a few of the Movie Clip's methods listed under Actions (such as `stop()`, `play()`, and `goto`), you'll find them all under Objects, Movie Clip (shown in Figure 7.4). Keep in mind that when you understand the way to use methods, you can figure out all these. That is, you always use the form `clipName.`*`method(parameters)`* (or just *`method(parameters)`* when targeting the current clip). However, it makes sense to step through a few of the more interesting Movie Clip methods now.

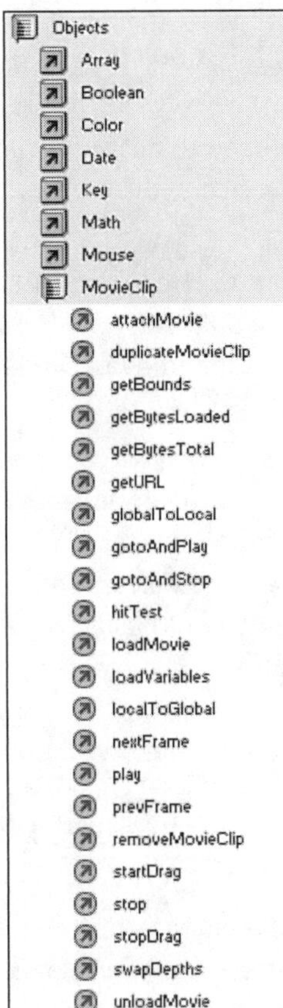

Figure 7.4 *All of the Movie Clip's built-in methods (listed under Objects in the Actions panel).*

`attachMovie()`, `duplicateMovieClip()`, and `removeMovieClip()` let you create (and delete) clip instances at runtime. You'll see how to use all these in Chapter 11, "Objects," as well as the Dynamic Slide Presentation workshop.

`getBounds()` will return any clip's dimensions, which effectively ascertains a clip's size. Because a clip's dimensions include four values (`xMin`, `xMax`, `yMin`, and `yMax`), `getBounds()` actually returns a value in the form of a generic object (which contains all four values). In Chapters 11 and 12, "Homemade Objects," you'll learn how a generic object maintains multiple values, and in the

"Mapping" workshop, you'll use `getBounds()` in a practical exercise.

`getBytesLoaded()` and `getBytesTotal()` are used to ascertain file-size information on `.swfs` being loaded dynamically through `loadMovie()`.

`getURL()` is commonly used to create a hyperlink. However, in Chapter 14, "Interfacing with External Data," you'll see how it can also exchange data to server scripts, JavaScript, and even Director or Authorware.

`globalToLocal()` and `localToGlobal()` are fancy ways to covert a point (x and y coordinate) in one clip instance to the equivalent point in another clip instance. As you recall from Chapter 1, different clips' coordinate systems vary. These methods perform a sort of "exchange rate" on coordinates. Just as you could ask, "How many dollars is 100 yen worth," `globalToLocal()` answers the question, "If a point is 100x 100y in this clip, what is that same point in another clip?" The catch is that the parameter you supply must be in the form of a generic object because it contains two values (one for x and one for y). You can avoid `globalToLocal()` by making calculations manually—it's just harder that way.

`hitTest()` is used to determine whether one point is within the shape or bounds of a particular clip. For example, you can determine whether or not the user has clicked on a graphic portion of a movie clip—effectively making a clip act like a button. Also, `hitTest()` can tell you whether one clip is currently intersecting another. This is, by far, one of the greatest enhancements in Flash 5. We'll use it in several workshops including "Creating Custom Cursors," "Working with Odd-Shaped Clickable Areas," and "Creating a Multistate Button."

`swapDepths()` will exchange the level number of one clip with another. Although clips loaded through `loadMovie()` (or placed on stage using `attachMovie()`) start with a particular level number, `swapDepths()` doesn't change these level numbers. It only applies to the "natural" stacking that occurs when you place clips on top of each other (or use Modify, Send to Back, for example). Also, it works only on multiple clips in a particular timeline.

That pretty much covers the more interesting Movie Clip methods. Obviously, learning which one is which is just a start. You'll get plenty of practice with practically all these in upcoming chapters and workshops.

Referencing Clips and Targeting

Now that you know about accessing clips' properties, variables, and methods, you'll want to make sure that you target the correct clip. Targeting was covered generally in Chapter 1, but it won't hurt to revisit the topic and apply it to what you've learned in this chapter. Basically, you can set/get properties and variables or assign methods to any clip you want—you just need to be clear which clip (or which timeline) you are targeting.

Relative and Absolute Referencing

The section on targeting in Chapter 1 was extensive in covering the concept. Now we'll look at targeting (or referencing) clips very specifically. As anyone who's studied physics knows, "everything is relative." When you're in a car driving beside a train, it can seem the train is barely moving—or even moving backward. The train could be going backward relative to your perspective, when in fact relative to the Earth the train is moving forward quite fast—just not as fast as your car. The concept is called "frame of reference," or starting point. Frame of reference applies to Flash when you think about a script's starting point. If you put a script in a keyframe, your starting point is the timeline in which the keyframe resides. If that's inside a clip, your starting point is the timeline inside that clip. Placing a script on a button is similar to keyframes because you're starting point is the timeline where the button is placed. When you place scripts on clip instances it gets a little weird. Scripts *on* clip instances behave the same as if they were *in* that clip (like a keyframe or button in that clip). It makes sense when you think about it, but it's also easy to incorrectly assume that you're starting at the timeline in which the clip is sitting. Figures 7.5 and 7.6 show how frames of reference work.

Now that you know to be clear about your starting point (that is, where the script is written), we can explore the different types of relative and absolute references. The list below shows several ways to target the rotation property of a `frontWheel` clip instance that happens to be inside the "car" clip instance. Inside "frontWheel" are many instances of a Spoke symbol—and they're named `spoke1`, `spoke2`, and so on (as Figure 7.7 shows). Remember, it's the instance names—not the symbol names—that matter when you target clips.

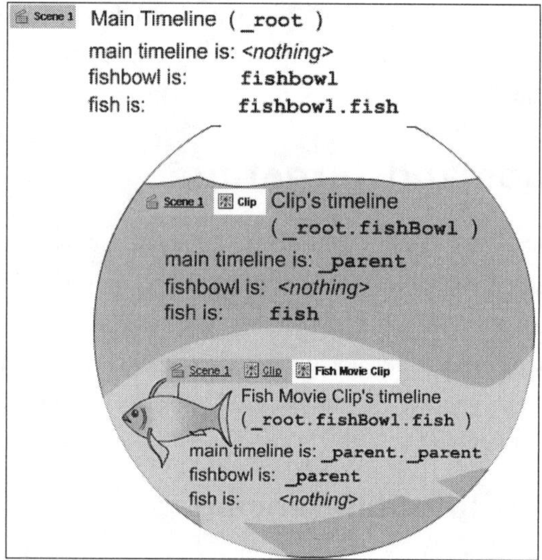

Figure 7.5 *Since your frame of reference is from outside the bowl, the fish appears to be "in water, in the bowl."*

Scripts on buttons or keyframes are "in" the main timeline.

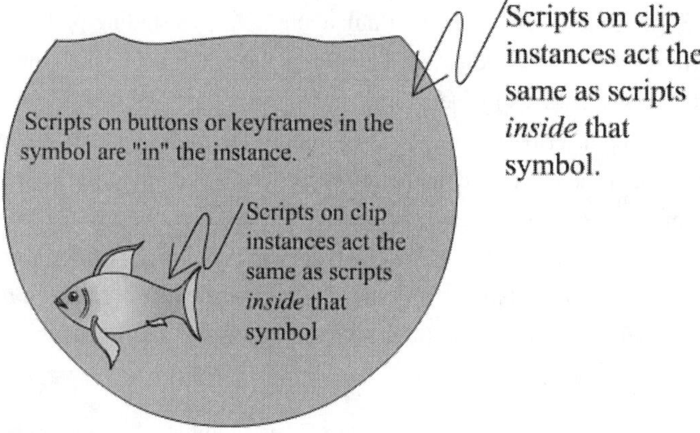

Figure 7.6 *Scripts attached to clip instances (or to keyframes in the clip) act as though they are "in" that timeline.*

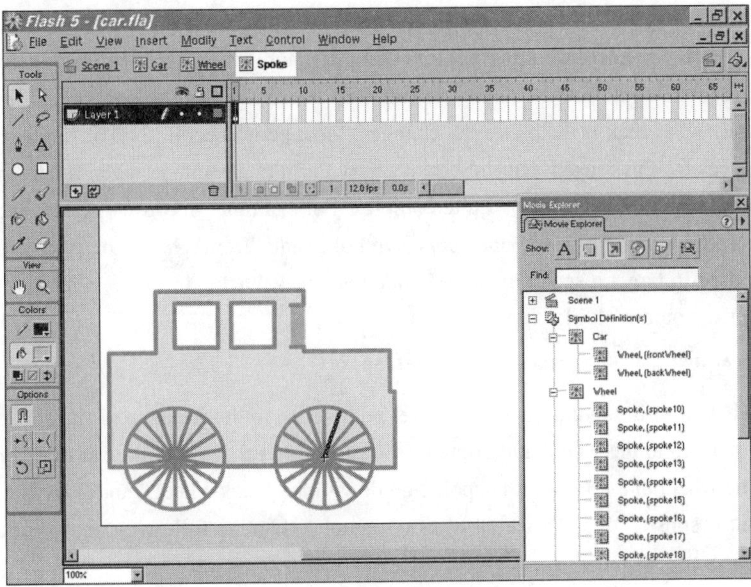

Figure 7.7 *Regardless of how many times the Spoke symbol is used, you can target an individual instance by its instance name.*

From a button or keyframe script on the main timeline:

Relative: `car.frontWheel._rotation`

Absolute: `_root.car.frontWheel._rotation`

From a button or keyframe in the car symbol or from a script that's attached to the car instance in the main timeline:

Relative: `frontWheel._rotation`

Absolute: `_root.car.frontWheel._rotation`

From a button or keyframe in the frontWheel symbol or from a script that's attached to the frontWheel instance inside the car instance:

Relative: `_rotation`

Absolute: `_root.car.frontWheel._rotation`

From a button or keyframe in the spoke symbol or from a script that's attached to one of the "spoke" instances in frontWheel:

Relative: `_parent._rotation`

Absolute: `_root.car.frontWheel._rotation`

It might seem that I was redundant by including the way to express an absolute reference in each example, but this will drive home the point that absolute paths are identical no matter what your frame of reference. They're hard-wired in that they will break if the hierarchy changes. Most people pooh-pooh absolute references for this reason, but they have a very definite advantage when relative references would otherwise be quite complex. For example, if you wrote a script attached to a clip inside one spoke symbol inside "frontWheel" that was supposed to target a spoke instance inside the "backWheel" instance, a relative reference would look like this:

```
_parent._parent._parent.backWheel.spoke1
```

That is, from the clip inside a spoke, go up once to the instance of the spoke, go up again to the wheel that contains the spoke, go up again to the car that contains the wheel that contains the spoke, go down into "backWheel," and then down into "spoke1." This is arguably more complex than the following absolute reference:

```
_root.car.backWheel.spoke1
```

Relative references work great when the resulting path is short or direct. I could target a neighbor's house relatively as "down the block and across the street." But to use a relative reference to my friend across the country, it would become a nightmare—an absolute reference would probably be better.

Another big consideration is that when you place a script inside a master symbol, that script will be present in every instance you create. Remember, you can only target instances of clips. If a script is targeting another clip relatively, each instance (of the master symbol) will do the same thing. If a script targets one clip instance absolutely, multiple copies of the script (caused from multiple instances of that symbol on stage) might be redundant, but it won't target more than one clip. Let's say you put a script in the first frame of the master wheel symbol. Consider a relative script: `spoke1._xscale=200`. This will cause the "spoke1" in both the "frontWheel" and "backWheel" instances to get wider. Actually, if you use the wheel symbol ANYWHERE else in the entire movie, its "spoke1" will grow too. Compare this to using the absolute reference `_root.car.frontWheel.spoke1._xscale=200`. Naturally, this script will execute once for every instance of the master wheel symbol used, but the result is that it will affect only one thing: the "spoke1" that's inside the "frontWheel" that's inside the "car" that's placed in the main timeline.

It's not that one method is better than the other; it's just that they have different results. As much as this might sound like a defense of absolute references, that's not the case. There's need for both absolute and relative. That said, I definitely try to use relative references as much as possible. They tend to enable you to make drastic changes to your movie at the last minute without extensive script rewrites.

Dynamic Referencing

When you know a clip's instance name or relative location, absolute and relative targeting is suitable. However, you might not want to hard-wire every target reference. For example, assume that you have seven box clips (one for each page of a slideshow) and that you want them moved to the right when the appropriate page of a slideshow is active. In other words, you have something like Figure 7.8 where invisible buttons are placed on top of the seven boxes. The user will be able to jump to any page (by clicking a box on the left) or they'll be able to advance to the "next" (or "previous") page by clicking the arrow buttons. The clip instances are named `box_1`, `box_2`, and so on. It's easy enough to target each box from the individual invisible buttons placed on top of each one. But the arrow buttons must be able to target the clips dynamically. If you're on page 1 and you click the right arrow button, you want `box_1` to move to the left and then `box_2` to move to the right. But when you're currently on page 2, the same right arrow button should then move `box_2` left and `box_3` to the right. (All this in addition to telling the slideshow movie clip to go to the next frame.) The point is, the right arrow button will need to do the same basic operation (move boxes), but it should do so slightly different depending on the current page. We need to refer to a "box_*x*" clip dynamically (where "x" depends on the current page).

In pseudo-code, the script on the right arrow button should be

```
Set box_currentFrame's _x to 0 //current Frame being the current frame in
the slideShow
Make the slideShow go to the next Frame

Now, set box_currentFrame's _x to 50 //now that "currentFrame" has
increased.
```

But you can't just say `box_currentFrame._x=0` because the clips are only named `box_1`, `box_2`, and so on. We can ascertain the `_currentframe` property of the slideshow clip (using `slideShow._currentframe`). The closest guess that makes sense (but won't actually work) is `("box_"+slideShow._currentframe)._x=0;`.

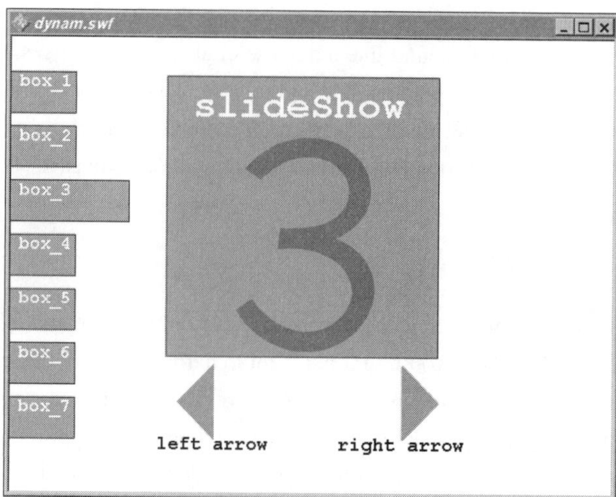

Figure 7.8 *In this example, the arrow button will dynamically target an individual box clip in the left column.*

The only problem is that while `"box_"+slideShow._currentframe` indeed evaluates to "box_1" (if `slideShow`'s current frame is 1), this result is a string (not a reference to a clip instance). That is, we don't say `"box_1"._x=0`, we say `box_1._x=0`. Sorry to show all these ways that *don't* work, but it helps to see the issue at hand.

The solution is easier than the explanation of how it works. Here's how you do it:

```
_root["box_"+slideShow._currentframe]._x=0;
```

If you said: `_root["box_"+2]`, notice the result of concatenating `"box_"` and `2` will be a string `"box_2"`, but when this string is placed in brackets that immediately follow a target path(`_root` in this case) Flash will try to find the clip instance with that name in the path given. In actuality, every timeline has a special kind of array (called an associative array) that contains the name of each clip present. In Chapter 10, "Arrays," you'll learn more about arrays and associative arrays.

Naturally, you don't need to know that much about associative arrays to start referring to clips dynamically. Just specify the path (like `_root`) and follow that—not by a dot—but by a square bracket that contains an expression that results in a string matching the name of the clip you want to target (`_root["box_"+2]`). Notice that targeting the `_root` timeline is an explicit target. If the clip whose name you were building dynamically existed in a nested clip, you could use `_root.subClip[stringExpression]` (where "stringExpression" resulted in a string that matched a clip name in the `subClip`'s timeline. However, to make a dynamic reference to a clip that's in the current timeline, just use the keyword `this`, which will target the current timeline. So, you could use `this[stringExpression]`. Now you have your object and you can proceed with the "...dot-property," "...dot-variable," or "...dot-method." The finished script (shown earlier in pseudo-code) looks like this:

```
on (release) {
  _root["box_"+slideShow._currentFrame]._x=0;
      slideShow.nextFrame();
      _root["box_"+slideShow._currentFrame]._x=50;
}
```

This code first figures out which box instance to target by combining `"box_"` with the value of `slideShow._currentFrame`, and then it sets the `_x` of the correct box clip to `0`. Next, it makes `slideShow` advance to the next frame. Finally, it targets another `"box_x"` in `_root` to set its `_x` to `50`. But at this point (now that `slideShow` has advanced), the value for `slideShow._currentFrame` has increased, so a different box is targeted (and moved to an x position of `50`).

The more streamlined version that follows is a lot less complex than the solution I originally developed. Just to see another way to solve this task (and to review other concepts, such as loops), check out this other solution:

```
on (release) {
    slideShow.nextFrame();
    for(i=1;i<8;i++){
        _root["box_"+i]._x=0;
    }
    _root["box_"+slideShow._currentFrame]._x=50;
}
```

In this solution, the first line sends `slideShow` to the next frame. Then in the for-loop statement I set *all* seven "box_" clips' `_x` back to zero. Finally, I set the correct box's `_x` to 50. I admit that this solution wasn't eloquent, but it's still good for review.

As I said, you can start writing expressions that result in a dynamic clip name and, as long as you put it between brackets that immediately follow a path, it works great. You'll learn more about what's really happening when you study arrays. Just don't forget the syntax is

`path[string].property` not `path.[string].property`.

Notice that you don't use a dot after the path when the brackets are present.

It might look like we're targeting clips by name, but notice that their names are never between quotes. This is because clips are a data type. You can only target a clip with a string using the bracket reference. Realize, too, that as a data type clips can be stored in variables. You could have one variable containing a string (`myName="phillip"`), another containing a number (`myAge=36`), and still another containing a movie clip reference (`myClip=_root.someClip`). I say "reference" to a clip because like other reference data types discussed in Chapter 4, "Basic Programming in Flash," (compared to "value" or "primitive" data types), movie clips are objects. After you assigned `myClip` to reference the `someClip` instance, you could say `myClip._alpha=50` and the original would change. I mention this because you'll quite often want to store references to clips in variables, but you need to remember those variables only contain "pointers" to the original. We'll store clip references in variables in the "Working with Odd-Shaped Clickable Areas" workshop (as well as other times throughout the book).

Summary

Although it might seem that you learned several aspects of movie clips in this chapter, the truth is that you learned one basic concept: the syntax "targetPath.clipInstanceName.property". The part "dot property" could change to "dot variable" or "dot method" for slightly different purposes. Actually, home-made variables are best understood as homemade properties. And methods are simply functions that are assigned to individual clips. (Properties just "are" and methods "do something.")

You also learned how each timeline (or target path) contains an array full of all the clips present. This enables you to dynamically refer to clips by building their names dynamically with an expression. The syntax was "path[stringName].property".

The best part of this chapter was that every concept about movie clip instances is totally transferable to the concept of objects generally. When you learn more about objects in Chapters 11, "Objects," and 12, "Homemade Objects," you'll see the same concepts of instances, properties, and methods. From now on, each chapter will keep expanding on the same themes.

{ Chapter 8 }

Functions

Now that you can write complex statements and affect clip instances by changing their properties, it's time to learn to modularize your scripts. Placing the same (or very similar) script on several buttons is a cry for help. Every time you copy and paste the same block of code, a little voice should be saying "No!" In Chapter 3, "The Programmer's Approach," we discussed *why* you want to reduce repeated code. Now you'll see one great way to do it: functions.

Among all the benefits of functions, the core benefit is that you can store code in one place and access it as much as you want. Type it once, use it a million times. This chapter will introduce other benefits as well as show you how to create functions.

In addition to learning how to use homemade functions just as you use Flash's built-in functions, in this chapter you will write functions that do the following:

- Act as subroutines, thus eliminating repeated code
- Accept parameters so that they can perform differently based on different situations
- Return values so that they can be used within expressions
- Act as custom methods (for your own purposes)

You'll see all three uses for functions (subroutines, returning values, and acting like methods). As you might have noticed, functions can do more than simply reduce repeated code—but that's the main thing. Regardless of how you use them, functions always take the same form.

How to Use Functions

Functions involve two steps: writing the function and then using the function. We're going to discuss using functions first, which might seem like I'm putting the cart before the horse. However, because Flash's built-in functions are already written, it's easy to look at using those. Also, this way, when you do write your own functions, you'll already know how to use them. Suffice it to say that you can't start using a homemade function unless you write it first…and if you just write a function (but never use it), nothing happens.

Using Built-in Functions

To get this far in the book, you've already learned *something* about the built-in functions. In addition to the brief explanation in Chapter 4, "Basic Programming in Flash," you actually used a few functions in Chapter 5, "Programming Structures." For example, to ensure that an expression was treated like the number data type, we used the Number() function as in `Number(anExpression)`. This evaluates the string "anExpression" as a number. If the expression in parentheses evaluated as `"112"`, the entire expression (`Number("112")`) would evaluate as `112`.

In Chapter 5, we also looked at the methods of the Math object (square root and sine, for example). These are—at their core—functions too, but we'll return to methods later in this chapter. For now, let's consider only the conventional functions listed in the Actions panel (as in Figure 8.1).

Regarding all the built-in functions, consider two things: how they are used in expressions or statements and what they do. Any time you want to call (that is, execute) a function you simply type its name and parentheses using this form: `functionName()`. Functions' names are always followed by parentheses. Not only does this make them easy to identify, but—more importantly—the parentheses provide a means for you to provide an optional parameter (also sometimes called an *argument*). The `getTimer()` function is complete without parameters. `getTimer()` returns the elapsed milliseconds since the movie started, so it doesn't need any additional information. The `Number()` function, however, requires a parameter. It needs to know what expression to evaluate as a number. Another function that requires a parameter, `String(expression)`, will return a string version of *`expression`*.

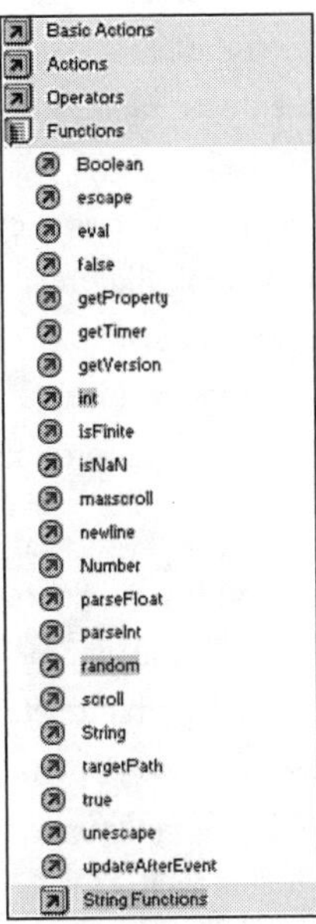

Figure 8.1 *Flash's conventional functions as listed in the Actions panel.*

Now you know how to use a function: call its name followed by parentheses, which may or may not accept parameters. As for what they do, it's important to understand that the built-in functions do *nothing* except return values. They don't perform an assignment as a statement does. That is, if `myVar` equals the string `"11"`, the expression `Number(myVar)` not only has no effect on `myVar` (it'll stay `"11"`), but by itself `Number(myVar)` is practically meaningless because it's only an expression and not a statement. The function only *returns* a value so you can use the function within a larger expression or statement. For example, `myVar= Number(myVar)` will first perform the function on the right side of the equal sign and return (into its place) a number version of `myVar` (so the statement becomes `myVar=11`). Then the equals will perform the assignment (and `myVar` is changed). It's simply a way to write an expression that changes depending on what the function returns.

Imagine a function that returned the effective temperature based on the wind chill. (By the way, we could write such a homemade function.) In that case, you'd need two parameters (current temperature and wind speed). Multiple parameters are separated by commas. Calling the homemade function would look like this: `effectiveTemp(40,20)`. We could build the function so that it arbitrarily establishes the first parameter is current temperature and the second is wind speed. Even after we build such a function, we can't just call the function because we need a place for the answer to go—that is, by itself `effectiveTemp(40,20)` doesn't really *do* anything. One logical thing you can do is call this function within a larger expression, which would look like this: `"It's only 40 degrees, but it feels like it's "+effectiveTemp(40,20)+"!"`. You could also call the function within a statement to assign the result that's returned to a variable: `realTemp=effectiveTemp(40,20)`. The thing to remember is that all built-in functions do one thing: return values.

Another point that should be clear is that the parameters you provide can be hard-wired (such as `40` or `20`), or they can be variables (such as `curTemp` or `curSpeed`) and the value of the variables will be used instead. The parameters could actually be the result of expressions (such as `TempSum/NumSamples` or `speedInKilometersPerHour*.62`). Whatever is placed in the parentheses will be evaluated. Finally, consider that expressions can include calls to functions that return values. Therefore, one parameter might invoke a function and whatever is returned from that function would be used in its place. These examples are completely legitimate: `realTemp=effectiveTemp(curTemp,speedInKilometersPerHour*.62)` and `realTemp=effectiveTemp(Number(temperatureString), Number(windSpeedString))`. Notice the `Number()` function that's nested in place of a parameter. Just remember all that you learned in Chapter 5 about writing complex expressions and the nested parentheses should be easy to track.

Using Homemade Functions

Using homemade functions is practically identical to using built-in functions. You call homemade functions in the same way that you call built-in functions: `functionName(optionalParams)`. The difference is that homemade functions can do other things besides *just* return values. You can design your homemade functions to return values if you want. Also, if you want your function to accept parameters, you need to build them that way. So, calling homemade functions is identical to calling built-in functions. However, when we get to writing our functions (later this chapter), you'll find that homemade functions can do a lot more than the built-in ones—you just have to write the script to make them perform the operation that you have in mind.

There is one slight difference in how you call homemade functions. In the case of the built-in functions, you can call them any time, any place—on a button, in a clip's keyframe, wherever. Homemade functions are written in keyframes. It can be a keyframe in the main timeline or inside a nested clip. Because homemade functions are "in" a particular timeline, they need to be targeted. If you are calling the function from any keyframe or button located in the same timeline as your function, you can call that function by simply typing its name (`functionName()`). (That is, technically, a relative reference.) However, if you are "in" another timeline, you have to precede the name of the function with a target path. Maybe you have a function in the main timeline and you want to call it from inside a clip. Just use the absolute reference `_root.functionName()`. If the clip is only nested one level deep, you could alternatively call the function with the relative `_parent.functionName()`. The concept of targeting should be very familiar to you. All the same information you learned about targeting properties, variables, or methods of clips in Chapter 7, "The Movie Clip Object," applies to calling functions…relative and absolute references. (You can learn more about targeting in Chapters 1, "Flash Basics," and 7.)

In Chapter 7, you also learned that many built-in Actions are really methods of the Movie Clip object. Methods are functions that are applied to individual instances (of clips, in this case). For instance, as a method, `someClip.gotoAndStop(2)` will cause an instance named "someClip" to jump to frame 2. When you write homemade functions, you can choose to write them in a keyframe of the main timeline or in a keyframe of any master symbol. Naturally, you'll need an instance of the clip containing the function if you want to call it. When calling such functions, you always precede the function name with a path to that function. The syntax of such a call looks the same as when applying methods to clips. That is, *`someClip`*`.gotoAndStop(2)` is the same form as *`someClip.myFunction()`* (where "myFunction" is the name of a homemade function that exists in a keyframe of the clip "someClip"). Not only do they "look" the same, but homemade functions can act like built-in methods if that's how you design them. This is a great way to leverage the knowledge you already have. Instead of trying to learn lots of different things, I think it's best to learn a few things really well, and then everything else can be understood in relative terms.

Creating Homemade Functions

Now that you know how to call functions (that is, how to use them), we can look at how you write them. The concepts of accepting parameters, returning values, and acting like methods should start to really make sense when you apply them to a purpose. You'll not only learn how to write functions, but also how they can help you. It's not as though this were an exercise in learning vocabulary words such as *parameters* and *methods*; rather, you will get to the point where you can reach for these tools as needed to solve problems.

Basics

Functions are written in keyframes. I find it much easier to type in the basic form while in Expert Mode. Here's the skeleton form:

```
function myFunction(){
}
```

The word "function" is *always* used as is. Next, you type the name for your function—anything you want as long as it's one word. (Keep in mind, you can't use words that are already part of the ActionScript language for your function name.) Parentheses always follow the function name. If you expect to receive any parameters, you must provide each with a temporary one-word name (separated by commas when you have more than one parameter). Finally, the opening and closing curly brackets enclose your entire script. Within the script for the function, you can use the name given for any parameters and it will evaluate as the value for that parameter. For example, consider this start of a function that accepts a parameter:

```
function doubleIt(whatNum){
}
```

In this case, the function name is "doubleIt." If you call this function (from elsewhere), you'd say `doubleIt()`. Because this function can be called while providing a parameter, the call would actually look like `doubleIt(12)` or like `doubleIt(getTimer())`. Calling the function effectively jumps to the function, sending with it the value of the parameter. Once at the function's script, the value provided as a parameter is referred to by using the parameter name (in this case, `whatNum`). If the parameter's value happens to be `12`, `whatNum` is `12`; if the parameter is `1203`, `whatNum` is `1203`. This is just like any variable (you refer to their values by referring to their name). In the preceding example, you can refer to `whatNum` anywhere within the function, and you'll be referring to the value of whatever was passed as a parameter. You'll see how to apply parameters in a moment, but for now just understand these two basic forms (functions that accept parameters and those that don't).

You're about to see the four basic applications of homemade functions. Then you'll have a chance to create functions that solve problems.

Functions as Subroutines

The first type of function we're going to write is unlike built-in functions because it won't return a value. A *subroutine* is one or more lines of code that you want to execute from more than one place in your movie. Perhaps you have several buttons that do the same basic thing. Instead of putting the same script on each button, you can call the same function from each button. The advantage (in addition to reducing the amount of typing) is that your code is centralized. If there's a bug or you want to make an adjustment, you need to do it in only one place (in the master function) and not on each button's call to the function.

Consider the example from the "Dynamic Referencing" section in Chapter 7 (shown in Figure 8.2).

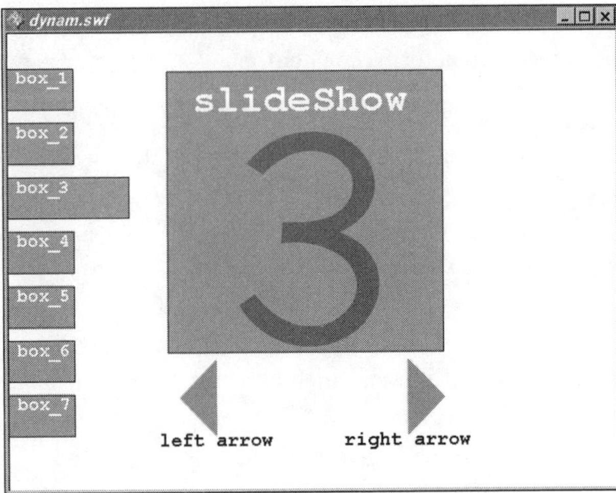

Figure 8.2 *Moving all seven "box_" clips can be done in a for-loop that references them dynamically.*

There were "forward" and "back" buttons that, in addition to moving to the next or previous frame of a clip, also set the _x position of seven clips ("box_1," "box_2," and so on) to zero. The code for the "forward" button was as follows:

```
on (release) {
    slideShow.nextFrame(); //move slide show ahead
    //Move all the boxes back to 0
    for(i=1;i<8;i++){
        _root["box_"+i]._x=0;
    }
    _root["box_"+slideShow._currentFrame]._x=50; //set cur box to 50
}
```

Notice that the "back" button code was almost identical:

```
on (release) {
    slideShow.prevFrame(); //move slide show back
    //Move all the boxes back to 0
    for(i=1;i<8;i++){
        _root["box_"+i]._x=0;
    }
    _root["box_"+slideShow._currentFrame]._x=50; //set cur box to 50
}
```

In addition to the "back" and "forward" buttons, there were seven invisible buttons on top of the box clips that had code that was nearly identical. Each of the seven buttons covering the box clips had code like this (although the parameter for `gotoAndStop()` was different for each button):

```
on (release) {
    slideShow.gotoAndStop(1); //move slide show to frame 1
    //Move all the boxes back to 0
    for(i=1;i<8;i++){
        _root["box_"+i]._x=0;
    }
    _root["box_"+slideShow._currentFrame]._x=50; //set cur box to 50
}
```

The only difference in each of the seven buttons was that the frame number used in the `gotoAndStop()` method was different: 1, 2, 3, and so on. But the rest of this code is the same as the "forward" and "back" buttons.

This is clearly a case in which a function can serve to eliminate redundant code. The script in each button is identical except for the first line (and, as you'll see later, the first line is even similar enough to be moved into a function that accepts a parameter). For now, let's move the repeated code from each button into a function. In place of the code that's moved, we simply call our function. So, you can simply create a function in frame 1 of the main timeline:

```
function moveBoxes(){
}
```

Then, paste (between the curly brackets) the code taken from each button. The finished function will look like this:

```
function moveBoxes () {
     for(i=1;i<8;i++){
          _root["box_"+i]._x=0;
     }
     _root["box_"+slideShow._currentFrame]._x=50; //set cur box to 50
}
```

Finally, you simply need to call this function from each button. The "next" button becomes

```
on (release) {
     slideShow.nextFrame(); //move slide show ahead
     moveBoxes();
}
```

The "back" button becomes

```
on (release) {
     slideShow.prevFrame(); //move slide show back
     moveBoxes();
}
```

And each invisible button looks like this:

```
on (release) {
     slideShow.gotoAndStop(1); //the 1 is different in each button
     moveBoxes();
}
```

Notice that in place of the code that was moved to the function, a call to the function is used instead. That is, `moveBoxes()` is used in place of the code that was removed.

Because the code is in only one place, it can be modified quickly. For example, if it turns out that there are more than seven "box" clips to move, we can modify that for-loop in the function.

The process of writing a function is to first identify a need and then solve it. In the case of a function that serves as a subroutine, the need is to reduce redundant code. The solution involves extracting that portion of the code that's repeated, moving it into a function, and—in the place from which it was extracted—calling the function. It's fine to start scripting and later notice that some code is repeated. When you find yourself copying and pasting code, bells should ring in your head saying, "time to consider a function." I often build my first version of a script using a rather hard-wired approach. After I get it working, I walk through the code and try to identify portions that are duplicated. Then, I try to move the duplicated code into a function instead.

As you're about to see, the repeated code doesn't even have to be identical. It can simply be similar. The bells that ring in your head can also be useful if they identify portions of your code that follow the same pattern. Just think about pseudo-code. If the explanation of what's being achieved in your code (the pseudo-code) can be generalized, you can probably write a function instead. For instance, in the preceding example, we didn't extract the very first line in each button because they were different. One used `nextFrame()`, another `prevFrame()`, and each of the seven invisible buttons used a different parameter for `gotoAndStop()`. Although this might seem unique for each button, it can actually be generalized. In pseudo-code, the general version of the first line for *each* button is "jump slideShow to a new frame." The trick is translating the pseudo-code. You'll see that the solution is to use a parameter.

Making Functions That Accept Parameters

Writing a function that accepts parameters is quite easy. Doing it effectively is just a bit more work. First, consider the form

```
function myFunction(param){
}
```

Whatever value is sent as a parameter when calling this function (as in `myFunction(12)`) can be referred to by using the variable name `param`. Inside the function (between the curly brackets), you can refer to that parameter name (`param`, in this case) and you are really referring to the value sent from the function call. It's like if you order a steak cooked "well done." Consider that the cook always performs the "cookIt" function. The parameter is "doneness." It doesn't matter whether you call this function by saying cookIt("wellDone") or cookIt("rare"), there's always a "doneness" parameter. It just happens that the value for doneness varies.

One common reason to make your function accept parameters is that you don't really want to perform the *exact* same procedure every time, but rather you want to perform a slightly different procedure each time. Just like the "cookIt" function, you'd like some variation available. Let's try to further consolidate the script in each button from the last example. The "next" button uses `slideShow.nextFrame()`, the "previous" button uses `slideShow.prevFrame()`, and the seven other buttons use `slideShow.gotoAndStop(x)` (where "x" is 1 through 7). Although this might look like three distinct scripts, they can easily be consolidated. Without changing what we've already coded in `moveBoxes`, we can add a feature to this function. Namely, we can make it accept a parameter that serves as the destination frame for the `slideShow` clip. That is, `slideShow.gotoAndStop(`*`destinationFrame`*`)` will work great if "destinationFrame" evaluates to the correct number. We'll just send a number when we call the `moveBoxes()` function (as in `moveBoxes(2)`) and name the parameter `destinationFrame`. Check out the finished function:

```
function moveBoxes (destinationFrame) {
    slideShow.gotoAndStop(destinationFrame);
    for(i=1;i<8;i++){
        _root["box_"+i]._x=0;
    }
    _root["box_"+slideShow._currentFrame]._x=50; //set cur box to 50
}
```

Notice that only the very first line and the second line have changed (the rest remains untouched). Now that this function accepts parameters (namely, the frame to which you want `slideShow` to jump), we can adjust the various calls to this function. (By the way, only when you make a significant change to the function—like adding a parameter—do you need to modify every call to that function—usually edits will occur only in the function itself and not in the calls to the function.) The seven buttons are easy to adjust. In each button, remove the line that starts `slideShow.gotoAndStop()` and change `moveBoxes()` to `moveBoxes(1)` for the first button, `moveBoxes(2)` for the second button, and so on. For the "forward" and "back" buttons, you need to first remove the first line (either `slideShow.nextFrame()` or `slideShow.prevFrame()`). Then when calling `moveBoxes()`, you need a value for the parameter. You can't just hard-wire something like `moveBoxes(2)` because that will *always* jump to frame 2. The "forward" button should (in pseudo-code) "jump to the current frame plus one" and the "back" button should "jump to the current frame minus one." We can write an expression in place of the parameter that results in the frame to which we want to jump. The call from the "forward" button will look like this: `moveBoxes (slideShow._currentFrame+1)`. The "back" button will use `moveBoxes (slideShow._currentFrame-1)`. The expression `slideShow._currentFrame+1` can be translated as "slideShow's current frame plus one."

Finally, there's one slight problem with the solution I've outlined. Namely, it's possible to press the "forward" button when you're already on the last frame of "slideShow" or press the "back" button when you're on the first frame. Therefore, the value that is sent as a parameter can be too high or too low. Inside the function, the line `slideShow.gotoAndStop(destinationFrame)` will attempt to jump to frame zero or to a frame number greater than the maximum. Nothing detrimental happens, but it's worth addressing this issue…for practice, if nothing else. (Ideally, we'd just make the buttons dim out and become inactive appropriately—and you'll do just that in the Slide Show workshop.) Without going through the work to inactivate buttons there's another simple fix for this issue. Inside and at the top of the `moveBoxes()` function, add the following two if-statements:

```
if(destinationFrame==0){
  destinationFrame=1;
}
if(destinationFrame>slideShow._totalFrames){
  destinationFrame=slideShow._totalFrames;
}
```

Translated, the first if-statement says that if the value for `destinationFrame` happens to be `0`, reset `destinationFrame` to equal `1`. The second if-statement checks whether `destinationFrame` is greater than the `_totalFrames` property of `slideShow` and if so, it sets `destinationFrame` to equal `_totalFrames`.

Just because `destinationFrame` is a parameter that's accepted doesn't prevent us from changing its value after we're inside the function. This solution resolves the minor flaw in the original function. Here's the final function in case you want to attempt to rebuild the example from chapter 7:

```
function moveBoxes (destinationFrame) {
  if(destinationFrame==0){
    destinationFrame=1;
  }
  if(destinationFrame>slideShow._totalFrames){
    destinationFrame=slideShow._totalFrames;
  }
```

```
    slideShow.gotoAndStop(destinationFrame);
    for(i=1;i<8;i++){
        _root["box_"+i]._x=0;
    }
    _root["box_"+slideShow._currentFrame]._x=50; //set cur box to 50
}
```

It's both typical and desirable to put the bulk of your code in functions and then make the calls to that function as minimal as possible. Remember, you can invoke any function as many times as you make calls to it.

Even though this sample function accepted a parameter and used that parameter's value directly (as the frame to which we jumped), parameters don't have to be used so directly. The parameter can control what part of a function to skip or execute. For example, a function could perform several very different procedures depending on the parameter accepted. Consider this example:

```
function doSomething(whatToDo){
  if (whatToDo=="eat"){
    //place code for "eating" here
  }
  if (whatToDo=="sleep"){
    //place code for "sleeping" here
  }
}
```

If the function is called with `doSomething("eat")`, just the code within the first if-statement is executed. Notice, too, that if you called `doSomething("cry")`, neither if-statement will be entered. Of course, you can also write nested if-else or if-else-if statements. The point I'm making here is that you can use the parameter to affect which part of the function is executed, rather than using the parameter's value directly within an assignment inside the function. I use this technique often for multipurpose functions, which act like a clearing house. Several different procedures go through the same function, but only execute a small portion of the function.

Making Functions That Return Values

Making a function that returns a value is as simple as adding a line that starts with `return`. Following the word `return`, you can type a hard-wired number, a variable, or an expression—the value of which will be "returned" to wherever the function was called. Consider this basic form:

```
function doubleIt(whatNum){
  return whatNum*2;
}
```

Now, from anywhere in your movie, you can call this function. Because this function returns a value, the place where you call the function turns into the value that's returned. So, `trace(doubleIt(12))` will display `24` in the output window. You could also say this:

```
theAnswer=doubleIt(22);
trace("Two times 22 is "+theAnswer);
```

One important note about the word `return`. In addition to specifying what is returned (to wherever the function is called), this will jump out of the function. That is, if there are more lines of code after `return` is encountered, they'll be skipped. This is actually kind of nice even if you're not trying to write a function that returns a value. For example, an if-statement at the top of a function could cause the rest of the function to be skipped when a particular condition is met. We looked at this technique in Chapter 5 and compared it to `break`—which only jumps out of an enclosed loop (not the entire function the way `return` does).

The main thing to remember about functions that return values is that you'll probably want to call them from within a statement. Simply writing the script `doubleIt(12)` doesn't really do anything because the answer (the value `24` that is returned) is not being used anywhere. There's no rule that says you have to use what's returned from a function. It's just more likely that when you call a function that returns a value, you will want to use that value somehow. Compare it to using a slot machine (you "call" the slot machine function by pulling the arm). Normally, you would take the winnings that are "returned," but if you want, you can just watch the pretty shapes spinning.

Let's look at a more practical example than my `doubleIt()` function. We can write a simple function that uses a currency exchange rate to calculate the value in U.S. dollars for a price given in Canadian dollars. The idea is that anytime you're given a price in Canadian dollars, you can call the `convert()` function (with the value in Canadian dollars as a parameter) and the value in U.S. dollars will be returned into the place the function is called. For example, you can call this function like so:

```
Trace("20 dollars Canadian is really "+convert(20)+" in US dollars");
```

This function is explored in great detail in the "Currency Exchange Calculator" workshop, but here's a finished version:

```
function convert(amountInCAD){
  exchangeRate= 0.62;
  return amountInCAD*exchangeRate;
}
```

The only reason I use the variable `exchangeRate` is that I want a clear and easy way to adjust that value (because it obviously varies). You could consolidate this into one line if you simply used `0.62` in place of `exchangeRate` in the second line. Actually, you could also add some fancy features that rounded off the answer. When you see the "Currency Exchange Calculator" workshop, you will see all kinds of fancy features—such as making the answer appear in "money format" ($1.50, not 1.5, for example). The methods of the Math object explored in Chapter 5 (as well as the String object that you'll see next chapter) will make this process relatively simple. As with all functions, those that return values aren't particularly difficult to write. The effort comes in designing a good one. You'll build your skills with practice.

Finally, it's not necessary that a function that returns a value must also accept parameters. It just makes sense when you want the function to do something *with* a value you provide.

Using Functions as Methods

Built-in functions can be called from anywhere by simply referring to the function name (as in `Number(anExpression)`). Unlike built-in functions, for homemade functions, you have to target the timeline where the function exists. Often, I write all my general purpose functions in the main timeline. If I want to call such a function from within a clip or nested clip, I have to remember to include `_root.` before the function's name (as in `_root.convert(12)`). As previously mentioned, a function that's written in a keyframe of a different timeline needs to be targeted as well. You could actually have two different Movie Clips each with a function named `myFunction()` in their first keyframe. These functions could produce entirely different results. Within either clip, simply calling the function (as `myFunction()`) would work great. If you were outside the clip or wanted to target the `myFunction()` of another clip, you'd have to precede the name with a path. For example, `_root.someClip.myFunction()` would execute the `myFunction` inside the clip with an instance name of "someClip".

To understand creating functions that perform like methods, recall what a method is. A method is a function that is applied to a single instance of a movie clip. (Actually, methods are functions that affect objects—but the object with which we're most familiar is a movie clip instance.) The "Action" `gotoAndStop(1)` is really a method because it is applied to the timeline in only one clip at a time. If you design them right, custom functions can act just like methods.

Let's write a function that serves as a method. I'd like a method called `grow()` that will increase both the `_xscale` and the `_yscale` properties of a clip (it's always such a pain to set *both* these because there's no "`_scale`" property). First, make a clip by drawing a circle, selecting it, and choosing Convert to Symbol. Then go inside the master clip and attach this script to the first frame:

```
function grow(){
  _xscale+=10;
  _yscale+=10;
}
```

Translated, this says, set the `_xscale` to `10` more and set the `_yscale` to `10` more. Which `_xscale`? Because no clip is targeted, the clip itself will grow. Now, this function can be called from anywhere inside the clip simply by saying `grow()`, but I want to do it from the main timeline. Drag a few instances of this clip to the main timeline, and then name each instance something unique (maybe `circle_1`, `circle_2`, and so on). Now, in the main timeline, create two buttons, one with this script:

```
on (release) {
  circle_1.grow();
}
```

The other button's script can be

```
on (release) {
  circle_2.grow();
}
```

Check out Figure 8.3.

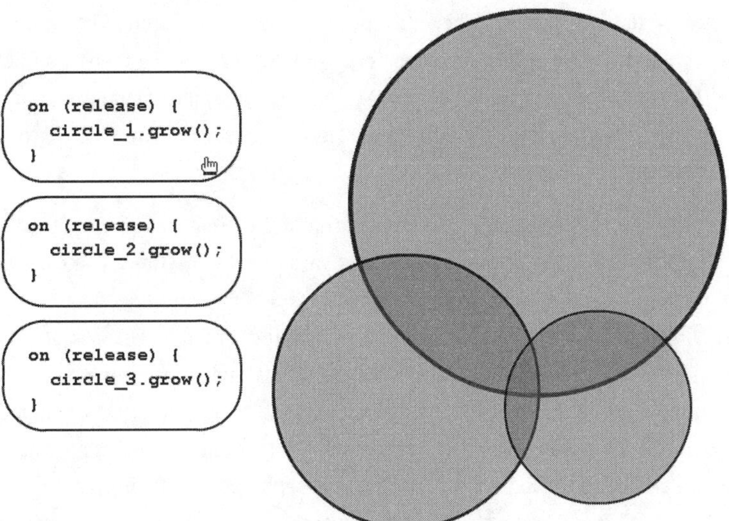

Figure 8.3 *A function inside the master symbol acts like a method of each instance.*

It looks exactly like applying a method to a clip (like you might do `circle_1. nextFrame()`).This example really does behave like a method for one important reason. The function refers (relatively) to the clip in which it is contained. I don't think this is a hard-and-fast rule of what makes a custom method, but for a function to act like a method, I think it's fair to say that the function has to affect the clip it's inside. All methods are functions—not all functions are methods. When functions are unique to the clip in which they're contained, you can think of them as methods.

Local Variables

The variations of functions (acting like methods, returning values, accepting parameters, and acting like subroutines) are all part of the same thing: functions. They're not even exclusive concepts. For example, you can have a subroutine that accepts parameters. The differences are in the way you use the functions you create. Local variables are another concept related to functions. You can use local variables in any type of function, but you don't have to.

Local variables are used just like any other variable except they exist only while inside the function. Similar to the way a named parameter has a value only while you're inside the function, local variables can be accessed only from within the function. The only real benefit of local variables is that they cease to occupy any memory after they're used. This concept of "good housekeeping" is not terribly important until your movies become very complex—and even then, it's likely that the user's computer memory (RAM) is large enough to make the issue almost nonexistent. But it's worth understanding, because there's no reason to use more memory than you have to.

Normally, after you assign a value to a variable (like `username="phillip"`), a small portion of RAM is dedicated to that variable. At any time, you can ascertain the value of `username`. Even if you're in another timeline, you can access the variable by preceding its name with the path to the variable. That variable will "live" forever—even if you reassign it to an empty string (as `username=""`, for example). If you are done with the variable, you can use the `delete` statement to remove it from memory (`delete username`). Depending on your application, you might want the variable to "live" forever. Perhaps you're tracking a user's score and you don't want to flush it from memory. Just remember that even if you stop using a variable, it's still occupying a portion of RAM (unless you delete it). Such "normal" variables can be considered global variables in that they're available at any time and from anywhere (that is, they're not "local").

All variables are safe, yet temporary, storage for data. They are temporary in that when you restart the movie, they are gone (or at least reinitialized). Some variables are used so briefly that you should consider making them local variables. A local variable does occupy RAM, but as soon as you leave the function that RAM is released and the variable ceases to exist. The way that you declare a local variable in a function is by using `var`. There are two ways; you can either say `var tempVar` (where `tempVar` will be the local variable) or `var tempVar="initial"` (where `tempVar` is the local variable and you're assigning a value from the get-go—to, in this case, the string `"initial"`). Then, from anywhere inside the enclosed function, you can refer to the variable by name (you don't need to proceed with `var`).

A perfect example of where I should have used a local variable was for the `exchangeRate` variable in this function:

```
function convert(amountInCAD){
  exchangeRate= .62;
  return amountInCAD*exchangeRate;
}
```

Because `exchangeRate` was used only once for convenience—and never again outside the function—a local variable would have been more appropriate. It would look like this:

```
function convert(amountInCAD){
    var exchangeRate= .62;
    return amountInCAD*exchangeRate;
}
```

Just that simple `var` before the first use of the variable makes it local. (Also, remember that you won't be able to access the value of a local variable from outside the function.)

Here's a great analogy to understand local variables. Just remember that variables are for storage. If you're baking a cake, you'll likely need to mix all the dry ingredients before combining them with the wet ingredients. If you use a bowl to temporarily hold the flour, salt, baking powder, and so on, the bowl can be considered a local variable. You put all the dry ingredients in one bowl, mix them, and then finally pour the whole bowlful into *another* bowl that contains your eggs, milk, vanilla, and the rest. The dish in which you bake the cake is more like a regular (global) variable. You pour the whole cake mixture into this dish, bake, and serve inside the dish. You want the baking dish to stick around for a while. This analogy is best for thinking about local variables. Often you want a place to temporarily store information (the dry ingredients or the exchange rate, for example). Then when you're done, you don't need the variable (or bowl) anymore. The truth is that if you never use a local variable, you'll probably never know the difference. It becomes an issue only when you're storing (unnecessarily) an enormous amount of data in a global variable. In any case, now you know how to declare a local variable!

Applying Functions to Previous Knowledge

Now that you've seen most of the ways built-in and homemade functions behave, it makes sense to review some previously covered concepts, which happen to apply seamlessly to functions. This section is almost a summary of functions—and that's how you should see it. Here's a chance to solidify a few concepts you've heard over and over.

Review Built-in Functions

Built-in functions all return values. Some people actually define a "function" as only something that returns values. But we've seen that homemade functions don't have this requirement—Flash's built-in functions do. If you simply remember that all built-in functions return values, you'll also remember that they are used within expressions or statements. They don't create statements by themselves.

Almost all the built-in functions follow the form `functionName(optionalParam)`. Some accept more than one parameter. Both `true` and `false` are functions in that they return true or false, respectively, but they don't use the parentheses. Use `true`, not `true()`. Finally, the two "functions" `scroll` and `maxscroll` are really "properties" of variables associated with dynamic text fields. If you have a variable (for example, `myText`) associated with a Multiline Dynamic Text field, the default `myText.scroll` is `1` (meaning that the first line appears at the top of the field). If you executed the script `myText.scroll=2`, you'd see the second line appear at the top of the field (effectively making it look like it scrolled down one line, as in Figure 8.4). Both `scroll` and `maxscroll` are definitely not functions. They look like properties in the form `variable.scroll`—but, unlike other properties, these two affect variables (not clip instances).

Finally, there is a whole set of "Actions" that act very much like homemade functions. All of Flash's Actions are either methods of clips or ActionScript statements. An example of an Action that's really a method is `nextFrame()`, which applies to a specific clip's timeline (or the current timeline when no clip is specified). The majority of the Actions, however, are really just statements. Most of these structural elements of the ActionScript language were covered in Chapter 5. Although we studied both methods and functions, realize that built-in examples of each exist within Flash.

This is a multiline
dynamic text field
associated with the
variable myText. The
script on the buttons to
the right simply change
the scroll property of
myText. It should appear

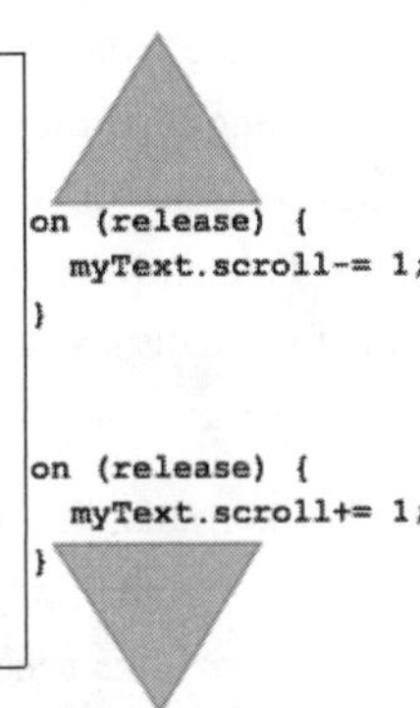
on (release) {
myText.scroll-= 1;
}
on (release) {
myText.scroll+= 1;
}

dynamic text field
associated with the
variable myText. The
script on the buttons to
the right simply change
the scroll property of
myText. It should appear
that this text scrolls

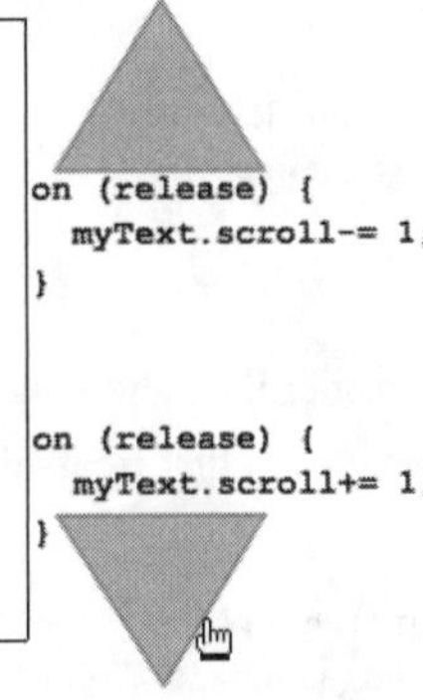
on (release) {
myText.scroll-= 1;
}
on (release) {
myText.scroll+= 1;
}

Figure 8.4 *You can make a Dynamic Text field scroll by changing the* `scroll` *property of the associated variable.*

Things to Remember

There are many things to remember when writing or calling functions. I think the biggest concept is that homemade functions are called by preceding the function name with a path to that function. Because functions are always written in keyframes, you simply need to target the timeline where it resides.

Naturally, functions that return values should be called from within an expression because the value that is returned will be returned to wherever the function was called. This concept has been explained, but realize that just because your function returns values, that doesn't mean it can't do other things, too. That is, a function can act as a subroutine (maybe setting the `_alpha` property of several clips) and when it's done, it can return a value. There's also no rule that says if a function returns a value, you have to *use* that value. You might have a function that does several things and then returns a value. If you simply call it by name—for example, `doit()`—the value that's returned never gets used but the function still executes (including all contained scripts). Because the function returns a value, you might normally use it within a statement such as `theAnswer=doit()`, but you don't have to.

Finally, don't forget all that you learned about data types in Chapter 4. When passing values as parameters, pay attention to the data type sent to and expected by the function. Also realize functions that return values only return values of the type you specify. For example, if the following function is called using `doit("one")`, you'll have trouble because the parameter being sent is a string and the function almost certainly expects a number.

```
function doit(whatNum){
  var newLoc=whatNum*10;
  someClip._x=newLoc;
}
```

Similarly, consider the following function, which returns a string. If you call it within an expression that treats the result as a number, you'll get unexpected results.

```
function getAlpha(){
  return "The alpha is "+curAlpha
}
```

You'll also have trouble if you call the preceding function with `someClip._alpha=getAlpha()`

The problem is that you're trying to set the `_alpha` of "someClip" to a string (where you can only set `_alpha` to a number). This is simply a case of mixing data types. You're trying to use apples in the orange juice maker, if you will.

Remember, too, that there's a movie clip data type. You refer clips by name but not a string version. That is, simply typing `someClip._x=100` will set the `_x` property of a clip instance called `someClip`. Notice that there are no quotation marks. The reason I'm reminding you now is that you can store a reference to a clip instance in a variable or as a parameter. For example, the following function accepts—as a parameter—a reference to a clip:

```
function moveOne(whichOne){
  whichOne._x+=10;
}
```

This function will work only when the movie clip data type is sent as a parameter. For example, if you have a clip instance named "red," you can use `moveOne(_root.red)`. If the clip is in the same timeline from which you call this function, you could use `moveOne(red)`. But notice that it's a reference to the clip (data type "movie clip"), not a string, that is being passed as the parameter.

Finally, an esoteric point should be made about the terms *argument* and *parameter*. In my opinion, they can be used interchangeably. Some people define parameter as the general term and argument as the specific term. That is, when you're not sure what the parameter's value is, it's still a parameter. After you are done analyzing and know the value, you call it an argument. So, a function can accept parameters, but when you call the function, you'll use a particular value as an argument. I'm only mentioning this definition so that you'll know *argument* and *parameter* are really the same thing. I'll try to use "parameter" throughout the book, but don't be surprised when you hear someone else say "argument."

Of course, there are countless other things to remember, but at this point, I think it makes the most sense to practice. Try to analyze a Flash movie you made in the past to see whether a function can reduce redundant code. Naturally, if it "ain't broke," there's little incentive to fix it. However, recognizing places in your own code that can be optimized is a great skill. If you're having a hard time finding flaws in your own movies, here are a few exercises to try out:

- Write a function that moves a clip instance (maybe a box) 10 pixels to the right. Create two different buttons that call this function.
- Adapt the preceding function to accept a parameter so that it can move the clip instance 10 pixels to the right or to the left—depending on the value of a parameter received. Make one button move the clip to the right, the other to the left.
- Write a different function that returns half of the value provided as a parameter. That is, if the function is called `half()`, calling the function with trace (`"Half of 4 is "+half(4)`) will result in "Half of 4 is 2" appearing in the output window.
- Write another function that acts like a method inside a clip. Make one that reduces the clip's `_alpha` or increases it. You can write two methods or one that accepts a parameter. In the end, you should be able to use buttons in the main timeline to target any particular instance (of this clip with the method) and you can reduce or increase the `_alpha`.

Summary

Functions are so useful that it's hard to imagine programming without them. It's possible (after all, you couldn't write functions in Flash 4), but functions mean that repeated code can be consolidated; that one block of code can behave slightly differently depending on the value of a parameter received; that values can be returned; and that you can create your own methods.

Throughout all these techniques, one thing remains consistent: The form of a function is always the same. Additional parameters will sometimes appear in the parentheses following the function name, and sometimes you'll return values, but the form is always the same. Just like if-statements and for-loops, you should start every function by typing the core form (always in a keyframe script) as

```
function anyName(){
}
```

Then you can fill in the space between the curly brackets and parameters if you want. Practically every workshop exercise involves a function, so get used to it! You'll learn to love the way that functions minimize typing.

{ Chapter 9 }

Selecting Text, Trapping Keys, and Manipulating Strings

Storing the string data type in a variable is straightforward enough. But manipulating a string can be much more difficult. After you have a string, you'll often want to change it, extract just a portion, or analyze the characters contained in the string. Perhaps you want to automatically capitalize the first letter in each word of a string. Or maybe you want to compare the user's input text to a list of correct answers. Using the features of Flash's String object, you can manipulate strings the way a word processor can "find-and-replace"—and much more.

In addition to exploring the ways to manipulate strings during runtime, this chapter includes information about both the Key object and the Selection object. The Key object lets you "trap" keypresses the user makes, so you know exactly which keys are being pressed. The Selection object lets you ascertain or set the portion of an editable field that's currently selected. Although most of the tricks learned in this chapter might at first seem dry or boring, they're actually very powerful and dynamic. For example, the Key object can easily detect when the user has multiple keys pressed, which has applications for games.

Specifically, in this chapter you will

- Manipulate strings using the String object
- Build dynamic HTML text

- Determine which keys are being pressed using the Key object
- Ascertain and set the selected area of a text entry field

The three unrelated objects (String, Key, and Selection) are included in this chapter for a few reasons. They're all special objects in that they don't follow all the rules of objects as do those discussed in Chapter 11, "Objects." Also, they're simple enough to fully cover in one chapter. Finally, you can probably remember all three as being related to the keyboard because that's how you type into input fields, press keys, and create strings. This final similarity is more serendipitous than practical. Realize the three objects are being discussed separately and not as part of the same concept.

String Object Form

I'll first explain the easy way to think of the String object and then I'll provide the messy details that—although important—will probably never affect you in any practical manner. The String object has several methods and one property—`length` (shown in Figure 9.1).

You can write an expression using the methods or property in this form:

```
anyString.method()
anyString.property
```

Recall that methods (like functions) always include parentheses that will hold optional parameters. The form above shows that a variable (`anyString`) that contains a string for a value can be used with any method or property. For example, the `toLowerCase()` method converts the string to all lowercase characters and returns the result. If `anyString` happens to equal `"Phillip"`, the following expression would return (that is, "turn into") `"phillip"`:

```
anyString.toLowerCase()
```

You could actually use `"Phillip".toLowerCase()`, but more likely you'd want to write an expression that changed based on the value of a variable (`anyString`). The form is quite simple, however.

The only property is `length`. (And, unlike properties of clips, this one doesn't have an underscore at the beginning of its name.) Using `anyString.length` returns the number of characters in the string (`anyString`).

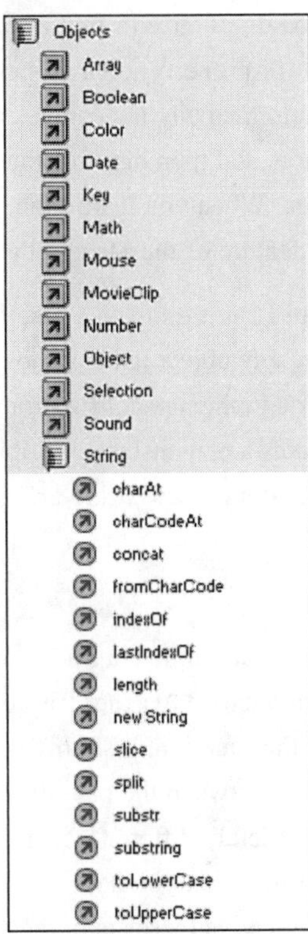

Figure 9.1 *All the String object's methods (and one property) are found in the Toolbox list of the Actions panel.*

It doesn't get much harder than that. Some methods require a parameter or two. For example, `charAt(index)` requires the parameter (index) to specify which character you're trying to get. For example, `"Phillip".charAt(2)` returns `"i"` (because the first character is located in "index" 0—it counts 0, 1, 2, 3, and so on). We'll look at some practical uses for the different methods in the next section. Notice, it really is pretty simple.

Esoteric String Object Details

Before we move on to more practical discussion, a few details need to be explained. First, all methods of objects require that an object has to be instantiated. In the case of the movie clip object, it simply requires that you have an instance onstage before you can refer to any properties or methods. However, the methods of the String object are special because you don't have to first instantiate the object manually. By simply using a method (or property) on a variable or string literal (like all the earlier examples), Flash automatically instantiates a temporary String object, does the method's operation, and then discards the object. You don't have to care because it's automatic. When you learn more about objects in Chapter 11, you might learn to love this feature of the String object.

You *can* instantiate a String object if you want. (But I can't think of a practical reason why you'd want to.) The way you instantiate any object (except movie clips, which are simply dragged to the stage) is through the `new` constructor. (Think of a "constructor" as something that constructs a new instance of object type—in this case, String.) Here's an example of creating a new string and placing the entire object into a variable:

```
myObjectVar=new String("phillip")
```

Even though I don't have a practical reason to actually instantiate a String object, I want to point out something confusing. The *function* called `String()` is completely different than `new String()`. In the case of the function, it simply returns a string version of whatever is passed as a parameter (between the parentheses). When you preface with the word `new`, you get a completely different result: a new String object. Just as the `Number()` function ensures that you have a number data type, `String()` ensures that the expression in the parentheses is in the string data type form.

Another very similar method is the `toString()` method, used like `whatever.toString()` to return a string version of `whatever`, as long as the data type of `whatever` is an object. The `toString()` method is almost identical to the `String()` function except that (as a method) it operates only on objects (Array, Color, and so on, as you'll see in Chapter 11). Depending on the type of object you're using the `toString()` method on, it will behave slightly differently. For example, when you `toString()` an array, each item *in* the array gets converted to a string individually (instead of just one big string). You'll learn more about arrays in Chapter 10, "Arrays." The point is that `toString()` is a little more refined in its behavior in comparison to `String()`. Generally, most of these details are very intuitive if you avoid using the `new` constructor and simply think of the `String()` function and `toString()` methods as ways to ensure that a variable is of the string data type.

Methods of the String Object Explored

You can use the String object to do some pretty fancy maneuvers. After walking through a few definitions, we'll look at a few examples of how to use them for practical tasks. You can actually learn quite a bit by exploring the tool tip and generic starter script that appears in the Actions panel (see Figure 9.2). The following discussion should give you a good background to the String object's methods before we exercise our expression-writing skills to use the String object.

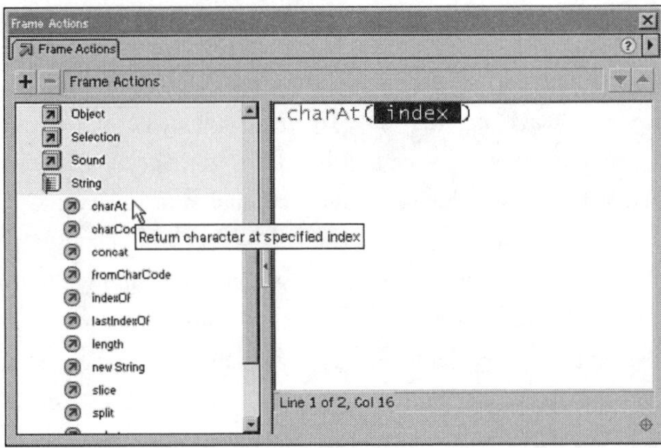

Figure 9.2 *In addition to information provided in the tool tip, methods appear in the script area with parameters selected (so you can replace them).*

Zero-Based System

While playing with the String object, you must remember that (as with arrays) counting begins with 0 (not 1). This is called a zero-based system. That is, the characters in `"Phillip"` are `"P"` in the zero index, `"h"` in the first index, `"i"` in the second index, and so on. Any time you specify an index in a string, you must start by counting 0, 1, 2, and so on. This "counting from zero" technique can mess you up when you consider the only property of strings (the others are methods): `length`. The expression `"Phillip".length` will return `7` even though the last character is in the sixth index. It's obvious when you think about it, but it often trips me up.

Extracting Portions of Strings

On with the fun! The three methods `slice()`, `substr()`, and `substring()` are different versions of the same basic method. These will return a portion of the string being operated on. Even though they're practically equivalent, each has a unique feature or two that makes it interesting. It might make sense to memorize one and then realize that the other two are available when your favorite becomes unwieldy.

For the following examples, assume that the variable `myString` equals `"ABCDEFGHI"`.

`slice(`*`start,end`*`)` returns all the characters from "start" to (but not including) "end." `myString.slice(2,4)` returns `"CD"`. That is, the character in the second index (`"C"`) to—but not including—the fourth index (`"E"`). Special feature 1: If, in either parameter, you want to include a number equal to the index of the last character but you don't know how many characters are present, just use `-1`. For instance, if you want all the characters from the second index through (but not including) the end, you could use `myString.slice(2,-1)`—which, in our example, would equal `"CDEFGH"`. Special feature 2: If you leave out the second parameter, you'll get all the characters from "start" through (and including) the last character. That is, `myString.slice(2)` returns `"CDEFGHI"`.

`substr(`*`start,length`*`)` returns a total of "length" characters starting with the one in the "start" index. `myString.substr(2,4)` returns `"CDEF"`. That's because the second parameter (`4`) specifies that a string of four letters will be returned, starting with the character in the second index (`"C"`). Special feature: If you leave out the second parameter, you'll get all characters from "start" through (and including) the last character—just like the `slice()` method.

`substring(`*`from,to`*`)` returns all the characters from "from" to (but not including) "to." `myString.substring(2,4)` returns `"CD"` because (just like the `slice()` method) the second index is `"C"` and all the characters to (but not including) the fourth index (`"E"`) would include just indexes two and three. The `substring()` method is the same as `slice` except the special features vary. Both have the option of leaving the second parameter blank (and getting a string from the one parameter provided through the end of the string). But only `substring()` has the feature that when you accidentally use a higher number for the first parameter, the higher and lower numbers are automatically swapped. That is, `myString.substring(4,2)` also returns `"CD"`. Also, using negative parameters will behave as though they were zeros. That is, you can't specify a "from" or "to" that are below the first index (`0`) or above the top index (`length-1`).

Just to make it confusing, there's an old deprecated *function* called `substring()`. As a function, it is used by itself (not attached to a string object). The best way to avoid confusion is to make sure that you never use this function. One way to keep track is that methods always appear after the string (like `myString.substring()`), whereas the `substring()` function's form is `substring(`*`string,start,length`*`)`. Just so you know what it does, the `substring()` function returns a total of "length" characters from the "start" spot (not index) in "string." Therefore, `substring(myString,2,4)` returns `"BCDE"`. Notice the `2` parameter is not an index but rather the second character (counting the way you would normally—starting with 1). As I said, just avoid using this and you won't get confused.

Extracting Characters, Changing Case, and Searching

Before we do a few exercises, let me introduce just a couple other methods. When you only want one character, you can use the `charAt()` method. `charAt(`*`index`*`)` simply returns the character in the "index" position. Therefore, `myString.charAt(2)` will return `"C"`. It's pretty simple, really. A sister method `charCodeAt()` is identical except instead of returning an actual string version of the character in the particular index, it returns the ASCII code for that character. The ASCII value for "A" is 65, "B" is 66, and so on. The code for "a" is 97, "b" is 98, and so forth. By the way, the old way to convert a string to uppercase was to find its ASCII value, (assuming it was greater than 96) subtract 32 (the difference between 97 and 65), and then convert back to the string value for the resulting code. (You're about to see that this is unnecessary now.) To convert an ASCII number back to a string, use `String.fromCharCode(65)`. Notice you don't use `fromCharCode()` in the same way you use other methods (attaching it to a particular string). In this way, `fromCharCode()` acts like all the Math object methods (which always appear `Math.`*`whatEverMethod`*`()` but with `String` verbatim).

The method `toLowerCase()` will return an all-lowercase version of the string being operated on. `myString.toLowerCase()` returns `"abcdefghi"`. Remember that none of these methods actually change the string itself. An assignment like this will however: `myString=myString.toLowerCase()`. Naturally, `toUpperCase()` will return an all-uppercase version of the string.

Finally, perhaps the most powerful methods of the String object are `indexOf()` and `lastIndexOf()`. These will search through your entire string for a pattern (either a sequence of characters or a single character) that you pass as a parameter. It will then return the index at which the pattern is first found. The difference between `indexOf()` and `lastIndexOf()` is that `indexOf()` starts from the beginning and searches forward, but `lastIndexOf()` starts at the end and searches backward. For example, `myString.indexOf("A")` will return `0` because "A" was found in the zero index. If the pattern provided as a parameter doesn't appear in the string, `-1` is returned. Optionally, you can specify that the search starts at a different spot than the very beginning or very end. You simply include an additional parameter, as in `myString.indexOf("xx",2)`, which starts from the second index and searches for `"xx"`. Using these methods, you can quickly find where any particular sequence of characters appears within a larger string. For example, you could first determine where the colon appears in the string `"username:phillip"` and then use `substr()` to extract just the characters before or after the colon.

```
theString="username:phillip";
spot=theString.indexOf(":");
if (spot<>-1){
  firstPart=theString.substr(0,spot);
  secondPart=theString.substr(spot+1);
}
```

Notice that because `substr()` includes characters only from its first parameter *to* (not including) its second parameter, I could use `spot` (the spot found using `indexOf()`) when assigning the value for `firstPart`. But when assigning `secondPart`, I wanted to start with one character past the colon (`spot+1`). Also, because I didn't include a second parameter, `secondPart` included everything from `spot+1` through the end. Notice that this code works no matter what the value for `theString`. For example, `"city:Portland"` works just as well. Finally, the if-statement uses the expression `spot<>-1` for a condition. Translated, it says "If it's true that spot is not equal to `-1`, then proceed." Recall that `-1` is returned when the `indexOf()` method can't find the character for which you're searching.

String Object Methods Applied

That was a nice warm-up example. Let's look at a few more complex solutions that involve a taste of some of the other things you've learned so far.

Let's say you want to ensure that the first letter in each word of a string is capitalized. The `toUpperCase()` method won't work because it will change every character! The following two functions achieve this goal. In pseudo-code: "Loop for as long as it takes to find all the blanks, and then whenever you find a blank, use the `toUpperCase()` method on just the character that follows the blank." Check out the two functions here:

```
function capitalizeWords(theString){
  var blankFound=-1;

  while ( true ) {
    theString=capitalize(blankFound+1,theString);
    blankFound=theString.indexOf(" ",blankFound+1);

    if (blankFound==-1){
      return theString
    }
  }
}

function capitalize(index, aString){
  return aString.substr(0, index) + aString.charAt(index).toUpperCase()
  ➥+aString.substr(index+1)
}
```

This actually took me quite some time to program, but (as always) I just did it one step at a time. I first built the function `capitalize()`, which will replace an individual character within a string (and return the result). The `capitalize` function receives both an index (that is, which character you want capitalized) and a string (that's the string you want changed). The one-line function builds a string by combining three parts: first the characters in front of the index (`aString.substr(0, index)`); then, an uppercase version of just the one character in the index (`aString.charAt(index).toUpperCase()`); finally, all the characters after the index (`aString.substr(index+1)`). The last `substr()` method doesn't include two parameters because I wanted everything from just past the index to the end (when you leave the second parameter blank, the method returns all characters through the end). Basically, the `capitalize()` function combines three parts: before the character, the character, and after the character. Only the character is turned to uppercase. Before I proceeded, I would test the function with a button containing this—hard-wired—script:

```
on (release) {
  trace(capitalize(7,"phillipkerman"));
}
```

When working, this will display “phillipKerman” in the output window. I tried a few more options, such as capitalizing the first letter or the last letter—the point being that I tested this function before moving on to the more complicated `capitalizeWords()` function.

After I got the `capitalize()` function working, I built `capitalizeWords()`. I wanted a loop that would go through an entire string and capitalize every letter that appeared after a blank. Because I didn’t know exactly how many times the loop would repeat, I made a loop that “while true” will loop forever. Notice within the loop that if the variable `blankFound` ever equaled `-1` (the if-statement `if(blankFound==-1)`), the line `return theString` would execute, which jumps out of the function. (Without this escape route, we could have had a true infinite loop on our hands—as discussed in Chapter 5, “Programming Structures.”) Remember that when using `indexOf()` and no match is found, `-1` is returned. So, the second line in the loop—the one that assigns `blankFound` to the index where a blank is found (`theString.indexOf(" ",blankFound+1)`)—will turn into `-1` when no more blanks are found. Notice that the optional parameter `blankFound+1` is provided in this `indexOf()` method (specifying where the search for blanks should start—not at the beginning). Without this, `indexOf()` would keep finding the *first* instance of `" "` but I wanted it to find one, and then find the next. To make sure that it doesn’t find the same blank twice, I simply say “start searching on spot past the last one found.” On each iteration of the loop, I reassign `theString` (the string passed as a parameter) to a new value. Specifically, I capitalize the character just past the last blank found using my `capitalize()` function created earlier (`theString=capitalize(blankFound+1,theString)`). The only funky thing is that in the first line I initialize the value to `blankFound` to `-1` so that the first time in the loop (when I capitalize character `"blankFound+1"`, I’m actually capitalizing the character in the `0` position (that’s the first character).

Naturally, this is easier to explain than it is to write (or to interpret). It’s interesting, though, that when I explained how it works, I did so in almost the reverse of the order in which it appears. That’s not a requirement, but in the case of the “while true” loop, I think the very first thing you must establish is a “way out.” I’ve heard robbers always establish their exit route before proceeding. It’s practically the same thing with loops (you don’t want to be stuck in an infinite loop). Also, because Flash doesn’t read the script in a linear order, you shouldn’t try to interpret my finished code that way either. You can go through line by line, but just realize that certain parts might repeat (in a loop) and you might need to jump around to other parts of the script (anytime a function is called).

Alright, that example was a bit of a doozy. Here's one that's a bit less involved.

The following function accepts a filename (such as `"sunrise.bmp"`) and returns a string in the form `"The file sunrise is a bitmap"` (or "jpeg" or "text file," and so on). The basic approach is to cut the string into two parts: the part before the period (the prefix) and the part after the period (the extension). Then we use a series of if-else statements to determine what file type the particular extension matches. Finally, we create the string "The file BLANK is a BLANK," but replace the two BLANKs with the prefix and file type, respectively. Here's the code:

```
function getInfo(filename){
  var dotLoc=fileName.lastIndexOf(".");
  var prefix=filename.substr(0,dotLoc);
  var extension=filename.substr(dotLoc+1);
  var filetype;
  if (extension=="bmp"){
    filetype="a bitmap";
  }else if (extension=="txt"){
    filetype="a text file";
  }else{
    filetype="an unknown file type";
  }
  return "The file \"" + prefix + "\" is " + filetype + ".";
}
```

Notice that I save a few local variables that I'll need within the function but nowhere else: the `dotLoc` (containing the "last index of" the period); `prefix` (using `substr()` to extract all characters from index 0 through `dotLoc`); and `extension` (using `substr()` again, but from the index `dotLoc+1` through the end). Then the if-else sequence checks `extension` against a few known file types and sets the filetype variable accordingly. The last else is a catch-all that simply sets `filetype` to "unknown". Also, just so that the string follows proper English and uses "a" and "an" appropriately, I included that part in the `filetype` variable. This technique is also useful when plural or singular words are being built on-the-fly—it eliminates the need for funky things such as "page(s)," for example.

To test this function, make a button with this code:

```
on (release) {
  trace(getInfo("sunrise.txt"));
  //or
  //onScreenVariable=getInfo("sunrise.txt");
}
```

You can probably see that what you've already learned about code structures (statements such as "if" and "while") plus homemade functions will all come in handy when you try perform elaborate maneuvers with the String object.

There are a couple methods of the String object that I've left out. In particular, I've left out the method `split()`, which is quite cool. It will convert a string into an array. You just specify a delimiter as a parameter (`myString.split(`*`delimiter`*`)`). If `myString` is `"phillip,david,kerman"`, `myString.split(",")` will return an array with three items (`"phillip"`, `"david"`, and `"kerman"`). We'll look at this method more in Chapter 10.

Finally, I left out the `concat()` method. It does the same thing as the + concatenation character except that it will never act like an addition operator (as + will when the two operands are both numbers). If `myString` is `"Phillip"`, `myString.concat("David","Kerman")` will return `"PhillipDavidKerman"`. By the way, you can have as many parameters as you want—just separate each with a comma.

Using HTML Text

One of the cool features in Flash 5 is that in addition to the regular anti-aliased text, you can display basic HTML text. HTML, which doesn't support anti-aliased text, is used in text files that display in a browser. Instead of containing actual formatted text (such as bold or italic), "tags" specify what kind of formatting is requested. The benefit is that every browser can interpret the tags instead of relying on a proprietary format (such as one company's word processor format, for example). In Flash, the benefit is that instead of formatting the text by hand (where it will be locked down when you export the movie), you can format text during runtime.

It helps to understand a little bit about HTML (which I will assume you know). Combined with the string manipulation you learned about earlier in this chapter, you can do some amazing things. For example, let's say the user types in his name and you want a text field to display "Welcome **Phillip**!" (and you want whatever name the user typed in to be bold). In HTML, that string would look like this:

```
Welcome <b>Phillip</b>!
```

Of course, you don't want the hard-wired "Phillip" but rather a variable. Therefore, you'll need a Dynamic Text field onscreen with its options set to display a variable (say, `message`) and set to HTML text (see Figure 9.3).

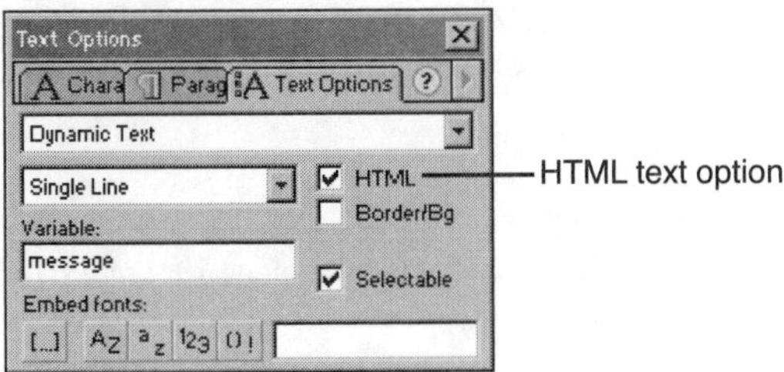

Figure 9.3 *To display text using HTML, it must be Dynamic Text (or Input Text) and have the HTML option selected.*

Then, assuming that you have established that `username` has a string in it (perhaps you had the user type it into another Input Text field with `username` associated), you can then use this code:

```
message="Welcome <b>" + username + "</b>";
```

I'll admit this might not look terribly exciting—but it really is! It means that dynamically generated text can include fancy (albeit pretty basic) formatting. Here's some simple code that displays the value of two variables (`verbalScore` and `mathScore`) in a visually pleasing column format shown in Figure 9.4:

```
message="Results:\r";
message=message+"Verbal Score: \t<i>"+ verbalScore +"</i>\r";
message=message+"Math Score: \t<i>"+ mathScore +"</i>\r";
message=message+"Total: \t\t\t<i>"+ Number(verbalScore+mathScore) +"</i>";
```

A couple of things to notice. Just as with literal quotation marks (`\"`), you can create literal return characters (`\r`) and tabs (`\t`). It might seem odd that such formatting goes inside the string part of the variable and not outside the quotation marks like the two variables do. Also, notice that I had to use the `Number()` function because `verbalScore+mathScore` would otherwise result in a concatenated string (because the other operators in that line of code are also strings). Finally, this code could easily be placed on one line. I did it this way because it's easier to see how the separate lines will appear. Basically, I'm saying "message=this+return," and then "message=what message equals already plus this + return," and then "message = what messaged equaled plus more + return," and so on. I'm just building it one line at a time and it's easier to read.

Results:
Verbal Score: *780*
Math Score: *800*
Total: *1580*

Figure 9.4 *Dynamically formatted text is possible (at runtime) when using HTML.*

Although HTML text has great potential, it's not a panacea. On one hand, you're limited to aliased (jaggy) text and a very limited version of HTML (only the tags `<a>`, `<b>`, `<font color>`, `<font face>`, `<font size>`, `<i>`, `<p>`, and `<u>`). On the other hand, there's no other solution like it. Possibly the coolest thing is that the HTML tag `a href` works. This means you can include hyperlinks within text fields. Even if the word moves (for instance, if the text field's contents change), the hot-word itself will remain hot. Try this code and then preview your movie in a browser:

```
message="This is <a href=\"http://www.samspublishing.com\"
➥target=\"_blank\">hot</a>";
```

Basically, this makes the word `"hot"` a hyperlink that opens a new browser window (`_blank`).

Selection Object

Even though the String object is not directly related to HTML text, they can be used together. The same goes for the Selection object. To fully apply the features of the Selection object methods (shown in Figure 9.5), you'll also need to use the String object.

The Selection object enables you to control selectable text fields. Input Text is automatically selectable, but you can also set the Selectable option for Dynamic Text as in Figure 9.6. You can control selectable fields in several ways. First, you can set or ascertain which field currently has focus. Only one field can be actively selected at a time, and that field is said to "have focus." In addition to setting or finding out which field has focus, you can also specify (or find out) which portion of that field is currently selected. The most obvious application for this is a situation in which you want to help a user fill out a form. Instead of making the user fill in a blank field, you can preselect a portion so that typing automatically replaces the selected text. Maybe the field says "Enter Name" and instead of making the user select the text (so the user can replace it with his name), you can select it for him.

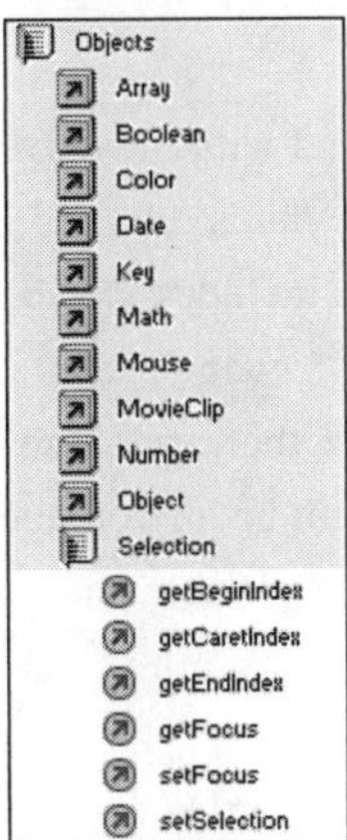

Figure 9.5 *There are only a few methods for the Selection object.*

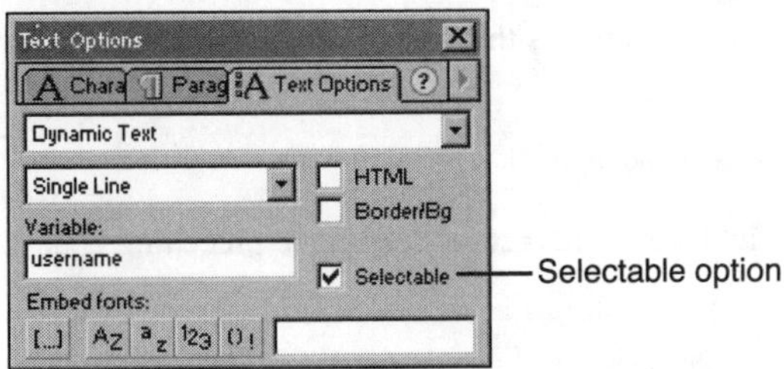

Figure 9.6 *Dynamic Text fields aren't automatically selectable the way Input Text fields are. You must choose the Selectable option.*

The most practical feature of the Selection object, however, is setting (or finding out) which input field has focus. When you learn to use the Key object to trap the Tab key (in the next section), you can force the next logical field to get focus when the user presses Tab. Finding out which field has focus is also useful in a situation in which you want to provide one prompt at a time to instruct the user depending on which field has focus. You can do all this and more with the Selection object.

Like the Math object, the Selection object never needs to be instantiated. You simply use "`Selection.`" verbatim for every use—`Selection.oneMethod()` `Selection.otherMethod()`. The list of methods is quite short. You can only set or get which field has focus, and set or get the portion that's selected in the field that currently has focus. We'll look at setting and getting focus first.

Getting and Setting Focus

`Selection.getFocus()` returns the variable name associated with the currently focused text field. The only catch is that the variable name that's returned is in the form of a string (not the actual variable), and it always includes the absolute path to that variable. On top of that, the path doesn't start "`_root.`" but "`_level0.`" (or `_levelx` where x is the level number where the variable resides). Simply finding the name of a variable (in string form) might be all you need. And, if you use the following code, you can extract just the variable name at the end of the string:

```
wholeThing=Selection.getFocus()
justVarName=wholeThing.substr(wholeThing.lastIndexOf(".")+1)
//or in one line:
justVarName=
➥Selection.getFocus().substr(Selection.getFocus().lastIndexOf(".")+1);
```

The fact that `getFocus()` always returns the string name for your variable means that you cannot do something like this:

```
Selection.getFocus()="Something new";
```

If the currently selected field were `_level0.message`, the preceding code would translate to this meaningless line:

```
"_level0.message"="Something new";
```

But you want

```
_level0.message="Something new";
```

The quick solution to this is to use the function `eval()`. That is, `eval("_level0.message")="Something new"` will assign the string `"Something new"` to the value of the variable itself. Therefore, the following line works as you might expect:

```
eval(Selection.getFocus())="Something new";
```

The last point regarding `getFocus()` is that if no field has focus it will return `"null"`.

As for the `setFocus()` method, you must specify a string form of the variable name whose field you want to set focus. For example, to set focus on the field containing the variable `message` (that resides in the root—not in a clip's timeline):

```
Selection.setFocus("_root.message");
```

Notice that the variable name is in quotation marks. Although `getFocus()` returns a string form starting with the level number, you can (if you want) use the hierarchy starting `_root`. Notice, too, that the preceding method doesn't return a value; rather, it goes ahead and sets the focus. It's almost like performing an assignment, but not quite.

Setting and Getting Selections

After you're sure about which field has focus, you can set (or find out) what portion of the field is selected. Before you use any of the following Selection methods, make sure that there is a currently focused field. Otherwise, the `setSelection()` method will have no effect and the various "getSelection" methods will return `-1`.

The `setSelection()` method is the easiest to understand. The form is `setSelection(`*`start`*`,`*`end`*`)` where "start" is the index at which you want the selection to start and "end" is the last character that is also selected. (Unlike `substr(`*`start`*`,`*`end`*`)`, which is not inclusive of the last parameter, `setSelection()` includes all the characters inclusively.) As with all the String object methods, Selection object methods are zero-based (meaning they start counting the first character as index 0).

To find out what portion of a field is selected, you can use the methods `Selection.getBeginIndex()` and `Selection.getEndIndex()`. These two are pretty self-explanatory, but just remember that if no field had focus or no characters are selected these methods will both return `-1` (instead of the index at which the selection starts or ends).

Finally, there's one last method, called `getCaretIndex()`, which returns the index in front of the blinking cursor. That is, if you click to start typing at the very beginning of a field, `Selection.getCaretIndex()` will return `0`. You can think of this as the index into which the user will start typing (when she starts typing).

The Selection object isn't terribly exciting. It comes in handy only when controlling selectable text fields. Later in this chapter, we'll use it in conjunction with the Key object. Just remember that with the Selection object, you must first have a focused field before you can select text. And, selecting a field (or finding out which fields are selected) uses a string version of the variable name.

Key Object

I keep mentioning that the three objects covered in this chapter are only related because you can use them together. If one of these objects is the most independent, it would have to be the Key object. (The main reason I've included it in this chapter is that—like both the Math object and the Selection object—you never need to instantiate it.) The Key object consists of just a few methods and several constants. Primarily the methods just allow you to ascertain whether a particular key is currently being pressed (whether it "is down") or, in the case of Caps Lock or Num Lock, whether a key "is toggled." The constants (simply properties that never change) are all associated with particular keys. That is, to check whether a key is pressed, you need to specify which key. Each key is a constant (such as Shift, Left Arrow, Delete, and so on).

Using the Key Object

To use the Key object, use the form `Key.isDown(`*`whichKey`*`)`, which returns either `TRUE` or `FALSE` where "whichKey" is either the Key object constant for that key, or the "virtual key code" for that key. Virtual key codes are almost identical to ASCII. However, because ASCII applies only to numbers and characters that appear in strings, virtual key codes are extended to include other keys such as Shift and Ctrl. What's really funky is that the virtual key code for an alphanumeric key happens to be the same as that key's uppercase ASCII. ASCII distinguishes between uppercase and lowercase, but includes only letters and numbers. Virtual key codes include all keys, but don't recognize any difference between uppercase or lowercase. The ASCII for "A" is 65 (same with the virtual key code for the A key). However, the ASCII for "a" is 97, but 97 happens to be the virtual key code for the "1" on a keyboard's number pad. The virtual key codes can all be found in Flash's ActionScript Reference Guide. For a practical example of the `isDown()` method, consider that the virtual key code for the Tab key happens to be `9`. Both of the two following expressions will return `TRUE` if the Tab key happens to be pressed:

```
Key.isDown(9);
Key.isDown(Key.TAB);
```

Notice that the form for a Key object constant is `Key.`*`THEKEY`* (where "THEKEY" is TAB, SHIFT, ENTER, and so on). A full list of the Key objects is shown in Figure 9.7 and you'll notice the constants are all uppercase. The key constants (as opposed to virtual key codes) simply make your code a little bit more readable. However, only a handful of key constants are available (the ones you'll probably use most commonly).

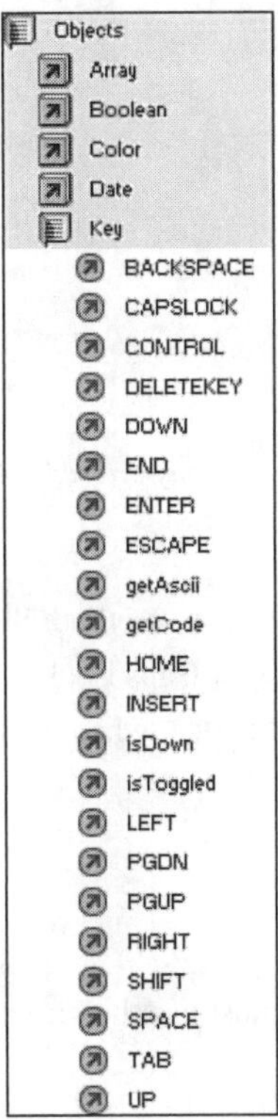

Figure 9.7 *All the Key object features (notice that most are just constants—the all-uppercase items).*

An important detail when using a Key object to check whether a key is down is to think about *when* you're checking. One logical place to check is within a `keyDown` clip event (see Figure 9.8). That is, when the user presses a key, you can check whether one key or the other is being pressed. You could also use the `isDown()` method within an `enterFrame` clip event (where you'd keep checking at all times). This will become more apparent when we try out some practical examples, but realize the method returns `TRUE` or `FALSE` based on the status of the user's keyboard at the time the script is executed.

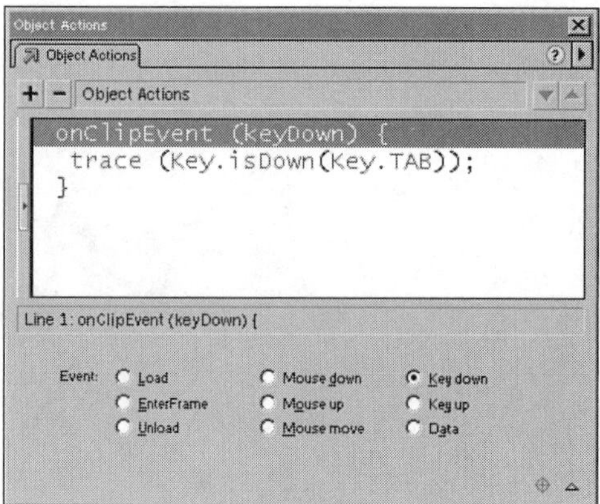

Figure 9.8 *A script that checks whether a particular key is currently pressed is logically placed within a* `KeyDown` *clip event.*

The other primary feature of the Key object is the `isToggled()` method. Similar to `isDown()`, this method tells you whether the Num Lock or Caps Lock is currently engaged. For example, both these expressions return `TRUE` when the Caps Lock is on:

```
Key.isToggled(20);
Key.isToggled(Key.CAPSLOCK);
```

Because there's no constant for the Num Lock key, you must use the virtual key code (`144`) to determine whether the Num Lock is on:

```
Key.isToggled(144);
```

By the way, if you don't feel like looking up the virtual key code for a special key that you'd like to trap, you can figure out what a particular key's code is by using the `getCode()` method. This method will return the virtual key code of the last key pressed. For example, the following script (attached to a clip instance) will display onscreen the virtual key code for any key pressed:

```
onClipEvent (keyUp) {
  trace (Key.getCode());
}
```

How do you think I determined that the Caps Lock key was `144`? I simply used this script, pressed the Caps Lock key, and saw a `144` display in the output window.

By the way, there's a similar method that lets you learn what the ASCII value for the last key pressed: `Key.getAscii()`.

Key Object Examples

Let's look at a simple example first and then move on to something more advanced. Let's say you want to let the user move a movie clip around the stage by pressing the arrow keys on his keyboard. The up arrow key moves the clip up, the down arrow key moves it down, and so forth. The following code can be placed on the clip instance:

```
onClipEvent (keyDown) {
var howMuch=2
  if(Key.isDown(Key.DOWN)){
    _y+=howMuch;
  }
  if(Key.isDown(Key.UP)){
    _y-=howMuch;
  }
  if(Key.isDown(Key.RIGHT)){
    _x+=howMuch;
  }
  if(Key.isDown(Key.LEFT)){
    _x-=howMuch;
  }
  updateAfterEvent();
}
```

You'll notice I used a local variable, `howMuch`, so that if I wanted to change the amount the clip moves for each keypress, I could change it in one place. I threw in `updateAfterEvent()` at the end so that regardless of the movie's framerate, this script would update the onscreen contents every time a key was pressed. Also, because this clip event waits for a "keyDown," the speed of execution is directly related to the "repeat rate" of the user's keyboard settings. You could change the clip event to "enterFrame," in which case the script would check which keys were down as frequently as the framerate (that is, 12 fps would "enter frame" 12 times a second).

You may have noticed if you tried the sample code that you can hold two arrow keys at the same time (for instance, down and right) to make the clip move diagonally. Let's add a feature that makes the clip move twice as fast when both the Shift key is pressed and an arrow key is pressed. Replace the line `var howMuch=2` with the following code:

```
var howMuch;
if (Key.isDown(Key.SHIFT)){
  howMuch=4;
}else{
  howMuch=2;
}
```

Notice that in this case I chose to simply establish `howMuch` as a local variable in the first line (without assigning it), and then I assign it a value of `4` or `2` based on whether the Shift key is selected.

That was a pretty easy exercise. A challenging exercise you can try—which would involve some major adjustments to this script—involves using the left or right arrows to rotate the clip and then using up and down arrows to make the clip move forward or back. When the clip is rotated 180 degrees, make it move down; when it's rotated 0 degrees, make it move up. The solution lies in considering that every time you move the clip, you really move it some x and some y. It just happens that (based on the rotation) sometimes the x is 0 or negative. All you need are the trigonometry methods of the Math object.

Here's the code:

```
onClipEvent (keyDown) {
var howMuchRotation=5;
  if(Key.isDown(Key.RIGHT)){
    _rotation+=howMuchRotation;
  }
  if(Key.isDown(Key.LEFT)){
    _rotation-=howMuchRotation;
  }
var howMuch=10;
var xChange=howMuch*Math.cos ((Math.PI/180)*_rotation);
var yChange=howMuch*Math.sin ((Math.PI/180)*_rotation);
  if (Key.isDown(Key.UP)){
    _x+=xChange;
    _y+=yChange;
  }
```

```
  if (Key.isDown(Key.DOWN)){
    _x-=xChange;
    _y-=yChange;
  }
updateAfterEvent();
}
```

Most of this is fairly straightforward, except the two lines in which I assign the value for `xChange` and `yChange` (the variables used to change the `_x` and `_y` positions of the clip). Basically, both `Math.sin()` and `Math.cos()` return a number between `-1` and `1`. The cosine of `0` degrees is `1` and `180` degrees is `-1`. Any midpoint is a fraction thereof. The cosine of `90` degrees (halfway between `0` and `180`) happens to equal `0`. The movie clip has a shape that looks like it's pointing to the right (as shown in Figure 9.9). If it's rotated `180` degrees (pointing left), I want the change in `_x` position (when moving "forward") to be `-1*5` (`5` being "how much"—that is, the full amount in the negative direction). If the rotation stays at `0` degrees, I want the change in `_x` to be `1*5` (so that it moves to the right). When it's `90` degrees, I don't want to change the `_x` at all, so `0*5` gives me zero. I can easily determine the factor to multiply `howMuch` by (between `1` and `-1`) just by calculating the cosine of the current rotation. If the rotation is less then `180` degrees, cosine will return a fraction of 1, which causes `howMuch` to be multiplied by a smaller number (meaning, the change in `_x` is proportionally less). The only hairy part is that you have to translate `_rotation` from its value in degrees to the equivalent value in radians (because Flash's Math object uses radians). As you recall from Chapter 5, you can translate degrees into radians by multiplying by `(Math.PI/180)`. The change in `_y` is calculated the same way but with sine. If the user presses the down arrow, I reduce the values for `_x` and `_y` instead of adding to them as is the case with the up arrow. Hopefully, this explanation gives you an idea of what went into the solution even if you can't immediately understand the code. Realize that you're coming in after the code is written, and in reality, you'll need to write the code from the ground up—so try to first just get the gist.

Here's one last example that's—admittedly—a bit hard-wired. I want to have three Input Text fields that tab from one to the next (and then back to the first). I'll need to use both the Key object to trap when the user presses Tab and the Selection object to force focus on the appropriate field. Notice I have four Input Text fields in my layout (see Figure 9.10).

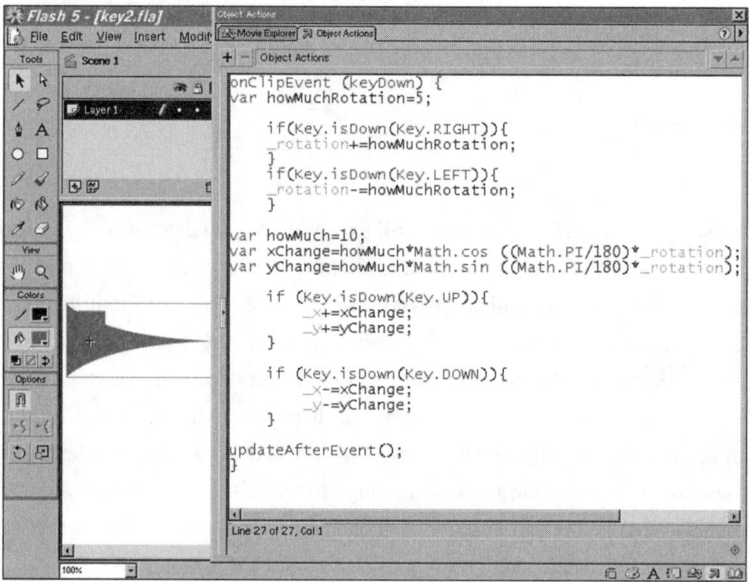

Figure 9.9 *When not rotated (0 degrees), the clip looks like it's pointing to the right.*

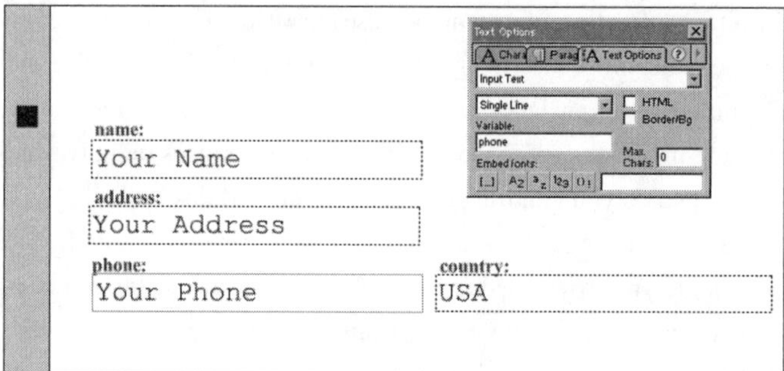

Figure 9.10 *Tabbing through these four Input Text fields will be controlled using the Key object.*

Each field has a variable (`name`, `address`, `phone`, and `country`, respectively). For better or worse, Flash will automatically tab through all Input Text fields in a logical order (from the top down, from the left to the right). This might be suitable most of the time, but this exercise overrides that behavior because (for this example) I never want the user to tab into the `country` field—the user can type into that field if he clicks there first, but he cannot tab in. To access the clip event

"KeyDown," you need a clip. So, the entire code for this exercise is attached to a dummy clip instance, used for no other reason than to have access to the "KeyDown" clip event: the black box off stage in Figure 9.10. Here's the code:

```
onClipEvent (keyDown) {
  if (Key.isDown(Key.TAB)){
    var curField=Selection.getFocus();
    curField=curField.substr(curField.lastIndexOf(".")+1)
    if (curField=="name"){
      Selection.setFocus("_root.address");
    } else if (curField=="address"){
      Selection.setFocus("_root.phone");
    } else {
      Selection.setFocus("_root.name");
    }
  }
}
```

The way this works is that first I use the Selection object's `getFocus()` to find out the current field's variable. Then, I use the String object's `substr()` in conjunction with `lastIndexOf()` to remove the path to the variable that is returned when using `getFocus()`. Finally, my "if-else-if" statement determines what field is next and uses `setFocus()` to force the focus to the correct field. Notice that I used a catch-all "else" (not "else-if") at the end because I want the user to be able to tab *out of* the `country` field if that's the current field (the user just can't tab into `country`). Actually, the plain "else" at the end means that if the focus is not in one of the other two fields (`name` or `address`), `name` always gets the focus. I could have 100 other fields and they'd all tab directly to `name` because "else" is a catch-all.

I'll be the first to admit that this solution is very hard-wired. After you learn about arrays in the next chapter, you could store all the field names in an array (in an order that matches the tab order you want), and easily find out what the logical "next" field is any time the user presses the Tab key. Just imagine how ugly the "if-else-if" statement would become if you had a couple dozen Input Text fields. So, even though I'm slightly ashamed of this solution, I'm proud of the fact it was a great way to exercise almost all the concepts covered in this chapter (so, don't discount this exercise because of a single flaw).

Summary

Wow, I think this chapter might be the most fun so far because not only did we explore new concepts, but they were easy to apply using our existing base knowledge. You got to see three unique Flash Objects: String, Selection, and Key. The main similarity of these objects is that they don't need to be instantiated the way other objects do. Actually, you could instantiate the String object, but you'll probably never want to. These are "no fuss" objects.

Using any string value as the object gives you access to some very fancy methods. Extracting substrings and changing case are just a couple things you can do to strings. The Selection object was all about finding or setting focus and finding or setting the portion of a selectable field that was currently selected. Finally, the Key object lets you find out which key (or keys) were pressed at any given time. Just for icing on the cake, you got to play with the dynamic formatting possibilities of HTML text.

If this isn't fun, I don't know what is!

{ Chapter 10 }

Arrays

Arrays are perhaps the single most exciting feature introduced with Flash 5. In the past, each variable could contain a string or a number—but just *one* string or *one* number. Arrays let you store as many individual values as you want, and they can be any data type. In addition to storing lots of information in one place (an array variable), you can quickly access any individual item to see or change its value. Plus the Array object has a host of methods that let you perform fancy operations on the contents of an array. For example, you can—almost instantaneously—sort the contents alphabetically if you want.

Although arrays are not the most advanced feature of ActionScript, they are perhaps the most valuable because they're so easy to use. If storing values in variables is convenient, storing lots of values in one array is invaluable. In addition to the useful operations you can do with arrays, you'll find that the syntax you learn (as with so much other syntax) is easily applicable to other parts of ActionScript.

In this chapter, you will

- Learn how arrays work and their benefits
- Build arrays using several techniques
- Access individual items in arrays (to ascertain or change their values)
- Explore all the methods for the Array object
- Learn how to create and use associative arrays

Unlike many topics covered in this book. we'll actually go through practically every detail of using arrays in ActionScript. For example, there are many topics I've left out of this book because they are either unlikely to ever serve you or they can be picked up easily based on the foundation knowledge you're acquiring. In the case of arrays, it's quite possible you'll use every conceivable aspect. For that reason, this chapter is quite detailed.

Array Overview

Arrays are simply another data type. Variables can contain strings, numbers, or other data types including arrays. Just as you can do "string" types of things to variables containing strings and "number" types of things to variables containing numbers, when your variable's value is an array, there is a unique set of "array" operations that you can execute. Strings and numbers are very familiar. Let's take an overview of the way arrays work.

The idea with arrays is that any one variable may contain multiple values—each in a unique address within the variable. Compare a plain variable containing a number or string to a studio apartment or single-person home. Assuming that only one person lives in any given apartment at a time, it's like a variable containing a string. You can replace the value in the variable or replace the person living in the apartment—but only one is in the variable or apartment at a time. If a regular variable is a single apartment, an array is like an apartment building. There might be 50 individual apartments in an entire building. Similarly, an array can have 50 individual locations for data (called *indexes*). Replacing the value in any one index is like replacing the resident in any one apartment.

Figure 10.1 *If a variable is like a house (that holds one person), an array is like an apartment building that holds many individuals.*

To continue with the apartment building analogy, it's possible to put different types of people in the different apartments. One apartment could even be used to store cleaning supplies. The storage concept is similar with an array. You could store a string in the first "index" of an array. In the second index, you could store a number. What's really wild is that you can store any kind of data type in the individual indexes of an array including arrays! That is, in the third index, you might have an array of 10 separate numbers. Compare this to one apartment being converted to bunk beds where four separate people could sleep.

Figure 10.2 *Each apartment (or index of an array) can contain several people (just as one index of an array can contain another array).*

Unlike apartment buildings, you can structure arrays without regard to physical limits. Your master array, for example, could be made up of 10 arrays, each containing 3 items. Each of the 10 arrays could contain students' personal information—maybe first name, last name, and age. If you decide to add a forth piece of information for each student, your 10 arrays will simply contain four items each. Consider the data in the table shown in Figure 10.3. All this data can be stored in one array variable. You could store an array of information in that fourth index—perhaps all the individual scores that each student has received on tests taken. Even if you don't have the same number of scores for each student, an array is perfectly suitable.

Arrays full of arrays (or "nested arrays") might seem complicated, but they actually help keep things organized in a couple ways. First of all, you may structure the data however you choose. You could have an array with 10 subarrays that each contain four items as in the 10 rows of four columns in Figure 10.3. Or, if you choose, you could have an array containing four items, which each contain

10 items each, as Figure 10.4 illustrates with its four rows of 10 columns. In this way, you structure data in a way that makes the most sense based on the nature of the data.

First name	Last name	age	score
Phillip	Kerman	35	100
Joe	Smith	28	89
Sally	Smith	30	91
Sam	Jones	19	74
Sandy	Miller	29	99
Bart	Brown	12	60
Andy	Anderson	29	80
Cindy	Corrigan	25	93
Damion	Dinkens	29	82
Mary	Miller	32	98

Figure 10.3 *All 10 rows of four columns each can be stored in one array variable.*

Phillip	Joe	Sally	Sam	Sandy	Bart	Andy	Cindy	Damion	Mary
Kerman	Smith	Smith	Jones	Miller	Brown	Anderson	Corrigan	Dinkens	Miller
35	28	30	19	29	12	29	25	29	32
100	89	91	74	99	60	80	93	82	98

Figure 10.4 *You can structure data in any format you want.*

Another way arrays (and nested arrays) keep things organized is by reducing the need for superfluous variables. Consider the relatively simple idea of 10 students each with four bits of information. To store all that information without arrays, you'd need 40 separate variables. Maybe something like this:

```
firstName_student1="Phillip";
lastName_student1="Kerman";
age_student1=35;
score_student1=100;
firstName_student2="Joe";
lastName_student2="Smith";
age_student2=28;
score_student2=89;
//and so on
```

Not only do you need to develop a workable naming convention, but you have to keep track of it. That is, you can't try to use the variable `student1_firstName` because the earlier convention was `firstName_student1`. With 40 separate variable names, there's a lot to track and many places to have problems. Arrays eliminate such issues entirely.

Array Creation and Manipulation

When you can see the benefits of arrays and you decide how to structure the data, you need to learn how to populate the array with the various values. After an array is created you'll need to learn how to manipulate its contents. Not only can you search and sort an array, but you also can add more items. Such array creation and manipulation are covered in detail in this section.

Creating and Populating Arrays

There are several ways to create a variable that contains an array. You can simply initialize a new variable as an array without contents, and populate the array later. Similarly, you can initialize an array of a specific dimension (that is, with a certain number of items). Finally, when you assign a variable's value to data that's in the form of an array, you can create and populate an array in one move. We'll look at all three ways to create arrays as well as how to add to an array already in existence.

The most basic form to make a variable become an array is

```
myArray=new Array();
```

This simply assigns the custom variable `myArray` the value of an empty array. The only thing this accomplishes is to prepare `myArray` so that you can start populating it. Although it's not the same thing, I think of this method as similar to the statement `var myLocalVariable`. All that statement does is say, "I'm about to start using this variable myLocalVariable and it's going to be local." It only makes sense to use the `new Array()` technique when you know you're going to need an array, but you don't know any of its contents yet. This just gets you set up with an array that you can mess with later.

Another—and, in my opinion, counterintuitive—way to initialize an array is the form

```
myArray=new Array(totalItems);
```

For example, `dozenThings=new Array(12)`. The parameter passed in parentheses establishes how many items are in this array. The twelve items in `dozenThings` (earlier) are null. The reason that I find this technique counterintuitive is that (as you'll see in a second) when you include multiple parameters in the parentheses it behaves as if you were creating and populating it in one step.

To create a new array *and* populate it with two or more items, use

```
stackedArray=new Array("first item", "second item", "third");
```

You can include as many initial values in the array as you want, but you must have more than one because a single item would indicate that you want to specify how many items an empty array should have (as above). For example, this could have unexpected results: `unluckyNum=new Array(13)` (because it will simply create a new array with `13` empty items).

Finally, the most direct (and probably the most intuitive) way to put an array into a variable is in the literal form

```
myArray=["item1","item2","item3"];
```

The brackets say to Flash, "These items are in the form of an array." You could also initialize an empty array as `myArray=[]`. This literal technique is the way that I usually create arrays (and it's the way I'll do it throughout the rest of this book).

Before we move on to accessing information stored in an array, let's talk about the data types you can put into the various indexes of an array. So far, I've been placing strings and numbers (strings being shown between quotation marks). Naturally, you can use variable names instead, and the current value for those variables will be in their place. For instance, `names=[firstname,lastname]` places the value for the variables `firstname` and `lastname` into the two indexes of the array `names`. You can also put references to clip instances, as in `myClips=[box,circle,_root.otherClip]`. If `box` and `circle` are clip instance names (in the current timeline) and a clip called `otherClip` exists in the main timeline, you've just stored references not to the string versions of clip names, but to the clips themselves. When you learn in the next section how to access one index at a time, you'll be able to refer to those clips and perform any operation that you can do when referencing clips directly.

In addition to strings, numbers, and instance references, you can store arrays. In this way, you can make an array full of arrays! Consider the following code sequence:

```
washingtonPolitics=["Governor Hansen", "Secretary White", "Attorney
➥Meier"];
oregonPolitics=["Governor Jones", "Secretary Stevens", "Attorney
➥Philips"];
californiaPolitics=["Governor Black", "Secretary Jackson", "Attorney
➥Smith"];
westCoast=[washingtonPolitics,oregonPolitics,californiaPolitics];
```

In the last line, the variable `westCoast` is assigned the value of an array with three items. It just so happens that the data type for each of these three items is array. As you're about to learn, you can quickly refer to the Governor of California by saying you want the first item in the third index of the `westCoast` array. (In reality, because arrays are zero-based, you start counting with zero, so you'd have to retrieve the zero item in the second index.) With this first example of an array full of arrays, I feel compelled to remind you that because arrays are reference variables (not primitive) they're copied by reference. Therefore, in this example, even after the variable `westCoast` is assigned, if you ever change any of the three "politics" arrays, you'll also be changing the contents of the respective index in `westCoast`. (If necessary, you can review the differences between primitive and reference variables in Chapter 4, "Basic Programming in Flash.")

Accessing Array Contents

As you just saw, populating arrays is pretty easy. Accessing the contents of previously created arrays is even easier. To access a particular array's contents, you need to be familiar with how that array is structured. For example, Figure 10.5 shows (on top) how our previous west coast politician example was structured: three arrays, one for each state. Just as easily, we could have had three arrays, but one for each job title instead. It doesn't really matter how we structure it, but when accessing individual items it's important to first know the structure.

[["Governor Hansen", "Secretary White", "Attorney Meier"],
["Governor Jones", "Secretary Stevens", "Attorney Philips"],
["Governor Black", "Secretary Jackson", "Attorney Smith"]]

[["Governor Hansen", "Governor Jones", "Governor Black"],
["Secretary White", "Secretary Stevens", "Secretary Jackson"],
["Attorney Meier", "Attorney Philips", "Attorney Smith"]]

Figure 10.5 *The same data can be structured however you want. The example on top is no better or worse than the one on the bottom.*

Now that you are familiar with the array's structure you'll find accessing items in the array (to see their values or change them) is very easy. We'll look at how to access individual indexes directly, and then look at how to use loops to step through all the indexes of an array.

Direct Access

Array items are accessed using what's called *bracket access*. The following expression will return the item in the first (the zero) index:

```
myArray[0];
```

Therefore, if `myArray` is first assigned the values using `myArray=["apples","oranges","bananas"]`, the expression `myArray[0]` returns `"apples"`. Simple, isn't it? The only thing to mess you up is the fact you must start counting with zero. I probably don't need to remind you (but I will) this bracket access simply produces an expression that returns the value in that index—but there's no assignment or change to the array. You could copy the second thing in `myArray` into another variable as so:

```
secondFruit=myArray[1];
```

`secondFruit` will be assigned the value `"oranges"`, but nothing changes in `myArray`.

To access the contents of an index in an array that's inside another array, the form is extended to

```
mainArray[indexOfSubArray][indexInSubArray];
```

Consider this example:

```
bookDataOne=["Teach Yourself", 587, 24.99];//title, page count, price
bookDataTwo=["ActionScripting", 500, 39.99];
allBooks=[bookDataOne,bookDataTwo];
```

After you understand the structure used (title, page count, price) to access the price for the first book, you can use `allBooks[0][2]`, or for the price of the second book, use `allBooks[1][2]`. To access the title of the first book, use `allBooks[0][0]`. If this way of referencing items in arrays inside arrays is confusing, consider looking at it in pieces. For example, to access the entire array for book 2, you'd simply use `allBooks[1]`. To access just the price from the simple array `bookDataTwo`, you'd use `bookDataTwo[2]`. But what is `allBooks[1]`, anyway? It's the same thing as `bookDataTwo`. Because `allBooks[1]` and bookDataTwo are interchangeable, you can say allBooks[1][2], and it's the same as saying bookDataTwo[2]. Because such nested bracket references use left-to-right associativity, allBooks[1][2] first performs the first part (allBooks[1]) and that turns into the array that then has its second index referenced.

What's cool about bracket reference is that you can use it for more than just accessing the contents of arrays. You can also refer to items and change them through assignments. For example, allBooks[1][1]=525 assigns the value of 525 to the second item in the second array, so that 500 changes to 525.

There's not much more to say about accessing the contents of arrays. Perhaps a few examples will solidify these points. Using the original data in allBooks, consider the following maneuvers.

This expression returns a number that is 10% less than the price for the first book:

```
allBooks[0][2]*.9;
```

If you want an expression that rounds off to the nearest cent (that is, the one-hundredth decimal), use

```
Math.round(100* allBooks[0][2]*.9)/100;
```

Notice that I multiply by 100, round off, and then divide by 100. The only flaw in this solution is that there are no trailing zeros; for 24.50, you'll get 24.5. To pad with trailing zeros, you'll have to convert to a string (and possibly use the String object's lastIndexOf() method and length property). These tricks are covered in the "Currency Exchange Calculator" workshop.

This statement takes 10% off the price of the first book and changes it in the array:

```
allBooks[0][2]= Math.round(100* allBooks[0][2]*.9)/100;
```

Loops

Even though accessing individual items in arrays is quite common, you'll also have the need to access each item in sequence. You already saw how to create an empty array or populate one. Later in this chapter, you'll learn all the methods available to add to, or otherwise change, arrays. If you populate your array by hand, going through each item is not much of a challenge because you'll know how many items are present. However, you might often add to arrays and never know precisely what items are present. In such cases, it's easiest to use a loop to go through each item. Even when you know how many items are in your array, a loop is often more efficient than writing a separate line of code to access each item individually.

Say you have an array called `vowels` that is initialized like this:

```
vowels=["A", "E", "I", "O", "U"];
```

A hard-wired (not ideal) loop could look like this:

```
for(i=0;i<5;i++){
  trace ("One vowel is " + vowels[i]);
}
```

Notice that using `vowels[i]` will extract items `0` through `4` from the `vowels` array as `i` varies from `0` through `4`. This example is hard-wired because the `5` means that the loop will always repeat five times (even if more items are added to the array later). You can improve upon this loop by using the for-in loop instead. A for-in loop will automatically step through all the items in an array.

```
for (i in vowels){
  trace ("One vowel is " + vowels[i]);
}
```

This alternative is easier because you don't have to include the three elements in a regular for-loop—namely, "init" (or `i=0`), "condition" (`i<5`), and "next" (`i++`). (These were all covered when we first looked at the for-loop in Chapter 5, "Programming Structures.") The for-in loop has a couple of funky attributes. First, nowhere do you specify that the iterant (`i` in these cases) will increment. In fact, the iterant actually decrements. It automatically begins at the highest index value (`4`, in the case of the `vowels` array) and then decrements through all the items in the array to zero. Often the fact that a for-in loop goes through the array in reverse order is not an issue. Just realize it works this way. Finally, to be fair, the initial for-loop I showed could be less hard-wired if, in place of `5`, you used an expression that resulted in the number of items in the array. You'll see later in this chapter that the `length` property (which you learned with the string object) can be used in exactly this way; `vowels.length` results in `5`.

Here's a quick example of a function that goes through the string passed as a parameter and replaces all vowels with an uppercase version of that character. So, `changeVowels("Phillip Kerman")` turns into `"PhIllIP KErmAn"` (notice that `"P"` and `"K"` were already uppercase).

```
function changeVowels(aString){
  var vowels=["A", "E", "I", "O", "U"];
  for (var spot=0; spot<aString.length; spot++){
    var aLetter=aString.charAt(spot).toUpperCase();
    var vowelFound=0;

    for (var i in vowels){
      if (aLetter==vowels[i]){
        vowelFound=1;
        break;
      }
    }
    if (vowelFound){
      aString=
      ➥aString.substr(0,spot) + aLetter + aString.substring(spot+1);
    }
  }
  return aString;
}
```

This example is worth walking through despite having arguably no practical use (I mean, how many times will you need to capitalize all the vowels in a string?). Anyway, after the array of vowels is created in line 2, a for-loop in line 3 goes through all the characters in the provided string (`aString`), one `spot` at a time. For every iteration of the main for-loop, the "charAt" the current spot is converted to uppercase and placed in the variable `aLetter`. Then the variable `vowelFound` is set to `0` (assuming at the start that the `aLetter` is not a vowel—but, of course, if it is, we'll find out shortly). While this one letter (`aLetter`) is being analyzed, we start another loop. This time, we use a for-in loop to go through all the items in the array of vowels (`vowels`). For every item in `vowels`, we check whether `aLetter==vowels[i]` (where `i` iterates from `4` down to `0`). Who cares that it's going backward because as soon as we find a match, we set `vowelFound` to `1` and break out of the current loop (the one looping through all the items in the `vowels` array). So, every time, the loop either finishes naturally and leaves `vowelFound` set to `0`, or finishes early and `vowelFound` is set to `1`. In any case, the next if statement performs a string replacement (of the letter in the current spot) if `vowelFound` is `1`. Notice that I don't bother extracting the letter in the current spot and changing it to uppercase, because I already did that when I first assigned `aLetter`'s value. Also notice that even letters that turned out not to be vowels were converted to uppercase because when comparing them to each item in `vowels`, they needed to be uppercase to match (as the `vowels` array contained all uppercase).

As an overview, this function steps through each character in the given string, compares this character to each item in an array of `vowels`, and when a match is found, makes a replacement to the given string. You'll have many more opportunities to write loops that work on strings (including the one that turns a number into a dollar value in the Currency Exchange Calculator workshop) and loops that work on arrays (when you need to loop through every clip onstage to see which one the mouse is covering in the Odd-Shaped Clickable Areas workshop).

Array Object Methods

Populating arrays and accessing their contents is quite convenient because you can store many different items in one variable. In addition, arrays are convenient because after they're created, ActionScript offers a host of methods that can perform very interesting modifications on that array (as shown in Figure 10.6). Besides the one property (`length`), almost all the Array object methods will actually modify the array itself. That is, `myArray.someMethod()` won't return a value—rather, it will *change* the contents of the array. Of course, `"someMethod()"` doesn't exist, but the types of methods available can be broken down into three general types: string-related, which convert arrays into strings or vice versa; populating, which add to or subtract from arrays; and finally sorting, which reorder the contents of your array. We'll look at the methods and related topics in that order.

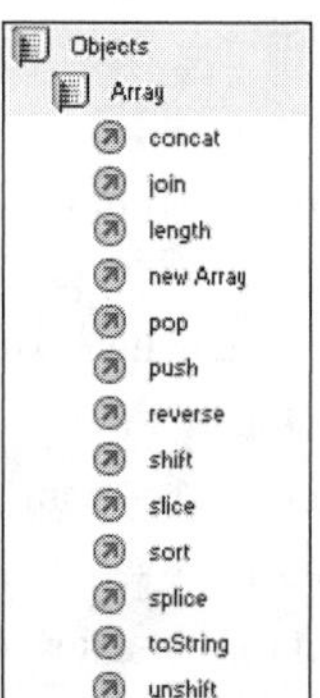

Figure 10.6 *All the methods for the Array object are listed in the Actions panel.*

String Related (`length`, `toString()`, `split()`, `concat()`, `join()`)

You won't find a listing of string-related array methods anywhere in the Flash help files. The topics you're about to learn are grouped together because I think they are either similar to String object methods or they involve converting strings to or extracting strings from arrays.

The only property available for arrays happens to be the same as the only property available for strings—namely, `length`. Although this might appear confusing, it's actually quite useful. If the object for which you're trying to get the length happens to be a string, you'll get a count of the number of characters. When the object is an array, you'll get the count of items in the array. Consider assigning a string to a variable as `myString="hot"` and assigning an array to a variable `myArray=["waffles", "pancakes", "cereal"]`. The following two expressions return 3:

```
myString.length;
myArray.length;
```

There's not much more to it, except to remember two points for both arrays and strings. First, `length` is a property (not a method) and, as such, doesn't include the parentheses that always follow methods. Second, because both arrays and strings are zero-based, the last character in a string with a "length" of 3 (or the last item in an array with a "length" of 3) is character (or item) 2.

The method called `toString()`—when attached to an array—will return a string version of the array. For instance, if a variable contains an array, such as `myArray=[1,2,3,4]`, the expression `myArray.toString()` will return the string `"1,2,3,4"`. One thing you can do with this method is quickly take an entire array and get a string that can be placed into a Dynamic Text field. Naturally, you could (with little more work) loop through the entire array and convert each item to a string. Perhaps you want to separate each item (being extracted from the array) with returns so that it appears in a Dynamic Text field like a column of data. As always, you can solve one task several different ways. You could either use a loop and concatenate each item with `"\r"` (for return) or write a function that replaces each comma with `"\r"`. The `toString()` method just gives you a quick and easy way to make a string. (By the way, objects introduced in Chapter 11, "Objects," can also use the `toString()` method.)

The `split()` method is actually a method of the String object. The reason I waited until now to introduce it is because this method takes a string (as its object) and returns an array. That is, if you take a string such as `myString="Phillip,David,Kerman"` and use this method (as in `newArray=myString.split()`), the result is that `newArray` is assigned the array value `["Phillip","David","Kerman"]`. The `split()` method uses commas (as a default) to separate the items in the string that is being operated on. If you want the `split()` method to use a different character as a delimiter instead of the comma, just supply the character as the parameter when using `split(`*`delimiter`*`)`. That is, if your string uses `"#"` for a delimiter (as in `myString="Phillip#David#Kerman"`), you can create the same array shown earlier by using `newArray=myString.split("#")`. This comes in handy when you have an external source of data that you want to use in an array.

In Chapter 14, "Interfacing with External Data," you'll learn how to load variables from server scripts, XML data sources, and text files. With the exception of XML data, external sources always provide data in the form of numbers or strings (not arrays). If you simply separate items with commas (or another delimiter), you can use `split()` to easily convert this loaded data into an array. Notice that I didn't say "quickly and easily" because the fact is `split()` tends to perform slowly. In fact, if you have a particularly long string that you're attempting to "split" into an array, it's possible that Flash will reach its 15-second timeout (mentioned in Chapter 5, when discussing infinite loops). It's probably faster to write your own loop that goes through a string and manually places items into an array—but it's more work.

The last two methods we'll explore in this section might seem identical, but they're actually quite different: `join()` and `concat()`. The `join()` method performs the opposite operation that `split()` does. That is, `join()` takes an array, converts each item to a string, separates each item with an optional separator (or comma), and finally returns the string. Actually, `join()` is almost the same as the `toString()` method except that with `join()`, you can optionally specify a different separator besides a comma. So, if a variable is assigned an array value, as in `myArray=[1,2,3,4]`, you perform the assignment `stringVersion=myArray.join("_")`. The result is that `stringVersion` will equal `"1_2_3_4"`. (When you use `join()` without a parameter, a comma will be used as the separator.) The `concat()` method will either concatenate additional items onto the end of an array or will concatenate two or more arrays (merging them into one). As a method, `concat()` is always attached to one array and takes (as parameters) the items you want to add to the array. If the parameters are individual values, they are added to the end of the array being operated on. For example:

```
odds=[1,3,5,7,9];
oddEven=odds.concat(2,4,6,8);
```

This creates an array `oddEven` with the value `[1,3,5,7,9,2,4,6,8]`. I suppose simply adding to the end of an array using `concat()` is convenient because you can use one line of code to add as many items listed as parameters.

The other way to use `concat()` is to concatenate one or more entire arrays to the end of another array. Consider this code:

```
vowels=["a","e","i","o","u"];
other=["y"];
odd=["q","z"]
all=vowels.concat(other,odd);
notOdd=vowels.concat(other);
```

First, notice that the first three variables contain arrays (even though `other` is an array with only one item). In the end, the variable `all` will equal `["a","e","i","o","u","y","q","z"]` and `notOdd` will equal `["a","e","i","o","u","y"]`. Notice also that when the parameters are arrays, the items in that array are added to the end of the array being operated on. Finally, you should notice too that the `concat()` method doesn't actually change the array, but rather returns a new array. I always find this method strange in that regardless of whether I want to add one item, several items, an array, or multiple arrays, I always must concatenate onto a base array. That is, you can't treat `concat()` like a function and say `concat(oneArray,otherArray)`. Because it's a method, you must say something more like `oneArray.concat(otherArray)`. (By the way, there's an identical `concat()` method that's used with strings.)

Populating in Order (`pop()`, `push()`, `shift()`, `unshift()`)

The rest of the methods we'll look at are different than all the others discussed so far this chapter. Both the populating methods (this section) and the sorting methods (next section) will actually change the array that they operate on. Methods earlier in this chapter will return values (either string or array data), but they don't actually change the array at hand.

The best way to understand these methods (`pop`, `push`, `shift`, and `unshift`) is to think of a spring-loaded tray dispenser that you might find in a cafeteria. With such dispensers, you can take a tray from the top of the stack and the next tray below rises to the surface for someone else to take. To replenish the dispenser, you can place one or more trays on top of the stack. Every time a tray is placed back on the stack, all the trays below are pushed down. Think of a starting array like a stack of trays (each item is a separate tray). Then the methods perform the following operations. Taking a tray from the top of the stack is equivalent to the `pop()` method because it will remove the last item in your array and return it (that item is returned and the array has that item removed). Placing trays on the top of the stack is the same as the `push()` method because it accepts one or more parameters that are placed at the end of the array. The `shift()` method is the same as `pop()` except that it removes the first item and returns it. Finally, `unshift()` is like `push()` except that it will add an item (or items) to the beginning of an array and push everything else to later indexes in the array. Check out Figure 10.7.

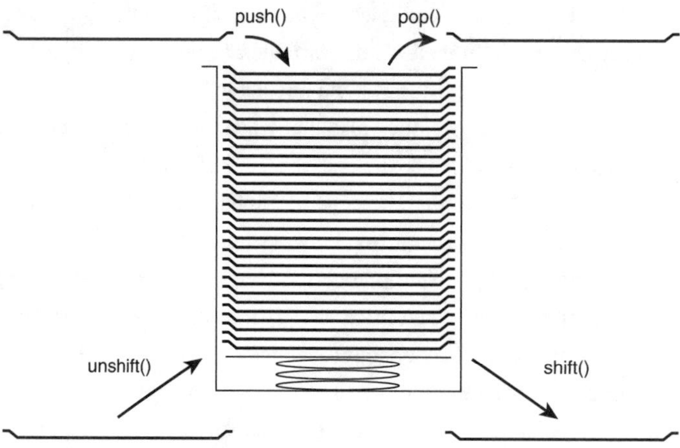

Figure 10.7 *To understand* `pop`, `push`, `shift`, *and* `unshift`, *you should think about a stack of trays.*

Although these four methods might seem useful only for a cafeteria simulation—they're actually quite useful. A great application to consider, and one that will help you understand how to *use* these methods, is a universal "back" button (like on a browser). Imagine that you give your users the ability to navigate to any section in your movie. For this example, let's say that each section is on a different frame number. In theory, this would be a simple case of pushing the frame number into an array any time a destination was navigated to, and popping the last value off the end of the array any time we wanted to go "back." Of course, it is slightly more involved, but here's what I came up with:

There is a button for each section to which the user can navigate as well as a "go back" button. Each navigation button invokes the custom function `go()` by providing the frame number to navigate to:

```
on (release) {
    go(5);
}
```

The "go back" button invokes another function:

```
on (release){
  goBack();
}
```

Then, I had the following code in the first frame of the movie:

```
history=new Array();

function go(where){
  history.push(where);
  gotoAndStop(where);
  stringVersion=history.join("\r");
}

function goBack(){
  if (history.length<2){
    return;
  }
  var discardCurrent=history.pop();
  go(history.pop());
}
```

Let me explain. First, the variable `history` was initialized as an empty array when this frame was reached (because the first line is not contained within a function, it executes when the frame is reached). We will be populating the `history` array via the `go` and `goBack` functions. Then, any time the `go` function is called, the destination frame (given the parameter name `where`) is pushed onto the end of the `history` array. The same parameter's value is used to navigate (using `gotoAndStop(where)`) to the desired section of `themovie`. Finally, a variable `stringVersion` is created that contains all the items in `history`, separated by returns. The `stringVersion` variable is used in a Dynamic Text field onscreen for testing.

The `goback` function (with no parameters) starts off with a couple of error checks. First, if the length of the history array is less than 2 (that is, it only has one item), the function is exited using `return`. If there's only one item in the array, the user is currently in that section and there's nowhere to go back to. Next, we strip off the last item in the array (which is the frame that the user is currently viewing) and place it in a local variable, `discardCurrent`. Actually, I could have simply used `history.pop()` with no assignment, but I want you to remember that the `pop()` method returns a value. Lastly, I call the regular `go` function and pass (as a parameter) the value of the last item in the array. Notice that by using `pop()` to grab the last item in `history`, I'm also removing it. If you don't remove the last item, it will be put in there twice because part of the `go` function's script involves pushing the item back onto the end of the `history` variable.

Sorting

You just saw how `pop()`, `push()`, `shift()`, and `unshift()` can add or remove items from an array. Even though the following methods don't change how many items are in an array, they most certainly change the array because they reorder it. There are only two sorting methods: `sort()` and `reverse()`. The simple one is `reverse()`, which simply reverses the order of the items in the array.

```
myArray=[1,2,3,4];
myArray.reverse();
```

After these two lines execute, the value of `myArray` is `[4,3,2,1]`. Generally, I think `reverse()` has limited value. First of all, you're the one who designs the structure of the array. You can always deal with an array no matter whether it's forward or reverse. For example, you can choose between `pop()` and `shift()` to delete items or between for-loops and for-in loops. If an array needs to be reversed, I just wonder who put it in the wrong order, but now you know how to swap the order in one swift move.

The `sort()` method is actually very powerful. Without any parameters provided, the `sort()` method will reorder your array in alphabetical order. It's pretty cool.

```
myFriends=["Dave","Graham","Chandler","Randy","Brad","Darrel"];
myFriends.sort();
```

After these two lines, myFriend's value becomes ["Brad","Chandler","Darrel","Dave","Graham","Randy"]. If sort() worked so easy in practice, this would be the end of the section. However, it's super funky in the way it sorts arrays. Specifically, it always sorts alphabetically even if your array contains numbers. For example:

```
someNums=[4,2,1,444,2222,11111];
someNums.sort();
```

This turns someNums into [1,11111,2222,2,444,4], which is not exactly numerical order.

Another counter intuitive fact about the sort() method is that it treats uppercase letters with greater importance than lowercase. Consider this example:

```
someWords=["Zimbabwe", "zebra", "cat", "apple", "Arizona"];
someWords.sort();
```

This turns someWords into ["Arizona","Zimbabwe","apple","cat","zebra"].

I'm sure that I don't need to provide more examples to make you want to learn how to make the sort() method perform the way you want. I thought it was confusing at first to really understand how to control the sort() method. The good news is that you can make the sort() method reorder your array by following elaborate rules. For example, in addition to sorting numerically, or without regard to uppercase and lowercase, you'll see how you can make up your own sorting rules such as sorting by length, or putting all the even numbers first and then the odds. You can make sort() follow any rule you can think of.

The way to write a customized sort is to provide a homemade function as a parameter. One way is to call another function from inside the parameter:

```
myArray.sort(customFunction);
```

Notice that normally, you always call functions by including opening and closing parentheses following the function name, but not when calling the function as a parameter of the sort() method. The job of customFunction is to set up the rule for comparison (when sorting). This comparison function is detailed in a moment.

Another way is to provide a literal function as a parameter. The way this works is you write your entire customFunction right inside the parentheses. You can even put it all on one line if you remember to use semicolons to separate "lines" of code. Ignore the code in the function and just check out the form that this literal technique follows:

```
myArray.sort(function(a,b){return a-b;});
```

Notice that the portion in parentheses (`function(a,b){return a-b;}`) is almost identical to any other function you can write. Besides being all crammed onto one line, there's no function name. Because this function is used in only one place and not called from other parts of the movie, you don't need to bother naming the function. Regardless of whether you call a function (like the first example) or you write the function literally right inside the parentheses, it works the same. The reason to consider the literal technique is that the comparison function is useful only for establishing the "sorting rule," and will likely never have any other value. Writing a function that gets called is not as efficient because Flash makes that function available for the entire movie. For the rest of this section, you'll see examples of calling separate functions only because I think it's easier to read than having the function squeezed into the parentheses.

This function that I'm calling a "comparison function" serves to establish the rules that the sort method uses to decide how to reorder items in the array. The function always accepts two parameters (by convention, called `a` and `b`). You can pretend that these two parameters represent two items in the array that are being compared. Imagine that you want to sort numerically. What if `a` is `10` and `b` is `12`? Naturally, you want `12` to come after `10` (that is, `b` after `a`). What if `a` is `2` and `b` is `10`? In that case, you'll want `a` to come first. The comparison function that gets called from the `sort()` method has one job—to return a positive number, 0, or a negative number. The idea is that based on how you want the sort to order things, your comparison function returns a positive number when `a` should come after `b`, negative number when `a` should go before `b`, or zero when you don't care (and Flash) will just leave the two items in their original order.

Let's just look at the finished version of a comparison function that correctly sorts an array numerically (and then we can try some "what if" numbers):

```
myArray.sort(numerical);
function numerical(a,b){
  if(a>b){
    return 1; //a should come after b
  }
  if (a<b){
    return -1;//a should come before b
  }
  return 0; //if they get this far, just return 0
}
```

So, just looking at the comparison function called `numerical`, imagine `a` is `10` and `b` is `5`. The function returns `1`, which means `a` should come after `b`. So far, so good. If `a` is `12` and `b` is `14`, `-1` is returned, meaning that `a` should come first. It works!

In fact, although my example function is easy to read, it's unnecessarily wordy. Here's a more concise version that (when you try any "what if" numbers) works the same:

```
function numerical(a,b){
  return a-b;
}
```

If `a` is `10` and `b` is `5`, this function returns `-5` (which—by being negative—means that `a` should go second). As you can see, when you get fancy like this, writing this whole comparison function right inside the `sort()` method's parentheses is more manageable. `myArray.sort(numerical)` isn't quite as streamlined as `myArray.sort(function(a,b){return a-b;})`, especially when you consider the first way requires you have that `numerical` function as well.

I hope this exhaustive explanation is clear. There are only so many common sorting requirements (alphabetical, numerical, alphabetical without regard to case, and so on) and I've provided those later in this chapter. After you have these, you'll probably never need to *really* understand how `sort()` works. But when you want to do some unique sorting, you'll need to write your own comparison function. For example, you might have a requirement that items in an array are sorted by value but they could be saved in U.S. dollars, Canadian dollars, euros, and yen. It's totally possible—albeit complicated—to write a comparison function that translates all the values into one currency before making the comparison. Check out the "alphabetical without regard to case" example for a *taste* of how this could work. The point is that you can do it when you know how `sort()` works.

Here are a few examples of common sorting needs. You can use any of these in the form `myArray.sort(`*`functionName`*`)` where "functionName" is the appropriate comparison function. To try to really grasp the following examples, try some "what if" values for `a` and `b` and see whether you can determine whether the function returns a positive number, negative number, or zero.

Alphabetical without regard to case:

```
function caseInsensitive(a,b){
  return a.toUpperCase() > b.toUpperCase();
}
```

Reverse numerical:

```
function reverseNumerical(a,b){
  return b-a;
}
```

By length (shortest strings first):

```
function byLength(a,b){
  return a.length-b.length;
}
```

Finally, for a slightly odd one…this function (when used with the `sort()` method) puts the array in numerical order but with all the odd numbers first:

```
function oddFirst(a,b){
  aOdd=a%2; //set aOdd to 1 if a is odd
  bOdd=b%2; //set bOdd to 1 of b is odd
  if (aOdd==0 & bOdd==0){
    return a-b;
  }
  if (aOdd<>0 & bOdd<>0){
    return a-b;
  }
  if (aOdd<>0 & bOdd==0){
    return -1;
  }
  if (aOdd==0 & bOdd<>0){
    return 1;
  }
  return 0;//just in case
}
```

This final example shows that you really can write a comparison function for unique sorting needs.

Associative Arrays

To appreciate associative arrays, you must fully understand the value of arrays generally. You've learned in this chapter that arrays have two general benefits: You can store multiple pieces of data in a single structured variable, and you can perform interesting operations on the contents of arrays. Unlike arrays, which contain multiple single-item values in their indexes, associative arrays have *pairs* of values. That is, a regular array could contain three items (say, "Phillip", "Kerman", and 35), but an associative array could hold three pairs (say, first: "Phillip", last: "Kerman", and age: 35). The value for the item in the zero index is `"Phillip"` in either case, but items in any index of an associative array are referred to by their name—in this case `"first"`. It doesn't matter in which slot the pair `first:"Phillip"` resides, you can always find it by referring to `"first"`.

Although associative arrays make your structured data vastly easier to manage because you'll never need to remember in which index a particular item of data resides, there is one drawback. Namely, associative arrays cannot use the Array object's methods or properties. That includes the `sort()` method and the `length` property. About the only automated manipulation that's possible is looping using the "for-in" loop. You can actually manipulate an associative array's values in almost any way you want, but you'll just have to do it by hand.

Let's look at how to populate an associative array and then we can look at how to access values within the array. To create a new associative array with a few items, use the following form:

```
myArray={name:"value",nameTwo:"ValueTwo",thingThree:13};
```

Notice that each item in the array is a pair of name and value. The names are always written literally (with no quotation marks). It's weird because you might expect that such names would exist previously as variables. But in this case, `name`, `nameTwo`, and `thingThree` are all created on-the-fly and sit there with no quotation marks. Also, notice the entire array is surrounded by curly brackets (not the square brackets that you saw with regular arrays). Each item is separated by commas.

To access a value from within the array, you need to use the name associated with that value, not the index within the array. For example, `myArray["nameTwo"]` will return `"ValueTwo"`. The thing that freaks me out is that even though `nameTwo` was used verbatim when creating the array, you need to put it within quotation marks when trying to find the value within the array. In reality, associative arrays are less like arrays and more like objects (which we'll talk about more in the next two chapters). When creating an associative array, you provide arbitrary names for each item and Flash accepts them. You're really coming up with unique custom properties, but I think it's easier to think that you're coming up with names for the various items in the array.

Finally, you place a string between brackets to access the value of a particular item (really the value for the property—but, again, think *arrays*). This happens to be identical to the way that you referred to instance names within any timeline. When you knew the instance name, you just used it without quotation marks like `_root.someClip`. But when you wanted to refer to a clip dynamically, you built a string and placed that within brackets (as in `_root["circle_"+curCircle]`). Notice, dot access works when you know the clip name, but otherwise you need to use bracket reference. If it doesn't make your brain start melting, realize that in the earlier associative array, you can refer to the value of the "name" item by using dot syntax, as in `myArray.name`. Talk about coming around full circle!

We can save some of this discussion of objects for later chapters. Let's step back and look at a couple practical examples of building associative arrays (and accessing their contents).

Let's consider another way to store the data from an earlier example:

```
bookOne={title:"Teach Yourself", pageCount:587, price:24.99};
bookTwo={title:"ActionScripting", pageCount:500, price:39.99};
allBooks=[bookOne,bookTwo];
```

Without even considering whether this is the ideal structure or not, look at how amazingly easy it is to remember which item is which. Earlier, if we wanted to find the price, we had to remember "index 2." The page count was "index 1." (Not exactly intuitive.) In this case, when looking at either associative array (`bookOne` or `bookTwo`), we can access the price in the form:

```
bookOne["price"];
```

Is that easy or what? Because `allBooks` is still a regular array, you can access the nested elements in the ways the following examples show.

The first book's page count:

```
allBooks[0]["price"];
```

The second book's title:

```
allBooks[1]["title"];
```

By the way, in addition to accessing values of any item in an associative array, you can also change the values. For example, this changes the price of the first book to `29.99`:

```
allBooks[0]["price"]=29.99;
```

Finally, you can add new items to an associative array as arbitrarily as you created them in the first place. Consider this example:

```
myData={first:"Phillip",last:"Kerman",married:true}
```

Later I want to add an item:

```
myData["childCount"]=1;
```

At this point, `myData` equals `[first:"Phillip",last:"Kerman",married:true,childCount:1]`. It doesn't even matter whether the additional index was inserted at the end or not, because you can only refer to it by name (as in `myData["childCount"]`).

If you're like me upon first grasping associative arrays, you're probably thinking that regular (flat) arrays are practically worthless. But remember that associative arrays don't give you any access to all the fancy methods and length properties of regular arrays. In case you need to sift through all the items in an array, consider the following function that uses a "for-in" loop (which, additionally, counts the total number of items in the array).

```
function siftArray(theArray){
  var counter=0
  for (i in theArray){
    counter++
    trace(theArray[i]);
  }
  trace("total items: "+counter);
}
```

One interesting thing is that through each iteration of the "for-in" loop, you may think that `i` is an integer. Actually, `i` will become the name for each item in the array. Otherwise, the line using `theArray[i]` would break the rule about how items in associative arrays can be accessed only by item name (not index number). To see what I'm talking about, just change the first `trace` statement to read:

```
trace ("This item named "+ i + " has a value of " + theArray[i]);
```

Summary

My head hurts! Not from too much technical information, but from being so excited. Arrays are such an eloquent way to store and manipulate data, it's a shame that some people go through life without ever once experiencing their benefit. Seriously, arrays are awesome.

You saw how arrays could be structured to hold lots of discrete data in whatever way you want. Actually, the stage at which you design how to structure your arrays is the most challenging. As far as what you populate your array *with,* you learned it could be of any data type, including arrays. In this way, you could have an array full of nested arrays. After you populate an array with data, it is a snap to access and see or change any particular item. Looping through an array is a breeze, too.

This chapter detailed how to use every method made for arrays. Without repeating them all now, just remember that you can manipulate your arrays of data in any manner you want.

Finally, just to make things crazy, we looked at the topic of associative arrays. Although these arrays lack the methods that regular arrays offer, they give you a way to store name/value pairs within each index of an array.

Just think, an entire chapter without any puns such as, "arrays offer an array of great features."

{ Chapter 11 }

Objects

If you've gotten this far in the book, you've seen objects in several places. Instances of movie clips are the most basic type of object in Flash, and the best to learn from as you can *see* them onscreen. You've also seen several of the scripting objects (namely, Math, String, Array, Selection, and the Key object). Although you've already learned a lot about objects, there's more!

The objects introduced in this chapter are not only particularly practical, but also they all require the formal rules of objects such as instantiation. In this way, they make previously explored objects seem very forgiving in comparison, because you'll be doing things that were never required in the other objects. Luckily, these objects are well worth the additional effort.

In this chapter, you will

- Learn the rules of these formal objects
- Use the Sound object to "attach" sounds that can be manipulated using scripts
- Use the Color object to tint clips on-the-fly
- Use the Date object to perform any imaginable calculation involving calendars or time
- Use the AttachMovieClip statement to effectively drag clips from the Library using ActionScript

Formal Rules of Objects

Most of these concepts will appear familiar. For example, by now you know that objects have properties, which are basically just variables that contain data. Some properties have visual representations, such as a clip's `_alpha` property for example. Although the value for this property can be ascertained (as in `theClip._alpha`) and changed (as in `theClip._alpha=10`), some properties can be ascertained only. The set of properties for any object type is specific to the object. For instance, only the Movie Clip object has an `_alpha` property. Other objects have other properties—but they're all the same in that they contain values that can, sometimes, be modified.

In addition to properties, objects can have methods, which are functions that are applied to unique instances of an object. Methods are processes, whereas properties are just static attributes. So far, this should be a review. The concept that's a little bit new is that formal objects must be instantiated. In the case of clip instances (that is, Movie Clip objects), you simply instantiate them by dragging them from the Library. After each object has been instantiated, it has its own unique set of properties and the potential to have methods, such as `nextFrame()`, applied to them individually. The formal objects require that you instantiate them using a constructor function. All constructor functions follow this pattern:

```
new Object();
```

For this chapter we'll see the following constructor functions that instantiate different formal object types:

```
new Sound();
new Color();
new Date();
```

(By the way, instantiating a new movie clip using ActionScript during runtime uses a different technique that's discussed in the "Attach Movie Clip" section later.)

The key to remember with instantiating objects is that you must store the object in a variable, so saying `new Sound()` doesn't really do anything. However, `mySound=new Sound()` creates a new instance (in the form of the Sound object) and places it into the variable `mySound`, whose value is of the object data type. From this point forward, you can treat `mySound` like any object, referring to properties (`mySound.someProperty`) or using methods (such as `mySound.someMethod()`) in the same way you would treat a clip instance.

Until you build your own objects, that's about all there is to it. The trick is that you must instantiate an object and place it in a variable before you can start doing stuff with it or doing stuff to it. Now we can see the nitty-gritty details of four objects.

Attach Sound

This section probably could be called "The Sound Object." However, if there's one step that's easy to forget when using the Sound object it's the attach sound step, so maybe the section title will help you remember. Here's the process you take in order to use the Sound object.

Sound Object Basics

The idea is that by using ActionScript, you will effectively drag a sound out of the Library and start using it in your movie. Items in the Library that aren't used anywhere in your movie normally don't export when you publish your movie (which is a good thing considering that unnecessary sounds will especially add to the filesize). After you import the sound you intend to "attach" into the Library, you'll need to override the no-export feature by setting the Linkage in the Library's option menu (as in Figure 11.1).

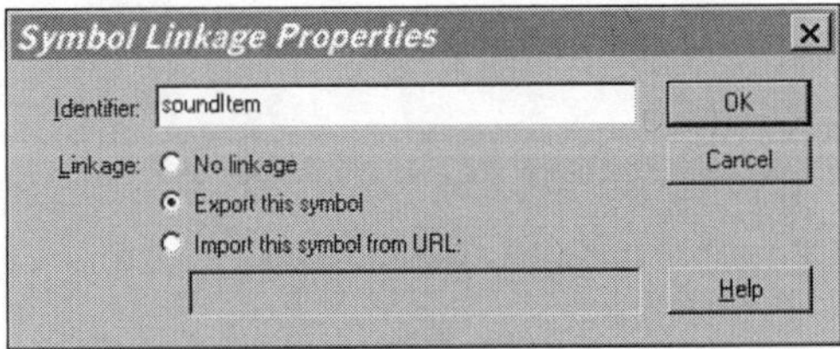

Figure 11.1 *A sound item is set to export (and given an identifier name) through the Library's Linkage option.*

All you need to do is select Export This Symbol and give it a unique identifier name (I'll use `"soundItem"` for my examples). Although we won't do it here, you can also Import This Symbol from URL but that requires you to build a shared library (a subject covered in my other book, *Sams Teach Yourself Flash 5 in 24 Hours*). In addition to causing your exported movie's filesize to grow, this sound will now download before subsequent frames load.

Now that we have a sound identified, we can start coding. You first instantiate a sound object and place it in a variable (I'm using `mySound`):

```
mySound=new Sound();
```

Before you can start using the Sound object methods shown in Figure 11.2, you need to attach the sound to this object.

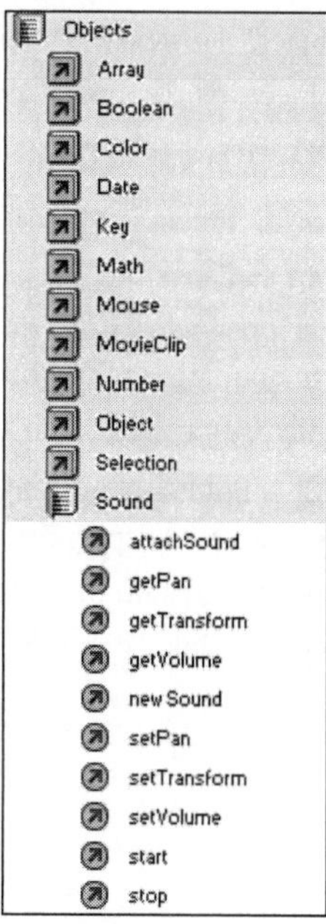

Figure 11.2 *The list of Sound object methods is short but they're powerful.*

The `attachSound` method lets you specify which sound (in the Library) you want to associate with this object.

```
mySound.attachSound("soundItem");
```

Notice that `"soundItem"` matches the name we gave the imported sound in the linkage settings. At this point, we can now start playing with the other methods. You'll likely want to start the sound so that you can hear all the changes you might make to the sound later.

```
mySound.start();
```

This will start the sound playing from the beginning of the sound file. Two optional parameters are included in this method. If you want to cut in and start the sound (not at the beginning), you can specify the number of seconds into the sound that you want to begin. That is, `mySound.start(10)` will start the sound 10 seconds in from the start. (Of course you shouldn't use this to skip past silence at the beginning of your sound: Any silence should have been removed before import as it adds unnecessarily to the filesize.) The second optional parameter lets you specify how many times the sound should loop. To make a sound play almost continuously, use `mySound.start(0,9999999)`. Notice that you still need something in the first parameter that specifies the delay until start time in order to use the second parameter.

The opposite of `start()` is obviously `stop()`. Use `mySound.stop()` to stop the sound. This is not "pause" in that if you later use `mySound.start()`, it will start over from the beginning. There are only a few other methods (shown in Figure 11.2), so let's look at them all.

Advanced Sound Controls

Although starting or stopping a sound isn't really fancy, you'll likely need to at least start a sound before using the other methods. While a sound is playing you can easily adjust its volume using `mySound.setVolume(`*`level`*`)` where "level" is an integer between `0` and `100`. Effectively this is a percent of the volume the user has her computer system and speakers set to. That is, `mySound.setVolume(100)` will play the sound at the full 100% of the user's computer settings. Conversely, `mySound.setVolume(0)` will make the sound silent. Keep in mind that `setVolume(0)` is different from `stop()` because the sound continues to play but at a volume of `0`. The default sound level is `100` and then you can lower it using `setVolume()`. If you ever need to ascertain the current level, just use `getVolume()`.

In addition to changing the volume, you can use pan to affect the balance between the left and right channels. Similar to the way a camera can pan left and right, you can cause the sound to seem to originate from the left or right. The `setPan()` method accepts a parameter ranging from `-100` (to pan all the way to the left) to `100` (to pan right). When the sound is sent to both speakers equally, the pan is `0`. So, when a sound is playing, you can use `mySound.setPan(-50)` and it will sound as if your audio has moved to the left. You can actually set the pan (as you can set the volume) even when a sound isn't playing, but you'll always need a Sound object on which to use the `setPan()` method. If you ever need to ascertain the current pan use `getPan()`.

Finally, the last Sound object method is called `setTransform()` (and its sister `getTransform()`). On the surface, this method appears very similar to `setPan()` because it controls how much sound is going to each channel. But it's actually a combination of setting the volume, setting the pan, and exactly which portion of the audio goes to each speaker. There are four factors that you specify when using the `setTransform()` method: how much left channel sound you want going to the left speaker (referred to as `ll` and ranging from `-100` to `100`); how much left channel is going to the right speaker (`lr`); how much right is going to the right speaker (`rr`); and how much right is going to the left speaker (`rl`). Through this method you have very fine control. By the way, all this changing of volume and pan actually overrides settings previously made through the `setVolume()` and `setPan()` methods.

Now for the funky part. Specifying the four settings (`ll`, `lr`, `rr`, and `rl`) would probably be easiest if you simply provided four parameters when invoking the `setTransform()` method. But it doesn't work that way. Instead, `setTranform()` accepts a single parameter in the form of *another* object that has four properties. The process involves first creating a generic object in a variable, setting the four properties (`ll`, `lr`, `rr`, and `rl`), and finally passing that variable (data type "object") as the parameter when calling `setTransform()`. Here's how you might do it:

```
transObj=new Object();
transObj.ll=100;
transObj.lr=0;
transObj.rr=100;
transObj.rl=0;
mySound.setTransform(transObj);
```

This script effectively sets the balance equal (left going to left and right going to right are both 100).

This assumes that `mySound` is already instantiated (and playing if you want to hear anything). After you have the variable (`transObj` in this case) that contains an object, you can change any of its four properties and then invoke the last line (`mySound.setTransform(transObj)`) to hear that change. Assuming that the `transObj` exists, you can send all the left channel's audio to the right speaker (and vice versa) by using the following code:

```
transObj.ll=0;
transObj.lr=100;
transObj.rr=0;
```

```
transObj.rl=100;
mySound.setTransform(transObj);
```

To make a stereo sound play as if it were mono, use this code:

```
transObj.ll=50;
transObj.lr=50;
transObj.rr=50;
transObj.rl=50;
mySound.setTransform(transObj);
```

Translated, this code says send half the left channel's sound to the left channel, and the other half to the right. Then send half the right channel's sound to the right and the other half to the left. The result is all sounds are evenly distributed to both speakers and it sounds mono.

Finally, if you need to ascertain the current transform, use `getTransform()`. The only tricky thing is that this returns another object. If you want to then specifically target one of the four properties, you can by using the dot syntax techniques of which you're so familiar. For example, to find out what percent of the left channel is going to the left speaker, use `mySound.getTransform().ll`. If you don't want to keep calling the `getTransform()` method, you can use code such as the following:

```
curTrans=mySound.getTransform();
trace("Left speaker is playing "+ curTrans.ll + "% of the left channel");
trace("Right speaker is playing "+ curTrans.lr + "% of the left channel");
trace("Right speaker is playing "+ curTrans.rr + "% of the right
channel");
trace("Left speaker is playing "+ curTrans.rl + "% of the right channel");
```

Controlling Multiple Sounds

I left out an optional parameter when first introducing the Sound object constructor function (`new Sound()`). Think of the parameter as the way to attach a sound to an instance. Then that instance and attached sound is independently controllable just like any other property of that clip. If you provide a reference to a movie clip as the parameter, the sound will be independently controllable. Otherwise all sound objects' volume will be the same. For example, here's how you can start playing two sounds and then control their respective volume levels:

```
sound1=new Sound(clip1);
sound1.attachSound("music");
```

```
sound1.start();
sound2=new Sound(clip2);
sound2.attachSound("narration");
sound2.start();
sound1.setVolume(50);
sound2.setVolume(80);
```

You'll need two clips onstage (`clip1` and `clip2`); two sounds in the Library with linkage set and identifiers (`"music"` and `"narration"`). When the sounds start, you'll hear their respective sounds change when calling `sound1.setVolume(`*`toWhat`*`)` and `sound2.setVolume(`*`toWhat`*`)`. It's weird because you'd think by having the two sound objects stored in two separate variables (`sound1` and `sound2`) you'd have independent control. Just remember, though, you need to attach the sound to a specific clip instance (by providing the clip as a parameter) to have such control. Lastly, variables (as always) are indeed part of the timeline where they're created (so you'll need to apply all that you know about targeting if you want to refer to them from other timelines). But interestingly, including a clip reference in the `new Sound()` constructor has no impact on targeting (so you don't need to worry about it).

The Sound object is pretty awesome. Unfortunately, you can't ascertain the total length of a sound or determine the current position in a sound while it plays. However, in conjunction with the `getTimer()` function, you can get pretty close. That is, if you know how long a sound is (because you imported it) and you know when a sound started (because you started it), you can store the start time in a variable (such as `startTime=getTimer()`) when you start the sound and then calculate the elapsed time in milliseconds any time by using the expression `getTimer()-startTime`. If you know the sound is 10 seconds long (10,000 milliseconds) and you find that `getTimer()-startTime` is greater than `10000`, then you know the sound has expired.

To use the Sound object, you just need to remember these steps:

1. Import a sound and set its linkage to export. Also, give the sound a unique identifier.
2. Instantiate the Sound object and store it in a variable by using the "new" constructor: `mySound=new Sound()`.

3. Attach a sound by referring to the identifier name given in step 1: `mySound.attachSound("identifier")`.
4. Start the sound and then use any of the other methods as you wish: `mySound.start()`.
5. Finally, when you're sure that you won't need the sound anymore, you can delete the variable containing the object: `delete mySound`. Although I don't believe a few unused sound objects will bring your movie's performance to a crawl, just as any variables, there's no reason to have more than you're using. (By the way, be sure to `stop()` the sound before you delete the variable, or you'll lose control of the sound.)

Color

Through scripting, you can use the Color object to apply color effects on clip instances the same way you can manually use the Effect panel. The process is analogous to using the Sound object. The Color object requires that you first instantiate an object through `new Color("clipToTint")` in which `"clipToTint"` is the clip you want to affect, and then use one of the two methods—`setRGB()` and `setTransform()`—to cause the clip to change. It really is that simple. It's just when you want to perform elaborate effects, there are additional details—as you'll see.

Simple Coloring

Here's the simple version of coloring a clip using the Color object. First, instantiate the Color object *and* specify a target clip:

```
myColor=new Color("theClip");
```

The variable `myColor` now contains the object, so the clip instance named `theClip` will be affected when we do the next step. (Notice that even though the clip is referenced between quotes, you can still use target paths as long as you remember the quotes.) At this point, you can color the clip using the `setRGB()` method. To tint it pure red, use

```
myColor.setRGB(0xff0000);
```

For green,

```
myColor.setRGB(0x00ff00);
```

Notice that the parameter used for the `setRGB()` method is in the form of a hexadecimal color reference. The first two characters `0x` act as a warning to Flash that what follows is in the hexadecimal format. So that's it! As long as you know the hex value for the color you intend to use, this works great. By the way if you want to learn more about hexadecimal color references, the easiest way is by exploring Flash's Mixer panel shown in Figure 11.3.

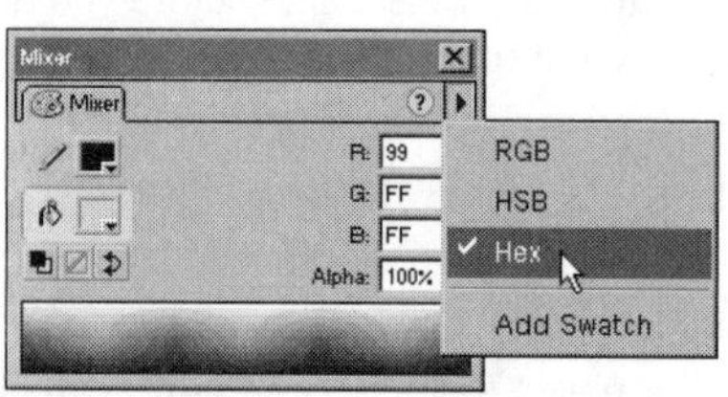

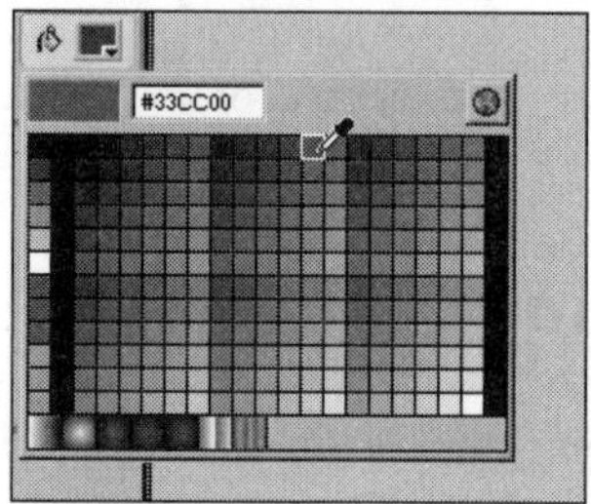

Figure 11.3 *You can change Flash's Mixer panel (left) to Hex or simply view Hex values any time you select a color swatch (right).*

Using RGB Values

In addition to providing a hex value (after `0x`) as the `setRGB()` method's parameter, you can provide a number between 0 and 16,777,215. The following three paragraphs include a detailed explanation of how you can specify colors in an intuitive (RGB) manner. 24-bit color includes 8 bits for each of the three colors red, green, and blue. This means that there are 256 shades for each color (0-255) because each binary digit is either "on" or "off." Eight binary digits—1, 2, 4, 8, 16, 32, 64, 128—all "on" adds up to 255. If they're all off, it adds up to zero. The highest number you can represent with twenty-four binary digits (three 8-bit colors) is 16,777,215.

An interesting method is used to relate 16 million different values to three colors. Blue always gets the first 8 bits (1 through 8 bits or 0-255). A value of 0 is no blue, and 255 is 100% blue. Something such as 128 is only 50% blue. To add green to the equation, 8 bits are still used, but they start at 9 and go through 16. So instead of ranging from 0-255 in one-step increments, green is defined with numbers between 256 and 65,280, which is 256 steps of 256 each. So every notch of green is 256; 256 is one notch of green, 512 is two notches of green, and so on. A number such as 522 is two notches of green and 10 notches of blue.

The way to see the breakdown of blue and green is to first extract the round 256 increments (256 goes into 522 twice; then the left over 10 is used for blue). Think about if blue went from 0-99 (in steps of 1) and green went from 100 to 1000 (in steps of 100). Because you extract the largest steps first and then the remainder, a number such as 600 would be a shade of green 6 units deep (and no blue), but a number such as 630 would be 6 units green and 30 units of blue. It actually works just like this except that instead of being based on 1s and 100s, it's based on 8 bit and 16 bit. Of course, red gets the last 8 bits, which means that it steps from 65,280 to 16,711,680 in 256 steps of 65,536 each. All this means is that it's next to impossible to intuitively specify colors using RGB—but we'll find a way.

The reason the previous concept is so difficult to understand is that we like to think of digits going from 0-9 (that is, in base 10). In our base-10 system, the far right digit is for "ones" (0-9), the second digit is for "hundreds" (0-9 again, but representing how many "hundreds"), and so on. Hexadecimal values do it in three pairs of characters RRBBGG. For example, the first two characters "RR" represents a number between 0-255 for red. The three 256-shade values for R, G, B are in the 24-bit system; they're just hard to derive. If you think in binary, though, it's probably easiest. Using 8 digits (for 8 bits), you can represent any number from 0-255. For example, 00000001 is 1, 00000010 is 2, and 00000011 is three. Each position in the 8-digit number represents a bit. To read the previous binary numbers, consider the far right digit as the "ones" (0-1), the second digit as the "twos" (0-1 representing how many "twos"), the third digit is for the "fours", and so on. Therefore you can count (in binary) 001, 010, 011, 100, 101, 111. Check it out... 1, 2, 3, 4, 5, 6 in binary!

For a 24-bit color, you need only to have 24 binary digits. The eight at the far right represent 0-255 for blue, the middle eight represent 0-255 for green, and the leftmost eight digits represent 0-255 for red (see Figure 11.4).

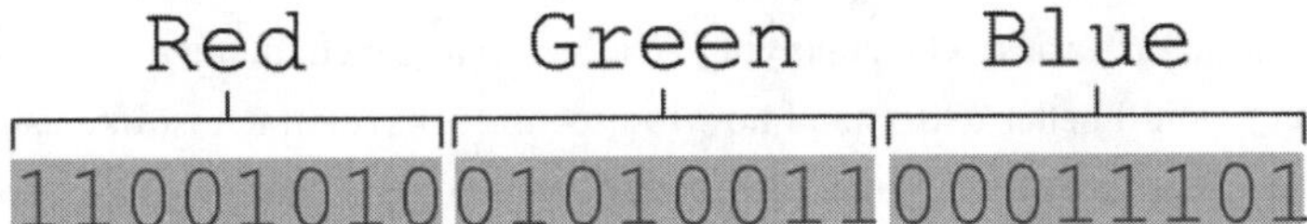

Figure 11.4 *A binary representation of a 24-bit number includes eight digits for each color.*

Finally, I can show you a quick way to convert RGB values (of 0-255 each) into binary at the same time that they can be used in the `setRGB()` method. That is, how do you turn `r=255`, `g=255`, and `b=255` (which is white) into a binary series of 24 ones or zeroes (that can, in turn, be used as the parameter passed when invoking `setRGB()`)? Assuming that `r`, `g`, and `b` are variables containing a number between `0` and `255`, you can use a bitwise shift operator to specify how many digits to the left you want the binary number to shift. That is, `5<<8` takes the binary version of `5` (`101`) and shifts it eight spots to the left (`10100000000`—that's `101` with eight zeros). This is exactly how to shift the value for green up eight places (or `g<<8`). Red needs to be shifted 16 places, so `r<<16` is used. Finally, the combined form looks as follows:

```
myColor.setRGB(r<<16 | g<<8 | b);
```

Notice that `b` (the value for blue) doesn't need to be shifted. The result of the entire expression in the parentheses is a binary number representing RGB by using eight digits for each color. In practice, you just need to make sure that your values for `r`, `g`, and `b` are between `0` and `255`; then simply use the previous method call as is.

Using the Color Transform Method

Naturally, you probably aren't satisfied with only 16 million different possible colors—you probably want to change the alpha of a color too. After all, I said you can use scripting to achieve the same results that the Effect panel can—and just look at all the things you can do with the Advanced option in the Effect panel in Figure 11.5. The `setTransform()` method allows you to modify any clip that has been associated with the color object in the same way the Advanced option of the Effect panel does. Of course, you could always just use the familiar `theClip._alpha=70` if you ever need to change the alpha of a tinted clip, but `setTransform()` can do even more than that.

Actually, if you understand the interface of the Advanced option of the Effect panel (which is easiest when applying an effect to a clip containing a raster graphic), you'll better understand how to use `setTransform()`. Just like using the `setTransform()` on the Sound object, you'll need to pass an object as a parameter. You first create a generic object, set its properties according to the effect you want, and then pass it when invoking `setTransform()`. The generic object has eight properties that correlate directly to the eight settings in the Effect panel. Of course we're not using the panel (that is the manual way), we're doing this with scripting—but it helps to consider these eight properties in relation to the panel (see Figure 11.6).

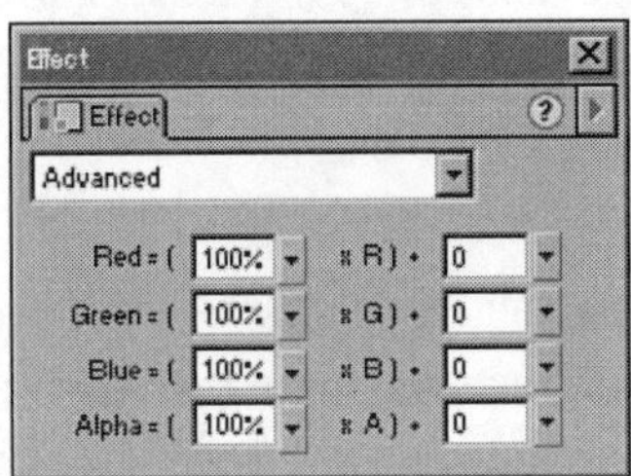

Figure 11.5 *The Advanced option in the Effect panel gives you fine control over tinting (especially with bitmaps).*

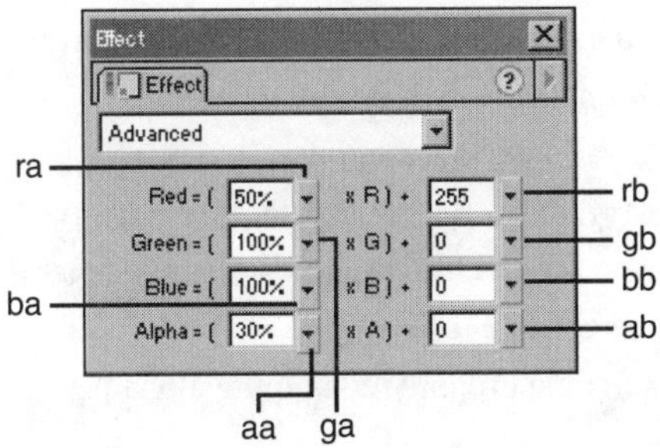

Figure 11.6 *The settings in the Advanced Effect panel are the same for the generic object passed to the* `setTransform()` *method.*

Here's a code sequence you might use to tint a clip 50% red and 30% alpha:

```
transObj=new Object()
transObj.ra = 50;
transObj.rb = 255;
transObj.ga = 100;
transObj.gb = 0;
transObj.ba = 100;
transObj.bb = 0;
transObj.aa = 30;
transObj.ab = 0;
myColor=new Color("theClip");
myColor.setTransform(transObj);
```

I see `setTransform()` as having two main benefits. You can change alpha of a clip and you can control subtle color shifts that are most apparent when the clip being colored contains a raster graphic (such as .bmp or .jpg). The fact that there are other ways to control alpha makes me think that the only real value for `setTransform()` is when manipulating raster graphics. The kinds of effects you can make are pretty cool, though.

Before we move on, let me just mention the two other methods `getRGB()` and `getTransform()`. The `getRGB()` method returns (in base 10) the last color value used on the object referenced. That is, `myColor.getRGB()` will return the color for the clip associated with the object stored in the variable `myColor`: specifically, a number between 0 and 16,777,215. By the way, a handy way to translate that number to binary is by using the `toString()` method but by providing a parameter. That is, `myColor.getRGB().toString(2)` will return (in the form of a string) the color value represented in binary. You can even use `toString(16)` to convert the number being operated on to hexadecimal. Check it out by including a Dynamic Text field onstage containing a variable value and use: `value=myColor.getRGB().toString(16)`. Finally, realize that the value returned when you use `getTransform()` is an object with eight properties. For example, if you want to ascertain the current alpha percentage, use `myColor.getTransform().aa` because `aa` is the property containing alpha percentage.

Date

The Date object gives you an easy way to store specific dates, ascertain the current date (and time), and find out details about any date (such as its day of the week). For example, I know I was born on a Wednesday—not because I remember, but because I can check it with the Date object. Basically, I created a new instance of the Date object with my birthday as the initial value. Then I used a method that returns the day of the week. Another interesting application is to repeatedly reassign a variable a new Date object (and use the current date and time for the initial value) and then you can display all the details of the current time (using a clock or calendar). It's even possible to accurately find the difference (in number of days) between two dates, and you don't need to know which are leap years or how many days any particular month "hath." (You know—"Thirty days hath September…")

Instantiating a Date

Similar to the Color and Sound objects, you always start by instantiating the Date object and then you can use methods on it. The variable you use to hold a Date object contains a snap shot of a moment in time. That is, a variable that contains the Date data type is only holding one moment in time. When you create an instance of the Date object, you can specify that moment (year, month, hour, second, and even millisecond if you want); or if you don't specify any date, you're given a date that matches the setting of your user's computer clock. Here's the form to create an instance with the current time:

```
now=new Date();
```

The variable now contains a Date object with the current time. You can provide up to seven optional parameters (to specify year, month, day, hour, minute, second, and millisecond). For example, this is how you create an instance that contains the U.S. Independence Day (July 4, 1776):

```
indyDay=new Date(1776, 6, 4);
```

That is, the year 1776, the month July (counting January as 0, February as 1), the fourth date in the month (which—surprisingly—starts counting with 1). I left out some optional parameters: hour, which counts from 0 (midnight) to 23 (11 p.m.); minutes (0-59 for every hour); seconds (0-59 per minute); and, milliseconds (of which there are 1,000 per second). Because the seven parameters are optional, you can leave them off if you want (though the order is important with the first parameter always referring to year, the second to month, and so on).

Manipulating Dates

After you've created a variable that holds your Date object, you can manipulate and view it through the various methods. Although quite a few methods are available (see Figure 11.7), there are only two general types—methods that "get" information from the date and methods that change or "set" elements within dates. Let's walk through some operations to get a handle on both types of methods.

Figure 11.7 *Although there are many methods for the Date object, they fall into two general categories—those that get values and those that set values.*

Getting Information from Dates

Several methods "get" specific information from a date. For example, the `getDay()` method returns the day of the week. However, because it returns a number between `0` (for Sunday) and `6` (for Saturday), you might first create an array with all the days of the week:

```
dayNames=["Sunday","Monday","Tuesday","Wednesday","Thursday","Friday",
"Saturday"];
```

Then you can easily determine the day of the week that the U.S. constitution was signed:

```
trace("Signatures were made on a "+dayNames[indyDay.getDay()]);
```

Because `indyDay.getDay()` returns a `4`, the expression `dayNames[4]` would return `"Thursday"`. It's almost as though it doesn't matter that `getDay()` starts counting with Sunday as `0` because when grabbing data from an array, we count the same way. (This isn't to say that it will never mess you up.)

Other methods are similar to `getDay()` such as `getYear()` (and its better half `getFullYear()`), `getMonth()`, and `getDate()` (which returns the number of the day in the month). It's unlikely that you'd really *need* these to ascertain the year, month, or date for a Date object that you created by specifying the date. However, they can be particularly useful when you're not sure of the date. For example, let's say that you want your Flash movie to display information about the current date in a Dynamic Text field. You can start with

```
now=new Date();
```

Then, if your text field contains a variable called `message`, you can use the following code:

```
monthNum=now.getMonth()+1;
dateNum=now.getDate();
yearNum=now.getFullYear();
message=monthNum+"/"+dateNum+"/"+yearNum;
```

By the way, `getYear()` returns the number of years since 1900 (so if you do a `getYear()` on a date in the year 2001, you'll get `101`). The method `getFullYear()` returns a 4-digit number (which naturally renders your Flash movie non-Y10K-compliant—but I wouldn't worry about it).

If you want to display the date in a format that's a little more wordy than 3/31/2001 (as previous), you can use a quick-and-dirty technique involving the `toString()` method. When used on a Date object, `toString()` returns the full date and time in the form:

Sat Mar 31 17:03:57 GMT-0800 2001

Although this is kind of nice, if you want something more readable, you could use a function such as this one:

```
function getNiceDate(whatDate){
  var dayNames=["Sunday",
  ➥"Monday","Tuesday","Wednesday","Thursday","Friday","Saturday"];
  var monthNames=["January","February","March","April","May",
  ➥"June","July","August","September","October","November","December"];
  var day=dayNames[whatDate.getDay()];
  var month=monthNames[whatDate.getMonth()];
  var date=whatDate.getDate();
  var year=whatDate.getFullYear();
  return (day+" "+month+" "+date+", "+year);
}
```

Just pass an actual Date object for a parameter, and you'll get a string back that follows a more traditional form than what you get with `toString()`. That is, `trace(getNiceDate(indyDay))` will result in `"Thursday July 4, 1776"` displayed in the output window.

The data maintained in a Date object is detailed down to the millisecond. However, because instantiating a new Date object (with `new Date()`) only takes a snap shot of the current time, in order to make a clock (that doesn't appear frozen in time), you'll need to repeatedly re-instantiate the date object. The ideal place to do this is inside an enterFrame clip event. So, if you have a Dynamic Text field (associated with a variable `theTime`) in a movie clip and you attach the following code to the clip instance, you'll have a nice digital clock (as shown in Figure 11.8).

10:45:51 PM

Figure 11.8 *You can easily make this digital clock display with a Dynamic Text field and in a Movie Clip.*

```
onClipEvent (enterFrame) {
  now=new Date();
  seconds=now.getSeconds();
  if (seconds<10){
    seconds="0"+seconds;
  }
```

```
  minutes=now.getMinutes();
  if (minutes<10){
    minutes="0"+minutes;
  }
  hours=now.getHours();
  amPm="AM";
  if (hours<10){
    hours="0"+hours;
  }else if (hours>12){
    amPm="PM"
    hours=hours-12;
    if (hours<10){
      hours="0"+hours;
    }
  }
  theTime=hours+":"+minutes+":"+seconds+" "+amPM;
}
```

The now variable is reassigned a new instance of the Date object and then used in most of the subsequent calculations. The `seconds` variable is set by applying the `getSeconds()` function to now. If `seconds` is less than 10 we just add a "0" in front of it so it still displays using two characters. The `minutes` variable is similar to `seconds`. In the case of `hours`, determining the actual hour is straightforward enough (`hours=now.getHours()`). I first assume it's AM (by setting `amPm` to "AM"), but if hours is not less than 10, I check if it's greater than 12...in which case I say `amPm` is "PM" and then take 12 off (that is, if it's 14:00 you subtract 12 to get 2 PM). Finally, I build the string called `theTime` that's displayed in a Dynamic Text field.

Naturally, the ugly part of this code is the error checking. That is, I go through extra work to make sure that numbers less than ten appear with a zero to their left. The important part to remember in this example is that the variable now is continually reassigned a new Date object (12 times a second if the frame rate is set to 12 fps). I don't think you'll see a performance hit from this code executing so frequently—but even if you did, it's a clock, so you'll want it to update frequently.

Setting Values in Dates

So far we've looked at using the Date object to store a moment in time and then use methods to peek inside. Although we haven't explored all these methods that "get" values returned, there's another set of methods that "set" values. These allow you to change any attribute of a date stored in a variable. For example, if you want to take today's date and find out the month and date for a day exactly two weeks from now, you can use the `setDate()` method. The `setDate()` method will change the date in the attached object to whatever number you provide as a parameter. If you provide "today plus 14 days" (that is, `getDate()+14`), you'll find the answer. Here's the code:

```
now=new Date();
fortNight=new Date();
fortNight.setDate(now.getDate()+14);
trace("Two weeks from now is: "+ fortNight.toString());
```

Notice that I could have simply used the `setDate()` method on my original date object (`now`). That is, `now.setDate(now.getDate()+14)`. Instead of getting confused with a variable called "now" that actually contained a date in the future, I came up with another variable name (`fortNight`). But it's important that before I try setting `fortNight`'s date, I had to instantiate the variable as a Date object (in the second line of code). Simply, you can only use methods on objects. Another important point is the `setDate()` method actually changes the object being operated on. This is performing an assignment without the equal sign. Finally, the cool part about `setDate()` (and all the other "set" methods) is that other elements in the object being operated on automatically update accordingly. That is, if you "setDate" to today's date plus 40 days (`now.setDate(now.getDate()+40)`), you'll find the object's month (found through `getMonth()`) has changed. Similarly, you'll find the year changes when you "setMonth" to the current month plus 13.

There's one last method that I want to describe. When you use the method `getTime()` on any Date object, the elapsed milliseconds between January 1st 1970 and the object being operated on will be returned. This might seem like a useless piece of trivia but it might come up on a quiz show some time. It also happens to be the most direct way to determine the difference between two dates. For example, if you knew one person was born five days after January 1, 1970 and another person was born 200 days after January 1, 1970, it's simple to calculate the difference in their two ages as 195 days. It's not that you care how many days apart from January 1st 1970 each birthday is—it's just a common reference point. In the following code sample, you see that we never really take much note as to how many milliseconds have past since 1970, we just find the difference between two dates. In fact, one of the dates used occurred before the magic 1970 date.

```
birthday = new Date(1969, 1, 12);
bicentennial = new Date(1976, 6, 4);
difference = Math.abs(birthday.getTime()-bicentennial.getTime());
millisecondsPerDay = 1000*60*60*24;
difference = Math.floor(difference/millisecondsPerDay);
trace ("Birthday was "+difference+" days before or after the
bicentennial");
```

Notice that no one really cares how many milliseconds have elapsed since January 1st 1970 (or, even that `getTime()` could result in a negative number if the date being operated on was earlier). Instead of calculating whether a birthday was before or after the bicentennial, I just calculated the absolute value of the difference. Absolute value (`Math.abs()`) always returns a non-negative number. Finally, to convert milliseconds into days, I divided by `1000*60*60*24` (which is based on the fact that there are 1000 milliseconds every second, 60 seconds every minute, 60 minutes every hour, and 24 hours each day). Instead of just dividing the `difference` by `millisecondsPerDay` I use `Math.floor()` to make sure to just extract the integer portion of the number. That is, I don't want to know that it's been 2698.958333 days—2698 is plenty. Using this same basic technique, you can accurately calculate the difference between any two days.

Attach Movie Clip

To be perfectly accurate, we've already discussed the Movie Clip object. However, by using the technique that follows, you can effectively drag instances of clips on to the stage entirely through scripting. This is almost identical to the Sound object. And, just like how you have to remember the `attachSound()` step with the Sound object, you must remember the `attachMovie()` step here.

If you want to use scripting to cause a clip instance to appear onstage during runtime, you must first set the linkage for that clip (as we did for sounds) and come up with a unique identifier. Then, all you do is call the `attachMovie()` function using this form:

```
targetPath.attachMovie("identifier", "newInstanceName", depth);
```

Where `"targetPath"` is a path to where the new clip will reside (like `_root`), `"identifier"` is the name you gave the clip through its linkage, `"newInstanceName"` assigns it an instance name (as if you typed it in manually through the Instance panel), and `depth` is the level number. (Most clips are on level 0, but when loading movies you can specify higher numbers and the clips will appear on top of others.) For example, if I have a clip who's identifier is "box", I could use

```
_root.attachMovie("box", "box1",0);
```

This will place an instance of the clip in the Library whose identifier name is set to "box" onstage. The clip's instance name will be box1. The following code will position and change the _alpha property of the clip:

```
_root.box1._x=190;
_root.box1._y=33;
_root.box1._alpha=50;
```

Looks pretty familiar, eh? Well, to explain this any further would probably insult your intelligence. We covered all the bases of Movie Clips in Chapter 7, "The Movie Clip Object." The only trick to remember here is the identifier that's set through the Library item's Linkage. Additionally, you can't put more than one clip on the same level. If you attach a clip and specify level 0, you can't put any other clips in that same level (nor can you load movies into that same level). Also, if you want to remove a clip that's been created using the attachMovie() function, you can use removeMovieClip() which is a *method* of the clip, so the form is

```
targetPath.instanceName.removeMovieClip();
```

Notice that you apply the removeMovieClip() method on a clip reference, the same way that you use any method, not on the identifier. For example, to remove the clip created previously, use the following:

```
_root.box1.removeMovieClip();
```

Finally, there's another confusingly similar method called duplicateMovieClip(). All you need to specify is the new instance name for the clip and the level number. For example, you can duplicate the box1 clip with

```
_root.box1.duplicateMovieClip("box2", 1 );
```

This method requires that an instance has already been instantiated (otherwise, you'd have no object to apply this method to). The good news, however, is the duplicateMovieClip() method doesn't require that you've previously specified the linkage and given the library item an identifier. Also, any scripts attached to the clip that's duplicated are contained in the duplicate. By the way, removeMovieClip() works the same way with clips created through the duplicateMovieClip() method.

Summary

We've looked at three traditional objects made for Flash—Sound, Color, and Date. In each of these, you first need to create an instance of the object (by putting it in a variable) and then you can use any of the object's methods. The three objects introduced in this chapter are a good representation of "formal" objects. So many other objects in Flash have special conditions that let you get away without instantiating them (the Math object and String object in particular). Also, we got to see a generic object when creating the parameter for the Sound and Color object's `setTransform()` method. Creating generic objects will be fully explored in the next chapter when we create our own custom objects. Our old friend the Movie Clip object was also touched on in this chapter when we looked at the process of "attaching" a movie clip. When you attach both a movie clip and a sound, you just have to remember to provide an identifier through the library item's linkage option.

If you ever have trouble grasping concepts about objects in general, remember that you can always think about what makes an instance of a clip an object. It has a set of properties that can be varied from instance to instance. And just like any object, there are a host of methods that can be applied to individual instances of clips. The other objects explored in this chapter are still objects; they just are not really visible.

{ Chapter 12 }

Homemade Objects

Now that you've seen a variety of objects built into Flash, it's time to make your own. The homemade objects you'll make in this chapter are almost identical to built-in objects such as Movie Clips, Sound objects, or the Date object: The instances of homemade objects you create can have properties and methods. What's more, all instances you create will maintain independent values for their properties.

In fact, homemade objects can be more sophisticated than those built into Flash because of a special feature called *inheritance*. After you design and build one object, it's possible to design new objects that share certain properties and methods of that object. For example, you could make a "bank account" object that includes a method to calculate interest. That same method can be inherited by another object (perhaps a "certificate of deposit" object). Through inheritance you can modularize code so that you're more productive.

You'll see the process of creating objects is relatively straightforward and consistent with everything you've learned. Designing a good object, however, will be where the challenge lies. The practical examples in this chapter should give you some ideas. Specifically, in this chapter you will

- Create simple objects that maintain unique values for properties in each instance
- Create custom methods for object instances

- Assign prototype properties so that one object type can inherit properties and methods of an another
- Change properties in "parent" objects so that the values of the same properties in their "children" will reflect the change
- Learn how to apply objects to practical Flash applications

Basic Objects

When you see how easy it is to make an object, you'll probably be surprised. In fact, when you created associative arrays in Chapter 10, "Arrays," you were actually making objects. Individual objects are simply a way to store multiple pieces of data. Creating associative arrays follows this form:

```
myData={age:35,height:72,citizenship:"USA"};
```

From this point, you could then access any item using the form:

```
myData["age"]=36;
```

Because an associative array is an object, it can be created (and accessed) accordingly. The following code achieves the same result:

```
myData=new Object();
myData.age=35;
myData.height=72;
myData.citizenship="USA";
```

You can still access individual items (which are probably best called *properties*) the same way as shown earlier (myData["age"]) or by using the dot-syntax with which we are so familiar (`myData.age`). This simply proves that objects are associative arrays (and vice versa).

Using Constructor Function

Imagine that you want multiple variables to contain objects, each of which contains properties for age, height, and citizenship. It would get rather involved to define all three properties every time you wanted to assign this object to a variable. Instead, you can create a function that serves as a constructor function (to instantiate new instances of the object):

```
function makePerson(age,height,citizenship){
  this.age=age;
  this.height=height;
  this.citizenship=citizenship;
}
```

Even though the `makePerson` function accepts three parameters, this function won't make a whole lot of sense if we call it as we would a normal function: (`makePerson(22,68,"Canada")`, for example. Notice that the three lines inside set three properties of "this." `this` is a keyword in Flash used in two ways. You can either use it to refer to the current clip (that you're "in"), or (as earlier) inside a function to refer to the object being created by that function. You're about to see how you create an object with a function, but if you just call the `makePerson()` function, it won't really do anything. Instead, we're going to use `makePerson()` as a constructor function (to "construct" an instance of an object). It will be called like so:

```
canadian=new makePerson(22,68,"Canada");
```

Basically, we're saying the variable `canadian` will contain a new instance of the object created in the `makePerson` constructor function, and then we send a few parameters to initialize property values. The reason for `this` in the constructor function is that we don't just want age set to `22` but rather `canadian`'s `age` will be set to `22`. We can keep calling the constructor function to make as many instances of the "makePerson" object that we want. For example:

```
mexican=new makePerson(33,70,"Mexico");
```

We've simply made a constructor function that serves to create multiple instances of an object. All we had to do was define the properties each instance would have automatically (`age`, `height`, and `citizenship`). In the end, you'll have two variables containing objects (`canadian` and `mexican`). Both have a set of three properties each. For instance, `canadian.age` is `22` and `mexican.age` is `33`. Placing all this code in the first keyframe will produce a structure of data visible through the Debugger as in Figure 12.1. Sometimes this might be the only way to see that they are working.

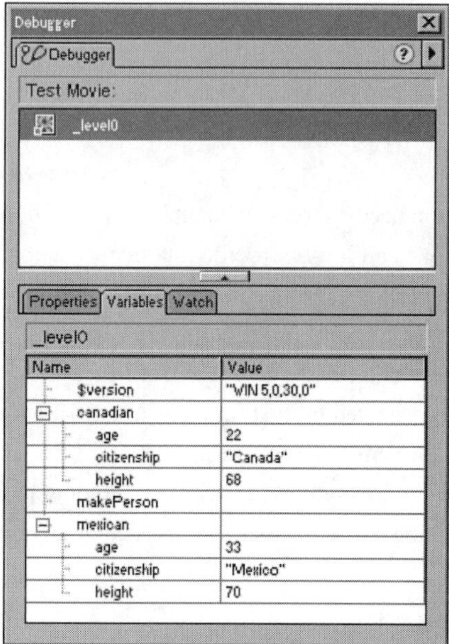

Figure 12.1 *Often the only way to see whether your objects are working is to use the Debugger.*

Making Methods

Now that you know how to create a constructor function, we can move on to creating methods. First, we'll make a method that's hard-wired for just one instance of our `makePerson` object, and then we'll improve on it.

You can add properties to a single instance with the form:

```
instanceVariable.newProperty=newValue;
```

For example, `canadian.favoriteBeer="Lager"` will create a `favoriteBeer` property and set its value to `"Lager"`. This isn't terribly exciting (or anything new, if you recall creating variables that acted like properties of clip instances). What's really wild is that assigning a property the value of a function creates a method. For example, consider this code:

```
function incrementAge(){
  this.age+=1;
}
canadian.haveBirthday=incrementAge;
```

Because incrementAge is really a function, the instance canadian now has a method called haveBirthday(). So, every time the script canadian.haveBirthday() is executed, the age property for the instance canadian is incremented.

Although this is pretty cool, it has the definite drawback of being hard-wired just to the canadian instance. Most likely, when you spend the time to develop a method, you'll want to be able to apply it to every instance of a particular type of object. After all, you're allowed to apply the nextFrame() method to any instance of a movie clip—so why not be able to apply the haveBirthday() method to every instance of the makePerson object? The way we just did it *will not* allow you to use mexican.haveBirthday(). We only specified this method for the one instance (canadian).

To create a method that will apply to every instance of a particular object, you use a special property, called prototype, that's built into every object. The prototype property is an object, so it has several properties of its own. You can individually specify as many properties of the prototype object (so as to create methods) by placing a function name into each one. The methods in the prototype object will apply to every instance spawned from the original constructor function. So, in the preceding script, instead of the line

```
canadian.haveBirthday=incrementAge
```

use this instead:

```
makePerson.prototype.birthday=incrementAge;
```

Translated, this says that the makePerson object's prototype now includes a property called birthday, which is assigned the value incrementAge. (Because incrementAge is really a function, this means we've made birthday() a method.) And because it's the special prototype property that we just added a property to, all instances created from makePerson will now have access to this method. Therefore, you can do both canadian.birthday() and mexican.birthday(). The result is that we've made a method for our makePerson object!

Remember that because the prototype property's data type is an object, it can contain multiple properties of its own. We've only added one property (a method really) to the makePerson's prototype property: "birthday." We can add more properties or methods.

```
function growAnInch(){
  this.height+=1;
}
makePerson.prototype.grow=growAnInch;
```

Notice this last line doesn't wipe away the "birthday" method already contained in `makePerson`'s prototype, rather we just added a new method (`grow()`).

So far, we've only talked about adding methods to your objects. However, if you want to add a property (not a method), you have to first decide whether this new property should be the same for each instance or whether it should be maintained individually for each instance. For example, if you decide that your `makePeople` object should include an additional property called `weight`, obviously each instance should have its own value for `weight` (that is, the `mexican` can weigh a different amount than the `canadian`). However, if you want to add a property such as `species`, it makes sense that this is the same for each instance. A property that's the same for each instance is more accurately called a *constant* (and as such could be written in all capital letters, such as `SPECIES`). Let me explain three different ways you can add properties.

To create a new property for just one instance of an object, use the familiar form: *`instance.newProp=value`*. If you want to create a new property that will be maintained individually for every instance created, you must go back to the original constructor function and add a line such as `this.weight=weightParam`. Finally, if you want to add a property that serves as a constant because it is the same for every instance, you need to add it to the `prototype` property:

```
makePerson.prototype.SPECIES="homo sapiens";
```

You might think that you could just hard-wire this `SPECIES` property inside the constructor function (that is, don't set `this.SPECIES` to a value passed as a parameter, but just hard-wire `"homo sapiens"`). Although this would serve to initialize the `SPECIES` property to the same value for each instance, it would still mean every instance could maintain a unique value for `SPECIES`. What's cool about adding the property to the `prototype` property is that later, with one swoop, you could change the value of the `SPECIES` property for all instances ever created (including those yet to be created). Simply execute the follow code:

```
makePerson.prototype.SPECIES="alien";
```

The previous analogies simply included physical human characteristics to—hopefully—make some concepts about objects clearer. The problem, however, is that it's nearly impossible to extrapolate this "makePerson" theme into a practical Flash application. Any time you work with objects (unless they are movie clip instances), it can be difficult because while you work, it's still kind of ephemeral. Ultimately, after you build an object, you can use it in conjunction with visual elements that appear onscreen. My suggestion is that you get very familiar with the Debugger (so that you can watch your variables as they change) and use `trace()` to test what you build every step along the way. For example, I typed the following block of code into the first frame of my movie, and then I opened the Debugger to watch my variables. Finally, I had some buttons (shown in Figure 12.2) to display expressions in the output window. This way I could be sure that all the code I produced was working.

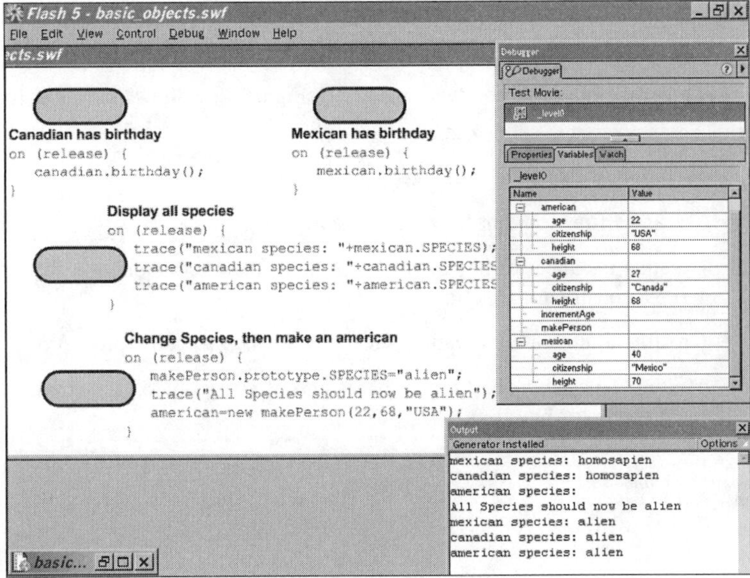

Figure 12.2 *Combining the Debugger and the* `trace()` *function along with rough buttons enables you to see how your objects are working.*

```
function makePerson (age, height, citizenship) {
  this.age = age;
  this.height = height;
  this.citizenship = citizenship;
}
canadian=new makePerson(22,68,"Canada");
mexican=new makePerson(33,70,"Mexico");
makePerson.prototype.birthday=incrementAge;
function incrementAge(){
  this.age+=1;
}
makePerson.prototype.SPECIES="homo sapiens";
```

As a review up to this point, the first five lines are the constructor function we first learned how to create. Lines 2-4 set properties that can be unique to each instance in the form `this.property=value`—where value can be passed as a parameter. Actually, the contents of the function itself aren't really important (it's just a regular function). The function becomes a constructor function only when we invoke it like one. We create an instance by saying `myInstance=new functionName()`, as in lines 6 and 7. Finally, we tapped into the object's `prototype` property. As an object itself, the `prototype` property allows us to assign values to as many named subproperties as we want. To create a method, we simply assign one of the prototype's properties the value of a function, as in line 8. Any other data type, as in line 12, will act like a global property (the value of which will be the same for every instance). Figure 12.3 shows the form for the various maneuvers we've looked at:

- Writing a constructor function
- Writing a function that becomes a method
- Creating instances of objects by invoking a constructor function the how to write a constructor function
- Creating a method by creating a property of the prototype property
- Making a global property (one that is part of every object) instantiated with the constructor function

constructor function:

```
function obj(param){
  this.prop=param;
}
```

function that will become a method:

```
function doIt(){
}
```

creating instances (by invoking "new" constructor):

```
inst1=new obj("x");          //inst1.prop == "x"
inst2=new obj("y");          //inst2.prop == "y"
```

making a method
(by putting a function inside a
property of the object's prototype property)

```
obj.prototype.myMethod=doIt;  //prototype.myMethod == a function
```

making a global property
(by putting any data type--except function--inside a
property of the object's prototype property)

```
obj.prototype.CONST="value";  //prototype.CONST == a string
```

Figure 12.3 *The syntax for the various maneuvers related to objects is shown.*

Inheritance

The `prototype` property can do more than simply maintain methods and global properties. You're about to see how you can write a generic method for one object, and then recycle that same method in another object. This is similar to the way you can write one generic function that you call from several places in your movie. It's different because you actually make one object inherit all the properties and methods of another. Consider how a child can inherit a base of attributes from his parent, but then goes on to develop his own. Similarly, we can write a generic object (with a set of methods) which then allows other objects to inherit (and thus recycle) the entire set of methods.

In the example that follows, you'll first create a "bank account" object that maintains a balance and interest rate for each instance. You'll write a method that compounds the interest on the current balance. Then, you'll make another object: a "certificate of deposit." Instead of writing a unique method to compound interest on the certificate of deposit object, you can just use the same method from the bank account object. The bank account object is the generic model. The certificate of deposit object inherits all the attributes (that is, the properties and methods) of the bank account object. See Figure 12.4.

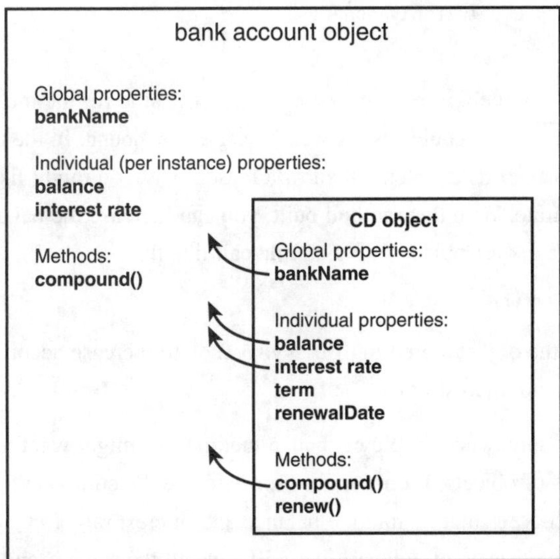

Figure 12.4 *The CD object will have all the same properties and methods of the bank account object plus a few of its own.*

In this way, the certificate of deposit object is everything the bank account object is and more. It might make your head spin to consider that you can have a deep hierarchy of objects that inherit attributes of others which, in turn, had inherited attributes from other objects. Although it's easy enough to explain how to do it, applying this knowledge is another matter entirely.

The way you build an object that inherits the methods of a parent object is actually quite simple. Consider this simple bank account constructor function that you might put in the first keyframe of a movie:

```
function bankAct(startingBalance,interestRate){
  this.balance=startingBalance;
  this.rate=interestRate;
}
```

To make an instance of this object (say, that you store in a variable called `primarySavings`), just use:

```
primarySavings=bankAct(5000,.04);
```

To create the `compound()` method for this object, use these two statements:

```
function multiplyAndAdd(){
  this.balance+=(this.balance*this.rate);
}
bankAct.prototype.compound=multiplyAndAdd;
```

In this case, there's no compelling reason to use a different name for the method and function; `multiplyAndAdd` could just as well be called `compound`. In the practical example at the end of this chapter, I'll show a reason why you might like to keep these names separate. With this method built, you can increase the balance in any instance of the `bankAct` object with a simple call like this:

```
primarySavings.compound();
```

This script will cause the object stored in `primarySavings` to increase according to its current `balance` and interest `rate`.

Now that we have this somewhat simple `compound` method, we might want to use it again for other types of objects. It only makes sense to use the compound method on other object types that maintain a balance and interest rate. Let's make a new object (a certificate of deposit) that will have all the same properties and methods of a `bankAct` object, but additionally, will have its own set of unique properties and methods. All certificates of deposit are bank accounts, but not all bank accounts are necessarily certificates of deposit. So, here's the constructor function for a CD object (short for *certificate of deposit*):

```
function CD(startingBalance,interestRate,lengthOfTermInDays){
  this.balance=startingBalance;
  this.rate=interestRate;
  this.term=lengthOfTermInDays
  var now=new Date();
  this.renewalDate=new Date();
  this.renewalDate.setDate(now.getDate()+this.term);
  this.longDate=this.renewalDate.toString();
}
```

In addition to initializing the properties `balance`, `rate`, and `term` (based on the parameters received), this function performs some Date object operations to set two other properties (`renewalDate` and `longDate`). In the fifth line a local variable (`now`) is assigned to the current time. The sixth line simply initializes `renewalDate` as a date object type (that is, its data type is object). Next `renewalDate` is reset by way of the `setDate()` method (pushing it out `term` days from now). Finally, in the last line, a string version of the `renewalDate` property is created, really just for readability because we'll never use this property within a calculation such as in the following method.

```
function extendDate(){
  this.renewalDate.setDate(this.renewalDate.getDate()+this.term);
  this.longDate=this.renewalDate.toString();
}
CD.prototype.renew=extendDate;
```

Notice that we don't ever *use* `longDate`, we just reassign it after adding `term` to the current `renewalDate`. The last line (outside the function) is the way we make `extendDate()` become a method (called `renew()`) of the `CD` object.

So far, we've built two objects (`bankAct` and `CD`) and a method for each. At this point, we could duplicate the code for `bankAct`'s `compound()` method and make an identical method for `CD`—however, I hate to repeat code I don't have to. We can specify that the `CD` object should inherit all the properties and methods built into the `bankAct` object. Notice that both objects have properties for `balance` and `rate`. Any time you inherit, all properties and methods are inherited. The fact that both `CD` and `bankAct` objects have some of the same property names doesn't really matter. When `CD` inherits from `bankAct` it simply supplements what it already has. If the same named properties exist (like in the case of `balance` and `rate`) they are not overwritten. Besides, both those properties need to be assigned uniquely when a new CD is instantiated. However, bankAct's compound() method is really worth inheriting as CD doesn't have that method but could easily use it. All this talk and it's so easy to do. To specify that the CD object will inherit all properties and methods of the bankAct object, use this code:

```
CD.prototype=new bankAct();
```

That's it. Translated, this simply says CDs are a subset of bankActs and shall inherit all properties and methods of bankActs. From this point forward, you can create as many CD objects as you want, and if you ever need to compound() the balance, you can do so, as the following sequence shows:

```
rainyDay=new CD(2000,.8,180);
rainyDay.compound();
```

The first line creates an instance of the CD and places it in the rainyDay variable. The second line invokes the compound method that was naturally inherited from the bankAct object (with the line CD.prototype=new bankAct();).

It's worth mentioning that there's another way to specify how one object will inherit everything from a "parent" object. Recall that any object has a prototype property that maintains all the different methods for that object. For example, CD's prototype has a property called renew (that occurred with the line CD.prototype.renew=extendDate;). Well, it just so happens that there is a property built-in to every object's prototype property! It's called __proto__ (notice the double underscores). I think it's easiest to think of this as similar to the relative reference _parent in that it identifies the object from which attributes were inherited. Specifically, instead of saying "CD should inherit everything from bankAct," we could have said that "CD's property called protoype has a property called __proto__, which is assigned the value of bankAct's plain prototype property." This tells Flash that all the methods in bankAct's prototype property shall be inherited through CD's prototype's __proto__ property. Both objects still have their own prototype properties filled with unique methods, but the special __proto__ property of CD's prototype shall point to bankAct's entire prototype property. So, the other way to specify that CD should inherit everything from bankAct looks like this:

```
CD.prototype.__proto__=bankAct.prototype;
```

(That's the same as saying CD.prototype=new bankAct().)Why am I even bringing this up if the first technique works? Well, you can use whichever technique you prefer to assign inheritance. Personally, I think the longer technique is clearer, despite being more complicated because you need to consider levels of hierarchy in the inheritance tree. It's often necessary to analyze an instance of an object after it's been created to determine its ancestry. If you look at the earlier variable called `rainyDay`, the only way to determine whether it's a `CD` object is to look at its `prototype` property. The only way to determine whether it's a `bankAct` descendant is to look at its `prototype`'s `__proto__` property. We'll use this technique to determine "who's your daddy," if you will, in the extended example of the next section.

Practical Example of Homemade Objects

For a practical example, let's consider a database full of products for sale through a music and video store. The start of a rough layout is shown in Figure 12.5.

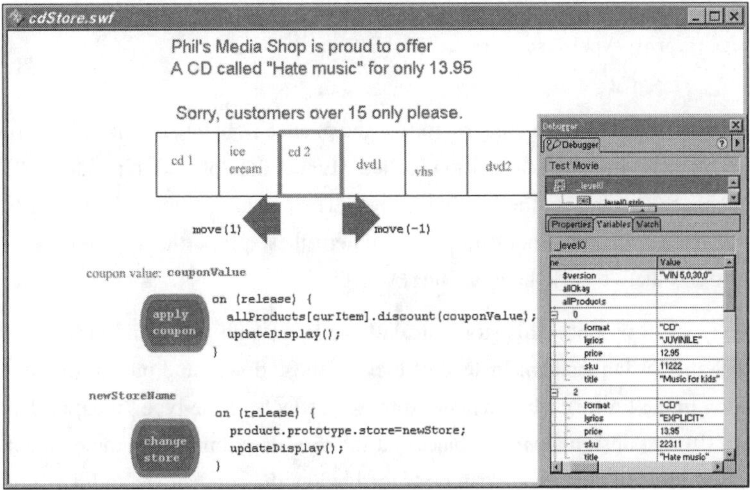

Figure 12.5 *This rough draft of our next exercise will explore every aspect of homemade objects discussed in this chapter.*

The basic features we're going to build include a way to first store the database of products in one big list and then to use the arrow keys to browse one item at a time. The selected product will have details such as its price and title provided in the text above. In addition, a button will allow a person to reduce the price by an amount indicated on a coupon. Finally, to demonstrate a global property, we'll be able to change the store name at any time. Obviously, this isn't the finished product, but should offer a great way to see how to apply objects. By the way, almost all the scripts are simply placed in the first keyframe. In addition, there are just a few buttons (such as the "next" and "previous" buttons) that call various functions such as `move()`. These are all shown within `mouseEvents` (such as `on (release)`).

First, we will design the objects. The most generic object will be called a "product." "Product" will contain both a `price` and a `sku`. In addition, we'll build a method that allows for a discount to be applied to the price. Here's the code to do what I've specified so far can be placed in the movie's first keyframe:

```
function product(price,sku){
  this.price=price;
  this.sku=sku
}
function coupon(faceValue){
  this.price-=faceValue;
}
product.prototype.discount=coupon;
```

The first function is the constructor for the `product` object and the second function (`coupon`) turns into a method (called `discount()`) placed in `product`'s `prototype` property in the last line shown. The `product` object is the most basic form from which all other objects will inherit these properties and methods (at this point there's only the `discount()` method).

The types of products this store currently sells are audio CDs and videos (in the VHS and DVD formats). Instead of locking those down (and preventing diversification in the future), I'll consider all these products of the type "media." To that end, I'll first design a `media` object that inherits everything from the `product` object. The following code can be placed below the code above and it will make the `media` object as a descendant to the `product` object:

```
function media(){
}
media.prototype=new product();
```

Notice the `media` constructor doesn't do much. For instance you might expect it to at least set a property or two. In the future I can make plain `media` objects that maintain their own properties but I have no plans for that now. Later, I could also create a method for the `media` object and all descendants would inherit that too (I'm not going to for this example). For now, I just want to ensure that all `media` objects (and their descendants) inherit everything from the `product` object.

Now I can make a separate object for audio CDs (`CD`) and one for videos (`video`) that both inherit everything from the "`media`" object type. Each will be a subset of the `media` object (and therefore the `product` object), so they'll have the `price` and `sku` properties to maintain right off the start. In addition, each object will have its own unique set of properties and methods. Let's just make the objects first:

```
function CD(title,lyrics,price,sku){
  this.title=title;
  this.lyrics=lyrics;
  this.price=price;
  this.sku=sku;
}
CD.prototype=new media();
```

The last line above establishes that `CD`s inherit everything from the `media` object.

```
function video(format,title,rating,price,sku){
  this.format=format;
  this.title=title;
  this.rating=rating;
  this.price=price;
  this.sku=sku;
}
video.prototype=new media();
```

Now that we have the constructor functions for video and CD objects and we've established that they inherit everything from media objects, we could create as many CD or video instances that we want. First I would like to write a method that works with either videos or CDs to determine whether the content is approved for children. If a video's rating property is not "R" and not "X," the `okayForKids` method (that we're about to build) will return true. Similarly, if a CD's lyrics property is not "EXPLICIT," the `okayForKids` method will return true. Initially, you might consider writing the `okayForKids` method for the `media` object. This makes sense when you consider that you want the same method to be able to be used with either object type. However, the decision as to whether it's "okay for kids" is based on a different property in each object. Instead, let's write two versions of the method. The following start has some problems that we'll address in a minute:

```
function okayForKids(){
  if (this.lyrics<>"EXPLICIT"){
    return 1;
  }else{
```

```
    return 0;
  }
}
CD.prototype.okayForKids=okayForKids;
function okayForKids(){
  if (this.rating<>"X" && this.rating<>"R"){
    return 1;
  }else{
    return 0;
  }
}
video.prototype.okayForKids=okayForKids;
```

The reason this solution won't work is that both the function declarations have the same name. Although it's desirable that both the *methods* are given the same name (so that we can invoke it the same way—`someCD.okayForKids()` or `someVideo.okayForKids()`)—we can't have two *functions* with the same name. Consider this modified (and usable) solution:

```
function notExplicit(){
  if (this.lyrics<>"EXPLICIT"){
    return 1;
  }else{
    return 0;
  }
}
CD.prototype.okayForKids=notExplicit;
function notX_notR(){
  if (this.rating<>"X" && this.rating<>"R"){
    return 1;
  }else{
    return 0;
  }
}
video.prototype.okayForKids= notX_notR;
```

Earlier in the chapter, I said the function that defines how a method will work can have the same name as the method, but it isn't always desirable. In this case, we made both of them different so that there would be no overlap.

One tiny thing to add is a store name property that can be changed (for all product objects and their descendants) in one move. Although we already have a method for the product object (`discount()`), we can add a global property (one that is *not* unique for every object instance) with the following line:

```
product.prototype.store="Phil's Media Shop";
```

That simply specifies a `store` property (and its value) for all product objects (and all descendants).

Finally, we can start making object instances! You can refer to the original constructor functions for both CDs and videos to make sure that the parameters passed make sense. Here are a few objects:

```
cd1=new CD("Music for kids","JUVINILE",12.95,11222);
cd2=new CD("Hate music","EXPLICIT",13.95,22311);
cd3=new CD("Musicals","MUSICAL",8.95,42311);
dvd1=new video("DVD","Explosion!","R",19.95,23122);
dvd2=new video("DVD","Colors","PG-13",19.95,2233);
vhs1=new video("VHS","Horses","G",9.95,2344);
```

Lastly, I want to store all my objects in an array so that I can step through them one at a time:

```
allProducts=[cd1,cd2,dvd1,vhs1,dvd2,cd3];
```

Now we can do a few exercises. Assume that we want to determine the price for the second product in `allProducts`:

```
allProducts[1].price;
```

Notice that we can grab the price property of an object by first referring to the array (full of objects).

If I want to discount the price of a product by `1.95`:

```
allProducts[1].discount(1.95);
```

The result is `cd2` now costs `12`.

Alright, you can see how easy it is to work with this storeful of objects. Let's build two arrow keys that simply step through each product and display data in a Dynamic Text field. Simply make one button containing `move(1)` (inside a mouse event, of course) and one with `move(-1)`. The `move()` function and the `updateDisplay()` function should be written as below in a keyframe of the main timeline:

```
function move (direction) {
  curItem -= direction;
  curItem=Math.min(allProducts.length-1, curItem);
  curItem=Math.max(0, curItem);
  updateDisplay();
}
function updateDisplay(){
  descript= allProducts[curItem].price;
}
```

Basically, the `move()` function increases or decreases the value for `curItem` in the second line. Also, by using `Math.min()`, `curItem` is assured to stay below the highest index in `allProducts`, and by using `Math.max()`, `curItem` is assured to stay at `0` or above. Then, the last line of the `move()` function calls the `updateDisplay()` function, which sets the variable `descript` to the `price` of `curItem`. The reason I didn't simply put the code from the `updateDisplay()` function inside the `move()` function is because I'd like to be able to invoke `updateDisplay()` from elsewhere as well. Finally, you'll need a Dynamic Text field associated with the variable `descript`. (Be sure to make this field a tall box with multiline and word wrap selected as in Figure 12.6, because we will be adding more information later.)

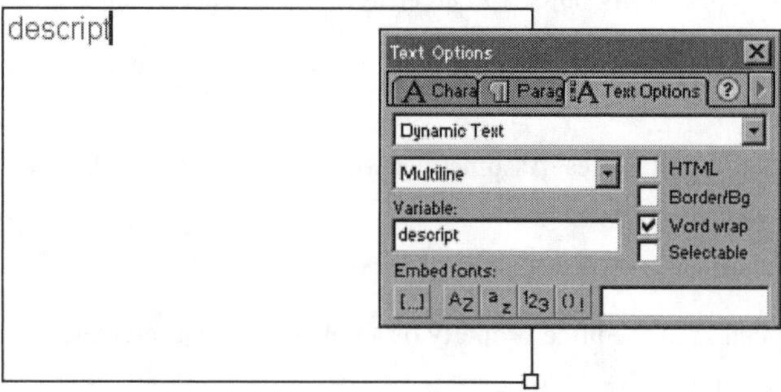

Figure 12.6 *Because the string we're going to display has lots of information, make sure to specify multiline and word wrap to accommodate it.*

Notice that the only data being displayed is the price. I'd like to display much more (such as its title, its type of media, and whether it's suitable for children). Check out the replacement version of the `updateDisplay()` function:

```
function updateDisplay(){
  var theObj= allProducts[curItem]
  descript= theObj.store + " is proud to offer \r";
  descript=descript + "A " + theObj.format;
  descript=descript + " called " + theObj.title;
  descript=descript + " for only " + theObj.price;
}
```

This `updateDisplay()` function needs to be called every time there's a change (that is, when the `move()` function is called) but in addition you should call this function right after you populate the array; the last line of the code in the first keyframe, after allProducts is initialized, should include a call to updateDisplay(). But it should work. Now that the structure has been built (and it's sound), we can start adding sophisticated features with ease. For example, if you want to add an additional warning when the product is not "okay for kids," it's rather simple to add the following if-statement at the end of the updateDisplay() function:

```
if (!theObj.okayForKids()){
  descript=descript+ "\r\r Sorry, customers over 15 only please."
}
```

Notice the exclamation point (logical not), which changes the meaning of the condition to if "not okay for kids."

You can keep adding features to this with little effort. To change the store name, just combine an Input Text field associated with a variable newStoreName with the following code in a button:

```
on (release) {
  product.prototype.store=newStoreName;
  updateDisplay();
}
```

Because store is a global property, this will change the value of store for every product object including descendants.

You can do the same thing to let users reduce the price of an item. Just make an Input Text field with the variable couponValue and make a button with this code:

```
on (release) {
  allProducts[curItem].discount(couponValue);
  updateDisplay();
}
```

Notice that both these buttons call the updateDisplay function.

Although this is pretty complete, I want to add one more variation for no other reason than to explore an application for the __proto__ property. Let's assume that our store wants to start selling food as well as media products. I'm going to simply make another object type equivalent to media and call it food. Later, I could make subobject types to food (the way CDs and videos were types of media), but I'm not going to go that far. This is all I did:

```
function food(name,price,sku){
  this.name=name;
  this.price=price;
  this.sku=sku;
}
food.prototype=new product();
```

Then, in the place where I instantiated all my objects, I simply created one more: `food1=new("Potato Chips",.55,12223)`. I also made sure to include it when I populated `allProducts`:

```
allProducts=[food1,cd1,cd2,dvd1,vhs1,dvd2,cd3];
```

Everything should still work, except that because the `updateDisplay` function includes the object's `title` and `format`, there's a problem in that `food` instances have only `name`, `price`, and `sku` properties. We can modify the `updateDisplay` to say (in pseudo-code), "If it's a media descendant, do what we were doing; otherwise, build a different string." The way to find out whether an object is a descendant of one object or another is to analyze its `__proto__` property. Based on our structure, the following statements are true:

```
cd1.__proto__==cd.prototype;
dvd1.__proto__==video.prototype;
cd1.__proto__.__proto__==media.prototype;
cd1.__proto__.__proto__.__proto__==product.prototype;
```

That is, the instance `cd1` has a `__proto__` equivalent, or direct parent, to the `cd.prototype`. Its parent's parent (`cd1.__proto__.__proto__`) is the `media.prototype`, and so on. We can also look at the ancestor of an object based on `food` (that is `food1.__proto__==food.prototype`). Finally, to apply this to the `updateDisplay` function, I chose to simply check whether it's a `media` object or a `food` object. It's a bit hard-wired, but the display that appears is naturally hard-wired because it's unique. Check out the revised version:

```
function updateDisplay(){
  var theObj= allProducts[curItem]
  descript= theObj.store + " is proud to offer \r";
  if (theObj.__proto__.__proto__==media.prototype){
    descript=descript + "A " + theObj.format;
    descript=descript + " called \"" + theObj.title;
    descript=descript + "\" for only " + theObj.price;
    if (!theObj.okayForKids()){
      descript=descript+ "\r\r Sorry, customers over 15 only please."
    }
  }
```

```
  if (theObj.__proto__==food.prototype){
    descript=descript + "A delicious " + theObj.name;
    descript=descript + " for only " + theObj.price;
  }
}
```

The coolest thing about objects is after they're built, you can add layers of features and significantly change your program without having things fall apart. The hard work is in designing the objects so that they make sense for your application. After they're built, they're easy to modify.

Summary

The truth is that you can live your whole life without once creating an object. You can also create simply amazing Flash sites without them, too. It's just that they're so darn convenient as a way to handle complex data. In the practical example we built, the code structure wouldn't need to be modified at all if you decided to add thousands of products. (Of course you'd have to instantiate those thousands of items and populate the `allProducts` array.) The visual representation of data stored in objects is a bit of work, but objects aren't supposed to create graphics for you. I see them as a ton of upfront work that pays back only when you can use them repeatedly.

As a quick review:

- You learned how to make custom objects.
- Create custom methods through the `prototype` property (which is an object in itself because it has multiple properties).
- Finally, when associating an object type's `prototype` with another object's new constructor function, you learned that all attributes were inherited.

{ Chapter 13 }

Smart Clips

Smart Clips are a sophisticated and convenient way to encapsulate code snippets in a form that can be shared and reused. A Movie Clip becomes a Smart Clip when you specify the parameters that you want the author to modify in each instance. Effectively, you're just extending the properties by which clip instances can vary from the built-in set of properties (such as `_alpha` and `_xscale`) to include anything you design.

Although you might have seen very advanced examples of Smart Clips (including those found in Flash's Common Libraries menu or that you've downloaded from the Macromedia Flash Exchange site), just because Smart Clips *can* be very advanced, they don't have to be. You can make a simple Smart Clip that serves to automate a small portion of just one project. The most important fact to realize is that everyone can make Smart Clips.

In this chapter, you will

- Learn all the steps involved to turn a Movie Clip into a Smart Clip
- Create adaptable parameters that the author can modify when using your Smart Clip
- Explore some practical uses for Smart Clips including improving productivity, assuring consistency, and centralizing code
- Build Custom User Interfaces that serve to replace the generic Clip Parameters panel with one you build in Flash

Before we begin this chapter, realize that Smart Clips are only used for authoring. After you build a Smart Clip, you can use it as many times as you want. You can even share it with others. It makes sense to do so because you might spend a lot of time making the Smart Clip really useful and adaptable to any situation. Because this means there are two authors, it makes sense to refer differently to the author who builds the original Smart Clip and the "using author" (that is, the person using a finished Smart Clip while building a Flash movie). After you build a Smart Clip, you could become the using author. In this chapter, I will refer to them differently—an author and a using author.

Standard Smart Clips

In Chapter 7, "The Movie Clip Object," you learned how to think of variables contained inside clip instances as homemade properties because you access and change them using the same syntax (`clip.property` or `clip.variable`). This concept will help when creating Smart Clips. The process involves specifying which clip variables (homemade properties) can be initialized through the Clip Parameters panel. Each Smart Clip instance can also have a unique starting value for any of these variables, just as each instance of a clip can have different starting values for any built-in property. Call them parameters, variables, or homemade properties—they're all the same, and with Smart Clips they're adjustable to the using author (see Figure 13.1).

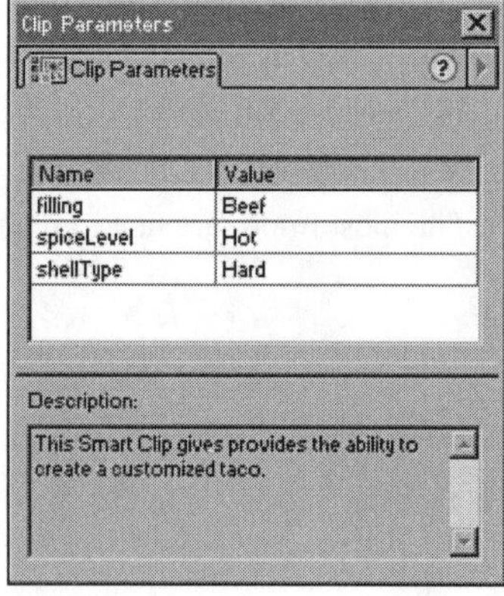

Figure 13.1 *The author can specify variables uniquely for every instance of a Smart Clip by using the Clip Parameters panel.*

The process of *using* a Smart Clip is simple: drag an instance onstage and set the initial values for the variables in the Clip Parameters panel. Then when the movie plays, it's as though each instance has a different `onClipEvent(load)` event to assign the values for each variable uniquely for each instance. What's the point? You could just write an `onClipEvent(load)` script for each instance, and you could avoid Smart Clips altogether. The problem, however, is that it's a lot more work and the process is less intuitive. (For example, you'd have to remember to include assignments for each variable.) Plus, a true Smart Clip lets you take advantage of the Clip Parameters panel and its description field (shown previously in Figure 13.1).

In addition to providing an error-resistant method for the using author to specify parameters, you can include the same base of code (through the master symbol in the Library) in Smart Clips. In this way, you can write one block of code that behaves differently depending on the values of the variables that have been initialized through the Clip Parameters panel. For example, the Smart Clip could contain Dynamic Text fields of a specific font and layout. If the values for the text field variables are specified in the Clip Parameters, each instance will display different text, but the font and layout will remain the same. Plus—just like any Movie Clip—if you make a change to the master in the Library (say that you change the font in the Dynamic Text field), you'll see that change in every instance. In this way, a Smart Clip can serve to establish consistent text styles. Another simple example is a clip with an animation of a ball bouncing. The ball will bounce as many times as the using author specifies for the `bounceCount` variable. They could have several instances of the same Smart Clip, but each would bounce a different number of times.

Let's first look at a couple basic Smart Clips and then we'll look at more advanced practical examples.

Making Smart Clips

Similar to a lot of programming, sometimes it's best to start by hard-wiring a prototype and then come back to clean up things, which makes the code more adaptable. Let's first go through some (non-Smart Clip) solutions to making individual clips behave differently.

Solutions That Don't Use Smart Clips

First, consider a Movie Clip with a 20-frame animation. In the last frame, place a script that reads

```
loopsRemaining--;
if (loopsRemaining) {
  gotoAndPlay (1);
} else {
  gotoAndStop (1);
}
```

(We'll keep this script for a few examples.) The first line of this decrements `loopsRemaining` by `1`. Assuming that the variable `loopsRemaining` is initialized with a value greater than `0`, this script will cause the clip to keep looping until `loopsRemaining` is reduced down to 0. Remember, if `loopsRemaining` is zero the condition is false, so it goes to the else part where `gotoAndStop(1)` executes. You can place two instances of this clip onstage and simply use the following script on each instance (not *in* the clip, but *on* the instance):

```
onClipEvent (load) {
  loopsRemaining=3;
}
```

Just change the value to which you're assigning `loopsRemaining` in each instance, and they'll repeat a different number of times.

So far, we don't have a Smart Clip and we can see it's slightly difficult to go through writing the `onClipEvent` script on each instance. Consider that you might not even need a Smart Clip but the preceding script is too difficult to trust all your using authors to execute—a Smart Clip would be more fool proof. Another (less than ideal) solution would be to first remove the entire `onClipEvent` (previous), name each instance (say `ball_1` and `ball_2`), and then from the first frame in the main movie, use a script such as this:

```
ball_1.loopsRemaining=3;
ball_2.loopsRemaining=5;
```

We still don't have a Smart Clip, and you can see this technique has its faults (namely, you have to name each instance and type the preceding script without error).

Finally, remove the script in the first frame so I can show you one other non-Smart Clip solution. Actually, this solution is not too bad although it's a lot of work. It also lets us explore a clip property that hasn't been mentioned previously (`_name`). In the first frame inside the master movie clip, we can write the following script:

```
loopsRemaining=_name;
```

Translated, this says "set loopsRemaining to the instance name of the clip I'm inside." To use this solution, you'll have to name the clips with names such as `"1"` or `"2"`. Plus, you'll have to change the script in the last frame to "go to" frame 2 (not 1). Otherwise, `loopsRemaining` will keep getting reassigned with the previous script. To get around the first problem, you could use a naming convention such as `"ball_1"` and use a String method such as `loopsRemaining=_name.subStr(5)` to extract just the portion of the name you need. Obviously, this is beginning to be a pain and has definite drawbacks like how we can't really use the first frame inside the clip and how we have to be careful what we name the instance.

Your First Smart Clip

Smart Clips offer the same basic features explored in all the preceding solutions—but we want the using author to specify the value for `loopsRemaining` in a very controlled and easy manner (that is, through the Clip Parameters panel). It's really quite simple to convert this clip into a Smart Clip. A Movie Clip becomes a Smart Clip when you Define Clip Parameters. If you first select our Movie Clip that uses the `loopsRemaining` variable and then choose Define Clip Parameters from the Library's Options menu, you'll be faced with the dialog shown in Figure 13.2.

From the Define Clip Parameters dialog, you can use the plus button to add variables that will be set-able by the using author. For this example, we'd simply press the plus button once and then double-click the `"varName"` that appears in the `Name` column and type **`loopsRemaining`**. Under the `Value` column, we'd double-click to replace `"defaultValue"` with `1` (meaning that if the using author never bothers to access the Clip Parameters panel, `1` will be used by default). Finally, leave the `Type` column in its default setting—meaning that the data type for this variable will be string or number. (We'll look at the other options in a minute.) That's all you need to do, but I want to mention a couple of other options in this dialog before we move on.

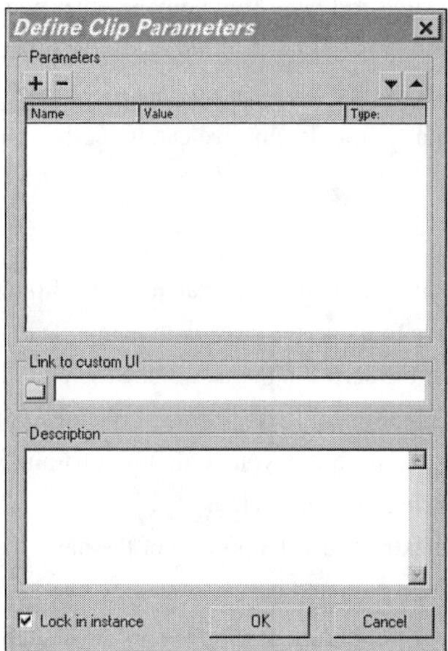

Figure 13.2 *The Library's Define Clip Parameters lets you specify which variables will be set-able in the Smart Clip.*

Normally, we want the using author to only change the values of variables, not variable names. The Lock in Instance option will prevent the using author from changing the name of the variables being edited through the Clip Parameters panel. Although I can't think of a practical reason for letting them change the name of a needed variable, unchecking Lock in Instance will also allow them to *add* variables through the Clip Parameters panel that provides an effective alternative to the `onClipEvent(load)` option I showed earlier.

Another option worth checking out is the Description field. Into this field you can write up a concise explanation of how to use the Smart Clip. It's a good idea to include information as to how to set each variable. For example, you could say something like "Use the `loopsRemaining` variable to specify the number of times you want the animation to loop."

Finally, we'll return to the Link to Custom UI feature later in this chapter when we use a Flash movie to replace the Clip Parameters panel.

By simply adding at least one variable through the Define Clip Parameters dialog, our Movie Clip turns into a Smart Clip evidenced by the new icon in the Library and the fact that the Clip Parameters panel is usable (see Figure 13.3).

If you drag three instances of this Smart Clip onstage, you can then set `loopsRemaining` for each one individually very quickly and easily through the Clips Parameters panel. (Be sure that your edits are accepted by clicking the stage after entering a value in to the Clip Parameters panel; otherwise if you test movie, the last saved value might be used instead.)

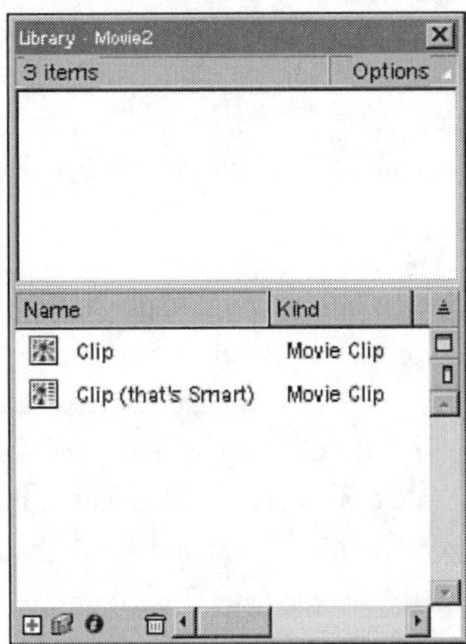

Figure 13.3 *When a Movie Clip turns into a Smart Clip, its icon changes in the Library (as shown in the second one listed).*

A Practical Example

Let's quickly build another simple Smart Clip as a quick review and so that you can see a more practical application: a template. Layout two Dynamic Text fields with placeholder text: one for a title and one for a subtitle. Make sure that the margins are wide enough to accommodate any likely content and pick a nice type face. Make sure that the title is associated with a variable `title` and the subtitle with a variable `subTitle` (Figure 13.4).

Select both blocks of text and convert them a Movie Clip symbol (F8). Confirm that the layout is satisfactory and use the Info panel to notate the x and y coordinates (making sure to use the center point indicated by a black box in the Info panel). Go inside the clip you just created and, in the first keyframe, use the following script to specify the initial location for the clip:

```
_x=150;
_y=229;
```

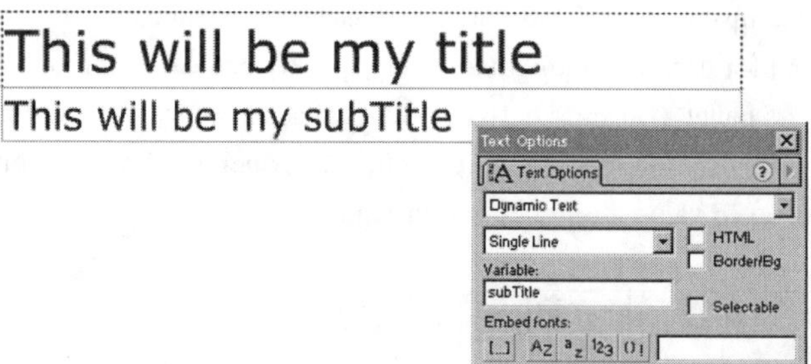

Figure 13.4 *The first Smart Clip we build will include Dynamic Text fields that we associate to variables.*

(But use whatever values you found through the Info panel.) Finally, we can make this a Smart Clip by Defining Clip Parameters. Just add `title` and `subTitle` to the name column for parameters. That's it! Anyone can now drag an instance onstage and define the content through the Clip Parameters panel, and the layout will be perfectly consistent. You can even make a global edit to the layout or font style by editing the master symbol. All the instances in use will retain their values for `title` and `subTitle`. (By the way, you'll need to test movie in order to see anything except your placeholder text in the two fields.)

Other Data Types

Before we move on to some advanced examples of Smart Clips, let's quickly explore the alternatives to the Default data type found when Defining Clip Parameters as shown in Figure 13.2, earlier in the chapter. The other data types are Array, List, and Object.

When you want the using author to populate the clip's variables with strings or numbers, just leave the option set to Default. However, as you know by now, other data types can come in handy. For example, you might want to let the using author set a single variable to an array. When you Define Clip Parameters, you simply specify that a particular variable shall be an Array. At that point, you can populate the array with default values by double-clicking on the field in the Value column. What's interesting about the Array type is that when the using author is populating the variable with values, he not only can change the default values you provided, but also he can add items to the array. None of the other data types (Default, Object, and List) let the using author add. A great example in which Array is a good choice is the Menu Smart Clip that ships with Flash (found under the menu Window, Common Libraries, Smart Clips). The using author is allowed to add as many items to the menu (which is to say, he's allowed to add items to the array).

When you want to give the using author a choice of several discrete options, select List. That is, Default lets him type anything he wants; Array not only lets him type anything, it lets him add items; but List only lets him select from a predefined list. For example, if you want to provide a choice of music genres but don't want the using author to type in just anything, you can instead offer a list of just Classical, Country, Rock, Jazz. In the Value column, you simply fill in what the options should be, and the using author can only select from a drop-down list. If you want something other than the first item—the zero spot—to be selected by default, provide an "offset" (see Figure 13.5).

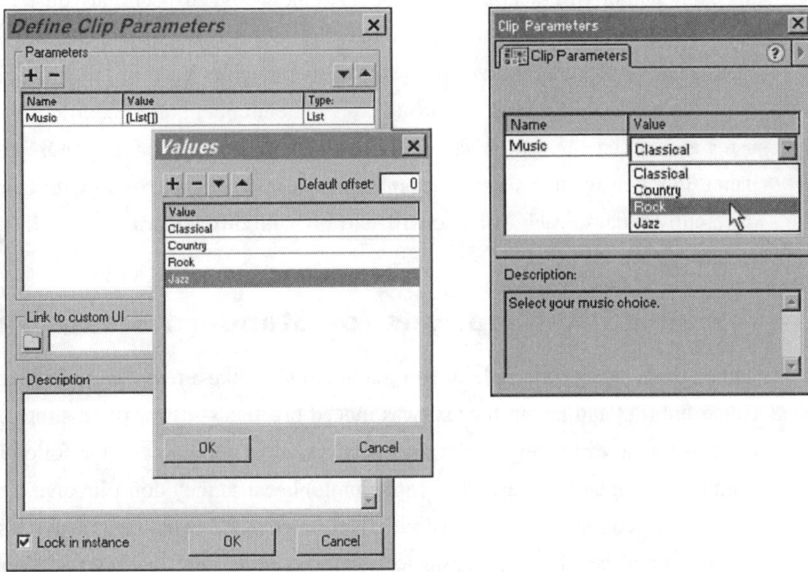

Figure 13.5 *Creating a "list" variable when defining Clip Parameters (left) gives the using author a limited choice (in the drop-down list on the right) when using the Clip Parameters panel.*

Finally, the Object type is convenient when you know that the variable used in your clip needs to be in the form of a generic object. Remember, generic objects are unique and hard-wired. We built generic objects to be passed as parameters in the `setTransform()` methods for the Sound and Color Objects in Chapter 11, "Objects," and they're the same as Associative Arrays (discussed in Chapter 10, "Arrays"). It's simply a data type that has multiple named properties (accessible either by `variableName["propertyName"]` or `variableName.propertyName`). Unlike the Array type, the Object type requires that you define the properties so that the using author simply defines the values for each property. In fact, you could just provide the using author several separate variables (all of the Default type), and then once inside the clip (say, in the first keyframe) write a script that builds an object by assigning properties based on the values provided. Selecting Object simply prevents the need to translate individual variables and instead creates a single variable with multiple properties (that is, an object).

As a quick review, we've seen that a Smart Clip is simply a Movie Clip for which the Define Clip Parameters option was used to specify clip variables that the using author will be able to manipulate. One would suspect that you'll be *using* those variables somehow inside the clip—such as within a Dynamic Text Field or in a script that utilizes the value of the variable. Each instance is unique in all the ways the different clip instances can be unique; but, in addition, the using author can change the value of all variables listed in the Clip Parameters panel. In this way, the using author makes each instance of a Smart Clip behave differently because each instance will start off with different values for all its variables.

Advanced Applications for Standard Smart Clips

Although the earlier example of using a Smart Clip like a template to impose a consistent font and layout for text was indeed practical—it was quite simple. Other practical examples aren't quite as simple. I'm going to call the following examples "standard" Smart Clips (not simple) because they don't involve the more advanced feature called custom UIs. A *custom UI* (which stands for User Interface) replaces the Clip Parameters dialog (and its rigid looking name and value columns) with a Flash movie that you have to build. It's the job of this other Flash movie (the UI) to set the necessary variables, but it can do so in a very graphic way. We'll make some in the next section, but I want to first show some advanced examples of the standard form. You don't need to try to follow along as we explore some of the possibilities.

In the Horizontal Slider workshop you'll build a slider that lets the user (not just the using author) interact by dragging it from 1 to 100 (as shown in Figure 13.6). After we build a somewhat hard-wired version, we turn it into a Smart Clip to allow the using author to specify four properties: the location of 1 (that's the minimum location for the slider), the location of 100, the initial location (so that the slider can default to a point other than 1), and the name for a function that the slider will continually call as the user slides the slider. Using a function makes it possible for the slider's value to be used to modify anything onstage—from another clip's alpha level to the overall sound level. This kind of function that a Smart Clip calls (back in the main movie) can be referred to as a *call back function*.

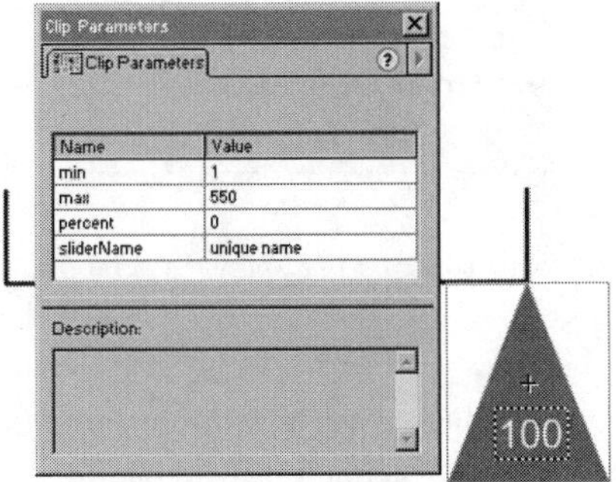

Figure 13.6 *In a workshop later, we'll turn a slider into a Smart Clip so that it can be reused.*

In the Tool Tip workshop, we build a Smart Clip where the using author can specify the exact string of text that should appear (when the cursor rolls over another object). The using author can drag as many instances of this Tool Tip Smart Clip as he wants.

Finally, here's an example of a Smart Clip I built for use in a real project. I used Flash in a presentation, but wanted another version (that the audience could download) that included speaker notes. The content for the notes would be loaded in from an external file (as you'll learn in Chapter 14, "Interfacing with External Data") because it wouldn't be written until later—plus I wanted to be able to modify it any time. Anyway, I made a Smart Clip not unlike the tool tip described previously, but instead of making the using author (me) specify *all* the text, I simply specified the section and subsection where it was being used. The loaded data included details as to which section and subsection it applied to, so my Smart Clip simply displayed (similar to a ToolTip) the data appropriate for that section. The result was that users can view the presentation and optionally click a Speaker Notes button to see additional information (see Figure 13.7).

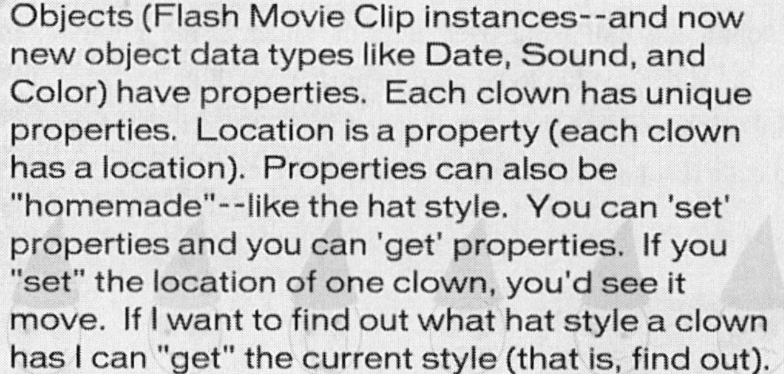

Figure 13.7 *In an actual project, I made a Smart Clip to display the appropriate speaker notes.*

Although these examples are not the only things possible with standard Smart Clips, I just wanted to make a point that you often don't *need* to build custom UIs.

Replacing the Clip Parameters Panel with Custom UIs

One of the most intriguing features of Smart Clips is the fact that you can assign an interactive Flash movie to play inside, and effectively replace, the Clip Parameters panel. The process involves first building a Flash movie, exporting it as a `.swf`, and finally pointing to the `.swf` through the Define Clip Parameters dialog. You'll have two files: an `.fla` file with the master Smart Clip in a Library and a `.swf` that plays inside the Clip Parameters panel. The `.swf` is called a custom UI and its filename is specified in the Link to Custom UI field shown in Figure 13.8.

By replacing the Clip Parameters panel, we have the opportunity to make something more usable. But most Smart Clips are perfectly suitable without a custom UI. So instead of leaping straight into building custom UIs, we'll first look at how to design them so that we're sure to use them appropriately. You'll see that custom UIs can be difficult to build—so it makes sense to make sure that they're necessary.

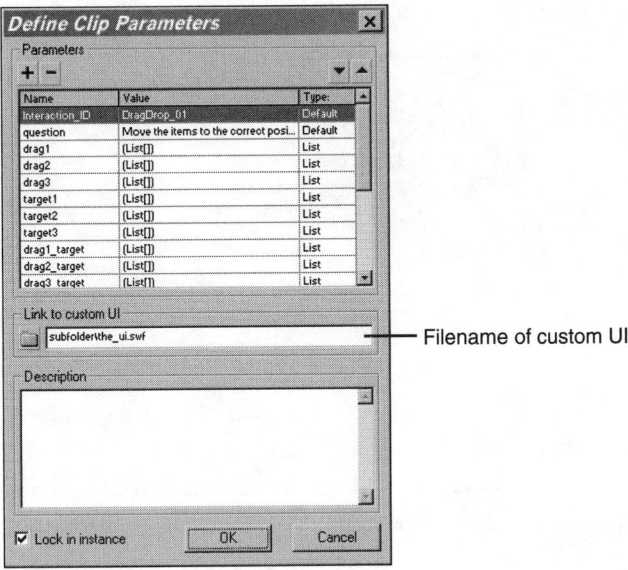

Figure 13.8 *The Link to Custom UI field points to an external file that will be used in place of the Clip Parameters.*

Designing Custom UIs

Naturally, the process of creating a custom UI is purely technical. To make a *good* custom UI is another matter. I think it's fair to say that the only time to create a custom UI is when the built-in Clip Parameters panel is inadequate. There are many situations in which this could occur. For example, making the using author set several variables through the standard Clip Parameters panel could be unreasonably tedious. In this case, an easier solution might be a graphic selection device such as a slider (see Figure 13.9). Or maybe you want to give the using author a taste of the selections he's making. If he's picking several colors, it might be nice to give him a preview so that he can visualize the results. Or, if he's selecting sounds, you could include a short audio sample. Finally, a perfect situation for a custom UI is when there is a series of complex selections the using author must make. For this case you could build a custom UI that served as a wizard—walking the using author through all the steps involved and even providing online help where appropriate. A good example of this approach can be found in the Smart Clips included with Flash's Learning Interactions (under Window, Common Libraries).

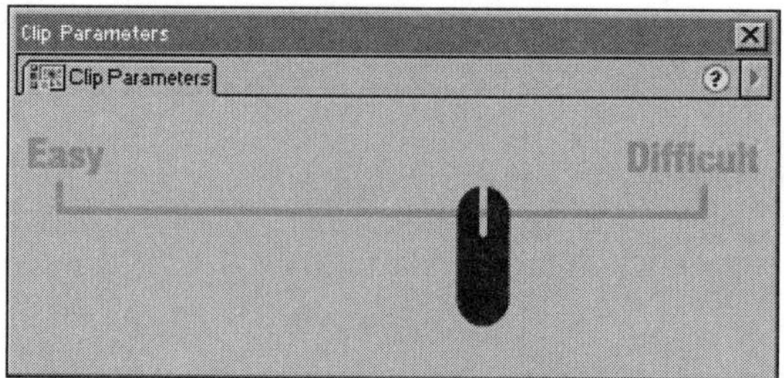

Figure 13.9 *A slider is just one graphic interface element possible to include in a custom UI.*

After you've determined that a custom UI is appropriate, you can take steps to design how it will function. The most important consideration is usability. Because the purpose of the custom UI is to provide some benefit not found in the standard Clip Parameters panel, you should make sure to make it easy for the using author. I suppose if you're building a Smart Clip for your own use, you can invest less time designing (at the expense of usability).

As it turns out, one of the most critical features that will make your custom UI more usable happens to be one of the most difficult to program. It's important for the custom UI to always indicate the current settings. For example, every button should include a highlight to indicate selected. This highlight should not only provide a clear indication at the time a selection is made, but also the using author should be able to return to the Clip Parameters and easily ascertain the current setting. After all, they might have several instances of the Smart Clip and want to check each one's settings. This round-trip feature (being able to leave and come back to a Smart Clip) is the difficult programming task. You'll see how to program it in the next section, but realize that it's also a matter of design how you choose to treat the graphic solution. Ultimately, making an intuitive custom UI takes more skill and creativity than simply programming it.

Building Custom UIs

Assuming that you've determined a custom UI is really necessary and you have a decent design, you can move on to really building it! First let's make a very simple one and then add some features. The concentration of this example is on making the custom UI, but we'll need a Smart Clip for whom the custom UI sets properties. You can use the simple bouncing ball Movie Clip used earlier. You'll want to create a file (maybe called `host.fla`), make sure it's saved, and then place this script in the last frame of the Movie Clip:

```
loopsRemaining--;
if (loopsRemaining) {
  gotoAndPlay (1);
} else {
  gotoAndStop (1);
}
```

The job of our custom UI will be to set the `loopsRemaining` variable. (Arguably, this Smart Clip doesn't really *need* a custom UI, but we're just doing it for practice.) Make sure that your Movie Clip is a Smart Clip by using Define Clip Parameters to specify that `loopsRemaining` is set-able by the using author. Finally, type **`myUI.swf`** in the Link to Custom UI field. You can also click the folder button and point to a file. However, besides the fact that we haven't made the UI yet, this feature always produces an explicit path where—for most situations—the relative path we typed in is more desirable. (By the way, in a workgroup situation, you could keep the custom UI in an explicit path on a server for everyone to share.)

Create a new file and save it as **`myUI.fla`** in the same folder as the host file. Finally, we can program it. Because we're basically replacing the standard Clip Parameters panel, we need to do what it was doing: setting variables. The only catch is that the variables that get exchanged with the host movie's Smart Clip need to reside in a movie clip that has an instance name of `xch`. You can have other variables in the UI file, but only the ones in the clip `xch` will become part of the Smart Clip in the main movie. This clip instance doesn't need anything graphic; it serves only to hold the variables that get used in the main movie. Although you can think of the `xch` clip as a surrogate of the actual Smart Clip, it doesn't need to have any correlation (in looks or function) to the Smart Clip—only that it contains the necessary variables.

We can make the fastest custom UI in history by creating an Input Text field associated with the variable `loopsRemaining` and then selecting the text block and converting to the Movie Clip symbol. Finally, just make the movie clip's instance name `xch` and export the movie as `myUI.swf` in the correct folder. Go back to the host movie and test it out by dragging two instances of the Smart Clip. Through the Clip Parameters panel you should see the Input Text field where you can specify a number of loops. Also, notice that you can keep the Clip Parameters panel open when you alternatively select the two Smart Clip instances onstage. Each should retain its `loopsRemaining` value. Pretty easy really.

Even if we try to spice it up with gratuitous effects (such as maybe text color), this custom UI is pretty simple. Let's change it so that we can encounter something more challenging. You can keep the `xch` clip—but change the text field to Dynamic Text (so that the user can't edit it). Make a button and create four instances in the main timeline lined up vertically. Place the following script in each button (changing the `1` to `2`, `3`, `4` for each button, respectively):

```
on (release) {
  pickLoop(1);
}
```

Now in the first keyframe of the main timeline, type this function:

```
function pickLoop(whatNum){
  _root.xch.loopsRemaining=whatNum
}
```

This achieves the task of changing `loopsRemaining` to whatever value is passed from the buttons that call `pickLoop()`. You can export the `.swf`, and it should work. However, when you test this from the host movie (the place where you should be testing this), there are two significant problems. Upon making a selection, the user is not given any graphic feedback as to which button was pressed. The other problem is when a user returns to view the current setting in a Smart Clip—he has no clue what the value is for `loopsRemaining`. We can produce a highlight on the currently selected button by creating another movie clip in the main timeline and calling the instance `arrow`. Then we just need a script in the `pickLoop` function to change the _y property of `arrow`. If the spacing is consistent, you could use a formula such as

```
arrow._y=46+75*(whatNum-1);
```

where 46 was the location for the top button and each button was 75 pixels apart. Or—in conjunction with an array full of discrete y locations—you could use an expression such as

```
var locs=[46,121,196,271];
arrow._y=locs[whatNum-1];
```

Each solution moves a clip instance (`arrow`) to point to the last button clicked—and the time to do this is inside the `pickLoop` function.

At this point, the custom UI should function as far as indicating a selection *after* you make it, but it still fails to appear with `arrow` in place upon returning to a previously edited Smart Clip instance. All we need to do is place the following script in an appropriate keyframe so that it executes every time a using author returns to edit the Clip Parameters:

```
pickLoop(_root.xch.loopsRemaining);
```

Basically, this script sends the current value of `loopsRemaining` (which is in the `xch` clip) to the `pickLoop` function. The problem with our custom UI is not that `loopsRemaining` is being lost (if you test it, you'll find that it is still there); but rather that the value of `loopsRemaining` is unknown when returning to the clip. However, if you place the preceding script in the first frame, it won't work! The issue is that Flash needs some time to send the variables from a Smart Clip instance to the Clip Parameters panel and then to your custom UI. The solution is to move everything in your custom UI out past frame 10 or so, and then invoke a function call (similar to the previous). One little catch is that the `xch` clip must be present in the first frame! The way I remember this rule is to imagine the Clip Parameters panel is attempting to set the variables that are part of the `xch` clip. Just like how any script can only set variables for clips that are currently present, the `xch` clip must be present at the very start so that the Clip Parameters panel can set the variables. I'm not sure if that's really the reason, but I simply place the `xch` clip in its own layer and make sure that it starts on frame 1. Actually, this is the best reason to consider *not* putting any graphics or buttons in the `xch` clip itself as you don't want the user interacting until everything is reinitialized.

The arrangement I'd recommend is as follows (and this will work for the previous exercise):

1. Place your dummy `xch` clip in frame 1 on its own layer.
2. In frame 1 of your `xch` clip's layer in the main timeline, place all the functions (such as the `pickLoop` function).
3. Make a new layer just for Actions, and in frame 10 make a keyframe that contains the reinitializing script (`pickLoop(_root.xch.loopsRemaining)`).
4. On frame 11, place a `stop()` script.
5. Place all your interactive elements (buttons for example) on frame 11.
6. Use the first 10 frames to display a "loading" message or an animation that serves to placate the using author who must wait for the reinitializing to occur.

Notice that you want to make sure that the user cannot interact while the custom UI is initializing, and that's why no buttons appear until frame 11. (Your loading message occurs before that.)

Although this example is admittedly simple, a more complex custom UI will have the same elements. You always need a clip named `xch` that holds the variables to be set in your Clip Parameters panel. And, unless your only means for the user to see his current settings is a text field, you'll need to initialize such highlights somewhere other than the first frame (I think frame 10 is a safe bet). After you understand these minimum features, you can move on to making more complex Smart Clips and custom UIs.

Keep in mind that the goal for any good Smart Clip (and custom UI, if needed) is to be something useful: for instance, a code snippet that can be used over and over. Although something that's particularly useful is worth investing time and effort to make it right, every Smart Clip is not necessarily hard to create. In practice, I've found that the majority of Smart Clips are built on a per-project basis. That is, you might need a special Smart Clip that's used throughout one Flash movie. As you saw early in this chapter, Smart Clips can be used as simple templates or style guides. A large number of the workshops later in this book involve creating Smart Clips because I want the code to be more usable. It turns out the Smart Clips we build won't have universal appeal: only that making it a Smart Clip means that the code is just a bit more adaptable.

If you do build a Smart Clip with a wide general appeal, you can share it with the Flash community. In Appendix B, "Making Flash Extensions for the Macromedia Exchange Web Site," you'll see how easy it is to turn a Smart Clip into a Flash Extension that can be downloaded from the Macromedia Exchange Web site (`http://www.macromedia.com/exchange/flash/`).

Summary

This chapter turned out to be more like a workshop and less like many of the earlier foundation chapters. That's because Smart Clips are more a feature of Flash than a language element of ActionScript. The only new concept was the "list" data type—which isn't really a data type but just another feature of the Define Clip Parameters dialog.

The concepts you learned in this chapter included how Smart Clips allow you to give the using author the ability to set initial values for any property, variable, or homemade property you specify. When you Define Clip Parameters, the Movie Clip magically turns into a Smart Clip. From that point forward, each instance onstage maintains its own values for the designated properties. The using author can change individual instance properties through the Clip Parameters panel (not to be confused with the Define Clip Parameters dialog in which you establish the properties that are set-able). Finally, if you go through the work to build a custom UI, you can use this Flash movie to effectively replace the Clip Parameters panel.

If you're left with any confusion as to the value of Smart Clips, don't worry. In the workshop portion of this book, you'll make plenty of them. It's not so much that you sit down and decide, "Today I'm going to make a Smart Clip." Rather, you can build some code and then say, "Hey, this would be way better as a Smart Clip because it would be adaptable for multiple instances."

{ Chapter 14 }

Interfacing with External Data

Flash is not an island. Data from outside sources can be included in a Flash movie. This means that even if the data changes after you upload your finished .swf file, your movie can reflect those changes, too. You can include timely information or make the movie appear customized to the individual user. The implications for such dynamic Flash sites are infinite.

In this chapter, we'll look at the main ways that Flash can interact with outside applications and data. I should note that there's a product, that isn't covered in this chapter, called Macromedia Generator that generates customized Flash `.swfs` on-the-fly—when visitors to your site request them. In this chapter, we will only look at ways to produce `.swfs` that adapt to outside data. There are extensive books and resources on how to use Generator, but I mention it here only so that I don't leave it out.

This chapter includes both detailed information and resources to get you started should you choose to develop your skills elsewhere. Specifically, in this chapter, you will

- Create external scripts that contain ActionScript code
- Load data from text files so that changes can be made without opening Flash
- Learn how to load data from or send data to server scripts (such as CGI or ASP)

- See how XML structured data can be incorporated in Flash
- Learn how JavaScript and Flash interact
- Get a foundation in using Flash movies inside Director or Authorware

External Scripts

In Flash 5, it's possible to store your scripts in external text files that are included when you export a `.swf`. Although all the *other* techniques covered in this chapter involve ways to import data while the movie plays, external scripts become locked inside the movie when you export. (It would be nice if changes to an external script could be reflected in a previously exported `.swf`, but it doesn't work that way.)

External scripts can still make you more efficient. If the same script is used in several places within one movie, and perhaps even used in several different movies, you can store that script in a single "external script" file. If at any time during production you find that you want to adjust or fix that script, you need to do it in only one place. Movies exported from that point forward would see the change—in every place where the script was used. Even though this feature is useful, I believe you can often be just as efficient by using more traditional techniques (things as simple as functions or Smart Clips). The only exception is when you want to use the same script throughout several movies without using *another* Flash feature called Shared Libraries.

Using external scripts is pretty easy—here's the process. In place of an actual script (that is, in a keyframe, button instance, or movie clip instance), refer to the filename where you plan to store the actual script. Macromedia suggests that you use a file extension of `.as`, but you can use `.txt` if you want—it's just a text file. (On my Windows machine, I've associated the `.as` file type with the Notepad text editor.) So, in the Actions panel, simply refer to the file after `#include`, as in

```
#include "somefile.as"
```

Notice that you don't put a semicolon at the end of this line! Also, you should realize that the content of this external script can be just a code segment (like the result of an event) or it can be the entire script (that is, including the event). So, attaching the following two scripts to two different buttons is totally legitimate.

One button:

```
on (press){
    #include "code_segment.as"
}
```

Another button:

```
#include "entire_script.as"
```

The only difference is that the file `code_segment.as` doesn't contain (and shouldn't contain) any event code—like `on (press)`. The file `entire_script.as` needs to contain the entire event because any scripts on buttons need to be surrounded by events. Actually, the contents of `entire_script.as` could include more than one mouse event, as so:

```
on (press){
    pressing=1;
}
on (release){
    pressing=0;
}
```

Just realize the entire contents of your external file will be placed in Flash exactly where you refer to them. Imagine the contents of the external script are pasted in place of the line starting `#include`.

There's not much more to say except to explain some practical concerns and potential applications. If you use Notepad to create your scripts, realize that you won't get all the enhancements (such as syntax coloring and error checking) that you do in Flash. There are some third-party and shareware text editors that can be customized to do syntax coloring, and because ActionScript is nearly identical to JavaScript, you can use any editor configured to edit JavaScript. It's still probably going to be easier in Flash. You might consider writing the script in Flash first, and then when you identify that using an external script would be more appropriate, just cut the script from Flash, in its place put the `#include` statement, and then paste the code into a text file. That way you not only know that the syntax is correct, but that the code works inside Flash.

Before we move on to the *really* dynamic features, let me just suggest a couple uses for external scripts. You might be building a site that jumps to different URLs (instead of using a more seamless approach involving `loadMovie()`) because you want the user to be able to use the browser's Back button. If you have a script that's either complicated or likely to need updating, you can put that script in an external script file. If you need to make a fix, the only drag is that you'll need to re-export all the `.swfs` in your site. But at least you won't need to make the *same* fix in each source `.fla`. Another thing external scripts are good for is building a code library. The truth is that storing scripts inside Flash, where you can copy and paste them into new movies, is almost the same thing. Except with external scripts, if you ever find an error in a script you use often, you need only re-export all the movies linked to that script.

I'm sure there are other ways to use the external script feature. In any case, I doubt they'll match the potential power of the other techniques shown in the rest of this chapter.

External Data Files

You just saw how you can store text files containing ActionScript in external files. But changes made to the external file after you export the `.swf` won't be reflected because they've already been included. The next technique you'll learn is how to store data in external files that aren't loaded until you request them at runtime. Specifically, your script can invoke Flash's `loadVariables()` method at any time to load variables from an external text file (or another data source, as you'll see in the "Server Scripts" section later in this chapter). By loading variables from a file at runtime, a Flash movie reflects the current values found in the file.

There are several ways to use the `loadVariables` statement. As a function (not as a method attached to a clip instance), you can use either of these two forms:

```
loadVariables(whatFile,targetClip,optionalMethod);
```

or

```
loadVariablesNum(whatFile,levelNumber,optionalMethod);
```

The difference between these two forms is simply that the first loads the variables into a named clip instance and the second loads the variables into a level number. Just replace "whatFile" with the name of the file containing the variables or a relative path to that file. Realize the file is really a URL when the movie's playing on a Web server. As such, relative paths use forward slashes (`/`). Also, although you're allowed to use explicit paths, you're restricted to using paths to files in the same domain where the Flash movie resides (apparently for security reasons). Anyway, it's easiest just to keep the data files in the same directory and simply refer to the filename (which is a relative path). "targetClip" is replaced with the clip instance name to where the variables will load. When using `loadVariablesNum`, you simply specify an integer in place of "levelNumber." After the variables load, they will either be part of a clip or a level number. To load variables into the main timeline, use either `_root` or `0`. Finally, we'll look at "optionalMethod" in the next section. Consider this example:

```
loadVaraibles("data.txt",_root);
```

This will load the data in a file called `"data.txt"` (which is adjacent to the Flash movie) and place all those variables in the root.

Just to show you some variation, the `loadVariables` function (shown earlier) can act like a Movie Clip method and I think it's slightly easier to read:

```
clipInstance.loadVariables(theFile);
```

To load variables from a file named "data.txt" into a clip named "myClip," use

```
myClip.loadVariables("data.txt");
```

To load this same file into a keyframe in the main timeline, use

```
_root.loadVariables("data.txt");
```

This last example has the same effect as `loadVariables("data.txt",_root)`. And, just so you know, `loadVariablesNum` doesn't work as a method.

We'll get to the format of this external file in just a minute, but there's a serious consideration when using any of the previous techniques: You must wait for the variables to fully load. Loading variables takes some time to complete because the data is actually traveling from your Web server into the Flash movie on the user's machine. The point is that if you start loading variables on, say, the first frame of the movie, you need a way to know when you can start *using* those variables because otherwise you'll get erroneous results.

Waiting for Variables to Load

There are two basic approaches to checking whether variables have fully loaded. When loading into the `_root` timeline, you need to keep checking whether the last variable in the data file has loaded. When loading into a clip instance, you can take advantage of the data clip event. Although you'll see that loading into the `_root` timeline is not as convenient when it comes to waiting for variables to load, it has the distinct advantage that when referring to variables in the main timeline, it's easy to proceed with `_root` or nothing if your script is *in* the main timeline. Variables in clips must include a target path, which can become cumbersome. Let's first look at waiting for variables to load into the main timeline, and then how to check that they've loaded into clips.

Loading Variables into the Main Timeline

Although I haven't explained the exact format of the external data file, it basically has a series of variable assignments (such as age=35, name=phillip). The variables and their values are loaded in order. So, if you put an assignment at the very end (such as `done=1`), you can be sure that all variables have been loaded when the variable `done` turns to `1`. So, in the first frame of a movie, use this script:

```
done=0;
loadVaraibles("data.txt",_root);
```

Then in frame 2 (in addition to putting a "loading" message onscreen), place this script:

```
if (done==1){
    gotoAndPlay(4);
}
```

This means if `done` is *not* yet `1`, it will just proceed to frame 3, where you can place this script:

```
gotoAndPlay(2);
```

It will go back to where it checks whether `done` is `1` yet. Get it? You first start loading all the variables, and then you keep checking whether the last assignment (that you purposely placed last—`done=1`) has occurred. This method works great, although it does take a few frames to pull off. Plus, you really should incorporate some "time out," so that if there's a problem and `done` doesn't turn into `1` after, say 45 seconds, you can display an error. To do this, you could add a line `startTime=getTimer()` in frame 1. Then in frame 3, change the script to read:

```
if (startTime+45000<getTimer()) {
    gotoAndStop("errorFrame");
} else{
    gotoAndPlay(2);
}
```

That is, the user will either keep looping back to frame 2 (which contains a script that might skip them ahead to frame 4) or they'll be sent to a frame that you've previously labeled "errorFrame" where the onscreen text could explain there was a problem.

This technique of waiting until variables are fully loaded is not overly complex. It's actually similar to many techniques people use to make sure that a movie has downloaded. That is, if it's fully loaded on frame 1, jump ahead to frame 3; but on frame 2, have a script that says go back to frame 1 (where you check whether it's loaded yet). Although this technique is manageable, it's not as nice as using the data clip event.

Loading Variables into Clips

When you load variables into a clip (instead of a level number or the `_root` timeline), you can place a script within a `onClipEvent(data)` event that won't execute until all the data is fully loaded. That is, on frame 1, start loading data into a target clip (such as `myClip.loadVariables("data.txt")`), and then include a `stop()` to keep the timeline from proceeding. Attached to the clip `myClip`, place a script like this:

```
onClipEvent(data){
    _root.play();
}
```

Basically, as soon as all the data is loaded, `play()` causes the main timeline to proceed. It's pretty simple in comparison to the other technique shown. Just realize that the disadvantage is that you must load variables into a clip instance, not a level number or the main `_root` timeline.

Data File Format

Although the data file that gets loaded via `loadVariables()` includes a series of variable assignments, its format is not like ActionScript as you might suspect. That is, the following is *not* a legitimate file format:

```
age=35;
name=Phillip;
```

Instead, the format of the data file must be formatted in what's called URL-encoded text. This is a standard format about which I'm sure that you can easily find more information. I'll give you the basics here. In URL-encoded text, the preceding data looks like this:

```
age=35&name=Phillip
```

Instead of spaces or returns between variables, an ampersand is used instead. There are other restrictions on certain characters that cannot be used without first being converted to legitimate URL encoding. It's not so much that returns are not allowed, but consider the following string:

```
age=35
&name=Phillip
```

In this case, age's value is "35/r/n". That is, 35, a return, and a line feed. (Actually, if I used a Macintosh to create this file, I might find that only the return and no line feed appears after 35). You'll see how you can use the preceding format in a later example. The point I wanted to make is that age's value isn't wrong, it just includes extra garbage that we don't really want (although we can remove it). If you're using a script to generate the text file automatically, it's probably no big deal to use the standard URL-encoded format (with no spaces). But if you're creating the data file by hand, it's much more legible if you can include returns. Consider these two examples:

Example of standard encoding:

```
total=3&page_1=First page&page_2=Page two&page_3=Last page
```

Example with extra lines:

```
total=3
&page_1=First page
&page_2=Page two
&page_3=Last page
```

Obviously, the second example is much more legible.

Another thing to always remember is that all values are strings. You don't need quotation marks, and even if you type a number (such as 35), it is read in as "35". You can easily convert any variable (after it is fully loaded) to a number version if you want. For example, age=Number(age) will reassign the value of age to a number version of age.

Examples of Using External Data Files

First, let's look at a simple example and then we can explore ways to make it more sophisticated (and, unfortunately, more complicated).

Let's say you want to make a movie that displays text that's imported from an external text file. Maybe you plan to have several different famous quotations for the user to read and you want to be able to update and add quotes without reopening the source `.fla` file. External data files are perfect for this.

Create a text file called `"quotes.txt"` and type the following text:

```
quote_1=A penny saved is a penny earned
&quote_2=Haste makes waste
&quote_3=It takes two to tango
```

(Notice the ampersand before each variable after the first.)

In the first frame of your Flash movie, type this script:

```
quoteClip.loadVariables("quotes.txt");
```

Save this file in the same directory as the "quotes.txt" file.

Into a Static Text field, type `"Loading"`, select the block of text with the Arrow tool, and convert it to a Movie Clip Symbol. Double-click to edit its contents and then insert a blank keyframe. In this new frame (2), create three Dynamic Text fields and make the margins very wide. Associate the variables `quote_1`, `quote_2`, and `quote_3` with each field. Return to the main timeline and attach the following script on the instance of the Movie Clip you just made:

```
onClipEvent (load) {
    stop ();
}
onClipEvent (data) {
    gotoAndStop(2);
}
```

Finally, make sure to name the instance of this movie clip `quoteClip` (because that's the clip we specified in the `loadVariables()` method). It should work great when you test it! (See Figure 14.1.)

Although this exercise should give you some ideas, there are a few things we need to analyze. First, how did we get away with having returns in the text file? Well, when you see the quotes onstage, you actually see the words plus an extra return—but that's not a problem because it's at the end of the line. If you were trying to display more text in a Dynamic Text field—something like `allQuotes=quote_1+quote_2`—you would actually get a return between the two even though that's not what you normally get when concatenating strings. It just so happens for this situation that there's no problem having extra returns. I'll show you how to remove the extra garbage at the end of the lines anyway.

A penny saved is a penny earned

Haste makes waste

It takes two to tango

Figure 14.1 *Loading variables from text files enables you to display their values inside Flash.*

You can also spice up this example slightly by using some skills you acquired earlier. You could include an additional variable in the text file that specifies how many quotes were in the file:

```
totalQuotes=3&quote_1=A penny saved is a penny earned
&quote_2=Haste makes waste
&quote_3=It takes two to tango
```

Notice that the value for the first variable (`totalQuotes`) doesn't have the extra return we would otherwise have to deal with. Now you can change the clip to contain just one Dynamic Text field associated with the variable `currentQuote`. Then, change the instance script to read:

```
onClipEvent (load) {
    stop ();
}
onClipEvent (data) {
    currentQuote=quote_1;
    currentQuoteNum=1;
    gotoAndStop(2);
}
```

Finally, you can use the clip's `totalQuotes` variable in conjunction with "next quote" and "previous quote" buttons. For example, here's a script for the "next quote" button:

```
on (release) {
          if (currentQuoteNum<totalQuotes){
            currentQuoteNum++;
            currentQuote=eval("quote_"+currentQuoteNum);
      }
}
```

Basically, knowing the value of `totalQuotes` allows us to make sure that the user doesn't go too far when pressing the "next quote" button. Also, the line `currentQuote=eval("quote_"+currentQuoteNum)` uses the `eval()` function to convert a string `"quote_"+currentQuoteNum` into the value of the variable it names. That is, if we simply said `currentQuote="quote_"+currentQuoteNum`, we'd see `"quote_2"` onscreen instead of the *value* for the variable `quote_2`. Another way to pull off the same effect is to use `this["quote_"+currentQuoteNum]`, which looks for a variable called `quote_2` that's contained in "this" clip.

I think the quotes example shows the potential of external data files. I have another sample script that does several additional maneuvers, which are not only useful but are also a good way to learn the concepts. Basically, I wanted to write a script that loads variables from a text file into the root timeline. However, I wanted to take advantage of the data clip event instead of the approach in which you keep checking whether the last variable has loaded. But the data clip event can be used only with variables loaded into Movie Clips. The script that follows takes all the variables loaded into a clip and moves them into the main timeline. In addition, I wanted the text file to include returns after each line to make it easier to read. But I didn't want those extra returns (and line feeds) to be part of the loaded variable. So, I needed to strip off any returns or line feeds at the end of the line. Here's the text file that is loaded in

```
totalNotes=4&note_1=The note for page one is here
&note_2=Here is the note for page 2
&note_3=On page three this note appears
&note_4=The fourth page has this for a note
```

I use `totalNotes` so that my Flash movie knows how many "note_" variables to load. Also, instead of remembering to strip off excess returns after the `totalNotes` variable, I figured it was still pretty legible to define `note_1` without first placing a return. The last thing to notice is that all my variables names (except `totalNotes`) follow the same convention—namely "thing_" followed by a number.

Here's the script that I attached to the clip into which the variables were loaded:

```
onClipEvent (data) {
    totalNotes=Number(totalNotes);
    for (var i=0; i<totalNotes; i++ ) {
        var thisOne=this["note_"+(i+1)];
        var lastChar=thisOne.charCodeAt(thisOne.length-1);
```

```
            while (lastChar==10 | lastChar==13 ) {
                thisOne=thisOne.substr(0,thisOne.length-2);
                lastChar=thisOne.charCodeAt(thisOne.length-1);
            }
            _root["note_"+(i+1)]=thisOne;
        }
        _root.nextFrame();
}
```

Let me explain each line. Because this is in a data clip event, none of this will occur until all the variables are loaded. First, I convert the `totalNotes` variable to a number because all variables loaded in will be strings. Next, I start a for-loop (which encloses everything except the very last line) that sets `i` to `0` and keeps incrementing `i` while `i` is less than the `totalNotes` variable. Notice the use of `var` in the for-loop statement because I want to discard this variable when done. Inside the loop (and every time the loop iterates), I set the temporary variable `thisOne` to the value of `this["note_"+(i+1)]`. Translated, the first time, I find the value of `note_1` (because `i` starts at `0`). Because the string `"note_1"` is in brackets, it returns the value of `note_1`. Now, with `thisOne` containing the value of `note_1`, I can start stripping return characters or line feeds from it. First, I put the last character into the variable `lastChar` and begin a while-loop that will continue "while" `lastChar`'s `charCode` is either `10` or `13` (the codes for linefeed and return respectively). Notice that the while-loop strips the last character for every iteration (and resets `lastChar` to the new last character). The last line in the for-loop assigns a value in the root timeline that's created dynamically from a string. I want to set the variable `_root.note_1`, and then `_root.note_2`, and so on, but because I'm building a dynamic expression within a loop, using `"note_"+(i+1)` won't work because it's just a string. Putting the string between brackets immediately following a target path will make it refer to an actual variable. Finally, after every "note" variable has gone through this process of stripping excess characters and moving into the root timeline, I have a simple `_root.nextFrame()` to get the main timeline to progress. You can test this script with the Debugger open to see that indeed it works. Keep in mind, this script includes two main features: strip excess returns and line feeds, and move the variables into the root timeline. I find both of these features useful in real projects.

Server Scripts

It might seem that we went through a lot of effort just to load text files that ultimately have to be edited by hand. They're not really *that* dynamic if you have to open the darn text file to make a change. Don't forget, it is indeed dynamic because you don't have to reopen the Flash movie—but we can do even more. For example, there are many scripting languages (such as CGI, ASP, and Perl) that in effect create URL-encoded strings based on dynamic information. Such scripting languages can easily interface with databases to produce different results depending on the current data in the database. The URL-encoded strings these languages produce can get into Flash several ways. Practicing with creating your own text files as we did in the previous section is not a waste of time because it mimics the process involved when you make Flash interface with server scripts.

I know just enough about this subject to work productively with others who are experts on the subject. My goal in this section is to give you the tools so that you can make your Flash movies talk to (and listen to) server scripts that someone else produces. Obviously, if you know a server script language, you'll be that far ahead—otherwise, you'll either need to study that subject further or work with someone who has. One big difference between loading variables from text files and loading variables from server scripts is that you can additionally *send* data from your Flash movie to the server script. We'll look at how in just a minute, but let me give you a quick overview of how server scripts work.

Here's my quick explanation. When a user requests an HTML file from your server, the server receives a request and then decides to send the HTML file along with any embedded images and `.swf` files to which the HTML refers to the user's machine. Some Web pages, however, are produced dynamically. The user requests a Web page and somehow, the server decides to send the user an HTML file that is created the instant that the user asks for it. Basically, it's as if the user says, "Give me a Web page," and the server says, "Hold on one second; let me make one fresh for you." Often the server will look at data in a database and deliver this customized HTML file based on timely information. Other times, the Web page the user sees is not just customized with timely information but it reflects the user's personal interests. How does the server know? One way the server knows what the user wants is based on information sent when the user makes a request. For example, if you visit a search engine, type something in the search field, and then press "search," the text you typed is sent to the server, which processes it and configures a Web page just for you.

The two ways (that apply to this section) of getting data to and from the server are called GET and POST. Both have their respective advantages and disadvantages. You might have noticed a tell-tale sign of the GET method because it will actually show the variables in the URL's address (like `http://www.server.com/searchengine.html?searchfor=flashbooks`). Check it out: that part after the actual HTML file looks like URL-encoded text—which is exactly what it is! In the case of POST, the data is still sent back to the server, but it's done stealthily; you won't see it in the URL address. Some servers are built around special applications that receive data from the users in the server's own proprietary way. Often you'll see your URL address end in something *other* than an HTML file (like `search.dll` or `search.cfm`). In those cases, the server is still configuring a Web page especially for you, but doing so might involve several steps. For example, before sending the user a Web page, the server might store information for statistical purposes about what was requested and then send a page back. I'm not going to (nor am I able to) explain all these technologies, but just realize data is sent from the user to a server which responds, eventually, with a Web page.

As long as the server is configured to send URL-encoded text back to Flash, you can easily have Flash ask the server for such a dynamic string of data. Flash taps into the standard GET and POST mechanisms to send data to a server and optionally get data back.

Consider these possibilities:

- Flash can send data to a server.
- Flash can ask a server for data.
- Flash can send data to a server and get data back.
- Flash can jump to another Web page at the same time that it sends data to a server.
- A server can send data to an HTML file, which in turn gives all the data to the Flash movie when it initially displays.

Instead of going through each scenario along with examples, I can summarize quite simply. The two gateways to GET and POST are through `getURL()` and `loadVariables()`. When you execute a `getURL()` hyperlink, you can optionally send all the variables currently in the `_root` main timeline by specifying either "GET" or "POST" as a third parameter. For example, `getURL ("other.html", "", "GET")` uses the GET method. Notice that because the second parameter is for an optional window parameter, if you don't plan to use this parameter you need to provide at least an empty string in its place. Keep in mind that most likely you'll actually specify a server application file (instead of `"other.html"`), which will not only accept the variables you're sending but, in turn, send an HTML file to the user. For example: `getURL("someapp.php","","GET")`. If you have only one custom variable in your main timeline (say, `username` and its value is currently `"phillip"`), this will perform the same function as typing the following into the URL address: `http://www.sameserver.com/someapp.php?username=phillip`. A good way to test whether the server script is responding correctly is to type the preceding URL into the browser's address bar. (Additional variables are, as with all URL-encoded text, separated with question marks.)

The only catch to notice in this example is that only the variables in the main timeline are sent in a URL-encoded string.

The way to load variables from a server into Flash is so simple that you're going to flip. You use the same `loadVariables()` technique explained earlier, but instead of pointing to a text file, you simply point to a server script. For example, `myClip.loadVariables("someapp.cgi")` acts the same as loading from a text file, but waits for the server to send URL-encoded variables into Flash. Keep in mind that this technique simply asks the server for variables. If you want to ask the server for variables by first sending all of what you have in Flash's main timeline, you simply provide either `"GET"` or `"POST"` as an additional parameter, as in `myClip.loadVariables("someapp.cgi","GET")`.

Without explaining how to write server scripts, they can be very easy. The most effort you'll invest is in deciding which variables will be sent from Flash (that is, what variables the server script will need) and then which variables need to be sent back to Flash (that is, what variables the server script will produce). I highly recommend using `loadVariables()` in conjunction with the data clip event (as we did in the last section). Otherwise, you have to make sure that the server script includes a variable at the end of each string indicating the entire set of data has loaded (and you have to wait for that variable to load).

Obviously, if you were expecting an extensive explanation of server scripting, you'll be disappointed. However, there are countless resources for topics such as CGI and PHP scripting. In my experience, you'll spend a lot of time working in Flash and—at the same time—the server scripting person will spend a lot of time in her databases and scripts. But simply getting the data to travel between Flash and a server is pretty nominal after you learn to use `loadVariables()` and `getURL()`.

XML

Even though using `loadVariables()` to import data (and `getURL()` to send data to a server) is quite powerful, the limiting factor is how you must format the data. Only name-value pairs are supported, which means you can only import or export variables and their values. Sometimes that is enough, but some types of data are more complex than that (for example, an object with its properties). In addition, the techniques we've seen in this chapter require that you carefully plan the structure of such data and stick to it. After all, Flash needs to know which variables are coming in and a server script needs to know which variables are being sent.

As a format, XML is not very exciting. It's not supposed to be. It's only supposed to be standardized so that data structured as XML in one program can be interpreted by another. In Flash, XML is interesting for two reasons. First, because it's extensible, even after you design a data structure, you can add levels of information without breaking what's already built. Second, it's a standard that many applications support. For example, any database program worth its salt can export a database in XML format. The exciting part is that through its extensibility, you can design your XML data to be as complex as necessary. Flash can import XML structured data, make sense of it (that is, parse out the elements it needs), and also modify or create XML data that can be sent to server applications.

Just like the other technologies in this chapter, the difficult part isn't exchanging data (in this case, as XML data), but rather designing an application to fill a particular need. I use an imaginary application to explain the foundation tools available for exchanging XML data. Again, the challenge for you will be to apply this knowledge to your own projects as appropriate.

First, let's look at the way some simple XML data is formatted. In my example, we'll load in data from a text file that contains XML-structured data. (It would be just as easy to load the same data from a server application that provides it in XML format.)

```
<ROSTER>
<STUDENT>
  <NAME>Phillip</NAME>
  <SEX>MALE</SEX>
  <GPA>4.0</GPA >
  <DEGREE>Photography</DEGREE>
</STUDENT>
</ROSTER>
```

XML separates the structure from the data (not unlike the code-data separation concept discussed in Chapter 3, "The Programmer's Approach"). Tags or, to use an XML term, nodes such as `<ROSTER>`, `<STUDENT>`, and `<GPA>` serve to provide arbitrary names for the data they enclose. For example, the value of the `<GPA>` node is `"4.0"`. You can have nodes inside of nodes, for instance `<NAME>`, `<SEX>`, `<GPA>`, and `<DEGREE>` are all "children" nodes of the `<STUDENT>` node (which is in turn a child node of `<ROSTER>`).

In this example, notice that enclosed in the "roster" node, is a "student." Inside the student node, there are four nodes (name, sex, GPA, and degree), each of which encloses a value. Depending on the level of the hierarchy, you can look at this data in different ways. For example, there's only one student in the roster. The name for the first student is "Phillip," his GPA is "4.0," and so on. This basic format can be extended to include more students as long as they are enclosed between the tags `<STUDENT>` and `</STUDENT>`. If they are going to be elements of the roster also, additional students must appear before the closing `</ROSTER>`. For example:

```
<ROSTER>
<STUDENT>
  <NAME>Phillip</NAME>
  <SEX>male</SEX>
  <GPA>4.0</GPA >
  <DEGREE>Photography</DEGREE>
</STUDENT>
<STUDENT>
  <NAME>Sally</NAME>
  <SEX>female</SEX>
  <GPA>3.81</GPA >
  <DEGREE>Painting</DEGREE>
</STUDENT>
</ROSTER>
```

This is a *very* basic structure for XML. Additional elements can be added at will. Not only more children of the roster node (`STUDENT`), but you can add children to the student node—perhaps a `GRADUATION_DATE` tag. Also, it's possible to add properties to any node. Properties are a good solution in cases in which the values for such properties aren't necessarily going to be part of the exposed data. For example, it's possible that there are two students with the same name, sex, GPA, and degree. To add a property, in this case a student ID number for each student node, you can change `<STUDENT>` to `<STUDENT ID="123">`. Additional properties are just added within the tag as in `<STUDENT ID="123" YEAR="Sophomore" EXPECTED_GRAD="1989">`. Later, you'll see how easy it is to extract such property values.

So far, we've just been formatting the data. There's at least one more detail that you need to add to an XML data file and that's a declaration at the top: `<?xml version="1.0"?>`. Besides being a requirement, the declaration ultimately means that the first node is really the first child. Notice that I include only the `version` property. There are other properties that you can include in the declaration that generally let you explain the overall structure and mode of operation—but this one is the minimum necessary. Here is a complete XML data source used for the following examples (that I'm saving in a file called `"my_data.xml"`):

```
<?xml version="1.0"?>
<CATALOG>
<SONG duration="2:50">
  <TITLE>Alec Eiffel</TITLE>
  <ALBUM>Trompe Le Monde</ALBUM>
  <LABEL>4AD</LABEL>
  <ARTIST>Pixies</ARTIST>
</SONG>
<SONG duration="5:16">
  <TITLE>Optimistic</TITLE>
  <ALBUM>Kid A</ALBUM>
  <LABEL>Capitol</LABEL>
  <ARTIST>Radiohead</ARTIST>
</SONG>
<SONG duration="2:37">
  <TITLE>Brass Monkey</TITLE>
  <ALBUM>Licensed to Ill</ALBUM>
  <LABEL>Columbia</LABEL>
  <ARTIST>Beastie Boys</ARTIST>
</SONG>
<SONG duration="2:43">
  <TITLE>I don't want to grow up</TITLE>
  <ALBUM>Adios Amigos</ALBUM>
  <LABEL>Radioactive Records</LABEL>
  <ARTIST>Ramones</ARTIST>
  <WRITER>Tom Waits</WRITER>
</SONG>
</CATALOG>
```

Before we jump into Flash to learn how to load all this data in, let me point out a few things. Also notice how there are spaces and returns to make this data more legible. The spaces are not within any tag, but between them. This will pose a problem if you're viewing the Flash movie in a Flash player prior to version 5.41. (In the first Workshop, you'll learn how to check what version the user has.) In the script that follows I include some error checking so that most spaces won't matter. However, the very first node ("catalog") must appear immediately following the declaration. It should read:

```
<?xml version="1.0"?><CATALOG>
```

Unless the first line reads as shown here, even my error-checking script won't work in the first releases of the Flash player (including the player that shipped with Flash and executes when you do a test movie). Basically, the first thing we'll do after the data is loaded is to determine the first child node. Placing `<CATALOG>` immediately following the declaration ensures that it's the first node (not a blank line that Flash can erroneously read in as a node).

To load this data into Flash, we need to use the XML object. The general procedure is instantiate the object, load data from an XML source, and then parse the data into a form that we can use inside Flash. Just like `loadVariables`, you want to make sure that the data is fully loaded before you start trying to use it—and naturally, there's a way to ensure that it's loaded. Here's a starter script that you could put in the first frame:

```
xmlObj=new XML;
xmlObj.load("my_data.xml");
```

This script simply creates an instance of the XML object, places it in the variable `xmlObj`, and then uses the `load()` method to start the import process. By the way, `"my_data.xml"` could just as easily be a URL address or a server application that returns XML structured data. Following the preceding code, we can add these two lines:

```
xmlObj.onLoad=parse;
xmlObj.ignoreWhite=1;
```

The first line is the XML object's equivalent to the data clip event. The line shown effectively says that when the `xmlObj` has finished its load process (started above), execute the following function called `parse()`, which is a custom function that we're about to write. If you simply want to advance to the next frame when importing is complete, you could change the line to read:

```
xmlObj.onLoad=nextFrame();
```

The line `xmlObj.ignoreWhite=1` sets the value for the `ignoreWhite` property to true. This property is supported only in Flash players version 5.41 and later. If your first node follows the declaration as explained earlier, you won't need to worry about this line.

So, that's really it! The first two lines made an object and started the import process, and then we added a function name that we want to execute when it's finished. Now we can write the `parse()` function, which will go through all XML data and extract parts that I can use in Flash. This is a common approach. Structure your data as you want it, load it in, and use only the parts you want. If you need to send it back to a server (the XML object allows you to *send* XML-structured data, too), you simply take the elements from Flash and build an XML structure that you send back to the server.

Here is the final script that steps through all the XML data and builds a string containing both the node names and the node values:

```
function parse(){
//MAIN NODE's XML OBJ:
mainNode = xmlObj.firstChild;
//MAIN NODE's NAME  ("catalog"):
mainName=mainNode.nodeName;

theString=mainName+"\r\r";

//ARRAY Of Children in MAIN (all the songs):
childrenOfMain=new Array();
childrenOfMain= mainNode.childNodes;

for(i=0;i<=childrenOfMain.length;i++){
    if (childrenOfMain[i].nodeName<>null){
        //NAME OF THIS CHILD (always "song"):
        theString=theString+"\r"+childrenOfMain[i].nodeName+"=";
//THIS CHILD's XML:
        thisChild = childrenOfMain[i];
        //ARRAY OF NODES in THIS CHILD ("title", "album", etc.):
        nodesOfThisChild = thisChild.childNodes;
            for(j=0;j<nodesOfThisChild.length;j++){
                //THIS TAG'S XML
                thisTag = nodesOfThisChild[j];
                //THIS TAG's NAME:
                thisName = thisTag.nodeName;
                    if (thisTag.nodeName<>null){
                        // & THIS TAG's VALUE:
                        thisValue=thisTag.firstChild.nodeValue;
                        theString=theString+thisName+":"+thisValue+" ";
                    }//if
            }//for
```

```
    }//if
}//for
}//function
```

Let me first explain this function in pseudo-code and then we can walk through each line. This script takes the first node ("catalog"), finds out how many subnodes (how many "songs") it has, and loops through each of those. Within each "song," it finds out how many subnodes it has and loops through each of those. Along the way, if any nodes appear as null, it means that Flash has simply found a whitespace that it erroneously interprets as a node (so, it's ignored). Throughout each of the loops, a variable `theString` is concatenated with names of all nodes and values for the ones that are three levels deep into the hierarchy (title, album, and so on). Sounds easy enough. While this script is relatively adaptable to any amount of data (if there were 100 songs, it would work just as well), it's built explicitly for a hierarchy that has one main node and tags with single values three levels deep. That is, the nodes within a song don't have any more levels of hierarchy, so those are treated as tags and simply taken for their values.

Although even the pseudo-code might seem complicated, we'll walk through this code because it's worth learning a couple properties included in the XML object. Each node within my data is treated as an XML object to utilize the XML methods and properties. You see in the first line of code that the variable `mainNode` is assigned the `firstChild` property of the original xmlObj. The first child is indeed the catalog, but realize its data type is an XML object. The variable `mainName` (in the next line) is assigned the value of the `nodeName` property of the `mainNode` object. That is, I pulled off the first child (it was an object), and then I found the `nodeName` of that child object. All that for the name "CATALOG" that starts the variable `theString`.

Next, I need to grab all the songs—that is, the child nodes of `catalog`. I create a variable `childrenOfMain` and initialize it as an array, and then extract the `childNodes` property from `mainNode` created earlier. Notice the expression `mainNode.childNodes` returns an array data type (not an XML object the way `firstChild` did, and not a string the way `nodeName` does). At this point, I start the main for-loop that steps through all the songs (literally the length of `childrenOfMain`). I want to extract one item (`i`) from the `childrenOfMain` at a time, but if that item turns out to be null, I'll just skip it. The `childrenOfMain` array could very likely contain more items than songs if Flash is reading whitespace. The if-statement's condition (`childrenOfMain[i].nodeName<>null`) alleviates that possibility. When I find a `nodeName` of an item in the `childrendOfMain` array that's not null (in our case, it will always be "SONG"), I concatenate that to `theString` (along with a return and an equal sign). Although the `nodeName` of this item in `childrenOfMain` is "SONG," I want to do some XML operations on it, so I take the item itself (in XML object form) and place it in the variable `thisChild`. Then I extract the `childNodes` property of `thisChild` and place it in the variable `nodesOfThisChild`. Remember, the `childNodes` property is in the form of an array. (This array contains an object for each node within a song—an object each for "title," "album," and so on.) Finally, I start *another* for-loop that steps through all the items in this `nodesOfThisChild` array. For each iteration, I place the current item (an object) into a variable `thisTag` (I call it a tag by preference only because I know this is the end of the road for nodes). Then I check the `nodeName` property for `thisTag`. If it's not null, I find the `nodeValue` property for the `firstChild` property of the `thisTag` object. Notice that I don't try to find the `nodeValue` for `thisTag`; rather, I find the `nodeValue` for `thisTag`'s `firstChild`. Realize that a variable containing the XML object data type can have properties, and those properties can have properties, and so on, and so on. Anyway, after I get the `nodeName` and `nodeValue` for the lowest level that I have dived, they are concatenated (with a colon in between) to the variable `theString`.

I recommend typing this script into the Flash Actions panel because the syntax coloring will help you separate the homemade variables from the built-in properties and methods. Remember that this script dives into only the first node of the XML data and then dives exactly two more levels deep. That is, from the `firstChild` (catalog), we get an array of `childNodes` (all the songs), and then (from each song) we get an array of `childNodes` (title, album, and so on), and then (from each of those nodes) we find their `nodeName` and `nodeValue` (`title` and "`Alec Eiffel`," for example). Your data structure could be deeper or shallower. If your data is deeper (say, each title has several nodes instead of a single value), you can continue to gather arrays of `childNodes` and analyze each one. If your data is shallower (for example, each song has one value and nothing more), you can ascertain the `nodeValue` earlier). Figure 14.2 gives you a visual way of looking at the data and the terms used.

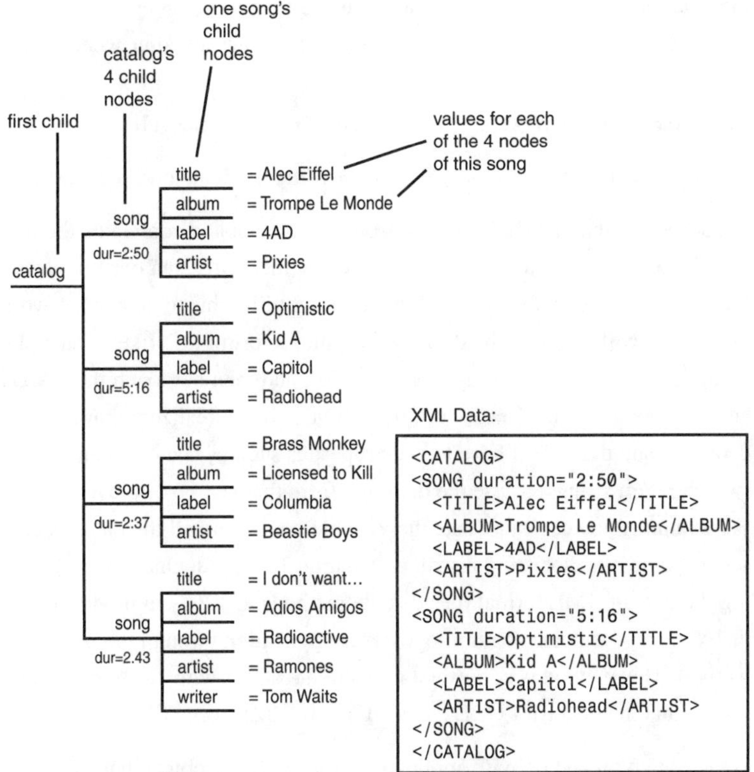

Figure 14.2 *A hierarchical view of the XML data (in the file on the right) shows that values are ascertained only for nodes three levels deep.*

So, although this script is pretty accommodating, it is locked to the hierarchy designed for this case. The entire source data is in the `xmlObj` if you ever need to dive through it again. Just realize that this script simply parses elements from the data (while ignoring nodes that come up `null`) so that it can display onscreen (in the `theString` variable).

If you noticed, in the XML data file, each SONG had a duration property (also called an *attribute*). Any node can have an attribute or attributes. To extract this information while parsing the data, use the `attributes` property to return an associative array of all the attributes. In our example, within the main for-loop, after you determine that the `childrenOfMain[i].nodeName` isn't `null`, you can extract all the attributes of `SONG` with the expression `childrenOfMain[i].attributes`. For example, if you want to add the `duration` information to our `theString` variable, just get the `duration` property from the attributes. You can add the following line of code directly after where `thisChild` is assigned:

```
theString=theString+"time: "+thisChild.attributes.duration+" ";
```

This code will make sense only if you know that such an attribute exists.

In addition to the methods and properties that we looked at already, there are a handful of methods that enable you to modify the XML data once it's inside Flash. Depending on the application, you might find this to be a lot of work. Often, you will just load the data, parse it into a form Flash likes (I just built a string, but you can build arrays for example), and then not touch the XML object again. If you keep the data for use in an XML object, realize that it's an object data type and that you'll have to use properties such as `nodeName` and `nodeValue` (which return strings) to use the data in a form that can be displayed onscreen. For example, you can't just take the variable containing all the data (`xmlObj`) and see its value by associating it with a Dynamic Text field. One advantage of leaving the data in XML format (besides the methods that let you modify the data) is that you can eventually send it to a server application through the `send()` method. This method is equivalent to using `getURL()` with `"GET"` or `"POST"` except that the data isn't URL encoded, it's in XML format.

We could go on and on with applications for the XML object, but I think it's fair to say that the work you will encounter involves designing solutions and building structures. The interchange between Flash and XML data sources is not super elaborate. This is also true with the XML Socket object. In fact, the XML Socket object has only six methods in addition to the new constructor function. Practically all the work to use this object will take place by the person writing a server application. Basically, the XML Socket object allows you to establish a persistent connection between a Flash movie and a server application. This means that you can make multiuser games or chat applications in Flash. The server can let people log on and manage who's currently chatting. Because the connection is persistent, it stays open until the server says so (or the Flash movie stops). The potential for this object is pretty great. Without actually providing much detail, here's a super-quick rundown of the methods for the XML Socket object. To begin a connection, use `connect()`. To indicate a function to execute when connected, use `onConnect()`. To send data, use `send()`. To close the connection, use `close()`; to indicate a function to execute when closed, use `onClose()`. Sounds pretty simple, eh? Within Flash it really is pretty simple, but the server application has to be written from scratch (in Java and by someone with extensive programming skills). I am unable to explain much more on this topic, but I will repeat: The hard part is for the programmer who writes the server application—not so much for the Flash person.

Hopefully you can see *some* of the potential for XML structured data. It's easy for me to say that most of the work really isn't *in* Flash, but rather in the way you design the XML solutions. It's true. You'll find your time is spent deciding how the data will be structured and then parsing out just the elements (node values) that you can use. It doesn't hurt, however to remember these key points that we covered.

- After you initiate the `load()` command, you'll likely want to identify a function to execute when it's finished loading—that is `onLoad=someFunction`. The only other way to really know the data has loaded is by continually checking whether the object into which you're loading has a loaded property of `true` (as in `if (xmlObj.loaded==true)`).
- Extracting nodes, their values, and their properties utilizes one of the following methods: `firstChild` returns an XML object; `childNodes` returns an array of all the nodes nested within a node; or `nodeName` and `nodeValue`, which both return strings.
- The XML Socket object is something entirely different than the XML object.

JavaScript

We've seen the gateway between Flash and text files, Flash and server scripts, and Flash and XML data. What else could you possibly want? Well, Flash can also have a meaningful "conversation" with JavaScript. That is, Flash can tell JavaScript to do things such as pop open a new window or display a message box (see Figure 14.3). Additionally, JavaScript can tell Flash to do things such as jump to a particular frame or assign a particular value to a variable. The interface between JavaScript and Flash has been around for several versions of Flash. If nothing else, it's a solid technology. However, let me just say that there are significant limits with specific browsers (most notably, Internet Explorer on Macintosh and Netscape 6 on all computers). I'm not going to list exactly which browser versions have specific limits, but rather provide an overall explanation of how the JavaScript/Flash interface works. Practically everything I show works, but I know that there are specific situations that could cause these scripts to fail.

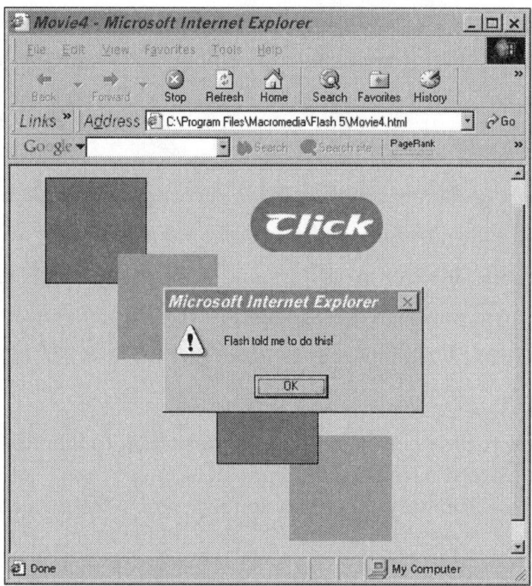

Figure 14.3 *Flash can communicate with JavaScript in many ways, including causing an alert message to appear.*

Quick and Dirty Method

The easy way to trigger a JavaScript function from Flash is through the `getURL()` statement. Instead of specifying a URL that you would otherwise hyperlink to, you include the following text:

```
javascript:myJavaScriptCode
```

`"myJavaScriptCode"` either calls a custom function that resides in the HTML page that hosts your `.swf` or it contains actual JavaScript code as is. For example, the following code will cause a dialog box to appear in the browser because actual JavaScript code is typed in verbatim:

```
getURL("javascript:alert('hi mom');");
```

Notice that within the string, a complete JavaScript code segment follows the word `javascript:`—including the semicolon that follows every line of code in JavaScript. This technique could get pretty complex when the JavaScript you want to trigger is more complex or involves several lines of code. Although you can type more elaborate JavaScript for `getURL`'s parameter, it can become pretty messy. Because the parameter is a string, you'll have to be careful to include only single quotation marks (as in the case of `'hi mom'`). For example, this code will cause a new window to open with a specified size and set of window features:

```
getURL("javascript: window.open('other.html',
➥'winName',' width=300,height=300,toolbar=no');");
```

You can see that it's beginning to get ugly. Consider how this would look with multiple lines! Instead of writing a ton of JavaScript inside Flash, you can simply trigger a custom function that resides in the HTML page. Because you can pass parameters from Flash, you can even make this function adaptable to multiple purposes. For example, in Flash you could simply call a homemade JavaScript function called `doit()`:

```
getURL("javascript:doit();");
```

Inside the HTML page that your Flash movie is embedded in, you would need a function called `doit()`:

```
<SCRIPT LANGUAGE=JavaScript>
function doit(){
    alert ('hi mom');
}
</SCRIPT>
```

The preceding code (in your HTML file) could include other functions as long as they reside between the `<SCRIPT>` and `</SCRIPT>` tags. You can also add more lines of code to the `doit()` function. Actually, you can do anything you want in JavaScript (according to the rules of JavaScript—which I won't cover in this book). The good news is that almost every skill you've learned about ActionScript can be applied to JavaScript (and vice versa).

The quick and dirty way to make Flash trigger JavaScript involves embedding `"javascript:"` in the `getURL()` statement. You can call JavaScript internal functions directly or trigger your own JavaScript functions. Although this might not work on very old browsers, it's probably the easiest way to make Flash talk to JavaScript. You can't, however, use this technique to make JavaScript control (that is "talk to") Flash. We'll see that next.

JavaScript Talking to Flash

Just as you can use ActionScript to ascertain clip instance properties, set clip instance properties, and apply methods to clip instances, you can use JavaScript to control a Flash movie and its included movie clips by ascertaining properties, setting properties, and applying methods. Again, the knowledge you've acquired up to this point will come in handy.

In a Web page, every image, Flash movie, form element, and so forth is an object. It's just that in JavaScript, you need to refer to the embedded object. To use any of the properties or methods of the "Flash object" (the embedded `.swf`), you use the form `flashObj.property` or `flashObj.method()`. Referring to the Flash object is analogous to targeting a clip instance. I'll show you how to target a Flash object in a minute. Because it's a little involved (you can't just say "flashObj," for example), we'll just write a function that returns the Flash object. The function will be called `flashObj()`. Therefore, if you ever type `flashObj()` in JavaScript, it will turn into a reference to the object (because that's what will be "returned" from the `flashObj()` function).

We can look at all the methods and properties now by using `flashObj()` in place of the actual Flash object.

Methods that target the main movie:

```
flashObj().Play()
```

Causes the movie to play (pretty easy, eh?).

```
flashObj().StopPlay()
```

Stops the movie (just like Flash's `stop()` method will—but from JavaScript).

```
flashObj().GotoFrame(num)
```

Of course, "num" must be replaced with an integer. Guess what "num" the first frame of a Flash movie is? Zero. That is, if you want to jump to frame 10, you use `flashObj().gotoFrame(9)`.

```
flashObj().Rewind()
```

Jumps to the first frame the way `gotoAndStop(1)` would from inside Flash.

```
flashObj().SetZoomRect(left,top,right,bottom)
```

Resizes the area zoomed in on by explicit values. You replace "left," "top," "right," and "bottom" with integers.

```
flashObj().Zoom(percent)
```

Resizes the zoomed area by a percentage specified in the parameter "percent."

`flashObj().Pan(x,y,mode)`

Pans the zoomed-in area (assuming that you're not zoomed all the way back). If "mode" is `0`, the "x" and "y" integers that you supply will be used as pixel values. If "mode" is `1`, "x" and "y" integers are used as percentage values.

`flashObj().LoadMovie(level,URL)`

Executes Flash's `loadMovie()`. Replace "level" with an integer and "URL" with a string specifying the address and name of the `.swf` file to load.

`flashObj().SetVariable(name,value)`

Sets a variable. You simply replace "name" with a string version of your variable and "value" with whatever value you want the variable to become. The only catch is your named variable will always become a string data type. (You can convert it to a number or any other data type—but from within Flash.)

`flashObj().TSetProperty("_level0", propCodeNum, value)`

Sets a property of the main movie. This is designed to target clips (and can be used that way as described in `TGotoFrame`, later), but if you simply target `"_level0"`, you'll affect the main movie. Each property (`_alpha`, `_x`, and so on) has a code number (found on the Property Code Numbers list later), so you just replace "propCodeNum" with the property's code number you want to set. Finally, "value" is replaced with the new value for the specified property.

Methods that target the main movie and return values:

`flashObj().TotalFrames()`

Returns the total number of frames in the movie.

`flashObj().PercentLoaded()`

Returns what percentage of the movie has downloaded. You'll learn that this is important because JavaScript is not allowed to "talk" to Flash unless it's entirely downloaded.

`flashObj().IsPlaying()`

Returns true or false, depending on whether the movie is currently playing or stopped.

`flashObj().GetVariable(name)`

Returns a string version of the variable specified in "name."

```
flashObj().CurrentFrame()
```

Returns the current frame number.

```
flashObj().TCurrentLabel("_level0")
```

Returns the current frame label name. (This method is really designed to ascertain the current frame label from a targeted clip, but providing the parameter "_level0" makes it target the main `_level0` timeline.)

```
flashObj().TGetProperty("_level0", propCodeNum)
```

Returns a string version of the property specified in "propCodeNum" (found in the Property Code Numbers list later). Targeting "_level0" makes this method return the specified property in the main timeline.

Methods that target clips:

```
flashObj().TGotoFrame("_level0/clip",frameNum)
```

Targets a clip instance (in this case, "clip" in the main `_level0` timeline) and causes it to jump to "frameNum," which you replace with an integer. Notice that the target you specify (in the first parameter) is a string that uses forward slashes instead of dots, and starts `_level0` instead of _root. The clip referred to here is the same as `_root.clip`, but that's not the syntax that you use in this method. (If the clip you're targeting has been loaded into a different level number, you can replace the zero as in `_level1` or `_level2`.)

```
flashObj().TGotoLabel("_level0/clip",label)
```

Causes a targeted clip to jump to a particular frame label (replace "label" with a string).

```
flashObj().TPlay("_level0/clip")
```

Makes a targeted clip play.

```
flashObj().TStopPlay("_level0/clip")
```

Stops a targeted clip.

```
flashObj().TSetProperty("_level0/clip", propCodeNum, value)
```

Sets a targeted clip's property (by setting "propCodeNum" to a number found on the Property Code Numbers list later) to a specified "value."

Methods that target clips and return values:

```
flashObj().TCurrentFrame("_level0/clip")
```

Returns a string version of the current frame number in the targeted clip.

```
flashObj().TCurrentLabel("_level0/clip")
```

Returns the label name for the current frame in the targeted clip.

```
flashObj().TGetProperty("_level0/clip", propCodeNum)
```

Returns a string version of the value for the specified property of a targeted clip. Replace "propCodeNum" with a number found in the Property Code Numbers list that follows.

Property Code Numbers:

```
0 _x
1 _y
2 _xscale
3 _yscale
4 _currentframe
5 _totalframes
6 _alpha
7 _visible
8 _width
9 _height
10 _rotation
11 _target
12 _framesloaded
13 _name
14 _droptarget
15 _url
```

Targeting the Flash Object

When in JavaScript, methods for the "Flash object" must be attached to the Flash object similarly to how methods are attached to clip instances in Flash. You can't just say `SetVariable("username","phillip")`; you must say something like `flashObject.SetVariable("username","phillip")`. However, referring to the embedded `.swf` file (the Flash object) is not achieved simply by saying `flashObject`. It's different for Internet Explorer and Netscape. To make it easy, and as promised, I'll provide a JavaScript function that will return the reference to the Flash object in the correct form. Then, any time you want to use a method, you simply use `flashObj()` as if it were the object itself (because the `flashObj()` function returns the object reference, it *is* the object).

Here's the function for the JavaScript portion of your HTML file (which goes after `</HEAD>` and before `<BODY>`):

```
function flashObj() {
    if(navigator.appName=="Netscape") {
        return document.embeds[0]
    } else {
        return window['flashObject']
```

```
    }
}
```

There are a couple assumptions made in this function that I can address. First, for the statement “return window[‘flashObject’]” (which references Internet Explorer) to work, you must provide `flashObject` as the name value for the `ID` parameter in the `OBJECT` portion of your HTML file. Your HTML should include the line `id=flashObject` as shown in Figure 14.4.

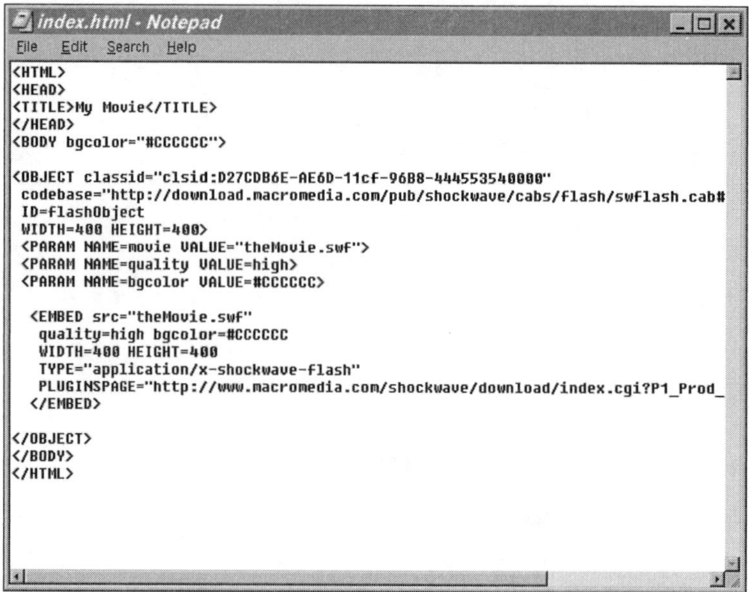


```
<HTML>
<HEAD>
<TITLE>My Movie</TITLE>
</HEAD>
<BODY bgcolor="#CCCCCC">

<OBJECT classid="clsid:D27CDB6E-AE6D-11cf-96B8-444553540000"
 codebase="http://download.macromedia.com/pub/shockwave/cabs/flash/swflash.cab#
 ID=flashObject
 WIDTH=400 HEIGHT=400>
 <PARAM NAME=movie VALUE="theMovie.swf">
 <PARAM NAME=quality VALUE=high>
 <PARAM NAME=bgcolor VALUE=#CCCCCC>

  <EMBED src="theMovie.swf"
   quality=high bgcolor=#CCCCCC
   WIDTH=400 HEIGHT=400
   TYPE="application/x-shockwave-flash"
   PLUGINSPAGE="http://www.macromedia.com/shockwave/download/index.cgi?P1_Prod_
  </EMBED>

</OBJECT>
</BODY>
</HTML>
```

Figure 14.4 *In the* `OBJECT` *portion of your HTML file, you need to provide an* `ID` *parameter in order for JavaScript to identify the Flash object.*

The `flashObj()` function also assumes that you have only one Flash movie in the Web page. To include more than one movie, and consequently allow this function to target a particular Flash movie, this function must be adjusted. The part for Internet Explorer is easy. Change the line `return window['flashObject']` to read `return window[whichObj]`, and type `whichObj` in the parentheses of the function so that the first line reads: `function flashObj(whichObj) {`. Then in the tag in which you specify the `.swf` file, if you make one movie's `ID` value `id=one_movie` and the other `id=other`, you can use `flashObj('one_movie')` or `flashObj('other')`, depending on which movie you want to target. For example, `flashObj('other').StopPlay()` will cause only that movie to stop.

For the Netscape portion, you need a script that determines what embed number the desired `.swf` has. That is, every movie is listed in an array, you just have to figure out which one is which. For example, if you know the first `.swf` was the one you gave `id=one_movie` and the second `.swf` was the one you gave `id=other`, you could use the series of if-statements shown in the Netscape portion of this completed version of the function:

```
function flashObj(objName) {
    if(navigator.appName=="Netscape") {
        var num=0;
        if (objName=='one_movie'){
            num=0;
        }
        if (objName=='other'){
            num=1;
        }
        return document.embeds[num];
    } else {
        return window[objName]
    }
}
```

Notice that Netscape doesn't use the `id=objectName` parameter, but because you want this function to work in either case, when you just supply an object name (like `flashObj('other')`), you can translate (for Netscape) the `objName` parameter provided into a number. If you have more embedded Flash movies, you'll have to add another if-statement for each one. By the way, I'm sure that it's possible to write a more efficient solution, but this should give you the idea (and it *does* work).

Workarounds

In addition to the way that Netscape and Internet Explorer vary in how they identify objects and the way you must remember to count frame numbers starting with frame `0`, there are a couple more bits of funkiness that I want to explain.

The Flash object methods that jump to a frame number or label effectively perform what Flash calls a `gotoAndStop()` (not `gotoAndPlay()`). Therefore, you can simply add an additional line of JavaScript that invokes the `Play()` method after jumping to a frame (if that's what you want).

Also, there are at least two JavaScript functions that have unpredictable results if Flash initiates them either directly or through a call to a custom function.

(Remember, Flash can execute JavaScript using `"javascript:..."` in a `getURL().`) These are `window.open()` and `location.href="page.html"`. As a workaround, you can make Flash invoke a custom function inside JavaScript, which instead of calling `window.open` or `location.href` directly, uses the `setTimeout()` function like so:

```
setTimeout("window.open('other.html')",0);
setTimeout("location.href='page.html'",0);
```

JavaScript's `setTimeout()` function accepts two parameters: first, a string version of the JavaScript code you want executed; second, the number of milliseconds that you want to wait before it executes. The `0`s in the preceding statements cause the enclosed scripts to execute right away (remember, it's a workaround—that's why it's so funky).

Finally, you don't want to let JavaScript try to perform any methods on a Flash object until it's fully downloaded. Luckily, the one method you *can* use before a movie is entirely downloaded is `PercentLoaded()`. You can place this function inside every JavaScript function to wait for the movie to download:

```
var movie_ready=="false";
if(movie_ready=="false"){
    while(movie_ready=="false"){
    if(flashObj().PercentLoaded() == 100){
        movie_ready="true";
    }
}
```

An even better solution involves making Flash (when the movie is entirely downloaded) invoke a custom function that sets a global variable indicating that the movie has downloaded. That is, in Flash use

```
getURL ("javascript:ready();");
```

Within the JavaScript, have this function:

```
function ready(){
    movie_ready='true';
}
```

That is, when this function is called, our homemade variable `movie_ready` will be set to `'true'`.

Also, in the HTML, include this in the BODY tag:

```
onLoad="movie_ready='false';"
```

To initialize movie_ready to 'false'.

Within every function that talks to Flash, insert this if-statement at the beginning:

```
if (movie_ready<>"true"){
    return;
}
```

Finally, attached to a clip instance in Flash, place this code:

```
onClipEvent(enterFrame){
  if(_root.getBytesLoaded()==_root.getBytesTotal()){
    getURL("javascript:ready();");
  }
}
```

This just keeps looping until everything has downloaded. Then JavaScript's ready() function is called that lets JavaScript know that it can start talking to Flash.

This solution will initialize movie_ready to "false". Then, (from inside Flash) when you've determined the movie is entirely downloaded, Flash will invoke the ready() function, which sets movie_ready to "true". Within every function, if movie_ready isn't true yet, JavaScript will return (effectively skipping the rest of the function).

There's actually a fair bit more that I can say about the JavaScript Flash interface. Instead, let me just give you a couple applications. One great application for JavaScript and Flash is to save cookies on the user's machine. This enables a Flash movie to reconfigure itself and appear in the same state as when the user last visited. We'll do a very simple application of this in the Workshop. Some people have also used JavaScript with Flash to offload some of the computations to JavaScript. Even though Flash has practically all the same functions available to JavaScript, in some cases it's faster to send the request to JavaScript, have it do the work, and then finally return the answers to Flash. Also, if you're delivering your movie as Flash 4 or Flash 3—believe it or not—most of these methods still work! (The following methods are the only ones that don't work in Flash 3: SetProperty(), GetProperty(), SetVariable(), and GetVariable().) The only difficulty in this process is that when you set or get variables, they turn into strings.

When I first started this chapter, I thought that perhaps the usefulness of JavaScript with Flash had faded away. But as I wrote, I came to the realization that there are still needs for these techniques. The best part of all is that because ActionScript and JavaScript are so similar, you can leverage the knowledge you've invested in learning Flash and apply it to JavaScript. If you do want to learn more, I have a paper and presentation available at `www.teleport.com/~phillip/flashforward2000/presentation/`.

Director and Authorware

I haven't always been a Flash junkie. I actually started using Authorware back in version 1.7. I've also been using Director for years (since version 3). Flash is awesome, but there are some things it simply cannot do. The good news is that you can play Flash movies within Director and Authorware. Both these tools have their respective advantages and disadvantages, but I can summarize what they offer over Flash in just a few paragraphs.

Flash can only send data back and forth to server scripts and JavaScript. (Alright, Flash can also load data from text files, but it can't write to those files.) This limit of Flash is not terribly significant except that it means all data collection from Flash must be done through server technologies. Both Director and Authorware enable you to read and write files on the user's machine. Additionally, they let you dynamically display practically any media type. For example, you can have Authorware display a .jpg file that's sitting next to the Authorware "movie" (called a *package*). If the .jpg file is replaced, the change is automatically reflected in the Authorware package. Without the server product Flash Generator, this is not possible in Flash.

In addition to interacting with external media formats and writing files, both Authorware and Director can interact with outside applications. Using third-party software called Xtras, you really can do anything: print high-resolution documents, view Acrobat files, pop open the CD drive, change the user's sound level—whatever you want. For example, I built an application in Director that lets you play any Beastie Boys audio CD and you'll see the lyrics appear in perfect synchronization (shown in Figure 14.5 and free to download from `www.teleport.com/~phillip/oldindex.html`).

Figure 14.5 *Director can talk to the user's machine like this CD player I made.*

The ultimate feature Authorware and Director have that Flash lacks is that these tools can display digital video! QuickTime, QuickTime VR, AVI, and (through Xtras) MPEG. I could go on with subtle things such as how performance can often be optimized to make Director or Authorware fly in comparison to Flash—but loading dynamic media (including video) and interacting with other programs summarizes it generally.

One of the media types that Authorware and Director support is Flash. In addition to just playing Flash movies in Director or Authorware, Director and Authorware can "talk" to Flash (and Flash can "talk back"). I'll give you an overview of the ways to incorporate Flash in both Authorware and Director.

Flash in Authorware

If you have a basic knowledge of Authorware you can easily import a Flash .swf (through the Insert, Media, Flash...menu option) and control how the movie plays or appears. In addition, Authorware can receive messages from Flash. Let's first look at how to control the Flash movie—that is, how to let Authorware "talk" to Flash.

Authorware Talking to Flash

There are more than 60 properties and methods of Flash that you can control from Authorware. There aren't even that many properties in Flash, but the additional control includes attributes that apply only when the movie plays inside

Authorware. For example, movies that play in Authorware perform best when Direct to Screen is selected. Turning off Direct to Screen allows you to place other graphics on top of the movie. The point is there are both features unique to Flash and those unique to Authorware (such as Direct to Screen) in every Flash movie contained in an Authorware file. If you peruse the "command reference" in the Authorware help files, you'll notice some commands have a syntax that refers to "icons" and others that refer to "sprites." The icon properties are those specific to Flash and the sprite properties are Authorware specific. It's not important that you memorize which is which, but knowing the difference explains why you're about to see two seemingly identical syntax forms.

To set a property that is unique to Flash for a Flash movie in Authorware, use `setIconProperty(IconID,#propName,value)` where "iconID" is a reference to the icon that contains the Flash movie. For example, if the icon's name is `"flash"`, you'd replace "iconID" with `@"flash"` (which returns the `IconID` for the icon with the name `"flash"`). Just like referring to clip instances in Flash, Authorware lets you refer to icons using their `IconID`. "#propName" must be replaced with a property (of which you'll find many in Authorware's help files). Property names are always provided as *symbols*, which is Authorware's term for data types that appear with a pound sign and never in quotation marks—such as `#rotation`, for example. Finally, "value" is the new value for the property you're setting.

The similar syntax for setting properties of a Flash movie that only apply to Authorware looks like this:

```
setSpriteProperty(IconID,#propName,value)
```

Ascertaining values for properties of Flash movies uses one of the two syntax forms shown here:

```
getIconProperty(IconID,#propName)
getSpriteProperty(IconID,#propName)
```

Just remember that because these functions return values, you probably use them in conjunction with an assignment like this:

```
curRotation:=getIconProperty(@"flash",#rotation)
```

Calling methods uses one of the following forms:

```
callIcon(IconID,#methodName,optionalParameter)
callSprite(IconID,#methodName,optionalParameter)
```

Notice that all available methods are referred to as symbols (for example, `callSprite(@"flashIcon",#gotoFrame,12)`).

Using these methods and properties from Authorware is fairly straightforward. You'll probably have to search a bit to find the appropriate properties from the available list, but when you find the one you need, it's easy to use. There are a few properties that require you to first indicate that they're allowed to be set. For example, you can't just rotate the contents of a Flash movie by using `setIconProperty(@"flash", #rotation, 180)` unless you've previously set the `#obeyScoreRotation` property (a property of Flash movies in Authorware) to `FALSE`. So the preceding rotation change will work only if this script is executed first: `setIconProperty(@"flash", #obeyScoreRotation, FALSE)`. Generally, however, setting properties from Authorware is pretty easy.

Flash Talking to Authorware

A Flash movie inside Authorware can't make any changes to the Authorware package itself. You saw earlier that Authorware can change properties of an embedded Flash movie—but not the other way around. However, you can send an "event" from Flash to Authorware, and if you've previously told Authorware to listen for such an event, you can also program Authorware to respond when the event is received.

The way to send events from Flash to Authorware is almost identical to the quick and dirty way of having Flash talk to JavaScript I mentioned earlier: Use the `getURL()` statement, and instead of a Web address, include a string that starts with `"event:"` (similar to the way you used `"javascript:"` earlier). Following the colon after "event," you include an event name; to provide parameters, include them after your event name separated by spaces. For example, consider this script in Flash:

```
getURL("event:flashTalking param1 param2");
```

When this script is executed, Authorware will receive an event with an `#eventNameSymbol` of `#flashTalking` and a `#paramListString` of `"param1 param2"`. You need to make sure Authorware is listening for and prepared to respond to events. Additionally, you need to sort out the data after it's inside Authorware because it all comes in one variable: a "Property List" (Authorware's equivalent to Flash's Associative Array).

First, to make Authorware listen for events, you simply need an Interaction Icon with icons placed to the right (hanging off of the Interaction Icon). This way you can set up a response for each piece of feedback that you want. One Response Type in Authorware is a button. If the user clicks the button, he gets feedback. Another Response Type is called Event—and that's the one you need here. As with any other Response Type, you can build the feedback and we'll do that next. If you simply place a Map Icon next to an Interaction Icon and select the Response Type of Event, you can edit the response by double-clicking on the letter "E" (as in Figure 14.6).

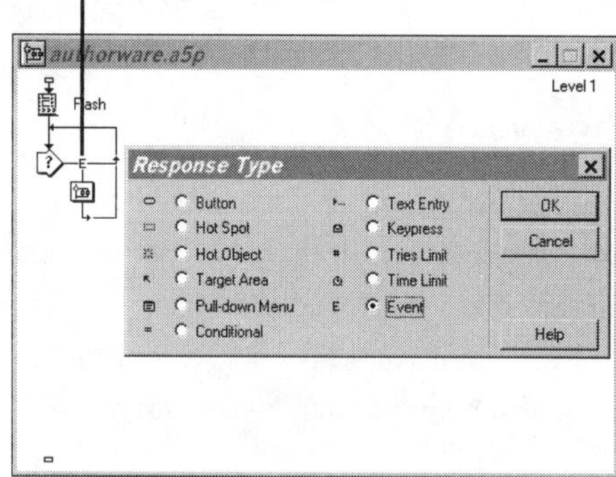

Figure 14.6 *The Event Response Type is selected and then properties (for this event) are reached by double-clicking the "E."*

In the Event tab of the Response Properties dialog, you select the sender for the event. Simply double-click the name listed for your Flash icon so that an "x" appears (if you have more than one Flash icon, they'll all be listed). Then, because we're sending "events," you need to double-click `event` from the Event Name list. Figure 14.7 shows the finished version of the Response Properties dialog.

Now, for the feedback and how to sort out the event data sent to Authorware. Inside the map with the Event Response, you can place any kind of feedback you want. For this demonstration, we'll just use a simple Display icon with the text "Authorware heard an event." At this point, if you test the Authorware file, you should see the display appear when the event is received. To sort out the data that's received, re-enter the Display icon and type this text:

```
{EventLastMatched}
```

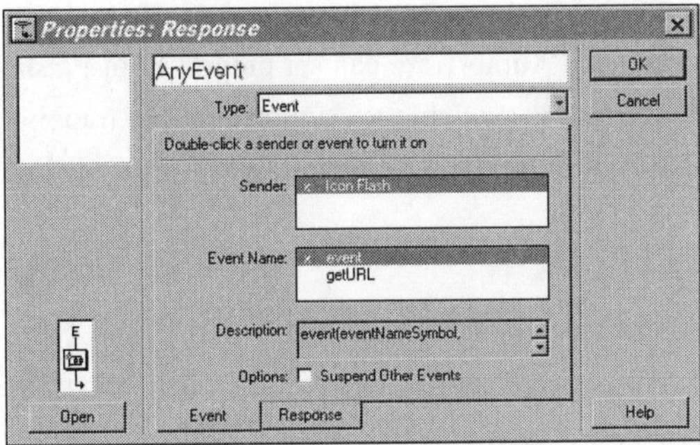

Figure 14.7 *The completed Event Response dialog box shows x's as displayed here.*

`EventLastMatched` is the variable containing all the data sent from Flash. Its form is a property list. Placing it between curly brackets causes Authorware to display the value for this variable. As a property list, this variable's value looks like an Associative Array. You'll notice several potentially interesting properties (when you see them all displayed as in Figure 14.8), but for now, let's just look at `#eventNameSymbol`.

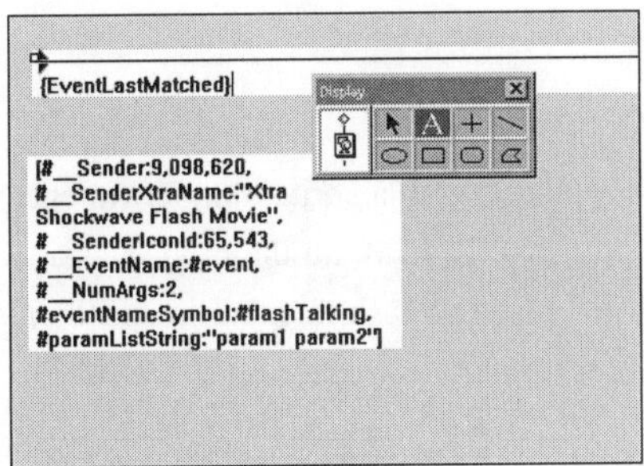

Figure 14.8 *The* `EventLastMatched` *variable (when between curly brackets) displays all the data received from Flash.*

If you simply create another text block with `{EventLastMatched[#eventNameSymbol]}`, you'll see the event name that was extracted from the entire `EventLastMatched` variable—and it should equal `"flashTalking"`. Finally, if you want access to the parameters, just grab the `#paramListString` that is `EventLastMatched[#paramListString]`.

You can see that with just a bit of Authorware experience you can make Flash send messages to Authorware, and Authorware can set properties of Flash movies. Not every feature of Flash is available to Authorware, but trapping messages *from* Flash means that Authorware can do anything as triggered from Flash.

Flash in Director

I suspect that if you're a "Director person," you probably didn't read the previous section (and similarly, no "Authorware people" are reading this). Maybe you use both Director and Authorware, in which case this section might seem slightly familiar. In fact, the way Director communicates with Flash is similar to but not the same as Authorware's method. As before, we'll look at Director controlling (or talking to) Flash followed by Flash talking to Director.

Director Talking to Flash

Director can control Flash in two basic ways. An individual Flash sprite on Director's stage can have any of its sprite properties ascertained (and many can also be set). The syntax in Director to return a property's value is

```
sprite(num).theProperty
```

To set a property, use

```
sprite(num).theProperty=newValue
```

Just remember that "num" has to be replaced with a sprite number (integer) and "theProperty" must be a legitimate property. To learn all the properties available (and to see all their current values), just place a Flash member in sprite 1, type this into the Message window, and press Enter:

```
sprite(1).showProps()
```

You'll see all the properties available (as in Figure 14.9).

This way you'll learn all the properties that can be used to replace "theProperty" in the syntax shown here. For example, from the more than 25 properties listed when you do a `showProps()`, you'll see rotation. Therefore, to set the rotation of the Flash sprite in channel 1, use

```
sprite(1).rotation=180
```

Figure 14.9 *Director's Message window will display all the properties available to a sprite when the* `showProps()` *function is called.*

Members have properties, too. To learn the properties available to a Flash member, first use

```
member("flashMemberName").showProps()
```

("flashMemberName" is the name of the member containing the Flash media.) You'll see many more properties available to a Flash member than a to a Flash sprite. It might also strike your interest that some of the member properties appear to be the same as the sprite properties. They might have the same name, but they're not identical. When you set a sprite property, you affect only that one instance (like changing a clip instance property onstage in Flash). When you change a member property, that change affects all instances that have been placed onstage and any that appear onstage. A member in Director is like a Library item in Flash. Therefore, if you change a member, you'll see the change reflected in each instance—just as if you change a Library item in Flash. The syntax to set or get a member property is

```
member("flashMemberName).propertyName
```

Pretty simple really. The only catch is that some properties cannot be set. You can ascertain their values, but you can't change them. Director will display a dialog that says, "Cannot set this property," in those cases.

Methods and Functions for Flash

In addition to the countless properties of Flash sprites and Flash members, Director's programming language, Lingo, provides additional control through sprite methods and member functions. For example, simple `play` and `stop` methods can be applied to Flash sprites. In addition, there are several Director-specific functions related to Flash. For example, the `findLabel()` function returns the frame number in a Flash movie for a given label name (provided as the parameter).

I'm not going to list all the functions and methods here, but because they're not always easy to find (not nearly as easy as the `showProp()` technique), I'll show you a great way to find them. The Categorized Lingo menu (found in any Director script window—as in Figure 14.10) has two categories with all the related functions, methods, and properties related to Flash members and sprites. The list is quite long, but when you find an interesting one, you can use the Flash online "Lingo Dictionary" to find more information.

Figure 14.10 *The Categorized Lingo menu provides the best access to all the Lingo related to Flash.*

Flash Talking to Director

Before I reveal the two main gateways through which Flash can talk to Director, let me provide this warning. If you want to make something really complex in Flash, fine. If you want to make something complex in Director, that's also fine. But if you want to use Flash inside Director, the best technique is to let Director do all the "heavy lifting" and let Flash be as simple as possible. Flash plays in a window on top of Director. Think of trying to hold a full cup of coffee and then think of trying to hold it while riding a unicycle. The additional level of complexity (besides being absurd) is just asking for trouble. Even if you make the Flash movie super simple (which you should), you might still need to send events to Director (and then let Director do the work), so let's see how.

There are two ways for Flash to trigger Director. Both ways use the familiar `getURL()` trick in which you provide something other than a URL as a parameter. Flash movies in Director can use either the `"lingo:"` or `"event:"` syntax. Using `"lingo:"` executes actual Director Lingo in much the same way the `"javascript:"` technique executes JavaScript. Using `"event:"` sends a custom event to the sprite that currently contains the Flash movie. The main difference is that `"lingo:"` gives you access to any built-in Lingo element or homemade handler in a Movie Script. The `"event:"` syntax provides quick and direct access to the behavior script attached to the particular sprite containing the Flash movie. You mighty find slight performance differences and even situations where one will appear to fail while the other works—I certainly don't know all the workarounds. But I can explain how to use both of them.

Using the `"lingo:"` technique, you can have Flash execute Director's built-in `alert()` function:

```
getURL ("lingo:alert(\"hi mom\")");
```

Basically, we just send a string (instead of a URL) and begin with `lingo:`, and then follow it with our Director Lingo code verbatim. Notice that because `alert`'s normal format is `alert("hi mom")`, you must include quotation marks, but we're placing them within the quotation marks required for the `getURL` parameter. The syntax `\"` inserts a literal quotation mark.

The same basic technique can be used to invoke a custom function (called a *handler* in Director).

```
getURL ("lingo:myHandler");
```

To use the preceding code, somewhere in a Director Movie Script you need a handler that looks something like this:

```
on myHandler
  alert("I heard Flash")
end
```

Additionally, you can pass parameters using this technique. In Flash's `getURL()`, include the first parameter that appears after the handler name and subsequent parameters after commas:

```
getURL ("lingo:myHandler \"stringParam1\"");
```

or

```
getURL ("lingo:myHandler \"stringParam1\", 33");
```

Notice that in the second example, I provide an extra parameter in the form of a number (not a string). Naturally, the Director handler will need to be adjusted to accept the parameters:

```
on myHandler oneParam, twoParam
  alert("one param was "&oneParam&" and the other "&twoParam)
end
```

Finally, for Flash to invoke a behavior attached to its host sprite, we'll use the `"event:"` syntax:

```
getURL ("event: theEvent");
```

Attached to the sprite holding this Flash media, you'll need a behavior script that looks like this:

```
on theEvent me
    alert ("Flash is talking")
end
```

Because this is a Director behavior, the keyword `me` is included for style (this is like Flash's `this`, which isn't always required).

This technique is similar to Director's `SendSprite()` function. To pass parameters in Flash, you need to separate the handler name from the first parameter and all subsequent parameters. Notice that this is slightly different than the `"lingo:"` syntax, which simply used a space to separate the handler from the first parameter. For example:

```
getURL ("event: theEvent, \"stringParam1\", 33");
```

This sends the values `"sringParam1"` and `33` as the first and second parameters, respectively. The updated behavior looks like this:

```
on theEvent me, param1, param2
  alert("Flash says "&param1&" and "&param2)
end
```

I'm sure that this section (and the last one on Authorware) was a complete bore if you've never touched those tools (and never plan to). But those of you with a past or future with these powerful tools should find this a great kickstart to incorporating Flash.

Summary

What can I say? This was a long chapter! It's the last one in the foundation section, and we're about to move on to some fun workshop exercises. It turns out that the material in this chapter was probably easier to grasp with the foundation you've already gathered. For example, even if you've never touched JavaScript or Director, you can probably make sense of most of the scripts provided. That's because we haven't just been learning Flash in all those other chapters, we've been learning programming! (Congratulations, you're now a programming geek.)

Seriously, this chapter showed you almost all the ways in which Flash can interact with the world around it. We started by including linked scripts when exporting a movie. Then we saw how Flash can read in data from text files. The same format was used when we learned how Flash can read data sent to it via a server script. The advantage to server scripts is that Flash could also send data (that is, all its variables) to the server, too. Although the standard technique (with `loadVariables()` and `getURL()`) used the URL-encoded format, we also took a dive into XML-structured data. We skimmed over the XML Socket object before looking at the ways Flash can be a good guest while inside Authorware or Director files. Even though I can't imagine any one human will ever have the need to use *all* these techniques, it's nice to be familiar enough to know what's possible.

{Part II }

Workshop

{Workshop} Introduction

Now we really get to *apply* the knowledge gained in the first part of the book. I can't imagine that you haven't touched Flash since starting the book, but in any case, you will now.

The first thing that I feel compelled to mention is that the code you'll find in the workshops ranges from flat-out bad to really good. The bad stuff is just there for educational purposes (so that we can fix it up). Even the good stuff should not always be considered the "best." There's always more than one way to achieve a result. I would never fault code if it worked. Certainly you shouldn't write code that's unmanageable, but there's a good argument for code that's clear to you. Often the examples shown are presented in a way that makes the most sense. I didn't make sacrifices just to make the code look pretty, but I didn't spend an inordinate amount of time streamlining it either. The workshops are intended to teach you a process of development as well as offer a chance to apply the topics covered in the first part of the book. (Please don't call me when you find a better way to do the same thing—consider that I'd be proud and leave it at that.)

Anyway, let me offer this quick overview of all the workshops.

1. "Ensuring That Users Have the Flash 5 Player." This no-nonsense workshop discusses some of the ways to make sure that your audience is equipped to see your Flash 5 creation. We also walk through an exercise using Flash itself as a way to determine player version.
2. "Faking Video." To answer one of the most frequent requests for Flash, this workshop shows how to simulate video inside Flash. You'll also make a simple slider and calculate percentages.

3. "Creating Custom Cursors." After two simple steps to make a custom cursor, this workshop goes on to make a Smart Clip and then a custom UI for that Smart Clip. It's a pretty involved workshop because you learn that you can't use buttons (even invisible ones) because they would conflict with any buttons that you try to place this Smart Clip over.
4. "Creating a Horizontal Slider." In this workshop, we make a Smart Clip version of a slider similar to the one built in the "Faking Video" workshop. As a Smart Clip, we make this as generic and universal as possible.
5. "Building a Slide Show." In addition to the slide show application that you build, you get your first introduction to using the `enterFrame` event as well as placing buttons inside Movie Clips so that you can disable them (by hiding the clip).
6. "Mapping." The general technique of mapping is applied to a contrived exercise but in a way so that you can apply it to other situations. Bring your math "thinking cap" to this one.
7. "Working with Odd-Shaped Clickable Areas." Although buttons are great, this exercise shows how movie clips (along with the `hitTest()` method) can serve as alternatives to buttons.
8. "Adapting Built-in Smart Clips." Not only does this exercise show you how to adapt the Menu Smart Clip that ships with Flash so that you can use it, you also learn a bit about the process involved including using the Debugger.
9. "Creating a Currency-Exchange Calculator." We turn a simple currency exchange calculation into a really usable application. There are some fancy string maneuvers and a simple use of the `loadVariables()` method.
10. "Creating a Tooltip Smart Clip." The basic concepts from the "Custom Cursor" workshop come into play, but we use `getTimer()` for the first time to add an optional delay.
11. "Creating a Digital Timer." In this workshop, we use the `getTimer()` in a most typical way—to make a digital stopwatch.
12. "Creating an Analog Timer." This workshop is really quite a snap after you have the code from the "Digital Timer" workshop. You just add visual hands to make a traditional analog stopwatch.
13. "Creating a Countdown Timer." We continue exploring traditional uses for `getTimer()` and add a few graphics to make this progress bar–type of timer. We also get to use math to calculate percentages.
14. "Using Math to Create a Circular Slider." This workshop doesn't look much different than a regular slider—it just follows a circular path. However, to calculate angles and draw arcs, we use several trigonometry functions from the Math object.

15. "Developing Time-Based Animations." In a simple example, we see how `getTimer()` can be used to ensure perfect synchronization—and how to effectively drop frames if the animation is not keeping up.
16. "Creating a Multistate Button." You'll make a button that behaves *exactly* like a system-level button used in standard programs (such as your browser, your word processor, and so on) by using a Movie Clip and ActionScript.
17. "Offline Production." We'll build an animation and then save the coordinates of each step so that it can be used in a time-based application.
18. "Creating a Dynamic Slide Presentation." Here we build an XML application that loads data dynamically to build a slide show with bullet points. It's an exercise in using XML-structured data as well as general template design.
19. "Creating JavaScript Cookies." You'll learn how Flash (through JavaScript) can read and write cookies so that the movie will remember the last settings a user made.
20. "Writing JavaScript Inter-Movie Communications." You'll make two Flash movies "talk" to each other by way of JavaScript.
21. "Fixing Broken Scripts." You'll be challenged to fix 10 faulty Flash files (that you download from `www.teleport.com/~phillip/actionscripting`). For each one, you'll be given a clue and the solution to make things right.

Naturally, each of these workshops involves many details requiring additional parts of ActionScript. After you complete them all, consider trying to rebuild them from scratch (without the book). I'll bet that many of you will find quicker or better ways to get them running.

{Part IIA }

Beginning Workshops

1 Ensuring That Users Have the Flash 5 Player
2 Faking Video
3 Creating Custom Cursors
4 Creating a Horizontal Slider
5 Building a Slide Show
6 Mapping
7 Working with Odd-Shaped Clickable Areas
8 Adapting Built-in Smart Clips

{ Chapter 1 Workshop }

Ensuring That Users Have the Flash 5 Player

It's safe to say that practically everything covered in this book is specific to Flash 5. This simply means that your audience must be equipped with Flash version 5 or later. Although it's possible to target older Flash players using the Publish Settings (Figure W1.1), selecting any option lower than Flash 5 causes most of the scripting capabilities to be off limits. It's actually possible to work in Flash 5 and deliver to Flash 4 or Flash 3—there are just so many details that we're not even going to discuss it. The fact is that at the end of 2000, more than 95 percent of all Internet users had at least the Flash 3 player. Although your Flash 5 movies won't work for these users, the solution outlined in this workshop will easily identify those users with anything less than the Flash 5 player and provide alternatives for them. These alternatives range from a link to Macromedia (so that they can upgrade) to channeling them to a different version of your Web page. The technique you'll learn in this workshop uses Flash to identify which version of Flash the user has.

Naturally, using Flash to test which version of Flash is installed assumes that users have at least *some* version of Flash. To provide a seamless experience for those 5 percent of users without any Flash player, you have a host of alternatives. Unfortunately, I don't think any solution is 100 percent foolproof. I'm not saying that the alternatives I'm about to present have inherent flaws, it's just that they also rely on technology that may not be functional. For example, if you try to use JavaScript to determine whether the user has the Flash player, it's possible that the user has turned off JavaScript in his or her browser. Anyway, there *are* some near iron-clad solutions to reach *any* user, even if they don't have Flash.

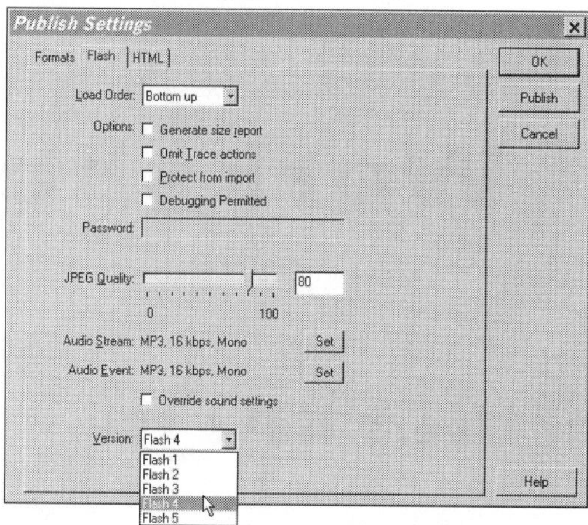

Figure W1.1 *You can target old versions of Flash using the Publish Settings, but you won't be able to use most Flash 5 features.*

First I'll provide a quick rundown of two non-Flash solutions and then walk through exactly how you use Flash to check which version of Flash is installed.

The non-Flash solutions use what's commonly called a "sniffer" script—an HTML file with scripts that attempt to sense what version, if any, of the Flash player is installed. The sniffer script is a file that serves as a gateway to redirect users to the appropriate content. Every user who visits your site always starts by visiting this gateway file. The file tries to determine whether the user can see Flash. If the user has Flash, he or she goes to the Flash version of your site (another page); if the user doesn't have Flash, he or she goes to the non-Flash version of your site. You can even send users to a third place if they have Flash but need to upgrade to the latest version. The non-Flash site can be as simple as a page that provides the users a link to Macromedia, where they can download the Flash player. The non-Flash site can also be as complex as the whole site built in HTML. The point is that the sniffer or gateway page sends the user to one of two places: the Flash site or the non-Flash site.

Macromedia has a nice set of instructions and sample files that will help you produce such a sniffer page. The Flash Deployment Kit (which can be freely downloaded from `www.macromedia.com/software/flash/download/deployment_kit/`) includes a gateway page (`enter.html`) and scripts in both

JavaScript and VBScript as well as plenty of documentation. Although there are lots of features, they all come down to how you use the "dispatcher." Basically, you just provide the appropriate parameters to the `MMFlashDispatch()` JavaScript function. You specify the URL for where your Flash content resides (the page where users with the appropriate Flash player automatically go), the minimum version of the Flash player required (say, version 5,41), whether you want to require the revision number (for example, 41) or just the major version number (such as 5), the alternative URL for those users who don't have Flash, the upgrade URL for those who have Flash but not the required version (this can be the same as the alternative URL), and finally, whether you want to remember (by way of a JavaScript cookie) when a user says he or she doesn't want to upgrade so that you don't even bother with this whole scenario the next time and instead automatically jump to the alternative URL. So really, you just specify the Web addresses to which you want to send users in different situations, and you're done. As you might expect, there are more details in the documentation that comes with the Flash Deployment Kit.

//

By the way, there's another nice set of scripts you can download from the Flash Exchange site (`www.macromedia.com/exchange/flash/`) called JavaScript Integration Kit for Flash. It's really more of a kit for Dreamweaver because everything is installed as Dreamweaver behaviors and commands. Included are controls to manage Flash movies with JavaScript (as covered in Chapter 14, "Interfacing with External Data") in addition to a Dreamweaver behavior called the Flash Dispatcher. The same dispatcher code from the Flash Deployment Kit is included in the JavaScript Integration Kit (but especially made for Dreamweaver). A big advantage of installing the JavaScript Integration Kit for Dreamweaver is that the code comes in the form of a Macromedia Extension. By using the free Macromedia Extension Manager program, you can easily manage various extensions (including this one). The reason I mention it is that you can make Flash Extensions that are also managed through this tool. It's nice for users because they can download and install Smart Clips, Flash Libraries, and Dreamweaver behaviors and manage them all through the Extension Manager. (In Appendix B, "Making Flash Extensions for the Macromedia Exchange Web Site," I provide the resources so that you can distribute Smart Clips in this manner.)

Before we get into the main workshop, I want to mention a suitable alternative to Macromedia's set of sniffer scripts. Colin Moock has produced the Moock Flash Player Inspector (or Moock FPI) which provides a similar set of alternatives to the Flash Deployment Kit. You can download the Moock FPI from `www.moock.org/webdesign/flash/detection/moockfpi/`.

Because this is a workshop, we're going to step through an exercise. The following exercise assumes that your user has at least the Flash 2 player. We'll create a Flash sniffer that redirects the user if they have anything less than Flash 5. This exercise is based on a Flash file that comes in the Flash Deployment Kit called `detectFlash.fla`. We'll build our own version of this file following these steps:

1. In a new file, select File, Publish Settings…. Under the Formats tab, make sure that Flash is selected. Select the Flash tab and select Flash 4 from the Version drop-down menu (as shown in Figure W1.1).

2. In frame 1, place the following script:

   ```
   atLeastFlash4 = "1";
   ```

   This script simply sets a variable, which will be ignored in any version of Flash lower than 4. That's because Flash 4 was the first version to introduce variables. (Notice that many of the ActionScript components are highlighted in yellow, meaning that they're unavailable because you changed the Publish Settings to Flash 4.)

3. Insert a blank keyframe in frame 2 and place this script:

   ```
   if (Number(atLeastFlash4)==1) {
   } else {
     tellTarget ("flashThreeButton") {
       gotoAndStop (2);
     }
     stop ();
   }
   ```

   Basically, if the variable `atLeastFlash4` is indeed `1` (as we just set it in frame 1), nothing really happens and we'll proceed like normal to frame 3. Because versions before Flash 4 don't support `if` statements, this script will be effectively ignored. Actually, Flash 3 and earlier versions don't ignore `if` statements, they execute only the `else` part of the statement. Why, I don't know. What happens is that any version before Flash 4 will execute the `tellTarget()` and `stop()` methods contained in the `else` portion of the statement. The `tellTarget()` method is the old way to attach a method to an individual instance. Translated to Flash 5, the script says `flashThreeButton.gotoAndStop(2)`. We'll make a clip with the instance name `flashThreeButton` that will jump to frame 2 for these (less than Flash 4) users. Finally, the `stop()` method just prevents our main timeline from going any further.

4. Let's build the clip for users of Flash 3 (and earlier). Select Insert, New Symbol.... Select Movie Clip and name this clip "Flash3."

5. You should be inside the Flash3 symbol. In frame 2, insert a keyframe and draw the shape for a button. Convert the shape to a button symbol (select it, press F8, and select Button). Attach the following script to the button:

```
on (release) {
  getURL ("http://www.macromedia.com/shockwave/download/index.cgi?
➥P1_Prod_Version=ShockwaveFlash", "_blank");
}
```

   Notice that the Web address should appear on a single line. The idea is that if the user doesn't even have Flash 4, they'll see this button, which will take them to Macromedia where they can upgrade. You may also want to center the button instance within the Flash3 symbol.

6. In frame 1, place a `stop()` script. Now the clip will normally sit in frame 1 (effectively as an invisible clip) and jump to frame 2 only when the button appears. You can place more content in frame 2—such as the message, "click the button to upgrade." If you want the user to automatically jump to the Macromedia site, you can take the `getURL()` code from the button and place it in frame 2. However, if you do this, it might be unclear to the user what is happening.

7. Drag an instance of the Flash3 symbol that we just made to frame 2 in the main timeline (remember, we just did a New Symbol and not a Convert to Symbol, so there's no instance on the Stage yet). Give this invisible clip an instance name of `flashThreeButton`.

8. Now that we've taken care of the sub-Flash 4 users, let's see whether the user has Flash 5. Insert a blank keyframe in frame 3 and place the following script in that frame:

```
playerVersion = eval("$version");
revision = substring(playerVersion, 5, 1);
if (Number(int(revision))<Number(int(5))) {
  tellTarget ("flashFourButton") {
    gotoAndStop (2);
  }
} else {
  getURL ("flash_five_content.html", "_self");
}
stop ();
```

   The first line assigns the variable `playerVersion` equal to the old `$version` variable that was introduced during the Flash 4 era. Unlike most variables, you can't just say `playerVersion=$version` because that dollar sign is not a legitimate way to start a variable name. The `eval()` function evaluates the value of the built-in `$version` variable. The form returned to the `playerVersion` variable looks like this: `"WIN 5,0,30,0"` (Figure W1.2).

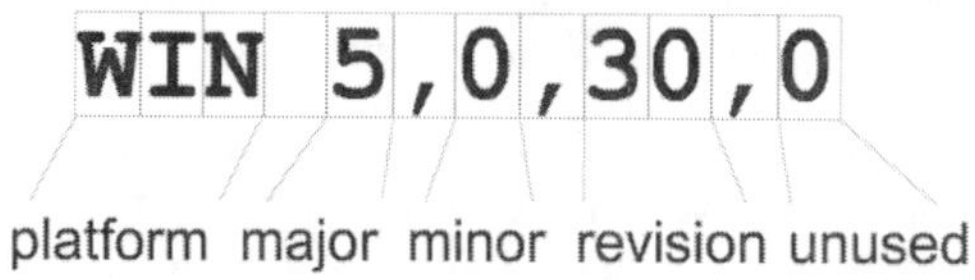

WIN 5,0,30,0

platform major minor revision unused

Figure W1.2 *The* `$version` *variable contains five key elements.*

The `$version` variable is a very specific string with information about the platform, the major version, the minor version (which is rarely if ever updated), the revision (also sometimes called the "patch" version, which is updated occasionally to provide added features and bug fixes—for example, the `ignoreWhite` XML property was introduced in `5,0,41`), and the last number which isn't even used. What might mess you up is that we assign the variable `revision` using the `substring()` *function* (not the preferred—and only available in Flash 5—`substring()` *method* of the String object). This function behaves differently as discussed in Chapter 9, "Selecting Text, Trapping Keys, and Manipulating Strings." The `if` statement in line three simply checks whether an integer version of `revision` is less than 5 or not. If it is, we tell the `flashFourButton` clip (that we're about to build) to go to frame 2, where the user will see a button to upgrade. Otherwise (if the version number is not less than 5), we do a `getURL()` to jump the user to our "real" HTML page with Flash 5 content. Just replace `flash_five_content.html` with the name of the HTML file that contains your Flash 5 content.

//

If you ever need to use the Flash 4 `substring()` *function* to ascertain the revision number, simply use `substring(playerVersion, 9, 2)`. An issue that might really freak you out is that the `$version` variable wasn't released with the very first version of Flash 4. The earliest versions of the Flash 4 player won't recognize this variable. However, it's not a problem because the `if` statement in line three will still work. Also, notice that the `int()` function is used to convert the `version` string to a number that can be used in a conditional statement. That's simply because Flash 4 didn't have the `Number()` function.

9. Now let's make the `flashFourButton`. Just duplicate the symbol called Flash3 (and rename it Flash4), then change any Flash3-specific text contained in the symbol. Make a new layer and drag an instance of the Flash4 symbol onto the Stage. It doesn't matter that this instance will start in

frame 1; it just must be present at the time `tellTarget()` is called. Make sure to give the symbol an instance name of `flashFourButton`.

10. At this point, you can export or publish the `.swf`.

We have just made a Flash 4 movie that acted like a sniffer to sense for sub-Flash 5 players. Those folks with Flash, but not Flash 5, are redirected. Those users with Flash 5 won't notice much at all because they'll jump to the right page.

There's one last task you may have to resolve: making sure that your Flash 5 users have the latest revision of the Flash 5 player. For example, you may really *need* to take advantage of a new feature (or lack of bug) in the 5,0,41 version of the player. Once you're in Flash 5, this is a simple task.

Although the Flash player doesn't get patched terribly often, several features and bug fixes were introduced in 5,0,41, so it's worth checking for this version. You can see the entire list of issues with the first Flash 5 player in Macromedia's technote 14732; you can see the corresponding enhancements made in version 5,0,41,0 and later in the technotes 14716, 14719, 14957, 14958, 14964, 14985, 14986, and 14987 (which pretty much explain how all the issues in technote 14732 were resolved). To view any of these technotes, type the address `www.macromedia.com/go/` and add the technote number at the end (for example, `www.macromedia.com/go/14987`).

You can use any of the `String` object methods on the built-in `$version` variable (which, unlike in Flash 4, can be used as-is and doesn't require the `eval()` function). Consider these five expressions to extract key portions of the `$version` variable:

```
//form:  WIN 5,0,30,0
platform=$version.substr( 0, 3 );
major=$version.charAt(4);
minor=$version.charAt(6);
revision=$version.substr(8,2);
unused=$version.charAt(11);
```

These String object methods should look familiar if you've read Chapter 9. Basically, I just came up with five custom variables to represent each portion of the `$version` variable. Most likely, you'll just need the line `revision=$version.substr(8,2)` to extract the revision number of the player because this is the portion that is updated most often.

//

Personally, I'm a paranoid person. The preceding scripts are not guaranteed to work if the Flash version numbering system ever changes. For example, what if there's a Flash 10? Although most Web sites created today will probably need an overhaul that far in the future, here are a couple of alternatives to parsing individual elements from the `$version` variable. By using the `indexOf()` method, we can find the location of the commas and then set our `minor`, `revision`, and `unused` variables:

```
var startMinor=$version.indexOf(",",5)+1;
var endMinor=$version.indexOf(",",startMinor);
minor=$version.substring(startMinor,endMinor);

var startRevision=$version.indexOf(",",endMinor)+1;
var endRevision=$version.indexOf(",",startRevision);
rev=$version.substring(startRevision,endRevision);

var startUnused=endRevision+1;
var endUnused =$version.length;
unused=$version.substring(startUnused, endUnused);
```

If nothing else, this example provides a good reminder of how to use the `indexOf()` method.

Notice that all the expressions shown with the `$version` (string) variable return strings. You can always use the `Number()` function if you need to.

Now that you're familiar with the ways to ensure that your users have the Flash player, we can move on to much more fun workshops! This workshop was included because I really wanted to concentrate just on Flash 5; all the great Flash 5 movies you make will go unrecognized if you can't upgrade your users.

{ Chapter 2 Workshop }

Faking Video

One of the most common questions I hear is, "How do I put a video in Flash?" Quite simply, you can't. Flash does allow you to import QuickTime videos, but only for the purpose of exporting QuickTime files with Flash media included. When exporting to the Flash player (that is, making .swfs), you cannot have video. However, if you consider "video" to be synchronized pictures and sound—sometimes you don't need traditional "video." If you just want a sequence of pictures (without synchronized audio), Flash can work quite well. That's what we'll do in this exercise.

1. First, we must convert our digital video into a sequence of bitmaps. Flash can import sequentially numbered bitmaps or other raster formats (such as `.jpg`). Most video editing software can export sequentially numbered still frames from a video, but you can also use Flash. In a new Flash movie, resize the stage to the same dimensions as the video you want to use, import a QuickTime video, extend the timeline by adding frames (F5) to accommodate the video's entire length. Then select the menu option File, Export Movie and from the Save as Type drop-down list, choose Bitmap Sequence (see Figure W2.1). Make sure that you export into an empty folder on a disk that has plenty of space. At this point, you can close the Flash file without saving because it was used only to create the bitmap sequence. (If you don't have a QuickTime video handy, you can follow along by creating a simple tween in Flash and exporting it as a bitmap sequence—just to get the idea.)

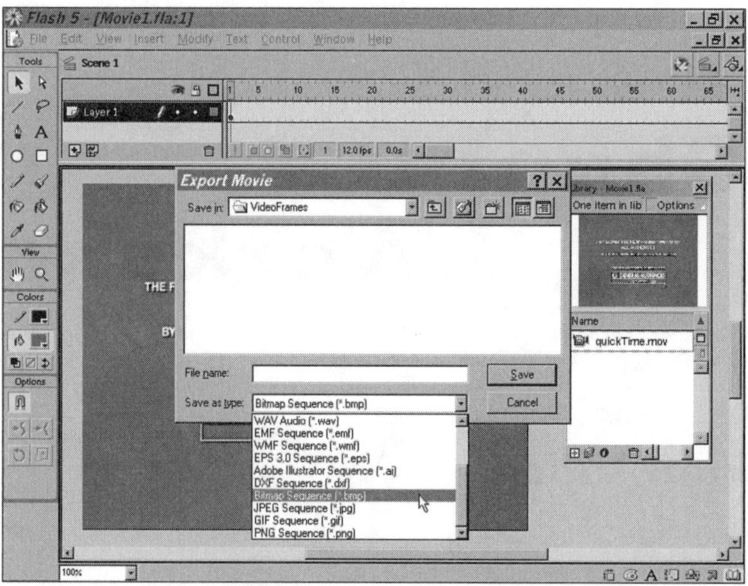

Figure W2.1 *Flash can export a sequence of video frames.*

2. In a new Flash file, we're ready to import the bitmap sequence. First select Insert, New Symbol; name it Video and leave it set to the default Movie Clip option. While inside the Video symbol, select File, Import and point to the *first* bitmap file from the sequence. If Flash notices that there are sequentially numbered files in the same folder, a dialog will ask whether you want to import all the images (answer Yes).

3. At this point, you just need to drag the Video Movie Clip to the stage anywhere in your movie and name the instance in the Instance panel. Some simple refinements you can make include placing a `stop()` script in the last frame of the clip. Also, in a separate layer of the Video MC, you can place two buttons: one with `play()` and another with `stop()`. Naturally, if you wanted to keep the play and stop buttons in the main timeline, their scripts would be `theClip.play()` and `theClip.stop()`, where "theClip" is an instance name you give the Video Movie Clip.

This Video clip is nice and all, but we came here to script! Besides, that was too easy. Let's add a slider that performs like Flash's red current frame marker: It not only moves from left to right while the video plays to indicate the video's position but—if dragged—it will make the video jump to another position.

4. First, we'll make the slider move. Inside the Video clip (and on a separate layer), draw a vertical rectangle that will become our slider. Convert it to a Movie Clip symbol called "Slider" (see Figure W2.2).

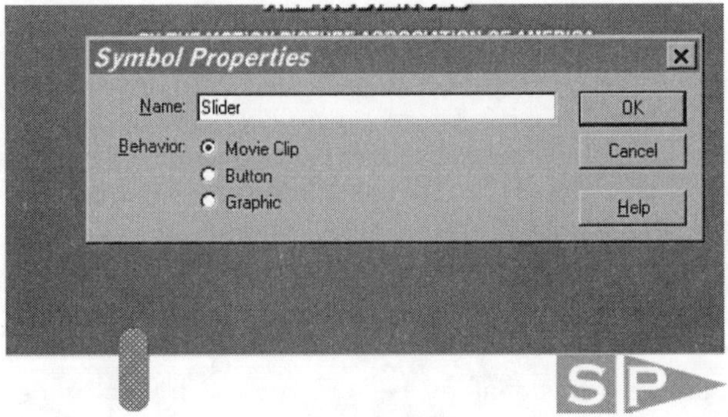

Figure W2.2 *In the Video clip, draw a vertical rectangle and convert it to a symbol.*

5. Use the Info panel to ascertain the desired minimum and maximum `_x` positions for this clip. To find the minimum `_x`, position the Slider symbol all the way on the left side of the stage and note the location of its center point; do the same for the right side of the stage to find the maximum `_x`. Make sure that the info panel is displaying the clip's center location; this is always used when setting a clip's position (see Figure W2.3).

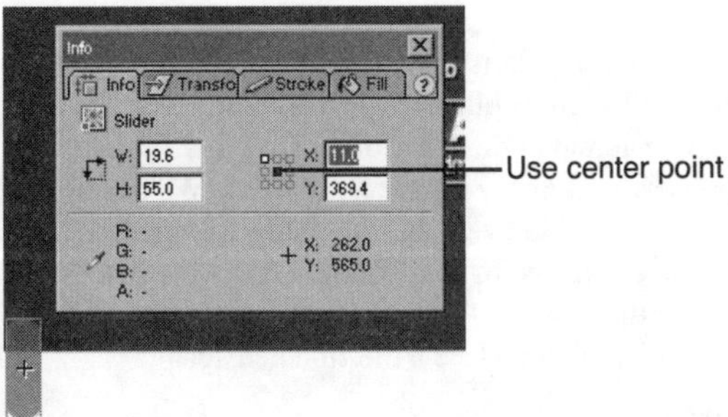

Figure W2.3 *Be sure that the Info panel displays the center point when gathering coordinate information.*

6. Attach this script to the instance of Slider in the Video clip so that our custom `min` and `max` variables are initialized. Use the numbers you gathered in step 5.

```
onClipEvent (load) {
  min= 11;
  max= 350;
}
```

7. Now we need to write the script that, depending on the current frame number, will reposition the slider to a proportional position between `min` and `max`. Sometimes the best way to write the formula is to first think of a few "what if" numbers. What if the current frame is 1? The clip should be at `min`. If there are 100 frames, when the clip is at 50 frames, the position should be halfway between `min` and `max`. These questions should help you analyze the situation and let you test your formula.

//

For the slider, consider this analogy. Let's say you're driving home from work. Your workplace is 10 miles from the ocean and your home is 30 miles from the ocean. Of course, I used easy numbers, but the point is that everything is relative to the distance from the ocean. Even though your total trip is 20 miles (the difference between 10 miles from the ocean and 30 miles from the ocean), you can't just say halfway is at 10 (half of 20—the total). You must, instead, say 10 plus the starting point of 10. It's easy to calculate that your halfway point is at 20 miles from the ocean. The reason I mention this is that the slider's minimum is not necessarily 0.

The pseudo-code for this formula is this: The percent complete `(current frame / total frames)` is multiplied by the total range `(max-min)` and then *added* to min. The actual code is as follows: `_x=min+(_currentFrame/_totalFrames)*(max-min)`. We're going to place this script inside an `enterFrame` event for the slider. However, realize that it's not the *slider's* current frame or total frames that we care about; rather, we are concerned with the Video's frames. Those two properties simply need to be preceded by `_parent`. Here's the finished script:

```
onClipEvent (enterFrame) {
  _x=min+(_parent._currentFrame/_parent._totalFrames)*(max-min);
}
```

8. Now, let's make this slider interactive so that the user can pick it up. In other workshops (such as "Odd-Shaped Clickable Areas"), you'll learn how to use the `mouseDown` clip event in combination with `hitTest()` to avoid buttons, but we'll just make a button for this exercise. We just need a button inside the slider. Double-click the slider to edit its master symbol, select the onscreen contents (the image of the slider), and covert it to a button symbol. Finally, place the following script on this button instance:

```
on (press) {
  dragging = 1;
}
```

```
on (release, releaseOutside) {
  dragging = 0;
}
```

//

Translated, this simply sets a variable in the slider clip called `dragging` to `1` or `0`. Notice that the `dragging` variable (referred to here on a button inside the Slider clip) will become part of the instance of Slider inside Video.

9. Now, when `dragging` is `1`, we can jump to a frame based on where the mouse is. Writing the formula is easy—translating it to Flash will take some effort. Again, let's start with some "what ifs." If the mouse is at `min`, we want to go to frame 1. If the mouse is halfway between `min` and `max`, we want to go to the frame halfway between 1 and the total number of frames. Here's an expression that results in the frame number to which we want to go: `((_xmouse-min)/(max-min))*_totalFrames`. That is, `totalFrames` is multiplied by the proportional position of `_xmouse`. What if `_xmouse` is the same as `max`? This turns into `1*_totalFrames`—perfect. (Try some other what-if numbers in the formula and you'll find it works as expected.) We're going to place that entire formula as the parameter for a `gotoAndStop()` method. However, although our formula correctly calculates the proportion, it can (and quite often will) result in a noninteger. The `gotoAndStop()` method *requires* an integer for a parameter. To make sure that it's an integer, we'll just put the formula within a `Math.floor()` method (discussed with other Math object methods in Chapter 5, "Programming Structures") before using it in a `gotoAndStop()`. We could place the `gotoAndStop()` (with formula) inside the clip's `enterFrame` event, but that will update only as frequently as the movie's framerate. Some users can really move the mouse quickly, and our movie should respond accordingly. The `mouseMove` event executes as often as necessary. Although the `mouseMove` event happens frequently enough, we want our script to execute only during those times when the user is dragging, or "if `dragging` is `1`". Finally, we need to precede all properties and methods with `_parent` when we want to target the Video clip (but leave the variables that are part of the clip alone—namely, `min` and `max`). Here's the finished formula attached to the instance of Slider in the Video clip:

```
onClipEvent (mouseMove) {
  if (dragging){
    theFrame=Math.floor((_parent._xmouse-min)/
➥(max-min)*_parent._totalFrames);
    _parent.gotoAndStop(theFrame);
    updateAfterEvent();
  }
}
```

//

Notice I threw in an `updateAfterEvent()` to make the onscreen contents redisplay. Also, instead of using the entire formula as a parameter, I first assigned the variable `theFrame`. Not only is this easier to read, but it allows for some subtle improvements we'll make later (in step 13).

10. At this point, it should work. The user will have an easier time grabbing the slider if the clip is stopped first. Also, the script that repositions the slider (in `enterFrame` event) updates only as frequently as the frame rate. So, the user isn't really dragging the clip, the clip is readjusting (in every `enterFrame`) to a new location. To make the performance snappier, just place `_x=_parent._xmouse` immediately above the `updateAfterEvent()` inside the `mouseMove` event. If you test it at this point, however, you might see the slider flicker. That's because your `_xmouse` is not perfectly coinciding with the location calculated by the formula used in the `enterFrame` script. We can "turn off" the `enterFrame` script while dragging simply by enclosing it within an if-statement. The improved `enterFrame` script is shown here:

```
onClipEvent (enterFrame) {
  if(dragging==0){
    _x=min+(_parent._currentFrame/_parent._totalFrames)*(max-min);
  }
}
```

11. Now, you just need to initialize `dragging` to zero in the load event. Just under where you assign `min` and `max`, place `dragging=0`.

12. At this point, it works pretty well. I just want to make one minor adjustment to account for those pesky users who like to trash what you build. Check out what happens when you drag the slider very quickly way off to the left or right. Not only does the slider go too far in either direction, the video often stops before reaching the beginning or the end. We can fix both issues.

13. To make sure that the video reaches the beginning (when the user moves too far to the left) or the end (when the user moves too far to the right), we write a script that checks for errors. It checks whether `theFrame` is less than 1 or greater than the total number of frames. Right underneath where `theFrame` is first assigned, place these two lines of code:

```
theFrame=Math.max(1,theFrame);
theFrame=Math.min(_parent._totalFrames,theFrame);
```

Translated, this says (after `theFrame` is assigned), make sure that it is either `1` or `theFrame`—whichever is greater. Also, make sure that it's either the total number of frames in the Video or `theFrame`—whichever is less. Using these Math object methods (covered in Chapter 5) makes sure that `theFrame` doesn't go below 1 or above the total number of frames.

14. To make sure that the slider doesn't go too far, we need to remove the line `_x=_parent._xmouse` and, in its place, put the same formula from inside the `enterFrame` clip. That is, `_x=min+(_parent._currentFrame/_parent._totalFrames)*(max-min)`. Now, even the most active users can't break it!

15. Finally, as you recall from Chapter 3, "The Programmer's Approach," the fact that we have the same formula in two places should make any programmer nervous. We can resolve this with a custom function (which you learned about in Chapter 8, "Functions"). In the place of both instances of the script (`_x=min+(_parent._currentFrame/_parent._totalFrames)*(max-min)`), place instead `updateSlider()`. Then inside the first frame of the slider (not the Video clip), place the following script:

```
function updateSlider(){
  _x=min+(_parent._currentFrame/_parent._totalFrames)*(max-min);
}
```

//

Remember that because the formula worked when attached to the instance of the slider, it will work just as if it were *inside* the slider. I'm not going to walk through it now, but I'm sure that you could figure out a way to place this script in the first frame of Video instead—you'd just have to adjust *all* targets. If you moved the script, `_parent` references would be removed, and `min` and `max` would need to be preceded with the slider's instance name (which we never assigned). In addition, the calls from the slider instance to this function would need to change to `_parent.updateSlider()`. It works now, but you can always adjust it. In the next few exercises, you'll learn how to convert a perfectly good (hard-wired) script to a Smart Clip. That usually involves moving scripts and changing targets.

If you wanted to improve this workshop, you could apply some of the techniques that you'll learn in the "Time-Based Animation" and "Offline Production" workshops. Specifically, it would be nice to make the playback speed of the video independent of the movie's framerate. That is, currently, the video will play slower or faster depending on the movie's frame rate.

Finally, after you build the Horizontal Slider Smart Clip in an upcoming workshop, you could use that (better) slider to control the video.

{Chapter 3 Workshop }

Creating Custom Cursors

Flash lets you make fairly sophisticated buttons with very little effort. The built-in Button symbol type is nice, but it allows only three visual states: Up, Over, and Down. In the Multi-state Button workshop, you'll learn how to include additional states such as "checked" for when the user has selected the button. In this workshop, you'll learn how to create custom cursors. Custom cursors not only tell the user that a button is clickable, they also provide clues about the type of button the user is presented with. A custom cursor can tell users whether they're supposed to drag the button or simply slide the button to the left or right.

This workshop shows you how to make a custom cursor in just a few steps. Then, the workshop takes what you built and creates a Smart Clip so that you can incorporate cursors in any movie you make. Finally, the workshop guides you through the steps to create a custom UI.

1. To start with, you need a Movie Clip containing the graphics for your cursor. Just draw anything you want and convert it to a Movie Clip symbol named "Cursor Graphic" (Figure W3.1). In this figure, the symbol is a hand with a pointing finger. Give the instance on the Stage an instance name of "hand."

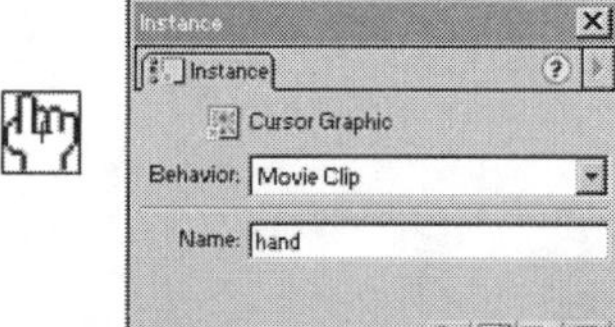

Figure W3.1 *Any graphic you place in a Movie Clip can become a cursor.*

2. Now we're going to write a script that we'll attach to the `hand` instance on the Stage. On the `mouseMove` event, we want the script to position the clip at the same point as the mouse. Although there's a property called `_xmouse` that can help us out in this script, it's important to understand that this property returns the location of the cursor relative to a particular timeline. For example, if your cursor is at the top-left corner of the Stage, `_xmouse` has an `_xmouse` and `_ymouse` of 0 (relative to the Stage). Relative to a clip whose center point is 0x, 0y, the cursor may be something quite different. So the script we write says "set the location of this clip to the location of the cursor within the main timeline":

```
onClipEvent (mouseMove) {
  _x=_root._xmouse;
  _y=_root._ymouse;
  updateAfterEvent();
}
```

   Notice that I included an `updateAfterEvent()`, which is best understood by testing what happens without this line (the clip won't play as smoothly).

3. Notice that the center of the `hand` instance coincides perfectly with the user's mouse. If you want to adjust the location of the cursor symbol, simply edit the master version of the symbol and move all the contents to a different location relative to the center (Figure W3.2). The center will still coincide with the user's mouse, but the graphics contained in the clip will appear in an offset location.

4. In a minute, we'll use `Mouse.hide()` to make the user's cursor disappear. The drawback to having a cursor present all the time in Flash is that the cursor remains onscreen when the user moves the mouse out of Flash's window. I want to make the custom cursor appear only when the user places the mouse pointer over an object (a button or a draggable item) and then restore the original cursor when the user rolls off the object. Although that may sound like a single action, it's really two: In addition to hiding and restoring the cursor, you must make sure that the `hand` instance is displayed or hidden accordingly. We'll do all that through a function.

Figure W3.2 *Moving the Movie Clip's contents relative to the center (the plus sign) affects where the graphic appears.*

Draw a square (with no stroke) and convert it to a Movie Clip called "Hot Area." You can set the clip's alpha so that it appears to be semitransparent. Also, give it an instance name of "hot." We will use this shape to define the area in which the cursor will appear. An invisible button (discussed in Chapter 1, "Flash Basics") would be a convenient solution because it has built-in mouse events for `rollOver` and `rollOut` (the events we'd like to trap). However, if we ever place an invisible button on top of another button, the script for the button underneath will be ignored. Because I'd like to use this Smart Clip anywhere (including on top of other buttons), the instance of `hot` will be used to define what area is "hot"—the area where the cursor should change. Because we're eventually going to make this a Smart Clip, we select both the `hot` instance on the Stage and the `hand` instance, choose Insert, Convert to Symbol…, call the symbol "Cursor Clip," and leave it as a Movie Clip.

5. If you test the movie, you'll find that it's broken; the `hand` instance doesn't match the cursor. That's because the instance of `hand` is now inside another clip. The script attached to the `hand` instance (`_x=_root._xmouse`) is wrong now because you actually want `_x` to be assigned to the `_xmouse` within the Cursor Clip. To fix the problem, simply replace `_root` with `_parent` in the code attached to the instance of Cursor Clip. While we're here, we can call a function that we're about to write that will hide or reveal the cursor when the mouse is over the `hot` clip. The function will be called `check()` and will reside in the first frame of Cursor Clip. We therefore add the line `_parent.check()` to the script attached to `hand`. The finished script looks like this:

```
onClipEvent (mouseMove) {
  _parent.check();
  _x = _parent._xmouse;
  _y = _parent._ymouse;
  updateAfterEvent();
}
```

6. Let's write the `check()` function. We can do it in steps. The pseudo-code is simply this: "If the mouse is on top of the `hot` clip, hide the real mouse and make the `hand` clip visible. Otherwise, reveal the real mouse and make the `hand` clip invisible." That's a lot to dive right into. Let's worry about how to determine whether the mouse is on top of the `hot` instance last. Here's a start for our `check()` function that resides in the first keyframe of Cursor Clip:

   ```
   check();
   function check(){
     onHot=true;
     if (onHot){
       Mouse.hide();
       hand._visible = 1;
     }else{
       Mouse.show();
       hand._visible = 0;
     }
   }
   ```

   The very first line calls the function so that we start checking even before the mouse starts moving. The function itself either hides the mouse—`Mouse.hide()` is a built-in function—and sets the `_visible` property of the `hand` instance to `1`, or shows the mouse using `Mouse.show()` and makes the `hand` instance invisible. This script is entirely dependant on the value of `onHot`, which must be replaced with an actual expression that results in `true` or `false` depending on whether the mouse is on the `hot` instance. Notice that the hard-wired line `onHot=true` causes the condition to be `true` always. We can test it now and if it works, change that line to read `onHot=false`. This is a great way to make sure that this part of our script works before we add complexity.

7. There happens to be a built-in Movie Clip method called `hitTest()`. Although you'll use `hitTest()` in the "Working with Odd-Shaped Clickable Areas" workshop, you won't use it now. It's a shame we can't use the method because `hitTest()` can easily tell us when the mouse is on top of the `hot` instance. We can't use that method because we need to make the `hot` instance invisible, and `hitTest()` doesn't work in that case. Instead, we'll first gather information about the size and location of `hot`, store it in a variable, and then make `hot` invisible. (By the way, `hitTest()` will work with clips set to `_alpha` 0, so we could do that, but we'll use a different solution anyway.)

   The good news is that we get to explore another method called `getBounds()`. This method returns a rectangle of any given clip instance. Because there isn't a "rectangle" data type, we use a generic object with four properties: `xMax`, `xMin`, `yMax`, and `yMin`. The coordinate values for the four extremes are relative to the timeline you provide as a parameter. Within the Cursor Clip, the coordinates of `hot` are different than the coordinates of hot within the main _root timeline. Right above the check() function in the first frame of Cursor Clip, type this script:

```
rect=hot.getBounds(this);
hot._visible=0;
```

The variable rect contains the coordinates of hot relative to the current timeline (Cursor Clip). For example, rect.xMax contains the coordinate of the left side of the hot instance (as measured within the Cursor Clip). The second line of code makes the hot instance invisible because we want it to disappear as soon as the movie plays.

8. Now we can finish the check() function. Remove the line onHot=true from the script you wrote in step 6 and replace the if statement's onHot condition with the following expression:

   ```
   _xmouse>rect.xMin&&_xmouse<rect.xMax&&_ymouse>rect.yMin&&
   ➥_ymouse<rect.yMax
   ```

   This expression says that if _xmouse is greater than the xMin of rect and less than xMax *and* if _ymouse is greater than yMin and less than yMax, then the mouse is within the rectangle defined by the hot instance. This statement doesn't look pretty, but it works perfectly.

9. At this point, you can drag instances of Cursor Clip into any movie, placing the semitransparent shape from the hot instance wherever you want a cursor to appear (Figure W3.3). However, if you resize any instance of Cursor Clip (for example, if you have a larger or smaller area you want the cursor to appear over), the Cursor Graphic clip will resize accordingly because it's inside the Cursor Clip you resized. Not only is this annoying, but unless you're allowed to resize the Cursor Clip it's not very useful at all.

10. Let's think what we need to do to resolve the resizing issue. Basically, we want the hand instance to resize itself in inverse proportion to the scale of the clip in which it resides. For example, if the instance of Cursor Clip on the Stage is resized to be really big, we want the hand instance to be resized small, and vice versa. The problem is a lot easier to solve when you think of it in those terms. The following code can be added to the first frame of Cursor Clip above the check() function:

    ```
    hand._xscale=(100/_xscale) * 100;
    hand._yscale=(100/_yscale) * 100;
    ```

    The way this code sets hand's scale to the inverse of the Cursor Clip's scale is based on the fact that no scaling is an _xscale and _yscale of 100. Let's try some "what if" numbers to see how this formula works: If _xscale of Cursor Clip is 100, then we want hand._xscale to be 100 too—(100/100) * 100 does equal 100. If Cursor Clip is scaled down 50%, we want hand to be 200%—(100/50)*100 does equal 200.

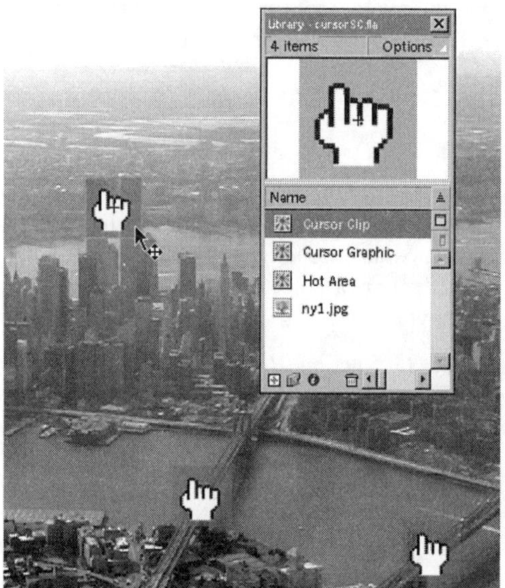

Figure W3.3 *You can use several copies of the clip to create cursors in different areas.*

11. The Cursor Clip appears to work great. Now is a good time to test it in a real-life situation. You may notice that if you place the Cursor Clip on top of a regular Flash button (for which you could write a script), the custom cursor flickers slightly. The problem is that our script says "hide the cursor" but the button says "show the standard button cursor." This problem appears only when you try to cover two or more buttons with instances of the Cursor Clip. Only one will work because each clip's script says, "if you're not within *my* rectangle, then show the cursor." Because the clips are in different areas, you will indeed be outside one clip's rectangle when you're within another's. We have to add a script that lets each clip reveal the cursor only once. If you restore the cursor with `Mouse.show()` only when you're exiting a clip's rectangle, the problem will be resolved. Again, it would be more convenient if we were using a button with its built-in `rollOut` mouse event, but we're not.

    To fix this bug, we'll use a custom variable we'll call `flag`. Programmers commonly need a variable that is switched on or off once or infrequently, and they call it a "flag." Think of the flag on some mailboxes that indicate whether you have outgoing mail. As soon as the mail carrier takes the mail, the flag goes down. The flag is a toggle for an event that occurs infrequently; the flag should not constantly go up and down. Outside of our `check()` function, we need a script that initializes `flag` to `0` (`flag=0`) so that `flag` is `0` at the start. Also, in place of where `Mouse.show()` is used in the `false` condition part of the `check()` function, we need an `if` statement like this one:

```
if (flag==0){
  Mouse.show();
  flag=1
}
```

Only if `flag` is `0` will the mouse be shown. Then we set `flag` to `1` so that it won't happen again until `flag` is `0` once more.

12. Finally, we must reset `flag` to `0` any time the cursor is indeed within this clip's rectangle. So right before the `else` in the `true` condition of `check()`, we add a line `flag=0`. Here's the finished script for the keyframe inside Cursor Clip:

```
rect=hot.getBounds(this);
hot._visible=0;
hand._xscale=(100/_xscale) * 100;
hand._yscale=(100/_yscale) * 100;
check();
flag=0;
function check () {
  if(_xmouse>rect.xMin&&_xmouse<rect.xMax&&_ymouse>rect.yMin&&
➥_ymouse<rect.yMax) {
    Mouse.hide();
    hand._visible = 1;
    flag=0;
  } else {
    if (flag==0){
      Mouse.show();
      flag=1;
    }
    hand._visible = 0;
  }
}
```

Now the script is quite solid. As long as you place the Cursor Clip on top of buttons, the button scripts will execute, and you'll only see the custom cursor graphic. You can do some other refinements, such as positioning the `hot` instance within Cursor Clip so that its top-left corner is centered. With this adjustment, when the author scales Cursor Clip, it appears to stretch to the right and down instead of scaling equally in all directions the way a clip with its contents centered will. You can also position the `hand` instance so that it's covered by the invisible button. You can even scale the instance to be so tiny that it won't get in the way. The script we added in step 10 restores the `hand` instance to its proper size anyway. Maybe you can think of more refinements; we're about to do many in the next section.

Now let's convert the Cursor Clip into a Smart Clip that allows the author using the clip to select from a variety of cursors. Keep in mind that we made the cursor in just two steps—it took several more steps to make the cursor really useful. It will take even more work to make it adaptable as a Smart Clip. In a real project, this investment is worth the additional time only if you can use the Smart Clip many times. Of course, it's worth the time now because we're learning.

1. First create an invisible Movie Clip. Select Insert, New Symbol..., name it "Invisible," and leave it as a Movie Clip. Don't draw anything in this clip. Go inside the Cursor Clip and drag an instance of "Invisible" from the Library. Consider placing this clip on its own layer so that it's easier to select by just clicking the layer name. Name this instance `hand` and copy to it the code attached to the original `hand` instance. Delete the old `hand` instance. The idea is that instead of having a particular cursor present in our Smart Clip, we'll use the built-in `attachMovie()` method to add the author's desired cursor at runtime.
2. We need a few cursors from which the using author can select. I created four: finger, grab, left-right, and up-down (Figure W3.4). Make four unique movie clips now, even if that means that you just draw something quickly.

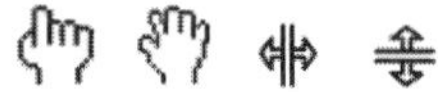

Figure W3.4 *We'll give the using author a choice of cursors.*

At this point, you shouldn't have any instances of the Movie Clips (finger, grab, left-right, or up-down) anywhere on the Stage. Inside Cursor Clip is the `hot` instance and an invisible clip that happens to have an instance name of `hand`. If you ever want to use the Smart Clip we're building in other projects, or if you want to share the Smart Clip, you're going to want to know about a great trick that ensures that all the components (including the four cursors we just made) are copied into other movies. Inside the Cursor Clip, make a Guide layer and place one instance of each clip on that layer. Even though objects in a Guide layer are not exported with the movie (and are not visible while you're working), placing objects in a Guide layer ensures that they are copied whenever you drag Cursor Clip into another movie. You can call the Guide layer "Just so they get copied."

3. To use `attachMovie()`, each cursor must have an identifier name. Individually set the Linkage for each cursor in the Library (finger, grab, left-right, and up-down). In the Linkage setting, select the Export This Symbol option and give it an identifier name identical to the symbol name (Figure W3.5). We select this option not so much because we need to export the clips (which will happen), but because `attachMovie()` requires an identifier name.

Figure W3.5 *To use* `attachMovie()`*, each clip must have an identifier name.*

4. Now we can write the script that decides which of the four cursors to use. The using author will ultimately specify this by setting a value for a variable. We can use the custom variable `pointerName` that we'll hard-wire at first and then have the using author specify using the Clip Parameters panel. Instead of trying to do it all in one step, we'll first try to make the variable work with a hard-wired script. At the beginning of the first frame in Cursor Clip, add the following two lines:

```
pointerName="grab";
hand.attachMovie( pointerName, "cursorInHand", 1 );
```

   The first line hard-wires `pointerName`, and the second line (including the four cursors we just made) "attaches" a new clip instance *inside* `hand`. This clip instance is a clip with the following details: an identifier named `"grab"` (because that's `pointerName`'s value), an instance name of `cursorInHand`, and residing in level 1 of `hand`.

5. Test it out! Now, we just have to remove or comment out the line in which we hard-wired `pointerName` and make the using author set this for us. Type `//` in front of the first line we added in step 4 so that it will be ignored. From the Library, select Define Clip Parameters…for Cursor Clip.

6. Click the plus under "Parameters" and then double-click varName to select it. Type `pointerName`. Instead of making the author remember the names of the four possible cursor choices, let's use the `List` data type (double-click `Default` under Type and select `List`). After `List` is selected, you should be able to double-click under the Value column and populate the list. Add the four names given as identifiers in step 3: finger, grab, left-right, and up-down (Figure W3.6).

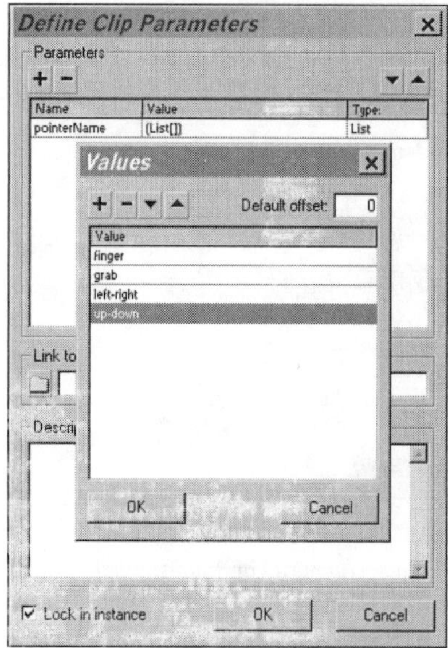

Figure W3.6 *The* `List` *data type allows the using author to select from a predefined list of cursor types.*

It's done! Yep, that was a lot of work, but check it out. Drag an instance of Cursor Clip—which is now a Smart Clip—into any movie you have. Using the Clip Parameters dialog, select the cursor of your choice. Use as many cursors as you want and mix and match the cursor choices. You can even resize the Cursor Clip, and the cursor won't get all whacked out of scale.

This particular Smart Clip is a good candidate for a Custom UI. For example, instead of making the using author select from a list of cursor names, you can show pictures of the cursors. You can even let the using author preview the cursor choices. The following steps show you how to extend this Smart Clip even further.

//

In addition to a tiny bit of math and some targeting issues, most of this workshop involved Flash features. Namely, the `_xmouse` and `_ymouse` properties, the `Mouse.hide()` and `Mouse.show()` functions, the Movie Clip methods `getBounds()` and `attachMovie()`, plus Smart Clips. We covered Smart Clips in Chapter 13, "Smart Clips," but this was your first chance to make something practical. We'll make more Smart Clips in upcoming workshops, including the next workshop, "Creating a Horizontal Slider." Remember that there are usually two steps involved: First make the clip work, even if it's hard-wired, and then convert it to a Smart Clip.

We need to build a Flash movie that lets the using author select from the different cursor choices. Specifically, we want the user to set the value for `pointerName`. When this Flash movie is finished, we can export it as a `.swf` and use it in place of the Clip Parameters.

1. Leave open the file you used to create the Cursor Clip Smart Clip and make sure that the Library is open. Start a new file by pressing Ctrl+N. Drag an instance of Cursor Clip into the new file. Save the original file as `cursorSC.fla` and then close it. Save the new file as `ui.fla` in the same folder as `cursorSC.fla`. The `ui.fla` file simply has four buttons, one for each of the four cursor choices. Ultimately, we'll use our plain Cursor Clip Smart Clip on top of those buttons. For now, delete the instance of the Cursor Clip (don't worry; it's safe in the Library of the new file). As you learned in Chapter 13, Custom UIs need space to initialize. So create a keyframe at frame 15 and create four horizontally aligned buttons as graphically as you want (Figure W3.7). You can also resize the Stage of this movie if necessary.
2. On each button, place a version of this script:

   ```
   on (release) {
     selectPointer(1);
   }
   ```

   For each button, change the parameter to read `1`, `2`, `3`, or `4`.
3. Draw some kind of highlight that will be used to indicate which cursor is currently selected. A simple orange square just bigger than the buttons will work fine. Convert this highlight graphic to a Movie Clip and name the instance on the Stage `highlight`.

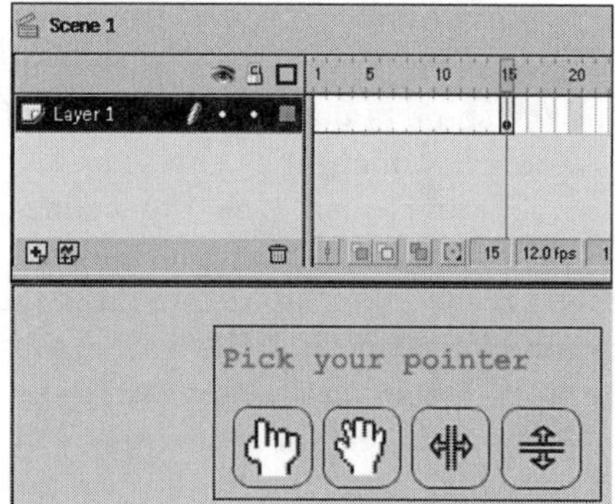

Figure W3.7 *The Custom UI has four buttons that won't appear until frame 15.*

4. Now we can write the `selectPointer()` function that the act of selecting each button invokes. The function sets `pointerName` and moves the `highlight` instance. To complete this function, we need something that translates the number (provided in the parameter sent when `selectPointer()` is invoked) to a name (which is needed in our Smart Clip for the value of `pointerName`). Yay! It's time for an array like the one you remember from Chapter 10. In the keyframe at frame 15, start with this script:

   ```
   stop();
   names=["finger","grab","left-right","up-down"];
   ```

   The first line prevents us from looping back to frame 1. The `names` array makes it easy to find any particular name. For example, if we want to know the name for the second `pointerName`, we just find the value in index 1.

5. We might as well make an array to contain the four locations for the `highlight` instance. You can position the `highlight` instance by hand in each spot and note the Info panel's x coordinate to acquire the clip's center. After you gather the values, leave `highlight`'s vertical position so that it matches the buttons, but move it either to the left or right, way off the Stage. In frame 15, add this line of code:

   ```
   locs=[35, 88.3, 141.6, 194.9];
   ```

   Use whatever values you found for your highlight. For example, `35` is the location in my movie when the `highlight` instance surrounds the first button. Because the vertical location is the same for all the buttons, the script has to change only the `highlight`'s `_x` property.

6. Now for the function. The previous two lines just sit in a keyframe script, so they execute only when that frame is reached. We want the `selectPointer()` function to move the highlight and store the value for `pointerName`. To make it easier when we get to making this Custom UI

restore old values, it's best to also store a value for pointerNumber. You'll see why this is important in step 8, when we make this Custom UI restore the old settings. Here's the selectPointer() function:

```
function selectPointer(whichOne){
  highlight._x=locs[whichOne -1];
  xch.pointerName=names[whichOne -1];
  xch.pointerNum=whichOne;
}
```

The first line is easiest: Simply set the _x property of highlight to the value found in the appropriate index of the locs array. Similarly, the second line sets the value of pointerName to the appropriate name. Actually, it looks like I'm setting the value of pointerName inside a clip called xch. Yep, Custom UIs must store all the variables you want to be part of the Smart Clip in a clip with an instance name xch. Finally, xch.pointerNum is saved for later.

7. Before we forget, let's make sure that we have a clip instance with the name xch. Make a new layer so that this clip will be present the whole time. You can use the Invisible Movie Clip that came in when you dragged Cursor Clip in. In any case, you need a clip in its own layer with an instance name xch.

8. To visually display the currently selected cursor for the using author, simply place the following script at the bottom of frame 15, below the selectPointer() function:

   ```
   selectPointer(xch.pointerNum);
   ```

   This line simply invokes the selectPointer() function when frame 15 is reached and supplies as a parameter the value of pointerNum currently stored in the xch clip. The statement makes sense only if xch.pointerNum has a value, which it will when the using author has previously chosen a cursor. Note that the statement doesn't cause any problems if this value is undefined, as it will be the first time.

9. Finally, since our restoration script (in step 8) doesn't occur until frame 15 you should put a "loading…" message or some other placating animation in the first 15 frames. Go ahead and drag the Cursor Clip Smart Clip on top of the four buttons. Use the Clip Parameters to choose an appropriate cursor. Don't get confused here! There's certainly no requirement that you use a plain non-Custom UI Smart Clip while you're producing the UI. I just thought it would be cool to put our Smart Clip to the test. This custom UI can have any crazy element you want; simply setting the value for pointerName is enough.

10. Save the file and export a .swf by doing a Test Movie. Close this file so that nothing gets mixed up and reopen customSC.fla. From the Library window select Cursor Clip and then select Define Clip Parameters. In the Link To Custom UI field, type the name of the movie we just exported—

in this case, `ui.swf`—and click OK. Now you can drag instances of Cursor Clip, and for each one use the Clip Parameters dialog to select the cursor of your choice (Figure W3.8).

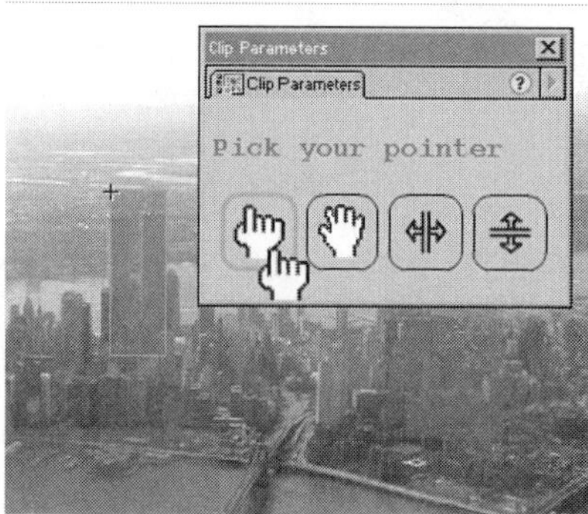

Figure W3.8 *When completed, our Smart Clip uses a Custom UI.*

This workshop shows that you can take a task that's easy to program and refine it—with a ton of work—to make it something really usable. Please realize that the purpose of this workshop was not *just* to make a cursor Smart Clip, but to explore and learn.

{Chapter 4 Workshop }

Creating a Horizontal Slider

This workshop explores a popular user interface control: the slider. Many users prefer to specify a number by using the seemingly continuous scale offered by a slider rather than by typing into a field. Some tactile learners may respond better to the sense of touch provided by a slider. Another benefit of using sliders is that sliders can be adjusted without taking your hand off the mouse.

This workshop has two parts. First we make a perfectly acceptable plain slider and then we convert it into a more usable Smart Clip.

Creating a Quick and Dirty Slider

1. Create a button that will serve as the slider the user is supposed to grab. Perhaps you'll want to use a vertical rectangle with rounded corners like the one you made in Workshop 2, "Faking Video." If the shape is particularly small, consider creating a large "hit" area for the button so that it's not too difficult for the user to grab the slider.
2. To make the slider movable, it must be a Movie Clip. Select the button instance you just made and convert it to a Movie Clip symbol called "Simple Slider." Now you have a button inside a clip.
3. Double-click the Simple Slider to edit its contents. Create a Dynamic Text field that reads `100` using `_sans` font. Associate the variable `percent` with this block of text. Make sure "Selectable" is not checked and that "Border/BG" is checked. Position the text right above the button as shown in Figure W4.1.

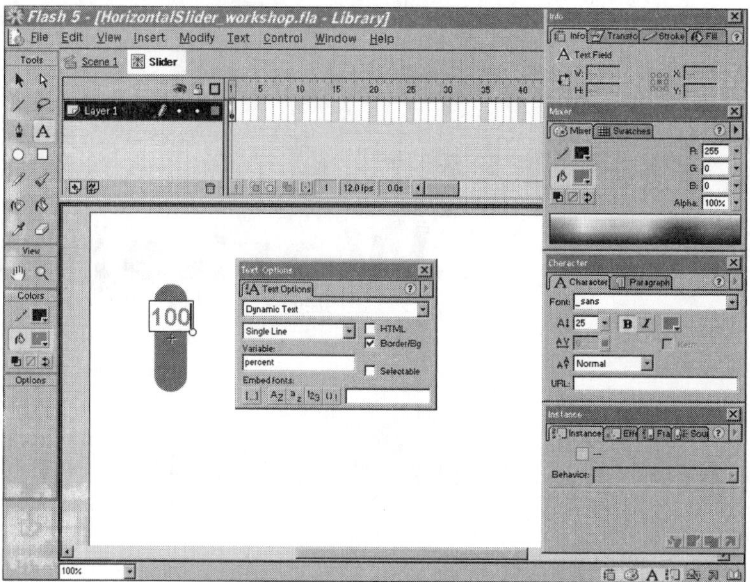

Figure W4.1 *The Dynamic Text field displays the slider's location as a percentage.*

4. On the instance of your button, place the following script:

```
on (press) {
  drag=1;
}
on (release, releaseOutside) {
  drag=0;
}
```

This script makes the button set the variable `drag` to `1` or `0`. The bulk of the code will be placed elsewhere; it's just that it's easiest to respond to mouse events using buttons. The only result of this script is that `drag` will change value, but that will trigger another script to kick in.

5. Return to the main timeline and select the instance of Simple Slider. Place the following script on the clip instance:

```
onClipEvent (mouseMove) {
  if (drag==1){
      _x=_root._xmouse;
  }
}
```

Translated, this script says that any time the user's mouse moves and the `drag` variable happens to be `1`, set the `_x` property of the clip to the location of the mouse (`_xmouse` within the `_root` timeline). Because we're setting the _x property of the clip in the _root timeline, we want it to match the user's mouse position in the _root timeline.

Test the movie. It works! In the next steps, we're going to fix a few things: The movie should move smoother, there should be minimum and maximum bounds, it shouldn't jump when you click the slider's left or right edge the way it currently snaps itself to the center of the mouse pointer, and the percent has to display in the Dynamic Text field. These are all easy tasks!

6. Throw in an updateAfterEvent() right before the close (}) of the if statement to make the movie play smoother.

7. To add bounds, use the Info panel to determine the minimum and maximum locations for the slider in the main timeline. Draw some vertical lines in the main timeline to represent the bounds. After you have the x coordinate values, place the following script above the mouseMove event on your slider (actually, the following code works fine if you place it below the event, but it makes more sense to have the load event come first):

```
onClipEvent(load){
  min=1;      //or your preferred minimum
  max=550;    //or your maximum
}
```

   In this code, replace the values for min and max with whatever the Info panel told you were your minimum and maximum values.

8. Inside the if statement of your mouseMove event and right above updateAfterEvent(), place this script:

```
if (_x>max){
  _x=max;
}
if (_x<min){
  _x=min;
}
```

   These two if statements make sure that the _x property doesn't go below min or above max. If you test the movie now, you should see that the slider is smooth and doesn't go past the bounds specified.

9. Now that we know the bounds involved, we can calculate percentage. The formula for percentage is simply "current position / total distance." Total distance is max-min, and current position is the slider's _x property. If your minimum is greater than 0 (suppose that the leftmost position is 220), current position is really _x-min. If the _x is right at minimum, the current position should be 0, which it will be if you simply subtract min from the _x property. Here's the formula you can place above the updateAfterEvent() script:

```
percent = (_x-min)/(max-min)*100;
```

Actually, to find just the integer portion of percent, you can use the Math Object's `floor()` method, which was discussed in Chapter 5, "Programming Structures." Replace the preceding code with this version:

```
percent = Math.floor((_x-min)/(max-min)*100);
```

The two remaining issues to resolve are the fact the slider snaps to the center of the mouse and that the percentage doesn't start displaying until the slider is moved.

10. The snapping is caused by the fact that we're positioning the slider's `_x` to the exact location of the `_xmouse`. If the user clicks the left side of the slider, we really want the slider to move to the `_xmouse` plus how far off center the user clicked. If the user clicks the right side, we want to subtract the offset. It's a subtle issue, but one that comes up often, especially when you make a homemade draggable Movie Clip: You can't just move the clip to the mouse's location; you'll have to subtract an "offset." To address the snapping, first add this code to the press mouse event script on the button that you made in step 4, right above `drag=1`:

```
offsetX=_x-_root._xmouse;
```

11. In the `mouseMove` event on the clip, change the line `_x=_root._xmouse` to read as follows:

```
_x=_root._xmouse+offsetX;
```

When the user clicks, we calculate the difference between `_x` and `_root._xmouse` and then we use that value by adding it to the clip's `_x` position.

> You may ask, "If we always *add* the offset, won't that make the slider appear to the right?" If the offset value is positive then, yes. Otherwise, when the offset is negative, adding it makes the slider appear to the left. Let's try some what-if numbers. Suppose that the slider is at `50`. If you start clicking at `45`, the slider should move to wherever the mouse is *plus* `5`. If you click at `55`, the slider should move with the mouse *minus* `5`. Actually, you can always add the offset because in the first case `50-45` is `5`. The second case `50-55` is `-5`. I always get messed up deciding whether to subtract `_xmouse` from `_x` or to subtract `_x` from `_xmouse`. Try a few what-if numbers, or use the trial-and-error method to work out the logic pretty quickly.

12. We have another step to complete before we can convert this slider to a Smart Clip and can really start using it. Place this code at the end of the `load` event on the slider instance, right before the closing curly bracket (`}`):

```
percent = Math.floor((_x-min)/(max-min)*100);
```

Although this statement is redundant (it also appears in the `mouseMove` event), it ensures that the percent is displayed at the very beginning.

13. We're about to convert this clip to a Smart Clip. In case you want to get off here and start using the clip as-is, realize that you can use the `percent` value anywhere in your movie. For example, if you have another clip on the Stage with an instance name `box`, you can add either or both of these lines of code right above `updateAfterEvent()` inside the slider clip's `mouseMove` event:

```
_root.box._alpha=percent;
_root.box._rotation=(percent/100)*360;
```

You can add this code right now because you have a perfectly suitable slider. Study Figure W4.2 for a full view of everything up to this point.

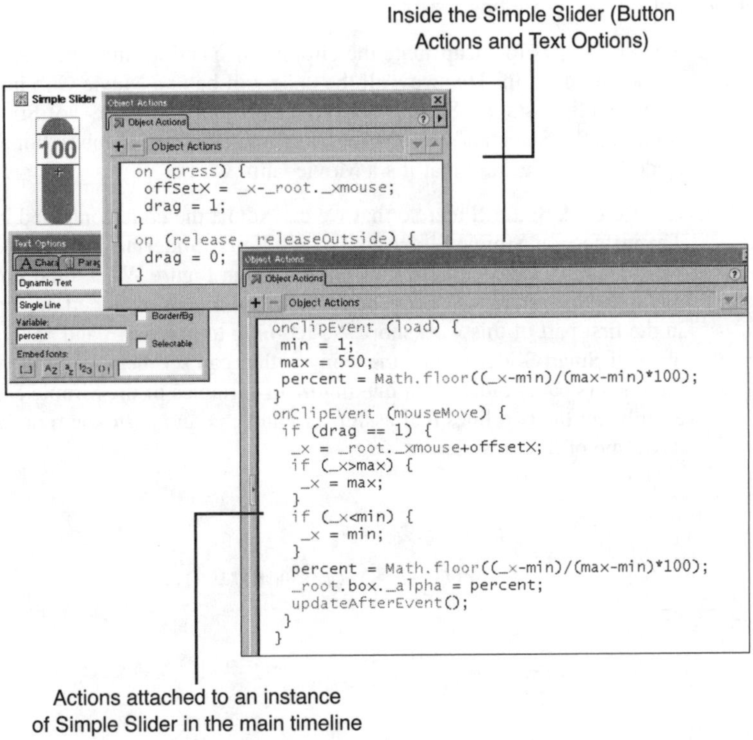
Inside the Simple Slider (Button Actions and Text Options)
Simple Slider
100
Object Actions
on (press) {
offSetX = _x-_root._xmouse;
drag = 1;
}
on (release, releaseOutside) {
drag = 0;
}
Text Options
Dynamic Text
Single Line
Variable:
percent
Border/Bg
Selectable
Embed fonts:
onClipEvent (load) {
min = 1;
max = 550;
percent = Math.floor((_x-min)/(max-min)*100);
}
onClipEvent (mouseMove) {
if (drag == 1) {
_x = _root._xmouse+offsetX;
if (_x>max) {
_x = max;
}
if (_x<min) {
_x = min;
}
percent = Math.floor((_x-min)/(max-min)*100);
_root.box._alpha = percent;
updateAfterEvent();
}
}
Actions attached to an instance of Simple Slider in the main timeline

Figure W4.2 *The Simple Slider contains ActionScript both in the master symbol and attached to the instance.*

Converting the Slider into a Smart Clip

We're about to make our slider slightly better. The limiting issues with the slider we built in the first part of this workshop include the following:

- All the code is attached to the clip instance on the Stage instead of inside the clip itself. The problem is that we can't drag additional instances of this clip from the Library without copying and pasting the code. If there were a bug in the code, it would be duplicated in each instance and would have to be fixed in all individual instances.
- The `min` and `max` variables are hard wired. Our Smart Clip will allow each instance its own `min` and `max` values, plus an additional variable for the starting percentage.

Here are the steps for making our pretty good slider into a very good Smart Clip that addresses the preceding issues:

1. The first step is to encapsulate the clip instance and its attached code inside another clip. This way, all the code will be *in* a Movie Clip instead of *on* an clip instance. Select the instance—and all the code—of Simple Slider on the Stage and convert it to a symbol. Call the symbol "Smart Slider" and make sure that it's a Movie Clip.
2. Double-click Smart Slider so that we can adjust the code contained in it. The instance of Simple Slider now inside Smart Slider has some code that we can adjust. Let's explore the code shown in Figure W4.3. First remove any lines that reference `_root.box` which you may have added in step 13 in the first part of this workshop. We're going to make `min` and `max` variables of Smart Slider so that the using author can set them using the Clip Parameters panel rather than making them variables of the Simple Slider. Simply cut the two lines that assign `min` and `max` and paste them in the first keyframe of Smart Slider.

```
onClipEvent (load) {
    min=1;
    max=550;
    percent = Math.floor((_x-min)/(max-min)*100);
}
onClipEvent (mouseMove) {
    if (drag == 1) {
        _x = _root._xmouse+offsetX;
        if (_x>max) {
            _x = max;
        }
        if (_x<min) {
            _x = min;
        }
        percent = Math.floor((_x-min)/(max-min)*100);
        updateAfterEvent();
    }
}
```

Figure W4.3 *Here is the script that needs to be improved when it's converted to a Smart Clip.*

3. Notice that the two lines that assign `percent` are identical. Remove the line starting `percent=...` inside the `load` event. Later, we'll write a script that takes care of assigning percent in the first keyframe of Smart Slider. At this point, you can remove the now empty `load` event. If you study the `mouseMove` event, you'll notice several variables that have to be adjusted, or "re-scoped," to target the correct timeline, most notably every reference to `min` and `max` needs to be up one level in the Smart Slider and not part of the Simple Slider where they are now. Instead of fixing everything here by adding `_parent` in front of each reference, select all the text between `if (drag==1){` and `updateAfterEvent()` (Figure W4.4) and cut it (do not delete it). Replace the cut code with `_parent.moveSlider()`. We'll write this function in a minute. The modified script on the slider instance should look like this:

```
onClipEvent (mouseMove) {
  if (drag==1){
    _parent.moveSlider();
    updateAfterEvent();
  }
}
```

The variables `min` and `max` will be part of Smart Slider so that they can be set using the Clip Parameters panel. The only thing that "happens" in this script is that, when the mouse is moved and `drag` is `1`, the yet-to-be-written `moveSlider()` function is invoked. The `moveSlider()` function will reside in the first keyframe of Smart Slider.

```
onClipEvent (mouseMove) {
    if (drag == 1) {
        _x = _root._xmouse+offsetX;
        if (_x>max) {
            _x = max;
        }
        if (_x<min) {
            _x = min;
        }
        percent = Math.floor((_x-min)/(max-min)*100);
        updateAfterEvent();
    }
}
```

Figure W4.4 *Here is the portion of the script to be cut and moved to a keyframe function.*

4. To create the `moveSlider()` function, enter the following script underneath the two lines that assign `min` and `max` in the first keyframe of Smart Slider:

```
function moveSlider(){
}
```

Between the two curly brackets, paste everything from your clipboard to form the following complete script:

```
function moveSlider(){
  _x = _root._xmouse+offSetX;
  if (_x>max) {
    _x = max;
  }
  if (_x<min) {
    _x = min;
  }
  percent = Math.floor((_x-min)/(max-min)*100);
}
```

At this point, the slider should still work—sort of. We simply moved the bulk of code to a function. Luckily, all the variables here don't need any adjustment the way `min` had to change to `_parent.min` on the old instance of Slider in the first part of this workshop. However, our `offSetX` has stopped working properly. Actually, we never assigned an `offSetX` of the new Smart Slider clip.

5. You have to adjust the script attached to the button inside the Slider clip. The variable `drag` is fine because that is used by the Slider clip itself. However, `offSetX` must be part of the Smart Slider. But simply changing the assignment to read `_parent.offSetX=_x-_root._xmouse` won't work entirely. (Try it out if you want.) It's not the difference between the slider's `_x` and the main timeline's `_xmouse`, but rather the difference between `_x` and the `_xmouse` of the Smart Slider's timeline. This line of code (found inside the `press` mouse event attached to the button instance inside the Slider symbol) has to read as follows:

   ```
   _parent.offSetX=_x-_parent._xmouse;
   ```

   I suppose we could have seen this coming. In the first part of this workshop, we had the Slider clip that either used its own variables or targeted the `_root` timeline. But back then `_root` was only "one level up." Now, with the instance of Slider *inside* the Smart Slider clip, the hierarchy isn't much different but `_root` no longer means "one level up," and we should use `_parent` instead (Figure W4.5).

6. One last fix and we'll be ready to make this clip a true Smart Clip! The percent isn't displaying correctly; it's being calculated fine, but it's part of Smart Slider now. You can fix this by accessing the Dynamic Text field inside the Slider symbol. Change the percent variable (with which the text is currently associated) to read: `_parent.percent` (Figure W4.6).

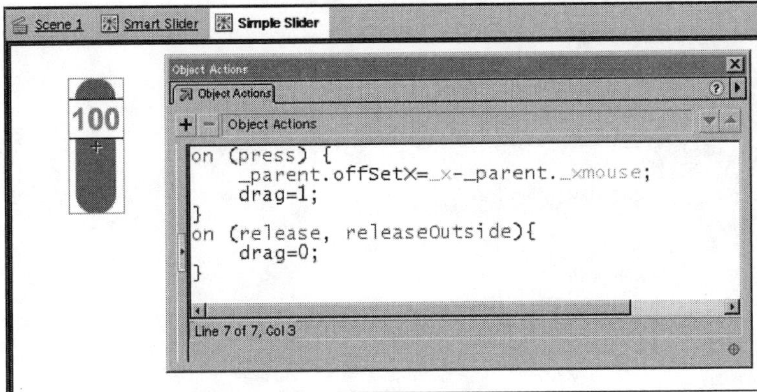

Figure W4.5 *The adjusted script on the button.*

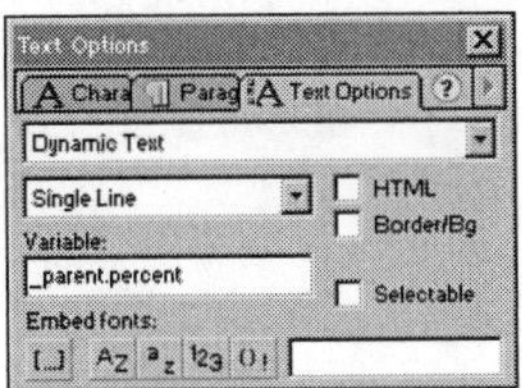

Figure W4.6 *One solution for displaying the correct* `percent` *is with a relative reference.*

7. We should make one more refinement before we convert to a Smart Clip. It would be nice to let the using author specify an initial value for `percent`. We should make sure that the slider not only displays the initial percent, but positions itself on the Stage accordingly. In the first keyframe of Smart Slider, type the following two lines of code directly after `min` and `max` are assigned:

```
percent=50;
_x= min+((max-min)*(percent/100));
```

   For now, `percent` is hard wired, as are `min` and `max`, for that matter. The second line sets Smart Slider's `_x` to `min` plus the `percent` multiplied by the range (`max-min`). We don't have to worry about making this value an integer using `Math.floor()` because there's no problem setting a clip's `_x` property to a float (a number that has decimal values).

8. After you test this out a few times to make sure that it works, we can turn Smart Slider into a Smart Clip so that the user can set `min`, `max`, and *initial* `percent`. Comment out the first three lines of code in frame 1 of Smart Slider to make the script appear like this:

```
//min = 1;
//max = 550;
//percent=50;
_x= min+((max-min)*(percent/100));
function moveSlider(){
  _x = _root._xmouse+offSetX;
  if (_x>max) {
    _x = max;
  }
  if (_x<min) {
    _x = min;
  }
  percent = Math.floor((_x-min)/(max-min)*100);
}
```

Commenting out these lines prevents us from overriding the values the using author supplies through the Clip Parameters panel.

9. Open the Library, select Smart Slider, and access the Define Clip Parameters dialog. Create three "parameters": `min`, `max`, and `percent`. Note that you can set initial values for each of these parameters as well (Figure W4.7).

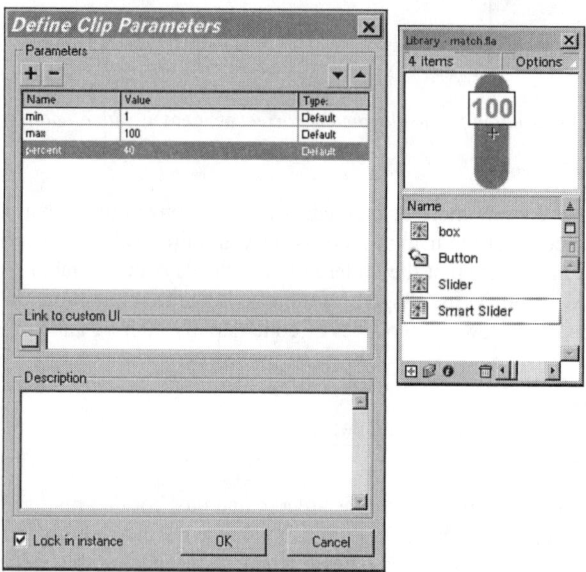

Figure W4.7 *Use the Define Clip Parameters dialog for the master symbol to enable the author to set these variables individually per instance.*

10. An overview of the main scripts is shown in Figure W4.8. The Smart Clip is complete. However, it lacks one tiny feature that could make the difference between something that's just cool looking and something that's very useful. We need a feature that links the slider to something onscreen. Although we can always ascertain the value of `percent` for any instance of this Smart Clip, it would be nicer if the slider itself sent a message to the Stage instead of us having to write a script that keeps asking the slider the value of its `percent`.

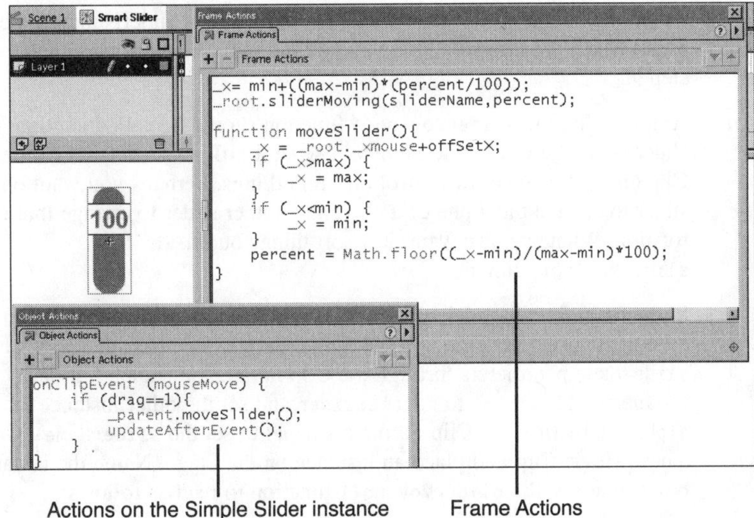

Figure W4.8 *The scripts for the first keyframe inside Smart Slider (top right) and the instance of Simple Slider (bottom left).*

To make this work, we'll need a function in the first keyframe of our main movie. No matter where we use the Smart Clip, it will send a message to this function in the `_root`. In the first keyframe of your main timeline, type this function:

```
function sliderMoving (whichSlider, howMuch){
}
```

The idea is that `sliderMoving()` can be invoked by any one slider, and there can be several. Passed as parameters will be a unique name `whichSlider` (that identifies which slider) and `howMuch` (the current percentage). Currently, this function doesn't do anything. If you want, you can add a line between the curly brackets that reads as follows:

```
trace("slider is moving "+whichSlider+" and "+howMuch);
```

For now, this statement tells us when a slider is invoking this function. We'll add more to this function later.

11. Making Smart Slider call this function is easy. Right before the close of the `mouseMove` event, type this line of code:

    ```
    _root.sliderMoving(sliderName,percent);
    ```

    This statement simply calls the `sliderMoving()` function in the main timeline. It sends as parameters the values of `sliderName` and `percent`. We haven't assigned `sliderName` yet, and we're not going to; the using author will do that using the Clip Parameters panel.

12. To let the using author assign sliderName, we just need to add that parameter through the Define Clip Parameters dialog. Add sliderName to the Smart Slider's parameters the way you did with the other parameters in step 9.

13. At this point, the `sliderMoving()` function should be called anytime the slider is dragged. It would be nice if several different instances of Smart Clip on the Stage could control different things. Perhaps you want one slider to change the alpha of a clip and another slider to change that clip's rotation. Whatever you want, just sort things out inside the `sliderMoving()` function.

    In the main timeline, delete all instances of the Smart Slider and start fresh by dragging two instances on the Stage. Set the `min`, `max`, `percent`, and `sliderName` parameters through the Clip Parameters panel. Set one instance's `sliderName` to `rotateSlider` and set the other instance to `alphaSlider` (use the Clip Parmeters panel to set the `sliderName`). Create a new Movie Clip and place an instance on the Stage. Name the instance box and adjust the `sliderMoving()` function to read as follows:

    ```
    function sliderMoving (whichSlider, howMuch) {
      if (whichSlider=="alphaSlider"){
        box._alpha=howMuch;
      }
      if (whichSlider=="rotateSlider"){
        box._rotation=(howMuch/100)*360;
      }
    }
    ```

    If you want to add more sliders, come up with a unique `sliderName` for each one and add another if-statement in the `sliderMoving()` function in order that uses the `percent` received as the value of `howMuch`.

14. We have one more step to make this Smart Clip complete. To make the initial percentage for any slider invoke the `sliderMoving()` function, even before the user even starts dragging, add the following script to the first keyframe in Smart Slider:

    ```
    _root.sliderMoving(sliderName,percent);
    ```

    Without this statement, my `alphaSlider` example could be given an initial percent of, say, 30, but the box instance wouldn't change its `_alpha` until I started dragging the slider.

Summary

In this workshop, you explored how to write a relatively simple script and then convert it into a Smart Clip. The process involved first creating a hard-wired script that worked to our satisfaction. Then we identified the aspects of the script that were not ideal—especially the fact that all the code was on the surface of the clip instance and that there were several hard-wired numbers. We also tried to think of generic applications for this Smart Clip, such as allowing the author to specify an initial percentage. All the variables that the using author would eventually access through the Clip Parameters panel must be "in" the main timeline of the clip itself. We simply moved the scripts to the first keyframe or used relative references such as `_parent` to make this possible.

For more information about relative references, refer to Chapter 1, "Flash Basics," and Chapter 4, "Basic Programming in Flash." General information about how to identify ways to improve scripts can be found in Chapter 3, "The Programmer's Approach." Writing functions was discussed in Chapter 8, "Functions." Finally, Chapter 5, "Programming Structures," covered if-statements, and how to write expressions such as our formula that determines percentage.

{Chapter 5 Workshop }

Building a Slide Show

After the last couple of workshops, this one will seem like a breeze. That doesn't mean that the results won't be impressive. In this workshop, you'll see how a little code can create a really nice effect. We're going to build a slide show that lets the user step through a series of images in a Movie Clip. Although the user can step forward and back in the slide show, instead of simply jumping to the next frame, we'll make the current page fade out and the next one fade up.

In addition to creating a slide show, you'll learn two general techniques: First, we'll use the `enterFrame` event to continuously make changes to the `_alpha` property of the current slide. We'll also look at a way to deactivate buttons so that when users view the first slide, they can't click the "page back" button. Similarly, when users are on the last page, they shouldn't be able to click "page forward." Although these two techniques are useful for *this* workshop, they'll also prove helpful in many of the workshops to come.

1. Create a Movie Clip with a separate image on each frame. Inside a new Movie Clip, insert blank keyframes as you import pictures or just draw something onto each frame. Consider creating a separate layer in which you draw a rectangle to serve as an outline (Figure W5.1).

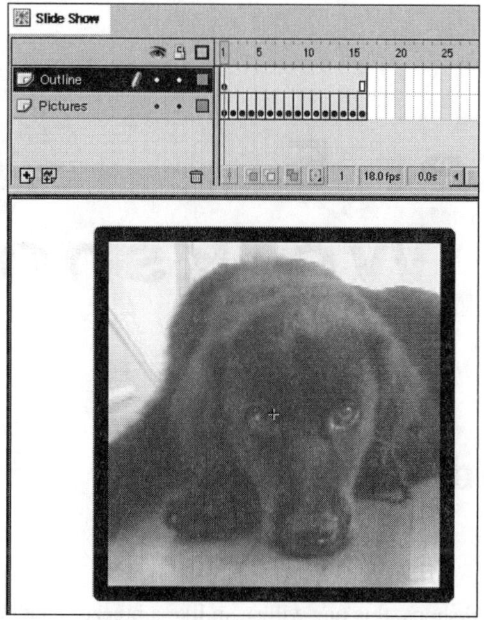

Figure W5.1 *Our slide show will be a simple Movie Clip with several frames.*

2. Drag an instance of this clip onto the Stage and give it an instance name of `slides`. Place the following script on the instance of `slides`:

```
onClipEvent (load) {
  stop ();
}
```

   This script simply prevents the slides from playing.

3. In the main timeline, draw a triangle that points to the right and convert it to a button symbol. Make a copy of this button and rotate the copy 180 degrees (Figure W5.2).

4. On each button, attach a version of the following script:

```
on (release) {
  _root.goPage(-1);//1 for forward, -1 for back
}
```

   In a minute, we'll write the `goPage()` function in the main timeline. Just make sure that for the "forward" button, you use `1` for the parameter. In the preceding script, we used `-1` because it's the "back" button.

Figure W5.2 *The same button symbol is used in two places, just rotated 180 degrees.*

5. Now we can write the `goPage()` function. Even though it's not going to be terribly complex, I'd much rather keep the buttons as simple as possible and place all the code in a function. In this way, we take advantage of one of the benefits of functions discussed in Chapter 8: that the same code can be accessed from several locations in the movie. Type this version of the function in the first keyframe of the movie:

```
function goPage(whichWay){
  slides.gotoAndStop(slides._currentFrame+whichway);
}
```

   This code simply uses the `gotoAndStop()` method to make the `slides` clip jump to a frame equal to its current frame plus either `1` or `-1`.

6. The clip basically works, but we're going to make the clip fade out first and then jump to the destination frame. To start, place the following script on the `slide` instance:

```
onClipEvent (enterFrame) {
  _alpha+=alphaChange;
}
```

   If the homemade variable `alphaChange` were `0` or `undefined`—as it will be if we never assign it—this script would have no effect. That is, if on every `enterframe` we assign the `_alpha` to be `0` more, nothing visually happens. Recall from Chapter 5 that saying `_alpha+=alphaChange` is the same as saying `_alpha=_alpha+alphaChange`.

7. Return to the `goPage()` function in the first keyframe and add a line of script that reads as follows:

```
slides.alphaChange=-5;
```

It's amazing how close to done we are. First, notice that regardless of the value of the whichWay parameter received in the goPage() function, we always want the slides instance's alphaChange variable to be negative. Also notice that goPage() is premature in making slides jump to a new frame—we don't want the page to advance until it's totally faded out. Finally, if you debug the movie and watch the properties for the slides instance, you'll see that once alphaChange is set to -5, the _alpha property continues to drop indefinitely.

8. Change the goPage() function so that it appears in its revised form as shown here:

```
function goPage(whichWay){
  slides.alphaChange=-5;
  slides.destinationFrame=slides._currentFrame+whichway;
}
```

Instead of actually making the slides clip "goto" a page, we set a variable in slides called destinationFrame which won't be used until the clip is ready to advance.

9. Now we can adjust the enterFrame script on slides. The first line is fine. We just need to keep checking to see whether _alpha has gotten low enough (say 0) at the point when we want to jump to the destination frame (either the next or the previous frame) and change alphaChange to a positive 5 so that it starts to fade back up. Check out the final version:

```
onClipEvent (enterFrame) {
  _alpha+=alphaChange;
  if (_alpha<1) {
    gotoAndStop (destinationFrame);
    alphaChange=5;
  }
  if (_alpha>100) {
    alphaChange=0;
  }
}
```

Basically, if _alpha ever goes below 1, we jump to the destination frame and set alphaChange to 5 so that the frame will start "unfading." The last if statement prevents _alpha from going past 100.

//

You may not think there's any harm in letting the clip's _alpha increase past 100. But if you let several seconds pass as it keeps increasing above 100 (to, say, _alpha 300), the next time the user clicks "forward" or "back" it will take just as long to come back down from 300 and then below 100 where you'll see the clip fade out again.

One other note: You just as easily could have written the two conditions for the `if` statements as `_alpha==0` and `_alpha==100`. Although this would work fine, I think the solution presented in the preceding script is "safer." What would happen if the `_alpha` skipped past `0` or `100`? It won't now with `alphaChange` being `-5` and `5`, but it could jump past such round numbers if you decided to start `alphaChange` at `-3`. Personally, I always prefer an `if` statement condition using > or < instead of == when doing so makes sense, of course.

10. This slide show works pretty well. Now we're going to add a feature that deactivates the appropriate buttons when you reach the beginning or end of the slide show. It turns out that the current version doesn't break when the user tries paging past either end because the `gotoAndStop()` method is ignored when you provide a frame number below `1` or above `_totalFrames`. I point out the fact Flash doesn't break only because you can often save yourself from writing error checking scripts (for instance, one that makes sure there's a next or previous frame to go to). Instead of writing such an error check in this exercise we will write a script that simply deactivates the buttons thus eliminating the issue entirely.

    All we need to do is place "dim" versions of the buttons underneath the real buttons and figure out a way to move or make invisible the real buttons. First, copy both buttons and Paste In Place by pressing Ctrl+Shift+V. Use the Instance panel to set both of the new instances to behave as Graphic symbols. Also make sure that the option for Single Frame is selected (Figure W5.3). We're not using Button behavior because the dim versions of the buttons should not include a cursor change or a script. And we're not using Movie Clip behavior because the button may have other "states" that translate into multiple frames as the Movie Clips loop naturally. The Graphic behavior is a good choice because of the selection of options available with that choice—in this case, the Single Frame option.

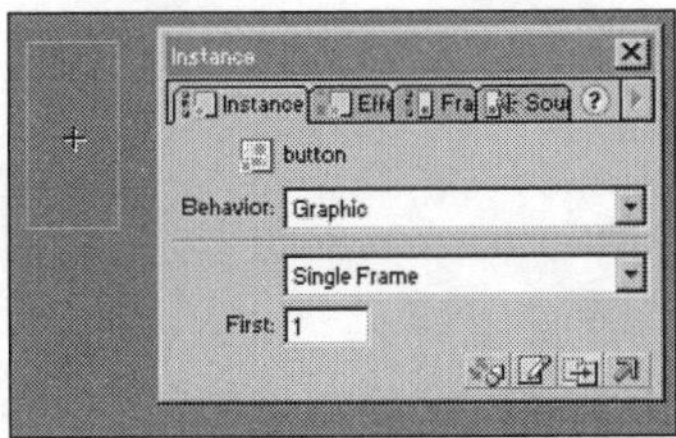

Figure W5.3 *A button instance can be given a Graphic behavior and be made to display just a Single Frame.*

11. Select both Graphic symbol versions of your buttons and use the Effect panel to change the Brightness or Tint to make "dim" versions of the buttons that look inactive. Finally, choose Modify, Arrange, Send to Back (or press Ctrl+Shift+Down-arrow) to push these dim versions behind the real buttons.

12. At this point, let's set the `_visible` property of each real button at the appropriate times. As you know, ActionScript can only set properties of Movie Clips—one way to remember this is that only clip instances can be named (and, hence, targeted by name). Anyway, those buttons have to be inside their own Movie Clips. Unfortunately, because each button has a different script, we can't make one Movie Clip with the button inside and then make a copy of the clip instance and rotate it because the button inside the duplicate would have the same script. My natural tendency would be to just make two Movie Clip symbols. Instead, we'll make a *super* simple Smart Clip that solves the problem. To that end, select the "next" button on the Stage and convert it to a Movie Clip symbol called "Button Clip." Delete the other button (the "back" button) on the Stage.

13. Go inside the master Button Clip and check out the script attached to the button: `_root.goPage(1)`. It's convenient that this script targets the `goPage()` function in our main timeline—no adjustment is necessary for the target. However, the script is passing `1` for a parameter, and we need one instance of this Button Clip to pass `1` and the other to pass `-1`. We can make this happen with a simple variable `buttonDirection` that is defined by the using author when we turn this clip into a Smart Clip. To accomplish this task, change the script attached to the button to appear like this:

```
on (release) {
  _root.goPage(buttonDirection);
}
```

14. To allow the using author to assign `buttonDirection`, open the Library, select Button Clip, and access the Define Clip Parameters dialog. Add a parameter called `buttonDirection` so that the author can set this parameter to `1` or `-1`. This Smart Clip is just for us, so we don't have to get fancy with a data type or even default values; you can just leave these options in their default settings.

15. The instance of Button Clip should be the "next" button. Access the Clip Parameters for that instance and set `buttonDirection` to `1`.

16. Drag another instance of Button Clip to serve as the "back" button which we removed in step 12. Set its `buttonDirection` to `-1`. Rotate it 180 degrees so that it points in the correct direction and position it on top of the dim version of the button.

17. Use the Instance panel to give each Button Clip instance on the Stage an instance name. Use `back` and `forward`.

18. When you test the movie, it should still work, although the buttons aren't hidden yet. Check out the diagram in Figure W5.4 for the layout. To make the dim versions of the buttons appear, we simply set the `_visible` property of the `back` or `forward` instances accordingly.

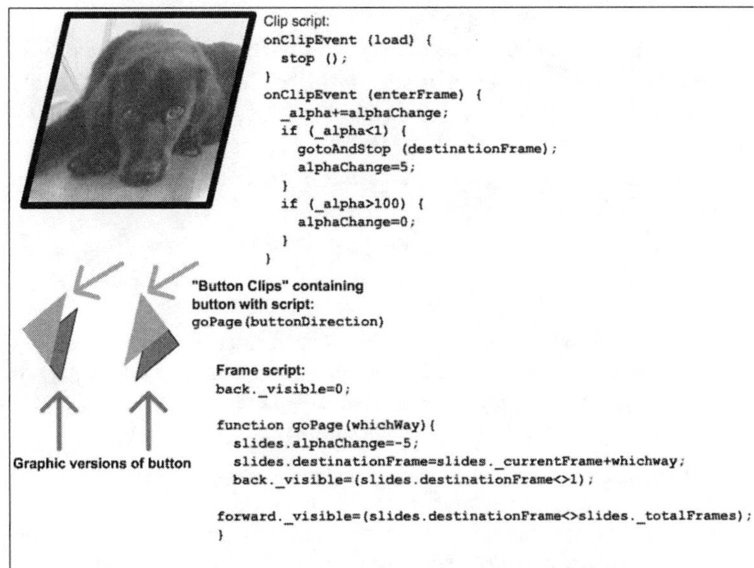

Clip script:
onClipEvent (load) {
stop ();
}
onClipEvent (enterFrame) {
_alpha+=alphaChange;
if (_alpha<1) {
gotoAndStop (destinationFrame);
alphaChange=5;
}
if (_alpha>100) {
alphaChange=0;
}
}
"Button Clips" containing
button with script:
goPage(buttonDirection)
Frame script:
back._visible=0;
function goPage(whichWay){
slides.alphaChange=-5;
slides.destinationFrame=slides._currentFrame+whichway;
back._visible=(slides.destinationFrame<>1);
forward._visible=(slides.destinationFrame<>slides._totalFrames);
}
Graphic versions of button

Figure W5.4 *This is the layout for Button Clips placed on top of dim Graphic versions of the plain button.*

19. Change the script in frame 1 to appear as follows:

```
back._visible=0;
function goPage(whichWay){
  slides.alphaChange=-5;
  slides.destinationFrame=slides._currentFrame+whichway;
  back._visible=(slides.destinationFrame<>1);
  forward._visible=(slides.destinationFrame<>slides._totalFrames);
}
```

The first line simply sets the `back` instance's visibility to 0 from frame 1. The last two lines in the `goPage()` function take care of hiding the buttons. You may have initially thought we'd do something like "if destination frame is 1, then hide back; otherwise, show back" and "if destination frame is the same as total frames, then hide forward; otherwise show it." But that would take two `if` statements and way more code. Instead, the solution in the preceding code sets the `_visible` property to the result of a logical expression, which is placed in parentheses for readability. Either slides.destinationFrame<>1 is true or it's false. When we're headed to frame 1, this statement is false and back is hidden. In any other case, the expression is true and back is shown.

//

This technique takes advantage of some of the simple expression-writing ideas you first learned about in Chapter 5. Remember that if you want to write a logical conditional expression using an equal sign (such as noMorePages._visible=(curFrame=lastFrame)), don't do it that way because a single equal sign performs an assignment. You must remember to use double equal signs instead: noMorePages._visible=(curFrame==lastFrame).

20. Finally, because I can't stop adding features, let's place a Dynamic Text field inside the master version of our slides clip that will display the current page number. Put it in a layer that's present for the entire timeline and associate it with the variable pageDisplay.

21. It makes the most sense to assign values to pageDisplay from the clip instance itself. In the load event, add the line pageDisplay="Page "+1+" of "+_totalFrames. In the enterFrame event at the point where _alpha bottoms out (right after where you set alphaChange to 5 and go to destinationFrame), add the following script:

```
pageDisplay="Page "+_currentFrame+" of "+_totalFrames
```

Naturally, we could keep touching things up forever, but things look pretty good now. When you build a good structure, making enhancements is usually easy. For example, creating the pageDisplay Dynamic Text field was a snap because the basic structure was well designed.

The main thing we learned in this workshop was how to use the enterFrame script to make changes repeatedly (in this case, to the _alpha property). In other workshops, including all the timer exercises (11–13) as well as the Time-Based Animation workshop (15), you'll learn how to use enterFrame to make changes only when necessary or desired instead of repeatedly, as we did in this workshop. Notice that one flaw of this exercise is that the speed of the alpha change is tied directly to the movie's frame rate. If you change the frame rate, the fade speed also changes. In later workshops, you'll learn ways to make animations based on time rather than on frame rate.

We also learned how, if we simply placed a Button inside a Movie Clip, we could effectively inactivate the button by hiding the clip. It turned out that we made a simple Smart Clip, too. The Smart Clip wasn't necessary to hide the button; we needed it so that two instances of the same clip could include different scripts (well, actually so that the script contained in the instance would pass a different parameter). This is a great example of a Smart Clip that isn't elaborate.

I think the best part of this workshop was that we created something that looks really cool, works really well, and took very little work. It just proves that simple solutions are sometimes best.

{Chapter 6 Workshop }

Mapping

In this workshop, you'll learn a valuable technique even though the exercise has limited practical value. Although mapping is a good concept to understand, this exercise involves a specific design that may or may not ever arise in the projects you build.

Mapping is the technique of translating coordinates from one space such as a tiny map to another space such as the territory represented by the map. Mapping is like those mechanical tracing arms that let you trace and scale at the same time. In this workshop, you'll do it with ActionScript.

Practical applications for mapping do exist. You may have a giant map of a city as well as a smaller one that the user can click on. Using mapping, you can calculate the location that was clicked and move the giant map proportionally to display the correct area. You can also use this technique with an assortment of sliders so that you can calculate the portion of a tall text field that should appear based on the location of a scroll bar. Finally, a really cool example of mapping is to make a magnifying glass that can be moved around the stage. In this workshop, we'll do an adaptation of part of a real project I worked on. The "boards" section of the 1999 `www.m-three.com` Web site included a mechanism that "zoomed in" on a snowboard graphic (Figure W6.1). When users move the crosshairs to the left, they "zoom in" on the left side of the large version of the board. When they move the cursor to the right, the board moves to the left to reveal the right side. The effect was pretty cool, but it didn't take a whole lot of work to program (to design, yes, but to program, no).

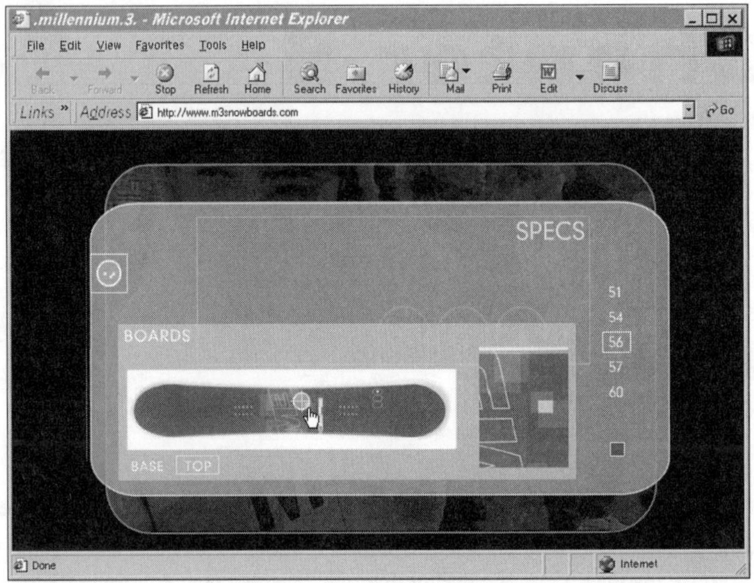

Figure W6.1 *In the original M3 Web site, users could inspect close-up views of the snowboards in a Flash movie that used mapping. Screen shots courtesy of Paris France Inc., Copyright © 1999 by MLY Snowboards.*

Here are the steps for mapping one image to another:

1. Either import a photograph or draw a large rectangle that contains a variety of colors and shapes (Figure W6.2). Convert the rectangle to a Movie Clip. Name the instance now on the Stage `big`.

2. Copy the `big` instance and paste it into a new layer. Resize the copy so that it's much smaller and can fit on the Stage. Name this instance `small`.

3. Draw a perfect square and scale it so that its width is a little less than half the height of the large rectangle (`big`). This square will define the viewable area. Place this square in a layer just above the layer containing `big`. Set the layer property for the layer containing the square to "Mask." Make sure that the layer that contains the `big` instance is set to "Masked" and the layer containing `small` is set to "Normal" (Figure W6.3).

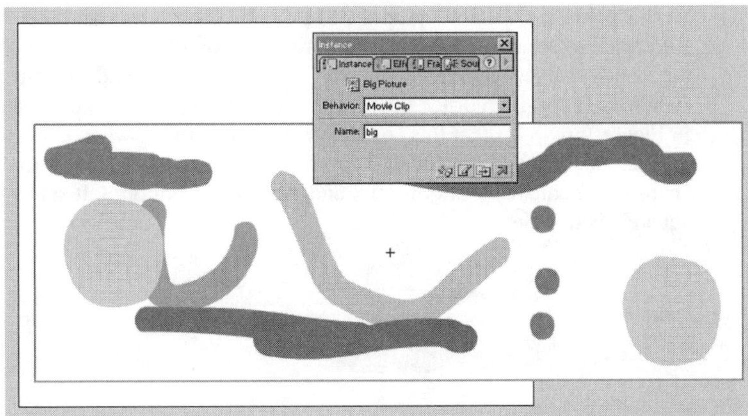

Figure W6.2 *A very large graphic or picture is turned into a Movie Clip with an instance name* `big`.

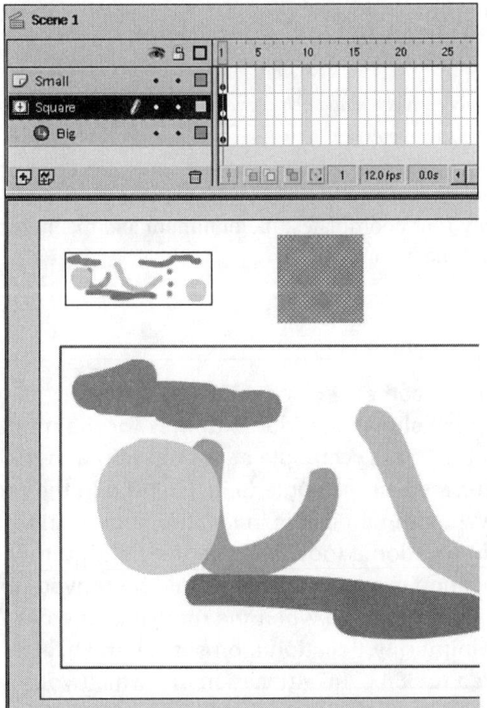

Figure W6.3 *The* `small` *instance is in a Normal layer, and the square shape is masking the* `big` *instance in the lowest layer.*

4. At this point, successively grab the `big` clip by each corner and use the Info panel to ascertain the `x` and `y` coordinates for all four extremes. Note the `x` and `y` values when `big` is moved all the way down and to the right (when `big`'s top-left corner snaps to the square's top-left corner as shown in Figure W6.4). Repeat this for the other three corners: when `big`'s top-right corner snaps to the square's top-right corner, when `big`'s bottom-right snaps to the square's bottom right, and when `big`'s bottom left snaps to the square's bottom left.

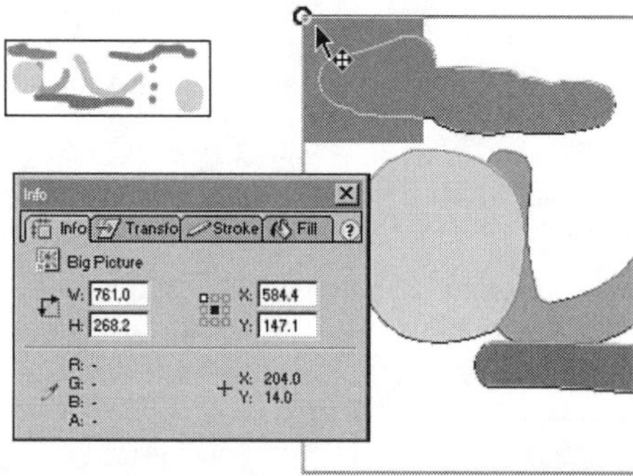

Figure W6.4 *We need to successively snap each corner of* `big` *to the square shape to gather the coordinates of the four extremes.*

5. Regardless of what you named the eight coordinates you gathered in step 4, there are really only four coordinates: the minimum and maximum `x` plus the minimum and maximum `y`.

The terms "min" and "max" can easily be confused, however. Consider Figure W6.5, which shows the four extremes for the mouse version (a, b, c, and d in the `small` rectangle at the top left) and the four extreme locations for the `big` rectangle (a, b, c, and d in the rectangles at the bottom). When the mouse is in location a on `small`, the instance `big` should be in location a (down and to the right). Similarly, when the mouse is in location d on `small`, `big` should be moved up and to the left (shown as d below). So when the mouse is at what I'd call a minimum x and minimum y (location a on `small`), the `big` instance should be moved to 584x, 147y (location a)—which you might call the maximum because those numbers are large. However, we're going to call these values the "minimum" because they correspond to when the mouse is in the "minimum" corner (a). You can call the numbers whatever you want, but just realize that clicking the top-left corner of `small` should move the `big` clip down and to the right.

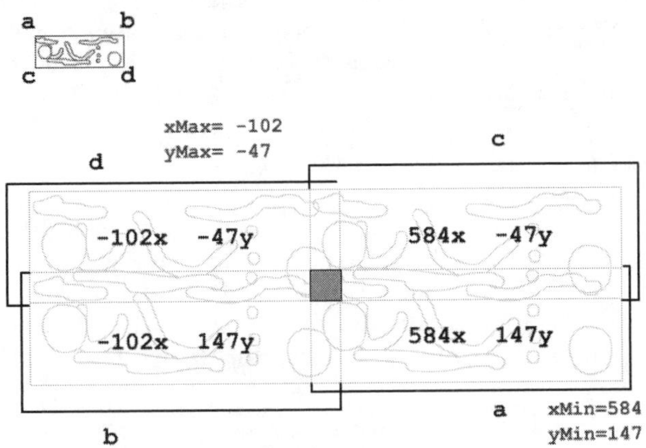

Figure W6.5 *This figure demonstrates how the four corners of the* `small` *rectangle are mapped to four extreme positions of the* `big` *rectangle.*

6. Now that we've gathered the four extremes for `big`, we can write a script attached to the `small` clip. Start by assigning some variables in a `load` event:

```
onClipEvent (load) {
  xMin=584;
  xMax=-102;
  yMin=147;
  yMax=-47;
  width=xMax-xMin;
  height=yMax-yMin;
}
```

   Naturally, you should use your own gathered values for the four variables. It may seem weird that these variables that define the extremes of the `big` instance are now part of the `small` clip. However, we're going to write a script that changes the location of `big`. Just remember that these six variables refer to the `big` clip.

7. Because we're going to be calculating a proportional location of the cursor (on top of `small`), we should gather some variables containing the coordinates of the four sides of `small`. Luckily, we can use the `getBounds()`

method, which was first discussed in Workshop 3, "Creating Custom Cursors." If we assign a variable (say `my`) to the `getBounds()` method of `small`, the variable `my` will become an object with four properties (`my.xMin`, `my.xMax`, `my.yMin`, `my.yMax`). Conveniently, we used similar names to contain the information about `big`. We just have to remember which one is which: `xMin` is for `big` and `my.xMin` is for `small`. We also have to remember that `my` is just one variable with four properties, and that the others are six separate variables. This is no problem if we can just keep them straight. The following script can be added inside the `load` event just below the script shown in step 6:

```
my=getBounds();
my.width=my.xMax- my.xMin;
my.height=my.yMax - my.yMin;
```

Notice that the first line assigns values to the four properties in the variable `my`. The `my` variable contains the generic object data type—as do associative arrays discussed in Chapters 10, "Arrays," and 12, "Homemade Objects." The last two lines simply add two new properties (`width` and `height`) to the variable `my`.

//

Another thing to notice is that the `getBounds()` method can accept a parameter specifying the timeline from which the coordinates `min` and `max` should be gathered. For example, `getBounds(_root)` finds the coordinates of the `small` clip in the main timeline. If you debug the movie and view the variables for `small`, you will see a difference between using `_root` and not using it. By leaving out the parameter, we're going to find the bounds of `small` relative to its own timeline! You might expect that we need the bounds relative to `_root`. Although you often will need the bounds relative to `_root`, in this case, we're just going to calculate the *proportional* location of the mouse. When we do, we have to remember to use only `_xmouse` and `_ymouse` (not `_root._xmouse` and `_root._ymouse`). It doesn't matter if you use `_root` everywhere or not, but you can't mix and match. The benefit of leaving it out will be more apparent when we assign a value for `percent` in a minute. I digressed here because you'll often provide `_root` as a parameter in the `getBounds()` method.

8. Now, let's set a variable when the user clicks so that we'll know when it's time to move the `big` instance. On the `small` instance, add these two events:

```
onClipEvent(mouseDown){
  clicking=1;
}
```

```
onClipEvent(mouseUp){
  clicking=0;
}
```

Any time the user clicks, the variable `clicking` will be assigned the value of `1`. Realize that because this is just a clip's `mouseDown` event and not the confusingly similar `press` event from a button instance, `onClipEvent()` executes when the user clicks anywhere! If you want to set `clicking` to `1` only when the user clicks on the clip, use the `hitTest()` method as shown in the following code. We'll cover `hitTest()` in more detail in Workshop 7, "Working with Odd-Shaped Clickable Areas."

```
onClipEvent(mouseDown){
  if(hitTest(_root._xmouse,_root._ymouse,0)){
    clicking=1;
  }
}
```

9. If you Test Movie, you won't see anything happen. Debugging the movie reveals that we're gathering all the variables we need, and that we know when the user is clicking, but we still have to repeatedly execute a script to move `big` to the proper location. A good place to write this script is in a `mouseMove` event. Attach the following script to the `small` instance:

```
onClipEvent(mouseMove){
  if (clicking){
    _root.big._x=_root._xmouse;
  }
  updateAfterEvent();
}
```

I hope it's apparent that this script only confirms that we can move the location of `big` while we drag. Other than that, it's worthless. Keep in mind that it's typical to confirm that things are working at every stage before proceeding. For something more productive, replace the preceding script with the following code, and I'll translate it:

```
onClipEvent(mouseMove){
  if (clicking){
    var xPercent=(_xmouse-my.xMin)/my.width;
    xPercent=Math.min(xPercent,1);
    xPercent=Math.max(xPercent,0);
    _root.big._x= xMin+(width*xPercent);

    var yPercent=(_ymouse-my.yMin)/my.height;
    yPercent=Math.min(yPercent,1);
    yPercent=Math.max(yPercent,0);
    _root.big._y= yMin+(height*yPercent);
  }
  updateAfterEvent();
}
```

In the first line inside the `if` statement, we determine the percent based on how far from `my.xMin` the mouse is divided by `my.width`. Notice that because all the values in the `my` variable were created relative to this timeline and not to `_root`, we need only calculate `_xmouse` and not `_root._xmouse`. This should explain why we didn't provide `_root` as the parameter of `getBounds()` back in step 7. After we calculate percent (it's actually a decimal number between `0` and `1` because we're not bothering to multiply by `100`), we make sure that we don't go past the bounds: `Math.min(xPercent,1)` returns `1` or `xPercent`, whichever is lower to make sure that `xPercent` isn't greater than `1`. Similarly, we use `Math.max()` to take the greater of `0` or `xPercent` so that `xPercent` never falls below `0`. Don't think that I made a typo: We're using `Math.min()` to make sure that `xPercent` isn't too *high*! I know that "min" implies a low number, but just try a few what-if numbers if this process is confusing. Anyway, after the percent is found, we apply it to `big`'s `_x` value by multiplying `xPercent` by the `width` of `big` and then add it to the `xMin` of `big`. This formula is similar to the techniques we used to gather the percent and then assign it in Workshop 4, "Creating a Horizontal Slider." In this case, we gather percent by using `small`'s coordinates and apply it using `big`'s coordinates. Finally, we do the same thing to assign `big`'s `_y` location.

At this point, the movie should work fine. However (as always), there's one subtle issue I think we should fix. Note that when you click once on the `small` instance, nothing happens. Only when you click *and drag* does the `big` clip start moving. You *could* simply copy the entire code inside the `if` statement in the `mouseMove` event (Figure W6.6) and paste it into the `mouseDown` event. Doing that, however, places the same code in two locations—yuck! Yes, a function is the solution.

```
onClipEvent(mouseMove){
    if (clicking){
        var xPercent = (_xmouse-my.xMin)/my.width;
        xPercent = Math.min(xPercent, 1);
        xPercent = Math.max(xPercent, 0);
        _root.big._x = xMin+(width*xPercent);
        var yPercent = (_ymouse-my.yMin)/my.height;
        yPercent = Math.min(yPercent, 1);
        yPercent = Math.max(yPercent, 0);
        _root.big._y = yMin+(height*yPercent);
    }
    updateAfterEvent();
}
```

Figure W6.6 *This portion of code can be moved to a function.*

10. Select the code shown in Figure W6.6 in the `mouseMove` event and cut it (don't delete). In its place, type `moveBig()`, which calls a function we're about to write. Inside the `mouseDown` event, type `moveBig()` as well so that the `mouseDown` event executes the same function. The two events should look like this:

```
onClipEvent(mouseDown){
  if(hitTest(_root._xmouse,_root._ymouse,0)){
    clicking=1;
    moveBig();
  }
}
onClipEvent(mouseMove){
  if (clicking){
    moveBig();
  }
  updateAfterEvent();
}
```

11. Because `moveBig()` is called without a path such as `_root.moveBig()`, we imply that the function will reside inside the clip itself. Therefore, we can write the following function in the first frame *inside* this master symbol:

```
function moveBig(){
  var xPercent=(_xmouse-my.xMin)/my.width;
  xPercent=Math.min(xPercent,1);
  xPercent=Math.max(xPercent,0);
  _root.big._x= xMin+(width*xPercent);

  var yPercent=(_ymouse-my.yMin)/my.height;
  yPercent=Math.min(yPercent,1);
  yPercent=Math.max(yPercent,0);
  _root.big._y= yMin+(height*yPercent);
}
```

Notice that you create only the framework for the function (`function moveBig(){}`) and then paste the code you cut in step 10 in between the curly brackets.

Now your movie should be complete!

//

By the way, there's an interesting way to write the `moveBig()` function for *just* the `small` instance. Currently, although the function is invoked in only the `small` instance (because that's the only clip with any scripts on it), the function actually resides in the master symbol (the same symbol used in the `big` instance). Therefore, the function is a bit redundant and is possible to invoke as either `small.moveBig()` or `big.moveBig()`—or for any other instance of this Movie Clip you happen to drag from the Library. Often, this is desirable because you want a function to behave like a homemade method for every instance, as you first learned in Chapter 7. First of all, there's no harm the way we have it because we never call `big.moveBig()`. But if you want to be slightly more efficient, you can move the entire `moveBig()` function from inside the symbol's first keyframe and paste the *entire* `moveBig()` function right before the closing curly bracket in the `load` event. In effect, this creates a method for an individual Movie Clip object in the same way we created homemade objects with methods in Chapter 12.

This workshop involved many specific steps. We used some hard-wired values that we gathered as well as some values calculated with the `getBounds()` method. Then we used those values to gather coordinates and determine proportional locations of the mouse compared to the `small` clip. Finally, we translated those found proportions to the `big` clip. For a challenge, try to replace the part where we assigned the hard-wired values for the extremes of the `big` clip. If you know that the `big` clip will initially appear in, say, the top-left location, you can use that information along with `big._x`, `big._y`, and `big.getBounds()` to ascertain the four extremes (`xMin`, `xMax`, `yMin`, and `yMax`). I'll put that solution in the downloadable version of this file available at `www.teleport.com/~phillip/actionscripting`.

{Chapter 7 Workshop }

Working with Odd-Shaped Clickable Areas

Flash buttons are the easiest way to trap mouse clicks. Buttons are simple and powerful. It's easy to include Over and Down states and even to define an odd shape that's clickable in the Hot state. Placing a script on a button opens up a variety of mouse events to which you can respond.

For all their greatness, buttons are fixed in their feature set: as soon as you want more, they become limited. For example, you can't change any property of a button the way you can with clip instances. In Workshop 5, "Building a Slide Show," we learned how to place a button inside a clip so that we could effectively hide the button by hiding the clip. Consider that for Workshop 6, "Mapping," we responded to the mouse without any buttons! Instances of Movie Clips give you access to clip events that include `mouseDown`, `mouseUp`, and `mouseMove`. The only catch is that clips all respond to mouse events regardless of where the event occurs—for example, the `mouseDown` event will be received by every clip instance regardless of where you click. However, if we use clips in conjunction with the Movie Clip object method `hitTest()`, we can determine whether the user has clicked on a particular clip.

This workshop involves a situation in which there are many individual shapes such as outlines of countries (Figure W7.1) that you want to become clickable. Instead of making each shape a separate button, we want to use Movie Clips because we want to change the properties of the shapes (such as `_alpha`) and we also want to "goto" particular frames. We don't want to use invisible buttons because each area would need its own button of a unique shape. We'll simply use the shapes of the clips themselves to establish the clickable areas.

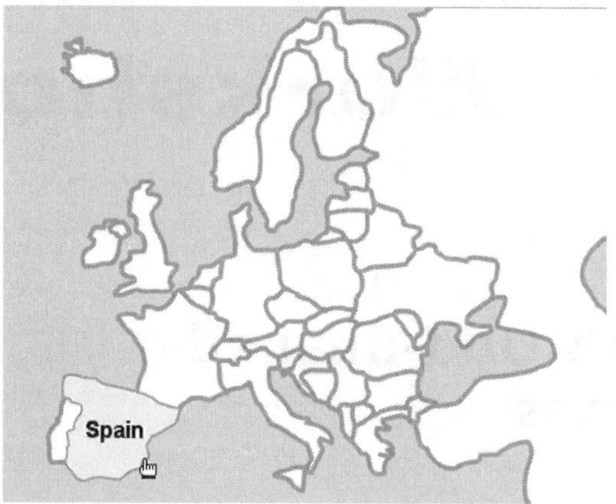

Figure W7.1 *You might need odd-shaped clickable areas when letting a user select individual countries.*

In addition to exploring the `hitTest()` method, this workshop exposes you to two specific techniques: First, we'll store references to all the clips in the movie in an array. Second, we'll use a single "monitoring" clip that responds to all mouse events (instead of placing the same script on each clip). This arrangement makes our work much easier.

Here are the steps for creating and managing odd-shaped clickable areas:

1. Draw a large, filled square. Set Stroke to at least 5 and use the Pencil tool with Pencil Mode set to Ink to draw squiggly lines (of a different color than the fill) to divide the square into sections (Figure W7.2).
2. Select everything you've drawn and choose Modify, Shape, Convert Lines to Fills. Then carefully select and delete the lines you just drew. The result is that you are chopping up the original square into sections. Pretend that these are the borders of countries.
3. Individually select each section and convert it to a Movie Clip (press F8). This is the one time when you can use the default "Symbol 1" name. In this example, we won't even name the instances!

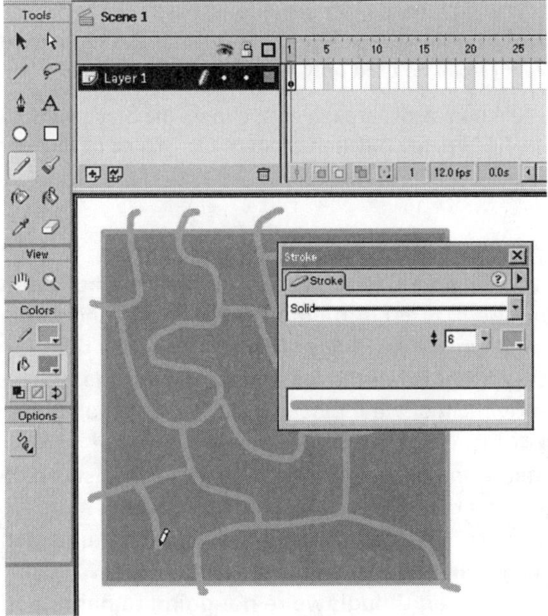

Figure W7.2 *We'll make odd shapes by drawing thick lines through a square.*

4. We're about to write the script that checks whether the mouse is on top of any clips. Instead of writing a script for each instance, we'll create a new clip that monitors all activity. The monitoring clip is a good idea because even if each instance only called a function, that would be a lot of tedious work. The crazy thing is that you may often find placing individual scripts on many instances performs better than the technique we'll use. (This workshop will be plenty snappy, but it's just something to know.) To create the monitoring clip, just create a New Symbol (press Ctrl+F8) and name it "Monitor," but don't draw anything in it because we'll just leave it invisible. Return to the main timeline and drag an instance of Monitor from the Library onto the Stage.

5. Now we can attach the following script to the instance of Monitor on the Stage:

```
onClipEvent (mouseMove) {
  _root.checkEm();
  updateAfterEvent();
}
```

This script simply calls the `checkEm()` function that we're about to place in the first keyframe of the movie. The `updateAfterEvent()` causes any changes made by `checkEm()` to immediately appear on the Stage. You might think that it would make more sense to just use `updateAfterEvent()` inside `checkEm()`. That *would* make sense except that `updateAfterEvent()` can be used only within a clip event.

6. The `checkEm()` function steps through each clip on the Stage and, if the mouse intersects the clip, the function changes the `_alpha` of that clip.

//

Normally, you'd probably prefer to target clips by name when setting their `_alpha` or using the `hitTest()` method. We're not going to name the clips. Instead, we'll write a script that loops through *all* the "objects" on the Stage (that is, all the instances) and for the objects that happen to be movie clips, we'll place a reference of that clip in an array. When `checkEm()` runs, it can simply step through the array. Consider if we did name the clips `country1`, `country2`, and so on. If we simply populated an array with a statement such as `allClips=[_root.country1,_root.country2]`, we could later target any individual clip using an expression such as `allClips[1]._alpha=50`. Even though we're not going to name our clip instances, we can still populate the array with references to those clips. Specifically, we'll step through the built-in array for `_root`, which contains all objects on the Stage.

In the first keyframe of the movie, type the following code:

```
allClips= new Array();
for (i in _root){
  if (typeof(_root[i])=="movieclip"){
    allClips[i]=_root[i];
  }
}
```

The variable `allClips` is an array. The `for-in` loop checks each object in the `_root` array and, if its `typeof()` is "movieclip," it adds an object reference to the `allClips` array. The function `typeof()` returns one of the following string description of the type of object supplied as a parameter: `string`, `movieclip`, `object`, `function`, `number`, or `undefined`. You can supply the `typeof()` function with an unknown data type and it will tell you what you have. Notice that not only is `_root` an address of a clip (the main movie's timeline), it also happens to contain an associative array with references to all the clips. Targeting clips dynamically was covered in Chapter 7 and associative arrays were covered in Chapters 10 and 12.

7. Now that the `allClips` array is populated, we can write the `checkEm()` script that is invoked every time you move the mouse. Let's first try the following script placed below the `for-in` loop you typed into the first keyframe in step 6:

```
function checkEm(){
  for (i in allClips){
    allClips[i]._alpha=30;
  }
}
```

   If you test this, you should see all the clips dim down to 30 percent alpha.

8. Obviously we want only one clip to dim out: the one with the mouse on it. The `hitTest()` method can help us figure out which clip that is. The form for `hitTest()` is `targetClip.hitTest(x,y,flag)` where `targetClip` is the clip you're checking, `x` and `y` are the coordinates of the point in question, and `flag` must be either `0` (when you only want to check whether the coordinates are within the square boundary of the clip) or `1` (when you want to check whether the coordinates are on top of the clip's outline—just its shape, as we're doing in this case). Finally, this method returns either `1` or `0` depending on whether the coordinates are within the clip's shape or bounds. Also, as you can with all clip methods, you can forgo the `targetClip` parameter to target the clip you're currently inside. To apply this logic to our function, we can put an `if` statement inside the `for-in` loop with the condition `allClips[i].hitTest(_xmouse,_ymouse,1)`. If that condition is `true`, we can set `_alpha` to `30`. Just for fun (and because we're so close to finishing), try the following script and see whether you can figure out the minor bug:

```
function checkEm(){
  for (i in allClips){
    if(allClips[i].hitTest(_xmouse,_ymouse,1)){
      allClips[i]._alpha=30;
    }
  }
}
```

   If you test this movie, you'll see that it works alright. However, once a clip's `_alpha` is set to 30, it never comes back up to 100. You can simply add an `else` clause to the `if` statement to solve the problem:

```
function checkEm(){
  for (i in allClips){
    if(allClips[i].hitTest(_xmouse,_ymouse,1)){
      allClips[i]._alpha=30;
    }else{
      allClips[i]._alpha=100;
    }
  }
}
```

//

By the way, because `allClips[i]` targets a clip, you can set any other property or use any other method with the form `allClips[i].method()` or `allClips[i].property`.

This script works perfectly. However, it can be streamlined in several ways. Although it's not a problem, notice that we're targeting the current clip by using `allClips[i]` in three places. You could simply add the line `var thisClip=allClips[i]` as the first line inside the for-loop and then use `thisClip` in the three places that use `allClips[i]`. Although this refinement is arguably useless, I wanted to point out you can store references to clips in variables just as `allClips` already includes several references.

I would personally opt for another refinement that many people might argue makes the function less readable. Just check out the following alternative to the `checkEm()` function, if for no other reason than to challenge your script-translation skills:

```
function checkEm(){
  for (i in allClips){
    if(allClips[i].hitTest(_xmouse,_ymouse,1)){
      allClips[i]._alpha=100-(allClips[i].hitTest(_xmouse,_ymouse,1 )*70);
    }
  }
}
```

It looks like our original function! We simply set each clip's `alpha` to the following expression:

```
100-(allClips[i].hitTest(_xmouse,_ymouse,1 )*70)
```

Because `allClips[i].hitTest(_xmouse,_ymouse,1 )` turns into either `1` or `0`, you can think of the expression as one of the following possibilities:

```
100-(1*70)
```

or

```
100-(0*70)
```

If `hitTest()` is `true`, we set the `_alpha` to `70` less than `100`; otherwise we set it to `100`. Again, this solution is not necessary, it's only an alternative.

9. Finally, we'll add a feature that determines which clip, if any, the user has clicked when the mouse button is pressed. Add this script to the Monitor clip instance:

```
onClipEvent (mouseDown) {
  _root.checkClick();
  updateAfterEvent();
}
```

   Now we just need to write a `checkClick()` function in the root timeline.

10. Try this version of the `checkClick()` function in the movie's first keyframe:

```
function checkClick(){
  for (i in allClips){
    if(allClips[i].hitTest(_xmouse,_ymouse,1)){
      trace ("You clicked "+allClips[i]._name);
      allClips[i]._xScale-=20;
      allClips[i]._yScale-=20;
      return;
    }
  }
}
```

Although there may be little practical value to this workshop the way it is (and to this function in particular), there are several lessons we can take away. In this `checkClick()` function, notice that because we're only doing something with the clip that matches and nothing to all the other clips, we can use `return` to stop looping as soon as something is found. In the `checkEm()` function, we set every clip's `_alpha` to either `100` or `30`. As it turns out, even when you have to loop through the entire array, the process goes quite quickly. After you learn more about `getTimer()` in the Timer workshops (11–13) and the Time Based Animation workshop (15), you'll be able to test the impact different script approaches have on performance. For example, I suggested that you could place the value of `allClips[i]` into the variable `thisClip` instead of constantly referring to `allClips[i]`. This change would certainly be worth the effort if performance noticeably increased because of the change. If you make 200 copies of the clips on the Stage, you'll start to see a slow down. In my tests, for example, I found that when I had 200 instances on Stage, the loop took as long as 100 milliseconds to complete (1/10 of one second). By trying different scripts, I reduced the loop to half that time. The point is that looping through an array is fast, but trying different scripts can often make it faster.

Remember that one of the main lessons in this workshop was to store references to clip instances in an array variable so that you can use the variable when you want to target instances.

We also learned the technique of using just one "monitoring" clip to capture all the mouseMove events. With much more work than we did in these steps, we could have attached a separate script like the following to each clip:

```
onClipEvent (mouseMove) {
  _alpha = 100-(hitTest(_root._xmouse, _root._ymouse, 1)*70);
  updateAfterEvent();
}
```

In addition to a possible improvement in performance, a single "monitoring" clip is better because making a change is easier when there's just one function or one clip to make the change to.

Finally, we also learned how to use hitTest(). In Workshop 16, "Creating a Multistate Button," we'll revisit hitTest().

{Chapter 8 Workshop }

Adapting Built-in Smart Clips

By now you should have enough skill to create your own Smart Clips. First of all, they don't need to be complex. Take for example the "forward" and "back" Button Clips created in Workshop 5, "Building a Slide Show." Even if you do need to invest a lot of work to create a Smart Clip, as we did in Workshop 3, "Creating Custom Cursors," you can often reuse the code so many times that you'll quickly see a return on your investment. But just because you *can* make a Smart Clip doesn't mean you have to reinvent the wheel.

Flash comes with several Smart Clips and countless others are available from the Flash community at the Macromedia Exchange for Flash (`www.macromedia.com/exchange/flash`). Most of these preexisting Smart Clips can be used as-is. However, you'll often find that you need to adapt them for your own purposes. One such example is the Menu Smart Clip (found under Window, Common Libraries, Smart Clips). It's pretty cool because you can simply specify the items you want in the menu using the Clip Parameters panel, and this Smart Clip configures a drop-down or pop-up menu that mimics the behavior found in system-level menus you've seen in other applications (Figure W8.1). However, that's all this Smart Clip does! If you want something to happen when a selection is made, or if you ever want to ascertain the current setting of the menu, you'll have to figure it out on your own. Alternatively, you could study this workshop because that's what we're about to do. We'll convert the Menu Smart Clip to suit our purposes. In the process, you'll learn the general approach you can take when tinkering with a preexisting Smart Clip.

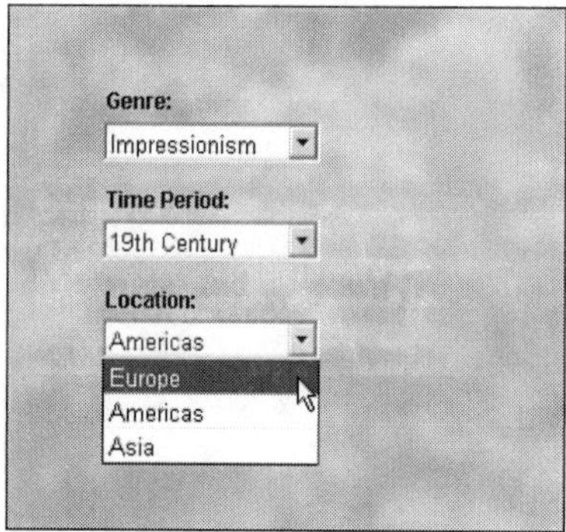

Figure W8.1 *The Menu Smart Clip lets you create customized drop-down menus for your movies.*

Follow these steps to adapt an existing Smart Clip to your own purposes:

1. Open the Smart Clips Library by selecting Window, Common Libraries, Smart Clips. Drag an instance of Menu onto your Stage. Close the Smart Clips Library because everything you need has been copied into your file.
2. Give the instance of Menu on the Stage the instance name `myMenu`. Debug the movie; as you know from Chapter 6, "Debugging," you may have to select Debug Movie twice. Select the `myMenu` instance listed in the Debugger as well as in the Variables tab (Figure W8.2).

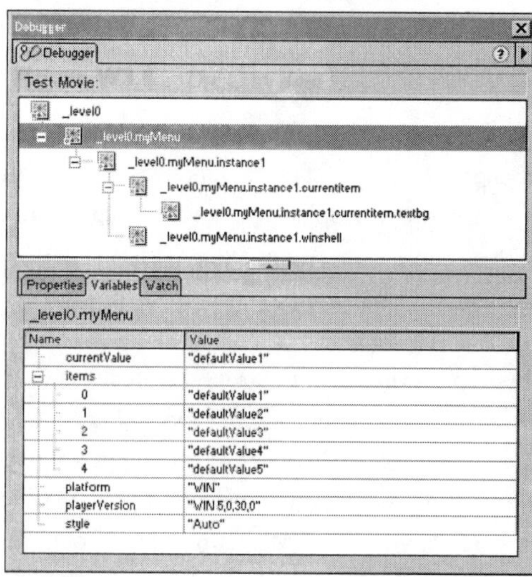

Figure W8.2 *We can analyze how the Smart Clip works by selecting the appropriate instance in the Debugger.*

3. Now interact with the menu in the movie that's playing and keep on eye on the Debugger. One thing that's interesting is that when the menu is open, you'll see many more instances present in the movie. That's because the code uses the `duplicateMovieClip()` method, which is similar to the `attachMovie()` method you'll learn more about in Workshop 18, "Creating a Dynamic Slide Presentation." The important variable to notice is `currentValue`. That variable always matches the name for the currently selected menu item.

4. Back in Flash, use the Clip Parameters panel to populate this menu with the following items: `Macromedia`, `Microsoft`, and `Macmillan`. Delete any excess items. When you test the movie, you should see that these three items are in the menu.

5. Create a button called "go" and attach the following script to it:

```
on (release) {
  if (myMenu.currentValue == "Macromedia") {
    getURL ("http://www.macromedia.com", "_blank");
  }
  if (myMenu.currentValue == "Microsoft") {
    getURL ("http://www.microsoft.com", "_blank");
  }
  if (myMenu.currentValue == "Macmillan") {
    getURL ("http://www.mcp.com", "_blank");
  }
}
```

   When the user clicks the "go" button, we check the `myMenu` instance's `currentValue` variable and then open a new browser window with the appropriate Web page. This script should work fine when you test the movie.

6. That wasn't too bad! Now let's add a feature that invokes the hyperlink using `getURL()` as soon as a selection is made and not after the user clicks the "go" button. To accomplish this, we'll have to do some snooping first. Double-click your instance of `myMenu` and notice a layer called "win" and one called "mac" (Figure W8.3).

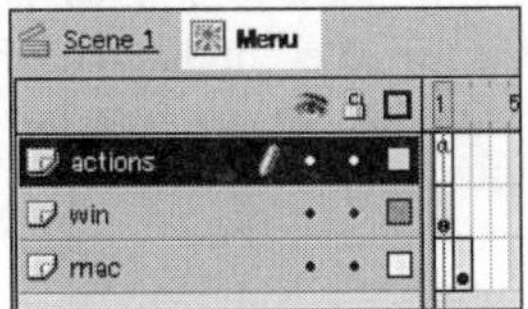

Figure W8.3 *The Smart Clip has a different nested clip in each keyframe.*

7. Move the red current frame marker between frames 1 and 2. Notice that there's a different graphic. In frame 1, there's an unnamed instance of the "menu-win" symbol, and in frame 2 there's an instance of the symbol "menu-mac." This is because the Smart Clip automatically displays the appropriate look-and-feel for your user's platform by grabbing the first three characters from the string returned using the `GetVersion()` function, which you first saw in the Workshop 1, "Ensuring That Users Have the Flash 5 Player." Debug the movie again, and you can see that, depending on your platform, the `_currentframe` property of `myMenu` is either `1` or `2` (Figure W8.4). By using the Clip Parameters panel, you can override the automatic platform selection by changing the setting for `style`. Go ahead and change it to Mac if you're on a Windows machine and vice versa. Then debug the movie again.

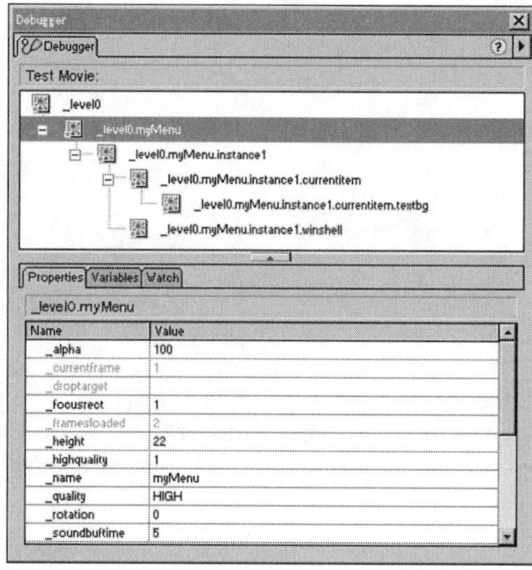

Figure W8.4 *We can use the Debugger to monitor properties including* `_currentframe`.

8. Although it is interesting to investigate how this clip was built, we need to dig further to solve the task at hand: trapping for an event that happens when the user changes the menu. When debugging, we can view how the instance of "menu-win" or "menu-mac" is behaving. The unnamed clip would be difficult to find in the Debugger, but because there's only one clip inside our `myMenu` clip, we can find it "one level deep" in the Debugger. There's only one clip at that level in the hierarchy, and it should be listed as `_level0.myMenu.instance1` or `_level0.myMenu.instance3`. Select this clip while you're debugging (Figure W8.5).

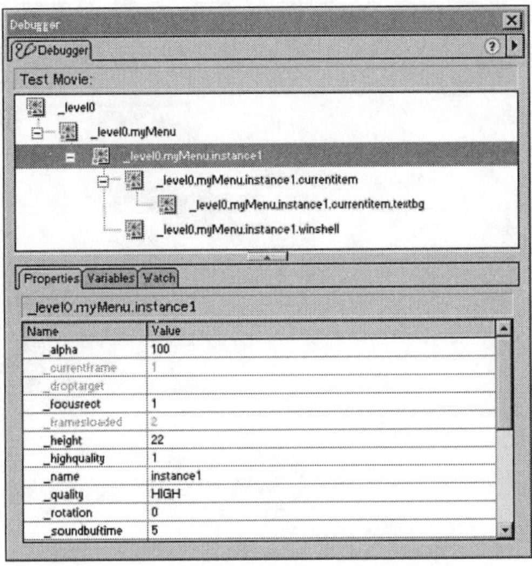

Figure W8.5 *When we analyze the nested clip ("menu-win" or "menu-mac"), we'll see its* `_currentframe` *property when the Menu Smart Clip is selected.*

9. Select the Properties tab in the Debugger so that we can monitor `_currentframe` while you make selections to the menu in the movie. The interesting fact is that the `_currentframe` is always `2` while the menu is open but falls back to `1` after a selection is made. If we just invoke a function every time the instance of "menu-win" or "menu-mac" reaches frame 1, we'll be set! Let's call a function that we'll store in the main timeline from frame 1 of those two symbols.

10. Because our script may not work perfectly on the first try, simply enter the symbol appropriate to your platform (unless, or course, you overrode the style parameter in step 7, in which case you should select the appropriate parameter now). Instead of digging deep into the clip, just edit the master version of "menu-win" or "menu-mac" from the Library window (Figure W8.6). Place the following script into frame 1:

```
_root.doit();
```

//

This code simply calls the function `doit()`, which we'll write and place in frame 1 of the main movie.

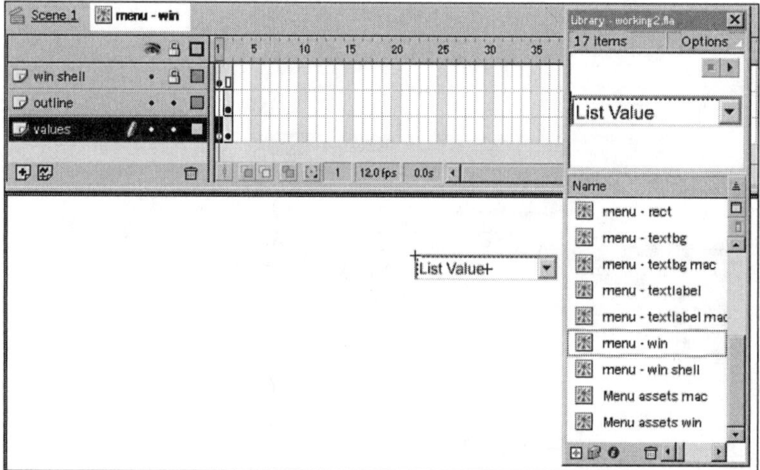

Figure W8.6 *The easiest way to edit the "menu-win" symbol is through the Library window.*

11. Return to the main timeline and copy the portion of code between the first and last curly brackets from the "go" button that we created in step 5.
12. In frame 1 of the main timeline, create the framework for `function doit(){}`. Then paste the code you copied in step 11 so that the function looks like this:

```
function doit(){
  if(myMenu.currentValue=="Macromedia"){
    getURL("http://www.macromedia.com", "_blank");
  }
  if(myMenu.currentValue=="Microsoft"){
    getURL("http://www.microsoft.com", "_blank");
  }
  if(myMenu.currentValue=="Macmillan"){
    getURL("http://www.mcp.com", "_blank");
  }
}
```

13. Although this function works alright, I don't like the fact that `doit()` is called at the very beginning before any selection has been made. However, it doesn't seem to be a problem because none of the `if` statement's conditions are met. My tendency, however, is to adjust the code we placed in frame 1 of "menu-win" or "menu-mac" so that it looks like this:

```
if (flag){
  _root.doit();
}
flag=1;
```

//

This a great use of a flag, which was first discussed in Workshop 3, "Creating Custom Cursors." Here's the way this flag works: The first time the script is encountered, `flag` is undefined, making the `if` statement's condition `false`. The last line sets `flag` to `1` so that next time (and all subsequent times) the line `_root.doit()` will execute.

14. After you place the `_root.doit()` call in the first frame of both "menu-win" and "menu-mac," there are some important remaining refinements. Specifically, I don't like how the first item in the menu appears as a default. I'd much rather see a message such as "Select..." appear in the menu field. This is an easy fix. Just open the Menu Smart Clip and, in the first frame, add this line of code above all the other code:

    ```
    currentValue="Select...";
    ```

    Although we could have placed this statement within a `load` event for the instance of `myMenu`, doing so wouldn't affect all menus. Perhaps you want a different default `currentValue` for each menu. If that is the case, you can use the `load` event or add `currentValue` as a parameter that the using author can edit through the Clip Parameters panel. Indeed, you can do a lot of different things, but for now, leave the `currentValue` assignment in the first keyframe as instructed.

There's one last issue that needs attention. If users make a selection from the menu (say, "Macromedia"), they'll navigate to that page. However, if users *begin* to make a selection by clicking to drop down the list but then change their minds and click off the list, our script still navigates to the most recent selection in the menu, and the users return to "Macromedia" in this case. This happens because our `doit()` function is called every time the menu is closed—even if the selection doesn't change. We can resolve this problem quite simply. If we save in a variable the last setting when the menu was open, we can check to see whether that value has changed before invoking the `doit()` function.

15. Repeat this step and step 16 for both the master symbols "menu-win" and "menu-mac." In frame 2, place the following script in either the "outline" or "values" layer. Do not place this script in the bottom layer because it doesn't have a separate keyframe for both frames 1 and 2.

    ```
    lastValue=_parent.currentValue;
    ```

    This script saves the value of `currentValue`, which is really a variable contained in the parent Menu clip.

16. In frame 1 of the same clip, change the script to read as follows:

```
if (lastValue<>_parent.currentValue){
  _root.doit();
}
```

    This script simply says to invoke the `doit()` function only if the `lastValue` variable is different than `currentValue`.

It's done! You can actually make more changes to this clip. Perhaps you want this Smart Clip to be totally self-contained so that there are no scripts in the main timeline. You'd just have to follow some of the same steps we took when converting the horizontal slider to a Smart Clip in Workshop 4, "Creating a Horizontal Slider." You can could also store all the addresses to which the menu navigates in an array and streamline the `doit()` function that way.

The intention of this workshop was not to show you the "ultimate menu." Rather, the purpose of this workshop was to show you some of the ways you can modify existing Smart Clips. You should also have learned some ways to analyze others' work. In particular, the Menu Smart Clip is a good one from which to learn because it exhibits many of the attributes of "good style" which were discussed in Chapter 3.

{Part IIB }

Intermediate Workshops

{Chapter 9 Workshop }

Creating a Currency-Exchange Calculator

The first eight workshops were relatively basic. Sure, there were plenty of new concepts and unique solutions to problems, but there wasn't all that much complex math or string manipulation, no homemade objects, and no interfacing with external data. If those first eight workshops were "basic," this workshop and the next seven will be "intermediate" workshops. As such, some of the steps are not explained as fully as they have been in the first workshops. Instead I'll try to reference where the topics were first covered. Don't worry, the remaining workshops won't be impossible, they'll just involve different topics.

In this workshop, we'll build a currency-exchange calculator. The user will be able to input any value and, based on the exchange rate, calculate the equivalent cost in another currency. As is true with many of these workshops, the finished product is not necessarily something you'll use as-is, but the process of working through the exercise will teach you some very valuable techniques. If you've read all the chapters in the Foundation, you'll no doubt recall the several times I referred you to this workshop. A lot is covered here. Specifically, you'll do some simple math and some slightly more complex math. You'll encounter some of the challenges when you have to convert numbers to strings. You'll also look at ways to improve the user experience by adding a feature that lets the user select from predefined exchange rates for different countries. Just to make it easy for us (and because exchange rates vary daily), we'll make it possible to load in the current exchange rates from external sources. Although you may never have to build a currency-exchange calculator again, I'll be willing to bet that you'll be able to use all of the topics covered here!

Consider the following description as the specification for this workshop. As you learned in Chapter 3, "The Programmer's Approach," after you have a detailed "spec," programming is almost routine.

> Provide the user with a way to convert values in one currency to the equivalent value in another currency. The user will be able to type any number into one field, adjust the exchange rate by typing into the "rate" field, and see the result after clicking a button labeled "convert." Additionally, you must format the value displayed in the standard money format: with at least one 0 to the left of the decimal, two decimal places shown at all times, and all fractional values rounded off to the nearest cent (the one-hundredth decimal place). Finally, the calculator must allow the import from an external source of several country's exchanges rates from U.S. dollars. The user will be able to select any country, and that country's exchange rate will automatically fill the "rate" field. Additionally, after any country's exchange rate has been selected, the user must be allowed to toggle between dollars and the other currency. For example, the user can toggle between "dollars to pounds" and "pounds to dollars" if the current rate is for British pounds. See Figure W9.1 for a rough layout. Finally, feel free to improve the interface for utmost usability where appropriate.

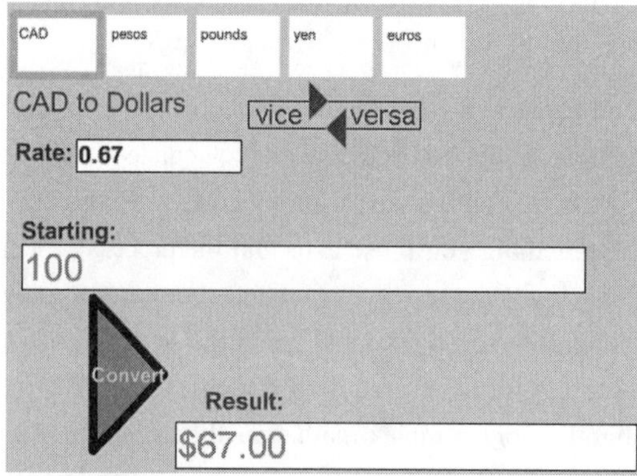

Figure W9.1 *We'll build a calculator based on a specification that includes this mock-up.*

Although this is a rather big task, realize that all great things are done in pieces. For example, we're not going to jump right in and have everything done after writing one script. Rather, we'll break things down and build each piece as we go. The whole time, we'll keep an eye out for approaches that might conflict with a future task. We'll do one thing at a time, but with an eye on the future. Luckily, this spec has been organized in a logical order with the simple tasks first. It will serve as the guide for the following steps:

1. Place two Input Text fields onscreen, one associated with a variable named `rate` and the other with a variable named `original`. Make sure that both fields have nice wide margins. Using the Text Options panel, set the Max. Chars option to something high, such as `20`. You may also opt for the Border/Bg option so the field remains outlined and easy to see. It's important that we allow the user to input only numbers and a period for decimals into these two fields (Figure W9.2) You can label these fields using additional plain Static Text.

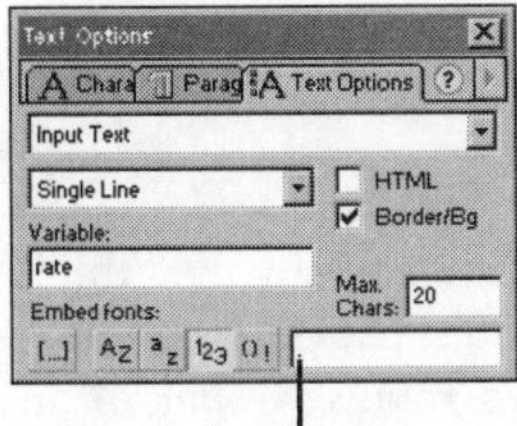

Figure W9.2 *You can limit input to just numbers plus individually identified characters.*

2. Create a Dynamic Text field (not an Input field because this field will be used to display the results) and associate it with the variable `result`. In the Text options panel deselect all of the buttons under Embed fonts (as this field will contain special characters such as the dollar sign).

3. Make a button called Convert and attach the following script to the button:

```
on (release) {
  result=original*rate;
}
```

Now you have a currency-exchange calculator! Pretty simple. If the `rate` is `.70` and you type `10` into the `original` field, pressing the Convert button puts `7` into the `result` field. Thank you and good night.

//

Not so fast. Although the preceding steps create a calculator that works there's more we have to consider. Try a `rate` like `.7` on an `original` value such as `10.95`. No doubt, the bug tester will determine that we're not rounding off to the nearest cent. We just need to write a `round()` function. But because the Math object already has a `round()` method, let's not use the same name for our function. We cannot use `Math.round()` directly because that function rounds to the nearest whole number. Consider the result of `0.7*10.95`. Currently, we're getting a result of `7.665`, but we want it to round to `7.67`. If you change the assignment to `result=Math.round(original*rate)`, you'll find that `7.665` rounds to `8`. However, we can still use `Math.round()` if we apply a fairly simply trick. Consider what happens if you first multiply `result` by 100 (you'd get 766.5), round that off (you'd have 767), and then divide by 100 (you'd get 7.67, which is what we want). Consider this verbose solution:

```
result=original*rate;
result=result*100;
result=Math.round(result);
result=result/100;
```

Although we could do this math in a slightly easier way, I think rounding off to specific decimal places might prove to be a useful utility for other projects (if not later in this workshop). Consider how this works: We used 100 to multiply and then divided by 100 because we wanted 2 decimal places. To round off to 3 places, we would use 1000. We'd use 10 for 1 decimal place.

4. Consider the relationship described in the preceding note as you type this homemade `rnd()` function into frame 1:

```
function rnd(num, places){
  var multiplier = Math.pow(10, places);
  var answer = Math.round(num*multiplier);
  return answer/multiplier;
}
```

This function accepts two parameters: `num` (for the number being rounded off) and `places` (for the number of decimal places). First we determine what we're going to multiply by (10, 100, 1000, or whatever). The `Math.pow()` method accepts two parameters: `base` and `exponent` so that the first number is raised to the power of the second number. In this example, if `places` is 2, 10^2 is 100. We then round off `num` multiplied by `multiplier` and place it in another temporary variable answer. Finally, we return the answer we just found divided by `multiplier`. This is exactly the process we need, and because it's now a function, we can use it any time.

5. To test the function we just wrote, change the script attached to the Convert button in step 3 to read as follows:

```
on (release) {
  result=rnd (original*rate, 2);
}
```

I suppose that you could have written this formula in two steps by first setting `result` to `original*rate` and then reassigning `result` to `rnd(result,2)`. The solution shown isn't too difficult if you remember that multiplication is performed first.

//

At this point, you might find that the `rnd()` function still doesn't work! `7.665` rounds off to `7.66`, but it *should* be `7.65`. There's nothing wrong with the logic used in the `rnd()` function—rather you're seeing an inherent problem with all computers when using floating-point numbers (decimal values). It's called the "rounding error" and it's unavoidable. Although we humans have no problem looking at a fraction such as `1/2` and deriving the accurate decimal equivalent of `0.5`, computers sometimes have problems. It's obvious when you consider a fraction like `1/3`, because the computer will need to round off a decimal like 0.333... (with repeating threes). But even fractions that should be expressed in simple decimals such as 7.665 will exhibit the problem. Our case of `10.95*0.7` exhibits the rounding error because the computer considers the answer to be 7.66499999.... You won't see it in Flash if you execute the script `trace(10.95*.7)`, but you will see it if you execute the equivalent code in JavaScript `alert(10.95*.7)` (see Figure W9.3).

Figure W9.3 *This pop-up box shows the full number.*

> If you investigate this subject, you'll find that there's actually a lot to it. You can avoid the issue entirely by simply using only integer numbers. However, dividing one integer by another will often create a floating-point number. The common practice is to avoid floating-point numbers as long as you can (through all your calculations) and at the very end display decimal values onscreen. For example, the exchange rate of `0.7` can be expressed as an integer if you use `7` and remember to divide the final answer by `10`. We're not going to go through that effort in this workshop, but it's worth considering. Instead we'll use a quick and dirty trick. Just realize the user doesn't care what's going on behind the scenes if, in the end, he sees the correct numbers onscreen.

6. The rounding error is small but quite annoying. To address it, I've developed this quick and dirty solution. Change the script on the Convert button to read as follows:

```
on (release) {
  var decimals=1;
  decimals+= (original.length- 1) - original.lastIndexOf( "." );
  decimals+= (rate.length- 1) - rate.lastIndexOf( "." );
  fudge=1/Math.pow(10,decimals);
  result=rnd ((original*rate)+fudge,2);
}
```

   Basically, I add a very small "fudge factor" to the floating-point product of original*rate that is always smaller than the total number of decimal places for both original and rate. In the first line, I initialize a local variable `decimals` to `1` (if no decimals are found, my fudge factor will still be `.1`—which will have no effect). In the second line, `decimals` is increased by the difference between the length of original (minus 1) and the last index of `"."`. So, if original is 10.95, I subtract `2` (the index where the last `"."` is found) from `4` (the length of `"10.95"` minus `1`) to determine that the number of decimal places is 2. In the third line of code, the number of decimals in `rate` is added to the decimals variable using the same expression. Finally, in the fourth line, I assign the `fudge` variable to the inverse of 10 to the power of all the decimals (`1/Math.pow(10,4)` returns `1/10000` or `.0001` for example). That fudge variable is added to the product of `original*rate` that is used in the `rnd()` function. Wow. All that work, and I still can't promise you'll never encounter the rounding error!

Although our homemade `rnd()` function works great, we still don't have displays that look like currency. We need "trailing" zeros to two decimal places and at least one zero that "pads" to the left of the decimal. Oh, and we need a dollar sign, too, but that's a piece of cake: `result="$"+result` (don't insert this code yet). It turns out that our needs are not all that uncommon.

7. In addition to `rnd()`, here are two other utility functions I've used for years in Director. They're translated here into ActionScript. We'll use both of them, so type them into the first frame script:

```
function pad(num, places){
  theString=String(num)
  for(i=0;i<places;i++){
    if (theString.length<places){
      theString="0"+theString;
    }
  }
  return theString;
}
function trail(num, places){
  var theString=String(num)
  for(i=0;i<places;i++){
    if (theString.length>=places){
      break;
    }else{
      theString=theString+"0";
    }
  }
  return theString;
}
```

These two functions help you turn a number into a string with a minimum number of digits. For example, you can use the `pad()` function to ensure that a number has at least `5` digits. For example, `pad(18,5)` takes `18` and returns a five-digit number. Returned, you'll have `00018`. Naturally, you use a variable for the first parameter. Similarly, the `trail()` function ensures that your string has a minimum number of digits but it adds zeros at the end.

//

I had an occasion to use the `pad()` function in a project that listed product numbers from a client's clothing catalog. Most items had three-digit product numbers, but several used only two digits. The items were supposed to be displayed as `004`, `089`, or `102`. Item numbers less than 100 had to be padded with zeros. I simply used the `pad()` function like this: `stringVersion=pad(itemNum,3)`.

Both the `pad()` and `trail()` functions loop through each character in the string. Until the desired number of places has been reached, the string `"0"` is concatenated to the end or beginning of the string that is returned. We'll use both of these functions within the `currency()` function that we're about to write to ensure that all decimal values have two digits.

8. Let's get started writing the `currency()` function. Although this function has to do several things, I know that all dollars should be at least one digit and that all decimals should be two digits. Type this function in the first keyframe:

```
function currency(num){
  //round it and make it a string
  var theString=String(rnd(num,2));

  //find where the decimal is
  var decimalLoc=theString.indexOf(".");

  //separate dollars portion from decimal
  dollars=theString.substring( 0, decimalLoc );
  cents=theString.substring(decimalLoc+1);

  //trail cents, pad dollars
  cents=trail(cents,2);
  dollars=pad(dollars,1);

  //return a nice string
  return "$"+dollars+"."+cents;
}
```

First we round off the number supplied as `num` and turn it into a string. Then we get the "indexOf" the decimal (that is, the location of the decimal). We use two variables to store `dollars` and `cents` respectively. Finally, the `pad()` and `trail()` functions are used to ensure that we have the minimum number of digits, using zeros if we don't. The whole thing is concatenated to return a nice-looking string with a dollar sign.

9 Now change the last line in the script attached to the Convert button to read:

```
result=currency((original*rate)+fudge);
```

This way, the new `currency()` function will be called (instead of just the `rnd()` function.

If you test this script, it appears to work only intermittently. Actually, if you didn't have the attitude of a cynic, you could easily think that the script works fine. Perhaps all the what-if numbers you've provided work out fine. But just try something as simple as a rate of .5 and an original value of 10. I get a result of $0.50—that can't be right! The solution is found in the fact that indexOf() returns -1 when the pattern being searched for (in this case ".") is not found. Therefore, our currency() function works only when the rounded number includes a decimal. Without a decimal, the decimalLoc variable starts off at -1 and the rest of the function falls apart.

10. To fix this bug, use this adjusted version of the currency() function:

```
function currency(num){
  //round it and make it a string
  var theString=String(rnd(num,2));

  //find where the decimal is
  var decimalLoc=theString.indexOf(".");
  var dollars;
  var cents;
  if (decimalLoc==-1){
    dollars=theString;
    cents="00";
  }else{
    dollars=theString.substring( 0, decimalLoc );
    cents=theString.substring(decimalLoc+1);
  }

  //trail cents, pad dollars
  cents=trail(cents,2);
  dollars=pad(dollars,1);
  //return a nice string
  return "$"+dollars+"."+cents;
}
```

This version of the function considers that when there's no decimal, the entire theString must be whole dollars; therefore cents must be "00". There's one last feature I suggest adding to the currency() function: When the dollars value goes above 999, it would be nice if commas appeared to separate every thousand. For example, $43009.95 should appear as $43,009.95. Instead of walking through the *entire* process of writing such a script, you can simply replace the last line in the preceding currency() function (the line staring return...) with this code:

```
var actualDollars="";
var thousands=Math.floor((dollars.length)/3);
var extra=(dollars.length)%3;
if (extra>0){
  actualDollars=actualDollars+dollars.substr(0,extra);
}
if (thousands>0){
  if (extra>0){
    actualDollars=actualDollars+",";
  }
```

```
    for (i=1;i<=thousands;i++){
      theseThree=dollars.subStr( extra + ((i-1)*3) ,3);
      actualDollars=actualDollars+theseThree;
        if (i<thousands){
            actualDollars=actualDollars+",";
        }
    }
}
//return a nice string
return "$"+actualDollars+"."+cents;
```

//

This code is gnarly, but let me explain the basic process. First we initialize the `actualDollars` variable that will ultimately contain the `dollars` portion of the result. Then we determine how many times 3 can be evenly divided into the length of our string and place the result in `thousands`. The variable `extra` is then assigned to the remainder of dividing our string's length by 3. For example, if the string is `"10000"`, `thousands` becomes `1` (the integer part of `5/3`) and `extra` becomes `2` (the remainder of `5/3`). If `extra>0`, we initialize `actualDollars` to equal just the first few characters of the string. For example, with the string `"10000"`, the first `2` characters are placed in `actualDollars` (those characters are `"10"`). Then, provided that there is at least one set of thousands (that `extra>0`), we place a comma after the `actualDollars` variable. In the example of the string `"10000"`, `actualDollars` is now `"10,"`. At this point, we're about to start the for-loop which keeps extracting the next three characters from our original `dollars` and attaches them to the end of the `actualDollars` string we're building. At the end of each loop, a comma is added, provided that we have more loops to go (if `extra>0`). Finally, we build our string using `actualDollars`, which now has commas appropriately inserted, and the original `cents` variable.

Now that the main functionality of the currency calculator is working, let's move on to loading preset rates from an external source.

11. Create a text file containing the following text and save it as `rates.txt` in the same folder as your working Flash file:

```
name_1=CAD
&name_2=pesos
&name_3=pounds
&name_4=yen
&name_5=euros
&rate_1=0.67
```

```
&rate_2=0.102
&rate_3=1.46
&rate_4=0.0086
&rate_5=0.934
```

The five `name_` variables describe the currencies; the five `rate_` variables contain the exchange rates from dollars to those currencies. The form is URL encoded. We'll have to eliminate the extraneous return characters at the end of each line. A discussion of URL encoding can be found in Chapter 14, "Interfacing with External Data." Now we can load these variables into Flash.

12. Currently, our movie is only one frame long. Select the first keyframe and move it to frame 2 (Figure W9.4). In frame 1, type the following script:

```
rateHolder.loadVariables("rates.txt");
stop();
```

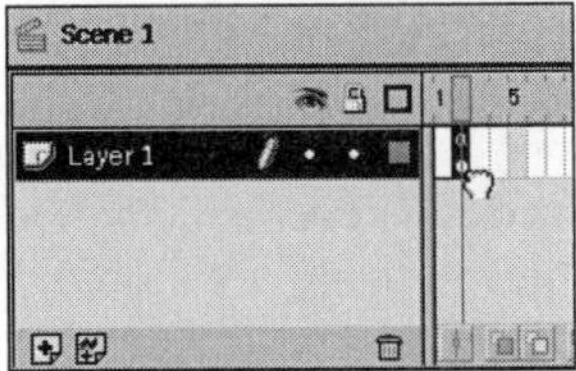

Figure W9.4 *We can move everything we built so far to frame 2.*

This script loads the variables found in the `rates.txt` file and places them in a clip instance called `rateHolder`. We haven't created that clip yet, but notice that I didn't name it the same as the variable `rate` because clips and variables with the same name would lead to problems and would be confusing. Using `stop()` means that the user will sit here on frame 1.

13. In frame 1, place a large text field onscreen containing the message `"Loading..."`. This message won't really be necessary when you're loading variables from a text file because the process will occur quickly, but you can always change the parameter in the `loadVariables()` function to provide for a server script that returned up-to-date values for the variables. Making that change would indeed necessitate the `"Loading..."` message.

14. We need an instance named `rateHolder`. Create an invisible Movie Clip as you did in Workshop 7, "Working with Odd-Shaped Clickable Areas." Create a new layer that spans both frames and place an instance of the invisible Movie Clip on that layer. Name this instance `rateHolder`.

15. To the `rateHolder` instance, attach this script:

```
onClipEvent(data){
  _root.nextFrame();
}
```

This script causes the main timeline to advance to frame 2 when all data has loaded.

16. We should add two additional features to the `data` event. First, it would be nice if all five rates and five names were part of the main timeline instead of always having to refer to them with expressions such as `_root.rateHolder.name_1`. To that end, add the following script inside the `data` event but before the `nextFrame()` method:

```
for (var i=0; i<5; i++ ) {
  var thisName=this["name_"+(i+1)];
  var thisRate=this["rate_"+(i+1)];
  _root["name_"+(i+1)]=thisName;
  _root["rate_"+(i+1)]=NumberthisRate;
}
```

This for-loop steps through all five names and rates and moves them into the main timeline.

//

By the way, the preceding script is hard-wired to expect exactly five items. A more dynamic solution can be achieved using a variable such as `totalItems` inside the text field the way we did in Chapter 14. Better yet, we can store all the data in XML format as we will in Workshop 18, "Creating a Dynamic Slide Presentation." The way the preceding for-loop works is that it first assigns the temporary variable `thisName` to `"name_"+(i+1)` because `i` goes from `0` to `4` in the loop. Because we want to dynamically refer to the value of a variable in the clip's own timeline, we have to place the string `"name_"+(i+1)` inside brackets that immediately follow the target path `this`. Then we assign a similarly named variable in `_root` to the value of `thisName`. This process is repeated for all five names. We do the same thing with the rates, too. Obviously, we could have done this without the temporary variables by using one-liners such as `_root["name_"+(i+1)]= this["name_"+(i+1)]`. You'll see why we did it this way in the next step.

17. Debug the movie and check out the values for the variables both in `_root` and in the `rateHolder` clip (Figure W9.5). (Debug twice if the debugger isn't currently open.)

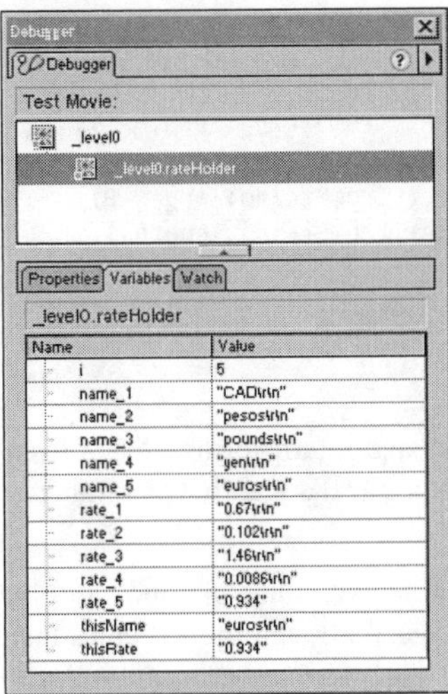

Figure W9.5 *A quick look with the Debugger reveals that our variables have loaded, but with "trailing garbage."*

18. The variables are the same, which proves that our script is moving the variables into the `_root` timeline properly. However, most of the variables contain the garbage characters "`/r/n`" at the end. We can remove these excess returns and line feeds the same way we did in Chapter 14. However, because this process might come in handy later, let's create a function that trims any excess characters from the strings passed to it. We'll convert both `thisName` and `thisRate` (by sending them to our function) before assigning the `_root` variables. In our `data` event, add two lines that call our yet-to-be-written function `removeExtra()`:

```
onClipEvent(data){
for (var i=0; i<5; i++ ) {
  var thisName=this["name_"+(i+1)];
  var thisRate=this["rate_"+(i+1)];
  thisName=_root.removeExtra(thisName);
  thisRate=_root.removeExtra(thisRate);
  _root["name_"+(i+1)]=thisName;
  _root["rate_"+(i+1)]=thisRate;
}
_root.nextFrame();
}
```

Although it's still possible to condense the six lines in the for-loop down to two, this code is very legible. We find the current name, remove extra garbage, and then assign the root variable. The following one-liner version is not as easy to read, but is perfectly acceptable:

```
_root["name_"+(i+1)]=_root.removeExtra(this["name_"+(i+1)]);
```

19 Place this code in the first frame of the movie:

```
function removeExtra(fromString){
  var lastChar=fromString.charCodeAt(fromString.length-1);
    while (lastChar==10 | lastChar==13 ) {
      fromString=fromString.substr(0,fromString.length-2);
      lastChar=fromString.charCodeAt(fromString.length-1);
    }
  return fromString;
}
```

This function simply removes any carriage returns or line feeds from the end of a line—just as we did in Chapter 14. It's just that as a function, we'll be able to call it from anywhere.

20. Debug the movie again and notice that the variables in your root timeline are nice and clean with no extra garbage. Although the variables inside `rateHolder` have the excess garbage, that's alright because we'll just use the ones inside `_root`.
21. From this point forward, all graphics will be placed on frame 2. Create five Dynamic Text fields associated with `name_1`, `name_2`, and so on.
22. Create a square button and place five instances of the button underneath the Dynamic Text fields you just created (Figure W9.6).

Figure W9.6 *Five button instances underneath five Dynamic Text fields will provide a way for the user to select preset exchange rates.*

23. On each button instance, write a version of the following script. Replace the parameter with 1, 2, 3, 4, or 5, depending on which button you're working with.

```
on (release) {
  preset(1);
}
```

This script simply calls the yet-to-be-written `preset()` function.

24. Before we write the `preset()` function, let's make a "selected" highlight for the buttons. Draw an outline rectangle with a nice thick stroke and make the size just bigger than the buttons. Convert this highlight graphic to a Movie Clip and name the instance `highlight`. Finally, use the Info panel to gather the x coordinates for the five possible locations of this highlight (when it highlights each button). Use a pencil and paper to write down those numbers.

25. Create the `preset()` function by typing this code inside the second keyframe:

```
highlightLocs=[42,122,202,282,362];
function preset(whichOne){
  curPreset=whichOne;
  highlight._x=highlightLocs[whichOne-1];
  rate=_root["rate_"+whichOne];
}
```

Notice that `highlightLocs` is an array defined outside the function (use the x coordinates you gathered in the last step. The `curPreset` variable is saved so that if we need it from some other part of the movie, we'll always know which preset is currently selected. The `highlight` instance has its `_x` property adjusted, and the variable `rate` displayed in the Input Text field we created in step 1 is updated.

//

Just to throw something out for fun (this is fun?), notice that the buttons in this example must be evenly spaced because the numbers in the `highlightLocs` array (starting with 42) are separated by 80 pixels. Consider the alternative statement below (that eliminates the need for the `highlightLocs` array entirely:

```
highlight._x=42+ (whichOne-1)*80;
```

Translated, this statement says that I want the `_x` property to be set to 42 plus 80 for every property greater than 1. It turns out that the array solution is best when spacing is not consistent. But just save this expression for the other times: *`minimum + (newInteger-1)*spacing`*.

At this point, the movie works quite well. Notice that you can always update the currencies included in the calculator or change the rates. At this point, we can add a seemingly endless list of refinements. These are generally just usability enhancements, but some are more critical than others. Here are the tasks that remain to be built:

- Display a text description such as "Dollars to Euros."
- Make a toggle button to change the direction of the conversion; for example, from dollars to Euros or from Euros to dollars.
- Remove the highlight and text description automatically as soon as the user enters his or her own `rate`.

- Replace the dollar sign `$` that appears when you're converting to dollars and replace it with the appropriate name or symbol of the currency to which you're converting, such as `Euros:`.

These enhancements should solve existing problems with the movie. Although these might not be the best solutions, the problems they present should definitely be addressed. It's usually best to identify the problems first and then work out solutions instead of simply specifying solutions. When you analyze the core issue, you can often find a better solution than the first one suggested. For this workshop, however, we're going to add the features listed.

26. To display a text description of the conversion process, create a new Dynamic Text field that's plenty wide and associate it with the variable `description`.

27. Add the following line to the end of, but still inside, the `preset()` function:

    ```
    description="Dollars to "+_root["name_"+curPreset];
    ```

    Notice the dynamic reference to the value of the appropriate `name_` variable.

28. The toggle button is a bit more complex. Create a button and attach the following script to its instance:

    ```
    on (release) {
      _root.toggle();
    }
    ```

    This script simply calls the `toggle()` function that we're about to write.

29. Select the toggle button, select Insert, Convert to Symbol..., give it a symbol name of "Toggle Clip," and leave the default Movie Clip behavior selected. Give the instance of this clip on the Stage the instance name `toggleButton`. Now we'll be able to inactivate this button at any time by simply setting `toggleButton._visible=0`.

30. Now we can write the `toggle()` function. In the keyframe on frame 2, write the following script:

    ```
    function toggle(){
      rate=1/rate;
    }
    ```

    This script simply inverses the current rate.

31. At this point, the toggle button works alright but it doesn't update the description. We need another variable that tracks whether we're going "to dollars" or "from dollars." We can name the variable `toDollars`; when

we're converting to dollars, `toDollars` will be `1`. When we're converting from dollars, we can set `toDollars` to `0`. By default, let's set `toDollars` to `1`. Place the following code in the keyframe on frame 2, outside any functions:

```
toDollars=1;
```

32. Inside the `toggle()` function, add the following line of code:

```
toDollars=!toDollars;
```

Translated, this statement says that `toDollars` is now equal to "not" `toDollars`. In this way, `toDollars` toggles between `1` and `0`.

You would be correct to assume that we're going to have to adjust the code where `description` is assigned. The `description` variable has to vary based on the value of `toDollars`. But realize that both the `toggle()` function *and* the `preset()` function make changes that require `description` to change. Therefore, we should write a single function that assigns a value to `description` that both `toggle()` and `preset()` can invoke.

33. In the keyframe at frame 2, write the following `updateDisplay()` function:

```
function updateDisplay(){
  if (toDollars){
    description=_root["name_"+curPreset]+" to Dollars";
  }else{
    description="Dollars to "+_root["name_"+curPreset];
  }
}
```

This function simply assigns the appropriate string to `description`.

34. To call the `updateDisplay()` function, simply insert the following code as the last line in both the `preset()` and `toggle()` functions:

```
updateDisplay();
```

The movie should work pretty well now. Believe it or not, there are still three features to add: the description, the toggle button, and the highlight that should all disappear any time the user enters his or her own rate. It's easy to make all these things appear empty initially, but we also have to turn them on and off. One final issue is making the dollar sign appear in the result only when appropriate.

35. First let's make the highlight, toggle button, and description appear hidden initially. Add the following script to the top of the script in frame 2, right above where we set `toDollars` equal to `1`:

```
highlight._x=-9000;
toggleButton._visible=0;
description="";
```

Notice that to hide the highlight, we move it way off to the side instead of setting its `_visible` property to `0` (which would also work, but we'd have to remember to set it back to `1` later). We take this approach because the `preset()` function only moves the `_x` property of `highlight` effectively making it visible.

36. To cause the toggle button to "come to life," add the following script to the `updateDisplay()` function:

```
toggleButton._visible=1;
```

All three components appear hidden at the start of the movie and appear when appropriate. Now we just need to figure out a way to make them go away. The moment at which they must hide themselves is when the rate field is edited by the user. What we'll do is create another variable that maintains the current rate set by either the `preset()` or `toggle()` function—not by the user. We can call that variable `currentRate`; if it ever changes, the three components `highlight`, `toggleButton`, and `description` have to hide. There's no "when the variable changes" event, however. The next best thing is the `enterFrame` event, where we can keep checking to see whether `currentRate` has changed.

37. We can write `enterFrame` scripts only on clip instances. Instead of creating a new invisible clip, let's use the `highlight` instance. I know it's weird, but we can store the new `currentRate` variable in `highlight` and, from there, monitor whether it ever changes. Write the following script attached to the `highlight` instance:

```
onClipEvent (enterFrame) {
  if (_root.rate<>currentRate){
    currentRate=undefined;
    _x=-1000;
    _root.description="";
    _root.toggleButton._visible=0;
  }
}
```

This script keeps checking to see whether the variable `rate` in `_root` is ever different than `currentRate`, a variable we'll maintain inside this clip. If they're ever not equal (the condition), the following four things happen: `currentRate` is set to `undefined`, causing it to be something different than `_root.rate`; the `highlight`'s `_x` is moved to `-1000`; `_root.direction` is cleared; and the `toggleButton` clip is hidden. In effect, this script waits until the user changes `rate` to something different than `currentRate`.

There's one more touch we have to add: We have to assign `currentRate` to the same thing as `rate` whenever the user uses `toggle()` or `preset()` to set `rate`.

38. To set highlight's currentRate to equal rate any time rate is set legitimately with toggle() or preset(), we could place a script in both the toggle() and preset() functions. But because both of these functions in turn call updateDisplay(), updateDisplay() is actually the best place to include the script. Place the following script within the updateDisplay() function:

    ```
    highlight.currentRate=rate;
    ```

39. Finally, the last touch to this giant project. We want the display to include the dollar sign only when we know that we're converting to dollars. This turns out to be a pretty easy fix. Replace the last line in the currency() function (where you return the nice string) with the following code:

    ```
    var prefix="";
    if (highlight.currentRate<>undefined){
      if (toDollars){
        prefix="$";
      }else{
        prefix=_root["name_"+curPreset]+":";
      }
    }
    //return a nice string
    return prefix+actualDollars+"."+cents;
    ```

    This script first sets prefix to "" (just in case). If the highlight instance has a currentRate, we assign prefix to be either "$" (when toDollars is 1) or the name of the currency plus a colon (when toDollars is 0). Yay! The string that is returned finally includes prefix.

Wow! If that wasn't fun, I don't know what is. Welcome to the more advanced workshops. Actually, this one was not only advanced, but long. The next workshops won't all be so involved. Here's a quick rundown of the techniques, both new and familiar, that came up in this workshop:

- The Math object: Math.round() was used to round off and Math.floor() was used to find the integer portion of a number. You can learn more about the Math object in Chapter 5, "Programming Structures."
- The String object: The length property, the subStr() method, and the ever-popular concatenation operator "+" were exploited. Chapter 9, "Selecting Text, Trapping Keys, and Manipulating Strings," covers many details of the String object.
- Operators such as % (modulo) and ! (logical NOT) were used. These operators are touched on in Chapter 5.
- Dynamic referencing of clips was used. Dynamic referencing is covered in Chapter 7, "The Movie Clip Object."

- We loaded data from external sources like we learned to do in Chapter 14.
- We hid clips that contain buttons to effectively deactivate the button, as we learned to do in Workshop 5, "Building a Slide Show."
- General approaches to programming and debugging techniques were reviewed. These techniques are covered in Chapter 3, "The Programmer's Approach," and Chapter 6, "Assigning Values," respectively.

{Chapter 10 Workshop }

Creating a ToolTip Smart Clip

In Workshop 3, "Creating Custom Cursors," you learned how to position a clip instance precisely where the mouse moved. You also learned how to turn it into a Smart Clip. This workshop is similar to that one in that we're going to move a clip to the mouse location, but this clip will contain text instead of a cursor graphic. The result is a feature commonly known as a ToolTip.

No doubt you've encountered ToolTips in many software applications, including Flash. In this workshop, we'll add several features to our ToolTip, including those common to system-level ToolTips plus a few extra features that will make our ToolTip unique. Naturally, the exact feature set for each instance of our Smart Clip will be adjustable through the Clip Parameters panel.

Like most workshops, this one starts off really easy and builds in complexity as we add specific features. Here are the steps:

1. Create a Dynamic Text field associated with the variable `text`. Make this field very wide so that it can accommodate any tip imaginable. I recommend turning off the Selectable and Border/Bg options in the Text Options panel.
2. Use the Arrow tool to select the text block and convert it to a Movie Clip symbol called Tip. Name the instance that's now on the Stage `tip`.
3. Double-click the Tip symbol to edit its contents. Use the Info panel to move the entire block of text to position 0, 0 inside the clip. The text block should be centered as shown in Figure W10.1. The idea is that when we position this clip, we will position the center point of the clip.

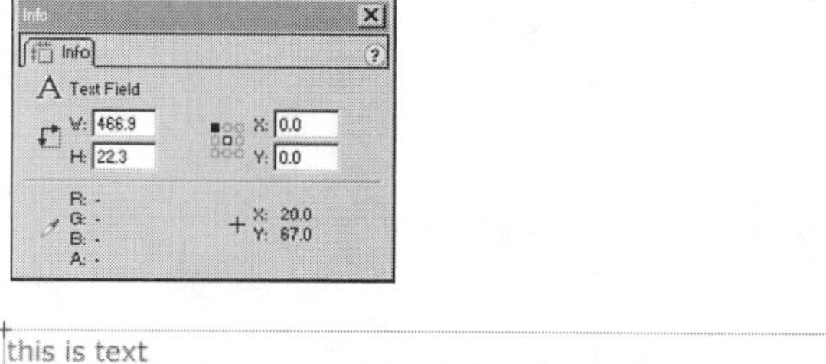

Figure W10.1 *Use the Info panel with the top-left corner option to position the Dynamic Text field inside the Tip symbol.*

4. Let's study a script that we *could* attach to the `tip` clip. Don't use this script, but study it so that we can determine what is lacking:

```
onClipEvent (mouseMove) {
  text = "This is a tip";
  _x = _root._xmouse;
  _y = _root._ymouse;
  updateAfterEvent();
}
```

   This script would indeed set the `text` variable and move the clip to where the mouse moved. However, we don't need the ToolTip to be visible at all times—only when the mouse is in certain areas. In addition, we could adjust this script so that it could be used from outside the clip (in a function perhaps). Then we could adjust the target for `text`, `_x`, and `_y` by preceding the function with `_root.tip`. I mention this only because ultimately we'll have several instances of a Smart Clip that do nothing but define the "hot" area and call a function that moves the tip.

5. Inside the Tip symbol, add the following script to the first frame:

```
text=""
_x=99999;
```

   This script effectively hides the entire clip when the movie starts. At this point, we're done editing the Tip symbol.

6. In the main timeline, draw a square, remove the stroke, and convert the fill to a Movie Clip symbol named HotArea. Although I would much prefer to use a button symbol to track when the mouse is in the correct area, we learned in Workshop 3 that this interferes with any other buttons over which we might want to place the ToolTip Smart Clip we're building. No big deal; later we'll just have to ascertain the bounds of the clip and then make it invisible.

7. From the main timeline, select the instance of HotArea and convert it to a symbol named Tool Tip. Leave it as a Movie Clip.

//

Converting the instance of HotArea to a symbol simply nests HotArea inside the Tool Tip symbol. Here are the reasons for the nesting. We need a clip inside our clip so that we can use the clip event `mouseMove`. Of course, our Tool Tip symbol is a Movie Clip, but we can't write scripts to attach to instances of the clip because these scripts will be created by the author using the Smart Clip. By writing the script on an instance that's inside our main symbol, we ensure that the script will be included automatically with each instance the using author creates. The only drawback is a slightly challenging task of targeting.

8. The process the using author follows is to simply drag Tool Tip from the Library and set a few parameters. The using author will also be able to resize the clip to specify a hot area. To make the resize process easy for the author, open the Tool Tip symbol and move the instance of HotArea so that its top-left corner is centered; use the Info panel to accomplish this task as you did in step 3.

Now everything is built—we just need to program it! The general design places most of the variables and scripts on the instance of HotArea that's nested inside the Tool Tip symbol. However, variables that the using author will identify through the Clip Parameter panel will be part of the instance of Tool Tip that the author drags onto the Stage. Let's first think of what variables the using author will be able to set and hard-wire them for now. First, the author should identify the text to appear in the ToolTip. Let's just call that `text`. Also, I'd like to give the author the option of either making the ToolTip "follow" the mouse when it's over the hot area or appear once and stay in place as most ToolTips do. That variable can be called `withMotion` and will be either `1` or `0`. Finally, we can provide a default delay before the tip appears, but if the author wants to increase or decrease that delay, he or she should be able to do so. We'll let the author set a variable `delay` that contains the number of milliseconds before the clip appears. If the author wants the ToolTip to appear instantly, he or she can set `delay` to `0`.

9. For now, hard-wire all three variables just described by placing the following script in frame 1 of the Tool Tip symbol:

```
text="This is a tooltip";
withMotion=1;
delay=500;
```

A `delay` of `500` translates to one-half of one second because there are 1000 milliseconds per second.

10. One last thing to remember is that the `tip` instance is outside our Smart Clip. This is a little bit hokey because otherwise the using author would have to remember to drag an instance of this clip onstage and remember to give it the instance name `tip`. Although this requirement would be fine for most situations (especially for Smart Clips that only you use), we're going to make this clip a little more universal. To that end, remove the instance of `tip` onstage and add the following script underneath the script you just wrote for the first keyframe inside `Tool Tip`:

    ```
    _parent.attachMovie("tip","tip",1);
    ```

    This script creates an instance called `tip` in the root level (or the level into which the using author places the Smart Clip).

11. To make the preceding script work, you must first set the linkage for the Tip symbol to export this symbol with an identifier of "tip." Select Linkage… from the Library's option menu and set the identifier now.

12. To make sure that the Tip symbol is copied into other files when you simply copy the Tool Tip symbol, create a new layer within the Tool Tip symbol. Drag an instance of the Tip symbol into this new layer. Resize the Tip instance as small as you can, place it in the same area as the instance of the HotArea symbol, and make the layer a Guide (Figure W10.2). We learned the Guide layer technique in Workshop 3.

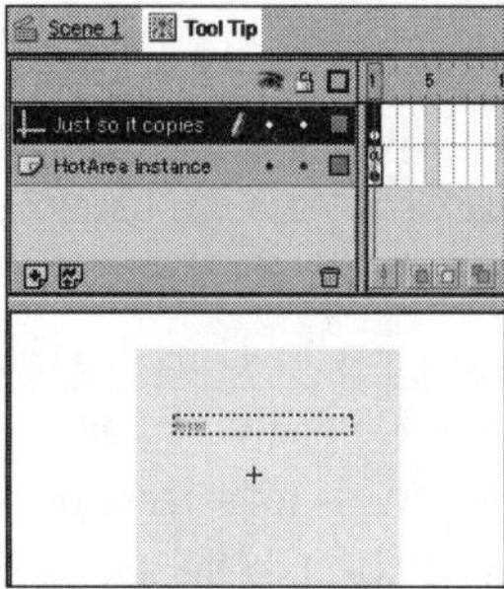

Figure W10.2 *Placing an instance of the Tip symbol in a guide layer ensures that it is copied even though it won't be used here.*

At this point, you may think the movie is not working because you won't see anything if you test the movie. Just remember that the Tip symbol contains a script that makes itself invisible by setting the `text` variable to `""` and its `_x` to `99999`. That's fine, but if you want to test it out, use the Debugger to see the `tip` instance created by the `attachMovie()` method.

//

If you have several instances of the Tool Tip symbol on the Stage, each instance will create an instance called `tip` because each contains an `attachMove()` method. This turns out not to be a problem because each time a new movie is attached, it wipes away the other movie because only one movie can be attached into each level number. If it freaks you out, you could use a flag as you learned to do in Workshop 3 and change the script inside the `Tool Tip` symbol to read as follows:

```
if (_parent.flag==undefined){
  _parent.attachMovie("tip","tip",1);
  _parent.flag="tip has been attached";
}
```

This script just calls `attachMovie()` once if the `flag` variable has not been set. Then it sets the `flag` variable so that no more `attachMovie()` methods in the other instances of the Tool Tip symbol will execute.

13. Let's move on to monitoring whether the mouse is over the instance of HotArea. Because we aren't using a button which could use the convenient `rollOver` and `rollOut` events, we can monitor the mouse by using either `hitTest()` or by gathering the bounds of the HotArea clip and then writing our own homemade hit test expression. It turns out that we can't use `hitTest()` because we're eventually going to set the instance of the HotArea symbol's `_visible` property to `0`. So we'll first save the bounds in a variable and *then* make it invisible. I've arbitrarily decided that it will be easiest to consider all coordinates relative to the timeline on which the user places the ToolTip Smart Clip. Normally, we use the `_root` if the user places the Smart Clip in the main timeline, but we really want just the `_parent` of the instance of Tool Tip, which is the same timeline to which the `tip` instance was attached. Let's calculate the bounds of `HotArea` relative to that timeline. Attached to the instance of HotArea inside Tool Tip, place the following script:

```
onClipEvent (load) {
  t=_parent._parent;
  rect=this.getBounds(t);
}
```

This script simply saves a variable as part of this instance of HotArea that contains size information for the shape: xMin, xMax, yMin, and yMax. We learned how to use getBounds() in Workshop 3 and Workshop 6, "Mapping." I also placed the main target space in the variable t (for target) because I want to reduce the amount of typing necessary. Remember that you can store references to clips (that is, timelines) in variables.

14. Now let's write the main script that determines whether the mouse is within the rect variable. Later we'll deal with how to react to such a situation—that is, how to display the text. Place the following script on the instance of HotArea:

```
onClipEvent (mouseMove) {
  x=t._xmouse;
  y=t._ymouse;
  onRect=(x>rect.xMin&&x<rect.xMax&&y>rect.yMin&&y<rect.yMax);
}
```

Notice how handy the t variable is. Without it, you'd have to type x=_parent._parent._xmouse in place of the first line. Actually, you save even more typing because the variables x and y store the mouse's x and y for use in the last line where onRect is assigned. That last line, by the way, uses a condition that's either true or false to set the value of onRect to true or false. Imagine what that last line would look like if you had to use _parent._parent._xmouse in place of each x and a similarly long expression in place of each y. If you debug the movie, find the instance of HotArea, and watch the variables, you'll notice that the onRect variable is set to true when the mouse is within the bounds of the instance of HotArea and is set to false when it's not.

15. Just being *on* the rectangle is important to know, but the tool isn't supposed to appear until the mouse has been on the rectangle long enough. Any time the mouse first enters the rectangle, we'll start timing. After enough time has expired, we'll make the ToolTip appear. We can use the enterFrame event to monitor whether enough time has passed. But first, we need a way to determine whether the mouse has just moved on or just moved off the rectangle. If we started timing every time the mouse is onRect, we would keep pushing the expiration time further out in the future because onRect stays true for a long time. Right before we set onRect, we can save the old value of onRect in another variable called was. If, after we set onRect, we notice that it's different than was, we know that onRect has just changed. Combining this information with whether onRect is now true or false, we can accurately determine when the mouse has entered the rectangle. Modify the mouseMove event attached to the instance of the HotArea symbol as follows:

```
onClipEvent (mouseMove) {
  x=t._xmouse;
  y=t._ymouse;
  var was=onRect;//the "old" onRect
```

```
  onRect=(x>rect.xMin&&x<rect.xMax&&y>rect.yMin&&y<rect.yMax);
  if (onRect==0&&was<>onRect){  // then just moved off
  }
  if (onRect==1&&was<>onRect){  // then just moved on
  }
}
```

This script first saves the old value of `onRect` in the variable `was`. After setting `onRect`, the script checks two conditions to see whether the mouse just moved on or just moved off the rectangle. Notice that both `if` statements must do more than just see whether the condition `was<>onRect` is `true`; that just tells us that something has changed. Also notice that the two `if` statements have no consequences. We'll put some scripts between the curly brackets in a minute.

16. We want to set a homemade variable `active=1` when the ToolTip should be on and `active=0` when the ToolTip should be off. But just moving the mouse onto the rectangle isn't enough to make the variable active. It's only enough to start timing. Before we display the ToolTip, we must wait until `delay` has expired. When the mouse rolls off the rectangle, we can set `active` to `0`. Add `active=0` to the `if` statement where the mouse moves off. But in the `if` statement where the mouse rolls on, simply set a variable `waiting=1` and another variable called `displayTime`. In pseudo-code, the value for `displayTime` is "now plus delay." See how `getTimer()` is used in the revised version of those two if statements that we started in step 15:

```
if (onRect==0&&was<>onRect){  // then just moved off
  active=0;
  waiting=0;
}
if (onRect==1&&was<>onRect){  // then just moved on
  waiting=1;
  displayTime=getTimer()+_parent.delay;
}
```

The move-off statement is easy: both our `active` and `waiting` variables are set to `0`. In the move-on statement, we set `waiting` to `1` so that we'll know it's worth checking whether it's time to become `active` and show the ToolTip. We also set `displayTime` to the current `getTimer()` value plus our `delay`, which is part of the `_parent Tool Tip` symbol based on the user settings.

//

If that last line of the script is confusing, realize that it doesn't matter what the current `getTimer()` returns—it could be `1000` or it could be `30000`. We just add the `delay` to this value. Consider how you might check out a book from the library for two weeks. Even if you had a wacky watch that showed the number of days since you were born (say 12,400), you could easily note the current "time" and add 14 days to find the due date for the book (12,414). In an `enterFrame` event, we will keep checking to see whether the current `getTimer()` is later than `displayTime` which is saved here and set `active=1` if it is. It's as if every day you checked your wacky watch to see whether 12,414 was showing.

17. The `enterFrame` script on the instance of HotArea starts with the following code:

```
onClipEvent (enterFrame) {
  if( getTimer()>displayTime){
    active=1;
  }
}
```

This code checks to see whether `getTimer()` is greater than `displayTime`. If so, we set `active` to `1`. In addition, we'll make the actual ToolTip appear in a minute. However, there are a couple of problems. What if you roll onto the rectangle and `displayTime` is set, but then you roll off? Eventually, `getTimer()` will be greater than `displayTime`. We need that `if` statement to include a condition that we still need a ToolTip (that you haven't moved off the rectangle). Although there are several ways to solve this problem, try this solution:

```
onClipEvent (enterFrame) {
  if( (getTimer()*waiting)>displayTime){
    active=1;
  }
}
```

Notice that if `waiting` is `0` (which it will be whenever the mouse rolls off), the expression on the left side of the greater-than symbol turns to `0` and most definitely is *not* greater than `displayTime`, no matter what that value is (as long as it isn't negative, which it never can be). By the way, we could have added an additional `if` statement to solve this problem—something like "if `waiting`, then if `getTimer()`..." and so on. But this current solution is pretty concise.

18. I'll bet you thought this step would never come—we're going to display the ToolTip! Right under the `active=1` statement in the `enterFrame` script created in the last step, add this code:

```
t.tip.text=_parent.text;
t.tip._x=x;
t.tip._y=y;
```

Pretty handy that we saved the correct target in the variable `t`. This script places the parent's text (which is set through the Clip Parameters panel) into the clip instance called `tip`, which we attached way back when. In addition, we're setting the `_x` and `_y` properties of `tip` to the `x` and `y` variables saved in the `mouseMove` event. In case you thought `x` and `y` should have been local variables (using `var`), now you can see that they must be available outside the `mouseMove` event.

At this point, the movie looks like it's working allright (though the tool tip doesn't go away which we'll address later). One problem is that the `enterFrame` script keeps executing over and over.

19. To optimize the `enterFrame` script, place the following script within the curly brackets of the `if` statement (maybe after `active=1`):

    ```
    waiting=0;
    ```

    After all, you're not waiting any longer. At this point, you can test the movie and see that the ToolTip appears correctly, but notice that it doesn't move with the mouse any more. In a way, this is good because we're going to give the using authors a `withMotion` option to specify whether they want the ToolTip to track the mouse. Even if you liked it before we added `waiting=0`, the problem was that updates were only occurring as fast as `enterFrame` occurred, which is based on framerate. When we finally add the `withMotion` option, we shouldn't be updating the ToolTip's location in an `enterFrame` event but rather in a `mouseMove` event.

20. To redisplay the ToolTip as fast as the user moves the mouse, add the following `if` statement at the bottom of, but still inside, the `mouseMove` event:

    ```
    if (active) {
      t.tip._x=x;
      t.tip._y=y;
      updateAfterEvent();
    }
    ```

    If `active` is set to `1` inside the `enterFrame` event, then every time the mouse moves, the location changes. If bells are ringing to tell you that we should move this code to a function, you must have read Chapter 3. Let's move the duplicated code to a function.

21. From the `enterFrame` script, cut the three lines that display the ToolTip; all three lines start with `t.tip`.... In their place, call the function `show()`. Here is what the current state of our `enterFrame` script should look like:

```
onClipEvent (enterFrame) {
  if( (getTimer()*waiting)>displayTime){
    active=1;
    waiting=0;
    show();
  }
}
```

Now we have to write the `show()` function that's being called here.

22. Before we write the `show()` function, let's also call it from inside the `mouseMove` event. Change the `if` statement we added in step 20 (the line that starts `if(active)`...) to read as follows:

```
if(active){
  show();
}
```

Now two different parts of our script are calling the same function.

23. Because practically all the code we've been writing has been on the instance of the HotArea symbol, calling a function such as `show()` means that it resides *inside* the HotArea symbol. Therefore, we could write the `show()` function in a keyframe inside this symbol. However, there's another way to include a function as if it is inside the clip: Write the whole function framework inside the load `clipEvent`! This approach may seem pretty crazy, but check out how we will write the `show()` function in this finished version of the `load` event, which is attached to the instance of the HotArea symbol we've been working on for so long:

```
onClipEvent (load) {
  t=_parent._parent;
  rect=this.getBounds(t);
  function show(){
    t.tip.text=_parent.text;
    t.tip._x=x;
    t.tip._y=y;
  }
}
```

The `show()` function looks as expected because we just pasted in the code extracted from the other events. What's strange is that it's totally enclosed in the `load` event. By the way, we could have achieved this end by writing the function in a keyframe inside this symbol. The way we've done it here is a little nicer because all the code is in one place.

24. The ToolTip movie should work pretty well, except that the text never disappears. To fix that problem, simply throw the following script inside the if-statement from step 16 in which we determined that the mouse just moved off the rectangle: in the `mouseMove` event, the part starting `if`

`(onRect==0&&was<>onRect)....` Right under where you set `waiting=0` and `active=0`, type this line:

```
t.tip.text="";
```

25. There are just two more steps before we can remove the hard-wired elements and turn this movie into a Smart Clip. We want the text to follow the mouse the way it does now only when the `withMotion` option is set to `1`. When the `enterFrame` event determines that it's time to show the text, it's fine to invoke the `show()` function. But we want to set `active` to `1` only when `withMotion` is `1`. Depending on whether `active` is `1` or `0`, the `mouseMove` event will or won't `show()` the ToolTip. Therefore, change the line in the `enterFrame` script from step 17 that reads `active=1` to read as follows:

    ```
    active=_parent.withMotion;
    ```

    Now only when `withMotion` is `1` will `active` be turned on. Remember in step 9 we hard wired `withMotion` to `1`. The ToolTip still appears once, but it won't move with the mouse unless the `withMotion` option is set to `1`.

26. Now use the Effect panel to set the `alpha` of the instance of the `HotArea` symbol to 30 percent and add the following line to the `load` event:

    ```
    _visible=0;
    ```

    The idea is that using authors can simply use this Smart Clip like an invisible button that they can place on top of anything for which they want a ToolTip. The Smart Clip must be partially transparent while authoring but invisible when the movie plays.

27. Assuming that everything works, you can go to the first keyframe of the Tool Tip symbol and remove the three hard-wired lines we added way back in step 9. Alternatively, comment them out like this:

    ```
    //text="This is a tooltip";
    //withMotion=1;
    //delay=500;
    ```

//

By the way, I actually tested all the code before writing this workshop. I tested it by hard-wiring `withMotion` to both `1` and to `0`. I also tried a few different `delay` settings. Although these settings will easily become part of the Clip Parameters, it was easy to test everything by just modifying the hard-wired elements. By testing it at this point, I knew that if something went wrong, there were fewer steps that could have contributed to the problem, making the movie easier to troubleshoot.

28. Finally, the end. Select the master Tool Tip symbol in the Library, choose Define Clip Parameters, and add the three variables `text`, `withMotion`, and `delay` (Figure W10.3). You'll probably want to set defaults that are usable as-is such as `1` or `0` for `withMotion` and `1000` for `delay`. The Define Clip Parameters process is detailed in Chapter 13, "Smart Clips," as well as in Workshop 3.

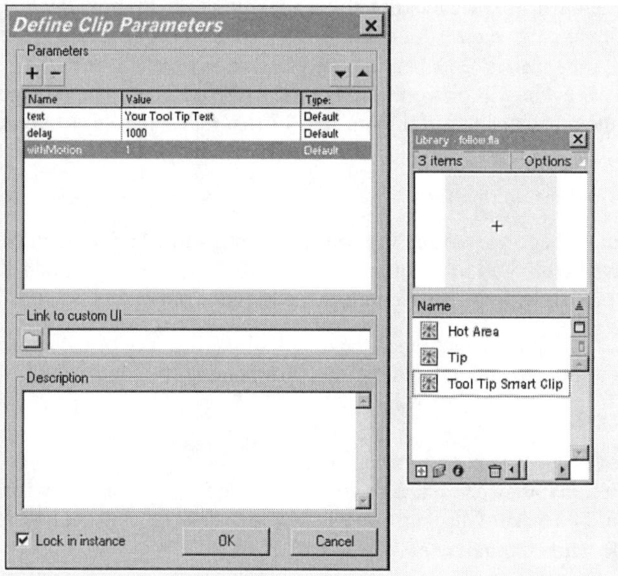

Figure W10.3 *Defining Clip Parameters may seem like an anticlimactic way to finish, but that's all it takes to turn this ToolTip clip into a Smart Clip.*

That's it! At this point, you should be able to place the ToolTip Smart Clip on top of any element in any movie and even stretch it from the right or the bottom to cover areas of different sizes. You can vary the `delay` time and, naturally, you make the text content for each ToolTip unique.

There are two reasons this workshop was so much work. First, we explored lots of variations, made mistakes, and took a long time analyzing—all to learn a few concepts. The other reason the workshop took a long time is because we made something really useful. We didn't make any compromises, we made it good. As you know, "good" generally means a lot of work.

{Chapter 11 Workshop }

Creating a Digital Timer

Using Flash's `getTimer()` function the way we did in Workshop 10, "Creating a ToolTip Smart Clip," is quite common. We saved the current `getTimer()` in a variable and then kept checking to see whether "enough" time elapsed by rechecking `getTimer()` and comparing that to the variable we saved at the start. In this workshop, we'll make a digital timer that the user can start, stop, and pause. To give the timer its functionality, we'll save the current `getTimer()` when the user starts the timer. Then, in every `enterFrame` event, we'll see how many milliseconds have elapsed since the start. We can then easily convert this value into hours, minutes, seconds, and even fractions of seconds.

This workshop should teach two concepts in particular: how to translate numbers between different formats (milliseconds into hours, for example) and how to use `getTimer()` in conjunction with the `enterFrame` event. Of course, in the end, we'll have a cool timer, the base code of which we'll use in Workshop 12, "Creating an Analog Timer" (Figure W11.1).

Here are the steps to follow to create a digital timer:

1. Create a new Movie Clip symbol called Timer. We want to make a clip that can be placed in any other movie.
2. Inside Timer (where you'll stay for the rest of the workshop), create a Dynamic Text field associated with the variable `display`. Make the field wide enough to accommodate about 10 characters based on whatever font size you use. I recommend the font `_typewriter` or another monospace

font because fonts that have variable widths make the timer jump around as it keeps changing.

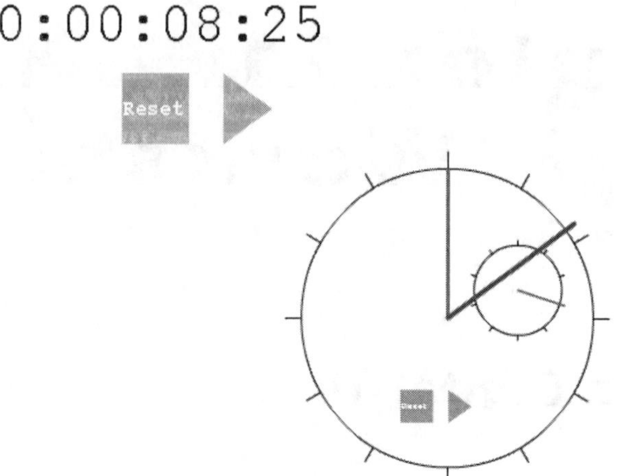

Figure W11.1 *The digital timer (left) and the analog timer (right) use the same code base.*

3. Draw a small box for the stop button and draw a triangle for the play button (Figure W11.2). Select both of these shapes and convert them to a single Movie Clip symbol called Controls.

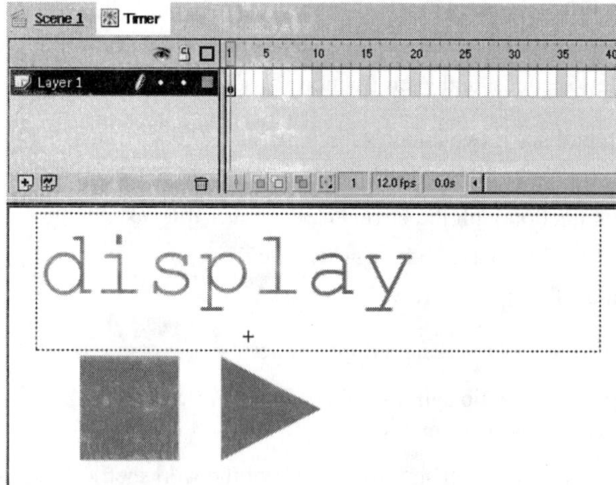

Figure W11.2 *The square will become the stop button and the triangle will become the play button.*

4. Double-click the instance of the Controls symbol to edit its contents. Insert a new layer and name one layer Stop and the other layer Play/Pause. Move the stop square shape to the Stop layer. In the Play/Pause layer, insert a keyframe by pressing F6 and change the square shape that's now in frame 2 to a pause button (two vertical lines as shown in Figure W11.3). In frame 2 of the Stop layer, insert a frame by pressing F5—not a keyframe because we just need the stop button shape to appear for both frames. Finally, in the Stop layer's keyframe, add this simple script: `stop()`.

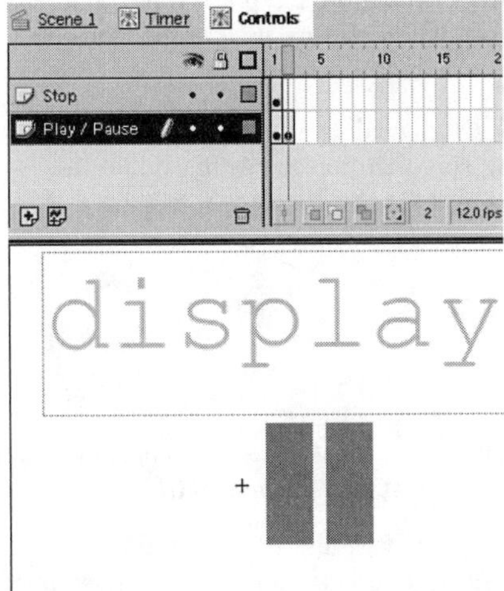

Figure W11.3 *The stop shape has its own layer, but the play and pause shapes appear in different keyframes of another layer.*

5. Now we're going to place invisible buttons on top of the three stop, play, and pause shapes. To do so, draw a square a bit larger than the shapes, convert it to a button symbol called Invisible, double-click the button to edit its contents, and drag the keyframe in the Up state to the Hit state (Figure W11.4).

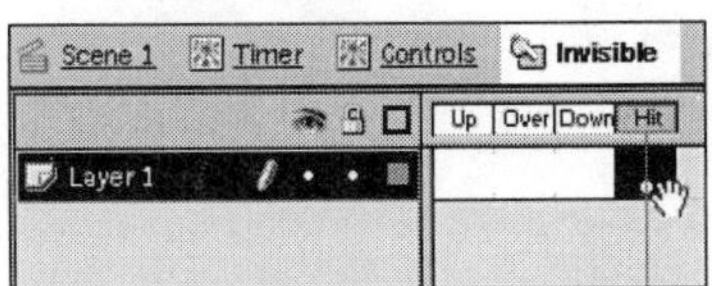

Figure W11.4 *You can make an invisible button by dragging the initial keyframe to the Hit state.*

6. Return to the Controls symbol by clicking "Controls" in the address bar. You should now have an invisible button that you can position on top of the stop button shape. Make sure that you move this button to the Stop layer. Attach the following script to this invisible button instance:

```
on (release) {
  _parent.stopTimer();
}
```

   In a bit, we'll write a `stopTimer()` function and place it in frame 1 of the Timer symbol, one level up from where we are now in the Controls symbol.

7. Copy the invisible button you just placed on stop and place it on top of the play button in frame 1, making sure that you're pasting it into the Play/Pause layer. Change the script for this instance to appear as follows:

```
on (release) {
  _parent.playTimer();
  nextFrame();
}
```

   Not only will this button call the yet-to-be-written `playTimer()` function, it also jumps to the next frame in the instance of the Controls symbol.

8. Make another copy of the Invisible button and paste it in frame 2 of the Play/Pause layer. Change the script on this instance of the invisible button to appear as follows:

```
on (release) {
  _parent.pauseTimer();
  prevFrame();
}
```

   This script calls the yet-to-be-written `pauseTimer()` function and jumps back to frame 1. Now we're done editing the Controls symbol.

9. Back inside the Timer symbol, attach the following script to the instance of the Controls symbol:

```
onClipEvent (enterFrame) {
  _parent.updateTimer();
}
```

   This script repeatedly calls the `updateTimer()` function that we're about to place in frame 1 of the Timer symbol. The only reason we're attaching this to the instance of Controls is that we want to use the `enterFrame` script, which is available only for clip instances. Furthermore, because there are no other clips present, it's just convenient to attach it here.

10. Now we can write a bunch of scripts in frame 1 of Timer. Let's start with this basic structure:

```
function playTimer(){
  startTime=getTimer();
  timing=true;
}
function stopTimer(){
  timing=false;
}
function updateTimer(){
  if(timing){
    display=getTimer()-startTime;
  }
}
```

This script is pretty basic. The `playTimer()` function saves off the current time in the `startTime` variable and sets another variable `timing` to `true`. The `stopTimer()` function simply sets `timing` to `false`. The `updateTimer()` function, which is called in every `enterFrame` event, no matter what, changes the `display` variable only on the condition that `timing` is `true`. It sets `display` to the current time minus `startTime`. If you drag an instance of the Timer symbol onto your main Stage and test this script, it should work fine—that is, if you like to watch the milliseconds count up. The pause button doesn't do anything yet except get you back to frame 1 in the Controls clip.

11. We can fairly easily convert the elapsed time (`getTimer()-startTime`) from its native milliseconds format into the more standard h:m:s:f (hours, minutes, seconds, fractions) format. Consider that there are 10 milliseconds per 1/100 of a second, 1000 milliseconds per second, 60000 milliseconds per minute, and so on. As you can see in the revised version of the `updateTimer()` function that follows, we also check whether the minute, second, or fraction portion of the time drops below 10. If it does, we pad with an extra `0`. For example, the display should read `0:01:30:09` for one minute thirty seconds and nine one-hundredths; it should not read `0:1:30:9`. Replace the `updateTimer()` portion of the script in frame 1 with this new one; leave the `playTimer()` and `stopTimer()` functions alone:

```
function updateTimer(){
  if(timing){
    elapsedTime=getTimer()-startTime;
    //hours:
    elapsedH=Math.floor(elapsedTime/3600000);
    remaining=elapsedTime - (elapsedH*3600000);

    //minutes:
    elapsedM=Math.floor( remaining/60000  );
    remaining=remaining - (elapsedM*60000);
```

```
    if (elapsedM<10){
      elapsedM="0"+elapsedM;
    }

    //seconds:
    elapsedS=Math.floor( remaining/1000);
    remaining=remaining - (elapsedS*1000);
    if (elapsedS<10){
      elapsedS="0"+elapsedS;
    }

    //hundredths:
    elapsedFractions=Math.floor ( remaining/10 );
    if (elapsedFractions<10){
      elapsedFractions="0"+elapsedFractions;
    }

//build the nice display string:
  display=elapsedH + ":" + elapsedM + ":" + elapsedS  + ":" +
elapsedFractions;
  }
}
```

This code probably looks much worse than it is. First of all, notice that none of this code will execute unless the `timing` variable is `true`—which is set accordingly in the `playTimer()` and `stopTimer()` functions. Once inside the script, we calculate the elapsed milliseconds and place that value in the `elapsedTime` variable. To determine how many full hours have passed, we place into the `elapsedH` variable just the integer portion of `elapsedTime` divided by `3600000` (the number of milliseconds in an hour). Then we have to calculate the remaining milliseconds. Suppose that 2 hours and 10 minutes have passed. If you know that there have been 2 whole hours, you only need the remaining 10 minutes' worth of milliseconds to calculate what's left over. The `remaining=elapsedTime - (elapsedH*3600000)` statement simply subtracts the whole hours just calculated (`elapsedH`) multiplied by the number of milliseconds in an hour from the original `elapsedTime`. For the remaining values `elapsedM`, `elapsedS`, and `elapsedFractions`, we first calculate how many full minutes or seconds or fractions remain and take that many milliseconds off the remaining variable so that each subsequently smaller value is based on what's left over. In addition, we start checking each value; if the value is less than 10, we insert a `0` in front of the value. (By the way, you could probably figure out a way to use the `%` modulo operator to calculate the remaining variable in all the cases above.)

At this point, the script works alright. We just need to add a few enhancements, including the `pauseTimer()` function. One of the biggest issues we have to rectify is that the play button seems to reset the timer every time it's clicked.

Naturally, the very first time we click the play button, we want to reset the timer, but if we have just paused the timer, we want the play button to effectively act like a "proceed" button and not a "reset" button. We can handle all of these issues simply by adding the variable `paused` that tells us whether the time has been recently stopped or paused.

12. Add the following function in the first keyframe of Timer:

```
function pauseTimer () {
  timing=false;
  paused=true;
}
```

    This function just stops the timing so that the display doesn't change and sets our new variable `paused` to `true`.

13. Change the `stopTimer()` function written in step 10 to read as follows:

```
function stopTimer(){
  timing=false;
  paused=false;
}
```

    In this version of the function. `stopTimer()` turns off `paused`. You could also add a line that makes the instance of Controls jump back to frame 1. Obviously, you'll need an instance name for the controls, but you could add something like `controls.gotoAndStop(1)`.

At this point, the clip should work pretty well. The two problems that remain are that the `playTimer()` function doesn't know or care whether `paused` is `true` or `false`. The second problem is that, initially, the display may not look like `0:00:00:00` (Figure W11.5). We'll make this easy fix first.

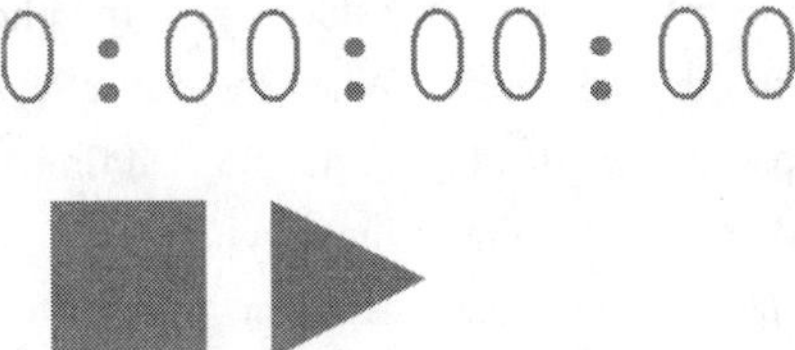

Figure W11.5 *The initial display should appear like this.*

14. In the first keyframe, add the following function:

```
function init(){
  display="0:00:00:00"
}
```

15. In the `stopTimer()` function, add the line `init()`. At the top of this frame script, outside of any functions, call the `init()` function by typing `init()`. With this call, the display appears cleared out when the user starts the movie or any time the user presses stop. Even though we could have written the one-line script `display="0:00:00:00"` that initialized the display in both the `stopTimer()` function and outside all the functions, I like keeping the script separate for two reasons: Edits need to be made in only one place and, if needed, we can call this `init()` function from other places. Both of these reasons that justify functions are discussed in Chapter 8, "Functions."

16. Finally, change the `playTimer()` function to appear as follows:

```
function playTimer () {
  if (paused){
    startTime=getTimer()-elapsedTime;
  }else{
    startTime=getTimer();
  }
  paused=false;
  timing=true;
}
```

    Notice that only if `paused` is `false` will `playTimer()` set `startTime` to `getTimer()`, which starts timing from this point forward. In the case in which `paused` is `true`, `startTime` is simply set to the `currentTime` minus `elapasedTime`, which was calculated the last time the `updateTimer()` function ran. Finally, `paused` is set to `false` and `timing` is set to `true`.

It's done. The scripting turned out to be relatively easy compared to how cool the result looks. You'll be thrilled to learn that you can use the bulk of this code in Workshop 12.

If you want a challenge exercise, try adding a "lap" function. Like a stopwatch, the `lap()` function would allow the user to click to stop the display from changing, but the timing would continue in the background. When the user clicked to proceed, the display would catch up and keep displaying the elapsed time since the user originally clicked play. I added that feature to the downloadable version of this file (at `www.teleport.com/~phillip/actionscripting/`) so that you can see one possible solution.

{Chapter 12 Workshop }

Creating an Analog Timer

In this workshop, we leverage the code we built in Workshop 12, "Creating a Digital Timer." That workshop created a timer that accurately calculated hours, minutes, seconds, and fractions of a second. In this workshop, instead of displaying those values as numbers, we'll display them graphically as a clock. We'll make a clip instance for each "arm" of the clock (hours, minutes, seconds, and fractions) and then we'll set their respective `_rotation` properties accordingly.

This is a really easy workshop!

1. Open the file containing the digital timer from the previous workshop.
2. Inside the Timer symbol, remove the Dynamic Text field containing the display.
3. Draw a large circle using a thick stroke and remove the fill. If you want to draw "hash marks" at 30-degree increments as shown in my version of the clock in Figure W12.1, you can, but it is not necessary to do so. Convert the entire shape to a symbol called Face.
4. Still inside the Timer symbol, draw a vertical line with a thick stroke. Convert the line to a symbol called Hand.
5. Double-click the Hand symbol to edit its contents. Use the Info panel to position the line so that the bottom of the line is aligned with the center of the clip. Using the top-left option in the Info panel, set x to 0 and y to a negative value equal to the line's height (Figure W12.2).

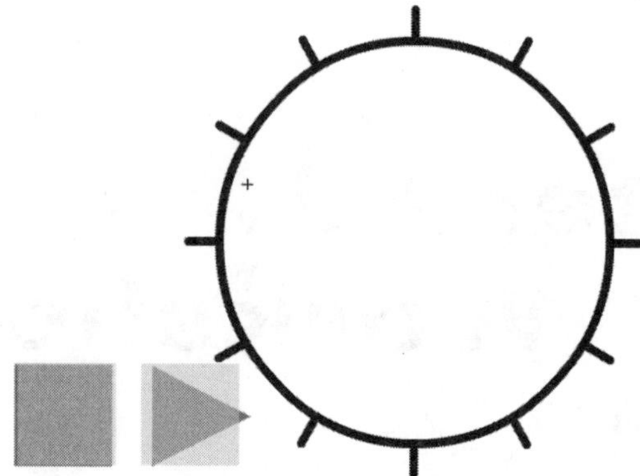

Figure W12.1 *The circle that will become the stopwatch face can include hash marks every 30 degrees if you want.*

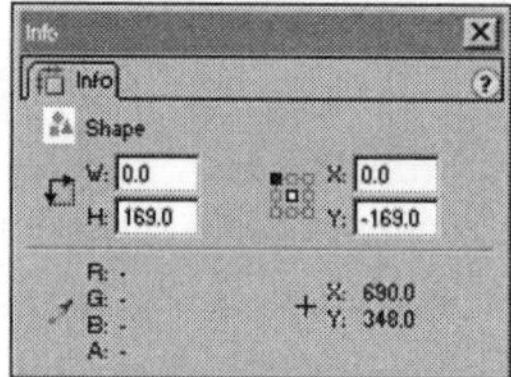

Figure W12.2 *Based on the line's height, we can make sure that the bottom of the line is centered inside the Hand symbol.*

6. Return to the Timer symbol to copy the instance of the Hand symbol. Paste an instance of the Hand symbol to create a separate instance for hours, minutes, seconds, and fractions. Name the different instances `h`, `m`, `s`, and `f`, respectively. You can also use the Effect panel to tint each instance differently.

7. Snap the bottom of the `h` clip to the center of the instance of the Face symbol. Adjust the clip's length by scaling it so that it's a little longer than the radius of the instance of Face. Send this clip to the back by choosing Modify, Arrange, Send to Back.

8. Snap the bottom of the `m` clip to the center of the instance of Face and adjust the length of the clip so that it's about the same length as the radius of the instance of the Face symbol. Send this clip to the back.

9. Snap the `s` clip to Face in the same way as you did the `m` clip and send it to the back.

10. Instead of snapping the `f` clip to the center of the instance of the Face symbol, first make a copy of the Face. Reduce the scale of this copy and place it on top of the larger instance of Face (Figure W12.3).

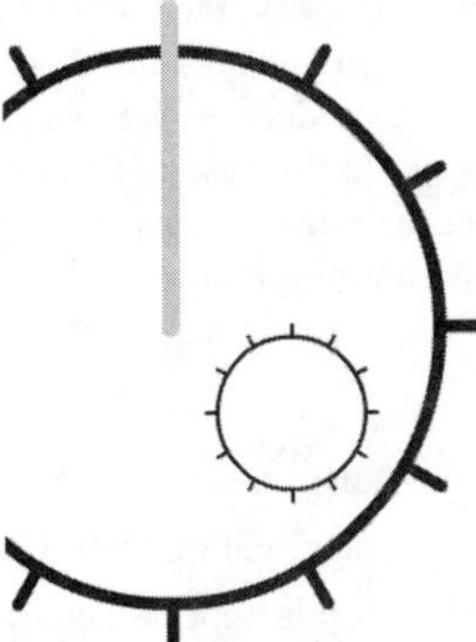

Figure W12.3 *The fractional seconds will be displayed on the smaller instance of the Face symbol.*

11. Snap the bottom of the `f` clip to the center of the small `Face` instance and adjust its length so that it's a little longer than the radius of the small face.

Believe it or not, we're almost done. All the graphics are built, and we just need to translate the values calculated in the `updateTimer()` function to `_rotation` values for the various hand clips.

12. Inside the `updateTimer()` function, remove or comment out each if-statement. Remember that these if-statements add a `0` in front of values less than 10. We'll need numbers, not strings, to calculate the rotation for the clock face. Remove or comment out the following parts of the `updateTimer()` function:

```
if (elapsedM<10) {
  elapsedM = "0"+elapsedM;
}
if (elapsedS<10) {
  elapsedS = "0"+elapsedS;
}
if (elapsedFractions<10) {
  elapsedFractions = "0"+elapsedFractions;
}
```

13. Also in the `updateTimer()` function, remove the line where `display` is assigned and replace it with these three lines:

```
h._rotation=elapsedH*6;
m._rotation=elapsedM*6;
s._rotation=elapsedS*6;
f._rotation= elapsedFractions*3.6;
```

We multiply hours, minutes, and seconds by 6 based on the fact that there are 60 of each per 360 degrees: 360/60 is 6. Try the what-if number 30 for minutes: 30*6 is 180, and that's exactly how many degrees we need the minute hand to rotate on the circle of the clock. In the case of fractions that are 1/100 of a second, consider that we want the `f` hand to go 360 degrees every second. Every 1/100 of a second must be multiplied by 3.6 or 360/100 because it takes 100 hundredths to make a whole second, or a whole circle in this case.

At this point, the movie works pretty well, but I know that on fancy stopwatches, the fractional second hand precisely displays a round fractional number. On the small clock face, the hand we've built for fractional seconds appears accurately, but the hand can often appear in odd locations, such as between hash marks. Just start and pause the timer a few times and see what I mean (Figure W12.4). We can't just change the hash marks because we'd need 100 marks around the circle. Even if we did, you'd find the hand won't touch each one because screen updates won't appear that frequently. Even if you cranked the frame rate up to 100 fps, it still wouldn't work.

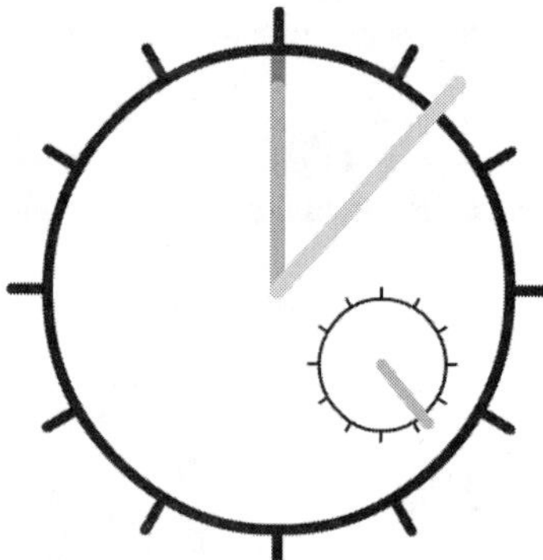

Figure W12.4 *The fractional seconds displayed don't always correspond to the hash marks on the small clock face.*

14. To address the fractional seconds issue, change the line in the `updateTimer()` function that assigns the `f` clip's `_rotation` to read as follows:

```
f._rotation= Math.round(elapsedFractions/10) * 36;
```

With this version of the formula, we'll always find the closest tenth of a second and set the rotation to 36 times that tenth because there are 10 36-degree units in a circle. The only problem now is that your hash marks may not represent tenths of a second. You can either make another version of the Face symbol and move the hash marks to every 36 degrees, or change the expression to this version:

```
f._rotation= Math.floor(elapsedFractions*.12) *30;
```

This version first calculates a round number of one-twelfth seconds and then multiplies by `30`, which is the number of degrees in the hash marks we added in step 3 to match our standard clocks with 12 hours per revolution.

15. One last touch is to modify the `init()` function to look like this:

```
function init(){
  controls.gotoAndStop(1);
  h._rotation=0;
  m._rotation=0;
  s._rotation=0;
  f._rotation=0;
}
```

The first line of this function works only if you gave the instance of the Controls symbol an instance name of `controls`. The other lines just make sure that whenever the user presses the stop button, the hands return to their original positions.

If I were you, I'd feel a little ripped off at this point. There wasn't much to this workshop. Okay, to make things interesting, let's add some audio for the seconds and fractional seconds. To do these next steps, you'll need one very short sound clip such as a click sound (I included one in the downloadable version of this workshop available at `www.teleport.com/~phillip/actionscripting/`).

16. We can use the Sound Object to make the click sound play once every second. Import a short sound and set the Linkage Properties to the Export This Symbol option. Give the symbol an identifier name of `sec` just as you learned to do in Chapter 11, "Objects," (Figure W12.5).

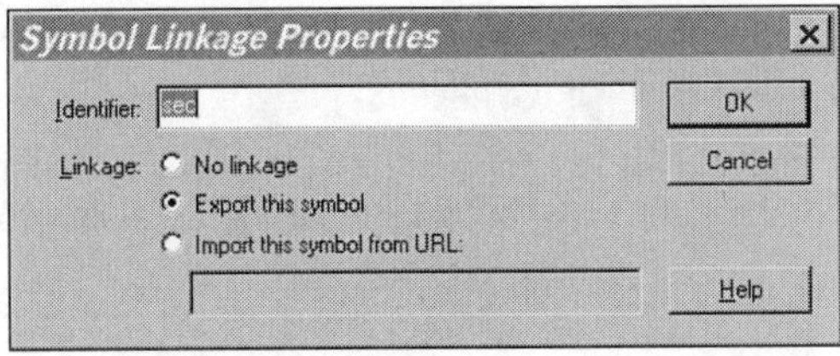

Figure W12.5 *To play the sound using scripting, we have to set its Linkage and give it an identifier name.*

17. Inside the `init()` function, add these lines of code:

```
sec=new Sound(this);
sec.attachSound("sec");
```

Notice that these statements won't actually start the sound, they just place the sound inside the variable called `sec`. The fact we're attaching the sound to the `this` clip means that you can have multiple instances of the `Timer` clip, each of which can maintain its own sound.

18. Anywhere inside the `updateTimer()` function *after* you set `elapsedS`, place the following `if` statement:

```
if (elapsedS<>lastS){
  sec.start();
  lastS=elapsedS;
}
```

This statement uses the `start()` method on the `sec` instance of the Sound Object. It does not call `start()` every time the `updateTimer()` function executes because `updateTimer()` executes many times a second based on the `enterFrame` event. As long as `elapasedS` is not equal to `lastS` (another variable we are introducing), `start()` starts the sound. It then sets `lastS` to the value of `elapsedS` so that next time this function executes, it will again be able to compare the new `elapsedS` and see whether it's truly a new value. Depending on your frame rate, the `updateTimer()` function will be executed many times per second.

At this point, you could take another, even shorter sound and follow steps 16 through 18 to make it play 10 times a second, or whatever the fractional display is displaying. However, I think this is a good example of where "faking it" is perfectly acceptable and more believable. We don't really have to make a sound play every tenth of a second. Instead, we can just record a loop that plays 10 clicks per second. Then, whenever the timer is running, we'll make that loop play; when the timer is stopped, we'll stop the sound. You just need a nice looping sound that makes 10 clicks a second when it's playing.

19. Import the looping sound and set its Linkage to Export. Use the identifier name `loopingClick` in the same way you named the sound in step 16.

20. In the `init()` function, add the following two lines:

```
loop=new Sound(this);
loop.attachSound("loopingClick");
```

This code simply creates another instance of the Sound Object in the variable called `loop`.

21. Now all you have to do is place the following script within the `playTimer()` function:

    ```
    loop.start( 0, 9999999999 );
    ```

    This script starts the `loop` Sound Object and makes it repeat many times.

22. Finally, place the following script inside *both* the `stopTimer()` and `pauseTimer()` functions to stop the sound:

    ```
    loop.stop();
    ```

That's it. It's kind of amazing that the fake way of just starting or stopping a loop is more believable than forcing Flash to carefully play a click sound for every fraction of a second. If you don't believe me, try it out. Just follow the steps to make the `sec` Sound Object play, but do it for fractions of seconds, which is related to the `elapsedFractions` variable.

This was a pretty fun workshop that extended the use of our `getTimer()` function. You lucked out because calculating the angles for the `Hand` instances was fairly straightforward. In Workshop 14, "Using Math to Create a Circular Slider," and to a lesser degree in Workshop 15, "Developing Time-Based Animations," you'll have to calculate angles based on trigonometry and the related issues of degrees versus radians, which are discussed in Chapter 5, "Programming Structures."

As far as the `getTimer()` function goes, Workshop 13, "Creating a Countdown Timer," shows how you can use it in a similar (but different) way. Actually, you'll see `getTimer()` many more times throughout this book.

{Chapter 13 Workshop }

Creating a Countdown Timer

This workshop combines the graphics of Workshop 4, "Creating a Horizontal Slider," with the timing calculations of the two timer workshops we just completed. It's actually a pretty easy workshop that proves you've been learning so far.

Quite simply, we're going create a Countdown Movie Clip that acts like a progress bar. From anywhere in the movie (say a button or a frame script) we'll be able to start the Countdown clip. The Countdown clip fills with a color until it's completely full and time is up. When you get the main functionality working, you can add refined graphics that make the clip look however you want. For example, you can make the clip graphic look like the hourglass shown in Figure W13.1.

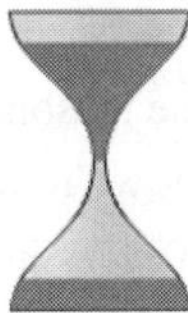

Figure W13.1 *Although we don't walk through how to make the hourglass timer, you'll be able to figure it out after doing this workshop.*

Follow these steps to create a Countdown timer:

1. Draw a wide rectangle (with both a fill and a pretty thick stroke). Select just the fill and convert it to a Movie Clip symbol called Strip. Name the layer Frame.
2. Select the instance of the Strip symbol and cut it, insert a new layer, and select Edit, Paste in Place. Name the instance `bar`. Name this new layer Strip and lock it so it doesn't get messed up during the next few steps.
3. Create a new layer and Paste in Place again to create another instance of the Strip symbol. Name this new layer Mask and lock that layer, too.
4. Arrange the layers so that Frame is on top, Mask is in the middle, and the original Strip layer is under Mask. Make sure that the Strip layer's properties are set to Masked (Figure W13.2).

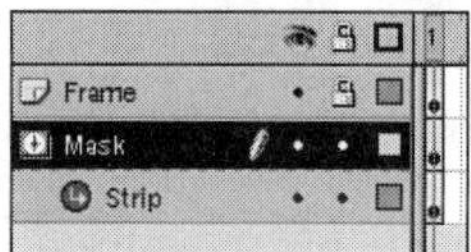

Figure W13.2 *The arrangement of layers is shown here.*

Now we've got the timer bar all built. The Mask layer will only reveal the bar in the area currently covered. So if we move the bar, the bar will be hidden. The Frame layer provides an outline so that the user can see the whole size of the timer bar.

We'll place scripts on the instance of `bar` (so, obviously, the Strip layer will need to be unlocked). The only thing we'll add later is a button or two (in a new layer) that will initiate the countdown. We'll need the `bar` instance to initialize a few variables in the `load` event and monitor the timing issues in the `enterFrame` event. In addition, we'll write a function that can be called from anywhere that will initiate the countdown. This function could be placed *inside* the Strip symbol, but instead we're going to place it on the `bar` instance. For one reason, we won't have to hunt around for different scripts. For another reason, we're using the Strip symbol elsewhere, and I don't want the same function in every instance we ever create. As it turns out, we're only using another instance of Strip in a Mask layer, which always renders all symbols to behave like Graphic symbols.

5. Select the instance of bar and attach this script:

```
onClipEvent (load) {
  max = _x;
  min = max-_width;
  total=max-min;
  _x = min;
}
```

Translated, this script first sets a variable max equal to the current _x. Then it determines that the min will be where it is now: max minus its _width. The total (the difference between max and min) is found. Finally, the current _x is set to the min calculated earlier. This bar will start all the way on the left and then move towards its max, where you positioned it onscreen, so that it looks like it's filling up the frame. At the end of this workshop, we'll look at other variations, such as making the bar move from right to left, emptying the frame instead of filling it up, and even making the bar move vertically.

6. Now we're going to add a function that can "start" this bar from anywhere in the movie. As you recall from Workshop 9, "Creating a Currency-Exchange Calculator," if you place the entire function structure function theName(){} within the load event, the function will act as though you wrote it in the first keyframe inside the symbol—but only for this instance. Add the following script just inside the load event, right after the _x=min; line but before the closing curly bracket:

```
function startNow(howLong){
  totalTime=howLong*1000;
  startTime=getTimer();
  timing=true;
}
```

If a script calls this function by using bar.startNow(10), the following three things will happen: The totalTime variable is assigned to 1000 times 10. The startTime variable is set to the current getTimer(). And the timing variable becomes true. Note that all these variables are part of the bar clip instance. In practice, calling startNow() allows us to specify a value in seconds for this timer to start counting down.

7. Any time timing is true, the enterFrame script must determine where the bar should be (based on how much time has elapsed and what the total distance to travel is) and must set the bar's location accordingly. Here's the entire script that gets placed on the bar instance to accomplish that:

```
onClipEvent(enterFrame){
  if (timing){
    percent=(getTimer()-startTime)/totalTime;
    if (percent>1){
      timing=false;
      percent=1;
```

```
    }
  _x=min+(percent*total);
  }
}
```

First notice that nothing happens unless `timing` is `true`. Then `percent` is assigned the value of the elapsed time (`getTimer()-startTime`) divided by `totalTime`. This isn't *really* a percent; it's a decimal value between `0` and `1`. To make it a true percent, we could just multiply by 100. Because "percent" is interesting only to humans, and because we're not displaying the percent, we won't bother converting it. In the last line of code, we set `_x` to the leftmost location `min` plus `percent` times `total`. For example, if `percent` is `1`, we'll multiply `total` by `1`, resulting in the whole `total`. Then we'll add that to `min`. Before we get to that line though, the `if (percent>1)` statement ensures that `percent` never stays above `1`, even though it *will* go over that value. Actually, the if-statement not only reassigns `percent` to `1` when it goes over `1`, it sets `timing` to `false` so that this becomes our last time in this part of the `enterFrame` script—at least until the timer is reset by the `startNow()` function.

8. Check it out: Create a new layer that contains a couple buttons and place a script like the following into one of the buttons:

```
on (release) {
  bar.startNow(2);
}
```

Use the same function call `bar.startNow(2)`, but use a different parameter to specify a different time.

This really was an easy workshop. Consider that you can make this timer trigger something else when it expires. You just need to place a script within that `if(percent>1)` statement. To test this logic out, try adding a line to the script, right after `timing=false`, that reads `trace("Time's up!")`.

If you want to make similar timeout clips that empty instead of fill up the frame or clips that move vertically, you just have to make an adjustment to the `load` event where you set `min` and `max`. Actually, if you want to make the timer bar vertical, you'll also have to change the `_x=min+(percent*total)` line inside the `enterFrame` script as well: change the `_x` to a `_y`.

Here are a couple sample variations of the timer bar. See whether you can figure out which one does what. Each `load` event is shown with the last line of the `enterFrame` script.

If this is in `load`:

```
max = _x;
min = max-_width;
total=max-min;
_x = max;
```

And if this is in `enterFrame`:

```
_x=max-(percent*total);
```

The result is that the bar starts fully filled and counts down by moving out of the way to the left. If you change the `enterFrame` part to read `_x=max+(percent*total)`, the bar will move to the right.

If this is in `load`:

```
min = _y;
max = min-_height;
total=max-min;
_y = min;
```

And if this is in `enterFrame`:

```
_y=min-(percent*total);
```

The result is that the slider is fully filled and counts down by moving out of the way in a down direction. It might make more sense to rotate the graphics 90 degrees.

If you really want to make the hourglass effect shown at the beginning of this workshop, you need two instances of `bar` with scripts. Call one instance `top` and the other `bottom` because they both can't have the same instance name. The only difficulty is in laying out the masking. Consider Figure W13.3 to see how it works.

After you have the masks and layers created, the top instance can start filled and move down out of the way. And the bottom instance can start out of the way and fill its area by moving up. If you're using a button to initiate the timer, you'll need to call both instances as shown here:

```
on (release) {
  top.startNow(4);
  bottom.startNow(4);
}
```

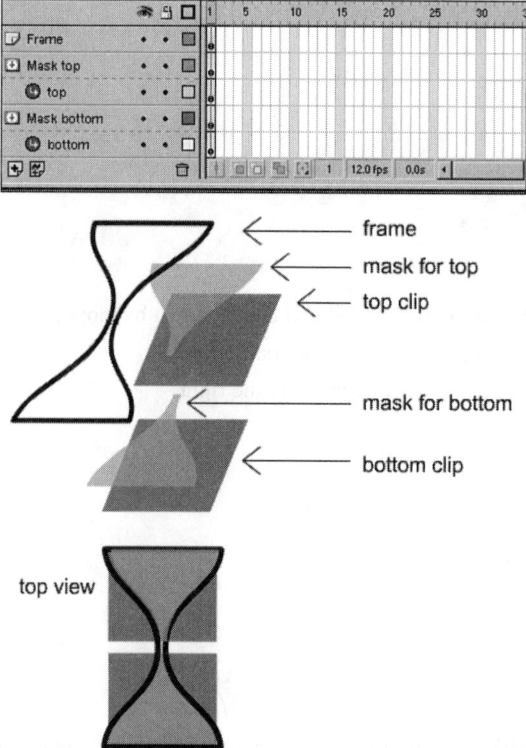

Figure W13.3 *The work involved to make an hourglass countdown is all in the layers and masks.*

Here are the critical portions of the scripts for both the top and bottom instances:

For the `top` instance's `load` event:

```
min = _y;
max = min+_height;
total = max-min;
_y = min;
```

For the `top` instance's `enterFrame` event:

```
_y = min+(percent*total);
```

For the `bottom` instance's `load` event:

```
max = _y;
min = max+_height;
total = max-min;
_y = min;
```

For the `bottom` instance's `enterFrame` event:

```
_y = min+(percent*total);
```

You can actually do a lot more with this kind of timing logic. For example, you could create a countdown timer that appears in analog form (Figure 13.4). Just like the hourglass version of the timer, all the work is in setting up the masks. After all, how difficult is it to set `_rotation` to `360*percent`? With the foundation you received in this workshop, you'll be able to figure out how to solve other similar challenges.

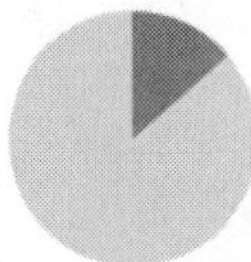

Figure W13.4 *Any kind of timer you can imagine, you can build!*

{Chapter 14 Workshop }

Using Math to Create a Circular Slider

By now, you're probably quite familiar with calculating percentages based on minimum and maximums. You're also probably quite comfortable writing scripts for the `enterFrame` and `mouseMove` events. This workshop involves using just a few trigonometry concepts to calculate angles and to specify locations around a circular path. Suppose that you have two known points such as the center of a clip and the current position of the mouse. Calculating the angle of a line drawn through those points is the main task in this workshop. Although the applications of such a trick can include creating eyeballs that appear to follow the mouse movements (Figure W14.1), we can actually use this knowledge for something more practical: a slider that moves along a curved path.

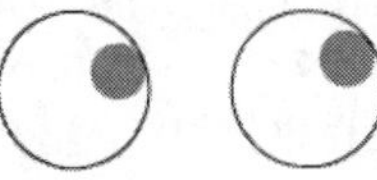

Figure W14.1 *Making eyeballs follow the mouse is one of the fun things you can do with math.*

It turns out that the actual math involved in this workshop isn't *that* bad. However, if you want, you can brush up on some of the Math Object methods discussed in Chapter 5, "Programming Structures," especially `Math.atan2()`, the first trigonometry function I learned to love.

Here are the steps for creating a curved slider:

1. To first get a sense of the formula we'll be using, create an eyeball shape: Draw a small dark circle inside a larger light circle, and make the dark circle touch the inside edge of the right side of the light circle (Figure W14.2).

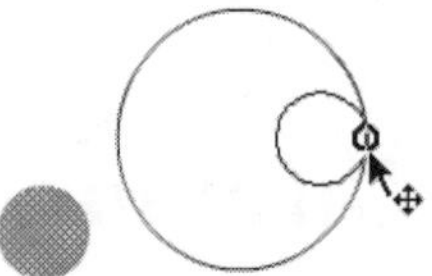

Figure W14.2 *Position the small dark circle inside the right edge of the larger circle.*

2. Select everything and convert it to a Movie Clip called Eyeball. Attach the following code to the clip instance:

```
onClipEvent (mouseMove) {
  var radians = Math.atan2(_root._ymouse-_y, _root._xmouse-_x);
  var degrees=radians/(Math.PI/180);
  _rotation=degrees;
  updateAfterEvent();
}
```

   Every time the mouse moves, this code will first assign the variable `radians` to the result of the `Math.atan2()` method. The two parameters provided to `Math.atan2()` are the x and y difference between where the mouse is and the center of Eyeball (for example, the y difference is `_root._ymouse - _y`). As you recall from Chapter 5, the `Math.atan2()` function returns an angle based on the length of the sides of a right triangle, even if those lengths are negative. Realize that for any angle you can draw vertical and horizontal lines to create a right triangle. Those two sides are provided for by the parameters in the `Math.atan2()` function. Also remember from Chapter 5 that the angle returned is in the form of radians.

   The second line of this script uses a standard formula to convert radians to degrees. Those degrees are used to set the angle of the Eyeball clip.

It's kind of cool: You can copy as many instances of the Eyeball clip as you want, and they'll all calculate the correct `_rotation` to follow the mouse pointer.

So we can make eyeballs, so what? For our slider, this bit of math will come in handy. While the user drags, we can calculate the angle from any known point—such as the center of the circle around which the user is dragging—to the mouse (Figure W14.3).

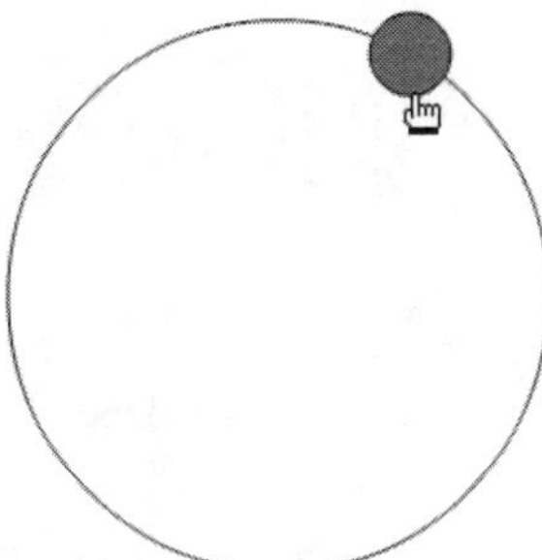

Figure W14.3 *We're going to make a dragable slider that follows the radius of a circle.*

With that angle in hand, we can calculate where the slider should be positioned. I want the user to be able to grab a small circle (think of the moon); as the user drags that circle, we position it in the correct place along a larger circle (think of the moon's orbit).

We could actually solve this exercise just by placing the moon off center within a clip (similar to the way the pupil was off center within the Eyeball symbol). However, this seemingly easier approach would require that any adjustments to the radius be made by editing the contents of our moon symbol. Besides, we've already learned how to rotate an off center symbol (the Eyeball). Positioning a clip on a circular path is entirely different.

3. In the main timeline, draw a circle. Don't bother making it a symbol, but instead note its center point and diameter (Figure W14.4). This circle will define the path for our slider.

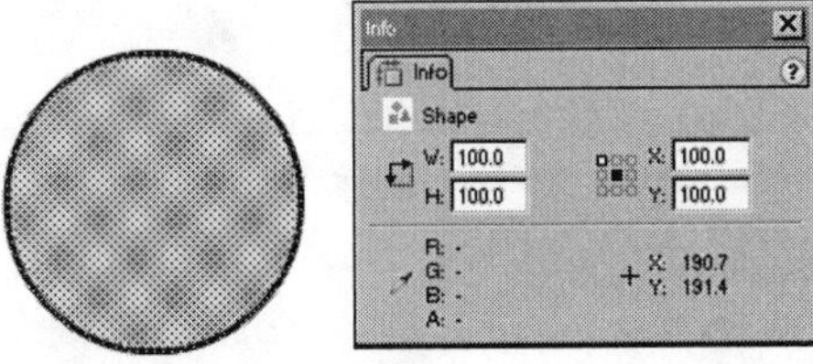

Figure W14.4 *Note the circular shape's diameter and position.*

4. Draw another medium-sized circle and convert it to a button symbol named Invisible. Go inside this symbol and drag the first keyframe to the Hit state so that it will be an invisible button.

5. Back in the main timeline, attach the following code to the invisible button instance:

```
on (release, releaseOutside) {
  dragging=false;
}
on (press) {
  dragging=true;
}
```

This code sets a variable called `dragging` to `true` or `false`, depending on whether the user is dragging the mouse.

6. Draw another small circle and position the invisible button on top of it. The idea is that we can make the clickable area bigger than the circle itself. Select both the small circle and the invisible button instance and convert them to a Movie Clip called Slider.

7. Back in the main timeline, we'll use those coordinates gathered in step 3. Select the instance of Slider and attach the following code:

```
onClipEvent (load) {
  centerX = 100;
  centerY = 100;
  radius = 50;
}
```

Naturally, you should set `centerX` and `centerY` to the center points of the circle you drew in step 3. Also, `radius` should be half the width of your circle. If we're going to position the slider clip along a specific point on a circle (once we know the angle), we need to know the center of that circle and its radius so that we know how far from the center of the circular path we want the clip to appear.

8. Now we can determine the angle between the center of the circle and the mouse pointer. Note, however, that this will prove to be only half our task. First draw a horizontal line and convert it to a Movie Clip symbol. Give this instance the name `line`.

9. Add the following code to the instance of Slider:

```
onClipEvent (mouseMove) {
  var radians=Math.atan2(centerY-_root._ymouse, centerx-
➥_root._xmouse);
  var degrees=radians/(Math.PI/180);
  _root.line._rotation=degrees
  updateAfterEvent();
}
```

This code should look familiar; it's the same code we put on the instance of the Eyeball symbol. Notice that the code uses the x and y coordinates of the circle shape that was initialized in the `load` event (`centerX` and `centerY`). Also realize that even if we changed the code where `_root.line`'s `_rotation` is set (to set the `_rotation` of the instance of the Slider symbol) the resulting movie wouldn't look very impressive because rotating a circle is not very interesting.

//

When you test the movie, the rotating line proves that we indeed know the correct angle. We just have to translate that angle to an x and y position for the slider. Although the "arc" functions `Math.asin()`, `Math.acos()`, `Math.atan()`, and `Math.atan2()` accept lengths of sides and return an angle, the regular trigonometry functions `Math.sin()`, `Math.cos()`, and `Math.tan()` accept angles and return proportional amounts of horizontal and vertical length. If we provide `Math.sin()` with an angle, it will return the vertical proportion. `Math.cos()` will return the horizontal proportion. When we multiply these proportions by `radius`, we can calculate where on the circle the instance of the Slider symbol should be positioned.

10. Modify the `mouseMove` event on the instance of `Slider` to appear as follows:

```
onClipEvent (mouseMove) {
  var radians=Math.atan2(centerY-_root._ymouse, centerx-
➥_root._xmouse);
  _x=centerX+Math.cos(radians)*radius;
  _y=centerY+Math.sin(radians)*radius;
  updateAfterEvent();
}
```

Notice that we don't bother converting to degrees. The `Math.atan2()` method returns radians and both `Math.cos()` and `Math.sin()` accept radians, so there's no need to bother with the "degrees" middle-man, if you will.

When you test this script, there are two significant problems remaining. First the slider circle appears to be 180 degrees off—it's always on the other side of the circular path. This is really only a matter of perception—sort of like how your eyes project images upside down on your retina and your brain flips them right side up. In addition, the instance of Slider moves even if we're not dragging because the `mouseMove` event executes any time the mouse moves.

11. To resolve one of these remaining issues, we need to add 180 degrees to the radians found. Naturally we don't really want to use degrees: Remember that half a circle is not only 180 degrees but pi radians. We'll just add `Math.PI` to the radians we find. The other part you'll notice in this final version of the `mouseMove` event is that all the code is tucked inside the `if (dragging)` statement, because we only want to execute this code while the user drags. Let's adjust the `mouseMove` event once again:

```
onClipEvent (mouseMove) {
  if (dragging){
    var radians=Math.atan2(centerY-_root._ymouse, centerx-
➥_root._xmouse);
    _x=centerX+Math.cos(radians+Math.PI)*radius;
    _y=centerY+Math.sin(radians+Math.PI)*radius;
    updateAfterEvent();
  }
}
```

Now that we let this code execute only while the mouse is being dragged and that we have adjusted for the half-circle offset, the movie works great. You'll probably want to position the instance of the Slider symbol so that it starts somewhere on the circle shape. By the way, you can adjust the radius and the center point for the circular path with ease in the `load` event.

To use this example as a slider that makes adjustments to something else onscreen, you just need to place some code right above the `updateAfterEvent()`.

12. Place a Dynamic Text field on the Stage and associate it with the variable `percent`.

13. Add the following line of code right above `updateAfterEvent()` inside the instance of Slider's `mouseMove` event:

```
var degrees=radians/(Math.PI/180);
_root.percent=degrees;
```

After converting to degrees (just to make this discussion easier to read), we set the `percent` variable so that we can watch the degrees change as we drag. Notice that when you test the movie, dragging clockwise from nine o'clock increases `degrees` from 0 to 180, but moving counterclockwise reduces a negative number from 0 to –180.

14. We can make the display of degrees appear continuous by inserting an if-statement between the two statements you inserted in step 13:

```
var degrees=radians/(Math.PI/180);
if (degrees<0){
  degrees=360+degrees;
}
_root.percent=degrees;
```

This code simply says that if `degrees` is less than 0, set degrees to 360 plus `degrees` (which is negative). That is, –180 (three o'clock) turns to 180, –90 (six o'clock) changes to 270, and so on (Figure W14.5).

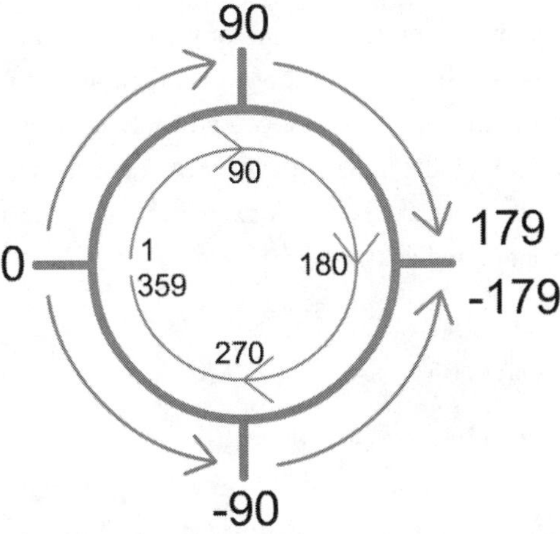

Figure W14.5 *The original degree values on the outside of the circle, including negative numbers, can be converted to all positive numbers as shown on the inside of the circle by using a simple formula.*

15. To make the `percent` variable show a number between 0 and 99, we can change the last line of the script to read as follows:

    ```
    _root.percent=Math.floor(100*degrees/360);
    ```

    This statement says that 360 divided into `degrees` times 100 gives us a percentage. If you want, you can add `1` outside the `Math.floor()` method if you want to display values from 1 through 100.

    You can just as easily use the `percent` value to set any property of any other clip. For example, if you have a clip named `it`, you can place the following script right after you assign `_root.percent`:

    ```
    _root.it._alpha=_root.percent.
    ```

16. If you don't like the fact that nine o'clock is where the scale starts, you can use the following technique to adjust the degrees found by any amount you want. Suppose that we want to subtract 90 degrees from every value to make twelve o'clock become the zero point. After all, before we converted to actual percent, twelve o'clock was displaying 90, as shown in Figure 14.5. To accomplish this task, subtract what you want (90 in this case), and our current if-statement will adjust for any negative numbers. Place this code right before the line starting `if (degrees<0)…`:

    ```
    degrees-=90;
    ```

> All this does is subtract 90 from degrees so that twelve o'clock is the zero point. As long as you do this *before* that if-statement, you can subtract any value from the degrees calculated.

This discussion was a little easier for you to read and for me to write after we converted to degrees. However, unless you are setting _rotation, which is the one part of Flash that requires numbers in degrees, you probably never need to convert to degrees. If you remember that there are 2*Math.PI radians in a circle, you can perform any of the code in steps 13-16. For example, here is the same exact code without ever translating radians to degrees:

```
radians-=(Math.PI/2);
if (radians<0){
  radians=(2*Math.PI)+radians;
}
_root.percent=Math.floor(100*radians/(2*Math.PI));
```

Notice that this code has one less line than the original version because we're not translating to degrees. The first line effectively subtracts 90 degrees from the radians found because Math.PI/2 is equivalent to 90 degrees. If radians is less than 0, we subtract radians from 2*Math.PI in the same way we subtracted degrees from 360 earlier. Finally, to figure out the percentage, we divide radians by 2*Math.PI instead of dividing degrees by 360.

With the exception of a little bit of math, this workshop turned out to be pretty easy. We'll use some of the same knowledge in the next workshop, "Developing Time-Based Animations," to rotate a clip and make it follow a path. But in that workshop, the main goal is to make sure that the clip rotates at a perfect rate, regardless of frame rate or the computer's performance. You'll get to use some of the same math, though.

{Chapter 15 Workshop }

Developing Time-Based Animations

Flash is a frame-based animation tool. As you know, just because you set the frame rate to 120 frames per second, doesn't mean that Flash will really display that many frames in one second. The frame rate you specify is more of a top end that Flash will not exceed. Even if you keep your frame rate down in the normal range of 20 fps, there's a good chance that Flash will occasionally take longer than one-twentieth of a second to display a frame. The standard practice is to just make sure that your movie performs adequately on a slow machine. But there's still no guarantee.

If you use audio set to stream, Flash will drop frames to maintain a constant rate of sound. However, this approach to maintaining a particular speed has its drawbacks as well. This workshop explores ways you can write your own code that effectively drops frames to keep up with a predetermined rate. This doesn't mean that you can actually reach the mythical 120 fps (Flash's maximum), but rather that you can make sure that your graphics stay on time. For example, you can designate that a circle will rotate fully in 10 seconds. On a super-slow machine, the circle might display only four times: at 0, 90, 180, and 360 degrees. On a fast machine, however, the circle might display at all 360 discrete angles. Regardless of the machine speed, however, one second after the clip starts, the circle will have made a full revolution. You'll learn how to accomplish this feat in this workshop.

We're actually going to make circles rotate as well as revolve around other circles. The techniques learned, however, can also be applied to animations that aren't so predictable and geometric. For example, in Workshop 17, "Offline Production," you'll first learn how to collect data for any kind of animation offline and then apply the time-based animation knowledge from this workshop.

This workshop starts our animation efforts with circles:

1. Start a new movie and set the frame rate to 24 fps.
2. Draw a circle that will become a graphic of the earth. Make sure that you include additional graphic elements that will allow us to see when this graphic rotates (Figure W15.1).

Figure W15.1 *Draw some shapes in the "earth" circle so that we'll notice when the circle rotates.*

3. Convert the circle into a Movie Clip called Earth. Place the following code on the instance of the clip:

```
onClipEvent(load){
  rpm=60;          //HARD WIRED
  degreesPerSecond=(rpm*360)/60;
  fps=24;          //HARD WIRED
  degreesPerFrame=degreesPerSecond/fps;
}
onClipEvent (enterFrame) {
  _rotation+=degreesPerFrame;
}
```

   This code isn't going to exhibit perfect synchronization. The `load` event starts by setting the `rpm` variable that specifies how many times per minute the clip should rotate. We will use this variable to specify how fast, based on time, this clip should rotate. We then easily translate revolutions per minute into the number of `degreesPerSecond`. The last two lines become problematic. First, hard-wiring `fps` is going to prove to be a hassle—and anyway, this movie should play the same regardless of the frame rate we specify. The last line of the `load` event accurately calculates the number of `degreesPerFrame` but bases its calculation on `fps`, which could easily slow down. The `enterFrame` script makes perfect sense *provided* that it is indeed executed 24 times a second.

//

> You can prove that this code doesn't work by first testing it and getting a feel for what 60 rpms looks like on your machine. Then change both the movie's frame rate and the `fps` value to, say, `90`. The movie won't play quite as fast unless you have a *really* fast computer. This approach, which simply adds to `_rotation` in every `enterFrame` event, assumes that each frame is entered on time.

4. Change the code attached to the clip to read as follows:

```
onClipEvent(load){
  rpm=60;       //HARD WIRED
  degreesPerSecond=(rpm*360)/60;
}
onClipEvent(enterFrame){
  now=getTimer();
  _rotation+=degreesPerSecond/(1000/(now-lastTime));
  lastTime=now;
}
```

   This `load` event is like the preceding one, but it contains much less information. The `enterFrame` script is a bit more complex. First we put the current `getTimer()` in a variable called `now`. Then we add the result of an expression to `_rotation`. Try the what-if possibility that we're supposed to rotate 10 degrees per second: If it's been two seconds since the last time we rotated, we should rotate 20 degrees. If it's only been 0.5 second since we rotated, we need to rotate just 5 degrees. To calculate how long it's been since the last time we rotated, we subtract `lastTime` from `now`. The formula works like this: if `lastTime` was five past the hour and `now` is six past the hour, you know that one minute has elapsed—but we're using milliseconds. If we divide 1000 into the number of milliseconds that have elapsed, we know how many seconds have passed. Then we divide that value into the number of degrees per second. (I think this formula is easiest to see when you try a few numbers.) Anyway, now that we have set the `_rotation`, we can save the current `now` into the variable `lastTime` so that the next time around we can calculate how long it's been since the last rotation.

   It should work really well. Try changing the movie's frame rate to 4 fps or 90 fps. The movie may play smoother or clunkier, but it always stays "on time."

5. We can extend this workshop to practice both our math and our skills with time-based animation. Select the instance of Earth and convert it to a Movie Clip called Clip with Earth.

6. Create another circle and convert it to a Movie Clip called Sun. Call the instance on the Stage sun.

7. Attach the following script to the instance of the Clip with Earth symbol:

```
onClipEvent (load) {
  rpm=20;        //HARD WIRED
  radsPerSecond=(rpm*Math.PI*2)/60;
  centerY=_root.sun._y;
  centerX=_root.sun._x;
  radius=Math.sqrt(Math.pow ( Math.abs(_x-centerX),2) +
  ➥Math.pow ( Math.abs(_y-centerY), 2 ));
}
onClipEvent(enterFrame){
  now=getTimer();
  radians=lastRad+(radsPerSecond/(1000/(now-lastTime)));
  lastTime=now;
  lastRad=radians;
  _x = centerX+Math.cos(radians)*radius;
  _y = centerY+Math.sin(radians)*radius;
}
```

Although this script is slightly longer than the earlier code on the instance of Earth, it's really the same idea. However, because we're not just adding to the `_rotation` property—we're actually positioning the `_x` and `_y` around a circle—we need the circle's radius and center point. In the `load` event, you see a hard-wired `rpm` value, but then instead of calculating `degreesPerSecond`, we calculate `radsPerSecond`. Figure that, for every revolution, we use `2*Math.PI` radians. The next two lines in the `load` event save the coordinates of the `sun` instance. The last line determines the `radius` as the distance between the `sun` instance and this instance (of Clip with Earth).

//

By the way, you can use the following general formula any time you want to calculate the distance between two points:

```
Math.sqrt(Math.pow(Math.abs(x1-x2),2)+Math.pow(Math.abs(y1-y2), 2 ));
```

In this syntax, `x1` and `y1` are the coordinates of one point, and `x2` and `y2` are the coordinates of the other point. For those of you who were awake in high-school Math class, this formula is based on the Pythagorean Theorem (which, yes, *does* come up in everyday life). Pythagoras said that with a right triangle, the square of the length of one side added to the square of the length of the other side will equal the square of the third side. For any two points, we can easily find the difference in x and the difference in y so that we can draw the straight sides of a triangle.

We can then raise those values to the second power (that is, we square them), and then add them together. Finally, we know that that sum is the square of the diagonal line connecting the two points; when we take the square root of that sum, we end up with the actual length. Figure W15.2 shows how the formula is derived. Notice that when finding the difference between two points, I use `Math.abs()` to ensure that the value is not negative. It turns out that this shouldn't matter because when you square a negative number, the result should be positive, but I'm leaving that formula in because it always shows distance as a positive number.

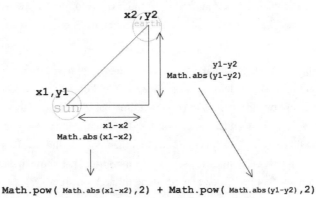

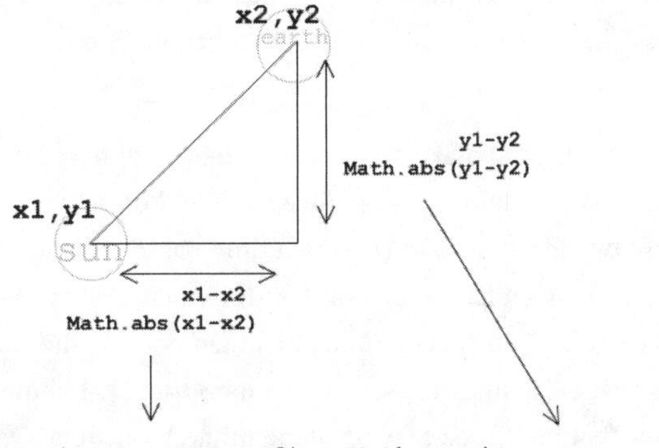

Figure W15.2 *Based on the Pythagorean Theorem, this diagram shows you how to determine the distance between any two points.*

Gee, we didn't even get to the `enterFrame` part of the script because we were having so much fun with math. Inside the `enterFrame` event, we first save the current `getTimer()` in the variable `now`. When we were adding to `degrees` in the instance of Earth, we simply said `degrees+=calculated amount`. With radians, however, we can't just say "add this to the current radians" because Clip with Earth doesn't have a "radians" property. We're calculating how many radians to add based on how long it's been since the last time we rotated, but we have to save that value in a variable to be used in the formula at the end of the event that translates radians into an x and y position. Anyway, we simply set a variable called `radians` equal to the `lastRad` (the `radians` from last time) plus the number of radians that should have occurred since last time (that is, `radsPerSecond` divided elapsed time in seconds: `radsPerSecond/(1000/(now-lastTime))`). The next two lines save the current value for `now` and `radians` in variables called `lastTime` and `lastRad` so that we can use them the next time around. Finally, in the last two lines, we set the `_x` and `_y` properties using cosine and sine, as you learned to do in Workshop 14, "Using Math to Create a Circular Slider."

The result is pretty neat. Notice that you can position the earth in any location, and it will determine the circular path to follow based on a circle drawn with its center at the `sun` and its radius equal to the distance between `sun` and the instance of the Clip with Earth symbol. Also notice that you can change the frame rate to anything you want, and the movie will always keep perfect synchronization (although the movie is sometimes jumpy when the frame rate is very low). You can also change either `rpm` value on the instance of the Clip with Earth or Earth symbols. We have successfully created an animation that is based entirely on time, not on frame rate.

What if you want to make an animation that's not based on math but you still want to make the animation time-based? We'll do that in Workshop 17. In brief, there are two basic steps to making a time-based animation that's not based on math: First you gather the coordinates for where the graphic you're animating should be at key moments in time, and then you use those values in an `enterFrame` event that keeps checking `getTimer()`. I know that explanation isn't complete, but you'll see how it's done in the Workshop 17.

{Chapter 16 Workshop }

Creating a Multistate Button

I love Flash as much as the next guy, but the built-in buttons are good only for a limited set of situations. If you need a button that has an Over state and a Down state, Flash's built-in buttons are great. But what about a "selected" state, such as a checkmark? We've solved this problem in other workshops by simply placing a clip instance on top of the button to represent the button being selected. But this solution doesn't work very well when you need to allow the user to select multiple buttons, as you do when presenting traditional check boxes (Figure W16.1).

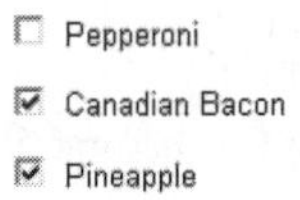

☐ Pepperoni

☑ Canadian Bacon

☑ Pineapple

Figure W16.1 *Traditional check box buttons include a "selected state" that Flash's built-in buttons don't provide.*

In addition to the problem of the lack of check marks, Flash's built-in buttons have only two options for the precise behavior a button exhibits: Track as Button or Track as Menu Item (Figure W16.2). When users click (and hold) on a button created with the default Track as Button option, they do only two things: let go *on top of* that button (and the click will register) or let go *off of* that button (and the click won't register). The Track as Menu Item option allows users to click and hold, drag, and then let go on a different button. If you have several buttons with graphic Over states, you can see the difference between these options when you test them out. Think of the difference between these options like this: The Track as Button option requires that the mouse is not pressed as you enter the space of the button. The Track as Menu Item option allows the mouse to be dragged into the button space.

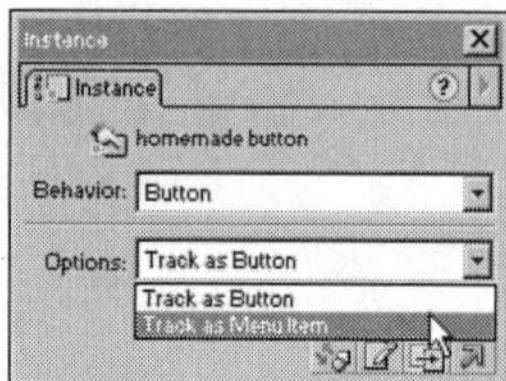

Figure W16.2 *Flash's built-in buttons behave differently depending on the options selected in the Instance panel.*

Unfortunately for us nitpicky people, neither option exhibits the precise behavior required of most system-level buttons. For example, try clicking and holding the close box in any open window. If you roll off, the button goes back to normal and as long as you keep holding the mouse down, you can't click any other button. If you keep holding the mouse and roll back over the close button, you can select it by simply letting go on top of the button. The built-in Flash buttons don't act this way. Alright, I don't lose sleep over the matter, but we can build our own homemade button that will accommodate these concerns and give us more control over the buttons by using a Movie Clip.

This workshop walks through one way to make such a button. It's a ton more work than just using the built-in buttons, but it's worth doing for the practice, if nothing else.

1. Start by building the pieces. Draw a circle for your button. Convert it to a Movie Clip symbol called Circle.
2. Select the instance of Circle and convert it to a Movie Clip called Button. Just the name of the clip is Button, not the symbol type. Now you have an instance of the Button symbol that contains an instance of the Circle symbol.
3. Double-click the instance of Button so that we can edit its contents. Inside the Button symbol, draw a graphic to be used as a highlight, such as an unfilled circle with a thick yellow stroke. Position the highlight so that it surrounds the clip of Circle. Select this shape and convert it to a symbol called Highlight. Give the instance of the Highlight symbol the name `highlight` as well.

4. We don't want `highlight` to be present at the start of the movie; we want it to appear only when the user rolls over the button. First select the `highlight` instance and cut it. Insert a new layer and name the layer Highlight; into this layer, paste in place the instance of `highlight`. We use a separate layer to help us select `highlight` after the next step.

5. Double-click the `highlight` instance to edit its contents. Drag the first keyframe to frame 2 so that nothing is on frame 1. Place the following script in frame 1:

   ```
   stop()
   ```

   Return to edit the contents of the Button symbol.

//

You can lock the Highlight layer so that it doesn't get messed up. There are two more clips to create that have the same properties as the `highlight` instance: one for a down state and one for a checked state. Both the `down` and `checked` instances will have nothing in their first frames except a `stop()` script, all their graphics will be in their second frames, and each will have a layer of their own in the Button symbol.

6. Draw the graphic for your down state; perhaps it's a dark version of the circle shape. Convert this graphic to a symbol called Down. Make its instance name `down` and place the instance in its own layer, also named Down. Finally, go inside the Down symbol, move the first keyframe to frame 2, and put a `stop()` script in frame 1. Return to edit the Button symbol and lock the Down layer.

7. Repeat step 6 for the checkmark state: Draw an *X* and convert it to a symbol named Checkmark. Make the instance name `checkmark`, put it in a layer called Checkmark, and edit its contents so that the graphic doesn't appear until frame 2 and so that there's a `stop()` script in frame 1.

Finally, we can arrange the layers and start scripting. You'll probably want the Checkmark layer to be uppermost, then the Highlight layer, then the Down layer, and finally the original circle clip's layer, which is probably named Layer 1. The stacking order depends on what kind of graphics and what kind of effect you want (Figure W16.3).

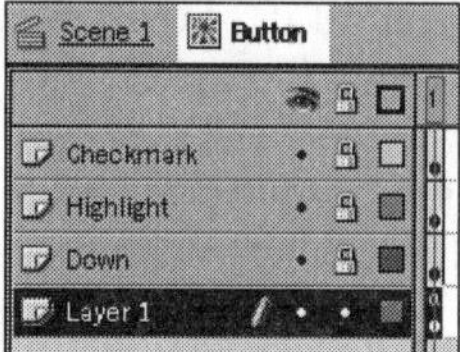

Figure W16.3 *Placing each instance in a different layer lets you control the stacking order and makes invisible clips easier to select.*

8. Now we can write most of our scripts for the rest of the workshop on the instance of the Circle symbol. Attached to the instance of the Circle symbol, place this starter script:

```
onClipEvent (load) {
  h = _parent.highlight;
  d = _parent.down;
  c = _parent.checkmark;
}
```

   All this script does is save a few very short variables that contain references to the `highlight`, `down`, and `checkmark` instances that are up one level from where this script executes. This code will save us some typing later when we want to set the properties of these clips.

9. Just to see how easy scripting this event can be, attach this script to the instance of Circle:

```
onClipEvent (mouseMove) {
  onMe=hitTest(_root._xmouse, _root._ymouse, 1 );
  h.gotoAndStop(1+onMe);
  updateAfterEvent();
}
```

   This script first sets a variable `onMe` to the value returned from the `hitTest()` method. If the mouse is currently on top of this clip, `onMe` is set to `1`; otherwise, it's set to `0`. Then the `h` clip jumps to frame 1 plus `onMe`. If `onMe` is `0`, the clip goes to frame 1 where there are no graphics. If `onMe` is `1`, the clip jumps to frame 2. You can test this out by placing two or more instances of the Button Movie Clip on the Stage.

Although there's nothing wrong with this script, it tracks only whether the cursor is over the clip. We want to track more things: We want to show the highlight only when the user rolls over this button and isn't currently clicking or dragging another button. We also want the `d` instance to jump to frame 2 when the user is clicking this button. To accomplish these tasks, we need to track two more variables. First, we'll use a variable `_root.clicking` to monitor whether the user is clicking *any* button. The variable `clicking` is `1` or `0` any time the user clicks. We'll use the variable `alive` to track whether the user is currently clicking *this* button. The variable `alive` is used to track not so much when the user is clicking, but whether the user clicks and drags off this button. For example, if the user starts by clicking this button, then rolls off without releasing the mouse, `alive` should remain set to `1`.

10. To start tracking these two new variables, we must first initialize these variables in the `load` event as follows:

```
onClipEvent (load) {
  h = _parent.highlight;
  d = _parent.down;
  c = _parent.checkmark;
  _root.clicking=0;
  alive=0;
}
```

    All we're doing is initializing both `_root.clicking` and `alive` to `0`.

11. Now add two more events as follows:

```
onClipEvent(mouseDown){
  _root.clicking=1;
  if (onMe){
    alive=1;
    d.gotoAndStop(2);
    updateAfterEvent();
  }
}
onClipEvent(mouseUp){
  alive=0;
  _root.clicking=0;
  d.gotoAndStop(1);
  updateAfterEvent();
}
```

    The `mouseDown` event first sets `_root.clicking` to `1`. If the user is on top of this button (that is, `if(onMe)` is `true`), then `alive` is set to `1` so that we'll know this button is the one that's currently being clicked and that no other button can be clicked. In addition, the `d` clip (the Down state) jumps to frame 2; a call to `updateAfterEvent()` is thrown in to make the movie perform quickly.

    The `mouseUp` event basically clears everything out. Later we'll add more to this event to check whether the user actually let go *on* this clip. The variable `alive` is set to `0`, as is `_root.clicking`. Finally, the `d` clip (the Down state) jumps back to frame 1.

Now we can adjust the mouseMove event. We still want to calculate whether the mouse is onMe, but deciding whether to display frame 1 or frame 2 of the two clips h and d is more complex. We want the highlight to appear only when the user rolls over this clip; that is, when onMe==1 *and* the user is not already clicking anything else (_root.clicking==0) or when this is the clip the user is clicking (alive is 1). For the Down state (the d clip), we want to see this graphic only if the cursor is over this clip (onMe==1) *and* this clip is alive.

12. Instead of writing several complex if statements that decide to either gotoAndStop(1) or gotoAndStop(2) in the two clips h and d, we can consolidate by writing expressions for parameters in the two gotoAndStop() methods. Because we know we're going to go to either frame 1 or frame 2, we might as well write an expression that evaluates to 1 or 2 depending on the conditions set forth in the previous paragraph. Here's the new mouseMove event script that accomplished this task:

```
onClipEvent (mouseMove) {
  onMe=hitTest(_root._xmouse, _root._ymouse, 1 );
  h.gotoAndStop(onMe+(_root.clicking==0||alive));
  d.gotoAndStop(1+onMe*alive)
  updateAfterEvent();
}
```

//

This code actually looks a lot easier than it is! The first line is the same as before. The equation for the h clip's goto parameter can be summarized by saying "onMe plus a condition." When that condition is true and onMe is 1, we'll jump to frame 2. If either onMe or the condition is false, we'll jump to frame 1. If both onMe and the condition are false, we'll try jumping to frame 0, which has no effect. The condition is simply that *either* _root.clicking is already 0 *or* alive is 1. This equation fulfills the description of the conditions that preceded this step. With this revised script, we'll never see the highlight if we're not on the clip, but then we'll only see it when either alive is 1 or _root.clicking is already 0.

The d clip's goto parameter is a little different. We simply add 1 to the product of onMe and alive. If either onMe or alive (or both) are 0, that product is 0 and we end up on frame 1: 1 plus 0 is 1. If *both* onMe and alive are 1, we jump to frame 2: 1 plus 1*1 is 2. Again, you could have done this with a bunch of nested if statements, but the resulting code wouldn't have been pretty.

The three remaining tasks are to get the checkmark working, to find a way to let the button trigger anything we desire (that is, to make the button do something besides look pretty), and to write a script that determines which button or buttons are currently checked.

13. To get the checkmark working, place this script as the first line inside the `mouseUp` event:

    ```
    c.gotoAndStop(onMe*alive+(c._currentFrame==1));
    ```

    This code really shows that you can avoid the if-statement if you try. If both `onMe` and `alive` are `1`, I want to jump to the frame that the `c` clip is *not* on. Assume that both `onMe` and `alive` are `1`, which is required if this button is to become checked or unchecked. The `gotoAndStop()` parameter can be summarized as "1 plus a condition." If the condition is `true`, we're going to frame 2: `1` plus `1` is `2`. If the condition is `false`, we're going to frame 1. The condition is that `_currentFrame` is already `1`. So when `c`'s `_currentFrame` is 1, the `true` condition makes the clip jump to frame 2; when `c`'s `_currentFrame` is 2, the `false` condition makes the clip jump to frame 1. It's pretty sneaky, but it works great.

14. To make any instance of our Button symbol invoke a unique function, we can use the same technique we used in Workshop 4, "Creating a Horizontal Slider." We'll make the Button symbol a Smart Clip that accepts as a parameter the unique name that is sent to the `_root` level when the script calls a function there. This is sometimes called a "callback" function because the Smart Clip is sending an event, or calling a function, in the host movie.

    Here's the final version of the `mouseUp` script for the instance of the Circle symbol in the Button symbol:

    ```
    onClipEvent(mouseUp){
      if (onMe&&alive){
        _root.button(_parent.id,c._currentFrame==2);
      }
      c.gotoAndStop(onMe*alive+(c._currentFrame==1));
      alive=0;
      _root.clicking=0;
      d.gotoAndStop(1);
      updateAfterEvent();
    }
    ```

    Just the first if-statement is new; the rest of the code is just for your reference. If both `onMe` and `alive` are `true`, an about-to-be-written function called `button()` is called. We send two parameters: the value of the `id` variable set using the Clip Parameters panel after we make Button a Smart Clip. We have to precede this variable with `_parent` because clip parameters are part of the Button symbol, which is one level up from this script that's attached to the instance of Circle. The other parameter is a condition that's either `true` or `false`. Based on this parameter, the `button()` function knows whether the button being pressed is being selected or deselected.

15. Select the Button symbol in the Library and add the variable `id` to make this a Smart Clip.

16. In frame 1 of the main movie, type this function:

```
function button(whatID,way){
  if (whatID=="coffee"){
    trace("coffee was clicked "+way)
  }
  if (whatID=="tea"){
    trace("tea was clicked"+way)
  }
}
```

    This code assumes that you've used the Clip Parameters panel to specify `id`s for a couple instances of the Button Smart Clip. For example, perhaps you gave one an `id` of `"coffee"` and another an `id` of `"tea"`. You just need to add an if-statement for any other `id`s you want to trap. Naturally, you can put any script you want inside the if-statement to replace the `trace()` function used here.

At this point, the movie works great. I'd like to add just one more function to the main timeline: Wouldn't it be nice to have a way to determine which of the buttons are currently checked?

17. Instead of giving every instance of the Button symbol an instance name, we can write a homemade method for the Button Smart Clip that returns whether or not the button is checked. In the first keyframe of the Button symbol, place this function, which is equivalent to writing a method for Button:

```
function getCheck(){
  if (checkmark._currentFrame==2){
    return (1);
  }
}
```

    When called, this function returns `1` only if the `checkmark` instance is on frame 2; otherwise, nothing is returned. Notice that this function has to refer to the clip instance `checkmark` and not to `c` because we're outside the instance of Circle where we came up with the `c` variable.

18. In the main timeline, draw a rectangle and convert it to a Button symbol. Attach the following code to the instance of this new button:

```
on (release) {
  theList = "";
  for (i in _root) {
    answer = _root[i].getCheck();
```

```
      if (answer) {
        theList = theList +":"+_root[i].id;
      }
    }
    if (theList<>"") {
      trace (theList);
    } else {
      trace ("none");
    }
  }
```

You'll have to adapt this script to your own use. In this version of the code, all that's happening is that a string named `theList` is being built and then output through `trace()`. The for-in `_root` loop steps through every clip in the main timeline. For each clip, we try to assign the variable `answer` to the value returned from calling the `getCheck()` method. You should recognize from Chapter 5, "Programming Structures," the `_root[i]` technique of targeting clips dynamically. Only instances of our Button Smart Clip will return anything; and only true when `checkmark` is on frame 2. When the `if (answer) statement` is `true`, we'll concatenate the `theString` string we're building with the value of the `id` variable. We get the `id` variable by dynamically targeting a clip: `_root[i].id`. At the end, we either display the `theString` variable or the phrase `"none"` if `theString` is still `""`.

This workshop turned into a ton of work considering that all we did was replace the built-in Flash button feature. By the way, you can add all kinds of additional features such as audio or animation just by editing the second frame in the clips `highlight`, `checkmark`, and `down`. If you want a cursor to go with this button, you can use the custom cursor we built in Workshop 3, "Creating Custom Cursors," or you can simply place an invisible button inside the Button Smart Clip. You don't even have to place any scripts on this button because we've already got that covered.

This workshop really just gave us a chance to practice the knowledge we've previously acquired. However, writing expressions as concisely as we did here hasn't been explored much. Quite often, expressions like the ones we used for the `gotoAndStop()` parameters can be more powerful than if-statements. Plus, you can always show off to other programmers during a "who's got the most concise code contest," which is a common occurrence in the programming community.

{Part IIC }

Advanced Workshops

{Chapter 17 Workshop }

Offline Production

This workshop combines offline production with time-based animation. As discussed in Chapter 3, "The Programmer's Approach," offline production is any procedure that's executed only during authoring. The process of creating still frames from a video (as we did in Workshop 2, "Faking Video") can be considered offline production. For this workshop, we will build a data string and output it using the `trace()` command. The text that appears in the output window will then be taken to another file and used in a time-based animation sequence. Making one file that gathers data and another file that uses that data might seem like extra work, but you'll see that both files can be quite simple. The file that acquires data has one simple job (gathering data) and the file that uses that data has a simple job, too (using the data).

Think about how a player piano accepts a roll of paper that has holes punched out of it. Imagine now that there was a special piano that punched the holes as you played on the keyboard. We're going to build a special Flash movie that produces the data for an animation and another movie that uses the data. After the data is produced, the offline movie that produced it can be discarded or saved for future jobs because it will have done its job.

1. Create a new file and save it as `offline.fla`. Draw a circle and convert it to a Movie Clip called Circle. Also name the instance of the circle on the Stage `circle`.

2. Make a simple animation using the `circle` instance in the main timeline. For this example, I made a tween that follows a Motion Guide (Figure W17.1).

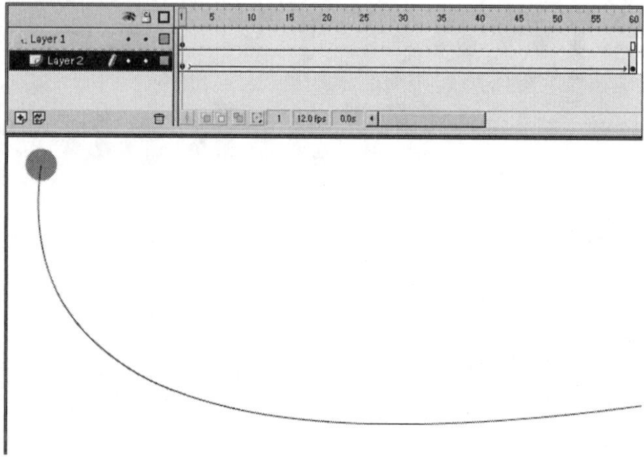

Figure W17.1 *Any animation will do, but I used a Motion Guide for this example.*

3. Create a new layer and draw a box in this layer. Convert the box to a Movie Clip. Attach the following script to the instance of this box:

```
onClipEvent (load) {
  xLocs = new Array();
  yLocs = new Array();
  flag=0;
}
onClipEvent (enterFrame) {
  xLocs.push(_root.circle._x);
  yLocs.push(_root.circle._y);
  if (_root._currentFrame==_root._totalFrames && flag==0){
    flag=1;
    trace("xLocs=["+xLocs.toString()+"]");
    trace("yLocs=["+yLocs.toString()+"]");
  }
}
```

The `load` event creates a couple of empty arrays to hold x and y locations, respectively. It also creates a variable `flag`, which will be set to `1` after all data has been gathered. In the `enterFrame` script, which executes once every time a new frame is displayed, the current _x location of the `circle` instance is added to the end of the `xLocs` array using the Array object's `push()` method. The same is done with the _y location in the `yLocs` array. The `if` statement checks a condition to see if both the `_currentFrame` is equal to `_totalFrames` and if `flag` is still `0`. If that condition is met, the `flag` variable is set to `1` so that string doesn't appear twice). Finally, a nicely formed string appears in the output window.

I say the string is nicely formed because it will be able to be used as-is to populate both array variables `xLocs` and `yLocs` in the second movie. The string includes three basic components: First, the variable name, an equal sign, and an open bracket: `xLocs=[`. Second, a string version of the array, which incidentally separates each value with a comma: `xLocs.toString()`. Finally, a closing bracket: `]`. Figure W17.2 shows what appears in my output window.

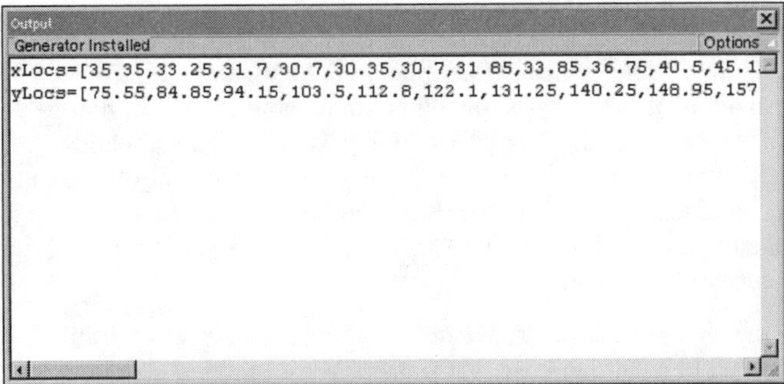

Figure W17.2 *The output window displays the string as we formatted it.*

4. Test this movie and copy the contents of the output window to the Clipboard. Return to the movie and open the Library window.

//

It turns out that if you have a lot of data in the output window—and I mean a *lot*—you may not be able to copy it all. I've noticed that this condition happens on the Macintosh more often than on Windows machines. Usually, you can get around this problem by using the output window's Save to File option. At the worst, you can shorten your animation for this workshop. In a real-world situation, you might have to gather the data in stages, maybe 100 frames at a time.

5. Create a new file called `online.fla`. Drag the Circle symbol from the old file's Library onto this file's Stage. Close the Library window.
6. Attach the following code to the instance of the Circle symbol in the new file:

```
onClipEvent (load) {
}
```

7. After the opening curly bracket, insert a return and then paste the text array declaration you copied from the other movie's output window in step 4. Add the last three lines of code shown here to the `load` event:

```
onClipEvent (load) {
  xLocs=[1,2,3,...];   //This is pasted in from the output window
  yLocs=[1,2,3,...];   //This is pasted in from the output window
  var fps=12;
  milPerFrame= (1000/fps);
  startTime=getTimer();
}
```

   The first two lines of the `load` event should contain the actual data, which will be much longer than what's shown here, assuming that your offline file had lots of frames. The last three lines should look familiar to you; they're from Workshop 15, "Developing Time-Based Animations." Here's a quick review: This code sets `fps` to the frame rate of our offline movie. The variable `milPerFrame` stands for "milliseconds per frame" and is calculated by dividing `fps` into 1000. Then the `startTime` variable is set to the current `getTimer()`.

8. For the `enterFrame` script, we just have to calculate which frame we're supposed to be on, and use that frame when extracting a value from the `xLocs` and `yLocs` arrays. Here's the script that accomplished that:

```
onClipEvent(enterFrame){
  now=getTimer();
  elapsed=now-startTime;
  frame=Math.floor(elapsed/milPerFrame);
  _x=xLocs[frame];
  _y=yLocs[frame];
}
```

   The code first determines the current time and puts that value in the `now` variable. Then the variable `elapsed` is assigned the *total* elapsed time. We are trying to determine which index of the array to use, so we need to know how long it's been since the start of the movie, not how long since the last time we entered this frame. After we know how much time has elapsed, we can set the `frame` variable to `elapsed` divided by `milPerFrame`. We use the `Math.floor()` method to ensure that we get a nice integer because we're about to use `frame` to indicate an index of an array. Then we just set `_x` and `_y` to the value found in the array `xLocs` or `yLocs`.

What's really cool about this workshop is that you can set the frame rate to anything you want in the online movie, and the animation will always play the same! Sure, if you lower the frame rate to something lower than what was used in the offline movie, the online movie will skip frames to keep on time, but that's a good thing.

Consider how you might use this technique to "record" your mouse movement. You could make another version of the offline movie that includes a dragable clip. As you drag the clip, the script records where the clip has been dragged. The only thing to remember is that you'll have to output all the variables gathered before you finish testing the movie. If you return to the authoring environment before you do that, all your variables will be reset.

The technique from this workshop is quite versatile. You can even use other programs to create the variables for the online version of the movie. Most animation tools have some sort of scripting capability to make that possible. You can even determine synch points in an audio file to use in Flash. When there's not a whole lot of data, you can just create the array of locations by hand. If it's just a simple animation, doing it by hand is easy. Actually, in the next workshop, "Creating a Dynamic Slide Presentation," we'll create a short list containing the location for a text bullet point that animates onto the Stage. No tweening necessary! Finally, realize that the array full of data doesn't have to be limited to x and y locations. You can automatically gather data about a clip's scale, alpha, or any other property.

{Chapter 18 Workshop }

Creating a Dynamic Slide Presentation

In this workshop, we'll explore two advanced topics: loading structured data in XML format and creating a dynamic screen layout on-the-fly. The project is to create a slide presentation that includes text and bullet points. Each "slide" is based on the same template, but the content of each will vary. In this project, every slide will have a title; a variable number of bullets; some "permanent content" such as the title, which stays on the screen while the slide is visible and the bullet points change; and some "post content" that appears after the last bullet point (Figure W18.1).

Structuring the data in XML format is only part of the task. We have to import that data, parse it, and then use it in an interactive Flash movie. When we're finished, the Flash movie will adapt itself to any XML file that has the format we design. With this approach, you can update the presentation simply by editing the XML file. This workshop isn't terribly intense, but surprisingly, designing the XML structure is probably the easiest part.

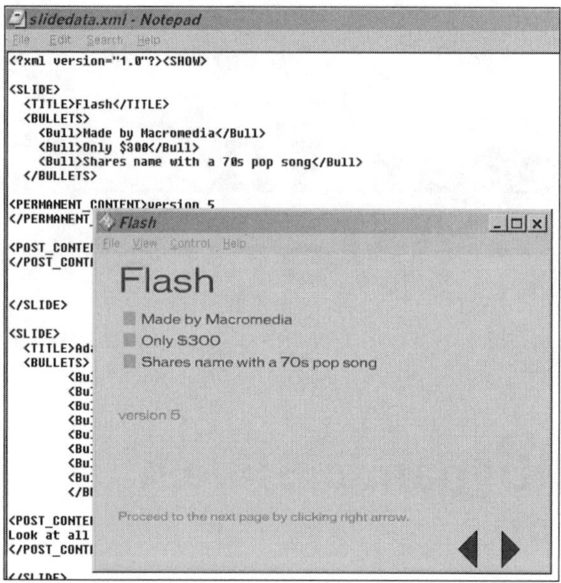

Figure W18.1 *In this workshop, we'll make a dynamic slide show that reads structured data from a file.*

1. First, let's structure the XML. For each slide, we need a title, permanent content, post content, and a variable number of bullets. So actually, the bullets tag will include subtags. Here's the starter format to consider:

```
<SLIDE>
  <TITLE>This is a title</TITLE>
  <BULLETS>
    <Bull>bullet one</Bull>
    <Bull>bullet two</Bull>
    <Bull>bullet three</Bull>
  </BULLETS>
  <PERMANENT_CONTENT>Stuff on the whole time.</PERMANENT_CONTENT>
  <POST_CONTENT>Stuff after last bullet.</POST_CONTENT>
</SLIDE>
```

   Notice that the "values" for `TITLE`, `PERMANENT_CONTENT`, and `POST_CONTENT` are all strings. The value for `BULLETS`, however, is a series of `BULL` children, which each have a value.

2. Use a text editor to create a file that contains several slides such as the one in step 1, but start the file with the following text on one line:

```
<?xml version="1.0"?><SHOW>
```

This code declares the file as XML and then starts the first tag SHOW. Each of our SLIDEs will be children of SHOW. After this line, place several SLIDEs that follow the form shown in step 1.

3. After the last </SLIDE>, insert a line that reads </SHOW>. This tag closes the <SHOW> tag that we opened in the first line.

4. Save the XML file as slidedata.xml. Details about how to create and format XML files can be found in Chapter 14, "Interfacing with External Data."

Now we need to load this XML data into Flash. In this workshop, we'll parse the XML data into Flash arrays. Although it's possible to load XML data and just leave it in its native XML format, we will store the data in arrays designed for easy access within Flash. We will modify the parsing script developed in Chapter 14, so the parsing won't be a ton of work. Besides, I want to remove all extraneous null nodes caused by white space in the XML file. Notice that there's no white space to contend with between the declaration and the first node, <SHOW>.

5. Open Flash and immediately save the default Flash file right next to your slidedata.xml file. Place some text onscreen that says "Loading...". In the first keyframe, place the following script:

```
stop();
loadFromFile();
function loadFromFile(){
  xmlObj = new XML;
  xmlObj.load("slidedata.xml");
  xmlObj.ignoreWhite=1;  //only post r41 player
  xmlObj.onLoad = parse;
}
```

The first line stops the timeline from proceeding. Then we call our loadFromFile() function. The function definition starts on line 3. Inside the function, we first instantiate the xmlObj variable as an XML object, which we'll use to hold all the XML data. The load() method is called and provided with the filename of our data file. By habit, I set the new ignoreWhite property to 1, but it turns out that the script that follows won't erroneously read white space as nodes, because we're going to load only the tags that match the ones we expect explicitly (TITLE, BULLET, and so on). (By the way, if you want to take advantage of the ignoreWhite property you'll want to ensure that the user's Flash player is later than revision 41.) The last line specifies that when the data has fully loaded, we will call the function parse(). That is, the onLoad property is assigned the name of a function that we still have to write.

6. The parse() function is a monster. It's actually a modified version of the script that's fully explained in Chapter 14. As we progress, I'll point out some of the differences between this version and the original. For now, this script goes in the first keyframe:

```
function parse(){
mainNode = xmlObj.firstChild;

//MAIN NODE's NAME  ("SHOW"):
mainName=mainNode.nodeName;
  if (mainName.toUpperCase()<>"SHOW"){
    //not the correct format
    return;
  }

  //ARRAY Of Children in MAIN (all the slides):
  childrenOfMain=new Array();
  childrenOfMain= mainNode.childNodes;

  allSlides=new Array();

  for(i=0;i<=childrenOfMain.length;i++){
    if (childrenOfMain[i].nodeName<>null){
      delete thisSlide; //from last time
      thisSlide=new Object();
      //thisSlide's form:
      //title:string,bullets:array,perm:string,post:string

      //THIS CHILD's XML:
      thisChild = childrenOfMain[i];
      //nodesOfThisChild is an ARRAY OF NODES in THIS SLIDE
      nodesOfThisChild = thisChild.childNodes;
      for(j=0;j<nodesOfThisChild.length;j++){
        //THIS TAG'S XML
        thisTag = nodesOfThisChild[j];

        if (thisTag.nodeName.toUpperCase()=="TITLE"){
          thisSlide.title=thisTag.firstChild.nodeValue;
        }//if
        if (thisTag.nodeName.toUpperCase()=="PERMANENT_CONTENT"){
          thisSlide.perm=thisTag.firstChild.nodeValue;
        }//if
        if (thisTag.nodeName.toUpperCase()=="POST_CONTENT"){
          thisSlide.post=thisTag.firstChild.nodeValue;
        }//if

        if (thisTag.nodeName.toUpperCase()=="BULLETS"){
          //THIS BULLET's CHILDREN (BULLs)
          bullets=thisTag.childNodes;
          all=new Array();
          for(k=0; k<bullets.length;k++){
            if (bullets[k].nodeName<>null){
              all.push(bullets[k].firstChild.nodeValue);
            }//if
            thisSlide.bullets=all;
          }//for
        }//if
      }//for
```

```
    allSlides.push(thisSlide);
    }//if
  }//for

  _root.gotoAndStop(2);
}  //function
```

This function differs from the parse() function in Chapter 14 in two main ways: In this version, we check for explicit nodeNames expected, instead of nodeNames that are simply not null. The second way this version differs from the original version is that the hierarchy in this example is one level deeper to accommodate the BULLs in each BULLET tag. In this function, the primary way to determine that we've found a legitimate node (that is, not a null node) is by comparing the nodeName to an expected value. For example, the following lines from the function check nodeNames to see whether they match what we expect:

```
if (mainName.toUpperCase()<>"SHOW"){
if (thisTag.nodeName.toUpperCase()=="TITLE"){
if (thisTag.nodeName.toUpperCase()=="BULLETS"){
```

In Chapter 14, we just checked to see whether the name was "not null," as in nodeName<>null. The version of the function we show here is limited to just these expected tag names. Because we don't know how many BULLs are in each slide, we do use the "not null" technique in the preceding function, but just for parsing the BULLs. You can see that in this line:

```
if (bullets[k].nodeName<>null{.
```

The main thing that's happening in this function is that when we find a nodeName that matches what we expect, we extract the nodeValue of the firstChild of that tag and place it in a property of a custom object (or "associative array"). Consider this portion of the preceding code:

```
if (thisTag.nodeName.toUpperCase()=="TITLE"){
  thisSlide.title=thisTag.firstChild.nodeValue;
}
```

If the condition is met, a property called title inside our custom object variable thisSlide is assigned the node value for the first child in this tag, which is the text for this TITLE. After we set all the properties of thisSlide, we stick thisSlide on the end of another array allSlides, as specified by the line towards the bottom of the script that reads allSlides.push(thisSlide). In the end, the allSlides array will have as many items as there are slides. The value of each index is a custom object with four properties: title, perm, post, and bullets. Each of the values for those four properties are strings, except for bullets which is an array that has as many items as there are BULLS in that particular slide. See the visualization of the array's structure shown in Figure W18.2.

```
AllSlides[

{ title:"txt", perm:"txt", post:"txt", bullets:["a","b","c"] },
{ title:"txt", perm:"txt", post:"txt", bullets:["a","b","c"] },
{ title:"txt", perm:"txt", post:"txt", bullets:["a","b","c"] },
{ title:"txt", perm:"txt", post:"txt", bullets:["a","b","c"] },
      ]
```

Figure W18.2 *Visualizing the structure of the* `allSlides` *array will help when we need to extract portions of the array.*

The other difference between this function and the `parse()` function shown in Chapter 14, "Interfacing with External Data," is in the hierarchy of the structure. In this version of the function, we have a `SHOW` with several `SLIDE` children. The children of the `SLIDE`s each have a value. However, this example goes one level deeper because one of `SLIDE`'s children, `BULLETS`, has its own children: several `BULL`s. The portion of the code that deals with this fact is shown here for explanation:

```
if (thisTag.nodeName.toUpperCase()=="BULLETS"){
  //THIS BULLET's CHILDREN (BULLs)
  bullets=thisTag.childNodes;
  all=new Array();
  for(k=0; k<bullets.length;k++){
    if (bullets[k].nodeName<>null){
      all.push(bullets[k].firstChild.nodeValue);
    }//if
    thisSlide.bullets=all;
  }//for
}//if
```

Because the `thisSlide.bullets` property is going to contain an array, we have to gather each item for that array. When we determine that the `nodeName` matches `"BULLETS"`, we enter the if-statement and then create two arrays: `bullets`, which will contain all the `childNodes` of `thisTag` (that is, all the `BULL`s), and `all`, which will contain all the `BULL` values that we find (that is, the text for each individual `BULL`). Then we loop through all the `BULL` items in the `bullets` array with a for-loop, and if `nodeName` is not `null`, we `push()` the `nodeValue` of the `firstChild` in `bullets[k]` into the array `all`. After the loop, we just assign `thisSlide.bullets` to the whole `all` array.

//

It's important to reassign `all` to a `new Array()` for every `SLIDE`. Otherwise, we'd be just adding `BULL`s to the `all` array from the last `SLIDE`. The same goes for the `thisSlide` object that is reinitialized for every `SLIDE` with the `thisSlide=new Object()` line, way up on top.

Finally, notice that when all the data has loaded, the `gotoAndStop(2)` script executes.

All this work to structure and parse the XML data is worth it. For one thing, you can use this slide presentation even if the data changes. As you're about to see, it's easy to do the rest of the work in Flash because we have a very nice array, `allSlides`.

7. Insert a blank keyframe into frame 2 by pressing F7.
8. On the Stage, create three Dynamic Text fields, each of which is associated with one of the following variables: `curTitle`, `curPerm`, `curPost` (Figure W18.3).

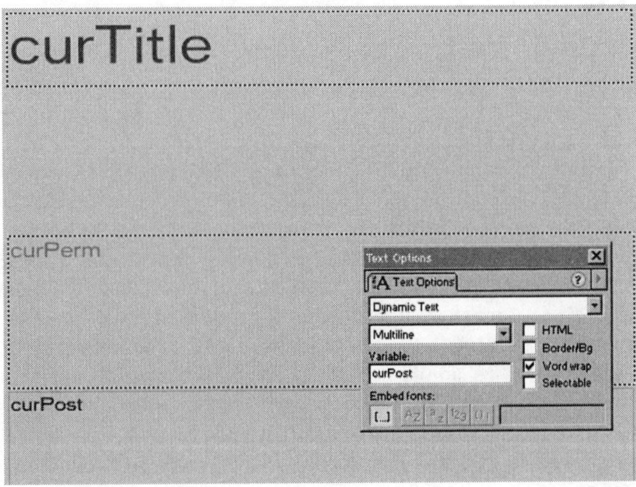

Figure W18.3 *We use three Dynamic Text fields to display the current values of three variables.*

9. Create a triangle-shaped button and make two instances of it—one pointing left and one pointing right. Place the following script on the right-pointing button instance:

```
on (release, keyPress "<Right>") {
  go(1);
}
```

For the left-pointing button, use this script:

```
on (release, keyPress "<Left>") {
  go(-1);
}
```

Now we just have to write the `go()` function that assigns the three variables `curTitle`, `curPerm`, and `curPost`. We'll worry about the physical bullet points later.

10. In the second keyframe, place the following script:

```
curPage=0;
go(0);
function go(dir){
  if ((curPage+dir>allSlides.length-1) || curPage+dir<0){
    return;
  }
  curPage=curPage+dir;
  curObj=allSlides[curPage];
  curTitle=curObj.title;
  curPerm=curObj.perm;
  curPost=curObj.post;
}
```

The first line initializes our `curPage` variable. I figure we'll start on page 0 since we want the data from the `0` index of `allSlides`. Then we call the `go()` function but supply `0` for a parameter so that we won't move forward or backward. Inside the `go()` function, the first if-statement determines whether we're paging past the end or beginning of the file by seeing whether `curPage` plus the `dir` parameter is not greater than the length of `allSlides` or less than `0`. Actually, we check to see whether it's higher than `allSlides.length-1`, figuring that if `allSlides` had `5` items (a `length` of `5`, or `5 SLIDES`), the last index would be `4`, or `length-1`. If the condition is `true`, we simply `return`. If you want to get fancy, you can hide the forward or back button when appropriate by placing each one in a clip, as we did in Workshop 5, "Building a Slide Show." After we get past the if-statement, `curPage` is incremented or decremented depending on the value of `dir`. Then we assign to `curObj` the value in the `curPage` index of the `allSlides` array. This step makes extracting individual properties of that item easier in the next three lines because we won't have to say `allSlides[curPage]` everywhere `curObj` is used. The last three lines show how easy it is to find the values in our array. The three onscreen variables display the correct strings.

When you test this out, it works. Of course, the bullets aren't appearing yet, and the post text that's supposed to wait until the last bullet has appeared isn't there yet.

11. To add the bullet functionality, we need a couple more pieces. Because we don't know how many bullets may appear on a slide, we'll make one Movie Clip and use the `attachMovie()` method to create as many instances as necessary. Create a wide Dynamic Text field and associate it with the variable `curBull`. Draw a box or circle as your bullet-point graphic and place it to the left of the Dynamic Text field.

12. Select both the `curBull` Dynamic Text field and the bullet graphic and convert them to a Movie Clip named Animated.
13. Select the instance of the Animated clip and convert it to a Movie Clip called Bullet. It is *this* clip that will be attached using `attachMovie()`.
14. Double-click the instance of the Bullet symbol so that we can edit its contents. Use the Info panel to position the instance of the Animated symbol so that its top-left corner is centered in the Bullet symbol (Figure W18.4).

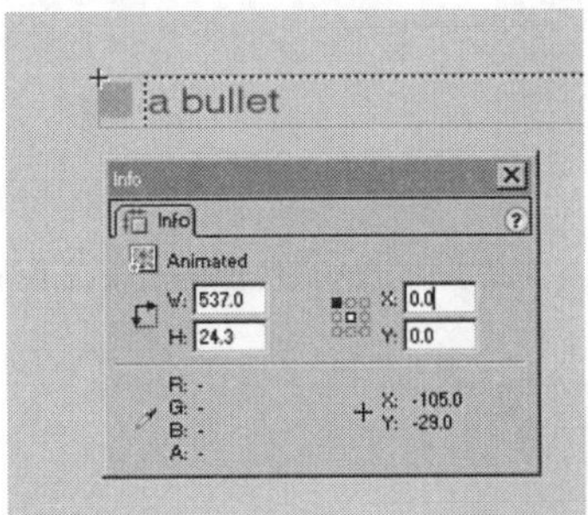

Figure W18.4 *Use the Info panel to adjust the top-left corner of the clip contained inside the Bullet symbol.*

15. Give the instance of the Animated symbol inside Bullet the instance name `anim`. We're going to need to set the value of `anim.curBull` if we want the text of the bullets to appear in the Dynamic Text field.
16. Back in the main timeline, let's gather a few locations so that the instance of Bullet can zoom onto the Stage. First, position the symbol of Bullet in the uppermost vertical location, right underneath the Title. Use the Info panel and note the y position of its center (Figure W18.5).
17. Copy the Bullet symbol instance and Paste in Place. Use the arrow keys to nudge the second instance of the Bullet symbol down until the spacing between the bullets looks appropriate. Use the Info panel to note the difference in y position of this second instance and write it on a piece of paper (Figure W18.6).
18. Select either instance of Bullet and move it off to the left side of the Stage. Note `x` for a series of about five positions that might occur if the instance of the Bullet symbol were zooming on the Stage. You can even make the Bullet go a little past its final location to suggest that it is settling in place with a little shake. This is the same offline process we will use in Workshop 20, "Writing JavaScript Inter-Movie Communications."

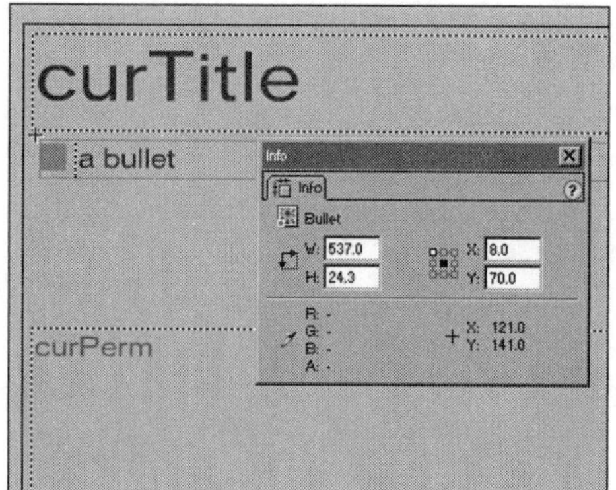

Figure W18.5 *We gather locations that are used in a scripted animation sequence.*

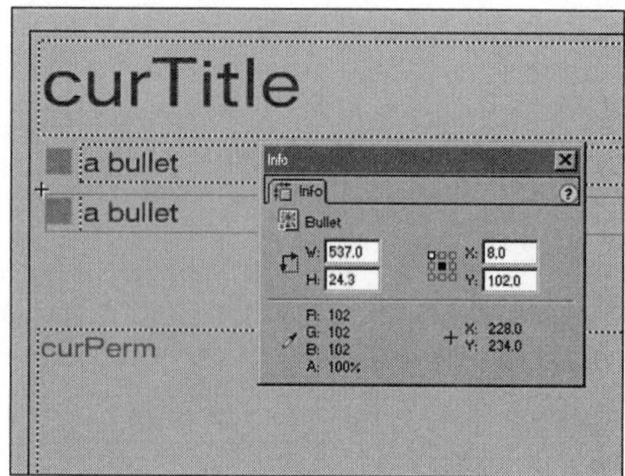

Figure W18.6 *We need to determine the vertical spacing between multiple bullets.*

19. Double-click to edit the Bullet symbol and attach the following script to the `anim` instance found inside Bullet:

```
onClipEvent (load) {
  myLocs=[0,-120,8,40,0,8];
  curSpot=0;
  moving=true;
  nextUpdate=getTimer();
}
onClipEvent(enterFrame){
  if (moving && nextUpdate<getTimer()){
    nextUpdate=getTimer() + 10;
    _parent._x=myLocs[curSpot];
    curSpot++;
    if (curSpot>myLocs.length-1){
      moving=false
```

```
      }
    }
  }
```

This script makes a time-based animation play once. Specifically, in the `load` event, we save the coordinates that you just gathered by placing them in an array called `myLocs`. Then `curSpot` and `moving` are initialized, and `nextUpdate` is set to the current `getTimer()`.

The `enterFrame` script starts playing the animation as long as the condition in the if-statement is `true`: if `moving` is `true` and the current `getTimer()` is greater than `nextUpdate`. Because both of these conditions are `true` at the beginning, `nextUpdate` is set to the current `getTimer()` plus `10`. You can change `10` to a higher number to create a longer delay between frames. The `_x` property of `_parent` is then set to the `curSpot` item in the `myLocs` array; because `curSpot` starts at `0`, the first item in the array is used. Notice that we have to position the `_x` of the `_parent`, which is the Bullet symbol, because it was the instance of Bullet that we placed on the Stage when we gathered the numbers in `myLocs`. Then we increment `curSpot`. The last if-statement simply checks to see whether we've run through all the items in the `myLocs` array, in which case it sets `moving` to `false` and the animation stops.

20. Back in the main timeline, delete all instances of the Bullet symbol. The code we just wrote is safe inside the master symbol.

21. We need a function that will instantiate an instance of Bullet on-the-fly; let's use `attachMovie()`. However, the method requires that the Movie Clip has its linkage set. Select the `Bullet` symbol in the Library and set its Linkage Properties to the Export this Symbol option. Give it the identifier name `bullet` (Figure W18.7).

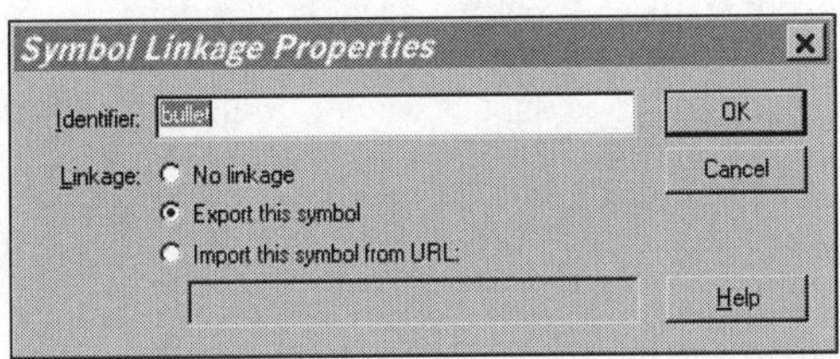

Figure W18.7 *Before we can use the* `attachMovie()` *method, we need to set the linkage and give the Bullet symbol an identifier.*

22. Place this function in frame 2's keyframe:

```
function doBullet(){
  if (curBullNum <curObj.bullets.length){
    curBullNum ++;
    attachMovie("bullet", String("bullet_"+curBullNum), curBullNum);
```

```
    _root["bullet_"+curBullNum].anim.curBull=
➥curObj.bullets[curBullNum -1];
    _root["bullet_"+curBullNum]._x=-9999;
    _root["bullet_"+curBullNum]._y=70+(( curBullNum -1)*32);
  }else{
    curPost=curObj.post;
  }
}
```

This `doBullet()` function first displays all the bullets. When all the bullets have displayed, it sets the variable `curPost`, which is the Dynamic Text field used to contain the post content. Let's step through this function. The if-statement first checks to see whether the variable `curBullNum` is less than the total number of bullets in this slide (the `length` of the array in the `bullets` property of the `curObj`). We'll have to initialize `curBullNum` to `0` in the `go()` function when we touch up that function next. Inside the if-statement, we increment `curBullNum` and then call the `attachMovie()` method. We attach the Bullet symbol, using its identifier of `"bullet"`, and give it the instance name `bullet_1`, where `1` is the value of `curBullNum`. The next time, the instance will be named `bullet_2`. The level number of the attached clip is simply `curBullNum`, just so that we know it's a unique level number. Next we set the `curBull` variable inside `anim` inside the newly instantiated clip. The line begins `_root["bullet_"+curBullNum].anim.curBull=...` because we want to target the clip dynamically; we can't just say `bullet_1.anim.curBull` because this script has to work for any clip, `bullet_2`, `bullet_3`, or whatever. We set the value of this `curBull` Dynamic Text field the same way we set the rest of the onscreen text. However, instead of saying `curObj.bullets` (which would give us the whole array of bullets), we say `curObj.bullets[curBullNum -1]`, which returns just the item in the index that's one lower than `curBullNum`. Remember that we've already incremented `curBullNum`, so it starts at `1`; but we need the `0` index first. We set the `_x` property of our new clip to `-9999` with the statement `_root["bullet_"+curBullNum]._x=-9999` (way off to the left). Then we need the starting y position and the value of the spacing between the bullets that we gathered back in step 17 to position the `_y` property correctly. In the code `_root["bullet_"+curBullNum]._y=70+(( curBullNum -1)*32)`, the initial y position is `70` and the spacing is `32`. Replace these values with the ones you found in step 17. This formula comes up in both Workshop 9, "Creating a Currency-Exchange Calculator," and Workshop 19, "Creating JavaScript Cookies."

23. We just have a little more touching up to do before we're finished. In the `go()` function, change the line that reads `curPost=curObj.post` to read as follows:

```
curPost="";
```

This statement simply clears the `curPost` text field and lets the `doBullet()` function take care of it.

24. We have to add a couple things to the `go()` function. You can place the following script anywhere within the `go()` function as long as it's after the if-statement. First, add a line that initializes the `curBullNum` variable:

```
curBullNum=0
```

25. Add the following for-loop to remove as many `bullet_x` instances that happen to have been instantiated:

```
for (i in _root){
  if (i.substr(0,7)=="bullet_"){
    this[i].removeMovieClip();
  }
}
```

This loop removes any clip instances that have an instance name starting `"bullet_"`, the same starting name we gave to each bullet clip instantiated in the `doBullet()` function. The idea is that when you click the arrow buttons, the `go()` function jumps you to the next slide. No bullets and no post text appear. Now we have to add a button that calls the `doBullet()` function.

26. In frame 2, draw a large rectangle over most of the screen. Select and convert the shape to a button called Invisible. Make this an invisible button by moving its Over state to the Hit frame as we've done so many times before.

27. Attach the following script to the invisible button instance:

```
on (release, keyPress "<Enter>") {
  doBullet();
}
```

Now you should be able to run the presentation. Click the invisible button or press Enter to view each slide in succession; press the arrow buttons to jump forward or back to a new slide.

You can add some nice touches by hiding the arrow buttons or the invisible button by first placing them inside clips, as you learned to do in Workshop 5.

This workshop was a lot of work, but realize that you can use the results of it over and over. Make a giant XML file full of whatever data or bullet points you want. You can also add other elements such as pictures and sound to this slide presentation. Generally, the work to make this project even better lies in good template design: You want something that's usable, expandable, and visually appealing.

{Chapter 19 Workshop }

Creating JavaScript Cookies

A common reaction to a long, drawn-out Flash introduction is to quickly click the Skip Intro button. Actually, the site `www.skipintro.com` exaggerates the issue. But it doesn't have to be this way: You can use a JavaScript cookie to store information about a user's activities and preferences and then retrieve the cookie later to adjust your Flash actions to that specific user.

Using cookies means that you can resist gratuitous animations or at least only show the user an introduction animation once. For example, you can write a cookie the first time a user views your introduction. For subsequent visits, the cookie can direct you to skip right past the intro so that the user doesn't even have the opportunity to click Skip Intro—you make that decision for him. In this workshop, we'll use a Flash movie to let the user specify his or her language of preference; we'll store that selection in a JavaScript cookie. If that user ever revisits your site, the preferred language will be restored by the cookie.

There's very little work to do in Flash, as you'll see:

1. In order for JavaScript to successfully "talk" to Flash the Flash movie needs to be entirely downloaded. Even though the first conversation between Flash and JavaScript will initiate from Flash, we still want to be certain the movie is entirely downloaded, so we'll just build a simple loading screen. In frame 1, place text that says "loading…" on stage. Also, place the following script in the keyframe:

```
if (getBytesLoaded()==getBytesTotal()){
  gotoAndStop(3);
}
```

This script will only jump the user to frame 3 when the movie is entirely downloaded.

2. Insert a keyframe in frame 2 and place the script: `gotoAndPlay(1)` so that if the user didn't jump ahead to frame 3, they will instead jump back to frame 1, where the download checking script will execute again.
3. Insert a keyframe in frame 3 and draw a button and create six instances of the button, stacked vertically and evenly spaced (Figure W19.1).

Figure W19.1 *Draw six buttons spaced evenly apart.*

4. On top of each button, place some text to specify a language choice. If this weren't a workshop, you'd actually spell out the name of each language *in* the native language—that is, you'd write *Español* instead of *Spanish*. But this is just an exercise, so don't waste your time fumbling for your Swahili dictionary.
5. To each button, attach a version of this script:

```
on (release) {
  setLanguage(1);
}
```

Arbitrarily establish that the top button is language 1, the second button is language 2, and so on. You must change the `setLanguage()` parameter for each button accordingly. Using a code number for each language will prove to be infinitely easier down the road.

6. Place the following code in the first keyframe of the movie:

```
getURL ("javascript:getCookie();");
language=Number(language);
function setLanguage(whatNum){
  language=whatNum;
  getURL("javascript:setCookie();");
}
```

The first line executes a JavaScript function called `getCookie()`. This yet-to-be-written function reads the current value for `language`, if there is one, and sets the `language` variable in our Flash movie. Because all Flash variables set from JavaScript are in string form, the second line simply converts `language` back to a number. The `setLanguage()` function that is called from all the buttons first sets `language` to the parameter received and then calls another function called `setCookie()`. This yet-to-be-written function will determine the current value of the Flash variable `language` and save that in a cookie.

7. We'll come back to Flash in a few minutes, so for now, save the movie and publish it. Open the `.html` file in a text editor so that we can edit some JavaScript.

8. Find the `OBJECT` portion of the HTML file and make sure that there's an item that reads `id=`. Either edit the text to read `id=flash` or add this item if it doesn't exist (Figure W19.2).

```
<HTML>
<HEAD>
<TITLE>working</TITLE>
</HEAD>
<BODY bgcolor="#FFFFFF">
<OBJECT classid="clsid:D27CDB6E-AE6D-11cf-96B8-444553540000"
 codebase="http://download.macromedia.com/pub/shockwave/cabs/
 WIDTH=300 HEIGHT=300 id=flash>
 <PARAM NAME=movie VALUE="working.swf"> <PARAM NAME=quality V
</OBJECT>
</BODY>
</HTML>
```

Figure W19.2 *Make sure that the* `id` *parameter is assigned within the* `OBJECT` *tag.*

9. Find the `EMBED` portion of the HTML file and make sure there's an item that reads `swLiveConnect=TRUE`. This will ensure that Netscape lets Flash interact with JavaScript. (Figure W19.3).

```
<EMBED swLiveConnect=TRUE src="Movie1.swf" quality=high bgcolor=#FFI
```

Figure W19.3 *The* `swLiveConnect=TRUE` *tag is necessary for the* `EMBED` *portion of the HTML.*

10. After the `</HEAD>` tag and before the `<BODY>` tag, type the following text:

```
<SCRIPT LANGUAGE=JavaScript>
<!--
//

//-->
</SCRIPT>
```

All the JavaScript we will write in this workshop will go between the first `//` and the last `//`.

11. In the JavaScript skeleton you just began, add the following function:

```
function flashObj() {
  if(navigator.appName=="Netscape") {
    return document.embeds[0]
  } else {
    return window['flash']
  }
}
```

As you learned in Chapter 14, "Interfacing with External Data," the `flashObj()` function is how we'll target the embedded Flash object.

12. Add this `setCookie()` function to the evolving JavaScript, too:

```
function setCookie(){
  var cookie_string=
➥"language="+flashObj().GetVariable('language')+ ";";
  var date_string = new Date("March 31, 2065");
  date_string = date_string.toGMTString();
  cookie_string = cookie_string + "expires=" + date_string;
  document.cookie = cookie_string;
}
```

The first line initializes the local variable `cookie_string` by concatenating `"language="` with the value of the Flash movie's `language` variable. The value for `language` is ascertained by using the `GetVariable()` method of the `Flash` object in JavaScript. Next, a local variable `date_string` is assigned to a date that's way in the future, in the form of a JavaScript `date` data type. The next line converts the date to a string using the `toGMTString()` method. Then `cookie_string` is concatenated with `"expires="` plus the `date_string`. Finally, the `cookie` property of this Web page is assigned the value of the string we just built.

Now that we have the process of setting the cookie out of the way, we can learn how to restore the cookie. As you recall, the first thing the Flash movie script does is try to `getCookie()`.

13. Place this `getCookie()` function in with the rest of the JavaScript:

```
function getCookie() {
  if(document.cookie == ''){
    return;
  }else{
    flashObj().SetVariable('language',
➥unescape(getCookieValue('language')));
  }
}
```

This code first checks to see whether the `cookie` property of this document is empty. If it is, it returns out of this function. If the cookie is not empty, it uses the `SetVariable()` method to set the `language` variable inside the Flash movie. The first parameter of `SetVariable()` is the variable name `'language'`, the second parameter contains the new value. In the preceding code example, however, you can see that the second parameter of `SetVariable()` is a call to another function called `getCookieValue()`. We'll write that function in a minute, but realize that the `cookie` property of a document can include several variables, each of which has a name and a value. You have to strip out just the value for the variable you want, which is what the `getCookieValue()` function will do.

14. Place this `getCookieValue()` function in with the rest of the JavaScript:

```
function getCookieValue(name){
  var wholeCookie = document.cookie;
  var firstChar = wholeCookie.indexOf(name);
  if(firstChar != -1) {
    firstChar = name.length + 1;
    var lastChar= wholeCookie.indexOf(';', firstChar);
    if(lastChar == -1){
      lastChar= wholeCookie.length;
    }
    return wholeCookie.substring(firstChar, lastChar);
  } else {
    return false;
  }
}
```

This function accepts for a parameter the `name` of the variable in the cookie that you are trying to find. We're passing `'language'` when we call this function, but we want the *value* of that variable. The first line sets `wholeCookie` equal to the entire `cookie` property of the document. The second line assigns to the variable `firstChar` the index in the `wholeCookie` string where `name` (that is, `'language'`) first occurs. The JavaScript `indexOf()` method is identical to Flash's version of that method, which was discussed in Chapter 9, "Selecting Text, Trapping Keys, and Manipulating Strings." If `firstChar` is not `-1`, which means that the first character wasn't found and we'd just return `false`, we execute line four in which we set `lastChar` to `1` more than the length of `name` (`'language'`). Because the cookie string looks like `"language=1;"`, we want to take the part right *after* the characters `'language'`, plus `1` more for the equal sign. Then we set `lastChar` to the index of `";"` but provide the optional parameter `firstChar`, which specifies where to start searching. We don't really need the first instance of `";"`—we're looking for the first one *after* `firstChar`. In case `lastChar` is `-1`, that is, `if (lastChar==-1)`—meaning that no semicolon was found—we just figure that `lastChar` is equal to the length of the whole cookie. We actually don't need to worry about this possibility because we were careful to put a semicolon at the end when we wrote the cookie. However, this `if` statement makes the function a little more versatile. Finally, the line `return wholeCookie. substring(firstChar,lastChar)` extracts just the value portion of the desired variable name and returns it.

At this point, the script actually works, but you might not know it. We need the Flash movie to display the current value for `language`. We should be able to set a language, restart the browser, return to the same page, and notice that the language is where we left it. The Flash movie itself gives us no indication that the JavaScript is working. By the way, if you want, you can throw an `alert()` command, which is the JavaScript equivalent to Flash's `trace()` statement, at the end of the `setCookie()` and `getCookie()` functions, like this: `alert(document.cookie.toString())`.

15. Back in Flash, let's make a highlight that points to the current language button. Draw a triangle that can point to a button. Convert it to a Movie Clip called Pointer. Position the pointer to the left of one button so that it can be moved up and down to point to other buttons (Figure W19.4).

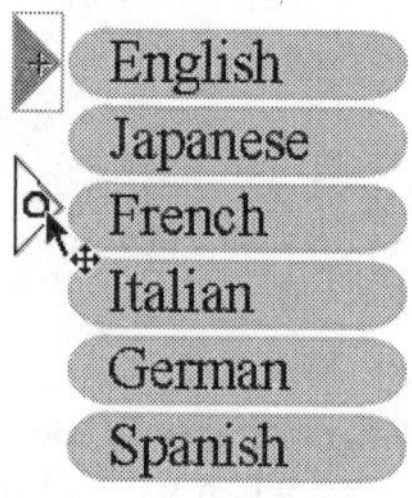

Figure W19.4 *The Pointer symbol should be able to point to any button in the list simply by changing its _y property.*

16. Move the Pointer clip all the way up and off the Stage while keeping its x position constant. Hold the Shift key when you drag to do this. The following script changes only the _y property of the clip:

```
onClipEvent (enterFrame) {
  if (_root.language<>0){
    _y = 50+((_root.language-1)*30);
    }
}
```

This script repositions the instance of Pointer any time `language` is not 0 (`if(language<>0)`). The formula you see here is based on my layout: The _y position of the instance of Pointer must be at `50` when it's pointing to language 1. The language 2 button is `30` pixels lower; each subsequent language button is `30` pixels lower than the one above it. This is the same basic formula that we used to position the highlight in Workshop 9, "Creating a Currency-Exchange Calculator": `minimum + (newInteger-1)*spacing`.

Now when you test this movie in a browser, the pointer will initially appear off-screen. After you set a language, the pointer will always reposition itself when you return to the Web page.

Perhaps the best part of this workshop is the realization that most of what you've learned in this book is applicable to JavaScript.

{Chapter 20 Workshop }

Writing JavaScript Inter-Movie Communications

We know that JavaScript can talk to Flash and that Flash can talk to JavaScript. But what about one Flash movie talking to another Flash movie? Even though it can't be done directly, it's easy to do. We can simply have one movie tell JavaScript to tell the other movie something. Sort of like two siblings who refuse to talk to each other directly: "Mom, tell my sister that I'm not talking to her."

The two Flash movies in this workshop will send messages to each other. The end result is not a particularly interesting-looking Web page, but it will give you a rather good understanding of what's possible. I once worked on a Web page that contained many separate frames, including a small Flash navigation control movie. I wanted a lot of audio for both background music and incidental rollover sound effects. But because the different pages within the site needed to reload the Flash movie, the same controller would reload and cause the background music to pause. To fix that problem, I kept all the audio in a separate Flash movie that never reloaded. So I had the navigation Flash movie and its buttons telling JavaScript to tell the audio Flash movie when to play the sounds. It was only a little bit of extra work, but it meant that the audio never paused between pages.

In this workshop, we won't be doing anything fancy except proving to ourselves that we can get Flash movies to talk to each other through JavaScript.

1. In Flash, start a new file and save it as `left.fla`. Select Modify, Movie and set the dimensions so they are taller than wider, such as 200 wide by 400 tall.
2. On the Stage, place some static text that reads *Left Side*.
3. Create an Input Text field and associate it with the variable `message`.
4. Copy and paste this Input Text field and change it to a Dynamic Text field. The user will be able to edit the first field, but the second field will be used to display values. Both are associated with the same variable name (which won't be an issue when we nest one inside a clip).
5. Select the Dynamic Text field and convert it to a Movie Clip. Give the instance on the Stage the name `received`. Now we really have two variables: `_root.message` and `_root.received.message` (Figure W20.1).

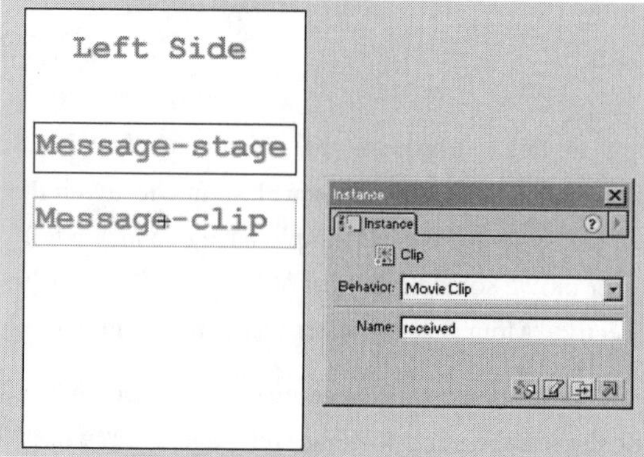

Figure W20.1 *In this movie, there's an Input Text field on the Stage and one inside a clip.*

6. In the main timeline, draw a shape for a button, such as an arrow shape that points to the right. Convert this graphic to a button.

Now we can do some scripting. The idea is that the user will be able to type into the input field and then click the button. This action will tell JavaScript to take the value from the `message` Input Text field and set the `message` variable in the *other* Flash movie. We'll build the other movie, which we'll call `right.fla`, in a minute, but there's so much identical stuff in these two movies, including the scripts, that we'll finish `left.fla` and do a Save As to create `right.fla`.

7. Attach this script to the button:

```
on (release) {
  getURL ("javascript:fromLeft();");
}
```

This script simply invokes a custom yet-to-be-written JavaScript function called `fromLeft()`.

8. Now we can do a little bit of offline production. Position the `received` clip off the Stage to the right without changing its vertical location. Use the Info panel to note the `x` position of the clip when it's off the Stage. Now move the clip so that it's halfway on the Stage; note this `x` position. Move the clip to its final resting place and note this `x` position. Move the clip a little bit too far to the left and note the `x` position. Move the clip back so that it's just to the right of its final position and note the `x` position. Finally, place the clip where it should land and note the `x` position. You should have about six coordinates written down. Use those numbers when you customize the following script which you should attach to the instance of `received`:

```
onClipEvent (load) {
  message="";
  lastMessage="";
  moveLocs=[260,180,100,90,110,100]
  moving=false;
  _x=-1000;
}
```

Basically, this script clears the `message` in the Dynamic Text field and clears another variable called `lastMessage`, which is used to monitor when `message` has changed. The `moveLocs` array is full of the x coordinates you just gathered; replace the values you see here with your own numbers, just as you did in Workshop 17, "Offline Production." The variable `moving` is set to `false` and the _x property is set to some location offscreen. Most of these variables will make more sense when you see the `enterFrame` script in the next step.

9. Add the following script to the `received` instance:

```
onClipEvent(enterFrame){
  if (message<>lastMessage){
    lastMessage=message;
    moving=true;
    spot=0;
  }
  if (moving){
    _x=moveLocs[spot];
    spot++;
    if (spot==moveLocs.length){
```

```
            moving=false;
        }
    }
}
```

The first `if` statement checks to see whether `message` has changed recently by checking whether it's equal to `lastMessage`. If it's different, `message` must have changed, and the next three lines of code are executed. The `lastMessage` variable is updated with the new value of `message`, `moving` is set to `true`, and `spot` is set to `0`. The second `if` statement is entered only if `moving` is `true`. If `moving` is `true`, then the `_x` property is set to one of the values in the `moveLocs` array; specifically, the value in the index `spot`, which was just set to `0`. Then `spot` is incremented. The next `if` statement checks to see whether `spot` has reached the end of the `moveLocs` array; if it has, `moving` is set back to `false`.

> This entire script really has nothing to do with JavaScript. It's just going to be cool when JavaScript changes the `message` variable of this clip it will animate on the screen. If you want to see the script work without JavaScript, place two buttons on the Stage: one with the script `received.message="hello"` and the other with the script `received.message="goodbye"`.

10. Save the `left.fla` movie and test it to export a `.swf`. Then select File, Save As.... Name the new file you're creating `right.fla` and make the adjustments described in the next four steps to `right.fla`.
11. Change the static text to read *Right Side*.
12. Make the button point to the left (if your button is an arrow shape).
13. Change the script on the button to read as follows:

```
on (release) {
  getURL ("javascript:fromRight();");
}
```

14. Change one line in the script attached to the instance of `received`. The `moveLocs` array should contain the x values for the locations of an animation that appears to start on the *left* side of the screen. Here are the numbers for my animation:

```
moveLocs=[-35,30,100,120,90,100];
```

15. Save the `right.fla` movie and test the movie to create a `.swf`.

16. Now we need an HTML file that contains both movies. You can simply publish both the `right.fla` and the `left.fla` movies, open one HTML file with a text editor, and copy all the code from `<OBJECT>` up to and including `</OBJECT>`. Open the other HTML file and paste the copied code after the closing `</OBJECT>` tag in the second file. Typing a series of dashes "----" between the two tags will separate the two movies so they appear side-by-side instead of on top of each other. Alternatively, you can use an application such as Dreamweaver, which makes inserting two Flash movies into a single HTML file quite easy. You can even place each Flash movie in a different cell of an HTML table (Figure W20.2).

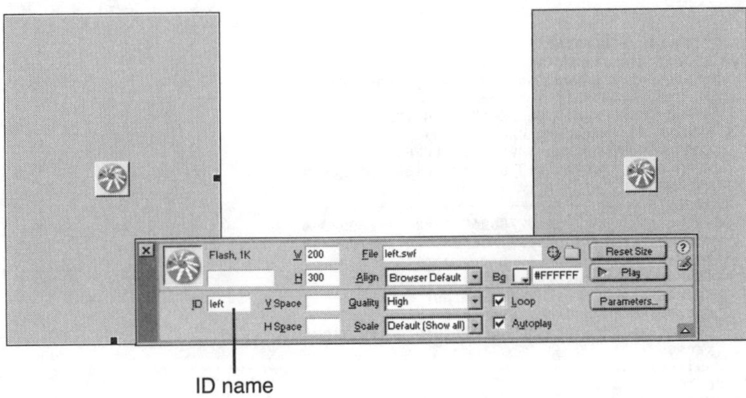

Figure W20.2 *Dreamweaver makes it easy to insert Flash movies into an HTML file; it also provides ID names.*

17. There's an important step we need to take before we get into the JavaScript: The `left.swf` file needs the `ID` of `left` and the `right.swf` needs the `ID` of `right`. Figure W20.3 highlights where this is done in the HTML file. If you're using Dreamweaver, you can actually specify an `ID` for any inserted object using the Properties window. Also, be sure to remember to include the line `swLiveConnect=TRUE` in the `EMBED` portion of the HTML.

18. Now for the JavaScript. All we really have to write is two functions: `fromRight()` and `fromLeft()`. Make a script section after `</HEAD>` and before `<BODY>` by typing the `<SCRIPT LANGUAGE=JavaScript>` and `</SCRIPT>` tags. All the JavaScript functions will go between these. In addition to these two functions, we should include a standard utility function that lets us properly target the correct Flash object, especially because there are two objects:

```
function flashObj(objName) {
  if(navigator.appName=="Netscape") {
    var num=0;
    if (objName=='left'){
      num=0;
    }
```

```
        if (objName=='right'){
          num=1;
        }
        return document.embeds[num];
      } else {
        return window[objName]
      }
    }
```

The `flashObj()` function was covered in Chapter 14, "Interfacing with External Data."

```
<BODY bgcolor="#FFFFFF">
<p><OBJECT classid="clsid:D27CDB6E-AE6D-11cf-96B
 codebase="http://download.macromedia.com/pub/sh
 WIDTH=200 HEIGHT=300 id="left">
    <PARAM NAME=movie VALUE="left.swf">
    <PARAM NAME=quality VALUE=high>
    <PARAM NAME=bgcolor VALUE=#FFFFFF>
    <EMBED src="left.swf" quality=high bgcolor=#
    </EMBED>
  </OBJECT> ------------------------------------
<object classid="clsid:D27CDB6E-AE6D-11cf-96B8-4
 codebase="http://download.macromedia.com/pub/sh
 width=200 height=300 id="right">
    <param name=movie value="right.swf">
    <param name=quality value=high>
    <param name=bgcolor value=#FFFFFF>
    <embed src="right.swf" quality=high bgcolor=
    </embed>
  </object></p>
</BODY>
</HTML>
```

Figure W20.3 *However you do it, the* `ID` *tags for the* `.swf` *files must be set properly.*

19. Now add these two functions to the JavaScript:

```
function fromLeft(){
  flashObj('right').
➥SetVariable('_level0/received/:message',
➥flashObj('left').GetVariable('message'));
}
function fromRight(){
  flashObj('left').
➥SetVariable('_level0/received/:message',
➥flashObj('right').GetVariable('message'));
}
```

This code is easier to read the way it appears here, but you can write both of these functions on a single line within the function. Let's look at just the `fromLeft()` function: First we target the `'right'` Flash movie and use the `SetVariable()` method on it. We're going to set the `message` variable in `received` to whatever the `message` variable of the `'left'` Flash movie is. In pseudo-code, here's what we're doing: "For the `'right'` movie, set `_root.received.message` equal to the `'left'` movie's `message` variable."

//

The only really ugly thing about this approach is when you're targeting a variable contained in a clip, as we are here with the variable `_root.recieved.message`. We can't use the dot syntax that we love. Instead, we have to use the old "slash syntax" which uses level numbers and forward slashes instead of dots. This is simply because the methods for the Flash object (in JavaScript) were developed before Flash 5's dot syntax. In our case, the targeted clip is in level 0 (`_level0`). If we had used `loadMovie()`, `attachMovie()`, or `duplicateMovieClip()` to create the `received` clip inside Flash it might have resided in a level number (higher than 0) and we'd have to target it accordingly (for example `_level1`). Level numbers aren't that big of a deal. The killer is that you must separate the path *to* the variable from the variable name with a colon. For example, if `'_level0/received/'` is the path to the variable, you must insert a colon before specifying the name, like this: `'_level0/received/:message'`

Despite its ugly syntax, this script should work pretty well (Figure W20.4).

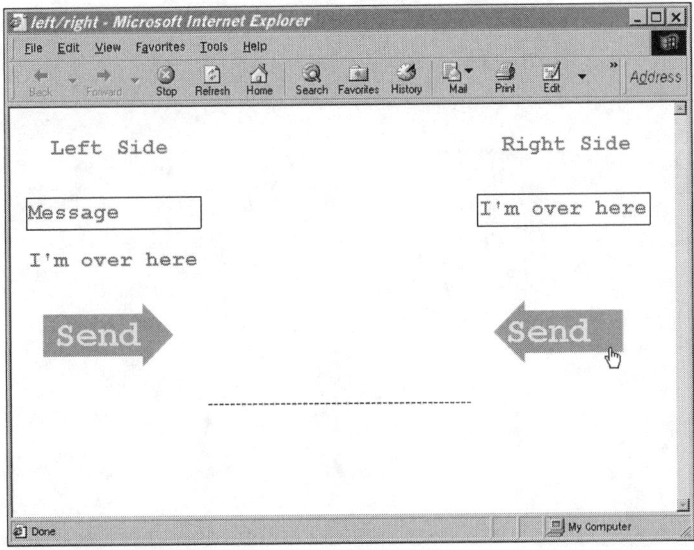

Figure W20.4 *The finished project shows that Flash movies can send messages to each other by way of JavaScript.*

You can do a lot more with JavaScript and Flash, but this workshop and Workshop 19, “Creating JavaScript Cookies,” should get you started using some of the material in Chapter 14.

{Chapter 21 Workshop }

Fixing Broken Scripts

In Chapter 6, you learned some of the ways to debug movies. In this workshop, you're given the chance to put those skills to work. Your task is to first download the "broken" Flash files (found at `www.teleport.com/~phillip/actionscripting/`) and then fix the errors that I have purposely included in them. None of these files will work without adjustment. Most of the fixes are simple—once you track them down.

The files you'll work with in this workshop either don't work at all or they work incorrectly. For each file, you'll find a description what's *supposed* to happen in the following sections. Then, if you choose to peek, you'll find a clue to the problem. Finally, I provide the solution and a short explanation. The difficulty of the problems in these files ranges from simple to quite difficult. (It's actually hard to gauge how difficult it is to find and fix a bug.)

One thing to remember in your real projects is that most bugs require only a simple fix. Sometimes the fix is very involved, but usually, it's just a minor oversight you made while programming. In this workshop, the "harder" bugs to fix usually require a little more digging to find. For example, you may have to edit the script for a button that's inside another clip. For every bug you find, you should feel *really* good about your debugging skills. If nothing else, you'll be rewarded with a movie that functions.

Card Flip

The file ("01_card_flip.fla") is just the start of a card-game movie that could evolve to be three-card monte. Although this file will take many steps to finish, the current version is supposed to allow the user to click on any card. The card then animates by reducing its `_yscale` until it reaches `0`. Then it's supposed to increase its `_yscale` until it reaches the normal `100` again, where it stops. Don't worry about showing the face of the card—we have bigger problems! The current version appears to scale down alright, but then it seems to scale up forever! Inside the Main Clip symbol is a script on the invisible button that triggers a variable on the clip instance of the Card symbol. See whether you can find and fix the bug.

Hint

The error is probably different than it appears. If you edit the master version of the Card symbol and place an odd graphic shape inside the rectangle shape (as shown in Figure W21.1), you'll see that the next time you test the movie, the error is *not* that the `_yscale` increases too much, but rather that it starts to decrease and keeps decreasing below `0` (where it will appear upside down). Don't worry about `_yscale` going above `100`; make sure that it never goes below `0`, and you'll be on the right track.

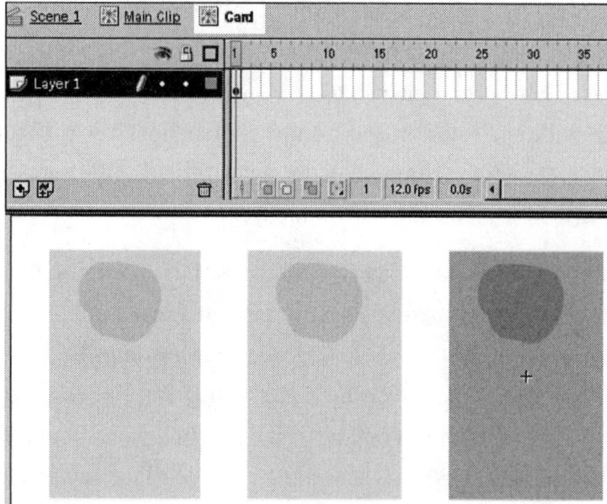

Figure W21.1 *Placing a splotch on one part of the card provides a clue to the exact problem.*

Solution

The problem can be found in the script attached to the instance of the Card symbol inside the Main Clip symbol. The variable `direction` starts at `-12` and is supposed to turn to `12` when the `_yscale` reaches `0`. The problem is inside the `enterFrame` script: The `if` statement checks to see whether `_yscale` is equal to `0` or `100`. The problem is that if `_yscale` jumps by `12` for each `enterFrame` event (while it's animating), then it will jump right past `0`. Change the first condition from `_yscale==0` to `_yscale<0`. Test the movie, and you'll see that the other `if` statement must be fixed, too. Change its condition to `_yscale>100`. Finally, you'll want to make one more touch. In addition to the other two statements in the `if(_yscale>100)` statement, add one that reads `_yscale=100`. This statement ensures that when `_yscale` goes past `100`, it is set back to `100`.

By the way, another solution is to change both values for `direction` (`12` and `-12`) to a number that divides evenly into `100`—perhaps `10`. But for this workshop, I think that's a poor solution because it will change the "speed" of the animation.

Card Snap

In this broken file (02_card_snap.fla), we've added quite a bit to the preceding Card Flip file (although we're not playing three-card monte yet). We're successfully assigning a unique random number to each "card_" instance's `cardNum` variable. I even threw in a Dynamic Text field, which is just for testing purposes because you don't want the user to know the value of `cardNum` for each card. The file works, but what I want is the card to animate when it's clicked. Actually, I had this grandiose plan to make the card change `_yscale` based on a scripted animation technique such as we used in other workshops. At the right moment (when the card's `_yscale` is low enough), I wanted to make the card jump to a frame within its 11-frame movie. I think most of it is built right, but I can't get it to start animating!

Hint

The entire solution is a matter of targeting variables correctly. Here's another clue: The solution involves changing the script on the invisible button.

Solution

Here's the problem: In the first frame's script, we're assigning the variable `cardNum` as part of the instance of the Clip w/Card symbol. Inside that instance, our button is referring to the `cardNum` variable as if it were part of the `card` instance contained in Clip w/Card. Just change the script on the invisible button so that it assigns the value of `card.animateTo` to the value of `cardNum` and not to `card.cardNum`. The script should look like this:

```
on (release) {
  if (card.flipped==false){
    card.animateTo= cardNum;
  }
}
```

When you get it working, study the way the scripted animation works. I think this version looks much snappier than the previous file, which just changed the `_yscale` a little bit at a time. This comment has nothing to do with the bug; it just points out another example of scripted animation.

Circle Move

This is a pretty easy one, but it it's likely to trip up even the most experienced ActionScripter. In the file ("03_circle_move.fla") you'll find three instances of the *same* Movie Clip—but only two bounce back and forth when you test the movie. Naturally, the master symbol contains another clip, so that the `enterFrame` script we're using isn't duplicated on the surface of each instance on the Stage. That is, when you fix the script, you'll have to fix it in only one place. For some unknown reason, the green circle never bounces back the way the red and blue instances do. What's so different about the green clip? How can you fix it so that they all bounce back and forth?

Hint

Drag another instance of the Clip w-Circle symbol and chances are very good that it will be broken too. Here's another clue: Review the solution from the "Card Flip" broken script, earlier in this workshop.

Solution

The reason both the red and green instances bounce back and forth is because I carefully placed their x coordinates at 210 and 100 respectively. Because they're moving by 10 or -10 each enterFrame, both will eventually reach precisely 550 and 0, which are the two extremes. We don't really want to check whether the _x position *equals* 550 or 0, we only care whether it's above 550 or below 0. The if statement should use a greater-than and less-than comparison operator. The finished version is shown here:

```
onClipEvent (load) {
  direction=10;
}
onClipEvent (enterFrame) {
  _parent._x+=direction;
  if(_parent._x>550){
    direction=direction*-1;
  }
  if(_parent._x<0){
    direction=direction*-1;
  }
}
```

It's true that I was being deceptive by artificially making the red and blue circle work when, in fact, almost any clip would fail with this script. However, you'll quite often write a script that appears to work for your conditions and *only* for your conditions. As soon as you take a script that works fine under certain conditions to another situation, errors often pop up. So, in fact, this kind of thing will probably happen to you eventually. However, if your tests are exhaustive, you should find such bugs.

Multiple Choice

The file ("04_multiple_choice.fla") is a great example of a dynamic multiple-choice quiz. You simply assign the variables question, answer1, answer2, answer3, and correctNum, and the text is displayed onscreen. This code could be expanded to load questions from a server or a text file. You can have lots of questions and even report the score at the end of a quiz. If only it worked! It's a shame it doesn't because we even have a highlight for the button that the user clicks, and a way to color the Dynamic Text field for feedback with HTML colored text. The only problem is that *any* answer is considered correct. Here's a free hint: Salem is the capital of Oregon. Please fix my quiz.

Hint

The entire problem is one missing character that should be included somewhere in the `attempt()` function. Okay, the problem is found in the `if` statement's condition.

Solution

This one gets me *all* the time! The `if` statement condition should use the comparison `==` not the assignment `=`. The way it is now, `whatNum` is assigned to `currectNum` every time. I don't know whether the bug would have been easier to solve if I had moved the statement `highlight._y=highLocs[whatNum-1]` to the end of the `attempt()` function. If I did that, the highlight would always move to the correct button, and not to the button the user clicked.

Rotating Box

Don't ask me what the practical use of this movie is—maybe a "Wheel of Fortune" game? If you open then test the file "05_rotating_box.fla" you'll find that you can set the box in motion by clicking either arrow button. When you click the Stop button, the next time the `_rotation` reaches a point that's evenly divisible by 90, the box should stop (Figure W21.2). I added some visual feedback for when the user clicks the Stop button—much like how a public bus might have a lighted sign saying, "stop requested," so that you don't keep requesting that the bus make the next stop. That's just a little touch that makes this movie more usable. The problem seems to be related to the seltzer—I can't seem to make the box stop on that one. Actually, if you start by pressing the left button, you won't be able to stop it on apples either. Obviously, when you investigate the solution, don't get hung up on the seltzer and apples choices; try to find why the box isn't working generally.

Hint

Uncomment the line `_root.test=_rotation` attached to the instance of the Box symbol by deleting the two forward slashes (`//`). You'll also need to place a Dynamic Text field on the stage associated with the variable `test`. This should answer why the long-winded condition in the `if` statement (`_rotation==0||_rotation==90||_rotation==180||rotation==270`) isn't working. Here's another clue: The solution requires a different condition in the `if` statement. Consider the modulus operator (`%`) and re-read the phrase "evenly divisible by 90" in the preceding movie description.

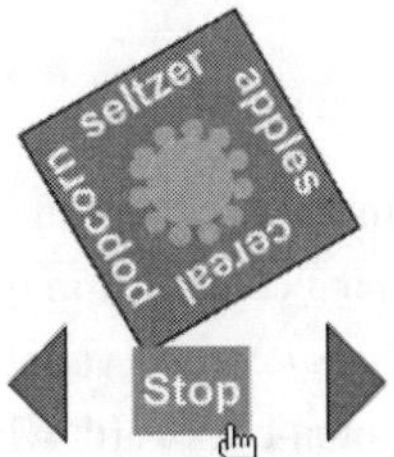

Figure W21.2 *Despite having little or no practical value, the goal of this movie is to enable the user to stop the box in one of four rotations.*

Solution

Like most solutions, the one I'm going to give you isn't the only one. All you need to do is to change the condition in the `if` statement to `_rotation%90==0`. In pseudo-code, this condition says, "the remainder of `90` divided into `_rotation` is equal to `0`." Here's the finished version of the `enterFrame` event:

```
onClipEvent(enterFrame){
  stopLight._visible=stopRequested;
  _rotation+=direction;
  if (stopRequested){
    if (_rotation%90==0){
      direction=0;
      stopRequested=0;
    }
  }
}
```

Word Float

I'm not really sure where I'm headed with this project, but the "06_word_float.fla" file doesn't seem to let me get any farther than where I am. All I want is for the five instances (`word_1`, `word_2`, `word_3`, `word_4`, and `word_5`) to contain the five individual words in my `arrayOfWords` array variable. The entire script is in frame 1, but it doesn't seem to work right. Please help!

Hint

This bug is almost too easy for a hint, but here's one: The first index in an array is 0.

Solution

The easiest solution is to change the instance names from word_1 through word_5 to word_0 through word_4. When targeting the variable word contained in the dynamically referenced clip (this["word_"+w].word), the w iteration variable is going from 4 down to 0. (Remember that for-in loops count backward, which doesn't have much to do with the problem but is an interesting tidbit.)

If, for whatever reason, you don't want to rename the instances (maybe those names are being used elsewhere or it's too much work to change them), there is another solution. Unfortunately, changing the statement that assigns the word variable to read this["word_"+w+1].word=arrayOfWords[w] won't work. The w iteration variable is not exactly usable as-is. Instead, you could initialize a variable such as counter and then increment it within the for-loop. But see if you can find the error in this code:

```
counter=0;
for (w in arrayOfWords){
  counter++;
  this["word_"+counter].word=arrayOfWords[w];
}
```

You'll see the problem if you test it: counter is going from 1 to 5 and w is going in the opposite direction from 4 to 0. Here's one of many possible alternatives that work:

```
counter=arrayOfWords.length+1;
for (w in arrayOfWords){
  counter--;
  this["word_"+counter].word=arrayOfWords[w];
}
```

Yellow Box

Here's another practically useless project as it is, but wait until you see it run! Right now, if you open and test the file "07_yellow_box.fla" nothing happens, but when you fix the syntax errors, the yellow box will rotate constantly and, as you move the mouse, it will change its `_xscale` and `_yscale` based on where the mouse goes. Please make it work. There's only a tiny bit of code, and it's all on the instance of the yellow box.

Hint

Make sure that the Colored Syntax option is selected from the Actions panel options arrow (Figure W21.3).

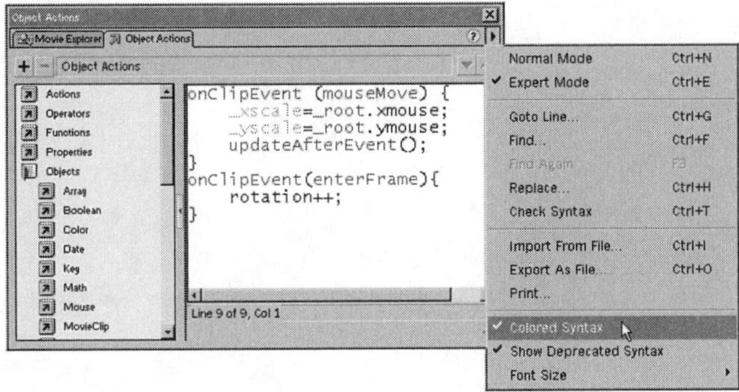

Figure W21.3 *If the Colored Syntax option is selected, you'll have an easier time fixing the bug.*

Solution

The solution is pretty easy. The `_xmouse` property appears incorrectly as `xmouse` (the underscore is also missing from `_ymouse` and `_rotation`). The best way to avoid this bug in the future (if you don't have a perfect memory and frequently make typos) is to leave the Colored Syntax option selected. Properties will then appear as green text. This exercise just underscores how important syntax really is.

Click and Hold

The file "08_click_and_hold.fla" isn't so much broken as it is lacking. How can you make the arrow buttons on the outside keep moving the box as the user clicks and holds the buttons? The various mouse events are covered: The regular "click" buttons respond to the `release` event, and the "click and hold" buttons respond to both the press and release events separately. That's cool. But we need more. When the file is finished, the box should keep moving while the user clicks the "click and hold" buttons.

Hint

This fix comes down to a need for an enterFrame script. It also makes sense to have an additional variable. Leave amount for use in the move() function, but create another one called movingAmount for use in conjunction with your enterFrame script.

Solution

One solution to this problem takes very little typing. It involves first changing the startMove() function inside the load event so that the function does only one thing: sets the value of movingAmount to the value of the direction parameter you receive multiplied by 3. Here's what the startMove() function should look like:

```
function startMove (direction) {
  movingAmount=direction*3;
}
```

Then add the following enterFrame script:

```
onClipEvent (enterFrame) {
  _x+=movingAmount;
}
```

This script simply keeps adding to the _x property the value of movingAmount, which is normally 0. Finally, consider adding a response to the releaseOutside event on the two buttons so that if the user clicks, rolls off, and then releases, the box doesn't keep moving. One button's fix would look like this:

```
on (release, releaseOutside) {
  box.startMove(0);
}
```

Notice the additional releaseOutside event. We're using an additional variable (movingAmount) so as to not conflict with the amount variable. If the enterFrame script also used amount, a simple click on either "click" button would start the box moving (and it would keep moving). If you want the Dynamic Text to reflect both numbers, you can simply place the line `amount=direction*3` somewhere inside the `startMove()` function.

Objects

Don't worry, the broken script found in the file "09_objects.fla" doesn't have much to do with objects. It deals instead with a common problem that arises when using objects. In this movie, I want a representation for each wheel of each vehicular homemade object that gets instantiated. In the first frame, you can see that I'm trying to put instances of my vehicle object in the variables `bicycle`, `car`, `unicycle`, and `truck`. Then I want to use `attachMovie()` to both place an instance of the Vehicle Shell symbol for each vehicle and, inside each vehicle, place an instance of the `Wheel` symbol for each wheel in that vehicle.

Just to see how the movie is working or not working, I placed a button inside the `Wheel` symbol that displays which wheel is being clicked. The problem is that I seem to get only one wheel for each vehicle—but I want to see as many wheels as necessary (as is shown in Figure W21.4). The thing that kills me is that when I debug the movie, all my objects are instantiated properly (as Figure W21.4 shows). Please make the wheels appear to spread out horizontally. Consider peeking at the hint because you'll still be left with a nice challenge; even when you know *where* the script has to be adjusted, there's still a lot of work to do the adjusting.

Hint

Right after you execute the `attachMovie()` method for each wheel inside the `for` loop (`for (w=1; w<allObjects[i].wheels+1; w++)`), you must reposition the newly created wheel by setting its _x property. Right now, all the clips are indeed appearing, but all have the same x coordinate so they're stacked. It's the same basic thing that happens in scripts that set the _y property of each vehicle or `object_x` clip. Study this line of code for an idea of what you have to do:

```
this["object_"+objectCount]._y=30*objectCount;
```

We want to set the _x property of the newly created `wheel_x` instance. With dynamic referencing, however, it's not so simple.

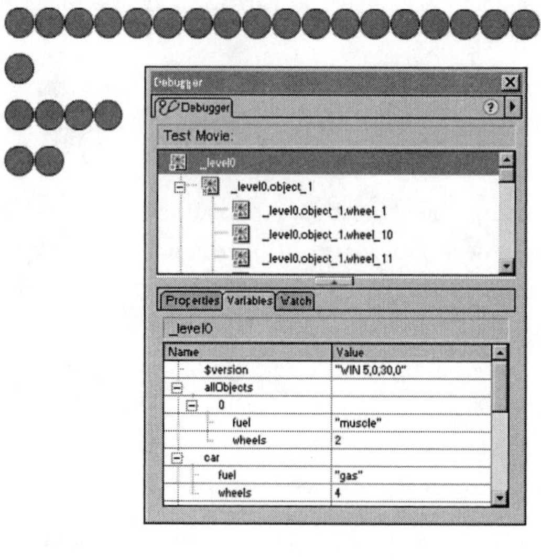

Figure W21.4 *When the file is corrected, you should see a circle for every wheel in every object.*

Here's another hint: The pseudo-code for the statement you have to write is: "Set the `x` of the new wheel inside the current vehicle to 20 pixels more than the last one," or "set the `x` of the wheel `wheelCount` inside the object `objectCount` to 20 times `wheelCount`."

Solution

Right underneath the line that starts `this["object_"+objectCount].attachMovie(...` place the following statement:

```
this["object_"+objectCount]["wheel_"+wheelCount]._x=20*wheelCount;
```

Pretty ugly, eh? Re-read the pseudo-code provided in the "Hints" section if necessary.

Move Multiple

How can so little code have so many errors? The file "10_move_multiple.fla" has two buttons that simply call my `move()` function, which is supposed to move each circle 10 pixels in the direction requested. I'm sure I'm targeting the correct circle_ clip because I re-read the dynamic referencing section of Chapter 7. However, I can't even test the movie without the output window rearing its ugly head. Make it go away and make the circles move.

Hint

After you fix the syntax error by putting semicolons in place of the commas in the for loop, you have two more fixes to make! I'll give you one: We're supposed to be changing the _x property of each circle. Add ._x after the this["circle_"+i] and you'll only have one more fix to make.

Solution

First, change the commas to semicolons in the for loop (I mistakenly use commas all the time). Next, notice that although we're targeting the correct circle_ clip, we're not specifying what property we want to change. It's likely that we want to change the _x property. Finally, the loop doesn't loop enough times. More specifically, it loops only when i is less than 4. We want it to keep looping while i is less than or equal to 4. There are a few other fixes you could make to solve this problem, but changing < (less-than) to <= (less-than or equal to) will do it. Here's the finished version of the move() function:

```
function move(direction){
  total=4;
  for(i=1;i<=total;i++){
    this["circle_"+i]._x += direction*10;
  }
}
```

Summary

That was fun wasn't it? It sure was fun for me *breaking* the scripts. Fixing them should be quite rewarding and very educational. I tried to expose some of the common problems programmers have with ActionScript. Errors in the following categories are common: targeting (both for variables and properties), syntax, logic flow, and array indexes. Of course, there are countless ways to solve any problem, but you must realize that there are even more ways to do it wrong! It's not easy to program, but with deliberation and patience, you have proven that you can do it.

{Part III }

Appendices

{ Appendix A }

Equivalents

There's always more than one way to solve a programming task. In addition to subjective personal taste, some solutions are actually better than others. I won't go as far to say the information in this appendix exhibits techniques that are better or worse than any others—but it does show you alternatives to many deprecated Flash 4 functions. In addition, several workarounds that were developed during the Flash 4 era are now unnecessary. Finally, some of the most common mistakes (at least that I make) are listed at the end of this appendix.

Alternatives to Deprecated Code

The following ActionScript components are either officially deprecated (meaning they are being phased out) or they should be. I've provided alternatives to the following components.

tellTarget()

The direct equivalent to `tellTarget()` is `with()`. Here are two equivalent code snippets:

```
//this code:
tellTarget ("aClip") {
 play ();
}
```

```
//is the same as this code:
with (aClip) {
 play ();
}
```

Neither method is actually necessary. Notice that the following one-line code is the same as the preceding two-line version:

```
aClip.play();
```

Both `tellTarget()` and `with()` are more convenient when you want several statements to execute in the targeted clip, because you can place as many lines of code as you want between the curly brackets. Notice that while inside the curly brackets, you don't need to precede each method with a targeted clip.

call()

In the past, `call()` was the next best thing to functions. You simply used `call(`*`frameNum`*`)` or `call("`*`frameLabelString`*`")` (where "frameNum" is an integer or "frameLabelString" is a string). The result was that all the scripts contained in the targeted frame executed as if you had entered that frame, without really going to that frame. It effectively achieved the modular benefit of using functions, but because there were no functions, `call()` was the only way. Even though all this history is interesting, there is no reason to use `call()` ever again. After you learn functions (as you did in Chapter 8, "Functions,"), you won't need `call()`.

ifFrameLoaded()

This outdated method will return `true` or `false` depending on whether the frame number passed (as a parameter) has loaded or not. The `_framesloaded` property can be used as an alternative to return the number of frames loaded. You should also check out the methods `getBytesLoaded()` and `getBytesTotal()` that return very detailed information about the download process.

toggleHighQuality()

This unwieldy old "action" was a real pain! Sure, it was nice to be able to change between low and high quality (usually dropping down to low quality right before a complex animation and then back up to high quality when it was over). The problem was that you had to track the current quality so that you didn't accidentally "toggle" it from high to low when you wanted to go the other way around. Now there's a property, `_quality`, which can be both ascertained and set using the standard property setting syntax. The property can be set to `"LOW"`, `"MEDIUM"`, `"HIGH"`, or `"BEST"`. By the way, you can only set `_quality` globally for the entire movie (and not selectively for individual clip instances).

eval()

I'm not prepared to say that `eval()` is never needed, but its old use—to retrieve the value for a dynamically named variable—is unnecessary. That is, you can build a variable name dynamically such as `"loc_"+curNum`—but this returns a string. To return the value of the variable `loc_1` (assuming that `curNum` is currently `1`), you can use either of these two expressions:

```
eval("loc_"+curNum)
this["loc_"+curNum]
```

The keyword `this` can be replaced with a target to a timeline. This topic is covered further in the "Dynamic Referencing" section of Chapter 7, "The Movie Clip Object."

Logical Operators (`and`, `or`, and `not`)

The `and`, `or`, and `not` operators have been replaced with `&&`, `||`, and `!`, respectively.

String Comparison Operators (`eq`, `ge`, `gt`, `le`, `lt`, and `ne`)

In the past, when writing conditional expressions involving strings you had to use the `eq`, `ge`, `gt`, `le`, `lt`, and `ne` operators (which stand for "equal to," "greater than or equal to," "greater than," "less than or equal to," "less than," and "not equal to"). They have been replaced with the standards (==, >=, >, <=, <, and `!=`), respectively.

String Functions

All the old string functions have been replaced with methods of the String object. You can recognize the difference in the syntax. The old functions use `functionName("aString")` and the new methods use `"aString".methodName()`. It's a little confusing because some of the new methods have the same names. However, the syntax always follows this form. In Chapter 9, "Selecting Text,

Trapping Keys, and Manipulating Strings," you can learn all the String object's methods.

Some people have found that certain older string functions actually execute faster than the new methods. You might consider performing a benchmark test. To compare two blocks, place `startTime=getTimer()` above and `trace("It took "+getTimer()-startTime+" milliseconds")` below one solution and compare the results when you do the same with another block of code.

int()

This old function returns the integer portion of the parameter passed (in the parentheses). The replacement is `Math.floor(someNum)` where "someNum" is the number that you want to convert to an integer. Realize that an integer is returned, so to change the value inside the `someNum` variable, use

```
someNum=Math.floor(someNum);
```

This topic is covered in Chapter 5, "Programming Structures."

random()

Although most of the replacements shown in this appendix are easier to use than their old counterparts, `random()` was pretty nice the way it was. The code `random(10)` would return an integer between `0` and `10`, inclusive. Calling `Math.random()` returns a decimal number between `0` and `1` (not including 0 or 1). Here's an expression that was explained in Chapter 5:

```
Math.random()*((max-min)+1)
```

This expression returns a number and decimal between `min` and `max`, inclusive. (You need to set `min` and `max` or replace them with hard-wired numbers to use this expression.) Pass the entire expression as a parameter in the `Math.floor()` method to turn it into an integer.

No More Funkiness

In the era of Flash 4, programmers had to be resourceful to get Flash to do amazing things. Flash's simplicity actually made it more difficult because it was limited. There are plenty of creative workarounds that programmers used to employ in Flash. Many of those workarounds are no longer needed. I don't want the following to sound like a list of cautions. I'm just trying to provide alternatives (that are usually easier) to some popular old tricks.

Two-Frame "Updater" Movie Clips

When all you had were keyframe and button scripts, there was no intuitive way to execute code repeatedly. You created a two-frame Movie Clip with code in the first frame's script and a `gotoAndPlay(1)` script in the second frame. As fast as that Movie Clip could loop, the code contained in the first keyframe would execute. Usually such clips would contain no graphics—they were only used for scripts. The alternatives available now are found in the clip events `enterFrame` and `mouseMove`. Actually, `mouseMove` executes as fast as the user can move his mouse, so for some scripts this is definitely better than any alternative.

The truth is that I still consider reaching for the old stand-by, the two-frame Movie Clip. For example, if I'm building a Movie Clip that will be used several times in the movie, it's not so simple to use a clip event. Clip events are placed *on* clip instances (not inside the master symbol). I would certainly shy away from copying and pasting my code on every instance of a clip just to have access to a clip event. That would mean the code is repeated (which we don't want for the reasons discussed in Chapter 3, "The Programmer's Approach"). You *can* write code once (inside a Movie Clip) that traps a clip event, but it needs to be attached to a nested clip. I'll often drag an invisible clip inside another Movie Clip so that I can then place scripts on the instance of the invisible clip. (That's the point at which I consider the two-frame option instead because I'd need only one Movie Clip.) Anyway, the problem with attaching a script to an instance of an invisible clip nested inside another clip is that you have to target variables and properties in relative timelines. That just means you have to concentrate when targeting—which isn't *that* bad—but you should see the dilemma.

Drag Invisible Movie Clip to Ascertain Mouse Position

Before the introduction of the `_xmouse` and `_ymouse` properties, the old trick was to make an invisible Movie Clip that the user started dragging (even without clicking) from the start of the movie. If you ever needed to ascertain where the mouse was, you'd just check the position of that clip. You'll likely hear about this technique only when listening to a few Flash old-timers chew the fat—it's totally unnecessary with Flash 5.

Pseudo Arrays

Before arrays, each variable could have only one value. In the past, you had to maintain several variables, such as loc_1, loc_2, and loc_3, and then access individual ones using something like eval("loc_"+num). Now with arrays, you can store as many individual values in one variable as you want, so a single variable (of the array data type) can maintain several values. Learn all about arrays in Chapter 10, "Arrays."

URL-Encoded Data Instead of XML-Structured

There are still plenty of reasons to use URL-encoded data (as discussed in Chapter 14, "Interfacing with External Data"), but with the potential of XML, you can load much more organized data. Just realize that it's available.

The Oldest Ones in the Book

I make as many (if not more) mistakes as the next person. Here are some of the errors that I find myself making all the time. (By the way, the Fixing Broken Scripts workshop includes exercises involving most of these.)

You Can't Set _currentframe

Try as you might, this property is read only. You can always ascertain the current frame number, but you just can't set it through this property. You can't just say _currentframe=10 and expect anything to happen. If you want to jump to another frame, you must use gotoAndStop(). Instead of someClip._currentframe=10, use someClip.gotoAndStop(10).

You Can Jump Only to Integer Frame Numbers

When you calculate a frame number to jump to, you must make sure that the expression evaluates to an integer. You can use Math.floor() to ensure that an expression is an integer. For example, a script such as gotoAndStop(percent*_totalframes) will work only if the expression (percent*_totalframes) evaluates to an integer. Use gotoAndStop(Math.floor(percent*_totalframes)) to make sure.

There's a Big Difference Between = and ==

As you learned in Chapter 5, = performs an assignment (as in myScore=100—which assigns myScore the value of 100) and == creates a comparison expression that evaluates to true or false (as in `myAge==35`—either it's `true` or it's `false`). This messes me up when I mistakenly use a single = in the conditional of an if-statement. I cannot think of a logical time when you'd want to use something like this:

```
if(myAge=21){
    //this script is faulty!
}
```

The code placed between curly brackets will *always* execute, because `myAge` will turn into `21`.

For-Loops Use Semicolons, Not Commas

This tip falls in the "the syntax has to be legit" category—which is obvious, but still easy to mess up. I find myself constantly writing for-loops like this:

```
for(i=1,i<=10,i++){
    trace("if I've told you "+i+" I've told you a million times");
}
```

Luckily, a syntax error appears in the output window when I test the movie because the commas inside the parentheses should be semicolons. I guess I just get so used to separating parameters sent and received in functions by using the comma that I want to use it in the for-loop. Perhaps this tip will save you a fraction of the time I've wasted making the error.

{ Appendix B }

Making Flash Extensions for the Macromedia Exchange Web Site

Macromedia's free Extension Manager makes it easy for Macromedia customers to install behaviors for Dreamweaver and Smart Clips or Libraries for Flash. Although the install process for Flash extensions is not much more than copying files to the appropriate folders, distributing files as an extension makes the entire process very easy for the end user. The end user needs to download only one file (a compressed "package") and double-click it to install. Managing installed extensions is also a simple process. All the installed extensions are categorized and listed in the Extension Manager. From there, the end user can view details about every extension and temporarily disable or remove them. It's quite simple for the end user and not much more work for you to build your own. You can then share your creations with the Flash community. Macromedia even serves up the files that you submit to its site.

How It Works

Here are the details.

You can package and distribute any set of files; but generally, you'll likely distribute .fla files containing artwork or Smart Clips, Custom UI .swf files (to go with the Smart Clips), Publish templates, ActionScript (text files with the .as extension), or Generator objects. There are a few more categories (called "types") for extensions, but really, you can distribute any kind of file.

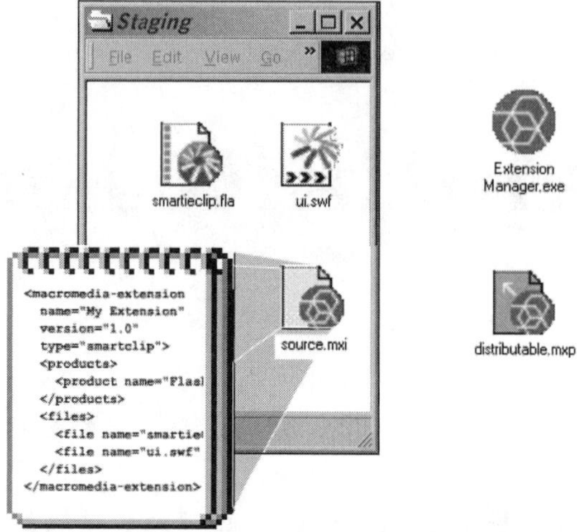

Figure B.1 *The "source.mxi" file specifies which files are to be included when you "package" using the Extension Manager to create the "distributable.mxp" file.*

The first step is to build this file or set of files that you want to distribute. Prepare all the files in the form you plan to distribute. In other words, if you're distributing .swf files you need to export the .fla files accordingly. Place all these files in an empty folder on your hard drive. In the same folder, write an "extension installation file," which is nothing more than an XML-structured text file with an .mxi extension that identifies the files you want to distribute along with other details such as the folders into which the files should install.

The following section outlines most of the details for writing the .mxi extension installation file. After it's written, you simply run the Extension Manager and select File, Package Extension…. You'll be prompted to name the "package" that will be created. Extension packages are single files that contain compressed versions of all your files along with the installation instructions. This single .mxp package can be distributed to anyone with the Extension Manager. Generally, people download these .mxp files from the Macromedia Exchange Web site, but you should definitely test your .mxp file before distributing it. To find the link where you can upload your finished .mxp file to the Exchange Web site simply select File, Submit Extension (from the Extension Manager program).

The MXI File Format

The following contains most of the details necessary to make the .mxi file for Flash extensions you build. You'll find more details in the Macromedia document `http://download.macromedia.com/pub/exchange/mxi_file_format.pdf`. Although I encourage you to read that document, it contains a lot of additional details that apply only to building extensions for Dreamweaver and UltraDev.

Here is the skeleton (or minimum) form of an .mxi file:

```
<macromedia-extension
 name="Name for your Extension"
 version="1.0"
 type="smartclip"
>
 <author name="Your Name" />

 <products>
  <product name="Flash" />
 </products>

 <description>
  <![CDATA[
   This is the description.
  ]]>
 </description>

 <ui-access>
  <![CDATA[
   You get to the installed files by selecting
   Window > Common Libraries > Phillip.
  ]]>
 </ui-access>

 <files>
  <file name="smartieClip.fla" destination="$flash/Libraries"/>
  <file name="ui.swf" destination="$flash/Libraries"/>
 </files>

</macromedia-extension>
```

Notice that everything appears between two tags (`<macromedia-extension` and `</macromedia-extension>`). You should notice also that the opening macromedia-extension tag isn't really a complete tag until the `>`, which appears after the line `type="smartclip"`. That's because `name`, `version`, and `type` are attributes (think "properties") of this tag. This is the minimum set of attributes. You simply change the values that appear as strings after `name` and `version` to whatever you want. You must use one of the following values for type because that value affects the icon that appears in the Exchange Manager (see Figure B.2). Here are the possible values for type: "smartclip", "actionscript", "lesson", "sample", "library", "generatorobject", "publishtemplate", "utility", "keyboardshortcut", and "suite".

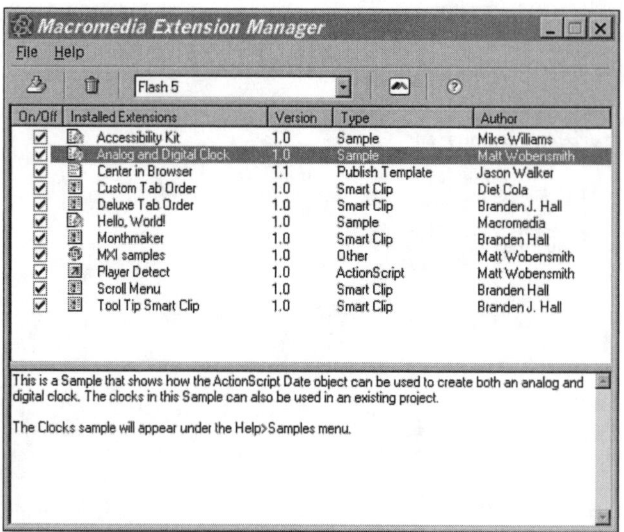

Figure B.2 *The Extension Manager lists all installed extensions, each with its type and associated icon and description.*

The next tag, <author name="Your Name" />, can simply be changed to your name. This also appears in the Exchange Manager.

The products node can include additional attributes for the product tag. The earlier example simply shows the name attribute (in this case, "Flash" as extensions can also be made for other Macromedia products). For example, the optional version attribute specifies the version of Flash (or whatever product) for which the extension was designed. There are two other optional attributes (called primary and required). The range of values for these two is "true" or "false". Primary is only necessary for extensions that work with more than one product (like Dreamweaver *and* Flash). If Required is set to "false", it allows users without the product listed to install the extension. (Leaving this attribute out will default to "true".) Here's an example of a version of the products node that requires Flash version 5:

```
<products>
    <product name="Flash" version="5" />
</products>
```

The next two nodes (`<description>`) and (`<ui-access>`) are very straightforward. You simply place text (between `<![CDATA[` and `]]>`) that will appear in the bottom half of the of the Extension Manager. The description should include helpful information about the purpose of your extension, but it can be any text. The `ui-access` portion should include directions for the user to find the installed extension. For example, if extension filename is "Phillip.fla" and it was copied into the Libraries folder adjacent to Flash, the user will find it by selecting Window, Common Libraries, Phillip. You should provide such instructions because the end user might not know where to start looking (because he's installed it via the Extension Manager—not Flash). You should also know that you can use HTML codes, including ` ` for a nonbreaking space and `<br>` for line break, to format how the description and `ui-access` text will appear to the end user.

The next node (`<files>`) is where you list the files to be installed. The two required attributes for each file are `source`, which is the path to the file adjacent to where the .mxi file resides, and the `destination` on the user's machine. The source is quite simple—you just name the file you want copied. Naturally, this file must be in the same folder as the .mxi file at the time it's packaged. There are two interesting details about the `destination`. First, notice that it's a relative path, rather than an explicit path. The `$flash` is a "token" (in this case, like a variable) that refers to the installed path of Flash on the user's machine. Generally, you need to place files only in subfolders adjacent to Flash. (You'll find information about creating your own tokens in the next paragraph.) The second interesting detail about the `destination` attribute's value is that you do not include a filename, because the installed file will have the same filename as the `source` file. An optional attribute `platform` allows you to specify files to be installed only for `"win"` or `"mac"`. The other optional attribute is `shared`, which identifies (with the value `"true"` or `"false"`) whether the file is shared among other extensions. What this means is that if a file is identified as `shared="true"` (because it's used by several extensions) and the end user removes just one of the extensions, the shared file is not removed.

One other node was not shown earlier because it's optional. That node is `<file-tokens>`, and it allows you to create different install locations that are either hard-wired or based on the end user's selection. Here are examples of the two forms:

```
<file-tokens>
 <token name="automatic"
  definition="c:\windows\desktop" />
 <token name="theirChoice"
  prompt="the Smart Clip"
  default="c:\windows\desktop" />
</file-tokens>
```

Both examples contain the `name` attribute. The token in the first example can be referred to in the `destination` attribute of any files being installed as `"$automatic"`. For example, you could use `destination="$automatic"` inside a `file` tag and the file would be copied to the user's desktop. Obviously, such hard-wired paths have problems on other platforms. The alternative in the second form is to provide a user with a prompt from which he can select a folder from a standard dialog (as in Figure B.3).

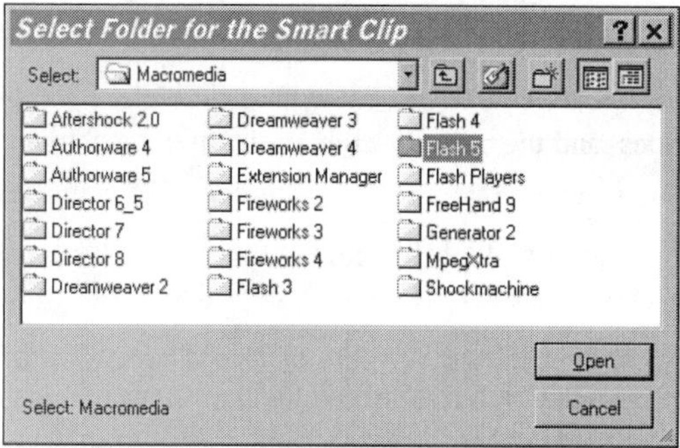

Figure B.3 *Letting the user select a folder (which becomes a "token") presents a dialog like this one.*

When using the prompt attribute (as in the second token), the prompt you provide is always concatenated at the end of the generic "Select Folder for" string. So, in the preceding example, "Select Folder for the Smart Clip" will appear. When using the `prompt` attribute, you can also specify a default directory in which the dialog will start. Making your own tokens is pretty neat but realize that there are other built-in tokens (that you can find in the Macromedia documentation) and it's really rare that you'll *need* to install files anywhere but in a subfolder of the Flash folder. The coolest part is that the Extension Manager will remove files regardless of where they were installed when the user disables or removes them.

{ Index }

Symbols

B

C

D

E

F

G

H

I

J-K

L

M

P

Q-R

S

U

V

W-Z

Other Related Titles

Sams Teach Yourself Macromedia Dreamweaver 4 in 24 Hours
Betsy Bruce
ISBN: 0-672-32042-8
$24.99 US/$37.95 CAN

How to Use Dreamweaver 4 and Fireworks 4
Lon Coley
ISBN: 0-672-32041-X
$29.99 US/$44.95 CAN

Sams Teach Yourself HTML and XHTML in 24 Hours, Fifth Edition
Dick Oliver
ISBN: 0-672-32076-2
$24.99 US/$37.95 CAN

Sams Teach Yourself JavaScript in 24 Hours, Second Edition
Michael Moncur
ISBN: 0-672-32025-8
$24.99 US/$37.95 CAN

Sams Teach Yourself ColdFusion in 21 Days
Charles Mohnike
ISBN: 0-672-31796-6
$39.99 US/$59.95 CAN

Sams Teach Yourself Dreamweaver UltraDev4 in 21 Days
John Ray
ISBN: 0-672-31901-2
$39.99 US/$59.95 CAN

How to Use Macromedia Flash 5
Denise Tyler and Gary Rebholz
ISBN: 0-672-32004-5
$29.99 US/$44.95 CAN

Applying Flash Character Animation Studio Techniques
Lee Purcell
ISBN: 0-672-32199-8
$54.99 US/$81.95 CAN

Sams Teach Yourself Active Server Pages 3.0 in 21 Days
Scott Mitchell and James Atkinson
ISBN: 0-672-31863-6
$39.99 US/$59.95 CAN

SAMS

www.samspublishing.com

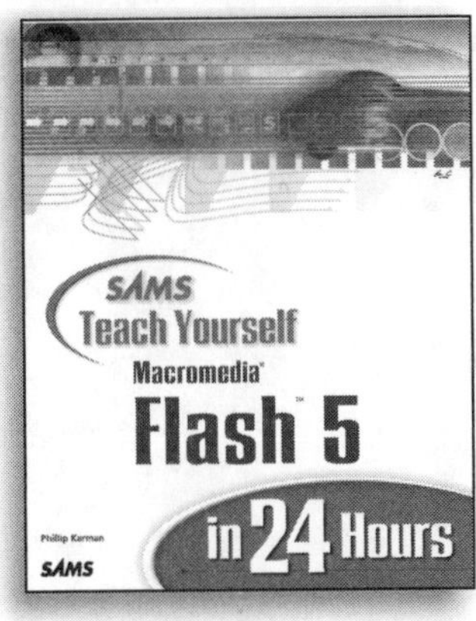

Sams Teach Yourself Flash 5 in 24 Hours
Phillip Kerman
ISBN: 0-672-31892-X
$24.99 US/$37.95 CAN

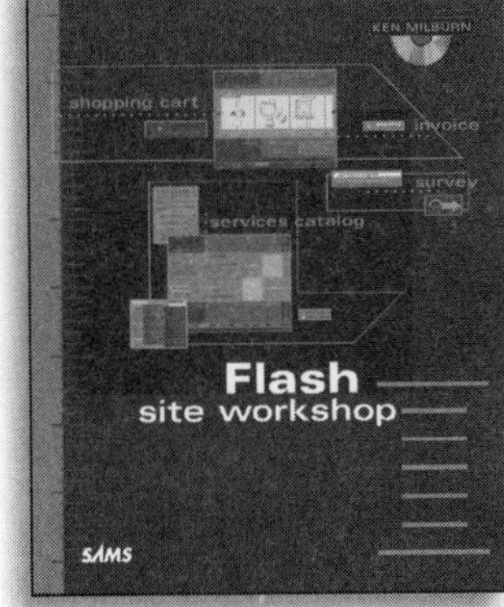

Flash Site Workshop
Ken Milburn, Oncall Interactive
ISBN: 0-672-31999-3
$49.99 US/$74.95 CAN

Flash for the Real World: E-Commerce Case Studies
Steve Street
ISBN: 0-672-32079-7
$49.99 US/$74.95 CAN

All prices are subject to change.